Y0-DFL-810

South-East Asian Social Science Monographs

# Human Resources in Development along the Asia–Pacific Rim

# Human Resources in Development along the Asia–Pacific Rim

*Edited by*
Naohiro Ogawa, Gavin W. Jones,
*and* Jeffrey G. Williamson

*Nihon University President's Grant for
Specified Interdisciplinary Research,
'The Sources of Economic Dynamism in the
Asian and Pacific Region'*

SINGAPORE
OXFORD UNIVERSITY PRESS
OXFORD NEW YORK
1993

Oxford University Press, Walton Street, Oxford OX2 6DP
Oxford New York Toronto
Delhi Bombay Calcutta Madras Karachi
Kuala Lumpur Singapore Hong Kong Tokyo
Nairobi Dar es Salaam Cape Town
Melbourne Auckland Madrid
and associated companies in
Berlin Ibadan

Oxford is a trade mark of Oxford University Press

Published in the United States
by Oxford University Press, New York

© Oxford University Press Pte. Ltd., Singapore, 1993

All rights reserved. No part of this publication may be reproduced, stored in a retrieval system, or transmitted, in any form or by any means, without the prior permission in writing of Oxford University Press. Within the UK, exceptions are allowed in respect of any fair dealing for the purpose of research or private study, or criticism or review, as permitted under the Copyright, Designs and Patents Act, 1988, or in the case of reprographic reproduction in accordance with the terms of the licences issued by the Copyright Licensing Agency. Enquiries concerning reproduction outside these terms and in other countries should be sent to the Rights Department, Oxford University Press, at the address above

British Library Cataloguing in Publication Data
Data available

Library of Congress Cataloging-in-Publication Data
Human resources in development along the Asia–Pacific Rim/edited by Naohiro Ogawa, Gavin W. Jones, Jeffrey G. Williamson.
p. cm.—(South East Asian social science monographs)
Includes bibliographical references and index.
ISBN 0-19-588596-1 (Hard cover)
1. Asia—Economic policy. 2. Pacific Area—Economic policy.
3. Asia—Population. 4. Pacific Area—Population. 5. Human capital—Asia. 6. Human capital—Pacific Area. 7. Education—Asia.
8. Education—Pacific Area. 9. Medical care—Asia. 10. Medical care—Pacific Area. I. Ogawa, Naohiro, 1944– . II. Jones, Gavin W., 1940–
III. Williamson, Jeffrey G., 1935– . IV. Series.
HC412.H86 1993
304.6′095—dc20
92-17954
CIP

Typeset by Indah Photosetting Centre Sdn. Bhd. Malaysia
Printed by Kim Hup Lee Printing Co. Pte. Ltd. Singapore
Published by Oxford University Press Pte. Ltd.,
Unit 221, Ubi Avenue 4, Singapore 1440

# Foreword

SOCIAL, economic, and political changes have dramatically altered the global situation in recent years. The Asia–Pacific region as a whole has achieved strong economic growth, and its potential has drawn a great deal of attention from all over the world.

This economic dynamism in the region is thought to be due, at least in part, to the region's overall success in human resource development. Many countries in the region have succeeded in lowering their mortality and fertility, improving their societal infrastructure, and raising educational levels, although there are considerable intra-regional variations, and some countries have not lived up to their potentials. Considering the prospect of the region as a whole, it seems fitting to call the coming century 'the age of Asia and the Pacific'.

In 1987, a group of researchers under the leadership of Professor Naohiro Ogawa of Nihon University began a three-year research project, 'Sources of Economic Dynamism in the Asian and Pacific Region: A Human Resource Approach', under the auspices of the Nihon University President's Grant for Specified Interdisciplinary Research. In 1989, an international symposium for specialists in this field was held as one of the ceremonial events of the centennial of the foundation of Nihon University. This volume, the product of these research endeavours, is a scholarly 'symposium' in its own right, seeking to shed new light on the economic dynamism in Asia and the Pacific from a human resource perspective.

I would like to thank all parties for their contributions to the success of this undertaking.

*Tokyo*  
*December 1991*

SHIGENORI KINOSHITA  
PRESIDENT  
NIHON UNIVERSITY

# Acknowledgements

THE editors wish to acknowledge the sustained support of Nihon University at all stages of the research project and conferences on which this publication is based. Without their vision this book would never have been published. Our contributors have been most co-operative in responding to deadlines and to requests for editorial amendments. The Cartography Unit in the Research School of Pacific Studies, Australian National University, prepared the diagrams. Finally, we wish to warmly thank Daphne Broers-Freeman, Publications Officer of the Demography Program, Research School of Social Sciences, Australian National University, for her invaluable editorial and administrative assistance in bringing the manuscript to publication standard.

*Tokyo, Canberra, and Cambridge*  NAOHIRO OGAWA
*December 1991*  GAVIN W. JONES
  JEFFREY G. WILLIAMSON

## Note

Throughout this volume, all references to dollars ($) are to US dollars, unless otherwise specified.

# Contents

| | |
|---|---|
| *Foreword* | *v* |
| *Acknowledgements* | *vii* |
| *Tables* | *xiii* |
| *Figures* | *xix* |
| *Notes on Contributors* | *xxi* |

**1 Introduction**    1
Naohiro Ogawa, Gavin W. Jones, and Jeffrey G. Williamson

| | |
|---|---|
| An Overview | 1 |
| Links to the New Endogenous Growth Theories | 3 |
| Increased Diversities in the Demographic Transition in Asia | 5 |
| Human Capital Deepening along the Asia–Pacific Rim | 7 |
| Some Unanswered Questions | 11 |

**PART I POPULATION CHANGE, HUMAN RESOURCE DEVELOPMENT, AND ECONOMIC TRENDS: AN OVERVIEW**    19

**2 Demographic Change and Human Resource Development in the Asia–Pacific Region: Trends of the 1960s to 1980s and Future Prospects**    21
Naohiro Ogawa and Noriko O. Tsuya

| | |
|---|---|
| Introduction | 21 |
| Demographic Change in the Asia–Pacific Region: Trends and Prospects | 23 |
| Interrelations between Demographic Changes and Socio-economic Factors | 49 |
| Subregional Differences in the Role of Human Resources in Asian Economic Growth | 54 |
| Conclusion | 64 |

## 3 Development Trends: A Comparative Analysis of the Asian Experience — 66
Burnham O. Campbell

The Long-run Structural Perspective — 66
Background: The World Scene in the 1980s — 81
Indices of Performance in the 1980s — 83
Comparative Economic Policies — 98
Future Prospects and Concerns — 113
Conclusion — 123

### PART II HUMAN CAPITAL DEEPENING AND CHANGING LABOUR MARKETS — 127

## 4 Human Capital Deepening, Inequality, and Demographic Events along the Asia–Pacific Rim — 129
Jeffrey G. Williamson

Sources of Growth along the Asia–Pacific Rim — 129
Age Distributions, Dependency Rates, and Accumulation Responses — 132
Mortality, Life Expectancy, and Human Capital Responses — 139
The Inequality Connection — 141
A Brief Glance at Some Historical Experience with Schooling — 147
Schooling, Inequality, Dependency Rates, and Culture — 152
A Concluding Remark — 158

## 5 Economic Growth Performance of Indonesia, the Philippines, and Thailand: The Human Resource Dimension — 159
Ernesto M. Pernia

Introduction — 159
Macroeconomic Performance — 160
The Human Resource Dimension — 165
Cross-country Analysis — 170
Conclusion — 173

## 6 The Feminization of Labour in the Asia–Pacific Rim Countries: From Contributing to Economic Dynamism to Bearing the Brunt of Structural Adjustments — 175
Lin Lean Lim

Introduction — 175
Trends in Female Labour Force Participation — 175
The Supply Responses of Women — 193
Growing Labour Feminization and Growing Vulnerability — 201
The Policy Implications — 207

## CONTENTS

| | | |
|---|---|---|
| 7 | **Labour Force Developments and Emerging Human Resource Policies in Japan**<br>Kenichi Furuya and Robert L. Clark | *210* |
| | Introduction | *210* |
| | Education and the Quality of the Labour Force | *210* |
| | Ageing of the Labour Force | *214* |
| | Labour Force Composition | *217* |
| | Employment Contracts and Compensation Policy | *222* |
| | Conclusion | *224* |
| | **PART III  EDUCATION IN DEVELOPMENT: CASE-STUDIES** | *227* |
| 8 | **Dilemmas in Expanding Education for Faster Economic Growth: Indonesia, Malaysia, and Thailand**<br>Gavin W. Jones | *229* |
| | Introduction | *229* |
| | Trends in Labour Supply, Employment, and Education from the 1970s to 1990s | *229* |
| | What Is the Appropriate Rate of Expansion of Secondary and Higher Education? | *237* |
| | Likely Future Trends and Their Implications: Indonesia | *243* |
| | Conclusion | *254* |
| 9 | **Demographic Change, Household Resources, and Schooling Decisions**<br>Andrew Mason | *259* |
| | Introduction | *259* |
| | Household Time | *262* |
| | Educational Expenditure | *273* |
| | School Enrolment | *277* |
| | Conclusion | *280* |
| 10 | **Education, Earnings, and the Self-employment Choice: A Study of the Male Chinese in Peninsular Malaysia**<br>David Demery and Andrew Chesher | *283* |
| | Introduction | *283* |
| | A Model of Employment Choice | *284* |
| | A Model of Earnings | *286* |
| | Previous Studies | *287* |
| | EPU–DOS Household Income Survey | *288* |
| | Estimation | *294* |
| | Results | *297* |
| | Summary | *309* |

## PART IV HEALTH AND AGEING — 311

**11 Socio-economic Development, Child Health Care, and Infant Mortality Change in Thailand** — 313
Noriko O. Tsuya, Naohiro Ogawa, Napaporn Chayovan, and Siriwan Siriboon

Introduction — 313
Data and Methodology — 315
Trends of Infant and Child Mortality Levels, 1972–1987 — 317
Changes in Indices of Economic Development and Health Expenditures — 321
Differentials of Infant and Child Mortality — 322
Logit Analysis of Changes in Demographic and Socio-economic Covariates of Infant Mortality — 324
Logit Analysis of Demographic, Socio-economic, and Health Care Determinants of Infant Mortality — 338
Conclusions and Implications — 343

**12 Health Status of the Elderly and Their Labour Force Participation in the Developing Countries along the Asia–Pacific Rim** — 349
Naohiro Ogawa, Noriko O. Tsuya, Malinee Wongsith, and Ehn-Hyun Choe

Introduction — 349
The Elderly in the Asia–Pacific Region: Demographic Profile and Socio-economic Status — 351
Labour Force Participation and Health Status of the Aged: A Micro-level Analysis — 358
Conclusion — 370

**13 Summary and Synthesis: Towards a Model of the Asia–Pacific Rim Success Story and the Role of Human Resources** — 373
Warren C. Robinson

The Individual Contributions — 373
Conclusion: Next Steps in Research — 386

*Bibliography* — 388
*Index* — 410

# Tables

| | | |
|---|---|---|
| 2.1 | Index of Demographic Transition for Selected Countries in Asia and the Pacific, 1960/5–1985/90 | 27 |
| 2.2 | Index of Demographic Transition for Selected Countries in Asia and the Pacific, 1990/5–2020/5 | 29 |
| 2.3 | Total Fertility Rates for Selected Countries in Asia and the Pacific, 1960/5–1985/90 | 31 |
| 2.4 | Life Expectancy at Birth for Selected Countries in Asia and the Pacific, 1960/5–1985/90 | 35 |
| 2.5 | Levels of Urbanization for Selected Countries in Asia and the Pacific, 1960–1990 | 38 |
| 2.6 | Age Structural Changes for Selected Countries in Asia and the Pacific, 1960, 1990, and 2025 | 42 |
| 2.7 | Annual Growth Rates of Labour Force Aged 20–29 by Sex for Selected Countries in Asia, 1985–2025 | 48 |
| 2.8 | GNP Per Capita at Market Prices for Selected Countries in Asia and the Pacific, 1960–1985 | 49 |
| 2.9 | Primary School Enrolment Ratios for Selected Countries in Asia and the Pacific, 1960–1985 | 50 |
| 2.10 | Secondary School Enrolment Ratios for Selected Countries in Asia and the Pacific, 1960–1985 | 51 |
| 2.11 | Female Labour Force Participation Rates for Selected Countries in Asia and the Pacific, 1960–1985 | 52 |
| 2.12 | Proportion of Labour Force in Agriculture for Selected Countries in Asia and the Pacific, 1960–1985 | 53 |
| 2.13 | Estimated Degree of Association between Selected Socio-demographic Variables and GNP Per Capita, 1960–1985 | 54 |
| 2.14 | Increase of National Income, Labour Force, Physical Capital, and Educational Capital in Japan, 1905–1960 | 57 |
| 3.1 | Per Capita Income Comparisons, 1960–1987 | 67 |
| 3.2 | Structural Changes in Output, 1965 and 1987 | 70 |
| 3.3 | Structure of Exports, 1982 | 72 |
| 3.4 | Educational Effort (Enrolment Ratios), 1965 and 1986 | 74 |
| 3.5 | Capital–Labour and Productivity Ratios, 1960–1987 | 77 |
| 3.6 | Demographic Developments, 1950–1990 | 80 |

| | | |
|---|---|---|
| 3.7 | Real Growth Rates, 1977–1989 | *84* |
| 3.8 | Export Performance, 1975–1988 | *86* |
| 3.9 | Resource Mobilization, 1975–1988 | *90* |
| 3.10 | Debt Indicators, 1975–1988 | *93* |
| 3.11 | Consumer Price Index (CPI) Inflation Rates, 1972–1989 | *95* |
| 3.12 | Monetary Deepening (M2/GNP), 1965–1988 | *97* |
| 3.13 | Government and Fiscal Policy, 1977–1988 | *100* |
| 3.14 | Monetary Policy, 1977–1988 | *105* |
| 3.15 | Real Interest Rates, 1982–1988 | *107* |
| 3.16 | Exchange Rate Policy, 1980–1989 | *110* |
| 3.17 | Future Demographic Developments, 1990–2025 | *117* |
| 4.1 | Sustainable and Transitional Components of Japan's Growth According to Denison and Chung | *130* |
| 4.2 | Past, Present, and Future Dependency Rates along the Asia–Pacific Rim | *133* |
| 4.3 | Exploring the Dependency–Labour Participation Rate Impact on Growth along the Asia–Pacific Rim | *134* |
| 4.4 | Exploring the Dependency Rate–Savings Rate Connection along the Asia–Pacific Rim | *136* |
| 4.5 | Life Expectancy at Birth along the Asia–Pacific Rim, 1965 and 1985 | *139* |
| 4.6 | The Kuznets Curve and the Virtuous Asians | *143* |
| 4.7 | Inequality and Growth: Which Drives Which? | *145* |
| 4.8 | Growth in Educational Enrolment by School Level and Countries by Income Class, 1960–1981 | *148* |
| 4.9 | Has East Asia Always Invested More in Schooling? Twentieth-century Secondary School Enrolment Ratio | *150* |
| 4.10 | Estimates of Secondary School Expenditure and Components, with the Price of Teachers Exogenous: 35 Countries, 1960–1980 | *154* |
| 4.11 | The Determinants of Secondary School Enrolment and Expenditure with Regional Dummies: 35 Countries, 1960–1980 | *157* |
| 4.12 | Why Were Commitments to Secondary Education So Different in South Korea and Brazil in the Early 1970s? | *157* |
| 5.1 | GNP Per Capita | *161* |
| 5.2 | Real GDP Growth Rates | *161* |
| 5.3 | Sectoral Distribution of GDP | *162* |
| 5.4 | Sectoral Distribution of Labour Force | *163* |
| 5.5 | Adult Literacy Rates and Gross Enrolment Ratios | *166* |
| 5.6 | Health, Nutrition, and Fertility Indicators | *168* |
| 6.1 | GNP Per Capita and GDP Growth Rates in Selected Asia–Pacific Countries | *176* |
| 6.2 | Labour Force Participation Rates: Male and Female | *177* |
| 6.3 | Relative Growth of Male and Female Employment in Manufacturing, Trade, and Services, 1970s | *178* |

| | | |
|---|---|---|
| 6.4 | Structure of the Economically Active Population by Major Occupational Groups and Sex, 1970 and 1980 | 180 |
| 6.5 | Unemployment Rates by Sex, 1975, 1980–1987 | 183 |
| 6.6 | Unemployment Rates by Sex and Age-group | 185 |
| 6.7 | Growth Indices of Male and Female Total Employment | 187 |
| 6.8 | Female Share of Paid Employment in Non-agricultural Employment and Average Annual Growth Rate of Female and Male Non-agricultural Employment, 1980–1986/7 | 188 |
| 6.9 | Female Share of Employment and New Job Creation in Manufacturing, Services, and Trade, Restaurants and Hotels, 1980–1986/7 | 189 |
| 6.10 | Female Share of Self-employment in Non-agriculture | 191 |
| 6.11 | Average Annual Rates of Net Rural Out-migration and Net Urban In-migration by Sex | 195 |
| 6.12 | Female Labour Force Participation Rates by Age-groups | 199 |
| 6.13 | Wage Rates and Earnings for Male and Female Manufacturing Workers, 1980 and 1985 | 202 |
| 7.1 | Distribution of Labour Force by Highest Level of Educational Attainment | 212 |
| 7.2 | Job Tenure by Sex and Firm Size | 213 |
| 7.3 | Labour Force Growth Rates | 214 |
| 7.4 | Ageing of the Japanese Labour Force | 215 |
| 7.5 | Age Distribution of Employed Persons | 216 |
| 7.6 | Labour Force Participation Rates | 218 |
| 7.7 | Male Labour Force Participation Rates: Selected Asian Countries | 218 |
| 7.8 | Labour Force Participation Rates for Men Aged 65 and Over: Selected Developed Countries | 219 |
| 7.9 | Female Labour Force Participation Rates: Selected Asian Countries | 219 |
| 7.10 | Distribution of Labour Force by Type of Worker | 220 |
| 7.11 | Annual Bonus Divided by Monthly Earnings | 223 |
| 7.12 | Proportion of Employees Who Are Part-time Workers | 223 |
| 7.13 | Mandatory Retirement Age by Size of Firm, 1989 | 224 |
| 8.1 | Indonesia: Index of Growth of Labour Force Age-groups, 1985–2000 | 230 |
| 8.2 | Indonesia, Thailand, and Malaysia: Change in Employment by Occupation, 1970–1985 | 232 |
| 8.3 | Trends in Mean Years of Schooling of the Labour Force | 236 |
| 8.4 | Proportion of Age-group Enrolled in Secondary and Higher Education: Comparison of ASEAN Countries with South Korea and Japan | 237 |
| 8.5 | Percentage Distribution of Occupations of Employed Population at Each Educational Level: Indonesia, Thailand, and Malaysia, 1985 | 238 |

| | | |
|---|---|---|
| 8.6 | Percentage Distribution of Educational Level of Employed Population in Each Occupation Group: Indonesia, Thailand, and Malaysia, 1985 | 240 |
| 8.7 | Summary Results of Educational Projections | 245 |
| 8.8 | Projection of Employment by Industry: Indonesia, 1985–2000 | 246 |
| 8.9 | Proportion of Employment in Professional, Managerial, and Clerical Occupations to Total Employment within Major Industries: Indonesia, Malaysia, and Australia | 247 |
| 8.10 | Shift–Share Analysis of Change in Employment in Occupational Groups: Indonesia, 1971–1985 | 248 |
| 8.11 | Projection of Employment by Occupation: Indonesia, 2000 | 250 |
| 8.12 | Trends in Absorption of Better Educated, 1985–2000, Assuming No Change in Industry–Occupation Matrix (that is, Assumption (1) in Table 8.11) or in Occupation–Education Matrix | 252 |
| 9.1 | Single Headship by Sex and Age-group among Selected Asian Countries | 266 |
| 9.2 | Labour Force Participation by South Korean Women, 1983 | 269 |
| 9.3 | Working Status of Employed South Korean Women, 1983 | 270 |
| 9.4 | Impact of Children on Per Capita Household Disposable Income | 271 |
| 9.5 | Expenditure on Education: Selected Results | 274 |
| 9.6 | Impact of Children on Educational Expenditure by Households | 275 |
| 9.7 | Impact of Children on School Enrolment: Thailand, 1981 | 278 |
| 9.8 | Impact of Children on School Enrolment: South Korea | 280 |
| 10.1 | Descriptive Statistics | 289 |
| 10.2 | Exogenous Variables: Descriptive Statistics for All Occupations | 298 |
| 10.3 | Exogenous Variables: Descriptive Statistics for Sales and Service Workers | 299 |
| 10.4 | OLS Earnings Regressions, Full Sample Dependent Variable: Log of Post-tax Annual Earnings | 300 |
| 10.5 | OLS Earnings Regressions, Paid Employed Dependent Variable: Log of Post-tax Annual Earnings | 301 |
| 10.6 | OLS Earnings Regressions, Self-employed Dependent Variable: Log of Post-tax Annual Earnings | 302 |
| 10.7 | OLS Earnings Regressions, Sales and Service Workers Dependent Variable: Log of Post-tax Annual Earnings | 303 |
| 10.8 | Maximum Likelihood Estimation: All Occupations | 305 |
| 10.9 | Maximum Likelihood Estimation, Sales and Service Workers: Reduced Form Results | 307 |

| | | |
|---|---|---:|
| 10.10 | Maximum Likelihood Estimation: Sales and Service Workers Structural Model | 308 |
| 10.11 | Predicted Probabilities of Self-employment | 309 |
| 11.1 | Life-table Estimates of Infant, Child, and Under-five Mortality per 1,000 Live Births in Thailand for Selected Time Periods | 317 |
| 11.2 | Cumulative Proportions Surviving at the Beginning of Interval ($l_x$): Births in Thailand during 1982–1987 and in Japan in 1955 and 1962 | 319 |
| 11.3 | GNP Per Capita and Indices of Health-related Government Expenditure Per Capita and Private Consumption Expenditure Per Capita at Constant (1972) Prices: Thailand, 1970–1984 | 321 |
| 11.4 | Life-table Estimates of Infant, Child, and Under-five Mortality by Selected Characteristics: Births during 1977–1987, Thailand | 323 |
| 11.5 | Definitions and Descriptive Statistics of Covariates Used in Logit Analysis of Infant Mortality: Births during 1970–1974, Thailand | 325 |
| 11.6 | Definitions and Descriptive Statistics of Covariates Used in Logit Analysis of Infant Mortality: Births during 1982–1986, Thailand | 326 |
| 11.7 | Estimated Coefficients and Standard Errors from Logit Analyses of Infant Mortality Utilizing the Model with Demographic and Socio-economic Covariates: Births during 1970–1974 and 1982–1986 in Thailand | 332 |
| 11.8 | Estimated Coefficients and Standard Errors from Logit Analyses of Infant Mortality Utilizing the Full Model: Births during 1982–1986 in Thailand | 334 |
| 12.1 | International Comparison of the Proportion of the Population Aged 65 and Over, 1985 | 351 |
| 12.2 | Familial Support Ratios for Selected Asian Countries, 1985 and 2025 | 353 |
| 12.3 | Labour Force Participation Rates for Males and Females Aged 60 and Over in Selected Countries, c.1980 | 355 |
| 12.4 | Labour Force Participation Rate of the Elderly by Age, Sex, Urban–Rural Residence, and Health Status: Thailand in 1986 and South Korea in 1988 | 359 |
| 12.5 | Logit Regressions Coefficients for Labour Force Participation of Old Persons Aged 60 and Over: Thailand, 1986 | 362 |
| 12.6 | Means and Standard Deviations of Explanatory Variables Introduced into the Logit Regressions | 363 |
| 12.7 | Profile of Computed Age-specific Labour Force Participation Rates for the Elderly in Thailand | 364 |
| 12.8 | Logit Regressions Coefficients for Labour Force | |

|  | Participation of Old Persons Aged 60 and Over: Thailand, 1986 | 366 |
|---|---|---|
| 12.9 | Means and Standard Deviations of Explanatory Variables Included in Male and Female Participation Equations | 367 |
| 12.10 | Logit Regressions Coefficients for Labour Force Participation of Old Males Aged 60 and Over: South Korea | 368 |
| 12.11 | Means and Standard Deviations of Explanatory Variables Introduced into the Participation Equation: South Korea | 369 |

# Figures

| | | |
|---|---|---|
| 2.1 | Observed Relationship between Average Annual Rate of Population Growth and GNP Per Capita Growth among 13 Selected Asian Developing Countries, 1965–1985 | 24 |
| 2.2 | Index of Demographic Transition for Four Subregions, 1960/5–1985/90 | 26 |
| 2.3 | Link between Demographic Transition and Agri-industrial Transition among 11 Selected Asian Countries, 1965–1985 | 28 |
| 2.4 | Index of Demographic Transition for Four Subregions, 1990/5–2020/5 | 28 |
| 2.5 | Observed Relationship between the Level of Urbanization and the Log of GNP Per Capita among Selected Countries in Asia and the Pacific, 1985–1990 | 39 |
| 4.1 | Actual, Transitional, and Sustainable Growth Rates in Japan, 1971–2001 | 131 |
| 4.2 | Why the Dependency Rate Effect Might Be Estimated as 'Weak' | 138 |
| 4.3 | Primary School Enrolment Rates: 1830–1975 | 149 |
| 4.4 | Japanese Secondary Enrolment Ratio: Secondary School Age 12–17 | 151 |
| 4.5 | Skill Investment Demand and Supply: The Uncertain Role of Inequality | 152 |
| 5.1 | Schooling and Economic Performance | 167 |
| 5.2 | Health and Economic Performance | 169 |
| 6.1 | Female Labour Force Participation Rate by Age in Selected Industrialized or Newly Industrializing Asian Economies, 1982 | 197 |
| 6.2 | Female Labour Force Participation Rate by Age in Selected South-East Asian Countries | 197 |
| 6.3 | Female Labour Force Participation Rate by Age in Selected South Asian Countries | 198 |
| 8.1 | Trends in Share of Professional, Managerial, and Clerical Employment Over Time: Selected Countries | 234 |

| | | |
|---|---|---|
| 8.2 | Share of Professional, Managerial, and Clerical Employment by Level of GNP Per Capita: Selected Countries | 235 |
| 8.3 | The Possible Effects of Overeducation in the Workplace | 256 |
| 9.1 | Mental Age, Birth Order, and Family Size | 260 |
| 9.2 | Average Household Size: Thailand | 263 |
| 9.3 | Adults per Child in Thai Households with Members Aged 0–4 | 264 |
| 9.4a | Children Living in Non-intact Households: Households Headed by Males | 267 |
| 9.4b | Children Living in Non-intact Households: Households Headed by Females | 268 |
| 9.5 | Adults per Child in Intact and Non-intact Households: Thailand | 268 |
| 9.6 | Percentage Decline in Per Capita Household Income: Impact of an Additional Child | 272 |
| 10.1 | Earnings–Age Profiles by Years of Education | 290 |
| 10.2 | Earnings–Age Profiles by Employment Type and Years of Education | 291 |
| 10.3 | Earnings–Age Profiles by Occupation and Years of Education | 292 |
| 10.4 | Earnings–Age Profiles by Occupation and Years of Education | 293 |
| 11.1 | Test of the Weibull Model: Infant and Child Mortality in Thailand, 1982–1987 | 320 |
| 12.1 | Proportion of the Population Aged 65 and Over Residing in Rural Areas in Selected Asian Countries in the Early 1980s | 354 |
| 13.1 | The Asia–Pacific Model of Successful Development | 382 |

# Notes on Contributors

BURNHAM O. CAMPBELL is Project Fellow, East–West Population Institute, East–West Center, Honolulu, Hawaii, United States.

NAPAPORN CHAYOVAN is Associate Professor, Institute of Population Studies, Chulalongkorn University, Bangkok, Thailand.

ANDREW CHESHER is Professor, Economics Department, University of Bristol, United Kingdom.

EHN-HYUN CHOE is Vice-President, Korea Institute for Health and Social Affairs, Seoul, Republic of Korea.

ROBERT L. CLARK is Professor and Interim Head, Division of Economics and Business, North Carolina State University, Raleigh, North Carolina, United States.

DAVID DEMERY is Senior Lecturer, Economics Department, University of Bristol, United Kingdom.

KENICHI FURUYA is Professor, College of Economics, Nihon University, Tokyo.

GAVIN W. JONES is Professor, Division of Demography and Sociology, Research School of Social Sciences, Australian National University, Canberra, Australia.

LIN LEAN LIM is Adviser on Women Population and Development, Labour and Population Team for Asia and the Pacific, ILO Regional Office for Asia and the Pacific, Bangkok, Thailand.

ANDREW MASON is Research Associate, East–West Population Institute, East–West Center, Honolulu, Hawaii, United States.

NAOHIRO OGAWA is Deputy Director, Population Research Institute, and Professor, College of Economics, Nihon University, Tokyo, Japan.

ERNESTO M. PERNIA is Economist, Asian Development Bank, Manila, the Philippines.

WARREN C. ROBINSON is Professor Emeritus, the Pennsylvania State University, University Park, Pennsylvania, United States.

SIRIWAN SIRIBOON is Researcher, Institute of Population Studies, Chulalongkorn University, Bangkok, Thailand.

NORIKO O. TSUYA is Associate Professor, Population Research Institute, Nihon University, Tokyo, Japan.

JEFFREY G. WILLIAMSON is Professor, Department of Economics, Harvard University, Massachusetts, United States.

MALINEE WONGSITH is Associate Professor, Institute of Population Studies, Chulalongkorn University, Bangkok, Thailand.

# 1
# Introduction

Naohiro Ogawa, Gavin W. Jones, and
Jeffrey G. Williamson

### An Overview

As most readers of this volume know, the market economies along the western rim of the Pacific Basin herein called the Asia–Pacific Rim have registered extremely rapid growth by any international standard. The growth has been fast when compared with that of post-World War II Latin America, South Asia, Africa, Europe, or North America, and fast even when compared with the pre-World War II economic histories of the Western industrial nations. A quarter of a century ago, hardly anyone would have predicted that Japan would be the world's largest manufacturer of automobiles in 1990, that South Korea would be a major centre of steel production and shipbuilding, that Taiwan and Malaysia would be leading exporters of semiconductors to world markets, or that Thailand would be a centre of dynamic growth in South-East Asia. If present trends continue, by the end of the twentieth century the Asia–Pacific Rim will produce more than one-fifth of the world's GNP, comparable in size with the share produced by Western Europe or North America. A vast change indeed since 1960 when the region produced only slightly more than one-tenth of the world's GNP, while North America was responsible for more than one-third. Part of this dramatic realignment of market size can, of course, be attributed to more rapid rates of population growth along the Rim, but mostly it can be attributed to per capita income improvement relative to the rest of the world.

This impressive growth performance certainly has not gone unnoticed by analysts and policymakers looking for lessons to apply to slower-growing regions and countries. America, long accustomed to the leadership role in the world economy, looks on with nervous envy and debates the sources of its lagging productivity growth, as living standards and productivity in Japan converge on those of the United States. The World Bank urges the rest of the Third World to mimic the export-oriented growth strategies which have been such an apparent success, first in South Korea and Taiwan, and now in Thailand and elsewhere south along the Rim.

The question continues to be much pondered: What have been the sources of this spectacular economic dynamism along the Asia–Pacific Rim? Growth theorists, economic historians, and development economists have yet to agree on the answers to this question—first raised in a different context by Adam Smith more than two centuries ago—but all seem to agree that the answers must be embedded somewhere in the following list of factors: (i) substantial investment in infrastructure; (ii) an efficient absorption of advanced technology; (iii) a stable political environment; and (iv) an impressive commitment to human capital formation. This volume stresses the last of these four factors, although it argues that they are closely interrelated.

It must be stated at the outset that human resource development along the Asia–Pacific Rim is intimately tied to population dynamics. As extensively discussed by Ogawa and Tsuya in Chapter 2 of this volume, the region has been undergoing a dramatic demographic revolution which parallels its spectacular economic growth. Although by 1990 almost 59 per cent of the world's population is located in Asia, population growth rates have been declining very rapidly in the past quarter century, especially in East Asia and parts of South-East Asia. These trends have had important implications for what is called human capital deepening.

The most obvious is that during the later stages of the demographic transition, the labour force continues to grow for some decades after fertility declines, causing the labour force participation rate to rise. These events contribute to development by enabling per capita income to rise as workers become a larger share of the population. Part of this effect is due to a favourable change in the age distribution, and part of it is due to the rise in married women's participation in labour markets as their time devoted to childrearing declines. In addition, households and nations are likely to find it easier to set aside resources for accumulation when the 'dependency burden' declines. A number of the latecomers along the Asia–Pacific Rim are now in the midst of these stages of the demographic transition when these economic advantages can have their most important impact. In contrast, Japan has entered a more mature demographic phase of ageing which has unfavourable implications for its future economic performance.

Although such forces have been and will continue for some time to be important, the impressive commitment to human resource development along the Rim cannot be explained solely by these transitional demographic connections. Other forces have been at work: even after adjusting for favourable demographic conditions, the Rim appears to maintain a higher commitment to human resource development than does most of the rest of the world. Thus, East Asia has higher levels of literacy and educational attainment, and invests more in both, than does Latin America, even after controlling for level of development.

Furthermore, this distinctive regional characteristic has had a long history. In the case of Japan, for example, approximately 45 per cent of the population was literate even before the Meiji Restoration in 1868. A compulsory educational system was established in 1872. Subsequently, primary school enrolment rose at an unprecedented rate—even when compared with nineteenth century industrializing nations—reaching 100 per cent in 40 years. This rapid increase in school enrolment contributed to widening and strengthening the human resource base which, in turn, facilitated the adaptation of advanced technologies borrowed from the West during the early industrial revolution in the late Meiji period. The story has been repeated during the twentieth century by Japan's followers along the Rim.

## Links to the New Endogenous Growth Theories

Four ideas emerge from the previous section which bear repeating since they have recently attracted the attention of growth theorists. First, there is a close connection between demographic dynamics, human capital deepening, and economic growth. Second, many of the countries along the Rim had a history of early commitment to human resource development prior to the post-1960 boom. The region has long been viewed as relatively scarce in natural resources and capital, but relatively abundant in human resources. Third, the heavy commitment to investment in human capital has involved active government intervention. Fourth, the same heavy commitment to investment in human capital has generated externalities, for example, human resource development along the Rim helps account for the rapid adaptation of imported technologies and thus rapid advance in productivity. Each of these ideas has served to motivate a resurgent interest in formal theories of growth.

A recent survey of the literature began with the statement that 'after more than a decade of quiescence, growth theory may once again be entering a period of ferment' (Romer, 1986). The old theory of economic growth in the 1960s assigned all steady state growth to exogenous factors: the rate of technological advance and population growth. The new theories endogenize one or both of these processes. Most relevant to this book, the new theories endogenize the rate of technological advance through human capital accumulation, most notably through formal schooling or through informal skill development on-the-job.

While empirical practitioners reading these pages might tend to be impatient with such a simplification, the new endogenous theories of growth do have some powerful implications which might help make some sense out of the economic performances along the Rim since about 1960. The crux of the matter is as follows: the old growth models of the 1960s assumed constant returns to scale to capital and labour jointly, but decreasing returns to either considered separately. Thus, rapid capital accumulation cannot produce rapid output growth for very long in such models. Decreasing returns could be offset in such models, of course, if exogenous technological change was allowed to grow at increasing rates, but such a device would hardly offer any real explanation for the prolonged economic boom along the Rim. The new theories offer an endogenous explanation by including human capital in the production function, either as an explicit factor of production, or indirectly as a process of learning new technologies, or both. A frequent attribute of the new theories is a role for public intervention when human capital formation generates externalities.

Arrow (1962) started the thinking on these issues in terms of learning-by-doing, and the important issues here are ones of excludability and rivalry. Any input, like skilled labour, is rivalrous if when used at one workplace it cannot be used at another. The important insight offered by Arrow, and extended by Romer, is to stress that human capital does not involve only the accumulation of rivalrous skills. Non-rivalrous forms of human capital also exist, for example, basic scientific knowledge, blueprints, designs, and modes of efficient production. Such forms of human capital can be used over and over at a multiplicity of sites with no limit on duplication. Thus, in the learning-by-doing models the accumulation of human capital generates externalities, having its influence on the level of technology.

If some human capital inputs are non-rivalrous, and may be duplicated easily, how can the full social return to their accumulation be captured by private agents, either (to take education as an example) through formal schooling by individuals or through on-the-job worker training by firms? One way to ensure equality between private and social returns is by excluding duplication by patents, restrictions on migration of workers with skills, or by monopoly. But such 'solutions', certainly common to many nations, suppress the rate of growth. Another way is through public intervention since human capital in such models has all the attributes of public goods. Public intervention may take place directly by subsidizing the supply of human capital, or it may take place indirectly by twisting the terms of trade to favour the expansion of those sectors in which learning-by-doing is most promising (Krugman, 1987; Lucas, 1988).

All of these new theories of endogenous growth stress that the rate of physical capital accumulation is an increasing function of the level of human capital. Furthermore, Uzawa (1965) and, more recently, Lucas (1988) have explored the implications of models where the rate of human capital accumulation is an increasing function of the level of human capital. An important variant on this kind of thinking is offered by Azariadis and Drazen (1990) who developed a model of threshold externalities. Educational investment has permanent effects on long-run growth potential since it influences the stock of available knowledge which can, in fact, be passed on to the next generation. However, there is likely to be a threshold of human capital: below it an 'underdevelopment trap' confines the economy to slow growth; above it, explosive growth is possible. Thus, for a given level of GNP, large differences in initial human capital endowments from the historical past imply very different current growth performance, that is, growth is dependent on the mechanisms by which the present situation was reached and history matters.

Empirical support for the new endogenous theories of growth appears to be quite favourable. For example, Azariadis and Drazen (1990) find that no country has grown fast in the post-World War II decades without high initial levels of human capital (proxied by literacy) relative to initial GNP. Those countries starting with a poor human capital endowment remained poor, while those countries with a favourable human capital endowment converged on the leaders. Baumol et al. (1989: Chap. 9) find the same. Barro (1991) also finds that when initial levels of human capital per capita are held constant, there is an inverse correlation between initial GNP and subsequent growth (that is, convergence). However, countries with higher initial human capital endowments have higher investment to GNP ratios. Thus, if human to physical capital ratios are initially high, a country's subsequent economic performance will feature high rates of physical capital investment and rapid per capita income growth. Indeed, Barro (1991: 417–18) shows these results to be especially true of countries along the Rim like South Korea and Japan, whose growth rates were raised by as much as 1.5 per cent per annum due to above average schooling levels in 1960.

Thus, the new theories of endogenous growth seem to offer strong motivation for the focus of this volume; human resource development made an important contribution to the spectacular growth observed along the Rim over the 1960s to 1980s, and it will make an important contribution in the 1990s and beyond as well.

## Increased Diversities in the Demographic Transition in Asia

The peak of population growth in Asia was recorded during the second half of the 1960s. At the regional level, however, there have been substantial differences in the tempo of reduction of population growth rates. In the late 1960s, Asia's three subregions had comparable annual population growth rates: 2.42 per cent in East Asia, 2.52 per cent in South-East Asia, and 2.40 per cent in South Asia. Two decades later, the average annual population growth rates were 1.31, 1.92, and 2.34 per cent, respectively. What accounted for these increased regional differences in the tempo of changes in the population growth rates in Asia?

As regards fertility, the magnitude and speed of fertility transition and their underlying mechanisms in many parts of Asia since the 1960s have been truly unique. It is a familiar theme in the population and development literature that economic development is, in general, inversely associated with the level of fertility. This generalization is based to a large extent on Western experience. However, evidence from many Asian countries indicates that relatively small subsets of developmental changes are enough to bring down fertility, and that a deliberately organized social effort to control fertility can have a significant influence on fertility reduction. Indeed, many developing countries in Asia have been heavily utilizing a host of modern contraceptive methods imported from advanced nations.

It should be stressed, however, that these mechanisms have varied markedly from region to region as well as from country to country. In East Asia, the demographically successful region, Japan is the forerunner of fertility transition. Japan managed to reduce its fertility level with unprecedented rapidity immediately after World War II. The other countries in East Asia such as Hong Kong and China also experienced comparable fertility declines, although at different time periods. In South-East Asia, Singapore is a showcase of success, cutting its fertility by half in one decade between the mid-1960s and the mid-1970s. Thailand, Indonesia, and Malaysia have been experiencing a substantial fertility decline since the 1960s. In sharp contrast to these countries in East and South-East Asia, fertility in all the countries in South Asia, except for Sri Lanka and some parts of India, shows no clear sign of the onset of fertility transition.

Mortality improvements usually take place before fertility reduction, but significant mortality decline occurred without accompanying substantial development in many parts of Asia. As a consequence of the spread of imported modern public health and medical technologies, the reduction in mortality has generally been rapid in developing Asia.

All the countries in East Asia and Singapore in South-East Asia have virtually completed their mortality transition. Although Thailand, the Philippines, and Malaysia had comparable levels of life expectancy at birth in the early 1960s, in the mid-1980s Malaysia has virtually reached the final stage of its mortality transition. On the other hand, the Philippines is lagging, while Thailand is quickly approaching the final stage. Although Indonesia is one of the last runners in mortality transition among the South-East Asian nations, its life expectancy has been improving at a pace similar to Malaysia and Thailand. By comparison, most of the countries in South Asia have low levels of life expectancy of around 50 years, indicating the necessity for more effective implementation of public health measures and better utilization of medical services, in addition to the general improvement in the standard of living through socio-economic development.

As a result of both pronounced fertility declines and remarkable mortality improvements among a number of countries along the Asia–Pacific Rim, the age composition of each of these nations has been changing markedly in recent years. The total dependency ratio has fallen substantially in almost all the countries in the region under review. From 1960 to 1990, Singapore had the largest reduction in its total dependency ratio (43 percentage points) among all the countries along the western rim of the Pacific Basin. Singapore is followed by South Korea (37 percentage points), Hong Kong (33 percentage points), Thailand (33 percentage points), and Malaysia (29 percentage points). All of these nations have already attained the status of NIEs or are approaching it rapidly. Moreover, Singapore's dependency ratio is currently the lowest among all the countries in Asia, followed by Japan, Hong Kong, South Korea, and China.

## Human Capital Deepening along the Asia–Pacific Rim

The economic–demographic literature considers several population-sensitive savings specifications (Kelley, 1988a). In the life cycle model, for instance, savings are affected by the need to finance the maintenance of children and retirement. In the income-distribution model, population growth can increase savings if the effect of a lower capital–labour ratio is to shift income to recipients of non-labour income, who are assumed to have a higher propensity to save. Apart from these theoretical models, the age-dependency model has been widely cited in the literature on population–savings rate linkages. The age-dependency linkage recognizes that a birth averted contributes to a decrease in consumption and an increase in savings, which in turn leads to capital formation. In view of the fact that both fast declines of the dependency ratio and rapid economic growth performance have occurred jointly in a number of the countries along the Rim, one can expect that the former has stimulated the latter through accumulation of savings and capital deepening in these countries.

During the 1970s and 1980s, a variety of econometric studies have estimated the impact of dependency rates on savings. On the basis of these estimated results, it can be easily conceived that the savings rate has increased strikingly as a consequence of the dramatic decline in the dependency ratio in each of these countries along the Rim.

The declines in total dependency rates induced primarily by reduced fertility have led not only to the rapid growth of physical capital per worker but also to human capital deepening in a number of countries along the Asia–Pacific Rim. The reduced total dependency ratio has facilitated a rise in spending on education at both government and household levels. Various econometric analyses contained in this volume provide substantial evidence for the validity of this dependency–education linkage. Williamson's Chapter 4, for instance, has examined cross-sectional data for 35 developing nations (including some Asian countries) and has shown that the reduction of total dependency contributed to a pronounced increase in public spending per secondary school student. The lower total dependency ratios resulted in very little increase in the secondary school enrolment ratios; fertility reduction, then, has induced an improvement in the quality of secondary school education on a per capita basis, but has not led to an expansion of enrolment. In addition to these macro-level results, a few micro level studies in Thailand and South Korea, reported in Chapter 9 by Mason, have also produced comparable results, thus providing additional support for the validity of the dependency–education connection in the countries along the Asia–Pacific Rim.

In addition to the human capital deepening effect resulting from reduced fertility, all the countries along the Rim with spectacular growth performance have seen a secular expansion of school enrolment over the last several decades. Japan, the Philippines, Thailand, and South Korea all underwent far steeper increases in their commitment to educational investment, compared with all the Western industrialized nations in the nineteenth century and almost all of the contemporary developing countries in Latin America and Africa. As discussed in Chapter 4 by Williamson, both historical and cultural factors may account for the regional differences in the magnitude of the strong commitment to schooling. The equality–schooling connection provides a plausible explanation for high investments in secondary schooling; income distribution in the countries along the Rim has been more equal than that in the other developing regions, and more egalitarian societies have had greater resources available for making a stronger commitment to education.

Pernia's Chapter 5, a cross-sectional analysis based upon data gathered from 12 developing nations in Asia, indicates a positive relationship between the mean number of years of schooling per worker and the growth rate of GNP per capita. The positive relationship is more pronounced among countries such as Hong Kong, Taiwan, South Korea, Malaysia, and Singapore, where the mean years of schooling of their workers imply secondary education or higher.

The foregoing discussion indicates that although it is difficult to determine to what extent the rapid expansion of educational systems has contributed to rapid economic growth, human resource development through schooling has greatly facilitated impressive growth performance in various economies along the Rim. In some of these countries, there have been an increasing number of imbalances between demand and supply in the labour market. In Thailand, for instance, double digit growth has been under way since the late 1980s and, as a consequence, the labour market at the middle level, particularly for those with secondary education, is expected to become very tight in the 1990s. While the demand for middle-level workers is projected to increase rapidly, the supply of these workers is expected to actually slow down during the period of the Seventh Development Plan (1992–6). As pointed out in Chapter 8 by Jones in this volume, Thailand has a very low gross enrolment ratio at the secondary level. Currently in 1990, the gross secondary enrolment ratio in Thailand is only about 30 per cent—a substantial wastage of educational potential from the almost universal enrolment at the primary level. The ratio in Thailand is much lower than those of other countries in the region: South Korea (94 per cent), Taiwan (91 per cent), Singapore (71 per cent), the Philippines (68 per cent), Malaysia (53 per cent), and Indonesia (39 per cent). Although Thailand has the potential to join the group of Asian NIEs in the 1990s, the wages of the middle-level workers are expected to rise rapidly, which will, in turn, erode the international competitiveness of Thai industries and services.

Jones's projection-based analysis draws upon data from Indonesia, Malaysia, and Thailand to shed light upon issues regarding the employment of the better educated. In Indonesia, over the 1985–2000 period, the growth of positions traditionally filled by the better educated, and of professional, managerial, and clerical employment in particular, is unlikely to cover the entire better educated segment of the labour force, with the result that there will be a 'pushdown' effect on the occupational distribution of the better educated. The same is likely to be true of Malaysia and Thailand as well.

These issues and problems with regard to the labour market reflect that crucial decisions still remain about appropriate rates of educational expansion and appropriate educational structures. The points of consensus emerging from a comparative study of a large number of rates-of-returns studies for various countries indicate that rates of returns tend to decline with increasing level of education (Psacharopoulos, 1973, 1985). However, Demery and Chesher in Chapter 10, using a highly sophisticated statistical tool, show that for Chinese males in Peninsular Malaysia, the returns to schooling rise with the level of schooling and are highest for the tertiary level.

Evidently, the rapid declines of fertility in the Asia–Pacific Rim countries contributed to the rapid increase in the proportion of women participating in the labour force, particularly as paid employees. Although female work-force participation in the region is not high compared with Europe or America, it is certainly higher than in South Asia, and rising faster; this, no doubt, helps to explain the stronger growth performance in East than in South Asia. In Japan, the proportion of married women aged 15–54 working as paid employees rose from 13 per cent in 1963 to 40 per cent in 1989. This rise has been the most rapid in the recorded experience of advanced nations. In spite of this dramatic change in female labour force participation, the status of Japanese female workers is notoriously low. A substantial proportion of these workers are marginal employees who are sensitively affected by short-run economic fluctuations as well as economic restructuring triggered by a series of oil crises and the fast appreciation of the yen against the world's major currencies.

Since the 1960s, female workers in developing Asia have been confronted with similar problems. While female participation contributed not only to the elastic labour supply at low cost but also the unique human resource qualities that fuelled the economic spurt of the countries along the Rim in the 1960s and 1970s, these women suffered from a wide range of problems arising from the economic reversal and structural adjustments of the 1980s. Adjustment processes in the Asia–Pacific Rim countries have been sex-asymmetric, in so far as they have subjected women more than men to greater economic and social vulnerability even as there has been increasing feminization of labour. Lim's Chapter 6 has attempted to approach these women-related issues in relation to three economic phases: (i) the boom years of the 1960s and 1970s, (ii) the world recession and debt crisis of the early 1980s, and (iii) the structural adjustments since.

In addition to women, the following two important segments of a population constitute the core of the vulnerable group who often miss the fruits of rapid economic development: children and the elderly. In some of the countries along the Rim, a considerable proportion of the labour force consists of school age children, and child labour is still a serious social issue. Moreover, children's productive and old-age security utilities are still crucial motives for a married couple to give birth to a large number of children in most Asian societies. Both infant and child mortality rates, though they have been on a downward trend in virtually all the nations along the Rim, are still high enough to imply a considerable wastage of human resources and therefore raise important policy issues for development planners. In the case of Indonesia, for example, various health policy measures have been incorporated in its development plan (Repelita V for 1989/90–1994/5) so as to lower infant mortality from 58.0 to 49.8 per 1,000 live births by the end of the plan period. A study on changing infant mortality in Thailand, which has been reported in Chapter 11 by Tsuya et al., shows that socio-economic development factors including the increased availability of medical care services play a major role in reducing the incidence of infant deaths.

As a consequence of their rapid fertility declines since the 1960s and mortality improvements since the early post-war years, several countries along the Rim have recently become increasingly aware of a wide range of ageing problems, and their ageing processes are expected to accelerate in the 1990s and beyond. Numerous adjustments will therefore be required at both societal and familial levels in these countries. At a macro-level, for instance, the pattern of public investment will be shifted from educational investment to health investment; there will be a change in overall labour force participation rates and in employment practices including the wage system. At an individual level, each elderly person has fewer children whom he or she can depend upon for old-age security; elderly people may need to modify their retirement plans.

In Chapter 7, Furuya and Clark discuss a variety of problems related to the utilization of elderly workers in the process of rapid economic restructuring in contemporary Japan, where the speed of population ageing is unprecedentedly fast. In the 1960s and 1970s, the Japanese economy enjoyed the entrance into the labour force of large cohorts who had relatively low wages, brought the latest training from the education system, and were more flexible in their job assignments. In the 1980s and 1990s, however, Japanese firms have been facing the prospect of dealing with relatively small entry-level cohorts and a large number of older, relatively highly priced workers. Furuya and Clark describe a series of policy responses and institutional changes made by both public and private sectors in order to adjust to an ageing labour force. These Japanese experiences are likely to provide a useful base for facilitating the formulation of effective ageing policies and programmes in other Asia–Pacific Rim countries in the 1990s and beyond.

In most of the developing countries along the Rim, the relative share of social security expenditure in GDP is still low, and a substantial proportion of the elderly are engaged in productive activities in order to earn income for themselves and their families. In a society where public income support is rarely provided for the elderly, the deterioration of their health conditions is often the onset of their retirement life. Ogawa et al. in Chapter 12 in this volume use two micro-level data sets gathered from South Korea and Thailand to analyse the relationship between the health status of the elderly and their labour force participation. Their estimated results show that the positive impact of health improvements upon participation is particularly strong in the case of elderly men in both countries. Because these countries are likely to undergo further improvements of mortality and morbidity at older ages in the years to come, this positive effect will be increasingly important with the passage of time.

In recent years, international labour migration has been an increasingly important element of human resource development and labour market adjustments in the Asia–Pacific region. In the 1970s, there were massive international labour flows from Asia to the Middle East. As a consequence of slower economic growth in the oil-exporting countries in the 1980s, however, labour migration from Asia to the Middle East has become increasingly difficult. Within Asia, there have been various flows of international labour migration, a well-known case being flows within the ASEAN region. Besides these international migratory movements, there has been a considerable flow of labour from developing Asia to Japan, Taiwan, and Hong Kong. Although no chapter in this volume has presented a detailed analysis of these new international migratory flows, Chapter 2 by Ogawa and Tsuya discusses labour migration from developing countries in Asia to Japan, and Chapter 6 by Lim touches upon various flows of female labour migration among the Asia–Pacific Rim countries.

## Some Unanswered Questions

As noted earlier, economic growth in the East Asian region can plausibly be explained by an emphasis on initial human capital endowments and more recent investments in human resources. A brief recapitulation of some of the trends in the NIEs from this perspective is in order. In the initial phase of growth, characterized by abundant labour and low wages, there were no market distortions which raised real wages in the modern sector above the supply price of labour. A steady growth in labour productivity in agriculture allowed a rapid transfer of labour out of agriculture and into the growing manufacturing sector. During this phase, labour productivity rose faster than real wages, thus permitting a rising rate of domestic savings and investment in the modern sector. Even when labour markets tightened, the rise in real wages was delayed, no doubt, partly because of the absence of strong and independent trade unions. Yet productivity gains proceeded apace and there was substantial upgrading in the educational and skill level of the labour force. The lag of wages behind productivity, despite its inequitable effects in holding down the rise in real incomes of workers, did have the advantage of raising the absorption of labour in the modern sector and minimizing unemployment and underemployment, resulting in a reasonably equitable pattern of growth.

Open economic policies and strategies of export-led industrialization were in conformity with underlying factor endowments and resulted in a rapid growth in the demand for labour. Government policy also contributed to the rise in the educational levels of the work-force. Labour was allocated to the more rapidly growing sectors, rather than into heavily protected industries, rent-seeking activities, or inefficient and low-productivity public sector activities, as it was in the overextended public sectors in many other developing countries.

The chapters to follow leave little doubt that human resource development has played a major role in the remarkable post-war economic development of the Asia–Pacific Rim. Four aspects of human resources which appear to have been crucial in the steady and rapid increase in labour productivity in East Asian development are (i) a disciplined and hard-working labour force, (ii) a high level of entrepreneurship, (iii) a deepening of human capital through education and training, and (iv) a rising participation rate for women. But many questions remain. Is the wide range of development performance in the region readily explained by differences in human resource development? Which aspects of human resource development have been crucial in the strong development performance? What is the relative importance of initial (pre- and early post-war) endowment of human resources on the one hand, and the speed of developing such resources since 1950 or 1960, on the other?

There is a danger of exaggerating the importance of human resources in development, just as there is in the case of any factor invoked to explain such a complex and far-reaching process. One statement that might meet with general acceptance is that human resource development is a necessary but not sufficient prerequisite for rapid economic development. However, the first half of the statement might meet with some dissent as can be expected. Windfall gains from rising oil prices have enabled some countries to achieve steep per capita income growth without much evidence of rapid gains in education, largely because international labour migration has helped fill the skill gaps in the workforce. Nutrition and health do almost inevitably improve in such a situation, but as a consequence rather than an initial cause of real income growth.

A number of the most successful East Asian countries, land-scarce and resource-poor as they were, were almost forced to rely on the accumulation of physical and human capital in order to succeed. But such a need does not always elicit the appropriate response, as some other land- and resource-scarce countries amply demonstrate. One of the key questions to be answered is why so many of the countries in the region did make an early commitment to major investments in human capital, thus helping to establish the preconditions for the rapid growth that followed.

There have been many efforts to look for commonalities between countries that will help explain the East Asian growth performance. Such commonalities can be at different levels: for example, factor endowments, demographic structure, cultural traits, forms of government, or macroeconomic development strategies. Is human resource development 'just another' of these possible explanatory factors, or is it integrally linked with some of the others, thus potentially playing a pivotal role?

The problem with the search for commonalities is that there are many exceptions. A few examples will suffice. The four Asian 'tigers'—South Korea, Taiwan, Hong Kong, and Singapore—all developed as resource-poor economies, for which the standard Hecksher-Ohlin prescription of developing labour-intensive activities, and then moving up the ladder of comparative advantage with capital accumulation was obviously appropriate. Raising the productivity of human resources is a key strategy in such labour-abundant economies. But the two front runners in the race to join the NIEs—Malaysia and Thailand—have different resource endowments and therefore different strategies may be appropriate (Lal and Myint, forthcoming).

This book has little to say about forms of government that are conducive to development, although it is frequently argued that a certain type of regime combined with some degree of executive and bureaucratic capacity is more likely than others to succeed in inducing economic growth. Many typologies have been developed to explore the relative success of different polities. Kim (1988) differentiates between polyarchy–democratic, socialist, and two kinds of authoritarian regime—civil and military. A 1990 World Bank-sponsored study on development differentiates between two kinds of autonomous polities (platonic and predatory) and two kinds of factional polities (oligarchic and democratic) (Lal and Myint, forthcoming). Dick (1974) found that in Asia, authoritarian governments performed slightly better than competitive ones, but not nearly as well as semi-competitive governments. Moreover, the authoritarian regimes performed better than the competitive ones only in countries with below-the-median GDP per capita.

If the concept of 'development' were expanded to incorporate aspects of political and social justice, the relative performance of the different kinds of regime would change. It may also be the case that at different stages of human resource development in a country, different kinds of political organization are optimal for development. Demands for greater democracy can be observed in many societies with swelling ranks of educated young people, but the extent of causality is difficult to determine.

Have policy or cultural traits been the more important reason for the observed strong improvements in labour productivity along the Pacific Rim? It has been commonplace to stress the Confucian ethic as an important ingredient of East Asian economic success, through its influence on work ethics, respect for authority, entrepreneurship, and valuation of education. Oshima (1988) notes that East Asian countries have longer working hours per week than the rest of Asia, and that these longer working hours have been maintained even as incomes rise. However, Belassa (1988), in his attack on cultural and social explanations for East Asian economic success as 'ex post hoccery', notes that as recently as the 1950s and 1960s the Confucian ethic was being advanced as a reason for the economic stagnation of the same economies. Belassa's argument that the divergent economic performance of countries with common cultural traits but different policy environments attests to the greater importance of policies than of cultural traits is persuasive, though it certainly does not close discussion on the role of cultural factors in development.

For economic growth, one question that deserves further analysis is the relative importance of the longer-term human resource endowment as against the recent dynamics of human resource development. Chesnais (1989: 6–7) notes that the progress in female literacy from early in the twentieth century to 1950 or so was much faster in East Asia than in the ASEAN nations (except Thailand) and that South Asian countries were much further behind. This hierarchy of educational progress was mirrored in the hierarchy of subsequent economic growth. As was pointed out earlier in this Introduction, investments in education and other human capital are more productive when past investments are larger; 'accumulation of knowledge and skills in the past eases the acquisition of additional knowledge' (Becker, 1988: 5). But how does it ease the acquisition of additional knowledge? Mechanisms that come to mind include the role of educated parents (especially mothers) in guiding their children's learning and progress through the different levels of the education system (illiterate parents would have only a vague notion of what a university is about); the ease of recruiting teachers of sufficient calibre to sustain a rapid expansion of the education system when the educational base is already fairly broad; and (perhaps more controversially) the role of an educated public in understanding the benefits from investing heavily in expanding the education system.

Compared to Indonesia or Malaysia, the educational 'base' is broader in countries such as Japan, the Philippines, and Sri Lanka. The failure of this to do either the Philippines or Sri Lanka much good in their development since the 1960s is no doubt explicable on the basis of such factors as inappropriate policy, economic mismanagement, poor terms of trade, tensions within the polity, and perhaps underinvestment in human resources in recent times. Any evaluation of human resource indicators in the 1950s would have to place the Philippines high on the list of East and South-East Asian countries in terms of literacy, prevalence of schooling, and levels of health and nutrition. A similar point can be made for Sri Lanka. Pernia's Chapter 5 in this volume shows that in the Asian context, both countries (especially the Philippines) are outliers in their slow economic growth when related to their human capital endowment expressed in mean years of schooling of the labour force. Their slide down the economic rankings has made it harder to maintain high levels of investment in human resources. But it may not be a matter simply of inability, but also of inappropriate priorities. The Philippine case is widely discussed in the chapters that follow; the Sri Lankan case is not. But both countries amply demonstrate that the benefits of a long period of building a strong human resource base can easily be frittered away. By the same token, just as West Germany's and Japan's economic recovery after World War II was facilitated by their human capital endowment and technical expertise, so too can the relatively high educational levels in the Philippines and Sri Lanka facilitate their economic development should they succeed in putting appropriate policies in place.

It can be hypothesized that there is an optimal path of educational expansion—a path that will differ from country to country—and that this path will be greatly influenced by past educational endowments. It is undoubtedly possible for a country with relatively weak educational endowments to overinvest in educational expansion, though in reality, the main problem may frequently be an inappropriate balance between different levels of the educational system, rather than the overall level of investment in education.

From a policy point of view, the issue of the appropriate mix of educational investment is crucial. Education is, in itself, a large and complex sector, and a general prescription (based for example on rates-of-returns studies: Psacharopoulos, 1985) that more education at whatever level will probably have a greater impact on productivity than most alternative investments will not (and should not) satisfy planners. It could be further argued (based again on rates-of-returns studies) that primary schooling should receive priority. Again, however, the prescription is inadequate, because primary schooling is already essentially universal throughout this region, and the studies have little to say about the returns to qualitative improvement in primary education as opposed to quantitative (and/or qualitative) improvement at other levels.

The beneficial effects of demographic trends on economic growth in the region since 1960 have been noted. They have come into effect through a number of mechanisms, including the faster rise in the average quantity and quality of education received by younger cohorts entering the labour force. This improvement in educational levels, in turn, affects the pace of change in fertility and mortality. The role of education (especially female education) is important in so many studies of fertility determinants that the endogenization of fertility in many recent growth models typically relies heavily on education as a determinant.

But it cannot be realistically claimed that all the mechanisms through which education affects fertility or through which it affects development are understood, nor can weights be confidently attached to the mechanisms that can be identified. There are individual-level effects of education and there are effects of a different order which result from having a schooled rather than an unschooled society. The problem is that schooling is such a multifaceted activity that its possible impacts can be at a variety of levels. It is not necessarily the content of education or the quality of teaching that is important, but simply the fact that increasing proportions of children are in school and the effect this has on familial roles and attitudes and in 'shaking up' a traditional society (Caldwell, 1980). Schooling may contribute to development through its effects on the subsequent productivity of those being schooled, or through more immediate effects on family and social relationships, for example, its effects on the status of women—effects which are recognized by traditionalists in some societies who fight bitterly to prevent mass education for girls, particularly at the high school level—or through its effects on personal qualities conducive to development, such as individualism and entrepreneurship.

The appropriate sequencing of educational and health investments is clearly a crucial issue, not touched on in the chapters that follow. The issue has two aspects. The first is the optimum timing of human capital investments *vis-à-vis* investments in physical infrastructure (roads, railways, telecommunications, urban infrastructure) and in basic rural development such as irrigation and extension work. An 'everything at once' strategy appears logical but is precluded by budgetary limitations; it may also be the wrong way to proceed given economies of scale and backward and forward linkages. The emphasis on human resource investments early in the development of many East and South-East Asian countries appears to have been correct in retrospect, enabling countries such as Japan and South Korea to rebuild physical capital quickly after it was destroyed by war.

The second aspect is the sequencing of human resource investments. The emphasis on the basics—mass literacy while sending students abroad for higher education, control of major endemic diseases—appears to have been correct in terms of current development theory (Colclough, 1982; Psacharopoulos, 1985). Thailand achieved a fair degree of basic literacy quite early but then lagged in expanding upper primary and secondary education. This lag was no doubt less costly to long-term growth because of the basic literacy already attained.

The success of East Asian countries, however, was based on much more than just an early emphasis on human resource investments. As Oshima (1987) has noted, there was a speed up in technological progress in these countries which gave them a head start in the 1950s and 1960s over other regions of Asia. The source of the technical progress was the early attainment of full employment, causing wages to rise faster than capital returns. This compelled entrepreneurs to accelerate the substitution of imported technologies for labour, thereby raising productivity and exports. In turn, technological progress called for better-trained workers and promoted the education of children so that they could cope with the demands of more sophisticated technologies. There was thus a kind of induced demand for education, and this may have been a better strategy of early development than providing education at the expense of capital accumulation and thereby slowing employment generation. If so, one could argue that the lag in provision of secondary education in Thailand compared to many other countries of the region may have been a more appropriate strategy than is generally thought: the induced demand for this level of education as a result of double digit economic growth since the late 1980s will now ensure that secondary education expands rapidly.

Finally, a range of equity issues deserve further attention. It may appear that nothing could be more equitable than providing universal primary school education (and thus literacy) and basic health care throughout a country. In general, indices of income distribution show less inequality in countries of the Asia–Pacific Rim than is the case, on the whole, in Latin America or South Asia. But great variation exists between countries of the Rim, and trends over time are going in different directions in different countries. Universal primary education does not, in fact, provide a completely level playing field on which children compete for further education according to their abilities. Quality differences between rural schools and those attended by the urban middle classes are often vast. The actual progression of children through secondary and higher education in South-East Asian countries continues to be strongly influenced by their socio-economic background (Jones, 1988b). Further improvements in the equity of access to higher education would undoubtedly promote more rapid economic development as well.

# PART I
# POPULATION CHANGE, HUMAN RESOURCE DEVELOPMENT, AND ECONOMIC TRENDS: AN OVERVIEW

# 2
# Demographic Change and Human Resource Development in the Asia–Pacific Region: Trends of the 1960s to 1980s and Future Prospects

Naohiro Ogawa and Noriko O. Tsuya

**Introduction**

IN recent years, increased attention has been drawn to the Asia–Pacific region which has achieved new prominence in economic growth performance, emerging as the most dynamic part of the world. Since 1960, the market economies of East Asia have been growing at average annual rates of 6 per cent or more on the basis of per capita income. Only slightly lower economic growth rates have been recorded by China and some of the South-East Asian countries during the corresponding period. In 1960, the share of world GNP for the East Asia–Pacific Rim countries was only 11 per cent. An estimate made in the early 1980s shows, however, that if the present economic trends continue, this share will double by the year 2000, thus being comparable to that of the Western European countries or the North American region (Economic Planning Agency, 1983).

Although there has been no consensus among development economists on definite answers to the question of how economic growth occurs, such remarkable economic growth in various parts of the Asia–Pacific region seems to be attributable to the following factors: (i) substantial investment in public and private infrastructure induced by a high rate of savings and effective means of allocating savings to productive investment; (ii) an efficient use of advanced technology imported from industrialized countries; (iii) a stable political climate; (iv) availability of better educated and trained human resources; and (v) an export-oriented development strategy in an era of favourable international trading environment (East–West Center, 1986). It is important to note, however, that although the manner in which these factors are organized accounts for the difference between good and poor economic performance, even in the East and South-East Asian economic success stories, there are substantial intercountry differences in terms of the importance of these factors in their developmental processes.

More importantly, most of these factors are closely linked to population change. In the recent past, the Asia–Pacific region has been undergoing rapid demographic change in parallel with its dramatic economic growth. For instance, the annual rate of population growth for East Asia declined from 1.98 per cent during 1960–5 to 1.31 per cent over the period 1985–90 (United Nations, 1989c). Over the same time period, the population growth rate for South-East Asia dropped from 2.37 to 1.92 per cent. By way of contrast, the annual population growth rate for South Asia has remained virtually unchanged at a 2.35 per cent level during the corresponding period. Although mortality improved remarkably in all of these subregions of Asia during the period in question, fertility reduction was even more pronounced in both East and South-East Asia, consequently leading to such large differences in population growth rates among the three subregions.

In the process of slowing population growth, the labour force continues to grow some years after fertility declines, thus increasing the percentage of the population engaged in productive activities. Moreover, as a result of reduced fertility, more economic resources can be allocated to those in the labour force in order to equip them with better physical capital. In addition, increased economic resources facilitate improvements not only in the coverage of the education programme but also its quality. A number of the countries in the Pacific Basin are now at a later stage of the demographic transition in which these economic advantages have been well appreciated. Newly industrializing economies (NIEs) such as the Republic of Korea (hereafter referred to as South Korea), Singapore, Hong Kong, and Taiwan are salient examples. Besides these Asian NIEs, developed countries in the Pacific Rim have also enjoyed high-quality human resources in their developmental processes. In the case of Japan, for instance, the college enrolment rate increased from 10.1 to 36.7 per cent over the period 1960–88 (Ministry of Education, 1989). This rapid increase in the enrolment rate for higher education has contributed to widening and strengthening the base of human resources which, in turn, has facilitated the adaptation of advanced technologies borrowed from the Western world in its post-war economic development. It is interesting to note that the common feature among all of the economically successful countries in the East Asia–Pacific region is that they are deficient in natural resources but rich in human resources. In contrast to these successful countries, other developing countries in the western part of the Pacific Basin have been slow in improving the quality of their human resources.

The series of economic crises triggered by the oil shocks and other unfavourable external developments required structural adjustments and stabilization measures in developing Asia as a whole, forcing human resource issues into the background in the latter part of the 1970s and in the early 1980s. Since the mid-1980s, however, there has been a resurgence of interest in human resource development and utilization along with concern about the issues of poverty, population growth momentum, and sustainable economic growth (Asian Development Bank, *Asian Development Outlook*, 1989).

In view of the fact that human resource development and population change are closely interconnected, this chapter discusses: (i) recently emerging trends of demographic change and its future prospects in the Asia–Pacific region, by drawing heavily upon data prepared in 1988 by the United Nations; (ii) intertemporal changes in the relationships between demographic factors and human resource development in the region; and (iii) the differences in the role of human resources in post-war economic development among the three subregions of Asia.

## Demographic Change in the Asia–Pacific Region: Trends and Prospects

*Population Size and Growth*

In 1960, the proportion of Asia's population to world population was 55 per cent, but it is now almost 59 per cent. This share is expected to increase continuously until the year 2000, after which it is projected to decline. At present, the total population size in Asia as a whole amounts to slightly more than 3 billion, and 43 per cent of them reside in East Asia, 15 per cent in South-East Asia, and 39 per cent in South Asia. As discussed earlier, because there has been a substantial disparity in the annual population growth rates among the three subregions since 1960, the proportion of the population in South Asia has increased by three percentage points during 1960–90. In contrast, the corresponding figure for East Asia has declined by four percentage points. These trends of the interregional differential in population growth are expected to continue until the 2010s. In 2025, the division of Asia's population is estimated to be as follows: 35 per cent in East Asia; 14 per cent in South-East Asia; and 44 per cent in South Asia (United Nations, 1989c).

Asia has the world's two most populous countries, China and India. In 1990, China's total population was slightly over 1.1 billion, and India's population size was fairly close to 0.85 billion, the sum of these populations corresponds to 38 per cent of the world's total or 64 per cent of Asia's total. The population of China accounts for 85 per cent of East Asia's total, while the Indian population amounts to 71 per cent of South Asia's total. Because of their sheer population size, changes in the population growth of these giants directly influence the populations of East and South Asia. In sharp contrast, there are a number of Asian countries with small populations. For instance, the Maldives' total population is only 0.2 million, and Brunei, one of the wealthiest nations in the contemporary world, has a population of 2.6 million. In the Pacific region, Niue has only 2,000 inhabitants (ESCAP, 1989). These figures indicate that there are vast differences in population size within the Asia–Pacific region.

The peak of population growth in Asia was recorded during the second half of the 1960s. However, the timing of population growth peaks varies considerably from country to country. Japan, Australia, New Zealand, and all the Asian NIEs had their peaks in the 1950s or even before that. Most of the ASEAN countries marked their peak years during the 1960s. The Asian and Pacific countries which have experienced average annual population growth rates below 2 per cent over the period 1960–90 include Japan, China, South Korea, Singapore, Australia, and New Zealand. Most of the ASEAN countries and all the nations in South Asia have had growth rates higher than 2 per cent.

Data gathered from 13 Asian developing countries are displayed in Figure 2.1. These data on population growth and on the growth of real GNP per capita over the period 1965–85 show a negative relationship between these two variables. The correlation coefficient between these two variables is −0.69. This result seems to suggest that the pace of economic development in Asian developing countries is, by and large, faster with slower rates of population growth. Such a conclusion, however, must be qualified because the net impact of population varies from nation to nation and over time (Kelley, 1988a). In some countries, population growth may, on balance, contribute to economic development; in many others, it will deter development; and in still others, the net impact

FIGURE 2.1

Observed Relationship between Average Annual Rate of Population Growth and GNP Per Capita Growth among 13 Selected Asian Developing Countries, 1965–1985

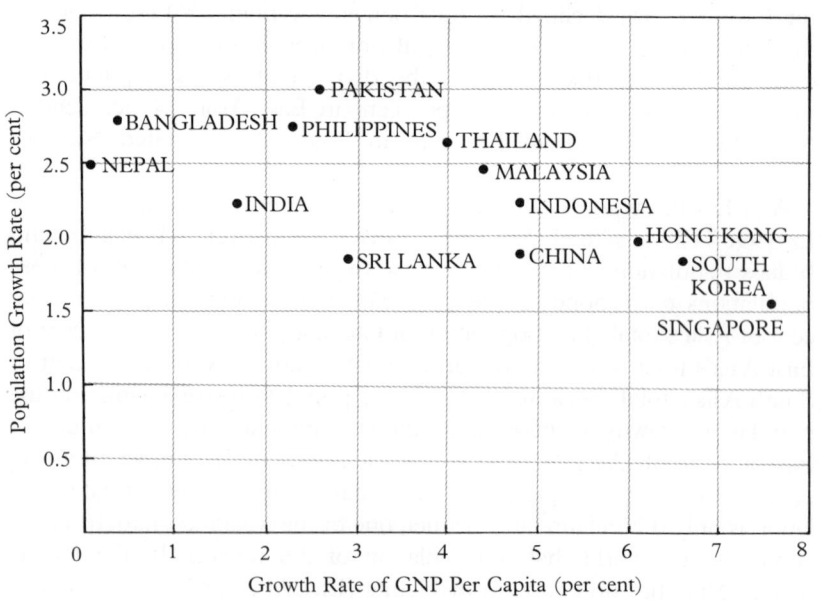

*Sources*: United Nations (1989c); World Bank (1987), *World Development Report 1987*.

will be negligible. During 1990–2025, the population growth rates of the Asian and Pacific countries are projected to fall further to a substantial degree. During the period 1990–2020, Japan, China, Hong Kong, South Korea, Singapore, Australia, and New Zealand are expected to have their average annual growth rates below 1 per cent. Almost all the ASEAN and South Asian countries are estimated to record their growth rates somewhere between 1 and 2 per cent. It should be stressed, however, that despite these anticipated declines of population growth rates, most of the countries in South-East and South Asia are expected to have a larger net increase in their populations in the 1990s to 2010s than that observed during the 1960s to 1980s. Such population increases are likely to generate immense pressure not only on the creation of employment opportunities but also on the more immediate requirements of health services, education, and housing in developing Asia.

*Diversities in the Demographic Transition in Asia and the Pacific*

Population growth rates are subject to changes in fertility, mortality, and migration, all of which play a vital role in the multidimensional process of demographic transition. A major characteristic of demographic transition in Asia is considered to be its quickness, compared with the experiences of Western countries (Leete, 1987). However, there are significant intercountry variations in the process of demographic transition in Asia and the Pacific.

To show the diversities of the degree of the demographic transition completed, a rough index of the transition process for the four subregions as well as for selected countries in each subregion has been computed, using the formula proposed by Cho and Togashi (1984). Although this index is by no means a perfect indicator of the degree of demographic transition, it still provides useful and concise information.

Figure 2.2 displays changes in this index for the subregions in Asia and the Pacific from 1960–5 to 1985–90, and Table 2.1 presents the corresponding values for selected countries in each subregion. Several points of interest emerge from the figure and the table.

First, a brief comparison of the four subregions, illustrated in Figure 2.2, reveals that although each subregion recorded a continuous rise in the degree of demographic transition completed during the last 25 years, there are substantial disparities in the tempo of the transition among them. In 1960–5, the value of this index was the highest for Oceania followed by East Asia by a wide margin. The difference between these two subregions, however, has diminished dramatically over time, particularly during the 1970s. In 1985–90, there is only a negligible difference between them. The remaining two subregions, South-East Asia and South Asia, were comparable in 1960–5, but the former has shown a more marked intertemporal increase in the degree of demographic transition completed than the latter. At present, South Asia is lagging considerably behind the remaining three subregions.

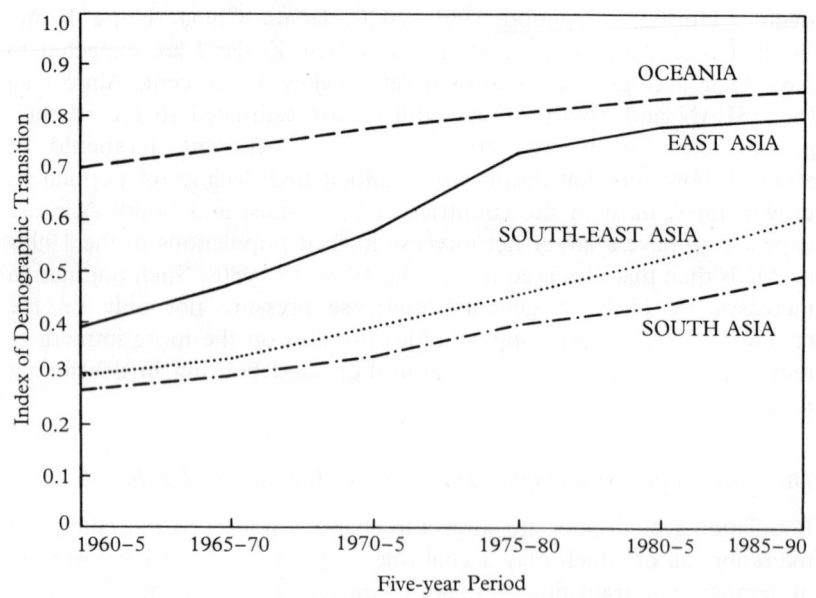

## FIGURE 2.2
Index of Demographic Transition for Four Subregions, 1960/5–1985/90

*Source*: United Nations (1989c).

Secondly, as shown in Table 2.1, on a country-specific basis, Japan and such NIEs as Hong Kong and Singapore (together with Australia and New Zealand) completed their demographic transition by 1985–90 with the highest values of the index among the countries under consideration. The rapid transitions achieved by Hong Kong and Singapore during 1960–75 were especially phenomenal. Moreover, another newly industrializing country, South Korea, is now very close to the completion of its demographic transition.

Thirdly, countries that achieved an intermediate level of completion (0.6–0.8) by 1985–90 are China, Sri Lanka, and the remaining three ASEAN countries. Among them, the rapidity with which the Chinese transition occurred between 1965 and 1980 was impressive. The degree of transition in all the South Asian countries except for Sri Lanka was still relatively low in 1985–90, and the tempo of the transition is also relatively slow. In fact, although India had a level of transition comparable to that of China during the early 1960s, the difference between them became increasingly larger over the next 20 years thereafter.

Figure 2.3 depicts the relationship between the annual rate of change in the index of demographic transition and the annual rate of change in the share of labour force in agriculture. Data displayed in this graphical exposition have been gathered from 11 Asian countries, covering the period 1965–85. Clearly, there exists a negative relationship between the two variables. The simple correlation between them amounts to −0.66. This result appears to suggest that the demographic and industrial transitions have been proceeding hand in hand in Asia.

TABLE 2.1
Index of Demographic Transition for Selected Countries in Asia and the Pacific, 1960/5–1985/90

| Country | 1960–5 | 1965–70 | 1970–5 | 1975–80 | 1980–5 | 1985–90 |
|---|---|---|---|---|---|---|
| East Asia | | | | | | |
| Japan | 0.39 | 0.48 | 0.58 | 0.73 | 0.79 | 0.80 |
| South Korea | 0.89 | 0.92 | 0.94 | 0.99 | 1.00 | 1.02 |
| China | 0.43 | 0.54 | 0.62 | 0.77 | 0.84 | 0.90 |
| Hong Kong | 0.32 | 0.41 | 0.54 | 0.70 | 0.76 | 0.78 |
|  | 0.68 | 0.80 | 0.90 | 0.96 | 1.02 | 1.03 |
| South-East Asia | | | | | | |
| Singapore | 0.30 | 0.33 | 0.40 | 0.46 | 0.53 | 0.61 |
| Thailand | 0.71 | 0.84 | 0.92 | 0.99 | 1.01 | 1.02 |
| Philippines | 0.31 | 0.36 | 0.47 | 0.55 | 0.62 | 0.72 |
| Indonesia | 0.34 | 0.40 | 0.48 | 0.52 | 0.56 | 0.61 |
| Malaysia | 0.29 | 0.30 | 0.36 | 0.42 | 0.50 | 0.60 |
|  | 0.33 | 0.43 | 0.52 | 0.63 | 0.68 | 0.73 |
| South Asia | | | | | | |
| India | 0.27 | 0.30 | 0.34 | 0.40 | 0.44 | 0.50 |
| Pakistan | 0.29 | 0.32 | 0.37 | 0.44 | 0.47 | 0.54 |
| Bangladesh | 0.20 | 0.22 | 0.25 | 0.27 | 0.30 | 0.37 |
| Sri Lanka | 0.15 | 0.16 | 0.17 | 0.22 | 0.28 | 0.35 |
|  | 0.51 | 0.55 | 0.62 | 0.64 | 0.71 | 0.76 |
| Oceania | | | | | | |
| Australia | 0.32 | 0.41 | 0.54 | 0.70 | 0.76 | 0.78 |
| New Zealand | 0.84 | 0.88 | 0.92 | 0.97 | 0.99 | 1.01 |
|  | 0.80 | 0.85 | 0.89 | 0.94 | 0.97 | 0.99 |

Source: United Nations (1989e).

Note: The index of the percentage of the demographic transition completed was constructed using the following formula:

Index $= 0.40[(7.5 - \text{TFR})/5.3] + 0.40[1 - (75 - e_0)/43] + 0.20[u]$

where
TFR = total fertility rate per woman,
$e_0$ = life expectancy at birth, and
u = proportion of population urban.

## FIGURE 2.3
Link between Demographic Transition and Agri-industrial Transition among 11 Selected Asian Countries, 1965–1985

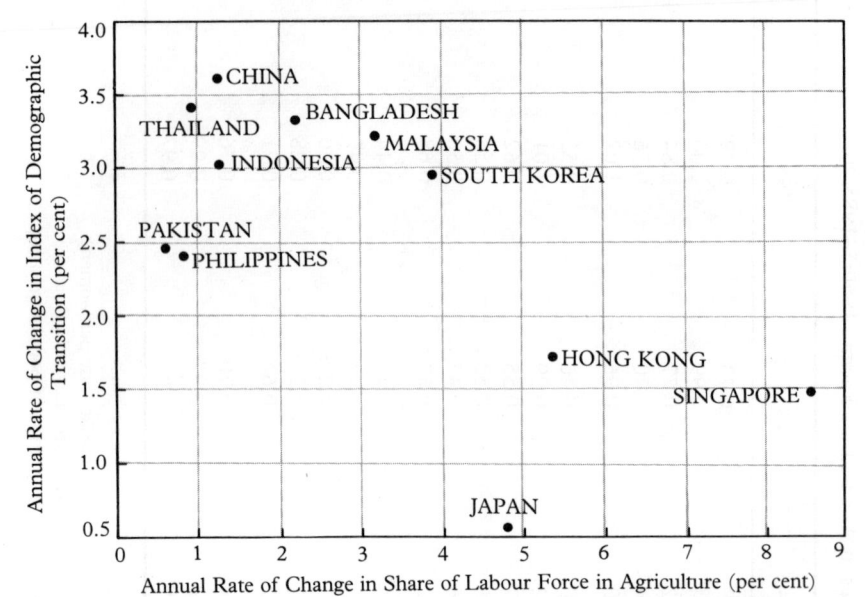

*Source*: Asian Development Bank (1988), *Key Indicators of Developing Member Countries of ADB*, Manila.

## FIGURE 2.4
Index of Demographic Transition for Four Subregions, 1990/5–2020/5

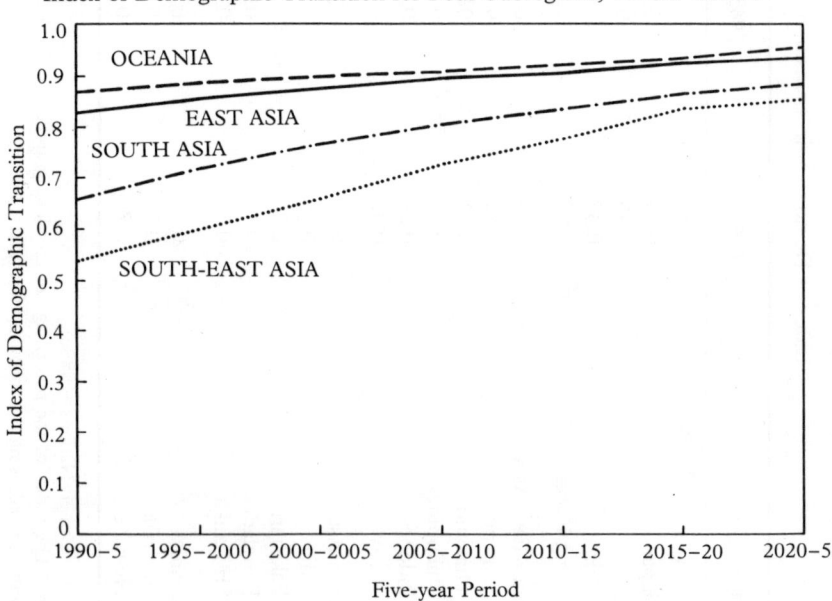

*Source*: United Nations (1989c).

TABLE 2.2
Index of Demographic Transition for Selected Countries in Asia and the Pacific, 1990/5–2020/5

| Country | 1990–5 | 1995–2000 | 2000–5 | 2005–10 | 2010–15 | 2015–20 | 2020–5 |
|---|---|---|---|---|---|---|---|
| East Asia | 0.83 | 0.86 | 0.88 | 0.90 | 0.92 | 0.93 | 0.95 |
| Japan | 1.02 | 1.03 | 1.03 | 1.03 | 1.04 | 1.05 | 1.05 |
| South Korea | 0.94 | 0.96 | 0.98 | 0.99 | 1.00 | 1.01 | 1.02 |
| China | 0.81 | 0.84 | 0.86 | 0.88 | 0.90 | 0.92 | 0.93 |
| Hong Kong | 1.05 | 1.05 | 1.05 | 1.06 | 1.06 | 1.06 | 1.07 |
| South-East Asia | 0.67 | 0.72 | 0.77 | 0.81 | 0.84 | 0.87 | 0.89 |
| Singapore | 1.03 | 1.03 | 1.04 | 1.04 | 1.06 | 1.06 | 1.06 |
| Thailand | 0.78 | 0.80 | 0.83 | 0.85 | 0.87 | 0.88 | 0.90 |
| Philippines | 0.67 | 0.72 | 0.77 | 0.82 | 0.85 | 0.90 | 0.92 |
| Indonesia | 0.66 | 0.72 | 0.77 | 0.81 | 0.83 | 0.86 | 0.88 |
| Malaysia | 0.78 | 0.83 | 0.88 | 0.91 | 0.93 | 0.94 | 0.96 |
| South Asia | 0.54 | 0.60 | 0.66 | 0.73 | 0.79 | 0.84 | 0.87 |
| India | 0.58 | 0.64 | 0.70 | 0.76 | 0.81 | 0.86 | 0.88 |
| Pakistan | 0.44 | 0.52 | 0.61 | 0.70 | 0.77 | 0.82 | 0.86 |
| Bangladesh | 0.40 | 0.46 | 0.51 | 0.59 | 0.67 | 0.72 | 0.77 |
| Sri Lanka | 0.79 | 0.82 | 0.85 | 0.86 | 0.88 | 0.90 | 0.91 |
| Oceania | 0.81 | 0.84 | 0.86 | 0.89 | 0.90 | 0.92 | 0.93 |
| Australia | 1.02 | 1.02 | 1.03 | 1.03 | 1.04 | 1.04 | 1.05 |
| New Zealand | 1.00 | 1.01 | 1.01 | 1.02 | 1.03 | 1.03 | 1.04 |

*Source*: As for Table 2.1.

In so far as the outlook of demographic transition in the four subregions is concerned, the values of the index of demographic transition are expected to continuously rise up to the year 2025, as illustrated in Figure 2.4. More importantly, the disparities among the four subregions will decrease substantially, particularly after the turn of the twenty-first century. A similar observation is also applicable to the country-level discussion. In the early part of the twenty-first century, the values of the index of demographic transition for all the countries listed in Table 2.2 are expected to exceed the 0.6 level. For instance, although the difference between Japan and Bangladesh was 0.67 in 1985–90, it is projected to decrease to only 0.28 in 2020–5. These results point to the converging trend in the levels of demographic transition in the Asia–Pacific Rim countries in the years to come. Caution should be exercised, however, with regard to the validity of this interpretation, which is heavily dependent upon the population projections prepared by the United Nations. How much confidence can be placed in these long-term projections? Demeny (1984) aptly describes them as speculative exercises rather than forecasts. These projections are fraught with uncertainty arising from difficulties in predicting fertility trends and from the fact that forecasting errors accumulate over time.

By changing the parameters attached to fertility, mortality and urbanization, the index of demographic transition has been recomputed with a view to testing its sensitivity. The recomputed results were considerably different from what has been presented above, but the findings obtained were virtually the same.

*Fertility Change*

Since the mid-1960s, the magnitude and tempo of fertility transition and their underlying mechanisms in many parts of East and South-East Asia have been truly unique (Duza, 1989). For this reason, Asia's fertility transition has received considerable research and policy attention. It is a familiar theme in the population and development literature that economic development is, in general, inversely related to the level of fertility. This generalization is based to a large extent on Western experience. However, a close examination of various European populations reveals little statistical evidence of an association between fertility declines and a specific level of socio-economic development (van de Walle and Knodel, 1967, 1980). Furthermore, evidence from studies of many Asian countries indicates that relatively small subsets of developmental changes are enough to bring down fertility (Knodel and Debavalya, 1978; Sun et al., 1978) and that a deliberately organized social effort to control fertility, which can be independent of narrowly conceived indicators of development, can have a significant influence on fertility reduction (Freedman and Takeshita, 1969). Moreover, to understand various subtleties in the process of Asia's fertility transition, some of the fertility theories and hypotheses formulated in the 1980s are called for (Duza, 1989). These include the demand theories of value and costs of children

(Easterlin, 1986), intergenerational reversing of the flow of wealth (Caldwell, 1982), and the 'ideational shift' hypothesis (Cleland and Wilson, 1987).

Because there are substantial inter- as well as intra-regional variations in trends of changing fertility among the Asian and Pacific countries, fertility changes during 1960–90 are examined by subregion and by country within each subregion. Table 2.3 presents intertemporal changes in the total fertility rate (TFR) over the period 1960–90 for the four subregions and 15 selected countries in Asia and the Pacific. Based on this table, several observations can be made.

First, among the four subregions, the extent to which fertility has declined during the 1960s to 1980s is most pronounced in East Asia, followed by South-East Asia. East Asia's TFR has decreased by 57 per cent, South-East Asia by 39 per cent, Oceania by 35 per cent, and South Asia by 22 per cent. In 1985–90, TFRs for both East Asia and Oceania are close to the replacement level of fertility.

Secondly, note from Table 2.3 that in East Asia, the demographically successful region, Japan is the forerunner of fertility transition. In fact (not shown in Table 2.3) Japan managed to reduce its fertility level with unprecedented rapidity (Hodge and Ogawa, 1991). Japan's TFR

TABLE 2.3
Total Fertility Rates for Selected Countries in Asia and the Pacific, 1960/5–1985/90

| Country | 1960–5 | 1965–70 | 1970–5 | 1975–80 | 1980–5 | 1985–90 |
|---|---|---|---|---|---|---|
| East Asia | 5.35 | 5.39 | 4.40 | 2.80 | 2.33 | 2.31 |
| Japan | 2.01 | 2.00 | 2.07 | 1.81 | 1.76 | 1.70 |
| South Korea | 5.40 | 4.52 | 4.11 | 2.80 | 2.40 | 2.00 |
| China | 5.93 | 5.99 | 4.76 | 2.90 | 2.36 | 2.36 |
| Hong Kong | 5.30 | 4.01 | 2.89 | 2.31 | 1.80 | 1.70 |
| South-East Asia | 5.89 | 5.79 | 5.26 | 4.79 | 4.28 | 3.58 |
| Singapore | 4.93 | 3.46 | 2.63 | 1.87 | 1.69 | 1.65 |
| Thailand | 6.42 | 6.14 | 5.01 | 4.27 | 3.52 | 2.60 |
| Philippines | 6.61 | 6.04 | 5.29 | 4.96 | 4.74 | 4.33 |
| Indonesia | 5.42 | 5.57 | 5.10 | 4.68 | 4.10 | 3.30 |
| Malaysia | 6.72 | 5.94 | 5.15 | 4.16 | 3.91 | 3.50 |
| South Asia | 6.03 | 5.96 | 5.70 | 5.27 | 5.14 | 4.72 |
| India | 5.81 | 5.69 | 5.43 | 4.83 | 4.75 | 4.30 |
| Pakistan | 7.00 | 7.00 | 7.00 | 7.00 | 7.00 | 6.50 |
| Bangladesh | 6.68 | 6.91 | 7.02 | 6.66 | 6.15 | 5.53 |
| Sri Lanka | 5.16 | 4.68 | 4.00 | 3.83 | 3.25 | 2.67 |
| Oceania | 3.94 | 3.54 | 3.19 | 2.85 | 2.64 | 2.57 |
| Australia | 3.28 | 2.87 | 2.54 | 2.09 | 1.93 | 1.85 |
| New Zealand | 3.79 | 3.22 | 2.79 | 2.20 | 1.96 | 1.90 |

Source: As for Table 2.1.

declined by one-half in only a decade, from 4.54 in 1947 to 2.04 in 1957. The other countries generally followed the pattern set by Japan. Hong Kong and China succeeded in halving their birth rate in approximately ten years, although at different time periods. The tempo of fertility reduction in South Korea was slower, but nevertheless its TFR was cut by one-half in 15 years from the early 1960s to mid-1970s. Though not indicated in Table 2.3, South Korea's TFR for 1988 was estimated to be 1.56 per woman, one of the lowest levels in all of Asia. In addition to South Korea, TFRs for Hong Kong and Japan are now considerably below the replacement level.

Thirdly, from the TFR changes in South-East Asia shown in Table 2.3, notice that while all the ASEAN countries under consideration experienced considerable fertility reduction during 1970–80, they show substantial differences in the trends of fertility during the period prior to 1970. Specifically, like many East Asian countries, Singapore is a showcase of success, cutting its fertility by one-half in one decade between the mid-1960s and the mid-1970s. Singapore attained below-replacement fertility in the late 1970s, the first case in Asia. Thailand's TFR dropped by more than 50 per cent during the period 1965–70 to 1985–90. Both Indonesia and Malaysia have been experiencing a gradual but steady fertility decline since the 1960s. In the case of the Philippines, the reduction of fertility has been under way at a slow pace, recording the highest level in the subregion in the 1970s and 1980s.

Fourthly, concerning changes in TFR in South Asia, note from Table 2.3 that except for Sri Lanka, whose fertility rate shows a trend of gradual but steady decline, fertility in all the other countries (India, Pakistan, and Bangladesh) shows no clear sign of the onset of fertility transition.

Fifthly, regarding TFR changes in countries in the Pacific, observe that the fertility level of the two countries (Australia and New Zealand) was already relatively low in the early 1960s with TFR being approximately 3.5. Although the tempo of decline since then has been gradual, TFRs for these countries had fallen below the replacement level by the early 1980s.

The foregoing discussion based upon Table 2.3 indicates that although all the Asian developing nations under review had extremely high fertility levels at the beginning of the 1960s, all the East Asian countries and many of the South-East Asian countries have been able to depress their fertility rates to a remarkable degree from the 1960s to 1980s, leaving South Asian countries far behind. Thus, the interregional differentials in fertility in Asia as a whole have expanded considerably during this period.

At the same time, the fertility transition observed in both East and South-East Asian nations has been substantially quicker than that in the developed countries. Moreover, their fertility transition has occurred at considerably lower levels of economic development, compared with that for industrialized nations. These fertility experiences of many Asian countries led to questions posed about the validity of the 'classical' model of demographic transition that regards socio-economic development as a primary prerequisite for the fertility transition. Evidence from such Asian countries as China, South Korea, Thailand, Indonesia, and Singapore seems to indicate that fertility decline can occur even at a relatively early stage of development, and that the decline may even facilitate development (Knodel and Debavalya, 1978; Hogan and Frenzen, 1981; Donaldson et al., 1982). However, this observation does not negate the importance of socio-economic development in the process of fertility transition. In fact, they interact with each other (Cho and Togashi, 1984).

As pointed out by Lapham and Mauldin (1985), holding the level of economic development constant, strong political commitment and national family planning programmes prove most crucial in defining the timing, magnitude, and tempo of fertility transition. The Asian experiences seem to substantiate the validity of this view. Some salient examples are the strict enforcement of one-child family policy in China since 1979, and the strong government effort to control population growth through a series of family planning campaigns in South Korea, Indonesia, and Thailand. This view also accounts for the Philippines' recent stagnation in the process of fertility transition. In addition, South Asian countries, except for Sri Lanka, have not yet succeeded in entering a fertility transition, although they all (including Sri Lanka) express the necessity of and actually attempt governmental intervention to promote fertility (and therefore population) control. This seems to indicate the lack of strong government commitment and the inefficiency and ineffectiveness of intervention measures, suggesting the need for further improvements in their population control programmes.

Although most of the governments of the Asian developing countries have been strengthening their family planning programmes to reduce their fertility levels as quickly as possible, the Malaysian government has adopted a 'pronatalist' policy in order to increase its population from 15 to 70 million by the year 2100 (Takeshita, 1987; Leete, 1989; Cheung, 1989). Since the late 1980s, however, the degree of its possible implementation has been seriously doubted. In another ASEAN country, Singapore, although its long-term demographic goal is to stabilize the population early in the twenty-first century, its fertility has kept on declining at a below-replacement level. To cope with this situation, the government implemented a programme in 1987 to motivate people through considerable monetary incentives to have more children (Saw, 1990). It will be interesting to see how this programme affects Singapore's fertility.

According to the medium variant of the 1988 United Nations population projections, all the countries listed in Table 2.3 are expected to either attain or approach very close to the level of replacement fertility by the year 2025. The timing of achieving the replacement-level fertility, however, differs pronouncedly from country to country. For instance,

China is projected to reach this level by the year 2000, Thailand and Sri Lanka by 2005, Indonesia and Malaysia by 2010, and the Philippines by 2020. The United Nations projections also indicate that slowing of the tempo of decline is likely to take place in all the countries with their fertility transitions completed or to be completed soon. They also show that the steepest declines will occur in Indonesia, Malaysia, the Philippines, and Thailand before the end of the twentieth century (Duza, 1989). Moreover, the medium variant of the United Nations projections has assumed the unlikelihood of any reversal of fertility among the countries with their current fertility levels below replacement.

*Mortality Changes*

In a process of demographic transition, mortality decline usually takes place before fertility reduction. Unlike the case of their Western predecessors, in many developing countries, including those in Asia, significant mortality decline took place without accompanying substantial socio-economic development. This was due mainly to importation of medical knowledge and technology from the West, and to the subsequent spread of ideas on public health and hygiene through governmental programmes. As a consequence of the spread of such imported modern public health and medical technologies, the reduction in mortality has generally been rapid in Asia and the Pacific since World War II. As in the case of fertility, there are also considerable differences in levels and trends of mortality changes within and among the four subregions.

Table 2.4 documents an overall trend of increasing life expectancy at birth for both sexes combined in the Asia–Pacific region during 1960–90. Life expectancy at birth is a summary measure of mortality at all ages in a population. It is independent of the age structure of the population and is therefore useful for making international comparison. To facilitate the discussions which follow, a life expectancy of 70 years is regarded as a criterion for the completion of mortality transition; this figure is close to the current average life expectancy among the developed nations in the 1980s.

Several points of discussion emerge from data displayed in Table 2.4. First, observe that the mortality transition had already been completed in the 1960s in two East Asian countries (Japan and Hong Kong), both of which are considered to have almost completed their demographic transition by 1980. Japan now enjoys the highest level of life expectancy in the contemporary world (Ogawa, 1986a, 1989a, 1989b). It can be seen that the tempo of increases in life expectancy has been very similar for all the East Asian countries under review except for China. Note that although the tempo of improvements and the degree of absolute gains are similar among all the four East Asian countries, there remain some, though not large, differentials between South Korea and the other two countries (Japan and Hong Kong). Furthermore, China's life expectancy has been on a rapid upward trend, gaining 20 years over the period 1960–5 and 1985–90. By 1990, the levels of life expectancy of

TABLE 2.4
Life Expectancy at Birth for Selected Countries in Asia and the Pacific,
1960/5–1985/90 (years)

| Country | 1960–5 | 1965–70 | 1970–5 | 1975–80 | 1980–5 | 1985–90 |
|---|---|---|---|---|---|---|
| East Asia | 51.0 | 60.2 | 63.8 | 66.5 | 68.4 | 69.9 |
| Japan | 69.0 | 71.1 | 73.3 | 75.5 | 76.9 | 78.1 |
| South Korea | 55.2 | 57.5 | 61.5 | 65.5 | 67.7 | 69.3 |
| China | 49.5 | 59.6 | 63.2 | 65.8 | 67.8 | 69.4 |
| Hong Kong | 67.6 | 70.0 | 72.0 | 73.6 | 75.4 | 76.2 |
| South-East Asia | 46.7 | 49.3 | 51.6 | 54.2 | 57.2 | 59.6 |
| Singapore | 65.8 | 67.9 | 69.5 | 70.8 | 71.8 | 72.8 |
| Thailand | 53.9 | 56.7 | 59.6 | 61.2 | 62.7 | 65.0 |
| Philippines | 54.5 | 56.2 | 57.9 | 59.8 | 61.9 | 63.5 |
| Indonesia | 42.5 | 45.1 | 47.5 | 50.0 | 53.5 | 56.0 |
| Malaysia | 55.7 | 59.4 | 63.0 | 65.3 | 68.0 | 69.5 |
| South Asia | 45.0 | 47.4 | 49.5 | 52.0 | 54.4 | 56.9 |
| India | 45.5 | 48.0 | 50.3 | 52.9 | 55.4 | 57.9 |
| Pakistan | 44.4 | 46.8 | 49.0 | 51.5 | 54.0 | 56.5 |
| Bangladesh | 40.6 | 43.3 | 44.9 | 46.6 | 48.6 | 50.7 |
| Sri Lanka | 63.5 | 64.2 | 65.0 | 66.8 | 68.9 | 70.3 |
| Oceania | 63.8 | 64.2 | 65.5 | 66.3 | 68.0 | 68.8 |
| Australia | 70.9 | 70.9 | 71.7 | 73.4 | 75.2 | 76.1 |
| New Zealand | 71.0 | 71.3 | 71.7 | 72.4 | 73.7 | 74.7 |

*Source*: As for Table 2.1.

South Korea and China are comparable, and both nations have virtually completed the mortality transition.

Secondly, concerning South-East Asia, data shown in Table 2.4 indicate that life expectancy at birth for both sexes combined has been rising substantially from the 1960s to 1980s. Moreover, among the five countries under consideration, the tempo of increases and the degree of absolute gains have been remarkable, but there have been considerable intercountry differentials among them. Clearly, Singapore, which had completed its mortality transition in the 1970s, is the forerunner among the five ASEAN countries. Although Thailand, the Philippines, and Malaysia were comparable with regard to their levels of life expectancy at birth in the early 1960s, in 1985–90 Malaysia has virtually reached the final stage of its mortality transition, whereas the Philippines is considerably lagging behind Malaysia, and Thailand is quickly approaching the final stage. Although Indonesia is presently the last runner in mortality transition among the five South-East Asian countries, its life expectancy has been improving at a pace similar to those of Malaysia and Thailand, and faster than that of the Philippines. It should also be noted that Indonesia's relatively high mortality accounts for its relatively low population growth rate as mentioned earlier.

Thirdly, as regards South Asia, it can be noted that Sri Lanka currently has a life expectancy much higher than the levels of the remaining three countries (India, Pakistan, and Bangladesh) and almost comparable to those of most ASEAN countries. On the other hand, life expectancy of the remaining three countries has been low, the level being around 50 years in the 1980s, indicating the necessity of more effective implementation of public health measures and better utilization of medical services, in addition to the general improvement in the standard of living through socio-economic development.

Fourthly, concerning the selected countries in the Pacific presented in Table 2.4, Australia and New Zealand have almost identical trends and levels of life expectancy throughout the period under consideration. Though their life expectancy, like those of many Western industrialized countries, has been at a very high level, it has not made much of an absolute gain from the 1960s to 1980s, thus distinguishing these two countries from the patterns of East and South-East Asian countries.

A careful examination of the data presented in Table 2.4 reveals that some of the countries with relatively high levels of life expectancy (approximately 65 years or higher) show a slower gain in the improvement of mortality. In addition to the three developed nations under consideration (Japan, Australia, and New Zealand), South Korea, Malaysia, and Singapore serve as a case in point. This may be explained by the fact that it is relatively easy and inexpensive to control infant and child mortality, while the reduction of mortality risk factors at middle and old age is more difficult and costly. Thus, when a population undergoes its mortality transition, substantial life expectancy gains generated at its early stage come from a rapid decline in infant and child mortality.

The validity of this view is further supported by the intertemporal change in the simple correlation between infant mortality rates and life expectancy at birth among the 15 selected countries under review from the 1960s to 1980s: $-0.97$ for 1960–5, $-0.97$ for 1965–70, $-0.96$ for 1970–5, $-0.95$ for 1975–80, $-0.95$ for 1980–5, and $-0.93$ for 1985–90. In 1985–90, the infant mortality rates of these sampled countries ranged from 5 in Japan to 119 in Bangladesh. Out of the 15 countries considered, 10 countries had their infant mortality rates higher than 50 per 1,000 live births in the early 1960s, but there are only three countries (Indonesia, Bangladesh, and India) having such high infant mortality in the late 1980s. Moreover, because higher infant mortality implies a greater wastage of human resources, some of the developing countries in Asia have included the reduction of infant mortality in their government development plans as one of the priority areas. In the case of Indonesia, for example, various health policy measures have recently been incorporated in its development plan (Repelita V for 1989/90–1994/5) so as to lower infant mortality from 58.0 to 49.8 by the end of the plan period (National Development Planning Agency, 1989).

The 1988 United Nations population projections show that the countries with relatively low levels of life expectancy will experience fast improvements in mortality, thus reducing the intercountry differentials in life expectancy. In the period 1985–90, for instance, the difference between Japan and Bangladesh amounts to 27.4 years, but by 2025 it is expected to decrease to 15.7 years. By the end of the 1980s, 9 out of 15 countries had already completed their mortality transition, but all the countries under consideration except for Bangladesh are likely to reach the end of their mortality transition by 2025. Thailand is expected to complete its mortality transition at around the turn of the twenty-first century, the Philippines in 2010–15, India in 2015–2020, and Indonesia and Pakistan in 2020–5.

These expected rapid declines in mortality in developing Asia and the Pacific imply that further declines in fertility should be ensured to avoid a continuing explosion of their populations which poses a serious threat to their development processes. In this context, increased research efforts on the possible effects of infant mortality on fertility demand should be encouraged. As pointed out by Bongaarts and Menken (1983), the probability of infant survival to adulthood, together with natural fertility, determine the supply of children. On this supply–demand relationship in fertility, some claim that besides being a fertility supply factor, the probability of infant survival is also a determinant of fertility demand since couples determine the level of their demand by taking the probability of infant survival into account (Easterlin, 1978). However, some question the feasibility of this possible interaction between fertility demand and supply, especially for developing countries (Lee and Bulatao, 1983).

*Urbanization*

Compared with the historical experience of developed nations, recent urbanization in developing countries has not been rapid. This is particularly the case in the Asia–Pacific region relative to other developing parts of the world (Pernia, 1988). In 1985, the level of urbanization in the world as a whole was 41 per cent. In the developing region it was 32 per cent as opposed to 72 per cent in the developed region. In Asia, it was estimated to be 28 per cent. Within Asia, the level of urbanization varied considerably: 29 per cent in East Asia, 26 per cent in South-East Asia, and 25 per cent in South Asia.

Table 2.5 presents the change in the level of urbanization over the period 1960–90 for the 15 selected countries in Asia and the Pacific. Except for a few countries such as Sri Lanka and Australia which experienced decreases in the levels of urbanization from the late 1970s to the early 1980s, all the countries listed in Table 2.5 have experienced secular increases in the proportion of the population residing in urban areas. We can also note in this table that only the following six countries have exceeded the 50 per cent urbanization level in 1990: Singapore (100 per cent), Hong Kong (93 per cent), Australia (86 per cent), New Zealand (84 per cent), Japan (77 per cent), and South Korea (72 per cent). Among these countries, South Korea's urbanization tempo has

TABLE 2.5
Levels of Urbanization for Selected Countries in Asia and the Pacific,
1960–1990 (per cent)

| Country | 1960 | 1965 | 1970 | 1975 | 1980 | 1985 | 1990 |
|---|---|---|---|---|---|---|---|
| East Asia | 25.0 | 26.4 | 26.9 | 27.6 | 28.1 | 28.6 | 29.4 |
| Japan | 62.5 | 67.3 | 71.2 | 75.7 | 76.2 | 76.7 | 77.0 |
| South Korea | 27.7 | 32.4 | 40.7 | 48.0 | 56.9 | 65.4 | 72.0 |
| China | 19.0 | 19.9 | 20.1 | 20.2 | 20.4 | 20.6 | 21.4 |
| Hong Kong | 89.1 | 89.4 | 89.7 | 90.6 | 91.6 | 92.5 | 93.2 |
| South-East Asia | 17.6 | 18.9 | 20.2 | 22.0 | 24.0 | 26.3 | 29.0 |
| Singapore | 100.0 | 100.0 | 100.0 | 100.0 | 100.0 | 100.0 | 100.0 |
| Thailand | 12.5 | 12.9 | 13.3 | 15.2 | 17.3 | 19.8 | 22.6 |
| Philippines | 30.3 | 31.6 | 33.0 | 35.6 | 37.4 | 39.6 | 42.4 |
| Indonesia | 14.6 | 15.8 | 17.1 | 19.4 | 22.2 | 25.3 | 28.8 |
| Malaysia | 25.2 | 26.1 | 27.0 | 30.5 | 34.2 | 38.2 | 42.3 |
| South Asia | 17.3 | 18.3 | 19.5 | 21.3 | 23.2 | 25.3 | 27.8 |
| India | 18.0 | 18.8 | 19.8 | 21.5 | 23.4 | 25.5 | 28.0 |
| Pakistan | 22.1 | 23.5 | 24.9 | 26.4 | 28.1 | 29.8 | 32.0 |
| Bangladesh | 17.3 | 18.3 | 19.5 | 21.3 | 23.2 | 25.3 | 32.0 |
| Sri Lanka | 17.9 | 19.9 | 21.9 | 22.0 | 21.6 | 21.1 | 21.4 |
| Oceania | 66.3 | 68.6 | 70.8 | 71.8 | 71.5 | 71.1 | 70.9 |
| Australia | 80.6 | 83.0 | 88.2 | 85.9 | 85.8 | 85.5 | 85.5 |
| New Zealand | 76.0 | 78.9 | 81.1 | 82.8 | 83.3 | 83.7 | 84.2 |

Source: As for Table 2.1.

been especially spectacular. The proportion urban was only 28 per cent in 1960, but it increased to 65 per cent in 1985. Furthermore, from 1960 to 1980, its growth rate was phenomenal with the peak during 1965–70. It should also be stressed, however, that among the remaining five countries with their levels of urbanization above the 70 per cent level in 1990, the pace of urbanization has been relatively slow.

From Table 2.5, it can also be observed that since 1970 the level of urbanization has been rising quickly among three ASEAN countries (Indonesia, the Philippines, and Malaysia). In South Asia, Bangladesh's urbanization pace has been rapid; its level has almost doubled during 1960–90. The remaining countries in South Asia have been experiencing a relatively slow urbanization process.

Urbanization is both an antecedent and consequence of development (Hauser, 1982). As displayed in Figure 2.5, cross-sectional data gathered from the 15 countries support this view. In this graphical exposition, a positive relationship between the level of urbanization and the logarithmic value of GNP per capita can be observed: the greater the log of GNP per capita, the higher the proportion urban, supporting the urbanization cycle hypothesis (Pernia, 1984). This hypothesis suggests that the 50 per cent level roughly marks the inflection point of the urbanization curve, with the 40–60 per cent range representing the

## FIGURE 2.5
Observed Relationship between the Level of Urbanization and the Log of GNP Per Capita among Selected Countries in Asia and the Pacific, 1985–1990

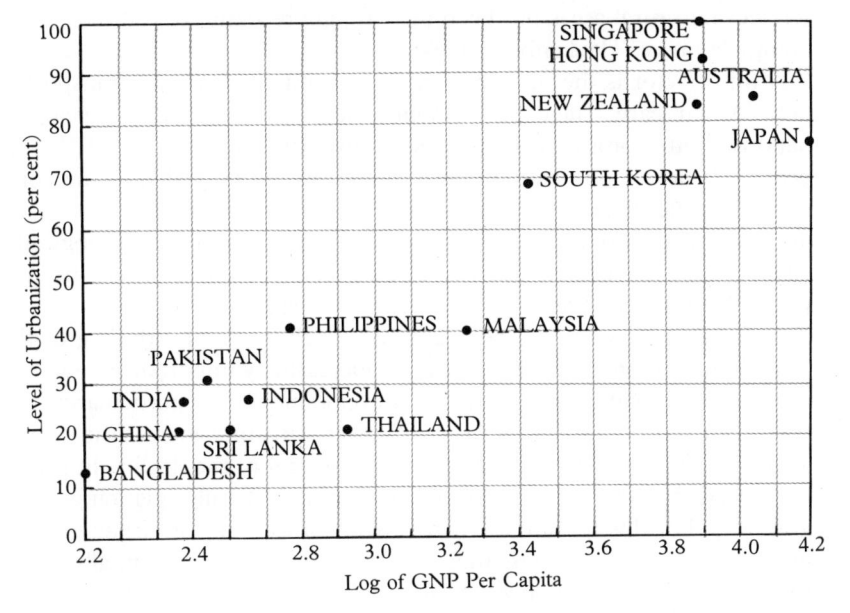

*Sources*: As for Figure 2.1.

phase of fastest urbanization. Furthermore, according to this hypothesis, South Korea is now in the deceleration phase of its urbanization process, whereas Malaysia and the Philippines are at early stages of the acceleration phase (Ogawa, 1985a).

This concept of the urbanization cycle hypothesis has been fully reflected in the 1988 United Nations population projections. The level of urbanization is projected to exceed the 50 per cent level for all five ASEAN countries by the year 2020, and for India and Pakistan by the year 2025. At the turn of the twenty-first century, South Korea's urbanization level is expected to catch up with that for Japan, and in 2025, the former will be 88 per cent as opposed to 80 per cent for the latter.

Although a number of studies (World Bank, 1982; Renaud, 1981) have demonstrated the robustness of the urbanization cycle hypothesis on the basis of cross-sectional data, the future scenario based upon the 1988 United Nations projections, in which this hypothesis is the key concept, is subject to uncertainties with regard to Asia's future urbanization.

One of the factors contributing to such uncertainties is that the international economic environment facing developing Asia in the 1990s and the twenty-first century is likely to be considerably different from what they have experienced before.

A second factor leading to the uncertainties is the pattern of urban development in the developing countries in Asia. As clearly distinct from the pattern of urban growth in the industrialized countries, urban areas in the Asian developing countries contain relatively small modern sectors and swiftly growing urban informal sectors with a rapidly growing population of urban squatters. Moreover, the extension of urban services into rural areas has been increasingly recognized in these developing countries (Hackenberg, 1980).

A third factor is the development of communications and transportation. At an early stage of economic development in the developed nations, both communications and transportation made urban living possible at lower population densities than would be viable in the contemporary developing countries in Asia. Furthermore, the means of information diffusion and transportation is much more technologically advanced in the present-day developing countries than when the developed countries were at initial development stages.

A fourth factor is the demographic mechanism of urban growth. Internal migration has come to play an increasingly important role in the growth of urban populations in developing Asia, particularly the ASEAN countries, partly because of lowered natural increase in urban areas (Ogawa, 1985a). One of the major sources of the decline in urban fertility is higher accessibility to government family planning programmes. For this reason, the components of a change in urban growth in the ASEAN region are thought to be different substantially from those of the more developed nations.

In preparing urban population projections for developing Asia, therefore, these factors unique to the developing part of Asia should be taken into account. Although they might follow the path of urbanization actually experienced by the developed countries, the simple application of the urbanization cycle hypothesis to Asia's pattern of urbanization poses some serious questions. Furthermore, because of the persistent pattern of diffused urbanization in the developing nations of Asia, it might prove easier to make assumptions about future trends for two or three urban categories than it would be to make a single assumption on the aggregate level of urbanization (Speare, 1984).

Although Asia's current level of urbanization is relatively low, urban growth rates have not only been high but the corresponding absolute increases have also been quite sizeable due to a large population base (Pernia, 1988). In many developing countries in Asia, while urban population growth has been rapid, because of high overall population growth rates, the growth of the rural population has been large enough to dampen the rise in urbanization levels. As a consequence of such rapid urban population growth, many of the Asian developing countries have the problems of urban primacy. Generally, the primate city is the national capital where both the population and major economic activities are highly concentrated. Thailand has the highest spatial concentration in the region, with over two-thirds of its urban population and a predominant share of overall economic activity situated in Bangkok. Other countries with high spatial concentrations are Bangladesh (30 per cent),

South Korea (41 per cent), and the Philippines (30 per cent) (Pernia, 1988).

Apart from urban primacy, the number of mega-cities with a population of 4 million and over is expected to increase in the years to come. In 1985, for instance, there were 20 mega-cities in Asia as a whole. There were 8 mega-cities in East Asia, 3 in South-East Asia, and 7 in South Asia (United Nations, 1985). In the year 2000, the numbers are projected to be 30 for the whole of Asia, 10 for East Asia, 5 for South-East Asia, and 12 for South Asia. By the year 2025, these numbers are estimated to be 59, 18, 9, and 24, respectively. These projected results point to the likelihood of a further increase in unrelenting pressure upon the well-being of urban residents in the developing countries in Asia in the 1990s and beyond.

*Age Structural Changes*

As a result of both pronounced fertility declines and remarkable mortality improvements among a number of countries in Asia and the Pacific, the age composition of each of these nations has been changing swiftly since the 1960s. As shown in Table 2.6, from 1960 to 1990, the total dependency ratio has fallen substantially in all the countries except for the two high-fertility countries (Bangladesh and Pakistan). The extent to which the dependency ratio for each country has decreased over this period is closely related to the magnitude with which its fertility has been lowered, as reflected in the intertemporal change in the young dependency ratio. Among the 13 countries which show a decline in the dependency ratio between 1960 and 1990, Singapore has the largest reduction by 43.2 points from 82.8 to 39.6. Singapore is followed by South Korea (37.3 points), Hong Kong (33.1 points), Thailand (32.7 points), and Malaysia (28.2 points). All of these countries have already attained the status of NIEs or are approaching it promptly. This may indicate that such faster declines of the dependency ratio have facilitated their rapid economic growth performance. Moreover, Singapore's dependency ratio is the lowest in 1990 among all the 15 countries under consideration, followed by Japan, Hong Kong, South Korea, and China.

The 1988 United Nations population projections, as shown in Table 2.6, indicate that the countries with high dependency ratios will face a considerable reduction of the burden placed upon the working-age population in the 1990s and beyond. In these countries, the declining dependency ratios are likely to facilitate their developmental process. In contrast, the countries with low dependency ratios are expected to undergo a substantial increase, mainly due to a rapid rise in the proportion of the elderly.

Table 2.6 also documents the changes in the aged dependency ratio for all the countries under consideration from 1960 to 1990. In the countries whose onset of fertility reduction was early, the changes in this ratio are most pronounced. Clearly, Japan has the largest gain from 9.0

TABLE 2.6
Age Structural Changes for Selected Countries in Asia and the Pacific, 1960, 1990, and 2025

| Country | 1960 Total | 1960 Young | 1960 Aged | 1960 Index of Ageing | 1990 Total | 1990 Young | 1990 Aged | 1990 Index of Ageing | 2025 Total | 2025 Young | 2025 Aged | 2025 Index of Ageing |
|---|---|---|---|---|---|---|---|---|---|---|---|---|
| East Asia | 75.1 | 66.6 | 8.5 | 12.8 | 47.1 | 37.8 | 9.3 | 24.6 | 46.8 | 26.6 | 20.1 | 75.7 |
| Japan | 56.1 | 47.2 | 9.0 | 19.0 | 43.3 | 26.5 | 16.8 | 63.3 | 63.5 | 24.8 | 38.7 | 156.1 |
| South Korea | 82.7 | 76.6 | 6.1 | 7.9 | 45.4 | 38.5 | 6.9 | 17.9 | 45.7 | 25.5 | 20.2 | 79.5 |
| China | 77.7 | 69.1 | 8.6 | 12.4 | 47.2 | 38.6 | 8.6 | 22.3 | 45.4 | 26.5 | 18.9 | 71.4 |
| Hong Kong | 77.6 | 72.6 | 5.0 | 6.8 | 44.5 | 31.8 | 12.7 | 39.8 | 58.4 | 25.2 | 33.2 | 131.6 |
| South-East Asia | 80.9 | 74.9 | 6.0 | 8.1 | 67.3 | 60.8 | 6.5 | 10.7 | 45.5 | 33.5 | 11.9 | 35.6 |
| Singapore | 82.8 | 79.0 | 3.8 | 4.8 | 39.6 | 31.9 | 7.7 | 24.3 | 55.4 | 25.7 | 29.7 | 115.5 |
| Thailand | 90.3 | 85.0 | 5.2 | 6.2 | 57.6 | 51.4 | 6.2 | 12.0 | 45.2 | 30.5 | 14.7 | 48.3 |
| Philippines | 91.0 | 85.2 | 5.8 | 6.8 | 76.9 | 70.9 | 6.0 | 8.5 | 46.7 | 36.5 | 10.1 | 27.8 |
| Indonesia | 77.0 | 71.1 | 5.9 | 8.3 | 63.7 | 57.4 | 6.3 | 11.0 | 44.8 | 31.5 | 13.3 | 42.3 |
| Malaysia | 94.9 | 88.2 | 6.6 | 7.5 | 66.7 | 60.3 | 6.4 | 10.6 | 47.3 | 33.5 | 13.8 | 41.0 |
| South Asia | 78.5 | 72.4 | 6.2 | 8.5 | 74.4 | 67.3 | 7.1 | 10.5 | 47.0 | 36.3 | 10.7 | 29.3 |
| India | 76.1 | 70.0 | 6.0 | 8.6 | 69.5 | 61.8 | 7.6 | 12.3 | 46.0 | 34.0 | 12.0 | 35.4 |
| Pakistan | 92.3 | 84.3 | 8.0 | 9.5 | 93.7 | 88.4 | 5.2 | 5.9 | 50.3 | 42.7 | 7.6 | 17.9 |
| Bangladesh | 80.8 | 74.1 | 6.7 | 9.1 | 87.9 | 82.5 | 5.5 | 6.6 | 46.0 | 39.2 | 6.8 | 17.4 |
| Sri Lanka | 84.1 | 77.4 | 6.7 | 8.6 | 60.5 | 52.2 | 8.3 | 15.9 | 50.8 | 32.5 | 18.3 | 56.3 |
| Oceania | 67.7 | 55.2 | 12.5 | 22.6 | 56.0 | 41.9 | 14.1 | 33.7 | 55.0 | 34.2 | 20.8 | 60.8 |
| Australia | 62.8 | 49.0 | 13.8 | 28.1 | 49.6 | 33.2 | 16.4 | 49.4 | 55.5 | 28.5 | 27.0 | 94.5 |
| New Zealand | 71.0 | 56.2 | 14.8 | 26.3 | 50.2 | 33.7 | 16.5 | 49.0 | 54.5 | 27.5 | 27.0 | 98.3 |

*Source*: As for Table 2.1.

in 1960 to 16.8 in 1990. Hong Kong and Singapore show considerable increases, although their 1990 levels are still low by the standards of developed countries. In 1990, Japan has the highest value, closely followed by New Zealand (16.5) and Australia (16.4).

A brief comparison of the index of ageing, however, yields a substantially different picture. Because the effect of fertility decline is immediately reflected in this index, a marked increase in the value of this index is observed among several developing countries under review, as presented in Table 2.6. Obviously, those countries which have shown a large increase in the aged dependency ratio have experienced a marked rise in their values of the index of ageing. These countries include Japan, Australia, New Zealand, Singapore, and Hong Kong. Among these five countries, Japan has the most aged population in 1990. Besides these industrialized countries and newly industrializing nations, South Korea, China, Thailand, Malaysia, and Sri Lanka have experienced a considerable increase in the index of ageing.

The foregoing discussion indicates that population ageing has been under way in all the countries in East Asia. Although its 1990 level (24.6) of population ageing is lower than that for Oceania (33.7), it is projected to rise to 75.7 by the year 2025, which is higher than the corresponding value for Oceania (60.8) (United Nations, 1989c). Moreover, Japan is expected to exceed the 100 level sometime during 2005–10, Hong Kong during 2015–20, and Singapore during 2020–5. In these countries, the number of those aged 65 and over will be greater than those aged 0–14 within the first quarter of the twenty-first century. Both South Korea and China are projected to be quickly catching up with Australia and New Zealand during 1990–2025. It is also interesting to note that although the four ASEAN countries (Indonesia, Malaysia, the Philippines, and Thailand) have comparable values of the index of ageing in 1990, three of them (Indonesia, Malaysia, and Thailand) are expected to undergo a fast process of population ageing in the early part of the twenty-first century, leaving the Philippines far behind. In South Asia, the process of population ageing is very slow; except for Sri Lanka, all the countries will have their values of the index of ageing below 40.

These projected results on the index of ageing suggest that the countries which have experienced or are undergoing the rapid fertility transition are likely to go through the process of population ageing in the 1990s and beyond. More importantly, primarily because the fertility transition in these Asian countries has been substantially quicker than in the developed countries, the speed of population ageing in the former has been and will be much faster than that observed in the latter. These Asian countries, therefore, need to swiftly shift the emphasis from the quantitative question of 'how many dependants' to the qualitative one of 'what kind of dependants' the working population has to support. In addition, the Asian societal structure and family organization are pronouncedly different from those of Western industrialized nations. Population ageing in Asia is also expected to advance at a lower level of economic development, compared with the case of the developed nations in the West (Jones, 1988a). Hence, Asia's process of adjustment to its age structural changes is likely to encounter a wide range of problems, both serious and unique, in allocating the support resources for a rapidly growing number of the elderly population (Ogawa, 1988a, 1990, 1992).

It is also important to observe that although the proportion of the elderly aged 65 and over in the total population in developing Asia is still considerably lower than that for the developed region, due to the large population size in the former, 46 per cent of the elderly in the entire world are currently residing in the three subregions of Asia in question. Because the urbanization level in these subregions is low, most of the elderly in Asia are living in rural areas where poverty is a serious problem.

It is axiomatic among demographers that declining fertility, not increased life expectancy, is the principal determinant of population ageing. It should be stressed, however, that the mortality effect on population ageing becomes increasingly strong as the process of demographic transition and economic development proceeds. In Japan, for instance, the fertility effect was approximately 10.5 times more dominant in inducing the ageing process than the mortality effect over the period 1950–70. During the period 1970–85, however, mortality declines contributed to the ageing of the Japanese population by about 22 per cent more than the fertility reduction (Ogawa, 1986a, 1988a, 1989b). In 1990, the mortality effect on population ageing seems relatively limited in most of the Asian countries, as compared with the fertility effect. However, if the trends in mortality improvements observed in the 1970s and 1980s continue in these countries, mortality at advanced ages will fall substantially in the 1990s and early part of the twenty-first century, thus making it a major source of population ageing. It is generally considered that the role of mortality improvements in inducing the ageing process becomes increasingly vital, especially when life expectancy at birth exceeds 70 years (Myers, 1988). In view of the fact that some of the developing Asian countries have already achieved a higher than 70-year life expectancy at birth, it can be easily conceived that in these countries the mortality effect will overtake the fertility effect before the end of the twentieth century or in the early part of the twenty-first century. This implies that development planners in these countries should pay greater attention to mortality changes in the 1990s and beyond.

Based upon the discussions above, it may be concluded that during 1990–2025 the Asia–Pacific region is likely to face two different problems, namely, population explosions and population ageing. In this sense, the nature of population problems in Asia and the Pacific will become increasingly heterogeneous towards the end of the twentieth century and in the early part of the twenty-first century. Moreover, within each subregion, the seriousness of these problems will vary from country to country over time. To cope with these problems, a different set of population and development policy measures will be required for each individual country at a different stage of development. Such policy adjustments, however, are thought to be difficult due to the fast fertility and mortality transitions under way.

*International Migration*

Since the mid-1970s, problems on international labour migration have become increasingly serious in the Asia–Pacific region. In the 1970s, there were massive international labour flows from Asia to the Middle East, particularly from countries in South and South-East Asia to oil-exporting countries. The estimated 900,000 guest workers in 1970 grew at 9 per cent per annum during the 1970s (Appleyard, 1984). As a consequence of slower economic growth in the oil-exporting countries in the 1980s, however, labour migration from Asia to the Middle East has become increasingly difficult.

Within each subregion, there is a flow of labour among the constituent countries—international labour migration within the ASEAN region being a salient example (Lim, 1986). It is of significance both in terms of the numbers involved and their economic importance to the ASEAN countries (Stahl, 1985): Singapore relies on Malaysia for a significant proportion of its labour supply; Indonesia supplies a great many workers to Malaysia and a smaller number to Singapore; and Thai and Filipino workers find employment in both Singapore and Malaysia. Filipinos are found in large numbers in Sabah (East Malaysia) while a number of Thai farm workers find seasonal employment in the northern states of Peninsular Malaysia.

Since the late 1970s, refugee migration from and within Asia stems mainly from the conflicts in Vietnam and Afghanistan. Refugees from Vietnam typically make nearby countries such as Thailand, Malaysia, and Indonesia their first countries of refuge, permanent settlement being made later in North America, Europe, and Australia. Even now in the early 1990s, a substantial number of boat arrivals from Vietnam are being reported from various countries of Asia.

Besides these international migration flows, there has been a considerable flow of labour from developing Asia to Japan since the mid-1980s. Presently, the Japanese government prohibits business firms from importing labour, except for those with highly specialized skills such as foreign language teachers and professional athletes. The proportion of foreign nationals in the Japanese labour force is estimated at only 0.0018 per cent, the lowest percentage among the industrialized nations (Abella, 1989). The corresponding figure for the OECD countries ranges from 2.8 per cent for the Netherlands to 9.4 per cent for Belgium.

It should be emphasized, however, that the number of undocumented and illegal labour migrants from developing Asia has been increasing at an alarming rate. The number of illegal foreign workers arrested by the

Japanese authorities was only 2,339 in 1983, but increased to 14,314 in 1988. Moreover, until 1987, the majority of these illegal foreign workers arrested had been women, but beginning in 1986, the number of male illegal foreign workers grew rapidly, exceeding that of their female counterparts in 1988. Most of these foreigners were unskilled workers, engaged in the service, manufacturing, and construction industries. Data for 1988 show that 38 per cent of them were from the Philippines, 21 per cent from Bangladesh, 17 per cent from Pakistan, 10 per cent from Thailand, and 7 per cent from South Korea. These percentages indicate that more than 90 per cent of the illegal foreign workers arrested were from the developing region of Asia, whose countries used to be the major exporters of labour to the oil-producing countries in the 1970s.

The following three factors are generally considered to have induced this rapid growth of labour migration from the developing parts of Asia. One is the increased income disparity between Japan and developing Asia due primarily to the appreciation of the yen. For example, in 1980, the differential in GNP per capita between Japan and the Philippines was 14:1. In 1988, it rose to 33:1. A second factor is related to Japan's slower growth of the labour force relative to the growth of labour demand. It is ironic, however, that although there has been a severe shortage of young workers since the mid-1980s, there has been a huge surplus of aged workers owing to the ageing of the labour force and the seniority-oriented wage system in Japan (Martin and Ogawa, 1988). A third factor is the differential responses among various industries to a wide range of structural adjustments required because of the strengthening of the yen against the world's major currencies, particularly the dollar (Shimada, 1989). As a result of the pronounced change in relative factor prices, many industries have managed to shift their production outside Japan by exporting capital to the sources of cheap labour. However, labour-intensive industries such as construction and services have been slow in adjusting themselves to these changes. Because the working conditions of these industries with low productivity are inferior to those of other industries with high productivity, young workers shy away from the labour-intensive industries. Consequently, in the construction industry, there are 4 million blue-collar workers, but approximately half of them are above 50 years of age (Shimada, 1989). Furthermore, the shortage of labour has become particularly serious among small-scale businesses in the industries with low productivity.

According to the data collected in 1988 from small-scale firms by the Ministry of International Trade and Industry (MITI), 58 per cent of the firms surveyed expressed an urgent need for importing unskilled workers from foreign countries (Ogawa, 1989c).

In the early 1990s, Japan's labour shortage problems are industry-specific. To a great degree, these problems may be solved through a series of adjustments in the labour market. It should be stressed, however, that because the absolute size of the labour force is projected to start diminishing from the end of the twentieth century (Ogawa et al.,

1988), these problems are likely to be further aggravated in the long run. In addition, although Japan produces 13 per cent of world GNP by importing a vast amount of natural resources and raw materials from different parts of the world, a number of tight restrictions and regulations are still imposed upon the inflow of various foreign goods and human resources. In view of this situation, since the late 1980s, there has been increasing pressure from the international communities upon Japan to remove these trade barriers. In response to such external pressure, the Japanese government has just begun exploring the possibilities of opening up its market.

It is often argued that one of the factors leading to Japan's prohibition of the importation of labour from foreign countries is the cultural one (Weiner, 1985; Lim, 1989a). It is well known that Japanese society is remarkably homogeneous (Hodge and Ogawa, 1991). For this reason, importing labour from foreign countries on a large scale may add a considerable degree of heterogeneity to Japanese society, thus disrupting its societal system. Data gathered from a nation-wide survey on internationalization conducted by the Mainichi Newspapers at the end of 1988 showed that out of 2,238 respondents, 45 per cent of them stated that it was desirable to import unskilled labour from foreign countries, while 48 per cent of them were against the idea of accepting such foreign workers. A multivariate analysis of this data set has identified, as one of the major determinants of accepting foreign workers in Japanese society, the degree of international exposure through personal contacts with foreigners and the purchase of foreign goods particularly imported from Asian NIEs. This statistical result suggests that because the volume of human contacts and the purchase of NIEs' products have been rapidly increasing in Japanese society since the early 1980s, if this trend continues, it is likely that the proportion of the Japanese population in favour of labour migration from developing Asia will rise over time.

The literature on international labour migration shows that by and large, labour demand in receiving countries tends to be the main determinant for the genesis of labour movements across national borders (Lim, 1988a). As shown in the data compiled in 1988 by MITI, Japan's demand for unskilled foreign workers has already been strong, so it may be said that it is unavoidable for Japan to open its doors to workers from the developing region of Asia. Caution should be exercised, however, with regard to Asia's potential for supplying labour to Japan. As displayed in Table 2.7, the growth of the labour force for the age group 20–29 is projected to decline substantially in many developing countries in Asia, due primarily to their declining fertility. This suggests that at the beginning of the twenty-first century when Japan's population ageing process accelerates, developing Asia may not have enough labour surplus to export to Japan. It is therefore possible that Japan will have to import labour from the other developing regions by 2010. In any case, the processes shaping international labour migration in this increasingly interconnected global economy are extremely complex and intricate, involving various dimensions such as economic, political, institutional,

## TABLE 2.7
### Annual Growth Rates of Labour Force Aged 20–29 by Sex for Selected Countries in Asia, 1985–2025 (per cent)

| Country | 1985–90 | 1990–5 | 1995–2000 | 2000–10 | 2010–20 | 2020–5 |
|---|---|---|---|---|---|---|
| Bangladesh | | | | | | |
| Male | 3.03 | 3.31 | 3.23 | 2.30 | 1.33 | 0.66 |
| Female | 5.31 | 5.93 | 5.06 | 4.49 | 3.70 | 3.20 |
| China | | | | | | |
| Male | 3.90 | 1.21 | −2.74 | −1.67 | 0.76 | −0.39 |
| Female | 4.26 | 1.55 | −2.55 | −1.48 | 1.05 | −0.14 |
| Hong Kong | | | | | | |
| Male | −1.24 | −2.09 | −0.78 | 0.10 | −0.66 | −0.87 |
| Female | −1.54 | −2.08 | −0.55 | 0.75 | −0.49 | −0.62 |
| India | | | | | | |
| Male | 2.25 | 2.02 | 1.34 | 0.53 | 0.16 | −0.67 |
| Female | 1.54 | 1.53 | 0.94 | 0.59 | 0.77 | −0.43 |
| Indonesia | | | | | | |
| Male | 2.46 | 2.73 | 1.41 | 0.37 | 0.23 | −0.15 |
| Female | 2.82 | 3.02 | 1.60 | 0.73 | 0.62 | 0.52 |
| Japan | | | | | | |
| Male | 1.29 | 1.88 | −0.07 | −2.04 | 0.65 | 0.99 |
| Female | 1.40 | 2.13 | −0.60 | −1.77 | 0.92 | 0.91 |
| South Korea | | | | | | |
| Male | 0.69 | −1.06 | −0.47 | 0.86 | −0.24 | −0.96 |
| Female | 1.03 | 0.30 | 0.93 | 1.78 | −0.03 | −0.58 |
| Malaysia | | | | | | |
| Male | 2.60 | 1.81 | 0.90 | 1.60 | −0.51 | −0.84 |
| Female | 2.33 | 2.48 | 1.77 | 2.56 | 0.15 | −0.32 |
| Nepal | | | | | | |
| Male | 2.38 | 3.84 | 3.20 | 1.77 | 1.80 | 0.92 |
| Female | 3.05 | 2.45 | 2.14 | 1.05 | 1.02 | 3.50 |
| Pakistan | | | | | | |
| Male | 2.58 | 2.23 | 2.05 | 2.78 | 0.97 | 0.46 |
| Female | 4.87 | 4.66 | 4.24 | 5.36 | 3.52 | 3.09 |
| Philippines | | | | | | |
| Male | 2.94 | 2.65 | 2.25 | 1.29 | 0.65 | −0.19 |
| Female | 1.25 | 1.56 | 2.14 | 1.85 | 1.65 | 0.91 |
| Singapore | | | | | | |
| Male | −2.27 | −2.56 | −1.75 | 0.12 | −0.27 | −0.68 |
| Female | −2.29 | −2.31 | −2.15 | 0.34 | −0.28 | −0.62 |
| Sri Lanka | | | | | | |
| Male | 0.73 | 0.38 | 1.04 | 1.80 | −1.24 | −0.08 |
| Female | 0.34 | 0.83 | 1.39 | 2.51 | −0.20 | 0.86 |
| Thailand | | | | | | |
| Male | 2.88 | 1.69 | −0.27 | −0.06 | 0.86 | 0.65 |
| Female | 1.77 | 1.00 | −0.93 | −0.31 | 1.25 | 1.54 |
| Turkey | | | | | | |
| Male | 2.42 | 1.78 | 0.30 | 1.11 | 0.63 | 0.26 |
| Female | 3.12 | 2.76 | 1.53 | 2.58 | 1.53 | 0.82 |

*Source*: United Nations (1988d).

and social factors. In addition, the configuration of world conditions is changing constantly. For these reasons, it is virtually impossible to make any definite predictions regarding the future international flows of labour to Japan.

In this section, the trends of various demographic factors in Asia and the Pacific from the 1960s to 1980s have been reviewed, and their future prospects examined. In the ensuing section, the discussion, focusing upon fertility and mortality, is on the interrelationships between the population variables and socio-economic development factors, based on cross-sectional data gathered from the Asia–Pacific countries.

## Interrelations between Demographic Changes and Socio-economic Factors

In this section, for 1960–80, trends of changes in the level of economic development, as reflected in GNP per capita, as well as changes in such human resource indicators as primary and secondary school enrolment ratios, the female labour force participation rate, and the proportion of labour force in agriculture are first looked at. Then changes in the degree of association between a level of economic development and socio-demographic characteristics of the population, namely, fertility, mortality, education, and labour force are examined.

TABLE 2.8
GNP Per Capita at Market Prices for Selected Countries in Asia and the Pacific, 1960–1985 (dollars)

| Country | 1960 | 1965 | 1970 | 1975 | 1980 | 1985 |
|---|---|---|---|---|---|---|
| East Asia | | | | | | |
| Japan | 467 | 917 | 1,930 | 4,990 | 9,870 | 11,270 |
| South Korea | 154 | 105 | 260 | 580 | 1,620 | 2,160 |
| China | – | – | 120 | 180 | 290 | 320 |
| Hong Kong | 331 | 531 | 890 | 2,160 | 5,210 | 6,120 |
| South-East Asia | | | | | | |
| Singapore | 438 | 525 | 960 | 2,540 | 4,570 | 7,590 |
| Thailand | 94 | 129 | 190 | 360 | 670 | 800 |
| Philippines | 251 | 188 | 240 | 370 | 700 | 580 |
| Indonesia | – | – | 90 | 210 | 480 | 530 |
| Malaysia | 270 | 307 | 390 | 820 | 1,680 | 1,980 |
| South Asia | | | | | | |
| India | 72 | 103 | 100 | 140 | 220 | 270 |
| Pakistan | 81 | 112 | 170 | 140 | 290 | 340 |
| Bangladesh | 59 | 72 | 100 | 130 | 140 | 150 |
| Sri Lanka | 151 | 160 | 170 | 220 | 260 | 380 |
| Oceania | | | | | | |
| Australia | 1,574 | 2,018 | 1,960 | 4,760 | 9,990 | 9,130 |
| New Zealand | 1,653 | 2,107 | 2,220 | 4,610 | 6,910 | 6,960 |

*Source*: World Bank (1988), *World Tables 1987*, Washington, DC.

Table 2.8 presents changes in GNP per capita for the Asian and Pacific countries under consideration. The table clearly shows the rapidity of economic development experienced in the region as a whole during 1960–85. The tempo of economic development of East and South-East Asian countries was considerably faster than that of South Asian countries, thus widening the income disparities between the countries over time. In 1960, New Zealand had the highest GNP per capita and the lowest GNP per capita was recorded by India. The income level for the former was 23 times higher than that for the latter. In 1985, GNP per capita for Japan (the highest country) was 75 times larger than for Bangladesh (the lowest country). In addition, it is interesting to note that according to the most recent *World Development Report* (World Bank, 1989), Singapore and Hong Kong were ranked as upper middle-income economies in 1986 but joined the high-income economies in 1987.

Tables 2.9 and 2.10 present changes in primary and secondary school enrolment ratios during 1960–85. These ratios express enrolment of all ages in primary or secondary schools as a percentage of the population

TABLE 2.9
Primary School Enrolment Ratios for Selected Countries in Asia and the Pacific, 1960–1985 (per cent)

| Country | 1960 | 1965 | 1970 | 1975 | 1980 | 1985 |
|---|---|---|---|---|---|---|
| East Asia | | | | | | |
| Japan | 103 | 100 | 99 | 99 | 101 | 102 |
| South Korea | 94 | 101 | 103 | 107 | 109 | 96 |
| China | 109 | – | 89 | 126 | 105 | 124 |
| Hong Kong | 87 | 103 | 117 | 119 | 107 | 105 |
| South-East Asia | | | | | | |
| Singapore | 111 | 105 | 105 | 110 | 108 | 115 |
| Thailand | 83 | 78 | 83 | 83 | 99 | 97 |
| Philippines | 95 | 113 | 108 | 107 | 114 | 106 |
| Indonesia | 71 | 72 | 80 | 86 | 107 | 118 |
| Malaysia | 96 | 90 | 87 | 91 | 95 | 99 |
| South Asia | | | | | | |
| India | 61 | 74 | 73 | 79 | 81 | 92 |
| Pakistan | 30 | 40 | 40 | 46 | 43 | 47 |
| Bangladesh | 47 | 49 | 54 | 73 | 62 | 60 |
| Sri Lanka | 95 | 93 | 99 | 77 | 98 | 103 |
| Oceania | | | | | | |
| Australia | 103 | 99 | 115 | 107 | 109 | 106 |
| New Zealand | 108 | 106 | 110 | 106 | 108 | 106 |

*Sources*: World Bank (1984), *World Tables*, 3rd edn., Baltimore: Johns Hopkins University Press; World Bank (1988), *World Tables 1987*, Washington, DC; World Bank (1988), *World Development Report 1988*, New York: Oxford University Press.

TRENDS OF THE 1960s TO 1980s AND FUTURE PROSPECTS 51

TABLE 2.10
Secondary School Enrolment Ratios for Selected Countries in
Asia and the Pacific, 1960–1985 (per cent)

| Country | 1960 | 1965 | 1970 | 1975 | 1980 | 1985 |
| --- | --- | --- | --- | --- | --- | --- |
| East Asia | | | | | | |
| Japan | 74 | 82 | 86 | 91 | 93 | 96 |
| South Korea | 27 | 35 | 42 | 56 | 76 | 94 |
| China | 21 | – | 23 | 56 | 43 | 39 |
| Hong Kong | 20 | 29 | 36 | 49 | 64 | 69 |
| South-East Asia | | | | | | |
| Singapore | 32 | 45 | 46 | 52 | 58 | 71 |
| Thailand | 13 | 14 | 17 | 26 | 29 | 30 |
| Philippines | 26 | 41 | 46 | 54 | 62 | 65 |
| Indonesia | 6 | 12 | 16 | 20 | 29 | 39 |
| Malaysia | 19 | 28 | 34 | 42 | 49 | 53 |
| South Asia | | | | | | |
| India | 20 | 27 | 26 | 26 | 31 | 35 |
| Pakistan | 11 | 12 | 13 | 15 | 14 | 17 |
| Bangladesh | 8 | 13 | 19 | 26 | 18 | 18 |
| Sri Lanka | 27 | 35 | 47 | 48 | 51 | 63 |
| Oceania | | | | | | |
| Australia | 51 | 62 | 82 | 87 | 85 | 95 |
| New Zealand | 73 | 75 | 77 | 81 | 81 | 85 |

Sources: As for Table 2.9.

of primary and secondary school age, respectively, and so they can sometimes exceed 100—due to enrolments outside the official ages for the educational level. From Table 2.9, note that primary education has become almost universal in Asia and the Pacific, except for such South Asian countries as India, Pakistan, and Bangladesh. Even in these countries in which primary education has not yet become universal, the proportion of population with primary education appears to be increasing steadily. In contrast to primary education, however, substantial differences in the extent of dissemination of secondary education can be found among the Asian and Pacific countries considered. Specifically, as shown in Table 2.10, a vast majority of the population has acquired secondary education in the three developed countries in the region (Japan, Australia, and New Zealand), and the quickness of the spread of secondary education in South Korea during 1960–85 is remarkable. Some countries have also made significant progress in spreading secondary education, if not as much as South Korea, whereas others have made very little progress.

Turning to changes in labour force variables, Table 2.11 presents changes in the female labour force participation rate during 1960–85. It can be noticed from the table that the female labour force participation

TABLE 2.11
Female Labour Force Participation Rates for
Selected Countries in Asia and the Pacific, 1960–1985

| Country | 1960 | 1965 | 1970 | 1975 | 1980 | 1985 |
|---|---|---|---|---|---|---|
| East Asia | | | | | | |
| Japan | 36.0 | 38.0 | 39.0 | 38.3 | 37.7 | 37.8 |
| South Korea | 17.2 | 19.8 | 32.1 | 33.3 | 34.1 | 34.0 |
| China | 37.0[a] | 35.3 | 41.7 | 42.4 | 43.2 | 43.2 |
| Hong Kong | 22.6 | 24.7 | 34.7 | 35.4 | 35.5 | 34.5 |
| South-East Asia | | | | | | |
| Singapore | 14.5 | 15.5 | 25.9 | 30.7 | 34.5 | 33.4 |
| Thailand | 49.8 | 46.3 | 47.3 | 47.1 | 47.1 | 45.9 |
| Philippines | 29.4 | 25.9 | 33.2 | 32.8 | 32.9 | 32.1 |
| Indonesia | 20.0 | 20.6 | 30.2 | 30.8 | 31.3 | 31.3 |
| Malaysia | 18.9 | 19.9 | 31.2 | 33.0 | 34.6 | 34.9 |
| South Asia | | | | | | |
| India | 27.3 | 27.0 | 29.7 | 28.5 | 27.2 | 26.2 |
| Pakistan | 5.7 | 5.6 | 9.1 | 9.8 | 10.4 | 11.4 |
| Bangladesh | 3.3 | 4.4 | 5.4 | 5.8 | 6.3 | 6.8 |
| Sri Lanka | 16.2 | 16.6 | 25.0 | 25.6 | 26.7 | 26.9 |
| Oceania | | | | | | |
| Australia | 20.2 | 23.5 | 31.2 | 34.4 | 37.5 | 37.8 |
| New Zealand | 18.7 | 21.1 | 29.4 | 31.6 | 34.0 | 34.5 |

Sources: World Bank (1984), *World Tables*, 3rd edn., Baltimore: Johns Hopkins University Press; World Bank (1988), *World Tables 1987*, Washington, DC.
[a] 1957 data.

rates have been increasing considerably in the 1970s and 1980s in many Asian and Pacific countries, particularly among the newly industrializing economies. In some other countries, the rates have been fluctuating over time, but the magnitude of such oscillations is fairly small. Altogether, it can be said that during the period 1960–85, there has been a substantial intercountry differential in the pattern of changes in the female labour force participation rates.

Table 2.12 presents changes in the proportion of labour force in agriculture during 1960–85. The countries under consideration show very different levels in their proportions of labour force engaged in agriculture owing to the fact that the region includes such city-state countries as Hong Kong and Singapore, and such developed countries as Japan, Australia, and New Zealand. Although there remain significant differences in the proportions *per se*, all the countries have experienced decreases in the proportion of the agricultural labour force during 1960–85, indicating an overall trend of increasing industrialization.

Next, changes in the strength of association of these human resource factors and demographic variables (discussed in the previous section)

TRENDS OF THE 1960s TO 1980s AND FUTURE PROSPECTS  53

TABLE 2.12
Proportion of Labour Force in Agriculture
for Selected Countries in Asia and the Pacific, 1960–1985 (per cent)

| Country | 1960 | 1965 | 1970 | 1975 | 1980 | 1985 |
|---|---|---|---|---|---|---|
| East Asia | | | | | | |
| Japan | 33.0 | 26.0 | 19.6 | 15.4 | 11.2 | 11.0 |
| South Korea | 66.0 | 58.3 | 49.1 | 42.8 | 36.4 | 36.0 |
| China | – | – | 78.3 | 76.3 | 74.2 | 74.0 |
| Hong Kong | 8.0 | 5.7 | 4.4 | 3.2 | 2.1 | 2.0 |
| South-East Asia | | | | | | |
| Singapore | 8.0 | 5.7 | 3.4 | 2.5 | 1.6 | 2.0 |
| Thailand | 84.0 | 82.1 | 79.8 | 75.3 | 70.9 | 71.0 |
| Philippines | 61.0 | 57.1 | 54.8 | 53.3 | 51.8 | 52.0 |
| Indonesia | 75.0 | 70.7 | 66.3 | 61.8 | 57.2 | 57.0 |
| Malaysia | 63.0 | 59.5 | 53.8 | 47.7 | 41.6 | 42.0 |
| South Asia | | | | | | |
| India | 74.0 | 74.0 | 71.7 | 70.7 | 69.7 | 70.0 |
| Pakistan | 61.0 | 60.0 | 58.9 | 56.8 | 54.6 | 55.0 |
| Bangladesh | 87.0 | 86.5 | 81.4 | 78.1 | 74.8 | 75.0 |
| Sri Lanka | 56.0 | 55.5 | 55.3 | 54.3 | 53.6 | 53.0 |
| Oceania | | | | | | |
| Australia | 11.4 | 9.6 | 8.1 | 7.4 | 6.9 | 7.0 |
| New Zealand | 14.7 | 13.2 | 11.9 | 11.5 | 11.2 | 11.0 |

Sources: As for Table 2.11.

are examined with the level of economic development. Table 2.13 presents the estimated Pearson correlation coefficient of the social and demographic variables under consideration. It can be seen from the table that GNP per capita has strong negative correlations with TFR, the infant mortality rate, and the proportion of labour force in agriculture. Furthermore, the degree of negative association between GNP per capita and the proportion of labour force in agriculture increased considerably during 1960–85. In contrast, the level of economic development is found to have strong positive correlations with secondary school enrolment ratio and life expectancy at birth. Meanwhile, the correlations between GNP per capita and the primary school enrolment ratio and the female labour force participation rate showed an intermediate level of association, although the strength of association of female labour force participation increased considerably during 1970–85.

From these findings, therefore, it can be supposed that all the demographic and human resource factors under consideration are closely associated with levels of economic development. It is, however, extremely difficult to determine the precise nature and direction of the causal relationships among these variables. Moreover, some of the relationships may need to be estimated simultaneously, while the others may

TABLE 2.13
Estimated Degree of Association between Selected
Socio-demographic Variables and GNP Per Capita, 1960–1985

| Variables | 1960 | 1965 | 1970 | 1975 | 1980 | 1985 |
|---|---|---|---|---|---|---|
| GNP per capita | 1.000 | 1.000 | 1.000 | 1.000 | 1.000 | 1.000 |
| Total fertility rate (TFR) | −0.657 | −0.737 | −0.834 | −0.771 | −0.702 | −0.689 |
| Life expectancy at birth | 0.717 | 0.710 | 0.761 | 0.751 | 0.757 | 0.773 |
| Infant mortality rate | −0.670 | −0.650 | −0.730 | −0.704 | −0.690 | −0.707 |
| Primary school enrolment ratio | 0.519 | 0.440 | 0.577 | 0.466 | 0.452 | 0.297 |
| Secondary school enrolment ratio | 0.755 | 0.774 | 0.884 | 0.833 | 0.798 | 0.763 |
| Female labour force participation rate | −0.104 | 0.028 | 0.140 | 0.229 | 0.296 | 0.312 |
| Proportion of labour force in agriculture | −0.694 | −0.712 | −0.813 | −0.829 | −0.848 | −0.895 |

*Sources*: As for Tables 2.4, 2.8, and 2.9.

encounter the multicollinearity problem. More importantly, the usefulness of modelling the interrelationship among population and socio-economic variables on the basis of intercountry aggregate data is often questioned (United Nations, 1981).

## Subregional Differences in the Role of Human Resources in Asian Economic Growth

In the previous section, it has been noted that both demographic and human resource factors are closely associated with overall economic development in the Asia–Pacific region. Emphasis, however, has been placed upon population variables. In this section, therefore, an attempt is made to discuss the role of human resource factors in economic development on a country-specific basis.

Several sources-of-growth studies on the US economy were undertaken in the late 1950s and throughout the 1960s (Schultz, 1961; Denison, 1967). These studies pointed to the importance of human capital in the process of economic progress. Encouraged by this well-known finding, many developing nations enthusiastically began to make strenuous efforts to strengthen their educational programmes as a means of uplifting their undeveloped economies. At one of the conferences held in Karachi in 1960, many Asian governments agreed on plans for seven years of free, compulsory public education by 1980. It is important to note, however, that more than one-third of these countries failed to achieve this policy target, and some of those which managed to meet this goal did so only by lowering the quality of education to a substantial degree (Oshima, 1986). Although it is difficult to pinpoint the reasons for the reduced enthusiasm for human resource development among some of the Asian developing countries since the early 1980s, it has been speculated that despite the fact that human development is a slow process, too much was expected from education in the short run (Oshima, 1986).

It should be stressed, however, that the extent to which education has contributed to economic growth varies from country to country in Asia. The intercountry differences in the magnitude of the contribution of human resource development to economic growth are partially reflected by the differentiation or widening gap in the average incomes of Asian countries, as discussed in the earlier section. In view of such intercountry income differences, it is fitting to review briefly the role of human resources in the post-war aggregate growth of the three subregions, by highlighting the experiences of a few selected countries in each subregion.

*East Asia*

Japan and then South Korea are discussed as representatives of East Asia. At the close of World War II, the Japanese economy was severely crippled and in shambles. In his paper presented at a conference in 1949, Warren Thompson, a noted American demographer, stated, after serving as a population adviser to General MacArthur:

Japan can no doubt increase her resources significantly through trade as she did in the past. Malaya will take a certain amount of Japanese goods—textiles, bicycles, rubber shoes, flashlights, etc.—for iron ore, rubber, and tin.... A similar trade with Indonesia, the Philippines, and other Asiatic countries should be possible.... On the other hand, Japan's competitive position in foreign trade will improve by a general increase in her industrial efficiency.... But it is by no means certain that this improvement will be rapid or that it will be sufficiently great to enable Japan to meet European and American competition in many lines where good machinery, efficient labour, and good business organization can offset lower wages in maintaining low unit costs.... I do not believe the means of relieving the pressure of population on resources which have been discussed above will do a great deal to help Japan within the next decade or two (Thompson, 1950).

In retrospect, it is easy to see where Thompson erred in not foreseeing Japan's miraculous economic recovery in the 1950s and 1960s. One of the sources of his misjudgement is related to the framework in which international economic relations were to be conducted in the post-war period. In addition, he clearly underestimated the magnitude of fertility reduction which occurred in the late 1940s and throughout the 1950s. More importantly, Thompson greatly underestimated the qualities of the Japanese labour force available subsequent to World War II. It has been pointed out in a number of studies (Oshima, 1982, 1983a, 1983b, 1986; Cummings, 1980; Ohkawa and Shinohara, 1979) that the rapidity of changes in the Japanese economy during the 1950s would not have been possible without the high quality of manpower which had originated in the pre-war decades. To further endorse the validity of this view, it is useful to compare, as shown in Table 2.14, intertemporal changes in the following four indicators: (i) national income, (ii) labour force (gainfully employed population), (iii) physical capital stock (national wealth), and (iv) educational capital stock. Over the period 1905–35, the labour force increased 1.2 times, from 25.6 to 31.4 million, while physical capital increased about 4.5 times, from 5.8 to 25.9 trillion yen during the same period. Also, the national income showed a pronounced increase: about 4.3 times, from 1.2 to 5.2 billion yen. More importantly, educational capital stock expanded by about 8.3 times from 0.31 trillion yen in 1905 to 2.56 trillion yen in 1935, thus exceeding the growth rate of all the other indicators (Okita et al., 1982). These statistics indicate that Japan placed enormous emphasis upon human resource development in the allocation of its resources during the pre-war period. In 1950, the average worker on rural farms had 7 years of schooling, while the average worker engaged in the urban industrial sector had approximately 10 years of schooling. These levels of educational attainment among these workers were by far the highest in Asia at that time.

Immediately after World War II, Japan pursued a policy of agricultural development which enhanced the work motivation of all peasants through institutional changes such as the Land Reform Act of the late 1940s, which in turn, reduced substantially the power and privileges of large landowners. It was the high level of educational attainment of the farm labour force and its technological experiences accumulated since the Meiji period that made these institutional changes extremely effective in enabling the peasantry to improve the productivity of the land when new opportunities arose (Oshima, 1982).

Due to the rapid expansion of agricultural production, Japan became self-sufficient in food, which in turn, converted the large deficits in the balance of payments to surpluses by the end of the 1950s.

These surpluses were used for the further importation of machinery for heavy industrialization in the 1960s. As was the case with agriculture, the high level of schooling among labourers, combined with industrial experience acquired from several pre-war decades, was a main factor in the efficiency of Japanese industrial development. As extensively discussed elsewhere (Ogawa and Suits, 1982; Ogawa, 1986b), a large part of the high-quality labour force absorbed into urban industrial sectors had been transferred from the rural agricultural sector because young rural workers could be released from agricultural activities

TABLE 2.14
Increase of National Income, Labour Force, Physical Capital, and Educational Capital in Japan, 1905–1960

| Year | National Income Amount (¥ billion) | National Income Index | Labour Force Amount (¥ million) | Labour Force Index | Physical Capital Amount (¥ trillion) | Physical Capital Index | Educational Capital Amount (¥ 10 billion) | Educational Capital Index |
|---|---|---|---|---|---|---|---|---|
| 1905 | 1.210 | 100 | 25.6 | 100 | 5.8 | 100 | 31 | 100 |
| 1910 | 1.559 | 129 | 26.2 | 102 | 8.0 | 138 | 47 | 152 |
| 1913 | 2.045 | 169 | 26.4 | 103 | 8.6 | 148 | 59 | 188 |
| 1917 | 2.035 | 168 | 26.6 | 104 | 8.5 | 147 | 73 | 236 |
| 1919 | 2.761 | 228 | 26.6 | 104 | 10.1 | 174 | 81 | 260 |
| 1924 | 3.026 | 250 | 28.2 | 110 | 17.6 | 304 | 110 | 367 |
| 1930 | 4.054 | 335 | 29.3 | 115 | 23.1 | 398 | 186 | 600 |
| 1935 | 5.234 | 433 | 31.4 | 123 | 25.9 | 447 | 256 | 831 |
| 1955 | 7.189 | 594 | 39.2 | 153 | 21.7 | 374 | 538 | 1,731 |
| 1960 | 11.822 | 979 | 43.7 | 171 | 39.8 | 686 | 711 | 2,286 |

*Source*: Ministry of Education (1962: 11).
*Note*: National income, physical capital (national wealth), and educational capital are expressed in 1960 prices.

through small-scale mechanization as well as the increased participation of middle-aged women in the farm labour force. As documented elsewhere (Ogawa, 1986b; Tsuya and Kuroda, 1989), however, net in-migration from non-metropolitan to metropolitan areas was at a high level from the late 1950s to the early 1960s, with its peak in 1961. One of the primary factors contributing to the decline in the volume of in-migration into the metropolitan area is a decrease in the number of potential out-migrants from the rural side due to the rapid decline in fertility which commenced from the late 1940s (Ogawa, 1986b). Moreover, as a result of massive rural–urban migration and fast urban growth, the household size became smaller and the family structure changed from the extended type to the nuclear type, thus leading to a further decline in fertility (Ogawa and Hodge, 1986; Hodge and Ogawa, 1991). These changes seem to indicate that the mobility transition proceeded in parallel with the fertility transition in post-war Japan.

Although it has hardly been touched upon in the literature on Japanese economic development, the baby boom cohorts born from 1947 to 1949 played a significant role in achieving the phenomenal economic growth in the 1960s. During the baby boom period, there were almost 2.7 million births every year. Immediately after the baby boom period, the cohort size shrank dramatically due to the decline in fertility. For instance, the size of the cohort born in 1957 was only 1.6 million. These large baby boom cohorts entered the labour force in the early 1960s, and contributed to the rapid growth of the Japanese economy as workers with low wages. Because Japan's industrialization in the early 1960s was still predominantly of the labour-intensive nature, these large cohorts were in great demand in the labour market.

Another important point which has received only limited attention in the literature is the dependency rate effect upon capital formation. An early 1980s study showed that the economic gain from one birth averted during 1950–70 amounted to a range of 0.4–1.7 million yen (1970 constant prices), depending upon the time horizon and discount rates used (Ogawa, 1981). After liberalization of the abortion law (Eugenic Protection Law) in 1952, the reported number of induced abortions increased significantly. Furthermore, although official statistics show that the reported number was slightly more than 1 million cases a year during the period 1952–61, one study (Muramatsu, 1978) estimates that there were probably another 3 million unrecorded cases every year in the early 1950s. Although it is impossible to accurately estimate the economic gain derived from the births averted by abortion, it can be easily considered that it was quite a substantial amount. In any case, the argument can be made that the economic resources saved by averting births were invested into the Japanese economy. Hence, the fertility change occurring from the late 1940s to the latter half of the 1950s provided a useful base for Japan's miraculous economic growth in the 1960s.

Once the rural labour surplus was depleted, full employment was attained in the Japanese economy in the early 1960s. In other words, the neo-classical type of wage determination became applicable to the urban industrial labour market. As one of the signs of full employment, wages of the lowest-paid workers (casual and day labourers) began to rise faster than the monthly cash earnings of production workers in manufacturing. The increased wages for the unskilled workers attracted more workers from agriculture, which in turn, led to a rise in total farm family incomes. By 1961, off-farm employment contributed nearly as much as farm incomes, and this share continued to rise steadily thereafter. These changes in the farm households induced further mechanization (tractorization) in agricultural production, and consequently, the output per worker in agriculture increased almost as much as industrial output per worker.

It is also important to note that the wages of female textile workers too began to rise faster than those of male machinery workers (Oshima, 1982). The increased female wages attracted more women from the home into the labour market, thus raising their participation in the labour force as paid employees. As a result of the rapid transformation of employment patterns and wage levels, the distribution of income started to improve substantially, as suggested by Kuznets' U-shaped relationship between income distribution and per capita income changes.

Japanese industrial growth in the 1960s accelerated with the replacement of labour by extensive mechanization and other technologies; this substitution process gradually being transferred from the primary industry to the secondary industry, and then to the tertiary industry in the late 1970s. These were the decades when the capital- and knowledge-intensive industries, particularly the heavy industries, were expanded and modernized with the latest technologies from industrialized countries. Because advanced technologies could be easily borrowed from abroad, it was human resources that were strategic to the growth of these heavy industries particularly in terms of selecting, adapting, and operating new technologies (Denison and Chung, 1976; Oshima, 1982, 1986).

It is also important to take into account the fact that when the industrial structure of the Japanese economy shifted to the capital- and knowledge-intensive type, the enrolment rate for secondary and tertiary education rose pronouncedly. Moreover, many economists have pointed out the important role played by in-service training and on-the-job day-to-day learning in the accumulation of skills and know-how of workers Furthermore, these skills and know-how acquired by the workers have been effectively and efficiently transmitted to other workers primarily because their workplace is usually in an egalitarian atmosphere rather than in surroundings where occupations are rigidly stratified on the basis of either social classes or modern labour union contracts.

The foregoing discussion suggests that demographic changes, human resource development, and economic growth have been closely interrelated in the process of Japan's post-war economic recovery. In his papers, Oshima (1983a, 1983b) has hypothesized that Japan's industrial development induced its rapid fertility reduction. He has argued that in the process of industrialization, the demand for higher education increased the costs of children, and the long-run benefits of children as a form of old-age insurance declined as a result of wider availability of the public support system as well as extended opportunities to save and invest in assets. He has also suggested that it was the spread of secondary education that played a crucial role in linking the industrial and fertility transitions. In view of the analysis presented in this section, however, Oshima's hypothesis seems to need a further modification to account for the process of Japan's post-war economic growth and demographic transition. In this context, the interaction model formulated by Cho and Togashi (1984) appears to be more relevant.

The discussion now turns to the case of South Korea. Like Hong Kong and Singapore, South Korea reached levels of literacy and education as high as those of Japan in the early 1950s. This is partly because under the Japanese dominance of 1910–45, more than 50 per cent of the primary school age population were attending public schools by the mid-1940s (McGinn et al., 1980). This percentage was much higher than those for the colonies of the Dutch, British, and French. More importantly, these public schools were of a high standard. It is interesting to note that as was the case for Japan, these schools emphasized Confucian values and vocational education, which in turn contributed to a strong work ethic and a bureaucracy dedicated to national development (Oshima, 1986).

The pattern of South Korea's post-war economic growth is highly comparable to that of Japan, although the former started approximately one decade later than the latter. South Korea emphasized agricultural development in the 1950s and 1960s, while labour-intensive, import-substitution industrialization was promoted in the 1950s, followed by the export-promotion strategy of the 1960s. In the process of pursuing industrial development, South Korea imported advanced technologies from the United States and Japan, and was assisted financially by the former.

*South-East Asia*

Most of the South-East Asian economies have grown rapidly in the 1970s and 1980s, although their growth rate has been less impressive than that for East Asia. Leaving aside Brunei which is an oil-rich country, the ASEAN countries have already graduated from the ranks of low-income countries (as classified by the World Bank) to those of middle- or upper middle-income countries. It is important to note, however, that differences in resource endowment and policy orientation make it difficult to generalize about why the ASEAN countries have been successful (Naya, 1987: 47–87). Despite such difficulties, one can still find some similarities. For instance, the ASEAN countries, excluding Singapore, are comparatively rich in resource potential, and primary products are the mainstays of their economies and export earnings. Furthermore, the ASEAN countries have open economies and trade has greatly contributed to their growth since the early 1970s. As a result of the rapid rate of growth of exports, their export-to-income ratios are considerably higher than the ratio for Japan (Campbell, 1987).

Peninsular Malaysia achieved full employment in the first half of the 1980s. It is interesting to note that in 1985 per capita income for Malaysia was nearly as high as that of South Korea, although literacy and schooling of the labour force were substantially lower.

In the 1950s, the Philippines started out strong with levels of literacy, schooling, and per capita incomes higher than those for South Korea. However, these two countries emphasized different development strategies. In the case of South Korea, agricultural development was stressed, while a capital-intensive industrialization strategy was pursued by the Philippines. Three decades later, the Philippines ended with lower growth rates, larger amounts of unemployed labour, and a wider range of income distribution than South Korea. Interestingly enough, Oshima (1980, 1986) has pointed out that these differences in the growth performance between the two countries may be attributable to the difference in ways of thinking formed through education during the colonial periods in these societies. In any case, the Philippine experience shows that high levels of human resource development are not a sufficient condition for ensuring success in economic development.

Thailand, which, unlike other ASEAN countries, was never occupied by Western powers has achieved the most rapid sustained growth among the ASEAN countries, mainly on the basis of agricultural production. Thailand began her development process in the early 1950s with the smallest amount of modernized manpower among the ASEAN countries and with nearly half the per capita income of the Philippines. In the early 1980s, however, the per capita income level of Thailand surpassed that of the Philippines, as shown in Table 2.8.

During the 1970s and 1980s, the South-East Asian countries have succeeded in providing primary education to nearly all their children (Wong and Cheung, 1987). A number of these countries, however, have been suffering from high rates of drop out and repeaters which are most pronounced at the primary level (Poapongsakorn, 1985; Jones, 1988b). In Indonesia, for instance, only one-half of the pupils who entered primary school graduated from sixth grade in the late 1970s. The repeater rate during the same period was approximately 12 per cent. In Thailand, 23 per cent of the children who entered primary school reached grade four in 1980, while the repeater rate was 11 per cent. Similar drop out and repeater patterns can be observed in both Malaysia and the Philippines. These high drop out and repeater rates seem to reflect the fact that the utility of children as part of the family work-force is high, particularly in rural areas. In contrast to these ASEAN countries, Singapore boasts a high retention of pupils in school. However, due to this educational achievement, Singapore is now facing problems of filling lower levels of the occupational structure with willing workers (Postlethwaite and Murray, 1980).

Formal education, particularly in the higher levels, was assigned the strategic task of producing the high-level manpower required for economic development. In South-East Asia, however, higher education enrolment has risen so rapidly that a large number of secondary, vocational, and university graduates are confronted with a high incidence of unemployment (Poapongsakorn, 1985). In addition, most of the university students come from relatively wealthy families, which implies that poor families are subsidizing well-to-do families through higher educational programmes.

The other educational problem in the South-East Asian countries is the maladjustment of the educational system to the needs of national development; it is often the case that the structure and content of education are a direct copy from advanced countries. Furthermore, these countries have a severe shortage of qualified teachers, so that their quality of education is considerably lower than that in the advanced countries (Jones, 1988b). It is reported that high school graduates in East Asian schools have almost the same level of education as college graduates in some of the other Asian countries (Oshima, 1986). Therefore, in assessing the contribution of education to economic growth, a production function approach for international comparison may yield misleading results.

Another problem is related to the seasonal fluctuations in the demand for labour in rural areas. In a country like Thailand, or the eastern regions of Indonesia, a substantial proportion of the agricultural labour force is unemployed during the long dry season. To enhance the level of utilization of the labour force, it is highly desirable to strengthen the irrigation system and drainage works, and also to encourage the development of various non-agricultural activities.

Nevertheless, despite these numerous human resource problems, South-East Asia has done considerably better in its post-war economic growth than South Asia. In the 1980s, however, the economic performance of the South-East Asian countries has varied partly because two of them are oil exporters and the others, oil importers, and partly because they adopted different domestic policies. Apart from differing oil price fortunes, most of them have been affected by the decline in commodity prices and slow growth in world trade (Campbell, 1987). As a result, except for Malaysia, they have had high debt service ratios since the mid-1970s. Debt relative to GDP has declined in Indonesia and Thailand, but has been rising in Malaysia and the Philippines. These countries have been experiencing at the same time an increase in their foreign resource ratios, and they have had very high net factor payment outflows. It should be noted, however, that the debt situations for these ASEAN countries are still incomparably more sound than those for Latin American NIEs (Hayami, 1987).

## South Asia

Most of the human resource problems in South Asia are similar to those discussed above in regard to South-East Asia. For instance, South-East Asia has had lower rates of open unemployment and underemployment, and higher rates of female labour force participation. One of the problems which is unique to South Asia lies in its social stratification, an extremely important factor in the human resource development of some of the South Asian countries such as India and Nepal. Because the labour force is stratified into a large number of occupational groupings, the flow of communication, contacts, or other forms of exchange of information and skills in the workplace are severely limited. This in turn hinders the diffusion of advanced technologies (Oshima, 1980, 1986).

The dualistic nature of educational attainment is another problem, India being a salient example. Partly due to India's concentration of industrialization on heavy industries, a considerable proportion of the labour force is concentrated on the upper educational levels. Although the literacy level of India is substantially lower than those in other developing countries, 8 per cent of its population aged 20–24 are enrolled in higher education; the corresponding figure for Sri Lanka is only 3 per cent. As a consequence of low industrial growth rates since the 1950s, India has been facing a large surplus of highly educated manpower, in contrast with too few in the lower echelons of education (Oshima, 1980, 1986).

Sri Lanka's strong emphasis on human investment rather than on material investment has long been an exceptional case in Asia. Sri Lanka has been providing free primary and secondary education, free health services, subsidized food, housing, and transport, and other welfare services. Through these programmes, Sri Lanka now enjoys the highest literacy rate in South-East Asia and South Asia, together with the highest level of life expectancy and the lowest income disparity. But its GNP per capita for 1987 was $400, which was substantially lower than the corresponding figure for the Philippines ($590). Sri Lanka's experience may suggest that the allocation of resources should be balanced between human and material investment (Oshima, 1986).

Although most of the South Asian countries are pluralistic societies, different from the rest of Asia in terms of culture, religion, and many other societal aspects, they surely could learn much from the experiences of East Asia and South-East Asia in terms of the interactive process of demographic factors, human resource elements, and economic growth. Nevertheless, attention should be drawn to the fact that despite their relatively poor performance in terms of total economic growth, the South Asian countries did much better (compared with the other Asian and Pacific developing countries) during the 1980s than they did during the 1970s (Campbell, 1987). The better performance of the South Asian countries during the 1980s seems to be attributable partly to a result of the slippage elsewhere in the Asian region, and partly to their improved economic policy. The latter is especially noteworthy; although these South Asian countries have been generally inward-looking and dependent upon primary product exports, they have, since the 1980s, been making strenuous efforts towards promoting trade liberalization and reducing government intervention. If these trends continue and the required policy reforms are adopted, South Asia will be able to make significant strides in increasing productivity and per capita income. Needless to say, better human resource development is likely to play a key role in facilitating such processes.

## Conclusion

Since the 1960s, the Asia–Pacific region as a whole has emerged as the most dynamic part of the world. Its economic growth performance has been spectacular and its demographic transition has been unprecedentedly fast. Within the region, however, there have been substantial differences in the degree of dynamism in both economic development and population change. Both East Asia and the Pacific are forerunners, followed by South-East Asia, whereas South Asia is considerably behind.

As the income gap among the countries in the Asia–Pacific region has widened pronouncedly since the 1960s, the differentials in the degrees of fertility and mortality transitions have expanded. The urbanization trends and patterns in these countries have also been increasingly diversified. In this chapter, it has been demonstrated that Asia's demographic transition, measured in terms of the index reflecting fertility, mortality, and urbanization levels, has been proceeding closely together with its industrial transition. More importantly, in the countries which have been successful in these transitions, human resource development has played a crucial role in generating demographic and economic dynamism, as shown on the basis of the experiences of selected countries in Asia's three subregions.

According to the 1988 United Nations population projections, such increased heterogeneity of the pattern of demographic change in the Asia–Pacific area is expected to diminish considerably in the 1990s and beyond. It should be stressed, however, that in the process of convergence of differentials in the demographic factors, the Asia–Pacific region is likely to simultaneously face two formidable problems: population explosion and population ageing. Particularly, because the speed of population ageing in the Asia–Pacific region will be remarkably fast as a result of its rapidly declining fertility and mortality, the process of adjustments required at both societal and familial levels will be extremely difficult. Undoubtedly, in each of these countries, human resources will play an increasingly important role in solving a wide range of adjustment problems likely to arise from these two population crises.

Apart from these population problems, international labour migration within the region is expected to be further activated in the foreseeable future because internationalization of production among the countries of the region will be further increased. It should be emphasized, however, that due to the complexity of a host of factors involved in labour movements across national borders, it is virtually impossible to predict the volume and direction of such flows of human capital in any systematic way.

From the discussions presented in this chapter, it is obvious that what has already been ascertained about the nexus between population change and human resources in Asia–Pacific development is still limited. Although McNicoll (1989) has pointed out that there is a common sentiment among demographers today that their field is saturated, the Asia–Pacific region continues to provide challenging and important research issues.

# 3
# Development Trends: A Comparative Analysis of the Asian Experience

Burnham O. Campbell

THIS volume is concerned with the role of demographic change and human resource development in Asian economic growth. Whatever effects demographic change and human resource development have had, those effects did not occur in a vacuum. They were influenced by and in turn influenced all the other determinants of economic performance. Thus, to provide background for the discussion of the specific impact of demographic and human resource variables, this chapter looks at the long-run changes in economic structure in the region and at the comparative performance of Asian developing countries since 1960, but particularly in the 1970s and 1980s. It further considers differences in the policies followed by the Asian developing countries in the rapidly changing world economic environment of the 1980s and relates these policies to the economic performance of each country. Finally, the implications of the developments described and of ongoing demographic and technological changes for the region's future are discussed.

## The Long-run Structural Perspective

*Trends in Economic Performance: Comparative Growth in Real Per Capita Income*

The remarkable performance of the Asian NIEs has received world-wide attention. The reason for this attention can be seen in Table 3.1, where, taking the US change as the base, they show along with Japan far and away the largest gains in relative per capita income from 1960 to 1987. The South-East Asian countries, other than the Philippines, and the Latin American countries included in the table, other than Argentina, also did relatively well. Brazil and Thailand were especially outstanding in this respect, with Brazil's improvement coming early on in the period and Thailand's throughout, with an increase in pace of late. Generally the socialist countries, both in Asia and in Eastern Europe, and the

TABLE 3.1
Per Capita Income Comparisons, 1960–1987

|  | Per Capita Income (dollars) 1960 | 1987 | 1987 Per Capita Income/ 1960 Per Capita Income 1960–87 | Relative Growth in Per Capita Income (US Base) 1960–87 |
|---|---|---|---|---|
| **Asian NIEs** | | | | |
| Hong Kong | 348 | 8,070 | 23.19 | 3.52 |
| South Korea | 152 | 2,690 | 17.70 | 2.69 |
| Singapore | 432 | 7,940 | 18.38 | 2.79 |
| Taiwan | 138 | 4,630 | 33.55 | 5.10 |
| **Other ASEAN** | | | | |
| Indonesia | 76 | 450 | 5.92 | 0.90 |
| Malaysia | 278 | 1,810 | 6.51 | 0.99 |
| Philippines | 165 | 590 | 3.58 | 0.54 |
| Thailand | 96 | 850 | 8.85 | 1.35 |
| **South Asia** | | | | |
| Bangladesh | – | 160 | 2.00[b] | 0.30 |
| India | 73 | 300 | 4.11 | 0.62 |
| Nepal | – | 160 | 2.20[b] | 0.33 |
| Pakistan | 81 | 350 | 4.35 | 0.66 |
| Sri Lanka | 142 | 400 | 2.82 | 0.43 |
| **Socialist Economies: Asia** | | | | |
| Burma | 61 | 200 | 3.28 | 0.50 |
| China[a] | 60–118 | 290 | 4.83–2.45 | 0.73–0.37 |
| **Selected Developed Countries** | | | | |
| United States | 2,817 | 18,530 | 6.58 | 1.00 |
| Japan | 458 | 15,760 | 34.41 | 5.23 |
| Australia | 1,586 | 11,100 | 7.00 | 1.06 |
| New Zealand | 1,576 | 7,750 | 4.92 | 0.75 |
| **EC Sample** | | | | |
| Italy | 690 | 10,350 | 15.00 | 2.28 |
| United Kingdom | 1,359 | 10,420 | 7.67 | 1.17 |
| **Latin America** | | | | |
| Argentina | 606 | 2,390 | 3.94 | 0.60 |
| Brazil | 206 | 2,020 | 9.81 | 1.49 |
| Mexico | 331 | 1,830 | 5.53 | 0.84 |
| Peru | 208 | 1,470 | 7.07 | 1.07 |
| **Africa** | | | | |
| Ghana | 198 | 390 | 1.97 | 0.30 |
| Kenya | 102 | 330 | 3.24 | 0.49 |
| Egypt | 129 | 680 | 5.27 | 0.80 |
| Nigeria | 78 | 370 | 4.74 | 0.72 |

(*continued*)

TABLE 3.1 (continued)

|  | Per Capita Income (dollars) 1960 | 1987 | 1987 Per Capita Income/ 1960 Per Capita Income 1960–87 | Relative Growth in Per Capita Income (US Base) 1960–87 |
|---|---|---|---|---|
| Socialist Economies: Europe |  |  |  |  |
| Hungary | 905 | 2,240 | 2.48 | 0.38 |
| Poland | – | 1,930 | – | – |
| Yugoslavia | 927 | 2,480 | 2.68 | 0.41 |

Sources: 1960 data from United Nations (1976); 1987 data from World Bank (1989), *World Development Report 1989*.

[a]The first estimate for China extrapolates to 1960 the annual average growth given for 1967–87 in the 1988 World Bank's World Tables and the second does the same for the annual average growth for 1965–87 given in the World Bank's *World Development Report 1989*.

[b]Based on the assumption per capita income in Bangladesh in 1960 was the same as in Pakistan and that per capita income in Nepal in 1960 was the same as in India.

South Asian and African countries included in the table lagged behind everyone else. Also, with noted exceptions, the industrial countries sampled did better in raising their relative per capita incomes than did the developing countries.

Since the industrial countries sampled began with much higher per capita incomes, this last point means income disparities have widened significantly between these countries and the South Asian, African, and socialist countries sampled as well as between these countries and the Philippines and Argentina. Basically, the beginning gap (1960) has remained about the same between the industrial countries and the other South-East Asian and Latin American countries sampled—though being reduced somewhat for the fast growers in these regions—and has been significantly reduced for the Asian NIEs. The NIEs have played the 'catch up' game very well indeed.

Clearly, there have been both striking success stories and dismal failures in economic performance in different parts of the world since the mid-1960s. Just as clearly, there remain very large disparities in per capita income and much to do in most of the developing world simply to achieve minimum standards much less begin catching up with the high-income countries.

The issue in Asia and the Pacific and elsewhere is: What accounts for the differences in relative growth performance shown in Table 3.1 or, in the same vein, what could trigger the cumulative increases and catching up so clearly needed? Easy generalizations do not seem likely, except possibly from the experience of the Asian NIEs and Japan. There are important similarities between these countries, but there are also important differences.

Perhaps the relatively poor performance of the Philippines compared to Thailand or the generally lacklustre outcomes in South Asia and Africa can offer a clue. While setting the stage for the discussion of the role of human resources and demographic change in the growth process, another goal of this brief review of economic performances and policies is to gain insight into the possible sources of the differences observed in Table 3.1.

*Changing Structure of Production and Trade*

With such wide variations in growth achievement, it is interesting to see if shifts in the production structure and the composition of trade give any clues about the sources of the observed differences in relative growth. Not unexpectedly, there is a definite positive correlation in Asia between the relative change in a country's real per capita income and the relative decrease in the share of national output originating in agriculture (Table 3.2). Leaving out the city-states, the two larger NIEs led the shift from low productivity agriculture to higher productivity industrial and service occupations. They, in turn, are followed by South-East Asia with the lower growth South Asian countries last.

Looked at country by country, Hong Kong has a developed country profile; South Korea and Taiwan have the basic NIE profile, with industry and the services sector growing as agriculture declines; Singapore is close to this pattern, but with an unexpected decline in its services sector; Thailand, Malaysia, the Philippines, Indonesia, Pakistan, and Sri Lanka have fairly similar transitional structures; and India is moving in this same direction, but with a larger share still in agriculture. Except for the Philippines and Sri Lanka, all these countries also show the expected growth in the services sector. One conjecture is that industrial growth in the latter two countries was 'hothoused' and did not take place naturally with complementary services sector growth.

Bangladesh and Nepal remain largely agricultural and have the smallest industrial sectors, but a minor shift to the industrial and services sectors is taking place. China occupies a world all its own, with both agriculture and industry having very high shares and the services sector, which can blossom only with a free market economy, being the lowest in the region. Generally, this imbalance results from the effects of planned resource allocation. Burma also occupies a unique place, with the only growing agricultural sector, the only declining industrial sector, and a declining services sector.

These changes are symptoms not causes of growth. They measure 'success' in the same way per capita income levels or real growth does. They do help in defining 'targets' since it is clear that if growth policies are working, the result will be a growth in demand for services, and the release of labour from low productivity in agriculture to higher productivity in industry. They also help in pinpointing laggards and fast

## TABLE 3.2
Structural Changes in Output, 1965 and 1987 (percentage share in GDP)

| Country | Agriculture 1965 | Agriculture 1987 | Percentage Change | Industry 1965 | Industry 1987 | Services 1965 | Services 1987 |
|---|---|---|---|---|---|---|---|
| **Asian NIEs** | | | | | | | |
| Hong Kong | 2 | 0 | −100 | 40 | 29 | 58 | 70 |
| South Korea | 38 | 11 | −71 | 25 | 43 | 37 | 46 |
| Singapore | 3 | 1 | −67 | 24 | 38 | 73 | 62 |
| Taiwan[a] | 18 | 6 | −67 | 41 | 51 | 41 | 43 |
| **South-East Asia** | | | | | | | |
| Indonesia | 56 | 26 | −54 | 13 | 33 | 31 | 41 |
| Malaysia | 28 | 22 | −21 | 25 | 38 | 47 | 40 |
| Philippines | 26 | 24 | −8 | 28 | 33 | 46 | 43 |
| Thailand | 32 | 16 | −50 | 23 | 35 | 45 | 49 |
| **South Asia** | | | | | | | |
| Bangladesh | 53 | 47 | −11 | 11 | 13 | 36 | 39 |
| India | 47 | 30 | −36 | 22 | 30 | 31 | 40 |
| Nepal | 65 | 57 | −12 | 11 | 14 | 23 | 29 |
| Pakistan | 40 | 23 | −43 | 20 | 28 | 40 | 49 |
| Sri Lanka | 28 | 27 | −4 | 21 | 27 | 51 | 46 |
| **Asian Socialist Economies** | | | | | | | |
| Burma | 35 | 37 | 6 | 13 | 16 | 52 | 47 |
| China | 39 | 31 | −21 | 38 | 49 | 23 | 20 |
| **Bench-mark Countries** | | | | | | | |
| Japan | 9 | 3 | −67 | 43 | 41 | 48 | 57 |
| United States | 3 | 2 | −33 | 38 | 30 | 59 | 68 |

Sources: World Bank (1989), *World Development Report 1989*; Asian Development Bank (1989), *Key Indicators of Developing Member Countries of ADB*.
[a]Beginning year for Taiwan is 1970. The share of agriculture in 1965 was 23 per cent; a breakdown of other shares comparable to that used in this table was not available in 1965.

movers. South Korea, Taiwan, Thailand, and Indonesia especially stand out in the latter respect and Nepal and Bangladesh in the former. Burma seems to have chosen to lag, so its policies cannot be called unsuccessful.

Finally, there should be some lessons in the Philippine experience. In 1965, the Philippines had the largest industrial and smallest agricultural sector in South-East Asia, ahead of Thailand and also ahead of South Korea. But, by 1987, the Philippines was in all aspects of structural change far behind South Korea and behind Thailand. Malaysia and Indonesia have also caught up with the Philippines industrially and moved ahead in terms of the drop in agriculture's share, where there was almost no change in the Philippines; and in services sector development since the services sector's share fell in the Philippines.

Turning to trade composition and utilizing a table covering the transitional 1970s produced for an earlier paper (Campbell, 1986: Table 3), given the above trends in industrial structure, as expected, share of primary products fell in every country for which data are available (Table 3.3). Of the countries left out, only Burma would have been likely to reverse this conclusion. However, the share of primary product exports remained very high in South Asia compared to South-East Asia and in South-East Asia compared to the NIEs. The forced pace of industrialization in the Philippines and Sri Lanka again shows clearly here.

Although, with the exception of Singapore, labour-intensive manufactures were generally higher in the NIEs than elsewhere, by the early 1980s most of the NIEs were already moving out of labour-intensive into physical and human capital-intensive exports. South-East Asia garnered some of this export business—with growth in the share of labour-intensive exports in all the subregion's countries, though held back in Indonesia by Dutch disease. The growth in labour-intensive exports was even greater as a share of Sri Lanka's exports, but, despite their relative abundance of inexpensive labour, the other South Asian countries experienced either no change or a slight decline in their share of labour-intensive exports.

As would be expected, the growth in physical capital-intensive exports was generally larger in the Asian NIEs as they moved up the structural change ladder. Force-feeding of this growth—now causing problems—seems to have occurred in South Korea. Also standing out is the generally higher share of physical capital-intensive exports in South Asia (especially India) than in South-East Asia. This reflects the difference between planned industrial growth in South Asia and the more market-led industrial growth in South-East Asia, and was kept going partly by the barter trade in these commodities between India and the Eastern European countries. Recent developments in Eastern Europe may spell an end to this trade, creating export problems for India in this sector. However, the most impressive changes in export composition show up in human capital-intensive exports—mostly electronics and/or other high tech goods. Increases here were large in all the NIEs and South-East Asian countries except Indonesia, but especially large in Malaysia, Singapore, and Hong Kong.

In sum, the changes in export composition between the regions parallel the changes in relative real per capita incomes. The expected movement in factor intensity from developed countries to the NIEs and from the NIEs to South-East Asia is apparent. The further movement of labour-intensive exports to South Asia also shows up. The experience reviewed shows human capital-intensive exports jumping over this step by step pattern into South-East Asia—though the composition within this category may be quite different in the NIEs and South-East Asia. Further, it highlights the ways in which policy (for example, the reversal

TABLE 3.3
Structure of Exports, 1982 (per cent)

| Country | Primary Products Export Share | Primary Products Percentage Change over 1970 Export Share | Labour-intensive Manufactures Export Share | Labour-intensive Manufactures Percentage Change over 1970 Export Share | Resource-based Manufactures Export Share | Resource-based Manufactures Percentage Change over 1970 Export Share | Physical Capital-intensive Manufactures Export Share | Physical Capital-intensive Manufactures Percentage Change over 1970 Export Share | Human Capital-intensive Manufactures Export Share | Human Capital-intensive Manufactures Percentage Change over 1970 Export Share |
|---|---|---|---|---|---|---|---|---|---|---|
| **Asian NIEs** | | | | | | | | | | |
| Hong Kong | 2.8 | −1.1 | 64.4 | −12.7 | 3.8 | −0.2 | 4.3 | 2.1 | 24.0 | 11.3 |
| South Korea | 8.1 | −14.4 | 39.3 | −13.1 | 11.4 | −2.9 | 27.8 | 23.4 | 13.2 | 6.9 |
| Singapore | 50.1 | −19.2 | 7.3 | −0.7 | 5.3 | 0.7 | 19.0 | 9.9 | 18.6 | 12.5 |
| Taiwan | 11.0 | −12.1 | 45.1 | 3.6 | 11.2 | −0.9 | 13.4 | 4.8 | 19.3 | 4.9 |
| **South-East Asia** | | | | | | | | | | |
| Indonesia | 94.4 | −3.8 | 0.6 | 0.0 | 3.4 | 2.6 | 0.5 | 0.3 | 0.6 | 0.3 |
| Malaysia | 71.5 | −1.6 | 3.5 | 2.3 | 8.1 | −14.2 | 2.4 | 0.5 | 14.2 | 13.5 |
| Philippines[a] | 73.6 | −24.3 | 12.9 | 11.6 | 5.1 | 0.5 | 1.8 | 0.6 | 6.6 | 4.2 |
| Thailand | 67.0 | −13.6 | 13.7 | 12.1 | 11.1 | −2.6 | 1.1 | 0.7 | 5.7 | 5.3 |
| **South Asia** | | | | | | | | | | |
| Bangladesh | 37.8 | – | 47.5 | – | 9.3 | – | 3.6 | – | 1.1 | – |
| India | 40.9 | −6.3 | 27.0 | −1.1 | 17.7 | 0.2 | 9.7 | −1.5 | 4.6 | 1.7 |
| Pakistan | 40.7 | −2.0 | 48.7 | −1.1 | 5.6 | 0.2 | 2.0 | 1.3 | 1.6 | 0.3 |
| Sri Lanka | 73.9 | −24.7 | 16.0 | 17.5 | 5.2 | 4.7 | 2.2 | 2.0 | 0.6 | 0.4 |

*Source*: Campbell (1986: Table 3).
[a] The Philippine primary product data have been adjusted upward to reflect the diversion of primary product to 'not elsewhere classified' in 1982; a result of government marketing programmes.

of the expected factor intensity of exports in the physical capital-intensive category in South Asia and South Korea's huge increase in share of physical capital exports) has been used to push this evolution along—in most instances with less than stellar results. The importance of human resources and education is also clear, especially in the rapid growth of human capital-intensive exports, where the education of females is particularly important, but also in the growth of labour-intensive manufactures outside the NIEs and of high tech exports in the NIEs.

It is within this framework of changing industrial structure and comparative advantage that human resource developments have been worked out and that demographic developments have made themselves felt. In looking at the 1990s and beyond, the feedbacks between relative demographic change, capital movements, and comparative advantage will be even more important as demographic profiles diverge ever more widely in the region.

*Changes in Human Capital*

The educational effort in 1965 and 1986, measured by enrolment ratios,[1] is used as a proxy for the change in human capital. This measure assumes that the stock of human capital relative to the population can be indicated by the current flow, that in making comparisons within a country over time the quality of education is unchanged, and that in making comparisons between countries the quality is the same in all. These assumptions, particularly the last, are rough approximations at best.

At the primary level, the positive relation between the beginning enrolment ratio (1965) and subsequent relative growth in per capita income is clear. The Asian NIEs had beginning ratios at or over 100 for both male and female populations (Table 3.4) and maintained ratios at or near this level in 1986. In this respect they were similar to Japan and the United States, the bench-mark developed countries shown. All the South-East Asian countries had lower but still relatively high beginning ratios for both male and female populations, but with a greater difference in favour of males than in the NIEs. By 1986 all had ratios essentially equal to or greater than 100 for both sexes. In South Asia, enrolment ratios for males varied considerably at the beginning, with India and Sri Lanka having enrolment ratios similar to those in South-East Asia. But all had very low ratios for their female populations. By the end of the period Bangladesh and Pakistan still lagged on the male side and all except Nepal and Sri Lanka lagged on the female side. Though data to show the exact changes are unavailable, the level of primary school enrolment ratios in Burma in 1965 was just below Thailand's and in China in 1986 these ratios were well over 100.

From a growth standpoint, it could be argued that a much greater priority be given education in the laggard countries. For example, it is interesting that the countries in which human capital-intensive exports

## TABLE 3.4
### Educational Effort (Enrolment Ratios), 1965 and 1986 (per cent)

| | Primary Male 1965 | Primary Male 1986 | Primary Female 1965 | Primary Female 1986 | Secondary 1965 | Secondary 1986 | Higher Education 1965 | Higher Education 1986 |
|---|---|---|---|---|---|---|---|---|
| **Asian NIEs** | | | | | | | | |
| Hong Kong | 106 | 105 | 99 | 106 | 29 | 69 | 5 | 13 |
| South Korea | 103 | 94 | 99 | 94 | 35 | 95 | 6 | 33 |
| Singapore | 110 | 118 | 100 | 113 | 45 | 71 | 10 | 12 |
| Taiwan | – | 100 | – | 99 | – | 90 | – | 23 |
| **South-East Asia** | | | | | | | | |
| Indonesia | 79 | 121 | 65 | 116 | 12 | 41 | 1 | 7 |
| Malaysia | 96 | 100 | 84 | 99 | 28 | 54 | 2 | 6 |
| Philippines | 115 | 107 | 111 | 106 | 41 | 68 | 19 | 38 |
| Thailand | 82 | 101[b] | 74 | 97[b] | 14 | 29[b] | 2 | 20 |
| **South Asia** | | | | | | | | |
| Bangladesh | 67 | 69 | 31 | 50 | 13 | 18 | 1 | 5 |
| India | 89 | 107 | 57 | 76 | 27 | 35 | 5 | – |
| Nepal | 36 | 114 | 4 | 104 | 5 | 25 | 1 | 5 |
| Pakistan | 59 | 55 | 20 | 32 | 12 | 18 | 2 | 5 |
| Sri Lanka | 98 | 104 | 86 | 102 | 35 | 66 | 2 | 4 |
| **Asian Socialist Economies** | | | | | | | | |
| Burma | 76 | – | 65 | – | 15 | – | 1 | – |
| China | – | 137 | – | 120 | – | 42 | – | 2 |
| **Bench-mark countries** | | | | | | | | |
| United States | 118 | 102[a] | – | – | 86 | 100 | 40 | 59 |
| Japan | 100 | 101 | 100 | 102 | 86 | 96 | 13 | 29 |

*Sources*: As for Table 3.2.
[a] Males and females are combined in the US data.
[b] 1985 figures.

increased the most in share in South-East and South Asia were the countries that had the highest beginning primary school enrolment ratios for females. However, that human capital is not the entire story is illustrated by the very high primary school enrolment ratios in China, the Philippines, and Sri Lanka relative to their per capita growth rate position and the relatively low enrolment ratios in Pakistan compared to its growth performance.

In looking at the performance of the economy for countries at development stages found in Asia in the 1960s, primary school enrolment ratios are much more indicative of probable success than secondary school ratios. However, once the industrialization process is under way, keeping it going depends more on secondary school enrolment and a growing pool of semi-skilled or skilled workers. Thus, though enrolments in 1965 at the secondary level were on average higher in the NIEs, the fact they were equalled or exceeded by many countries in other regions, that is, the Philippines, Sri Lanka, Malaysia, and India, is not surprising. Actually, all the Asian developing countries included in the table were far behind Japan and the United States in secondary school enrolment ratios in 1965.

By 1986, the NIEs had closed this secondary school enrolment gap, as was undoubtedly necessary given the changing structure of their exports and industrial production. Except for the Philippines, the South-East Asian countries remained far behind. One could venture that this lag may soon become a growth constraint to continued high growth rates in Thailand. In South Asia the level outside Sri Lanka began extremely low and generally remained there—though the increase in secondary school enrolment ratios in Nepal is certainly noteworthy. At this schooling level, in contrast to its very high primary enrolment ratios, China was more in line with South and South-East Asia in 1965.

It is safe to say that in all the Asian developing countries outside of the NIEs (and the Philippines) a major national priority must be the improvement of secondary school enrolment ratios if per capita incomes are to increase significantly. Enrolment ratios do not take account of quality differentials and having a relatively high secondary enrolment ratio is not a sufficient condition for successful growth, as the Philippines and Sri Lanka again show, but it seems a highly necessary one relatively early on in the development process.

To take the next step up the development ladder and become a modern economic society, a critical mass of highly educated individuals is required. In 1965, with the usual exception of the Philippines, which had outpaced Japan and the United Kingdom, no Asian developing country was close to the United States in this respect. The NIEs had the highest enrolment ratios, about half the level of Japan's. Elsewhere the ratio was 2 per cent or less, except for India's 5 per cent—which given India's population could provide the necessary critical mass for at least some of the activities requiring higher education, if the quality and kind of education measure up to the applied needs of these activities.

In the late 1980s, ignoring quality, only South Korea and the Philippines, with higher education ratios above Japan's, and Thailand seem to be raising higher education enrolment rates to appropriate levels. In Thailand, with open universities accounting for much of the gain, quality may be closer to the secondary school level, which would partly compensate for the relatively poor Thai showing at that level but leave an unacceptable higher education gap.[2] The continuing low ratios for Hong Kong and Singapore, particularly given their small population bases, are worrying. These countries will need to step up the service and high tech production ladder to keep per capita growth growing at previous high rates. Elsewhere, the low higher education ratios would soon become a growth constraint if development begins to take off—this is true in India as well since its ratio may give the necessary critical mass for research but not for nation-wide management and services.

*Capital–Labour Ratios and Economic Efficiency*

There is the expected close relation between the capital–labour ratio in 1983 and level of income per worker in 1986 given in Table 3.5, but in addition the capital–labour ratio is closely related to the relative change in per capita income growth between 1960 and 1987 (see Table 3.1). The first outcome follows directly from economic theory, reflecting the relation between capital–labour ratios and labour productivity. It would be expected as long as capital is not employed with much greater efficiency in one country than another. That will be briefly explored below. The second outcome, if the correlation between capital growth per worker and worker productivity holds, implies that relatively rapid growth was matched by relatively rapid capital accumulation per worker. In understanding the success stories, this implication directs attention to resource mobilization and the policies and factors favourable to above average resource mobilization.

GNP per worker and GNP per unit of capital are also shown in Table 3.5. As the capital–labour ratio increases, GNP per worker would be expected to increase but by decreasing amounts. Thus, output per unit of capital would be expected to fall. If this relation is found, other than pointing out that the extent of fall seems relatively small or large, there is little to be said. However, if a country with a higher capital–labour ratio also has a higher output per unit of capital than another country, either human capital accumulation is much greater in the second country or there are unexploited increasing returns or unexploited improvements in technology or economic organization in the second country.[3] If a country with a lower capital–labour ratio has a higher output per unit of capital than another country, then human capital must be greater or there must be unexploited improvements in technology or economic organization in the second country.

With these relations in mind and comparing all the countries with higher capital–output ratios than Malaysia as one group and all the countries with capital–output ratios below Malaysia's as the other, the following conclusions can be reached. First, all the Asian NIEs have both higher capital–output ratios and higher GNP per unit of capital ratios than Malaysia. If for this group of countries participation in world markets rules out any major unexploited economies of scale—a strong assumption for any point of time comparison—then Malaysia either uses on average less advanced technology, has relatively less human capital, or is less efficiently organized than the Asian NIEs. Given the similarity of their capital–labour ratios, the conclusion would seem especially strong for South Korea and Taiwan in comparison to Malaysia. The

TABLE 3.5
Capital–Labour and Productivity Ratios, 1960–1987

| Country | Relative Growth in GNP Per Capita (US = 1.0) 1960–87 (1) | Physical Capital–Labour Ratio ($'000) 1983 (2) | GNP per Worker ($'000) 1986 (3) | GNP/Physical Capital Stock[a] ($'000) 1985 (4) |
|---|---|---|---|---|
| Asian NIEs | | | | |
| Hong Kong | 3.5 | 24.7 | 10.03 | 0.41 |
| South Korea | 2.7 | 11.1 | 4.06 | 0.37 |
| Singapore | 2.8 | 38.6 | 11.08 | 0.29 |
| Taiwan | 5.1 | 13.0 | 5.99 | 0.46 |
| South-East Asia | | | | |
| Indonesia | 0.9 | 2.2 | 0.74 | 0.34 |
| Malaysia | 1.0 | 10.9 | 2.76 | 0.25 |
| Philippines | 0.5 | 3.4 | 0.81 | 0.24 |
| Thailand | 1.4 | 2.6 | 0.93 | 0.36 |
| South Asia | | | | |
| Bangladesh | 0.3 | 0.4 | 0.28 | 0.70 |
| India | 0.6 | 1.0 | 0.48 | 0.48 |
| Nepal | 0.3 | 0.4 | 0.25 | 0.62 |
| Pakistan | 0.7 | 1.3 | 0.66 | 0.51 |
| Sri Lanka | 0.4 | 1.7 | 0.66 | 0.39 |
| Asian Socialist Economies | | | | |
| Burma | 0.5 | 0.6 | 0.14 | 0.24 |
| China | 0.4 | – | 0.22 | – |

*Sources*: As for Table 3.2.
[a] Col. 3 ÷ Col. 2.

same result can be reached for South Korea *vis-à-vis* Taiwan and Hong Kong, especially, for the reason just noted, Taiwan. Finally, comparing the gap between Hong Kong's and Singapore's level of GNP per unit capital (Hong Kong's level being higher) with the gap between their capital–labour ratios (Hong Kong's ratio being lower), the former seems relatively large. Conversely, Singapore's level of GNP per worker is 10.4 per cent higher than Hong Kong's and this seems relatively small when compared to the fact that Singapore's capital–labour ratio is 56 per cent higher than Hong Kong's.[4]

Looking at the countries with much lower capital–labour ratios in 1983, since all had relatively low amounts of human capital, Bangladesh and Nepal were either using more advanced technology or their economies were better organized than Burma's. Similarly, Thailand was either using more advanced technology or, more likely, was more efficient than the Philippines; and Pakistan was the same relative to Sri Lanka. The same conclusion with the added possibility of increasing returns applies to all the other countries *vis-à-vis* Burma, to Pakistan *vis-à-vis* India, and to Thailand *vis-à-vis* Indonesia. Finally, with Pakistan, Sri Lanka, and India on the one hand, and the Philippines on the other hand; comparing the gap between their levels of GNP per unit of capital with the gap between their capital–labour ratios, the former seems relatively large. Conversely, the increase in GNP per worker seems relatively small. Of the countries covered, except for Burma, the Philippines gets the least output from its capital and, given its large amounts of human capital and access to modern technology, seems to have had the least well-organized economy.

It is also possible to make rough but interesting comparisons between countries in the two groups discussed. However, that is left to the reader. Such comparisons, as well as those made in the text, are obviously subject to numerous reservations and/or interpretations. However, the fact that the intercountry conclusions reached concerning the relative effectiveness of economic organization or adaptation of existing technology, also a measure of economic organization, are similar to those suggested by the analysis of a broad range of other criteria in subsequent sections of this chapter increases their credibility.

In any event, the growth laggards can be divided into two groups: those that are due to both lagging physical and human capital accumulation per worker and those due to ineffective use of their physical and human capital resources. In some instances, as noted, countries are members of both groups. The upshot is that there is much intra-Asian catching up to do, offering many opportunities for profitable movement of capital, if the capital is welcomed, towards the countries at the bottom and middle of the capital–labour ladder.

*Demographic Developments and Growth*

Demographic change can influence and be influenced by economic growth in a variety of ways, many of which are brought up in the following chapters. Without making any attempt to assign cause and effect and basing the analysis on the change in population growth rates between the late 1960s and the 1980s (Table 3.6), it is clear from comparison of Tables 3.5 and 3.6 that both the level of population growth at the beginning and the change in population growth rates over the period are directly related to relative growth performances over the period.

Population growth rates in the late 1960s were marginally lower in the NIEs than elsewhere and ended up clearly lower in the 1980s. Indonesia, Nepal, and Sri Lanka began with population growth rates at the NIE level, but the rest of the South and South-East Asian countries had much higher rates of population growth. By the end of the period, Thailand and China, the two fastest-growing economies outside the NIEs had achieved very large relative reductions in their population growth rates—though few would want to emulate the Chinese approach to accomplishing this outcome—and Sri Lanka's was at the NIE level. On this as on so many other counts, Sri Lanka did 'better' than its growth performance would indicate. Elsewhere, and this includes all the slowest-growing countries, population growth either increased, probably with improved health care in Bangladesh and Nepal, or remained at high levels even if decreasing. There seems a fairly clear lesson here.

Looking briefly at the dependency relations, as the demographic transition took hold, the total dependency ratio decreased significantly in the NIEs to levels considerably lower than elsewhere in the region between 1960 and 1990. This ratio also decreased in South-East Asia and China but remained much higher than for the NIEs. Marking the continued demographic expansion in South Asia, the total dependency ratio increased in Bangladesh, Pakistan, and Nepal and remained quite high in India. Only Sri Lanka showed a significant decline in total dependency.

Behind these shifts in the dependency rates are large declines in the young dependency ratio in the NIEs and most South-East Asian countries (and in Sri Lanka, Burma, and China) coupled with small increases or essentially no change in the aged dependency ratio. Together these relations would seem clearly to favour resource mobilization and human resource development in the NIEs over South-East Asia and in South-East Asia over South Asia. Except in Hong Kong and Singapore no major changes have occurred as yet in the aged dependency rate. That will come in the other NIEs and South-East Asia as the demographic transition continues.

The supporting role of labour market developments in the growth accomplishments of the Asian NIEs is often overlooked, but from 1950–5 to 1970–5 the growth of the labour force base in the NIEs was either the highest of any region or a close second. Thus, the NIEs' drive to development was supported by rapidly growing labour supplies, keeping real wages from growing more rapidly than productivity and so keeping profits and investment up. Beginning in the 1960s labour force base growth was also relatively high in South-East Asia, becoming the region with the most rapid growth from the period 1975–80 onwards.

TABLE 3.6
Demographic Developments, 1950–1990 (per cent)

| Country | Population Growth Rates 1965–73 | Population Growth Rates 1980–7 | Population 0–14 and 65+/ Population 15–64 1960 | Population 0–14 and 65+/ Population 15–64 1990 | Population 0–14/ Population 15–64 1960 | Population 0–14/ Population 15–64 1990 | Population 65+/ Population 15–64 1960 | Population 65+/ Population 15–64 1990 | Quinquennial Growth Rate in the Labour Force Base (Population 15–64) 1950–5 | 1955–60 | 1960–5 | 1965–70 | 1970–5 | 1975–80 | 1980–5 | 1985–90 |
|---|---|---|---|---|---|---|---|---|---|---|---|---|---|---|---|---|
| **Asian NIEs** | | | | | | | | | | | | | | | | |
| Hong Kong | 2.0 | 1.6 | 77.5 | 44.5 | 72.6 | 31.8 | 5.0 | 12.7 | 16.6 | 12.0 | 20.9 | 20.1 | 12.2 | 21.4 | 10.4 | 6.9 |
| South Korea | 2.2 | 1.4 | 82.7 | 45.4 | 76.6 | 38.5 | 6.1 | 6.9 | 8.3 | 12.4 | 11.2 | 14.6 | 18.4 | 14.7 | 13.8 | 11.0 |
| Singapore | 1.8 | 1.1 | 82.7 | 39.6 | 78.9 | 31.9 | 3.8 | 7.7 | 26.2 | 21.3 | 12.7 | 19.2 | 18.9 | 15.5 | 9.1 | 7.6 |
| Taiwan | 2.8 | 1.5 | 92.0 | 50.8 | 87.3 | 42.1 | 4.8 | 8.7 | 15.9 | 14.3 | 17.9 | 27.2 | 17.2 | 14.7 | 11.1 | 9.6 |
| **South-East Asia** | | | | | | | | | | | | | | | | |
| Indonesia | 2.1 | 2.1 | 77.0 | 63.7 | 71.1 | 57.4 | 5.9 | 6.3 | 10.0 | 9.4 | 8.7 | 11.2 | 16.1 | 12.3 | 16.1 | 14.6 |
| Malaysia | 2.6 | 2.7 | 94.9 | 66.7 | 88.2 | 60.3 | 6.7 | 6.4 | 12.9 | 12.1 | 15.4 | 17.4 | 14.5 | 18.9 | 13.3 | 15.2 |
| Philippines | 2.9 | 2.5 | 91.0 | 76.9 | 85.2 | 70.9 | 5.8 | 6.0 | 13.3 | 14.8 | 15.8 | 16.8 | 19.1 | 13.7 | 16.0 | 15.3 |
| Thailand | 2.9 | 2.0 | 90.2 | 57.6 | 89.5 | 51.4 | 5.2 | 6.2 | 13.1 | 12.5 | 12.6 | 16.2 | 18.7 | 22.5 | 17.1 | 14.4 |
| **South Asia** | | | | | | | | | | | | | | | | |
| Bangladesh | 2.6 | 2.8 | 80.8 | 87.9 | 74.1 | 82.5 | 6.7 | 5.5 | 10.0 | 9.4 | 8.7 | 11.2 | 16.1 | 12.3 | 16.1 | 18.8 |
| India | 2.3 | 2.1 | 76.0 | 69.5 | 70.0 | 61.8 | 6.0 | 7.6 | 10.1 | 10.4 | 10.6 | 11.7 | 12.9 | 13.1 | 12.8 | 12.7 |
| Nepal | 2.0 | 2.7 | 73.3 | 82.8 | 66.5 | 77.1 | 6.8 | 5.7 | 8.7 | 8.4 | 8.7 | 8.5 | 9.3 | 18.5 | 11.8 | 13.2 |
| Pakistan | 3.1 | 3.1 | 92.3 | 93.7 | 84.3 | 88.4 | 8.0 | 5.2 | 6.7 | 8.2 | 10.4 | 15.9 | 16.2 | 16.6 | 20.6 | 16.6 |
| Sri Lanka | 2.0 | 1.5 | 84.1 | 60.5 | 77.4 | 52.2 | 6.7 | 8.3 | 12.2 | 12.8 | 13.7 | 11.5 | 12.9 | 16.3 | 10.1 | 8.7 |
| **Asian Socialist Economies** | | | | | | | | | | | | | | | | |
| Burma | 2.3 | 2.2 | 80.3 | 70.3 | 74.2 | 63.3 | 6.1 | 7.0 | 5.8 | 8.4 | 10.9 | 11.5 | 13.1 | 12.9 | 12.2 | 14.4 |
| China | 2.9 | 1.2 | 77.7 | 53.9 | 69.1 | 38.6 | 8.6 | 8.6 | 3.4 | 4.3 | 9.1 | 15.2 | 12.0 | 14.3 | 15.6 | 12.1 |

*Sources*: United Nations (1989c); World Bank, *World Development Report*, various issues; Republic of China, Taipei, 1970, 1989.

But, since—except in Thailand from the mid-1970s to late 1980s—the right combination of policies to take advantage of this fact has not been found; the main result has been increased underemployment. Surprisingly, through 1970–5, growth in the labour force base in South Asia was considerably lower than in either the NIEs or South-East Asia. Thus, despite the large stock of underutilized labour in South Asia, the dynamic stimulus for labour-intensive production may have been greater in the latter regions.

In the 1980s these relations have reversed, with the growth rate in the labour force base in the Asian NIEs now lower than anywhere else in the region, with the exception of Sri Lanka. This provides a direct incentive for stepping up the technology ladder in production and for exporting capital to countries where labour force growth is still high or accelerating.

The latter would include all the South-East Asian countries, China (through 1985–90), Pakistan, and Bangladesh. Though several of these countries seem past their peaks, they in the 1980s had much more rapid growth in their labour force base than elsewhere in the region. Despite this rapid growth in Pakistan and Bangladesh and the large pool of underemployed labour in India, the more rapidly developing, more human capital-intensive, and more welcoming South-East Asian countries would likely be the preferred destinations for Asian NIE capital searching out relatively cheaper labour. With its labour force base growth now falling, but still relatively high—mind-boggling high in absolute terms—China is also likely to be a major recipient of such capital if China puts out the welcome mat again.

In summary, population and labour force growth rates are diverging and bringing dependency ratios along with them. Where they are low or falling, it means an ageing labour force and a relatively dwindling number of new entrants. Unskilled labour costs are bound to rise in relative terms in these circumstances. Where they are high or increasing, the opposite will occur. Thus, the location of labour-intensive production, the relative importance of secondary and higher education (which reduce effective labour costs by making labour more productive), and the movement of capital (both direct investment and financial capital), have been and will be affected by the economic impact of the demographic changes described.

## Background: The World Scene in the 1980s

Having established the long-run factors at work in determining the relative performance of the Asian developing countries, the stage is partially set for a detailed look at the relative performance and the policies adopted in the 1980s. To complete the setting, the world economic environment must be put in place.

The 1980s began with world inflation at a double digit rate and with real interest rates unexpectedly increasing, a real blow to countries borrowing on the opposite expectation. Then, very soon thereafter, the decade progressed to world recession, falling nominal and real world trade, worsening terms of trade—as commodity prices fell sharply—and record high real interest rates. The latter were accompanied by a steadily appreciating dollar, as the interest rate effects of the rapidly growing US fiscal deficit dominated the trade balance effects of the recession in the United States. As if there were not enough adjustment problems already for developing countries, at the same time, protectionism grew, fed by the impact of the stronger dollar on the US balance of trade and by demographic developments and high structural unemployment in most industrial countries, becoming more legalistic, subtle, and disguised than in the past. On the positive side, world inflation decelerated (somewhat slowly at first).

Except for the start of recovery from the recession, most of these circumstances continued into 1985, when the world economic environment began again to change dramatically, creating a new but generally more welcome set of adjustment problems for developing countries. Most important for the world environment was the record duration of continuing expansion, coupled with relatively low rates of inflation, in the United States and other major developed economies. Also, the US dollar dropped sharply *vis-à-vis* the yen and most EC currencies, helping some countries, especially the Asian NIEs, become more competitive but creating problems for those with large non-dollar debts and small non-dollar sales. Nominal interest rates along with real interest rates also fell sharply beginning in 1985, though the latter remained far above the levels of the 1970s. Then, in 1986, after trending down from 1980 on, oil prices fell by more than half, aiding most developing countries, again especially the Asian NIEs, and causing massive problems for oil exporters in Asia and elsewhere and difficulties for countries depending on workers' remittances from the Middle East.

After moving upward for two years during the cyclical recovery, commodity prices resumed their seemingly long-run decline in 1985, adversely affecting the predominantly agriculture- and mineral-based Asian developing countries outside East Asia. However, most commodity prices bottomed out by 1987 and with some important exceptions (for example, palm oil) have generally improved since. Prices in general fell further before starting up again in 1989 as the oil price also moved up from its low. Short-term interest rates also moved higher at the same time, as the US central bank and others concentrated on stopping inflation. One result is that the dollar's value has begun to appreciate again. Thus, the key prices affecting trade and capital flows have gone through one full cycle in the 1980s and are starting another upswing in the 1990s. On the positive side, the 1988–9 peaking, depending on the measure used, in the US budget deficit and the improvement in the US trade balance may help put off protectionist fervour (at least that directed elsewhere rather than towards Japan) in the United States for a while.

These more positive developments do not mean there were not plenty of uncertainties at the same time. The US and other world financial markets dodged a bullet in the 1987 stock market crash and may have to dodge another if the Japanese capital markets (and land values), the world's largest in dollar terms with yen appreciation, come down from their speculative crest. The revolutions taking place in Eastern Europe and the greater unification about to take place in Western Europe (at the end of 1992) have both increased the potential opportunities and the uncertainties faced by Asia's developing country exporters.

However, they have put the South Asian countries in a bigger bind. Concessionary financing now received by these countries could well be diverted to Eastern Europe and the barter trade with the Communist bloc that many utilized could end. Liberalization in Eastern Europe may force something akin to liberalization in South Asia. Similarly, unification that includes a unified tariff for Western Europe may bring about greater regionalization in Asia. Less positively, the renewed emphasis on Europe could end the focus on the 'Pacific Century' before it ever really had a chance to redirect relevant policies, which would ignore the longer-run realities.

Chief among these is the presence of over half the world's population in Asia. The most populous country, China, has added to the uncertainties faced by economic policymakers. Through June 1989, domestic liberalization, especially in agriculture, and consequent increased openness and growth gave China an increasingly active role in international trade and in capital markets, both as a recipient of direct investment and in the competition for financial resources. The Asian NIEs and Thailand were rapidly developing trading and investment ties with China, with Hong Kong by necessity, and with the others as an important aspect of their long-run policy. Much of this came to a halt with the post-Tiananmen Square domestic policy changes and the world's reaction to Beijing's clamp-down. Stresses were clearly building in the economy and would have required some policy shifts even had there been no political problems. The main result is a great deal of uncertainty about what kind of competitor and market China will be in the 1990s.

## Indices of Performance in the 1980s

### Real Growth in Total and GNP Per Capita in the 1980s

At the beginning of the 1980s—just before the 1982 recession—real growth rates mirrored the long-run interregional performances discussed above for real per capita incomes. The Asian NIEs led the way, followed by South-East Asia and then South Asia (Table 3.7). At this time the socialist economies were doing as well as South-East Asia.

Then in the slow growth period in the mid-1980s these relative positions were reversed, with China achieving the highest growth rate and many South Asian countries performing better than any South-East

TABLE 3.7
Real Growth Rates,[a] 1977-1989 (per cent)

| Country | Real GDP Growth (Average Annual Growth) ||| | Real Per Capita GDP Growth (Average Annual Growth) |||
|---|---|---|---|---|---|---|---|
|  | 1977-81 | 1982-5 | 1986-9 | 1989 | 1977-81 | 1982-5 | 1986-8 |
| Asian NIEs |  |  |  |  |  |  |  |
| Hong Kong | 10.8 | 4.7 | 8.9 | 2.5 | 7.8 | 3.4 | 10.9[c] |
| South Korea | 6.7 | 7.7 | 10.0 | 6.3 | 5.1 | 6.1 | 10.1 |
| Singapore | 9.0 | 5.4 | 7.7 | 9.2 | 7.6 | 4.2 | 6.0 |
| Taiwan | 9.0 | 6.1 | 9.4 | 7.7 | 7.0 | 4.5 | 9.6[c] |
| South-East Asia |  |  |  |  |  |  |  |
| Indonesia | 8.1 | 3.7 | 4.4 | 6.2 | 5.7 | 1.4 | 2.2 |
| Malaysia | 7.6 | 4.7 | 3.8 | 7.6 | 4.6 | 2.0 | 2.1 |
| Philippines | 5.4 | -1.6 | 4.6 | 6.0 | 2.7 | -4.0 | 2.0 |
| Thailand | 7.1 | 4.7 | 8.6 | 10.5 | 4.7 | 2.7 | 4.9 |
| South Asia |  |  |  |  |  |  |  |
| Bangladesh | 4.1 | 3.1 | 3.8[b] | — | 1.8 | 0.5 | 1.5 |
| India | 4.5 | 5.3 | 4.1 | 4.2 | 2.3 | 3.1 | 2.3[c] |
| Nepal | 3.2 | 2.9 | 4.5[b] | — | 0.7 | 0.2 | 0.6[c] |
| Pakistan | 6.5 | 6.5 | 6.2[b] | — | 3.3 | 3.3 | 3.1 |
| Sri Lanka | 5.7 | 5.0 | 2.0[b] | — | 3.8 | 3.6 | 1.3 |
| Asian Socialist Economies |  |  |  |  |  |  |  |
| Burma | 6.4 | 5.0 | 1.8[b] | — | 4.3 | 2.9 | -1.3[c] |
| China | 7.8 | 11.6 | 8.7 | 3.9 | 6.6 | 11.3 | 7.8[d] |

Sources: Asian Development Bank (1989) Key Indicators of Developing Member Countries of ADB; Far Eastern Economic Review (1990), various issues.
[a] All data are based on 1980 prices except for the 1988 growth in per capita GDP which is based on 1985 prices.
[b] Data are from 1986 to 1988 only.
[c] 1986 and 1987.
[d] 1986.

Asian country and as well as the NIEs. In effect, South Asia's independence of trade gave it a very brief advantage while China's performance resulted from its long overdue agricultural reforms. By this time, political and economic problems had taken the Philippines to the bottom of the growth list.

In the ensuing recovery period, China maintained the very high levels achieved and Thailand boomed, powered by sustained recovery in the developed countries. Growth rates picked up in the Philippines and Indonesia as well and by 1989 had also recovered in Malaysia. On the other hand, in South Asia real growth fell off, moving inversely to the rest of the Asian developing countries and revealing a dependence on by then slow-growing regions, for example, Eastern Europe, Iran, Iraq, or in Sri Lanka, the effects of ethnic unrest. Only India has a domestic market large enough to temporarily make import substitution pay—if there were sufficient domestic competition, which unfortunately there is not. The others must specialize and trade to have reasonable economic growth and the evidence suggests they have not been able to put in place the policies that would allow them to accomplish these goals. Burma, on a path all its own, achieved increasing isolation and even slower growth.

Since 1989, and with much public attention, growth has slowed sharply in China and, as a result of this, in Hong Kong. Growth is also off their record highs in Taiwan and South Korea, though remaining at high levels in world terms. With exports at the core of the decline and growing structural and labour problems, the slow-down in South Korea may last for a while. Only in Thailand do real growth rates remain at boom levels.

The importance of population policy or lack of it is clearly shown across the regions by the relation between total and per capita real growth. Having been through the demographic transition, the Asian NIEs generally garner most of their real GDP growth in per capita increases. In South-East Asia, where real growth is smaller and population growth larger but mostly slowing or falling, 40–60 per cent of aggregate growth often goes to keep per capita income constant, so that low growth often means backsliding in per capita terms. The Philippines, with the largest continuing growth in population in this sub-region, is worst in this respect. Except for Sri Lanka, the South Asian countries—where the demographic transition has not started or is barely under way—generally capture even less of the relatively slower growth they achieve in per capita terms, with the poorest country, Bangladesh, having the worst performance. Without population control these countries are very likely to remain in a low-income trap, sustained—at least in Bangladesh and Nepal—by international welfare programmes.

*Export Performance*

From the high levels of the late 1970s to the 1980–4 slow-down, export growth rates fell in every country (Table 3.8).[5] Up to that time, export

TABLE 3.8
Export Performance, 1975-1988

| Country | Growth Rate in Exports[a] (per cent) 1975-9 | 1980-4 | 1985-8 | 1988 | Terms of Trade (1980=100) 1987 | Per Capita Exports 1972-6[a] (dollars) | Percentage Change to 1987 | Relative Percentage Change (Thai=1.0) 1972/6-87 |
|---|---|---|---|---|---|---|---|---|
| Asian NIEs | | | | | | | | |
| Hong Kong | 21.3 | 14.1 | 22.8 | 30.3 | 106 | 1,340 | 545 | 1.63 |
| South Korea | 28.2 | 14.4 | 20.7 | 28.4 | 105 | 126 | 792 | 2.37 |
| Singapore | 20.7 | 11.8 | 14.5 | 37.0 | 102 | 2,109 | 420 | 1.26 |
| Taiwan | 25.0 | 14.0 | 19.4 | 12.4 | 126 | 335 | 718 | 2.15 |
| South-East Asia | | | | | | | | |
| Indonesia | 16.8 | 8.1 | 8.6 | 13.6 | 69 | 43 | 126 | 0.38 |
| Malaysia | 23.0 | 8.8 | 7.6 | 17.7 | 72 | 309 | 251 | 0.75 |
| Philippines | 12.2 | 3.7 | 8.5 | 24.5 | 98 | 51 | 78 | 0.23 |
| Thailand | 17.8 | 7.6 | 22.0 | 35.8 | 81 | 50 | 334[b] | 1.00 |
| South Asia | | | | | | | | |
| Bangladesh | 14.1 | 7.9 | 4.3 | 21.0 | 91 | 4 | 175 | 0.52 |
| India | 15.0 | 4.1 | 9.3 | 17.0 | 114 | 6 | 150 | 0.45 |
| Nepal | 12.9 | 10.9 | 11.4 | 25.8 | 93 | 6 | 50 | 0.15 |
| Pakistan | 14.2 | 6.4 | 15.6 | 8.4 | 99 | 14 | 186 | 0.56 |
| Sri Lanka | 13.7 | 9.3 | 1.2 | 8.1 | 96 | 36 | 133 | 0.40 |
| Asian Socialist Economies | | | | | | | | |
| Burma | 17.5 | 0.6 | -20.5 | -32.9 | 65 | 6 | 17 | 0.05 |
| China | 15.2 | 13.4 | 17.8 | 20.2 | 87 | 7 | 357 | 1.07 |

Sources: Growth rate in exports and per capita exports from Asian Development Bank (1989), *Key Indicators of Developing Member Countries of ADB*; terms of trade from World Bank (1989), *World Development Report 1989*.

[a] Annual averages.
[b] Estimated from actual export growth and estimated population growth.

growth rates were clearly higher in the NIEs than elsewhere. Surprisingly, the South Asian countries generally did as well as or better than the South-East Asian countries in 1980-4. South Asia's trade depends relatively more on barter and special circumstances than does trade elsewhere and so, as noted, is less responsive to changing market conditions. However, having had the disadvantage of starting from a lower level, doing as well means that no catching up took place.

With Singapore lagging initially, Asian NIE exports once more took off in the 1985-8 recovery period. However, with appreciation of its currency, the growth level fell rather sharply in 1988 in Taiwan. Except for Thailand, which was second only to Hong Kong for the entire period and to Singapore for the year 1988 only, the growth in exports was generally much lower in South-East Asia than in the NIEs in 1985-8. In fact, leaving Thailand out, three South Asian countries topped the South-East Asian countries in export growth in this period. Hopefully, this is a beginning in the reflection of policy reforms, especially in India. The expansion in all the South-East and South Asian countries (except Pakistan) in 1988 is impressive. China also achieved impressive high growth rates in the recovery period—ranking just behind Thailand—as the reforms carried out took hold. Burma was the only consistently negative performer, moving 'backward' rapidly.

Using exports per capita as a rough measure of export effort—and leaving out the city-states of Hong Kong and Singapore that by definition must have a high level of exports per capita—by the early 1970s Taiwan, South Korea, and Malaysia were already far ahead of the rest of developing Asia in this respect. In part, this can be attributed to necessity for the first two, since as small, resource-poor countries, they had no alternative to a major export effort if they wanted economic growth. Malaysia, on the other hand, is a resource-rich country with a relatively small population.

The South-East Asian countries other than Malaysia have much smaller export efforts than the Asian NIEs but in turn did much better in this respect than the South Asian countries (except Sri Lanka) and the socialist economies. Like Taiwan and South Korea, Bangladesh, Nepal, and to some extent Pakistan also fit the description of small, resource-poor countries but their export efforts were also very small in 1972-6, making clear that other factors besides initial resource endowments and size are involved.

From the 1970s to 1987, all countries except Burma increased their exports per capita—not difficult to do when inflation is factored in. However, in relative terms which partially adjusts for inflation,[6] the largest percentage increases—from the largest initial base and so no mean accomplishment—were in Taiwan and South Korea. China and Thailand came next, again ignoring the city-states. Lagging most in relative terms, were Burma, Nepal, and the Philippines, though all the other South Asian countries and Indonesia were also far behind the Thai bench-mark performance.

Just as in their growth performance, two characteristics of the countries at the bottom in exports per capita achievement are rapid population growth and/or welfare statism. Those at the top have all undergone the demographic transition. Clearly, the argument that fast population growth drives the economy towards greater economic growth is not supported in the data presented to this point. The further argument that it is the policies that are wrong, not the population growth, ignores the fact that the policies, especially welfare policies, are greatly influenced by population growth.

The terms of trade have supported the differences in growth rates and economic performance noted, making the most rapidly industrializing and fastest-growing Asian developing countries better off and the rest worse off in the 1980s. The terms of trade improved for all the NIEs. Outside this group, they worsened everywhere else. Unless exports have expanded enough to offset these changes, real imports must have fallen or debt increased.

In sum, export growth performance generally lines up with total and per capita economic growth performance. This fact has often been noted, but does not explain why some countries have opted for policies leading to more rapid export growth and others, policies that have penalized exports. The intent was not, it seems relatively certain, to reduce growth performance. Isolation from swings in the world economy may pay in some short-run periods, but, short-run set-backs notwithstanding, in most periods participation in the world economy yields higher growth rates.

As has often been argued, it may not be the participation *per se* that counts but the policies that must be in place to make such participation in the world economy a viable option. It is difficult to become and remain competitive in world markets without maintaining productive efficiency near the levels attained by other countries with similar factor endowments. Subsidies will not work in the long-run, unless they lead to increased efficiency and can be phased out. Human resource development cannot be much help in circumstances where the policies followed do not encourage productive efficiency.

## Investment and Resource Mobilization

Holding the efficiency of resource use constant and assuming Keynesian inflexibilities are not significant, the greater the proportion of output devoted to capital accumulation, the greater the growth in per capita income. Neo-classical growth theory would hold this to be a short-run relationship, but, if progress requires some embodiment, this relationship will hold for sufficiently long periods that the *ceteris paribus* assumptions of the neo-classical model will not hold. In any event, as Table 3.5 has shown, there is much evidence that large increases in the capital stock have been positively associated with high relative growth performance.

Since the Asian developing countries are not on the technological frontier, though South Korea and Taiwan are coming close, they have much catching up to do. Therefore, sources of increased productivity, mostly but not always embodied in new capital, are positively related to the savings ratio. Exceptions due to differences in the efficiency of employment of resources clearly exist, but they do not change the generally positive relation between savings rates, capital accumulation, and growth in real per capita income.

Thus, unless offset by even more rapid growth in the labour force, a higher ratio of gross domestic investment to gross domestic product (GDI/GDP) implies more rapid growth in capital per worker and so in productivity and per capita income. There is also a feedback here running from more rapid growth to higher savings ratios to higher investment ratios. How efficiently capital is employed matters, but for present purposes—whether caused directly or through the feedback loop—if a positive relation between economic performance and the investment ratio shows up, then the significance of the investment ratio is supported.

Gross domestic investment can be financed by domestic savings and by net capital inflows and transfers from abroad. Thus, gross domestic savings (GDS) limits the amount of GDI unless foreign credit is available. However, capital inflows may substitute for or supplement gross domestic savings. They will supplement GDS if they do not reduce the incentives (for example, the returns to savings) for domestic savings, a likely outcome where domestic capital markets are not well developed or where equity markets are very well developed and bond markets are not. In these circumstances, foreign inflows of capital will tend to provide funding for domestic investment otherwise not available. In most of the countries covered and mostly for the first reason—except in the Asian NIEs and Thailand where the second reason applies—capital inflows are likely to supplement not substitute for domestic savings. And, since the exchange rate effects of capital inflows are almost always limited by interventions, they are not as likely to penalize outward-looking industries as they might do in these same countries. In Table 3.9, the basic assumption is that GDS and the resource gap (net capital movements) are additive.

The investment ratio is generally highest over the period covered in the Asian NIEs, with Singapore on top, reflecting the role of public housing in that city-state, followed by South Korea. This ratio has also been relatively high, generally over 20 per cent, in Malaysia, Hong Kong, Taiwan, Thailand, Sri Lanka, Indonesia, and India. All of the high-growth countries are on this list. They are joined by the two oil exporters (Indonesia and Malaysia) and two countries in South Asia (India and Sri Lanka) with considerable government intervention and medium but falling growth rates. The relatively high investment ratio in the latter two countries emphasizes the fact that efficiency of employment of capital is also part of the story. China, in the only period for which data are available, as befits a centrally planned economy, also had a very high investment ratio.

TABLE 3.9
Resource Mobilization, 1975–1988 (per cent)

| Country | GDS/GDP[a] 1975–80 | GDS/GDP[a] 1984–8 | GDS/GDP[a] 1988 | GDI/GDP[a] 1975–80 | GDI/GDP[a] 1984–8 | GDI/GDP[a] 1988 | Resource Gap[a] 1975–80 | Resource Gap[a] 1984–8 | Resource Gap[a] 1988 |
|---|---|---|---|---|---|---|---|---|---|
| Asian NIEs | | | | | | | | | |
| Hong Kong | 30 | 25 | 28 | 28 | 30 | 33 | 2 | −5 | −5 |
| South Korea | 30 | 30 | 30 | 22 | 34 | 38 | 8 | −5 | −8 |
| Singapore | 42 | 41 | 37 | 33 | 42 | 41 | 9 | −1 | −4 |
| Taiwan | 32 | 20 | 24 | 30 | 34 | 33 | 2 | −14 | −9 |
| South-East Asia | | | | | | | | | |
| Indonesia | 21 | 27[b] | — | 25 | 26[b] | — | −4 | 1 | — |
| Malaysia | 26 | 28 | 29 | 27 | 36 | 39 | −1 | −8 | −10 |
| Philippines | 30 | 15 | 17 | 24 | 17 | 18 | 6 | −2 | −1 |
| Thailand | 26 | 24 | 28 | 21 | 23 | 28 | 5 | 2 | −1 |
| South Asia | | | | | | | | | |
| Bangladesh | 20 | 11 | 11 | 1 | 3 | 3 | 19 | 8 | 8 |
| India | 23 | 21[b] | — | 19 | 20[b] | — | 4 | 1 | — |
| Nepal | 14 | 18 | 20 | 8 | 11[b] | — | 6 | 7 | — |
| Pakistan | 17 | 17 | 16 | 6 | 8 | 9 | 11 | 8 | −8 |
| Sri Lanka | 26 | 24 | 23 | 11 | 13[b] | — | 15 | 11 | — |
| Asian Socialist Economies | | | | | | | | | |
| Burma | 16 | 15 | 15 | 13 | 12 | 11 | 3 | 3 | 3 |
| China | 33 | — | — | — | — | — | — | — | — |

*Sources*: World Bank Data Disc, Washington, DC: World Bank; Asian Development Bank (1989), *Key Indicators of Developing Member Countries of ADB*.
[a] Average annual or annual data; GDP = Gross Domestic Product; GDI = Gross Domestic Investments; GDS = Gross Domestic Savings.
[b] 1984–7.

Domestic savings ratios are highest for the Asian NIEs and the two oil exporters, Indonesia and Malaysia, with Thailand catching up quickly in recent years. Although all of these countries, except the oil exporters, depended on foreign financing in the late 1970s—except in Sri Lanka and India—by 1984–8 domestic savings were much more than adequate to finance their high investment ratios. Actually Thailand was a small net international borrower in this period but became a net lender in 1988. These high savings were generated by the private sector in Taiwan, South Korea, Hong Kong, and Thailand and generated by the public sector in Singapore, Malaysia, and (though less so) in Indonesia.[7]

With their savings efforts above average for the region and far above average for the developing world, it appears that net investment in these countries is constrained more by the return to capital than by domestic or imported savings. For the Asian NIEs in this group, given the decline in the growth rate of the labour force and resulting relative scarcity of labour, returns on capital invested domestically in labour-intensive industries must be falling relative to returns in similar industries elsewhere in the region. As long as the resulting capital outflow continues to be tolerated, such capital movements are likely to continue and to grow, especially to China and South-East Asia since India still blocks such inflows.

In India, the savings ratio is 'reasonable' but not large enough to cover present investment requirements. The difference is made up by grants and subsidized loans—neither of which have a great future in Asia. For India to begin to grow at a self-feeding pace, among many other requirements, a necessary one will have to be higher domestic savings or more willingness to borrow on market terms and to accept direct foreign investment. Sri Lanka has the highest dependency rate on external financing, spelling problems ahead.

Applying a much smaller share of resources to growth—so that only far above average efficiency could compensate in relative terms—are Pakistan, Burma, the Philippines, Nepal, and Bangladesh. All these countries except the Philippines have very low domestic savings ratios, much lower than their investment ratios. Both the investment and savings ratios started relatively high in the Philippines and then fell off sharply in the 1980s, with the decline in savings probably a result of inflationary expectations and general uncertainty about the future. But the investment ratio fell more[8] as domestic savings increasingly had to go to service the Philippine debt. Except for Pakistan, these countries have had growth problems, and growth is slowing even in Pakistan. It is worth noting that except for the Philippines these are the countries at the bottom of the educational effort list. All these countries have had and continue to have above average population growth.

In these low GDS/GNP countries, labour resources are going to be underequipped in both human and physical capital terms and successful growth must wait for the release of whatever is limiting effective capital accumulation. Generally, that seems to be domestic savings and/or economic efficiency. The latter must be considered since all, except the

Philippines, have managed to use foreign savings to achieve investment ratios, even though relatively low, that are considerably above their savings ratios.

In sum, the countries doing the best at domestic resource mobilization since the late 1970s were also the countries with relatively high growth rates in real per capita income. By the late 1980s all the Asian NIEs and most of the South-East Asian countries had high savings ratios and most had become capital exporters while all the South Asian countries had large resource gaps and low savings ratios.

*Debt and Foreign Savings Dependency*

The relative dependence on foreign savings in financing capital accumulation is one determinant of a country's debt situation. If foreign borrowing is not efficiently used so that debt grows more rapidly than GDP, then a debt problem is likely. This may be forestalled if subsidized debt terms keep servicing ratios low, but if the subsidized sources ever dry up so that old borrowing must be repaid and new borrowing must be at market terms, a debt or, if default occurs, a borrowing problem is sure to emerge.

In 1987, countries with very high debt/GNP ratios (Table 3.10) were the Philippines, Indonesia, Malaysia, and Sri Lanka. However, despite relatively low export and GNP growth, Sri Lanka is getting by with rapidly growing debt because it is borrowing on concessionary terms. But the Philippines and Indonesia clearly have a debt problem. Indonesia is a bit surprising in this context, especially given its excess of gross domestic savings over its gross domestic investment. Perhaps feeling safe in borrowing against its oil resources in the past could have led to dependency on continued borrowing to maintain the flow of external funds as oil revenues fell. Malaysia, another oil exporter, is on the borderline of a debt problem.

All three of these countries use 10 per cent or more of their output to service debt payments and, given that their debt/GNP ratios are growing, this is a required and not a voluntary buy-back (as in South Korea) of outstanding debt. The Philippines and Indonesia also have very high and growing debt service ratios, using one-fourth to one-third of exports just to meet debt payments, and they have very high and growing dead weight interest service ratios. On the other hand, Malaysia's debt service and interest service ratios have fallen and since Malaysia borrows at market rates and has an increasing debt/GNP ratio, this implies export growth has been sufficient to reduce the debt service ratio and also implies that past borrowing was put to good use.

The mid-level debt/GNP countries are South Korea, Thailand, Bangladesh, Nepal, Pakistan, and Burma. There are many different situations here. South Korea is rapidly reducing its once high debt/GNP and interest service ratios by advance payment of debt and export growth. At the present time, this country appears to have used borrowing more effectively than any other major debtor in the world.

TABLE 3.10
Debt Indicators, 1975–1987 (per cent)

| Country | Debt/GNP 1975 | 1980 | 1984 | 1987 | Debt Service/GNP 1975 | 1980 | 1984 | 1987 | Debt Service/Exports 1975 | 1980 | 1984 | 1987 | Interest Service/Exports 1975 | 1980 | 1984 | 1987 |
|---|---|---|---|---|---|---|---|---|---|---|---|---|---|---|---|---|
| **Asian NIEs** | | | | | | | | | | | | | | | | |
| Hong Kong | | | | | | | | | | | | | | | | |
| South Korea | 31 | 49 | 56 | 34 | 4 | 5 | 9 | 13 | 13 | 14 | 22 | 28 | 6 | 7 | 8 | 4 |
| Singapore | 15 | 19 | 19 | 22 | 2 | 4 | 6 | 4 | 2 | 2 | 4 | 2 | 1 | 1 | 2 | 2 |
| Taiwan | | 22 | 16 | 17 | | | | | | | | | | | | |
| **South-East Asia** | | | | | | | | | | | | | | | | |
| Indonesia | 36 | 33 | 44 | 80 | 3 | 4 | 6 | 10 | 14 | 13 | 25 | 33 | 5 | 5 | 10 | 14 |
| Malaysia | 20 | 22 | 63 | 74 | 2 | 3 | 18 | 14 | 5 | 5 | 29 | 20 | 2 | 3 | 8 | 7 |
| Philippines | 19 | 49 | 82 | 87 | 3 | 5 | 7 | 13 | 13 | 14 | 19 | 25 | 4 | 7 | 12 | 16 |
| Thailand | 9 | 26 | 48 | 44 | 2 | 4 | 7 | 6 | 12 | 15 | 25 | 21 | 4 | 6 | 9 | 7 |
| **South Asia** | | | | | | | | | | | | | | | | |
| Bangladesh | 13 | 32 | 41 | 54 | 1 | 1 | 1 | 2 | 16 | 7 | 14 | 17 | 5 | 4 | 7 | 7 |
| India | 16 | 11 | 17 | 19 | 1 | 1 | 1 | 2 | 13 | 8 | 18 | 22 | 4 | 3 | 7 | 8 |
| Nepal | 2 | 10 | 24 | 34 | 1 | 1 | 1 | 1 | 1 | 2 | 5 | 10 | 0 | 1 | 3 | 4 |
| Pakistan | 49 | 42 | 43 | 47 | 2 | 3 | 4 | 4 | 18 | 13 | 19 | 18 | 7 | 5 | 5 | 6 |
| Sri Lanka | 25 | 46 | 60 | 72 | 5 | 2 | 4 | 5 | 21 | 6 | 13 | 17 | 3 | 3 | 6 | 6 |
| **Asian Socialist Economies** | | | | | | | | | | | | | | | | |
| Burma | 9 | 26 | 46 | 47 | 1 | 2 | 3 | 2 | 17 | 20 | 53 | 59 | 5 | 8 | 19 | 22 |
| China | | 2 | 6 | 10 | | 1 | 1 | 1 | | 5 | 6 | 7 | | 2 | 2 | 3 |

*Source*: David and Lee (1989).

Thailand seems to be moving along the same path, but at an earlier stage, with the debt/GNP ratio and all the service ratios falling due to increased GDP and export growth and zero or negative net borrowing. Pakistan has also been using debt to accomplish growth, but with less success; its service ratios are lower than Thailand's because of more concessionary debt but they are not improving.

Bangladesh and Nepal are classic examples of concessionary borrowers and both are beginning to feel the effect—though at still low service ratios—of more market-based borrowing and of reduced export growth. If forced to borrow at market terms with no other changes, these countries would rapidly join the world's hopeless debt cases. Burma is an extreme outlier with very low service payments that balloon to extremely high service ratios relative to exports because of the country's extremely low and deteriorating export performance. The ability in all these countries to raise subsidized funds internationally, rather than speeding development, has seemed mainly to make possible the postponement of necessary reforms for short-run political gain.

At the bottom of the debt/GNP ladder are Singapore, Taiwan, India, and China. Singapore has such a high level of domestic savings that borrowing has not been a significant source of funds in the 1970s and 1980s. Taiwan is now a major net creditor and its debt reflects market opportunities. India has, at the expense of possible growth, restricted its borrowing largely to concessional funds. But (somewhat like Burma), even though the service of debt takes only a very small part of GNP, because exports and export growth are so low, its debt service and interest service ratios are relatively high. China has only recently become a borrower, so the growth in its debt/GNP ratio is rapid, and its borrowing is clearly on highly concessional terms. Actually China appears to have decided to use direct foreign investment rather than debt to transfer capital. India, of course, has cut off this source as well.

Thus, it seems no simple generalization will do; the ranks of both the most and least successful countries include many low debt countries and at least one of the highest debtors in each period. However, except for South Korea, it appears a low debt policy is best. This presupposes high domestic savings ratios. However, having a high savings ratio does not guarantee that a country will not have a debt problem. Indonesia certainly has one and Malaysia is close despite having above average savings ratios. Where both debt and savings ratios are low, as in most South Asian countries, growth is necessarily low unless China's alternative of high direct foreign investment is followed. But being willing to take on debt, as in three (Indonesia, Malaysia, and the Philippines) of the four South-East Asian countries and Pakistan and Sri Lanka, is by itself clearly not enough. The efficiency with which the debt is used is still the key.

*Financial Performance*

INFLATION RATES

Along with real growth rates, inflation rates provide a key index of economic performance. The twin goals of sustainable increases in real per capita income and price stability are difficult to achieve and often conflict. If either one is not met, there will be trouble ahead—though the costs and who is to bear the domestic burden of the costs of not meeting these goals are very different.

There are no Asian developing countries with the astronomical inflation rates of South America, but if double digit inflation is a 'warning' sign, then several Asian developing countries need to take heed. Often the implication of high inflation is poor economic management, usually an unwillingness to take any difficult steps 'now' for political reasons, whatever their long-run benefits. Thus, beyond the

TABLE 3.11
Consumer Price Index (CPI) Inflation Rates, 1972–1989 (per cent)

| Country | 1972–81[a] | 1982–8[a] | Second Quarter 1989 |
|---|---|---|---|
| Asian NIEs | | | |
| Hong Kong | 9.7 | 6.9 | 9.9 |
| South Korea | 17.3 | 4.3 | 5.7 |
| Singapore | 7.4 | 1.6 | 2.5 |
| Taiwan | 12.5 | 1.1 | 3.9 |
| South-East Asia | | | |
| Indonesia | 18.8 | 9.4 | 7.2 |
| Malaysia | 6.8 | 3.2 | 3.2 |
| Philippines | 14.1 | 16.4 | 8.8 |
| Thailand | 11.2 | 3.0 | 4.5 |
| South Asia | | | |
| Bangladesh | 22.4 | 17.5 | 10.6 |
| India | 9.0 | 8.1 | 8.4 |
| Nepal | 9.1 | 10.9 | 8.7 |
| Pakistan | 13.2 | 5.6 | 9.6 |
| Sri Lanka | 10.5 | 12.1 | 10.6 |
| Asian Socialist Economies | | | |
| Burma | 11.2 | 10.1 | – |
| China | – | 6.5 | 20.7 |
| Bench-mark Countries | | | |
| Japan | 9.0 | 1.6 | 2.7 |
| United States | 8.5 | 4.0 | 4.7 |

*Sources*: International Monetary Fund, various issues; Asian Development Bank (1989), *Key Indicators of Developing Member Countries of ADB*; *Far Eastern Economic Review* (1990), various issues.
[a]Annual averages.

immediate distribution effects, high inflation can be a symptom of economic mismanagement.

Countries with double digit inflation rates (Table 3.11) in the 1970s, in descending order, include Bangladesh, Indonesia, South Korea, the Philippines, Pakistan, Burma, Thailand, and Sri Lanka. By the 1982–8 period, only Bangladesh, the Philippines, Sri Lanka, Nepal, and Burma were in this group. All the countries failing to bring inflation rates down in keeping with the downward world trend are at or near the bottom of the growth list. Similarly, the countries with the lowest inflation rates in the 1980s, Taiwan, Singapore, Thailand, Malaysia, and South Korea, are all at or near the top of the growth list. China also had a relatively low inflation rate through much of the 1980s—though reported inflation rates in China are difficult to interpret—but this ended abruptly in 1989.

Except for the last group of countries, all the Asian developing countries, especially those in South Asia, had far higher inflation rates than the United States and Japan, placing a heavy burden on their exchange rate policies if they expected to remain competitive in these key markets. For the South Asian countries, this is one aspect of their greater emphasis on import substitution or inward-looking growth policies. Having placed less emphasis on trade expansion and on borrowing at market terms as a means of financing, they did not experience the same pressure to remain competitive in world markets. Therefore, they could afford the advantages, to their political élite at least, of inflationary policies.

MONETARY DEEPENING

Monetary deepening, measured by the M2 (currency, demand deposits, and time deposits) to GNP ratio, is an index of financial performance as well as of confidence in a country's economic management. Actually, monetary deepening is one of the outcomes of the financial development that usually accompanies successful economic development. The expectation is that it will increase in a supportive feedback relationship with economic growth up to a point and then, at high levels of financial sophistication and real income, begin to drop off. However, except possibly for the city-states, none of the countries considered has reached this point. For most, especially those near the bottom, the increased use of money or increased efficiency of resource use represented by an increase in the monetary deepening ratio implies an upward shift in their production function and thus an increase in their per capita income.

Relatively low deepening ratios, at any stage of development, reflect a relatively high preference for currency relative to demand deposits and/or a relatively high preference for consumption or non-monetary assets. Speculation, black markets, and government regulation can all contribute to a high cash preference. Lack of confidence in the government, especially in the government's ability and desire to control inflation and its general policy towards private wealth contribute to the preference for consumption and holding wealth in the form of real assets.

As shown in Table 3.12, monetary deepening is roughly correlated with economic development, with the levels highest in the Asian NIEs—except for South Korea—followed by Thailand and Malaysia. In addition to South Korea, where the level was and is surprisingly low, outliers include Indonesia and the Philippines on the low side and China on the high side. China's performance seems to reflect the lack of alternatives coupled with an expansionary monetary policy—the result is a powder keg with a burning fuse.[9]

Among the NIEs, all but South Korea show a significant increase in monetary deepening through the 1980s. In South-East Asia, significant increases occurred in Indonesia and Thailand. In the other South-East Asian and in the South Asian and socialist countries, the changes were small, nil (the Philippines), or negative (Pakistan and Burma).

For the countries with relatively low monetary deepening ratios and/or insignificant increases in the 1980s, past or present inflation rates or real deposit rates, to be discussed below, seem to be the culprit. However, in South Korea it may be the absorption of cash into the curb market that limits the total money stock relative to GNP.

TABLE 3.12
Monetary Deepening (M2/GNP), 1965–1988 (per cent)

| Country | 1965 | 1980–3 | 1988 |
|---|---|---|---|
| Asian NIEs | | | |
| Hong Kong | – | 94.5 | 159.1 |
| South Korea | 11.1 | 36.2 | 42.9 |
| Singapore | 58.4 | 71.9 | 84.4 |
| Taiwan | – | 74.4 | 143.7 |
| South-East Asia | | | |
| Indonesia | – | 19.3 | 31.2 |
| Malaysia | 26.3 | 61.0 | 67.1 |
| Philippines | 19.9 | 22.8 | 23.4 |
| Thailand | 25.6 | 42.5 | 66.4 |
| South Asia | | | |
| Bangladesh | – | 20.6 | 26.9 |
| India | 25.7 | 40.6 | 48.9 |
| Nepal | 8.4 | 25.1 | 31.9 |
| Pakistan | 40.8 | 38.6 | 35.7 |
| Sri Lanka | 31.4 | 29.5 | 31.7 |
| Asian Socialist Economies | | | |
| Burma | 29.0 | 29.1 | 28.9 |
| China | – | 34.9 | 70.2 |

*Source*: Based on Asian Development Bank (1989), *Key Indicators of Developing Member Countries of ADB*.

In sum, with some notable exceptions for monetary deepening, the financial performance indices covering the inflation rate and monetary deepening all fell in line—the latter positively and the former inversely—with growth performance and the ability to compete internationally and to effectively raise resources domestically.

## Comparative Economic Policies

*Introduction*

Given the wide swings in external circumstances since the mid-1970s just described, the performance of the Asian developing countries as they responded to the challenges presented makes an interesting and revealing story. Although—except for the obvious difference in fortunes of the oil exporters and importers and to a smaller extent the yen and dollar borrowers—the Asian developing countries faced roughly the same external factors, there were wide differences in their performances over the period covered. These partly resulted from differences in beginning resource endowments—a matter of luck and history for natural resources—and past policies for human and physical capital accumulation. However, given the comparative performance of countries with similar endowments and the fact that some of the least well-placed countries in terms of natural resources have achieved the highest growth rates, it seems clear that differences in the policies adopted or in the way they were implemented are most important in explaining the observed differences in performance. In this context, the macroeconomic, real exchange rate, the trade policies adopted, the degree and nature of the government's intervention in the allocative process, and the extent of competition encouraged were all significant.

There are at least three dimensions to economic policy that require attention. First, there is the enactment of institutional 'rules of the game'—ranging from anti-trust legislation to labour laws—that constrain economic activities. Second, there is the degree of intervention by the government in economic activities, whether directing resource allocation as in a command economy or by the licensing of production and other economic rights or by selective tax and subsidy policies. Finally, there are the fiscal, monetary, and exchange rate policies that set the domestic environment in which economic activity takes place. Unfortunately there is no adequate objective measure of the first and second dimensions across the region's countries. Thus, relative to these concerns, the government's role has to be inferred from limited empirical proxies and widely noted impressions.

Making this task even more difficult is the fact government intervention cannot be deemed all good or all bad. For example, if it is accepted that bureaucracy is 'inefficient' as a replacement for the market, that created vested interests align with bureaucrats to keep economic rents up and consequently efficiency is kept down, that welfare transfers and taxes needed to fund the bureaucracy and other expenditures reduce efficiency, etc., then beyond some level, government intervention or government expenditure can slow growth. But in order to provide goods and services with high externalities and to establish and enforce the rules that organize markets and constrain private self-interest in a socially acceptable manner, some level of government intervention is necessary and desirable.

*Fiscal Policies*

In the absence of other indicators, the government's direct as opposed to 'rule-setting' role is usually measured by its fiscal activities. The share of total government expenditures in GDP or of government capital expenditures in total capital expenditures or the share of taxes in GDP are all proxies of the extent of direct intervention. The government's macroeconomic role and attitude toward market versus directed allocation of resources is roughly measured by a country's fiscal budget position.

GOVERNMENT'S SHARE IN GDP AND GDI

The first index of the government's role is the share of government expenditures in GDP. While a higher than average share clearly indicates the government commands a relatively large share of the country's resources, this index must be treated with caution since it does not tell us whether or not they are used more efficiently than if they had remained in the hands of the private sector. Although the presumption is that the government is generally less efficient, if infrastructure needs have not been met or there is a large educational deficit, a relatively large government share could be a positive sign. And, if the share of government in GDP is lower than average, that does not rule out government control of economic activity through licensing or quasi-government enterprises.[10] Thus, a dual criterion combining the share of government capital expenditures in gross domestic investment (GDI) with the share of total expenditures will give more insight. The greater the relative amount of capital accumulation accomplished by the government, the more the allocation of this important part of the growth process is bureaucratized and unresponsive to market forces.

Where both the government share in the economy and in GDI are low, the presumption is that there is more competition and dependence on the market to engineer growth, so more flexibility and more growth, *ceteris paribus*. Hong Kong, South Korea, Taiwan, Thailand, and India meet this dual criterion (Table 3.13). The Philippines is close, though the share of the government in GDI is noticeably above the others. Except for India and the Philippines, these are all high-growth countries as the hypothesis advanced would suggest. In India and the Philippines, inefficiency attributable to government licensing of private investment and production is well known if not well documented.

Countries with low government shares in GDP and very high government shares in GDI would, on a priori grounds, appear the least likely to be successful. For whatever reason, they adopt policies that constrain

TABLE 3.13
Government and Fiscal Policy, 1977–1988[a] (per cent)

| Country | G/GDP 1977–81 | G/GDP 1982–4 | G/GDP 1985–7 | GCE/GDI 1986–8 | Taxes/GDP 1977–81 | Taxes/GDP 1982–4 | Taxes/GDP 1985–7 | Total Surplus (+) or Deficit (−)/GDP 1977–81 | 1982–84 | 1986–8 | Total Surplus (+) or Deficit (−)/GDI 1986–8 |
|---|---|---|---|---|---|---|---|---|---|---|---|
| **Asian NIEs** | | | | | | | | | | | |
| Hong Kong | 15 | 16 | 14 | 8 | 10 | 9 | 11 | −1.7 | −3.6 | 2.7 | 1 |
| South Korea | 17 | 18 | 17 | 9 | 16 | 16 | 16 | 0.8 | 0.6 | −0.3 | −1 |
| Singapore | 30 | 33 | 37 | 59 | 18 | 20 | 15 | −5.7 | −5.4 | 1.0 | 3 |
| Taiwan | 17 | 15 | 14 | 16 | 12 | 9 | 8 | −1.1 | −0.7 | −0.4 | −2 |
| **South-East Asia** | | | | | | | | | | | |
| Indonesia | 25 | 24 | 22 | 33 | 21 | 19 | 17 | −3.9 | −4.2 | −5.7 | −22 |
| Malaysia | 38 | 40 | 34 | 27 | 23 | 22 | 22 | −11.3 | −13.3 | −8.1 | −31 |
| Philippines | 15 | 13 | 15 | 21 | 11 | 10 | 11 | −1.5 | −2.0 | −3.5 | −24 |
| Thailand | 17 | 18 | 19 | 10 | 13 | 13 | 14 | −2.8 | −3.6 | −1.9 | −9 |
| **South Asia** | | | | | | | | | | | |
| Bangladesh | 16 | 15 | 11 | 51 | 7 | 7 | 7 | −7.6 | −6.1 | −6.1 | −44 |
| India | 14 | 15 | 17 | 10 | 8 | 8 | 0 | −3.1 | −4.3 | −4.9 | −21 |
| Nepal | 14 | 19 | 19 | 64 | 7 | 7 | 7 | −5.7 | −10.1 | −9.0 | −45 |
| Pakistan | 23 | 23 | – | 41 | 10 | 10 | | −10.6 | −6.6 | −8.0 | −48 |
| Sri Lanka | 36 | 35 | 40 | 82 | 19 | 18 | 19 | −14.5 | −14.0 | −15.4 | −54 |
| **Asian Socialist Economies** | | | | | | | | | | | |
| Burma | 14 | 14 | 14 | 25 | 11 | 9 | 8 | 1.7 | 0.7 | −3.1 | −23 |
| China | – | 15 | – | – | – | – | – | – | – | −0.7 | −2 |

Sources: As for Table 3.9.
Note: G/GDP = Government share in Gross Domestic Product; GCE = Government Capital Expenditures; GDI = Gross Domestic Investment.

private investment and are often not providing or maintaining the infrastructure needed to support the private economy. Bangladesh and Nepal fit this category and the hypothesis. Burma is close but has a much lower share of government capital expenditures in GDI.

Countries with high government shares in GDP and high ratios of government capital expenditures to total domestic investment would also be expected to penalize private enterprise in ways that will at some point limit growth. Sri Lanka is clearly in this category and Pakistan is close. It is a surprise to find Singapore in the same boat. The role of the Singapore government in providing public housing probably explains this result, but that does not mean the inflexibilities inherent in a large government share will not some day cause problems.

Finally, countries with high government shares in GDP and low in GDI could be seen as supporting the private sector. Malaysia is in this category, once again seeming to fit the hypothesis. Thus, except for Singapore, all of the high-growth countries have relatively small shares of government in GDI and in GDP. Which is cause and which is effect can only be guessed at, but the association between high growth and a relatively small role for government should at least give pause to those who want to emphasize government expenditures in stimulating growth.

TAX SHARES IN GDP

Deficits and government tax and non-tax revenues are conceptual substitutes. Social optimization would have governments equating the social marginal cost of funds with the social marginal benefits of government expenditures and substituting between the various sources of funds until the social marginal cost of funds raised in all ways is the same. Clearly, very few governments act in this way. Instead, the people making the decision equate their marginal cost of funds (or, if altruistic, their view of the social marginal costs) with the marginal benefits of expenditures as they perceive them and do the same for the alternative sources of funds. Social marginal costs and benefits and these personal marginal costs and benefits can differ widely.

The result is taxes are often too low in social terms, with government expenditures, especially capital expenditures, the opposite. Thus, a high share of taxes is not necessarily a bad sign, unless it is clear that the social marginal costs of raising the taxes exceed the social marginal benefits of using them. In more prosaic terms, if taxes are too low relative to GDP, either needed government expenditures—including human resource expenditures—go by the board or the government runs a deficit, with the associated problems discussed. And, if taxes are too high, by definition this means they will reduce incentives. Deciding the optimal cut-off point is an art not a science. For this reason it is useful to know that in the 1970s and 1980s the tax ratio in Japan has varied between 13 and 18 per cent and in the United States between 18 and 23 per cent.

Ranked in terms of the share of GDP used to pay taxes, relatively high tax burden countries, at around the US level, are Malaysia, Indonesia, Sri Lanka, and Singapore. South Korea and Thailand come next, in the Japanese range. The Philippines, Pakistan, Burma, and Taiwan follow, with ratios that reflect dependence on external borrowing in Pakistan and the relatively low share of government expenditures in GDP in the others. India, Bangladesh, and Nepal are the lowest tax burden (and the poorest) countries, but definitely seem to be both bypassing needed outlays, especially infrastructure and educational outlays, and depending too much on subsidized international borrowing.

However, there are no firm generalizations to be drawn from the analysis of comparative tax burdens. The highest-growth countries are not at either extreme, but the spread between them is great. At least at the levels found in the 1980s among the Asian developing countries, except possibly for Sri Lanka and Indonesia, it does not appear, where the tax burdens are high for their relative per capita incomes, that taxes provide major disincentives in the aggregate.

DEFICITS AND SURPLUSES

Relatively high government deficit to GDP ratios usually spell relatively greater problems with inflation or with foreign debt. Where the government deficit raises interest rates or increases relative inflation, it will also tend to appreciate the exchange rate and reduce the country's international competitiveness. The ultimate or net effect of a high deficit also depends on whether or not the deficit increases the government's share of output or decreases taxes and, if the share is increased, how efficiently the government uses the borrowed funds. Also, if the government's share is increased while avoiding the political test of tax raising, allowing short-run political manoeuvring at the expense of the future and putting off the pressure to make difficult policy choices; this is often a dangerous combination. Finally, whether raising expenditures or lowering taxes, the effect of a deficit depends on whether the funds are raised by borrowing domestically, printing money, or borrowing abroad.

The presumption is that funds borrowed by governments generally divert resources from more to less efficient uses. Where there are no alternatives—for example, taxes or user charges are ruled out because of low incomes or administrative problems—for meeting basic infrastructure requirements, this presumption could be wrong. Certainly very few regional developing countries can borrow much domestically so that high regional deficits usually must involve inflationary finance and the inflation tax or foreign debt that requires a future real transfer. Thus, the size of the government deficit relative to GDP is a measure of a country's policy effectiveness.

The basic assumption in the following discussion is that the higher the ratio of the government's deficits to national output, the greater is the sum of these negative effects. So, a higher ratio would be expected to be associated with a lower relative growth performance. Interventions that substitute for improving the deficit, if the deficit is politically vested, are likely to constrain competition, reduce trade, and generally make things even worse. This syndrome has reached major proportions in Latin America and is found in Asia as well.

Countries with deficits relative to GDP consistently much larger than usually considered acceptable—5 per cent is the most often mentioned 'warning' level in the international financial community—are Sri Lanka, Malaysia, Nepal, and Pakistan in that order of magnitude. Malaysia, however, has shown improvement in the late 1980s. Bangladesh is also above this warning level in all periods covered in Table 3.13. Thus, with the exception of India which is getting closer, all the South Asian countries are included in the high-deficit group.

Until the most recent period, when Singapore had one of the few regional surpluses, Singapore was in the above 5 per cent group as well. However, the other Asian NIEs have been at the low end of the deficit spectrum throughout the 1977–87 period, with South Korea having an average net surplus in the first two periods covered, Hong Kong having one in the last, and Taiwan very close to balance in all periods. The fact that Thailand was also consistently a low-deficit country and that China had a very low relative deficit for the one period data were available, lends further support to the notion that keeping the share of deficit spending down contributes to economic growth.[11] Again association does not show or prove cause but it is instructive, especially when compared with the high-deficit situation in most of the slow-growth South Asian countries. Burma and the Philippines are then the exceptions that prove the rule.

The relation between deficits and GDI in the 1986–8 period is even more strikingly related to growth performance. Basically, the assumption is the higher this ratio, the more private investment is penalized by government competition for funds. However, a relatively high deficit/GDI ratio does not necessarily mean that a country has experienced a relatively large substitution effect or even any substitution effect. A relatively high ratio can also arise because a greater share of government capital accumulation is financed by borrowing rather than taxation, in other words, by non-tax revenues, or because the government is borrowing to cover a relatively greater share of government consumption expenditures, creating dead weight debt.

So, whatever the source, the ranking of countries by the ratio of their government budget position to their GDI would be expected to have a clear inverse relation to their relative growth performance. The expected relation is clearly found. The Asian NIEs either do not have deficits or borrow through the government only a minuscule portion of their GDI. The same was true of China in 1986–8. Thailand also has a very low ratio of government borrowing to total investment expenditures, especially compared to the other South-East Asian countries.

With the exception of India, in the South Asian countries led by Sri Lanka, government fund-raising covered 40–50 per cent of GDI. Even if there is no substitution effect in these countries such dependence on deficit spending as opposed to taxation to finance government capital, or worse, government consumption expenditures spells both present and future trouble.

SUMMARY

The role of the government as measured by the relative size of the government sector has a widely varying relation to growth, with both high-growth and low-growth countries having low and high government shares in GDP. Although four of the six highest-growth countries had below average government shares, it appears the way government expenditures are financed and the extent of competition (and government regulation) are more important than who controls the productive resources.

However, the size of the central government deficit clearly does matter, if the close association between the share of the government sector's budget deficit or surplus in GDP and relative growth performance and relative inflation rates, is more than happenstance. Deficits (and inflation) are generally higher in South Asia and tend to be lowest, especially the total deficit, among the market economies of the Asian NIEs. This association carries over to the inverse relations between the share of the budget deficit in GDI and the relative growth performance. Put together, these results suggest keeping the financing of the government sector under control is a key to successful growth (though as derived they could equally suggest that successful growth is the key to keeping government financing under control).

*Monetary Policy*

Monetary policy, like fiscal policy, provides a measure of a government's economic attitudes and ability to respond effectively to changing economic conditions. In developing countries, monetary policy is often not independent of fiscal policy. For example, a common scenario is that inflation resulting from monetized deficit financing, often funded internationally, leads to an overvalued exchange rate, lower export growth, and increasing import growth, and finally to further international borrowing.

Thus, fiscal and monetary restraint and their opposites would be expected to go hand in hand. However, it is possible for a country with a large deficit to successfully pursue a tight money programme, keeping the inflationary impact of capital inflows down, or for a country with a fiscal surplus to have adopted an expansionary monetary policy, leading to inflation (though given the trade effects, this could not go on too long).

In the following discussion, monetary policy is measured by the relation between the rate of growth in the narrow (M1) money supply and the rate of growth in real output (from hereon $m$ and $q$ respectively). The greater the excess of $m$ over $q$, the greater the inflationary bias of monetary policy. This assumes that changes in income velocity do not act to offset the difference between $m$ and $q$. This possibility can be monitored in Table 3.14 by comparing the difference between $m$ and $q$ with the resulting inflation rate, $p$. If $(m - q)$ is greater than $p$, velocity has decreased and vice versa.

Some quick generalizations about monetary policy are possible from Table 3.14. First, there is the expected correlation between the growth rate of the money supply relative to the growth rate in real output, $(m - q)$, and the inflation rate, $p$. There are exceptions—Burma is the most exceptional—but the general relation is clear.

Second, with the exceptions easily noted in the table, the Asian NIEs generally had the smallest excess in money supply growth over real output growth. And, in South-East Asia, Thailand and Malaysia have kept their $(m - q)$ at levels comparable to the NIEs.[12] Thus, with the exception of China, all the high-growth countries adopted or have come to adopt policies of relative monetary restraint. Lack of monetary restraint has proved China's undoing.

At the other extreme, the slower-growth South Asian countries, with

TABLE 3.14
Monetary Policy, 1977–1988 (per cent)

|  | $m - q$ Annual Averages ||| $p$ Annual Averages |||
| --- | --- | --- | --- | --- | --- | --- |
| Country | 1978–82 | 1983–5 | 1986–8 | 1978–82 | 1983–5 | 1986–8 |
| Asian NIEs | | | | | | |
| Hong Kong | −1 | 13 | 11 | 10 | 3 | 5 |
| South Korea | 16 | 1 | 3 | 14 | 4 | 4 |
| Singapore | 4 | −2 | 2 | 5 | 1 | 0 |
| Taiwan | 11 | 3 | 11 | 10 | 1 | 1 |
| South-East Asia | | | | | | |
| Indonesia | 21 | 9 | 9 | 19 | 10 | 8 |
| Malaysia | 8 | −4 | 6 | 7 | 0 | 2 |
| Philippines | 4 | 19 | 16 | 11 | 26 | 7 |
| Thailand | 5 | −1 | 10 | 11 | 2 | 3 |
| South Asia | | | | | | |
| Bangladesh | 12 | 19 | – | 16 | 10 | 27 |
| India | 6 | 9 | 10 | 8 | 8 | 8 |
| Nepal | 11 | 8 | 16 | 7 | 8 | 13 |
| Pakistan | 10 | 3 | 10 | 9 | 7 | 5 |
| Sri Lanka | 12 | 12 | 12 | 16 | 12 | 10 |
| Asian Socialist Economies | | | | | | |
| Burma | 7 | 10 | −3 | 3 | 3 | 16 |
| China | 9 | – | 14 | – | – | 12 |

*Sources*: Money supply data are from Asian Development Bank (1989), *Key Indicators of Developing Member Countries of ADB*; real output (GDP) data are from Table 3.6 or its sources; inflation rates are from Table 3.10 or its sources.

India and Pakistan showing more restraint than the others, and the Philippines have had and still have a relatively large inflationary bias in their monetary policy. For the Philippines, a real monetary policy outlier, this is symptomatic of the problems leading to the country's poor growth performance. While fiscal measures do not show the way government intervention in the Philippines helped cause that country's problems, the monetary excesses brought about by 'crony' capitalism surely do. Finally, Indonesia has moved towards monetary restraint but is still somewhat given to excess money supply growth and greater than average inflation.

So, monetary policy like fiscal policy is closely related to the growth story. These policies themselves do not explain successful growth, but the factors that do lead to successful growth—especially an emphasis on competition, which for small countries means trade—force 'good' monetary and fiscal policies on countries.

*Real Interest Rates*

Real deposit and lending rates are determined by the inflation rate, an outcome of government policy, and by the nominal deposit and lending rates. In most Asian developing countries, the latter are sometimes set by the government and sometimes allowed to fluctuate within boundaries set by the government. Thus, real interest rates both carry out and reflect economic policy.

For example, if private domestic savings are to be stimulated, positive real returns must be expected. Where real deposit rates are continuously low or negative or vary widely between positive and negative returns, savings are likely to be low. Or, if real lending rates are low or negative, and especially if real deposit rates are also low and negative, the presumption is that capital resources have to be rationed by some other means than their cost. The other means is usually by government intervention, direct or indirect, and capital may not be efficiently employed. Where lending rates are less than deposit rates, borrowers are being subsidized and the government will almost always be involved in deciding who pays the cost and who gets the subsidy.

In the 1980s, real deposit rates have been highest of all and consistently positive in Thailand (Table 3.15). They have also been relatively high and positive in South Korea, Sri Lanka, Singapore, Taiwan, Malaysia, and, on the border, Pakistan. The effect of financial reform is clearly evident in Indonesia as deposit rates moved up from negative levels in the early 1980s to the Thai level after 1984. Thus, for the most part, real deposit rates in the high-growth countries encouraged savings and the efficient use of savings. Only Hong Kong for the short period covered is an exception.

The Philippines has had relatively low or highly negative real deposit rates, except in 1986–7. However, managing a relatively high real deposit rate in one two-year period is not likely to be sufficient to

TABLE 3.15
Real Interest Rates,[a] 1982–1988 (per cent)

| Country | Real Deposit Rate 1982–3 | 1984–5 | 1986–7 | 1988 | Real Lending Rate 1982–3 | 1984–5 | 1986–7 | 1988 | Real Lending Rate – Real Deposit Rate 1982–3 | 1984–5 | 1986–7 | 1988 |
|---|---|---|---|---|---|---|---|---|---|---|---|---|
| **Asian NIEs** | | | | | | | | | | | | |
| Hong Kong | *0.3* | 0.3 | — | — | *3.0* | 4.4 | — | — | *2.7* | 4.1 | — | — |
| South Korea | 3.8 | 7.2 | 7.3 | 2.9 | 5.5 | 7.6 | 7.3 | 3.0 | 1.7 | 0.4 | 0.0 | 0.1 |
| Singapore | 4.2 | 4.5 | 3.8 | 1.2 | 7.1 | 6.9 | 6.9 | 4.5 | 2.9 | 2.5 | 3.1 | 3.2 |
| Taiwan | *6.3* | *6.5* | *1.9* | — | — | — | — | — | — | — | — | — |
| **South-East Asia** | | | | | | | | | | | | |
| Indonesia | −4.4 | 9.2 | 10.1 | 9.7 | −1.7 | 4.5 | 14.2 | 14.1 | 2.7 | −4.7 | 4.0 | 4.4 |
| Malaysia | 4.2 | 7.1 | 4.2 | −2.6 | 5.3 | 9.3 | 8.6 | 4.7 | 1.1 | 2.3 | 4.4 | 7.3 |
| Philippines | 2.9 | −16.7 | 6.0 | 2.5 | 6.1 | −8.3 | 11.7 | 7.1 | 3.2 | 8.4 | 5.7 | 4.6 |
| Thailand | 6.5 | 11.4 | 7.7 | 5.6 | 13.9 | 17.2 | 14.0 | 11.1 | 7.4 | 5.9 | 6.4 | 5.5 |
| **South Asia** | | | | | | | | | | | | |
| Bangladesh | *1.0* | *1.4* | *1.7* | *2.7* | *1.0* | *1.4* | *4.7* | *6.7* | *0.0* | *0.0* | *3.0* | *4.0* |
| India | −2.1 | 3.0 | 1.6 | 0.9 | 6.6 | 9.5 | 8.2 | 7.7 | 8.7 | 6.5 | 6.6 | 6.8 |
| Nepal | −7.7 | −1.0 | −7.7 | — | 2.9 | 12.9 | −0.2 | — | 10.6 | 13.9 | 7.5 | — |
| Pakistan | *3.4* | *3.1* | *3.6* | — | — | — | — | — | — | — | — | — |
| Sri Lanka | 5.5 | 9.5 | 4.0 | −0.8 | 0.1 | 4.3 | 2.8 | −1.6 | −5.4 | −5.3 | −1.2 | −0.8 |
| **Asian Socialist Economies** | | | | | | | | | | | | |
| Burma | −4.2 | −3.8 | −15.7 | — | 2.3 | 4.2 | −0.6 | — | 6.5 | 8.0 | 15.1 | — |
| China | — | — | — | — | — | — | — | — | — | — | — | — |

*Sources*: Italicized data are from Asian Development Bank, *Key Indicators of Developing Member Countries of ADB*, various issues; and Asian Development Bank (1986), *Asian Development Review*, 4(2); remaining data are from International Monetary Fund (1987–9), various issues.
[a] Real rates are nominal rates adjusted for inflation (based on the country's CPI).

change the widely held expectations of low or negative returns to financial savings in the Philippines—perhaps a partial explanation of the country's low savings and monetary deepening rates.

Real deposit rates were lowest in Burma, Nepal, Bangladesh, and India. They were negative in every period in Nepal and Burma and low or very low in every period in Bangladesh and in every period save one in India. Not surprisingly, savings rates were also lowest in these countries. However, as with all individual variables, India's higher savings rate than Pakistan means real deposit rates are not the only determinant of savings rates.

In the same vein, Sri Lanka's high rate means that relatively high real deposit rates are not the only determinant of development. In fact, one reason why high real deposit rates are not enough for development in Sri Lanka is given by the excess of real deposit rates over real lending rates in that country in all periods. This sure sign of government involvement in the capital allocation process is also found in Indonesia, at least in the early stages of reform when only deposit rates were liberalized. In the early 1980s, real deposit and real lending rates were the same in Bangladesh and in the last two years they have been the same in South Korea. In fact, the margin is low enough to suggest government intervention in the allocation of funds throughout the 1980s in South Korea. This margin is also relatively low in Singapore and, in the early periods, in Malaysia and Hong Kong. For Singapore or Hong Kong, this outcome could easily be the result of greater financial industry competition and so efficiency, just as higher margins elsewhere, for example, in Nepal, Burma, India, Thailand, and the Philippines, may reflect the opposite considerations. For example, there is no way, even if there are several financial intermediary layers between the deposit and lending rates, for margins of 5 per cent or more to be free of economic rents.

*Real Exchange Rate Policies*

Another key policy variable is the real exchange rate which depends on a country's nominal exchange rate—generally under government control—and its rate of inflation relative to the rate of inflation of the country or countries included in the base of the exchange rate. Comparisons between real exchange rates and their movements over time reveal much about the success of government policies in managing international competitiveness, or, alternatively, about the degree of interest in being internationally competitive. Given that most of the exchange rates considered are not market determined, the effectiveness with which policy is carried out is demonstrated by a country's ability to constrain inflation to achieve the international goals indicated by changes in nominal exchange rates.

Observed changes in real exchange rates can result from policy changes, from outside developments affecting the balance of trade, capital flows and/or aggregate demand, or from domestic policies affecting the same variables and aggregate supply. They can also arise from changes in expectations influenced by all the foregoing. No matter how they come about, if one country's real exchange rate appreciates and another's depreciates, the second country becomes more competitive in world markets *vis-à-vis* the first. Only if export prices do not follow the general price level or decrease when the nominal exchange rate gains value will this not happen.

Table 3.16 shows the changes in real exchange rates for three periods, the first coinciding with the appreciation of the dollar and the last two (1985–8, 1988–9) with the dollar's depreciation. In this table a positive change is depreciation and a negative change is appreciation. Because a trade-weighted exchange rate and a trade-weighted inflation rate are not readily available for many of the Asian and Pacific developing countries, each country's exchange rates for the dollar and inflation rates relative to the US inflation rate are used in this table. This substitution may not distort too much since the United States would account for a large relative share of the weights in the desired indices and many regional trading partners have exchange rates tied to the dollar, and so cannot have too large a difference in inflation rate from the United States.

In 1980–5, all the included countries depreciated against the dollar in nominal terms. If nominal changes alone were considered, the Philippines, China, Indonesia, all of South Asia, and Hong Kong, in that order, would have gained a competitive advantage *vis-à-vis* the other Asian developing countries. However, only China, which had the most aggressive competitive improvement, Indonesia, Hong Kong, and Bangladesh achieved real depreciation greater than that of half the countries included. The others with large nominal depreciations lost any competitive advantage to their relatively high inflation rates. The Philippines showed the most slippage in this respect, followed by India, which was the only country with real appreciation in 1980–5, and Sri Lanka.

Joining the group increasing their relative real competitiveness were Thailand, South Korea, and Burma. Except for Burma and Bangladesh, all the countries increasing their competitiveness were high-growth countries. The other high-growth countries, Taiwan, Singapore, and Malaysia, kept their nominal rates more in line with the dollar and dropped in competitive position *vis-à-vis* the other Asian developing countries. However, all three achieved higher real depreciation than their managed nominal changes.

In the next period, 1985–8, even as the dollar depreciated sharply, several Asian developing countries achieved further nominal depreciation against the dollar, while the most rapidly growing, the Asian NIEs and Thailand, under pressure from the United States, had their currencies appreciate against the dollar. Indonesia, Nepal, and China stand out in the first group, but all the South Asian countries and the Philippines achieved substantial nominal depreciation.

In real terms, India achieved the largest competitive gain, turning a relatively small nominal depreciation into the largest real depreciation. Indonesia followed with an almost equally large real depreciation. Of the

TABLE 3.16
Exchange Rate Policy,[a] 1980–1989 (per cent)

| Country | Change in the Nominal Exchange Rate 1980–5 | 1985–8 | 1988–9 | Change in the Real Exchange Rate 1980–5 | 1985–8 | 1988–9 | Change in Real Exchange Rate – Change in Nominal Exchange Rate 1980–5 | 1985–8 | 1988–9 |
|---|---|---|---|---|---|---|---|---|---|
| **Asian NIEs** | | | | | | | | | |
| Hong Kong | 56.4 | 0.3 | 0.8 | 40.4 | −11.0 | −3.2 | −16.1 | −11.3 | −4.0 |
| South Korea | 43.2 | −15.9 | −8.4 | 32.4 | −18.6 | −9.1 | −10.8 | −2.6 | −0.7 |
| Singapore | 2.8 | −8.6 | −2.5 | 14.5 | −0.3 | −3.2 | 11.7 | 8.3 | −0.7 |
| Taiwan | 10.6 | −28.3 | −7.2 | 19.2 | −23.0 | −7.6 | 8.5 | 5.3 | −0.4 |
| **South-East Asia** | | | | | | | | | |
| Indonesia | 77.1 | 51.8 | 6.0 | 45.5 | 39.9 | 4.5 | −31.6 | −11.9 | −1.6 |
| Malaysia | 13.8 | 5.6 | 2.7 | 18.3 | 11.1 | 5.5 | 4.6 | 5.4 | 2.8 |
| Philippines | 147.8 | 13.4 | 4.0 | 27.4 | 2.9 | −3.2 | −120.4 | −10.5 | −7.2 |
| Thailand | 32.6 | −6.9 | 2.8 | 36.2 | −6.5 | 3.8 | 3.6 | 0.4 | 1.1 |
| **South Asia** | | | | | | | | | |
| Bangladesh | 81.2 | 11.7 | 3.2 | 35.1 | −2.8 | −4.3 | −46.1 | −14.5 | −7.5 |
| India | 57.4 | 12.5 | 19.8 | −11.1 | 41.7 | 10.6 | −68.4 | 29.1 | −9.1 |
| Nepal | 52.1 | 27.6 | 20.7 | 28.0 | −4.5 | 15.7 | −24.1 | −32.0 | −5.0 |
| Pakistan | 60.9 | 13.0 | 17.0 | 48.0 | 3.6 | 13.3 | −12.9 | −9.4 | −3.7 |
| Sri Lanka | 64.3 | 17.4 | 23.7 | 21.7 | −2.7 | 18.1 | −42.6 | −20.1 | −5.7 |
| **Asian Socialist Economies** | | | | | | | | | |
| Burma | 28.3 | −24.6 | 5.8 | 34.1 | −46.9 | −26.6 | 5.8 | −22.4 | −32.4 |
| China | 96.0 | 26.5 | 26.9 | 109.3 | −1.3 | 12.9 | 13.3 | −27.9 | −14.0 |

*Sources*: As for Table 3.11.
[a] In this table, depreciation has a positive sign and appreciation, a negative sign.

remaining group with large nominal depreciations, only Pakistan and the Philippines managed to improve their competitive position through low, real depreciation. While experiencing real appreciation and losing advantage in US markets, China, Sri Lanka, and Bangladesh still managed to gain a regionally more competitive position via their large nominal depreciation. Malaysia turned a relatively low nominal depreciation into the third largest real depreciation and so let changes in relative inflation rates improve its competitive position.

Allowing their competitive position to deteriorate in this period, despite relatively large nominal depreciations were the two poorest countries, Nepal and Bangladesh, and Sri Lanka. The fast-growing countries with nominal appreciation were reacting both to market forces, their growing balance-of-payments surpluses, and, as noted, to US pressure in letting their real exchange rate appreciate.[13] This same outcome in Burma on the other hand would seem to represent policy gone haywire, as would the 1988-9 real appreciation in the Philippines.

It is worth noting that in the most recent period the biggest real depreciations came in the South Asian countries where they were most needed. It is perhaps also significant that these countries greatly reduced the slippage between their nominal and real exchange rate changes—perhaps a hopeful sign that these countries are beginning to give more than lip service to the goal of increased international competitiveness.

*Trade Policy*

Although no readily available time series monitoring trade policies exists, since trade policies determine the basic openness of a country, they cannot be ignored. Probably the bottom line of relative growth performance is the extent to which production is carried out under competitive conditions. Countries whose domestic markets are too small to support much competition in production, can really only choose between a subsistence-level existence or an open economy. While it is possible, if the domestic market is large enough, to achieve a competitive environment without engaging in international competition, the experienced probability of doing so is very low. Since the 1960s, only Japan has successfully followed this route and only then with a large push from the United States.

The necessity of competing in domestic and world markets provides the incentives for economic efficiency and for keeping up with technological progress. It is ultimately not sufficient to emphasize and subsidize exports since this 'half-a-loaf' policy must sooner or later bring its own antidote in exchange rate appreciation or pressure to reduce resulting surpluses. Thus, openness is the key and a qualitative analysis of trade policies is appropriate.

On all counts, the most open countries are Taiwan, Hong Kong, South Korea, and Singapore. Hong Kong and Singapore have been low-barrier countries, both tariff and non-tariff, throughout the period covered in this chapter. In all these countries, participating in the international economy was the only realistic path to sustained growth and they set their trade policies accordingly. However, South Korea and Taiwan, especially the former, had until the 1980s placed emphasis on export promotion while constraining many manufactured and agricultural imports. They are now being forced to open the other 'half of the loaf'.

At the other extreme in terms of per capita income, it is clear that Bangladesh and Nepal had and have no choice but to improve their export effort or remain dependent on international welfare. It is also clear that they have not effectively taken steps to do so—Nepal perhaps because of its land-locked dependence on India.

It is further apparent that though they can delay the process, the small resource-rich countries such as Burma, the Philippines, Thailand, Malaysia, and Sri Lanka must at some point emulate Taiwan and South Korea if they want to raise per capita income acceptably. There is no option to external trade for sustained high-level growth in per capita income in these countries, though their resource endowments mean there is less pressure. The size of the domestic market and the variety of resources available are both insufficient to support a modern economy and the specialization of production needed for maximum gain through production or exchange. So far, however, only Thailand of the countries named is squarely on this path. Malaysia was on it, but has wandered off somewhat. All the rest restrain openness in numerous ways, with Burma positively abhorring it.

On the other hand, China, India, and Indonesia have more options. They have varying resource endowments but all have large domestic market potential. Indonesia is relatively resource-rich, but has, through the process now well known as the Dutch disease, kept back the growth of its manufactured exports and import-competing production until the decline in oil prices in the 1980s (when the Dutch cure had taken place). China and India are relatively resource-poor countries, though if conditions are right they are capable of food self-sufficiency.

All three have the option, as a step in the growth process, of using protection or inward-looking policy to develop the domestic market for manufactures and modern services. This would involve achieving sufficient competition domestically to increase productivity more rapidly than population growth and would be difficult to bring off without the increased specialization possible through trade and more importantly without the competitive pressure of having to compete internationally.

However successful initially, in all three of these relatively large countries, growth will reach a limit as the maximum economies of scale are attained and as isolation keeps them outside the loop of continual technological change. The limit will come soonest for the poorest, China and India, but at some point continued growth in all will require expanding trade to achieve the benefits of international specialization and to acquire the resources left out of their domestic base.

It is significant then that China, unlike India, where import substitution still holds sway along with all sorts of policies constraining domestic initiative and competition, has opted for relative openness and has been successful in greatly expanding its exports per capita, both in absolute and relative terms. As long as the Tiananmen Square (June 1989) events do not permanently reverse China's move towards openness, the Chinese have at least one wheel on the road to sustained growth. The formulation of trade policy in Indonesia has been split between engineering technocrats advocating more import substitution and economic technocrats advocating greater openness. The number of reforms instituted in the mid-1980s suggested the latter were winning, but of late trade policy in Indonesia seems to be falling between the proverbial two stools.

If market forces were allowed to rule in all of the above countries, demographic forces would play a large part in determining what goods and services are exported and imported and how the composition of trade changes over time. Whether or not a country has begun, gone through, or not started the demographic transition would be a major determinant of the rate of growth in the labour force and of the country's savings rate. Together, labour force growth and savings rates would be a major determinant of the capital–labour ratio and so, along with the path of response of the educational system and of comparative advantage in labour-intensive and human and physical capital-intensive goods. Demographic factors would also be key factors in determining the demand for and relative prices of non-traded goods (for example, housing) and so the equilibrium exchange rate. Interventions can offset these forces to some extent for some time, witness India's large physical capital exports, but the pressures created by ongoing demographic change will sooner or later surface. With this in mind, and given the policies now being followed and the options open as described above, in the concluding section of this chapter the effect of projected demographic changes on regional comparative advantage will be suggested.

## Future Prospects and Concerns

*Issues and Prospects*

Turning to the 1990s and beyond, there is concern that the continued slow-down in productivity growth in the industrial countries represents a long-run trend and one with ominous implications for growth in world markets, for the increase of protectionism, and, until recently, for hopes for a recovery in commodity prices. There are several different aspects to this situation.

For example, it is correct that average growth rates of industrial countries have been converging on the US rate rather than on the higher rates achieved by those nations now catching up with the United States. But still further behind and capable of a self-sustaining growth process at very high growth rates (witness China through much of the 1980s), if they get growth going, are countries containing well over half of the world's population. Catching up by these countries could sustain growth in world markets at present or higher rates for at least a century so the only grounds for trade pessimism would be concern about the ability of the developing countries to get their policies on target for growth.

Further, it seems apparent that the growth and unemployment problems besetting many industrial countries have some of the hallmarks of a bottoming out of a long-swing downturn. If so, the 1990s should be a period of general expansion, with growing world markets, and a great opportunity for adopting and pushing outward-looking, trade-oriented policies in the developing world.

This somewhat optimistic scenario ignores the building pressures for action on the environmental front, action that if effective must have world growth repercussions along with world distributional repercussions. It also presupposes that ever louder calls for increased protectionism never take hold since once in place they will prove extremely difficult to reverse. These protectionist developments arose partly from the policies made necessary by the birth of the welfare state in most industrial countries and the growth in unemployment resulting from the rapid expansion in the entering labour force in such countries in the 1980s. Both these sources of protectionist pressure are in the process of changing or disappearing.

Opposition at least to further expansion in the welfare state is increasing and there finally seems to be a growing conviction that something must be done about the US budget deficit—the key symbol of this particular issue. The demographic picture is also rapidly changing, with labour shortage at the early life cycle stages becoming or about to become the rule rather than the exception in most industrial countries, but most strikingly in Japan. Along with the ageing of the population and consequent emphasis on consumption, this is a change that may increase support for more openness. In sum, there is room for cautious optimism about the state of the world economy and of world trade in the remainder of the twentieth century. By the twenty-first century, however, there will be no avoiding the issues raised by the two PGs, population and pollution growth.

Central to any optimism is the assumption that the US budget deficit will be reduced. This deficit, along with the low US savings rate, has made the United States increasingly dependent on foreign financing. The capital inflows thus resulting from the interest rate effects of this deficit and from other attractive US returns kept the value of the dollar at levels too high for trade balance.

Although the political constraints on the budget deficit will remain, the 'peace dividend' that may arise from the events in Eastern Europe will make cutting expenditures somewhat easier. And, if the Federal Reserve continues its tight monetary policies, asset inflation may no longer serve as a substitute for real savings.

If these developments do not occur and other action—either increased protectionism or deflation would work in the short-run—is taken to improve the trade balance, the effect will be adverse for the developing countries. If protectionism is avoided—it cannot work in the long run—so that relative income adjustments are required to do the job and the United States has to make the income adjustment alone, unless monetary policy adequately compensates for reduced government expenditures or increased taxes, the effect could be a world recession.

Falling trade in a world recession could harm the developing country debtors more than lower interest rates would help them. In any event, improvement in the US trade balance, even in the midst of expanding world trade, means that net foreign investment must fall elsewhere—it will be deflationary wherever it occurs. This suggests the key role that could be played by the low-inflation, high-trade-surplus countries in helping the United States and the world adjust. Not only are Japan and West Germany involved, the Asian NIEs and the rest of the EC must play their part as well.

The required 'revolution' seems to be slowly under way in Japan and Japanese mercantilism may be gone by the twenty-first century. Further, the government has taken steps to increase domestic demand as export growth has fallen off. Together with the continued recycling of some of its surplus to the developing world, these developments suggest that Japan is on the right track.

Unfortunately, nothing so positive can be said about West Germany and the EC. There is still a danger that in 1992, when the EC's common tariff becomes a reality, there will be an extended shrinkage in world trade, especially Asian-European trade. This could be heightened if the Eastern European countries gain membership in or are favoured by the EC. However, when access to the (European) market for the laggard members begins to bring their per capita incomes closer to the market average, further trade diversion should become politically difficult and world trade should begin to grow once more.

*Demographic Trends: An Often Overlooked Factor*

There is one longer-run development that may possibly help the process of adjusting to changing comparative advantage and forestall the growth of protectionism. In the 1990s up to the 2010s the population of the industrial countries will age rapidly, with a steadily declining entering labour force following the passing through of the tail-end of the postwar baby boom.

A similar phenomenon has begun in some but not all Asian developing countries. Where it has begun, the entering labour force will continue to increase for 10-30 years at which time the populations of these countries will also begin to age. However, for some time to come the growth rate in the labour force between these countries and the major industrial countries will diverge, with the growth rate becoming zero in Japan (but, because of immigration, not in the United States) sometime between 1990 and 2010.

Specifically, the forecast growth rate in the labour force will be much lower for the Asian NIEs (Table 3.17) and will fall continuously from one five-year interval to the next until the year 2025, becoming negative for Singapore and Hong Kong in the second and for South Korea in the third decade of the twenty-first century.[14] However, Hong Kong's reversion to China can be expected to change this forecast for that 'country'. With regionally high beginning capital–labour ratios, these changes should further lower the relative returns to capital in the NIEs and further encourage the export of capital from the NIEs, if technological progress and capital upgrading does not take up the slack.

In South-East Asia, labour force base growth rates begin much higher than in the Asian NIEs and are quite comparable with each other, but will diverge considerably in the 1990s and beyond. Generally, the growth in the labour force base will be highest in the Philippines, with the difference increasing sharply in the twenty-first century. Malaysia's rate will remain closer to the Philippines' through 2005–10 and then fall towards Indonesia's and Thailand's. Unlike the NIEs, all these countries will have positive, if much lower, growth rates in their labour forces in the final decades covered in the table.

Clearly, there should be related changes in the relative cost of labour within South-East Asia, influencing the pattern of international trade and the industrial structure. Since the growth rate of the labour force base in South-East Asia will be several times the growth rate in the Asian NIEs throughout the period covered, the beginning differences in capital–labour ratios between these regions are likely to become wider and so provide further incentive to changes in the interregional pattern of trade and to the flight of labour-intensive production and accompanying capital southwards, especially to the Philippines.

The highest labour force growth rates of all will be experienced in Pakistan, Bangladesh, and Nepal up to at least the mid-2020s. These countries will start at levels near South-East Asia, but will have expanding or very high growth rates through the 1990s. The differential between these countries and most others in and out of South Asia will increase over most of this period. Sri Lanka will also experience an increasing labour force base growth rate through 2000, but will experience rapidly falling growth thereafter, beginning then to raise the relative cost of labour in that country compared to others in South Asia. Only India will experience a consistent decline in the rate of labour force base growth from the 1990s on, paralleling the experience of the Philippines in level and rate of decline.

Thus, except for India—a huge exception—the labour force growth rate will be larger in the South Asian countries than elsewhere and the differential will be increasing. With roughly similar and very low beginning capital–labour ratios, the relative cost of labour advantage in these countries should widen as well. Since participation rates are generally lower and rural underemployment generally higher in South Asia, the potential for effective labour force growth is truly great. Certainly the

## TABLE 3.17
### Future Demographic Developments, 1990–2025 (per cent)

| Country | Population 0–14 and 65+/ Population 15–64 1990 | 2000 | 2010 | Population 0–14/ Population 15–64 1990 | 2000 | 2010 | Population 65+/ Population 15–64 1990 | 2000 | 2010 | Quinquennial Growth Rate in the Labour Force Base (Population 15–64) 1985–90 | 1990–5 | 1995–2000 | 2000–5 | 2005–10 | 2010–15 | 2015–20 | 2020–25 |
|---|---|---|---|---|---|---|---|---|---|---|---|---|---|---|---|---|---|
| Asian NIEs | | | | | | | | | | | | | | | | | |
| Hong Kong | 44.5 | 44.4 | 40.7 | 31.8 | 28.8 | 24.6 | 12.7 | 15.6 | 16.1 | 6.93 | 5.69 | 4.52 | 4.14 | 2.95 | -0.69 | -2.76 | -5.08 |
| South Korea | 45.4 | 41.6 | 40.4 | 38.5 | 32.7 | 28.6 | 6.9 | 8.9 | 11.8 | 11.03 | 7.53 | 5.23 | 4.62 | 3.56 | 2.70 | 0.99 | -1.64 |
| Singapore | 39.6 | 39.4 | 37.9 | 31.9 | 29.5 | 25.0 | 7.7 | 9.9 | 12.9 | 7.56 | 4.49 | 4.65 | 3.59 | 3.06 | -0.49 | -2.62 | -4.75 |
| Taiwan[a] | 53.9 | 51.5 | 46.4 | 43.4 | 39.7 | 34.8 | 10.4 | 11.8 | 11.5 | 9.56 | 9.10 | 7.10 | 7.67 | 7.12 | 5.43 | 2.14 | 1.44 |
| South-East Asia | | | | | | | | | | | | | | | | | |
| Indonesia | 63.7 | 52.7 | 46.1 | 57.4 | 45.1 | 36.9 | 6.3 | 7.6 | 9.2 | 14.59 | 12.14 | 10.32 | 8.14 | 7.64 | 6.53 | 4.53 | 2.85 |
| Malaysia | 66.7 | 57.1 | 45.0 | 60.3 | 50.2 | 36.8 | 6.4 | 6.9 | 8.2 | 15.23 | 12.54 | 13.44 | 11.79 | 10.02 | 7.25 | 4.66 | 3.24 |
| Philippines | 76.9 | 66.2 | 55.0 | 70.9 | 60.1 | 48.1 | 6.0 | 6.1 | 6.8 | 15.33 | 15.09 | 14.80 | 13.59 | 12.19 | 10.38 | 8.45 | 6.82 |
| Thailand | 57.6 | 46.0 | 44.5 | 51.4 | 38.7 | 35.6 | 6.2 | 7.3 | 8.9 | 14.39 | 11.88 | 10.28 | 7.11 | 6.05 | 5.38 | 3.98 | 2.62 |
| South Asia | | | | | | | | | | | | | | | | | |
| Bangladesh | 87.9 | 76.0 | 66.1 | 82.5 | 71.8 | 61.0 | 5.5 | 5.1 | 5.2 | 18.81 | 18.39 | 16.92 | 15.46 | 15.22 | 14.44 | 13.12 | 9.75 |
| India | 69.5 | 65.5 | 56.9 | 61.8 | 57.1 | 47.7 | 7.6 | 8.5 | 9.2 | 12.69 | 11.48 | 12.15 | 11.37 | 11.41 | 10.01 | 8.24 | 6.46 |
| Nepal | 82.8 | 75.5 | 62.9 | 77.1 | 69.6 | 56.3 | 5.7 | 6.1 | 6.6 | 13.19 | 13.59 | 15.24 | 14.26 | 13.22 | 12.41 | 10.48 | 8.56 |
| Pakistan | 93.7 | 85.0 | 65.4 | 88.4 | 80.5 | 60.1 | 5.2 | 5.4 | 5.3 | 16.64 | 13.53 | 21.53 | 20.46 | 18.00 | 15.03 | 12.25 | 10.77 |
| Sri Lanka | 60.5 | 51.0 | 46.5 | 52.2 | 41.1 | 34.9 | 8.3 | 9.9 | 11.6 | 8.70 | 9.20 | 9.68 | 7.36 | 6.25 | 4.44 | 3.31 | 2.57 |
| Asian Socialist Economies | | | | | | | | | | | | | | | | | |
| Burma | 70.3 | 65.4 | 57.1 | 63.3 | 57.7 | 49.3 | 7.0 | 7.7 | 7.8 | 14.42 | 12.72 | 12.03 | 11.57 | 11.79 | 10.94 | 8.97 | 6.85 |
| China | 47.2 | 48.5 | 41.3 | 38.6 | 38.2 | 29.8 | 8.6 | 10.5 | 11.5 | 12.09 | 6.68 | 5.09 | 6.38 | 6.28 | 4.19 | 0.79 | -0.08 |

*Sources*: United Nations (1989c); Republic of China, Taipei, 1970, 1989.

[a] Taiwan data are based on the 1985 age–sex distribution and a variant of the constant fertility approach.

117

countries involved should become increasingly attractive locations for labour-intensive production, if their governments do not get in the way (except to close their large remaining educational gaps). Even in India, given the large amount of underemployment and relatively low participation rates, the slow-down in labour force growth may have little immediate effect on India's relative competitiveness in labour-intensive manufactures.[15]

Unless isolationism dies an unexpected death in Burma, labour force developments there are not likely to have much effect on trade patterns. Not so for China, where the growth in the labour force base in the world's largest population is relevant to everyone as long as China stays on the open economy path. According to forecasts, labour force growth in China will drop quickly to Asian NIE levels by 1990–5. However, the situation in China is similar to that in India and given the widespread underemployment and the very low capital–labour ratio in China, this may not put China at a disadvantage in labour-intensive products for some time to come. This conclusion implicitly assumes that interregional constraints on labour mobility are lifted in China; a possible outcome of the pressures arising from the very rapidly coming drop in labour force base growth.

In addition to relative rates of labour force growth, what happens to dependency ratios in future can play an important role in determining savings rates and thus the growth rate up to the mid-2010s through their effect on the rate of savings. At present, dependency rates are much higher for the South Asian countries, except Sri Lanka, than for the South-East Asian countries and for the South-East Asian countries compared to the NIEs, essentially paralleling the differences in savings rates between these regions. Between 1990 and 2010, dependency rates will fall everywhere, most of all in the South-East Asian countries but significantly in the South Asian countries as well, with positive savings rate connotations for all concerned. The result will be a region-wide convergence of population profiles but one that retains the present ordering of the level of dependency rates.

These changes in dependency ratios mask some wide swings in the relative importance of the age-groups supported. In all countries, except Bangladesh and Pakistan, the ratio of the over 65 age-group to the labour force base will increase through 2010, becoming highest in the Asian NIEs and China, Sri Lanka, and Burma. Generally, the increase will be small in South-East Asia and Nepal and India. At the same time the ratio of the population 0–14 to the labour force base will drop throughout the region. The largest declines will come in South-East and South Asia since the NIEs have already experienced most of their decline. Even with these large declines, the young dependency ratio in all the South Asian countries except Sri Lanka will remain far above the 1990 level in the NIEs. Primary education and child care will continue to be a major burden in this part of the world.

Relative to the developed world, where the ageing process is much more advanced than in any of the countries discussed above, these demographic changes will also be an important source of future economic change. The ageing societies in Japan, the United States—unless immigration offsets the ageing process—and Western Europe can be expected to place more emphasis on consumption and, because of relative labour scarcity, on increasingly human capital-intensive activities. The net effect should be growth in exports of all sorts of labour-intensive consumer goods (and of labour services) from the Asian developing countries to industrial countries, and from Asian countries slow in making the demographic transition to those more rapid in doing so. Trade in basic industrial commodities between developing countries should also be enhanced since their production will lose out to human capital-intensive activities in the industrial countries. Thus, ruling out the sort of immigration occurring in the United States as unlikely in Asia, a symbiotic relation, raising productivity all around, could result from the different demographic patterns in the future if trade policies adjust to allow it. Once again the importance of increased openness and the macroeconomic policies that support it is seen.

Although short-term movements in the value of most currencies *vis-à-vis* the dollar have encouraged the movement of production overseas from other industrial countries than the United States and while long-run differences in labour costs continue to do so for US direct foreign investment, the demographic trends just discussed are likely to have a more lasting effect. The relative scarcity of labour in the industrial countries and the consumption orientation of their ageing populations, suggest it will be increasingly profitable for firms in industrial countries to move to where the workers are to produce the goods consumed back home.

How this stimulus works out will depend on the attitudes of the potential recipient countries and these attitudes may be more receptive than in the past. Caught between the slow-down in external financial flows, both concessionary and market flows, increasing debt, and the rapid growth in their labour forces noted above, policies regarding direct foreign investment are likely to undergo a marked change. In fact China has concentrated on this form of capital transfer. Direct foreign investment, induced partly by relative population changes has also grown rapidly in South-East Asia. Only South Asia, where the needs are greatest, lags. But, this may change as the growing economic problems in the Middle East—due to the relative decline in oil prices—reduce the remittances sent home by South Asian workers and economic disruption in Eastern Europe wipes out South Asia's (especially India's) barter trade with that region.

*Evolving Comparative Advantage in Asia*

Whether or not the United States and other industrial countries get their policies right, so that the pressures for protectionism subside and their markets continue to grow, the demographic changes described and the economic development and spread of technical knowledge to come will continue to change comparative advantage. The future success of the Asian developing countries will depend on how well they adjust to and take advantage of the opportunities brought about by these changes and the extent to which they attempt to fend them off (that is, adopt inward-looking policies). Assuming no major increases or shifts in the structure of protectionism, the following region by region evolution of trade and comparative advantage might be expected.

The Asian NIEs are moving rapidly upmarket and will export more and more sophisticated human and physical capital-intensive goods to each other and to other developing countries, especially to South-East Asia and China. Their increasing penetration of the markets of industrial countries with mass-produced capital-intensive consumer goods should also continue. Their labour-intensive exports, on the other hand, can be expected to fall relatively in the 1990s and absolutely early in the twenty-first century. In aggregate, the NIEs may become significant net importers of labour-intensive goods—'may' because with present trade policies this would be impossible in the two largest NIEs, South Korea and Taiwan. And as they become increasingly specialized and sophisticated, intra-industry trade between the NIEs, especially in high tech products, should also grow.

Because of their present level of capital intensity and rates of capital accumulation and population growth, the Asian NIEs will not only be in a position to diversify; they will have to diversify to keep exports growing at a relatively high rate, whether to the industrial countries, to China (treating Hong Kong as separate from China) and Eastern Europe or to the Asian region generally. Even if trade policies in the industrial countries adjust to restrict such export penetration sector by sector, a likely possibility in the EC when the end of 1992 brings a diversity of products that are import-competing for the NIEs under a common tariff, they should be able to adapt in an amoeba fashion to the opportunities that must be open then.

The potential for increasing NIE interface with South-East Asia, also including intra-industry trade, is of growing importance and means trade policy, not only in industrial countries, but also in South-East Asia will be significant in the NIEs' future.[16] Finally, if the South Asian countries ever opt for growth and become truly outward-looking, they will provide a major opportunity for the NIEs, as the NIEs will for them.

Basically the problems in making all this come true involve the educational gap in Singapore and Hong Kong, the political uncertainty in Hong Kong, especially its relative independence after 1997, and to some extent Taiwan, the accumulation of past mistakes in South Korea's heavy industry and the associated centralization of economic power in the Chaebul, the response to environmental degradation in Taiwan, and the adjustment to growing agricultural imports in South Korea and Taiwan.

Based on the continued growth of capital intensity in the South-East

Asian countries, at a rate of increase slower than in the NIEs, but more rapid than in South Asia and most other developing countries, the expected movement in South-East Asian trade would be as follows: in spite of existing trade barriers, they should slowly but surely move away from depending largely on primary product exports to an increasing share for manufactured exports.

Thailand is already successfully doing this and should remain in the lead, but with a large remaining component of agricultural exports. The Philippines, if the proper policies are chosen and implemented, should be right behind, with, because of relative labour force growth, a greater emphasis on labour-intensive manufactures and, again, with a significant remaining component of agricultural (plantation) exports. Malaysia and Indonesia would be expected to follow in that order. Natural resource wealth and a relatively small beginning base should mean Indonesia would be the slowest to develop an important share for manufacturing exports. However, a demonstrated willingness to take the policy initiative may keep Indonesia ahead of the Philippines and move Indonesia ahead of Malaysia.

In spite of Indonesia's weight being so high in regional totals, it may be well into the twenty-first century before manufacturing exports dominate total exports for South-East Asia. Well before then, labour and human capital-intensive exports to both the NIEs and the industrial countries should grow rapidly. US, Japanese, and European direct investment have been and will remain important in speeding this process along, taking advantage of still relatively cheap and relatively well-educated labour supplies to produce goods for export to industrial countries and the NIEs. At some point soon, Thailand at least, will begin to export capital goods—in competition with the NIEs—as well as high tech goods and services. Like the NIEs, the South Asian market could become very important to South-East Asia.

Relative to either the NIEs or South-East Asia, South Asia has had a greater emphasis on exports to the socialist countries in Eastern Europe, to developing countries outside Asia, and to the Middle East. They may continue to export textiles, primary products, and some physical capital-intensive goods to these markets, but they may find the going difficult in Eastern Europe when they have to compete evenly with the rest of the world in these markets. That will be the case if the announced intentions of the Eastern Europeans to switch to free market economies are followed up. They may also increase their exports of textiles to the United States and the European Community under various quota arrangements—but, assuming China gets back on track, will have to compete directly with China in doing so.

Except for the last, these present and prospective trade patterns have little relation to the region's relative factor endowments, which would have placed great emphasis on labour-intensive manufactures and will place still greater emphasis on such exports. Rather these outcomes—statistically dominated by India—represent the effect of the planning and commercial policies adopted by India and most other South Asian countries. The only exception is Sri Lanka, but ethnic unrest has waylaid that country's liberalization efforts and moves to openness.

Without further movement to liberalize internally and externally, the prospects for South Asian export growth (and import growth) are not bullish. They are much more tied into the East European markets that have been growing more slowly than average and that are now in disarray. In the South Asian manufacturing or other sectors that have managed to achieve growing exports to the industrial countries, the products involved are greatly affected by voluntary export restraints and/or direct protection or by the decline in commodity prices. And, as noted, they do not trade with one another. Thus, one of the world's largest potential markets and competitors seems likely to remain largely on the sidelines for many years to come.

This was not so of China through 1989. Before Tiananmen Square (June 1989), China was becoming increasingly outward-looking and it seemed likely that China would in future compete effectively with South-East Asia in exporting labour-intensive goods to industrial countries and to the Asian NIEs and as a home base for industries in flight from these regions. China also would have been expected to do well in exporting resource-based and labour/human capital-intensive products to the same destinations, again in competition with South-East Asia and, to some extent, South Asia.

In the long run, China was expected to be a net importer of several primary products, benefiting the South-East Asian countries among others, and an excellent market for human and physical capital exports from the NIEs and later on the South-East Asian countries. But, given uncertainties involving what China will do now in the early 1990s, return to central planning or keep on the decentralized, market-oriented, open economy path carved out by Deng, it is very difficult to say what will happen. Even without the events of Tiananmen Square and thereafter to consider, the lack of experience with a Chinese role in regional and world markets makes any conjectures involving China's future role subject to much uncertainty.

In addition to continuing reforms and moving towards greater openness, China's future success will also depend on the effects of the abrupt demographic revolution being carried out on China's long-run comparative advantage and flexibility. In sum, if the 'planners' and 'isolationists' do not win the current political struggle and China gets its policies 'right' and demographic changes are on balance positive in their impact, then China will become a major competitor, major supplier, and major market on the world scene.

*A Note on Technology and the Future*

The potential impact of the continuing communications and information revolution and of the changed products and production techniques it makes possible is an important consideration in Asia's economic future. This revolution has led to the rapid dispersion of taste changes, the homogenization of tastes, so markets are more easily penetrated by outsiders, the rapid spread of other forms of new technology, and the more rapid obsolescence of existing technology. In fact, the combination of new developments in information systems with robotics is potentially so cost-saving it could reverse the present comparative advantage of many countries based on abundant labour. Clearly, the rapidly changing technological scene carries both a threat and a promise. Flexibility in response to these changes and adaptability in the face of uncertainty will be the keys to success.

Those countries that have achieved relatively high GDI ratios, that have an export orientation and have managed to make monetary, fiscal, and exchange rate policies support that orientation, and that have their educational support systems in place—as long as the planners do not try to outguess the market too often—should be able to avoid the threat and avail themselves of the promise. The NIEs, to varying degrees, come to mind. For the other Asian regions more will have to be done, though both the educational and policy framework seems to be in place in Thailand, and one or more of the necessary conditions seems to be met in the other South-East Asian countries. This is much less so for South Asia, where the challenge will be greater and lags in response to improved conditions longer, making the political road harder. If China gets back on course, then that mammoth country will increasingly participate in the ongoing technological revolution, with effects not easy to determine, but clearly important for the Asian world.

One benefit of being prepared to participate in the changing world technology is that large amounts of physical capital are not required for many of the new activities, an advantage for those countries with large populations and very low physical capital–labour ratios as in South Asia. Even with a relatively low per capita educational effort, India, for example, has the opportunity of acquiring the critical mass of trained people necessary for the production of new products and seems to be taking advantage of this fact. On the other side, Singapore has a problem in this respect. As part of China, Hong Kong's similar problem may disappear, but there will be plenty of other problems.

## Conclusion

In the long run, a country's development history and the contribution of demographic factors to that history depends on the initial resources available, on how technological change affects the relative value of these resources, and on the social and political institutions that shape the way a country utilizes its initial endowments to achieve growth. Within the framework established by these long-run factors, if the available data on international openness or the usual, intuitive ranking of countries by extent of government intervention are applied, it is clear greater openness and less government intervention are positively related to higher economic growth and to a generally better economic performance, including performance on most of the indices of welfare other than growth. Essentially, the greater the degree of competition, the greater economic welfare achieved. But whether necessary conditions themselves or part of the response to the necessary conditions, the relation between performances and policies reviewed also makes clear the importance of keeping fiscal deficits down, of restraining monetary growth, keeping real interest rates positive and successful management of the real exchange rate.

Demographic factors and human resource development have been seen to be important in many of the above contexts. Among other relations, the effects of differential rates of labour force growth and of changing dependency rates on both resource mobilization and comparative advantage were suggested and the positive association of both human resource development and slowing population growth with economic growth were noted. The following chapters will take up these issues and others, but it is important to remember that population and human resource policies cannot do much to achieve greater economic welfare unless supported by the economic policies set out above.

1. The ratio of the number enrolled in a given school level to the number that would be enrolled if all in the age classes 'normally' enrolled at that level were enrolled.

2. It is possible that many who did not complete their secondary education in the past have moved on to pursue a higher degree in the open university system, based on the substitution of work experience for secondary education.

3. There are many possible sources of this outcome, including differences in technological progress (including management techniques), the extent of international specialization, the degree of competition, and other incentive institutions.

4. The Singapore result could reflect the greater housing capital per worker in Singapore than elsewhere because of public housing and the relatively low measured value added from such capital in the public sector.

5. In fact, in 1985 exports were negative in all the South-East Asian countries and in India, Sri Lanka, and Burma. The fact that Singapore is on this list and that it had negative growth again in 1986 is probably a result of its neighbours' performance and the falling price of oil products.

6. On the basis of changes in prices only the oil exporters should show the greatest increase in relative exports given the terminal dates used, and the non-oil commodity exporters, the smallest increases. While these biases are apparent in the data, they seem less important than other sources of variation.

7. Indonesia's net capital outflow is a bit of a surprise, especially since Indonesia has a growing foreign debt, suggesting high levels of borrowing and even higher levels of investment outside the country. Perhaps this net outflow occurred at first because the oil shock windfall was too large to absorb easily in domestic investment but the reasons for its continuance are difficult to understand. As a low-income country with plenty of labour and a government that is liberalizing economic activity, the outflow of capital is surprising. One possible explanation could be the relative concentration of wealth in a few hands and the desire of the wealthy to diversify their portfolios.

8. This is the result of the Philippine debt situation, the generally high risk that lenders assign current Philippine loans, and the necessity of transferring capital abroad to meet debt service obligations—a possibly self-defeating scenario.

9. Already detonated in the informal markets.

10. The share of government in GDP is relatively low in the Philippines even though large blocks of output were until recently either marketed through government agencies or produced under government licences granting monopoly or near-monopoly rights.

11. China's position is somewhat surprising given its very high ratio of government expenditures in GDP and its spurt of inflation around 1989. Accounting procedures may well hide large off-budget or regional government deficits. Inflationary finance by regional governments and the new collective enterprises would not be traced in central government budget accounts or China's low deficit may reflect the relative importance of joint ventures with state enterprises, involving equity rather than debt financing.

12. Hong Kong, in the recovery period, has flirted with an inflationary monetary policy, but the excess of $m$ over $q$ has been largely offset by falling velocity. Taiwan's recent spurt based on balance-of-payments surplus has yet to be reflected in inflation. This means income velocity dropped sharply in Taiwan. If the funds leaving the income flow went into the stock market, they still have much inflationary potential.

13. Relative inflation increased South Korea's real exchange rate appreciation compared to its nominal appreciation in 1985-8—a result for which there is no political gain since policy discussion is always in terms of nominal rates in political circles (for example, the US Congress)—and turned Hong Kong's unchanged nominal rate into a large real appreciation, which for the reasons just suggested did not take the heat for nominal appreciation off Hong Kong either.

14. The UN forecasts for growth rates for 1990, 1995, and 2000 are most reliable since the population involved has already been born. The year 2005 is a transition point, but the sharp declines in most countries in 2010 and onwards reflect the optimistic 'middle' forecast of the UN.

15. This stock versus flow question is not easily resolved. A lower growth rate for the labour force means fewer applicants competing for the available jobs and, depending on the regional distribution of the growth, could mean excess demand for labour in some locales. Though the effect may largely be psychological in a country with India's extensive labour stock and underemployment, the impact on expectations of a tightening situation could be significant. With such rapid population changes going on, it would be useful to know more about the relative importance of flow changes versus stock situations.

16. Recognizing that for Singapore the interface is already extremely large.

# PART II
# HUMAN CAPITAL DEEPENING AND CHANGING LABOUR MARKETS

## 4
# Human Capital Deepening, Inequality, and Demographic Events along the Asia–Pacific Rim*

Jeffrey G. Williamson

### Sources of Growth along the Asia–Pacific Rim

IN the mid-1970s, Denison and Chung (1976) used sources of growth accounting to show *How Japan's Economy Grew So Fast*. The limitations to this kind of analysis are well known, but one chapter might be particularly useful to help organize this symposium's thinking about 'the sources of economic dynamism along the Asia–Pacific Rim'. Denison and Chung (1976: Chap. 12) posed this question: Could Japan's growth rate up to 1973–4 be sustained in the long run? They searched for the answer by decomposing the fast growth of the 1960s into that part of the performance which was sustainable in the long run and that part which was only transitional. The transitional part was attributed to its latecomer status, to special transitory demographic features, and to economic inefficiencies which had been mostly eliminated by the early 1970s. The result is reproduced in Table 4.1 while Figure 4.1 uses that information to trace out Denison and Chung's projections into the future. Figure 4.1 also plots Japan's actual growth performance since 1971 and, apart from the macroeconomic shocks around 1973–4, those projections were remarkably close to the mark. Both show a retardation across the 1970s, as Japan's economy approached the long-run sustainable growth path, and both show that much of the transition to the sustainable growth path was completed by the late 1970s. Furthermore, the slow-down also confirms the prediction made earlier by Ohkawa and Rosovsky even before *How Japan's Economy Grew So Fast* appeared (Ohkawa and Rosovsky, 1973: 232–50).

Not all of the Denison–Chung projected growth retardation into the

---

*The research assistance of Jonathan Morduch and Steve Schran is gratefully acknowledged. The helpful comments on earlier versions of this chapter by David Bloom, Anil Deolalikar, Takenori Inoki, Gavin Jones, Hiro Ogawa, Dwight Perkins, Henry Rosovsky, and participants at the January 1988 and November 1989 symposiums have improved it greatly.

TABLE 4.1
Sustainable and Transitional Components of Japan's Growth
According to Denison and Chung (per cent per annum)

|  | Contribution in Percentage Points 1961–71 ||| Year Transitional Contribution Expires (4) |
| Source of Growth | Total (1) | Sustainable (2) | Transitional (3) |  |
| --- | --- | --- | --- | --- |
| Growth | 9.56 | 3.24 | 6.32 | – |
| Labour | 1.78 | 0.68 | 1.10 | – |
| Employment | 1.09 | 0.33 | 0.76 | 1973 |
| Hours | 0.11 | −0.15 | 0.26 | 1974 |
| Age–sex composition | 0.19 | 0.11 | 0.08 | 1977 |
| Education | 0.35 | 0.35 | 0.00 | – |
| Unallocated | 0.04 | 0.04 | 0.00 | – |
| Capital | 2.57 | 0.86 | 1.71 | – |
| Inventories | 0.86 | 0.21 | 0.65 | 1976 |
| Non-residential structure and equipment | 1.44 | 0.38 | 1.06 | 1976 |
| Dwellings | 0.27 | 0.27 | 0.00 | – |
| International assets | 0.00 | 0.00 | 0.00 | – |
| Land | 0.00 | 0.00 | 0.00 | – |
| Advances in knowledge | 2.43 | 1.28 | 1.15 | 2002 |
| Contraction of agricultural inputs | 0.62 | 0.00 | 0.62 | 1982 |
| Contraction of non-agricultural self-employment | 0.19 | 0.00 | 0.19 | 1990 |
| Reduction in trade barriers | 0.01 | 0.00 | 0.01 | 2002 |
| Economies of scale |  |  |  |  |
| Measured in US prices | 1.14 | 0.42 | 0.72 | – |
| Income elasticities | 0.82 | 0.00 | 0.82 | 1995 |

*Source*: Denison and Chung (1976: 115, Table 12–1).

twenty-first century can be attributed to demographic, labour market, and human capital accumulation factors, but a good share of it can. Of the 6.32-percentage-point decline in the growth rate, they attributed 1.10 percentage points to labour force effects, 0.81 (0.62 + 0.19) percentage point to the exhaustion of inefficiencies associated with the demise of self-employment and the farm sector, and 1.71 percentage points to the slow-down in conventional accumulation. If the decline in conventional accumulation can be shown to be related largely to demographic and labour force events, then these three sources might account for almost half of Denison and Chung's projected slow-down in Japan's growth. That is certainly a big enough share to warrant the theme of this

## FIGURE 4.1
### Actual, Transitional, and Sustainable Growth Rates in Japan, 1971–2001

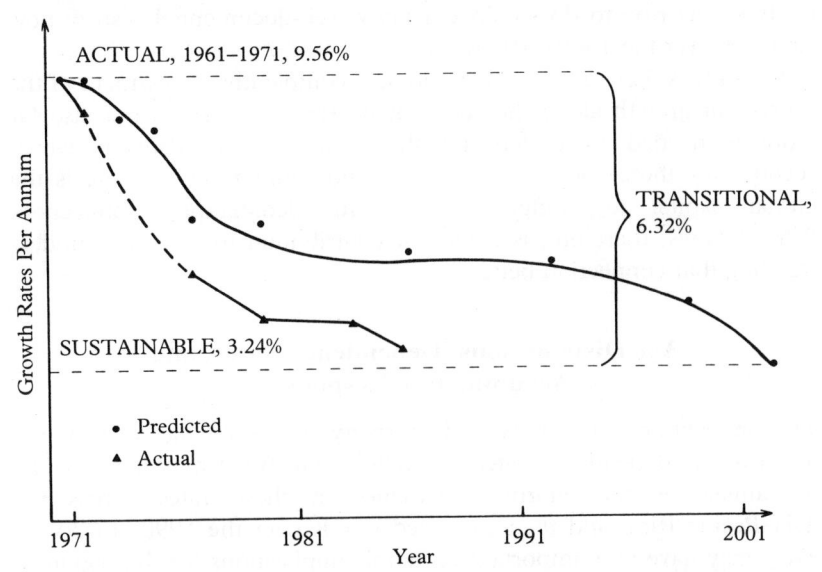

[Figure: Growth Rates Per Annum vs. Year (1971–2001). ACTUAL, 1961–1971, 9.56%. TRANSITIONAL, 6.32%. SUSTAINABLE, 3.24%. Legend: • Predicted, ▲ Actual]

*Source*: Denison and Chung (1976).

symposium, and it seems to be consistent with the hypothesis that a good share of the differences in growth performance along the Asia–Pacific Rim, or between it and Latin America, can also be explained by human capital and demographic forces.

There is another way to motivate this symposium's focus on human capital, namely, the recent theories of endogenous economic growth (Barro, 1989; Becker and Murphy, 1988; Lucas, 1988). These theories imply that if human to physical capital ratios are initially high, a country's subsequent economic performance will feature high rates of physical capital investment and rapid per capita income growth. Indeed, when Barro applied these theories to cross-national data spanning the period between 1960 and 1985, he showed that growth is positively correlated with schooling levels in 1960, and the correlation is very strong. This is especially true of countries like South Korea and Japan (Barro, 1989: 4–5), whose growth rates were raised by as much as 1.5 per cent per annum due to above average schooling commitments in 1960.

Denison and Chung, Ohkawa and Rosovsky, and the endogenous economic growth theorists have thrown down a challenge. What attributes of earlier economic and social history explain the above average commitment to human resource development, like schooling, in some countries and the below average commitment in others? What would be learned if this kind of analysis were applied in a comparative way to all of the economies—fast growers and slow growers, rich and poor—along the Asia–Pacific Rim? Oddly enough, very little comparative work of this sort has yet been applied systematically to the post-World War II economic history of the Asia–Pacific Rim. The time certainly seems ripe to do so since a fairly well-documented history now stretches over the 1960s–1980s.

Not only is there great value in doing a comparative assessment of the sources of growth along the Asia–Pacific Rim since 1965, but also far more is needed to understand the underlying mechanisms which account for these sources. One of the most important of these is the human capital deepening, inequality, and demographic connection. What follows, therefore, is a modest contribution to efforts in understanding that connection better.

### Age Distributions, Dependency Rates, and Accumulation Responses

The implications of fertility and mortality trends for age distribution patterns and dependency rates are well known. What may not be quite so familiar is the enormous variance in those rates across the Asia–Pacific Rim, and their projected trends over the 1990s to 2010s. They may have very important economic implications for the region so it would be useful to review the evidence once more.

Table 4.2 reports past, present, and future dependency rates. In it are summarized United Nations data for the share of populations aged 14 years or less, 65 years or more, and the two combined. The data were readily available for nine countries along the Rim.

The table does not show the fact that some of these countries have undergone important declines in their dependency rates over the 1960s to 1980s, and in such cases all of the decline appears to have been concentrated in the 1970s. Even so, the differences between Japan and the other eight nations are still enormous in 1980. Four of these are especially notable: the Philippines (whose dependency rate was 12.8 per cent higher than Japan's), Thailand (10.8 per cent higher), Malaysia (10.4 per cent higher), and Indonesia (11.7 per cent higher). These differences are very large even compared with the spectacular historical fall in Japan's dependency rate since 1950. China and South Korea also have higher dependency rates, though the differentials relative to Japan are not quite so high, 7.6 and 7.1 per cent, respectively. The rich city-states of Hong Kong and Singapore are much more like Japan.

Equally striking are the projected trends to the year 2010, and the correlation between those trends and the size of the 1980 differential with Japan's rate appears to be almost perfect. That is, dependency rates will have converged sharply along the Asia–Pacific Rim over the three decades following 1980. Indeed, every single country will have dependency rates below Japan's in 2010, a striking reversal in demographic features along the Rim. However, Japan will still have the lowest dependency rates among the young since all of the projected rise in its dependency rate will be attributable to the impressive increase in those

## TABLE 4.2
### Past, Present, and Future Dependency Rates along the Asia–Pacific Rim

|  |  |  |  |  | Ages 0–14 and 65+ |  |
|---|---|---|---|---|---|---|
| Country | Year | Age 0–14 | Age 65+ | Total | Country j Minus Japan | Year 2010 Minus 1980 |
| Japan | 1950 | 35.4 | 4.9 | 40.3 | | |
|  | 1980 | 23.6 | 9.0 | 32.6 | 0.0 | +4.3 |
|  | 2010 | 17.4 | 19.5 | 36.9 | | |
| China | 1950 | 33.5 | 4.5 | 38.0 | | |
|  | 1980 | 35.5 | 4.7 | 40.2 | 7.6 | −11.0 |
|  | 2010 | 21.1 | 8.1 | 29.2 | | |
| Hong Kong | 1950 | 30.3 | 2.6 | 32.9 | | |
|  | 1980 | 25.5 | 6.4 | 31.9 | −0.7 | −3.0 |
|  | 2010 | 17.5 | 11.4 | 28.9 | | |
| South Korea | 1950 | 41.7 | 3.1 | 44.8 | | |
|  | 1980 | 36.0 | 3.7 | 39.7 | 7.1 | −8.9 |
|  | 2010 | 23.6 | 7.2 | 30.8 | | |
| Indonesia | 1950 | 39.2 | 4.0 | 43.2 | | |
|  | 1980 | 41.0 | 3.3 | 44.3 | 11.7 | −12.8 |
|  | 2010 | 25.2 | 6.3 | 31.5 | | |
| Malaysia | 1950 | 40.9 | 5.1 | 45.5 | | |
|  | 1980 | 39.3 | 3.7 | 43.0 | 10.4 | −11.9 |
|  | 2010 | 25.4 | 5.7 | 31.1 | | |
| Philippines | 1950 | 43.6 | 3.6 | 47.2 | | |
|  | 1980 | 42.0 | 3.4 | 45.4 | 12.8 | −9.9 |
|  | 2010 | 31.1 | 4.4 | 35.5 | | |
| Singapore | 1950 | 40.5 | 2.3 | 42.8 | | |
|  | 1980 | 27.1 | 4.7 | 31.8 | −0.8 | −4.3 |
|  | 2010 | 18.2 | 9.3 | 27.5 | | |
| Thailand | 1950 | 42.5 | 3.0 | 45.5 | | |
|  | 1980 | 39.9 | 3.5 | 43.4 | 10.8 | −12.6 |
|  | 2010 | 24.6 | 6.2 | 30.8 | | |

*Source*: United Nations (1989b: 130–346, 'medium variant').

aged 65 and over. The distinction may matter not only to savings behaviour, but also to human capital accumulation. As Kelley has pointed out, 'in some countries we are beginning to see a decline in real per student expenditures on education at the same time that we observe an increase in real per capita spending on the aged [suggesting] a tension between generations in the allocation of the public purse' (Kelley, 1988b: 38).

What are the economic implications of these trends and differentials along the Rim? The crudest cut at this problem is reported in Table 4.3. Here GNP per worker is first calculated by applying the 1980 labour participation rate (percentage aged 15–64) to the 1981 GNP per capita estimates. Next GNP per capita in the year 2010 is calculated given the

TABLE 4.3
Exploring the Dependency–Labour Participation Rate Impact on Growth along the Asia–Pacific Rim

| Country | 1981 GNP Per Capita Index | | 1981 GNP per Worker Index Using 1980 Labour Participation Rate | | 2010 GNP Per Capita Using 1981 GNP per Worker Index and 2010 Labour Participation Rates | | Contribution to Growth Rate per Annum (%) |
|---|---|---|---|---|---|---|---|
| Japan | 10,080 | (1,000) | 14,955 | (1,000) | 9,437 | (1,000) | −0.23 |
| Singapore | 5,240 | (520) | 7,683 | (514) | 5,570 | (590) | 0.21 |
| Hong Kong | 5,100 | (506) | 7,489 | (501) | 5,325 | (564) | 0.15 |
| Malaysia | 1,840 | (183) | 3,228 | (216) | 2,224 | (236) | 0.66 |
| South Korea | 1,700 | (169) | 2,819 | (188) | 1,951 | (207) | 0.48 |
| Philippines | 790 | (78) | 1,447 | (97) | 933 | (99) | 0.58 |
| Thailand | 770 | (76) | 1,360 | (91) | 941 | (100) | 0.69 |
| Indonesia | 530 | (53) | 952 | (64) | 652 | (69) | 0.72 |
| China | 300 | (30) | 502 | (34) | 355 | (38) | 0.58 |

*Source*: World Bank (1983), *World Development Report*.
*Notes*: The 1981 GNP per capita figures are from World Bank (1983: 148–9), *World Development Report*. The labour participation rates are shares aged 15–64, from Table 4.2.

projected labour participation rate for that year, and assuming for the moment that GNP per worker remains unchanged. Finally, the implications of the drift in the labour participation rate from 1980 to 2010 on GNP per capita growth rates are reported. Note, first, the correlation between level of development and the growth rate impact. Poor countries along the Asia–Pacific Rim gain the most, while Japan, in fact, loses (confirming the Denison and Chung projections in Table 4.1). As it turns out, these demographic forces will also serve to help the slower growers (Indonesia, the Philippines, Thailand, and Malaysia, see Table 4.7), and in some cases they will help a lot.

The calculation in Table 4.3 is, of course, much too simple. It ignores the possibility that the decline in dependency rates everywhere along the Asia–Pacific Rim, with the important exception of Japan, might quicken the rate of growth in labour productivity. The latter would take place if capital deepening was stimulated by the decline in the dependency rate.

Is there any reason to expect that the decline in the dependency rate will stimulate accumulation and capital deepening everywhere along the Asia–Pacific Rim, outside of Japan? Around 1970, the answer would have been an unambiguous affirmative. At that time, the views of Coale and Hoover (1958) dominated. Coale and Hoover focused their attention on the impact of fertility decline, rather than population growth itself. A decline in fertility, they argued, lowers the number of young dependants (augmenting savings rates) and raises female labour participation rates, thus fostering economic growth. Coale (1986) repeated the point by showing that while population and per capita income growth may be poorly correlated, total fertility rates and per capita income growth are negatively correlated.

Leff's (1969) pioneering empirical study confirmed the impact of dependency rate effects on conventional savings, ignoring potential human capital responses. Two decades later, the profession is far less certain, but Coale, Hoover, and Leff would have suggested that present-day economists proceed as follows.

There have been a number of econometric studies which have estimated the impact of dependency rates on savings, and the estimated elasticity varies considerably from a high of $-1.49$ (Leff, 1969) to a low of $-0.13$ (Singh, 1975). Estimates for Asia alone appear to fall somewhere in the middle (Fry and Mason, 1982; Fry, 1984b; Mason, 1987a: 530, Table 4). What would the implications be of such estimates for the Asia–Pacific Rim? Table 4.4 offers some answers. There two counterfactuals are posed. First, what would each country's savings rate have been like had they had the advantage of Japan's lower dependency rate? Second, what will each country's savings rate be like given the projected decline in dependency rates everywhere along the Rim (with the exception of Japan)? The results can be summarized most conveniently if the 'middle' elasticity is viewed as most likely.

The implications emerging from Table 4.4 are striking. The slower growers would have enjoyed the most pronounced savings rate increases

TABLE 4.4
Exploring the Dependency Rate–Savings Rate Connection
along the Asia–Pacific Rim

| Country | Actual 1981 Gross Domestic Savings Rate (%) | Elasticity | Counterfactual Gross Domestic Savings Rate (%), Calculated at: Japan's 1980 Dependency Rate | UN Projected 2010 Dependency Rate |
|---|---|---|---|---|
| China | 28 | high | 35.9 | 39.4 |
|  |  | middle | 32.2 | 34.1 |
|  |  | low | 28.7 | 29.0 |
| Japan | 32 | high | n.a. | 25.7 |
|  |  | middle | n.a. | 28.6 |
|  |  | low | n.a. | 31.5 |
| Hong Kong | 24 | high | 23.2 | 27.4 |
|  |  | middle | 23.6 | 25.8 |
|  |  | low | 23.9 | 24.3 |
| South Korea | 22 | high | 27.9 | 29.3 |
|  |  | middle | 25.1 | 25.9 |
|  |  | low | 22.5 | 22.6 |
| Indonesia | 23 | high | 32.1 | 32.9 |
|  |  | middle | 27.9 | 28.3 |
|  |  | low | 23.8 | 23.9 |
| Malaysia | 26 | high | 35.4 | 36.7 |
|  |  | middle | 31.0 | 31.8 |
|  |  | low | 26.8 | 26.9 |
| Philippines | 25 | high | 35.5 | 33.1 |
|  |  | middle | 30.6 | 29.4 |
|  |  | low | 25.9 | 25.7 |
| Singapore | 33 | high | 31.8 | 39.6 |
|  |  | middle | 32.3 | 36.7 |
|  |  | low | 32.9 | 33.6 |
| Thailand | 23 | high | 31.5 | 32.9 |
|  |  | middle | 27.6 | 28.3 |
|  |  | low | 23.7 | 23.9 |

*Sources*: The 1981 actual gross domestic saving rates are taken from World Bank (1983: 156–7, Table 5), *World Development Report*. The counterfactuals use the dependency rates (ages 0–14 and 65+) in Table 4.2, and the elasticity of savings rates with respect to dependency rates are: 'high' (−1.49) (Leff, 1969); 'middle' (−0.80) (Adams, 1971); and 'low' (−0.13) (Singh, 1975)—all reported in Hammer (1985: 13).
n.a. = Not available.

had they had Japan's more favourable dependency rates: Malaysia, a gain of 5.0 percentage points in its savings rate; the Philippines, a gain of 5.6; Thailand, a gain of 4.6; and Indonesia, a gain of 4.9. If these countries were really savings-constrained, then the calculation implies that the slower growers along the Asia–Pacific Rim suffered significantly from high dependency rates. Assuming an incremental capital–output ratio (ICOR) of 4 : 1, it implies that Malaysia had a lower growth rate of 1.25 per cent because of it (5.0 × 0.25 = 1.25). Had Malaysia not had that disadvantage, it would have closed most of the 1960–81 growth gap between itself and Japan (4.3 + 1.25 = 5.55 versus 6.3 for Japan, see Table 4.7). According to UN projections, that disadvantage will have disappeared by the year 2010. If the dependency rate–savings rate connection holds, the implications are for future large increases in savings rates among the poorer nations along the Asia–Pacific Rim. In contrast, Japan's savings rate will decline by 3.4 percentage points. Again assuming an ICOR of 4 : 1, Table 4.4 implies that due to the dependency rate effect alone, growth rates in the poor, slower-growing countries will converge on Japan's: that is, Japan's 1961–80 growth rate would drop to about 5.5 per cent per annum by 2010 (once again consistent with the Denison and Chung projections in Table 4.1), while that of the four slower growers would rise to something like 5.3 per cent per annum.

These calculations are illustrative only, but they certainly suggest that the dependency rate–savings rate connection has great potential for the Asia–Pacific Rim. Unfortunately, however, very few development economists now believe this Coale–Hoover–Leff argument. First, the life cycle model underlying the calculations has come under attack (Hammer, 1985), especially for developing countries where the assumptions of the life cycle model are most likely to be violated. Second, recent econometric analysis suggests that the dependency rate effect is generally weak (Kelley, 1986), and that falling dependency rates raise savings only in fast-growing countries (Mason, 1988; Mason et al., 1986; Collins, 1989). Since so many of the East Asian countries were fast growers, the argument developed here may have more to recommend it. In any case, that part of the literature which rejects the Coale–Hoover–Leff argument has failed to appreciate the implications of that result. If savings and investment rates will be unaffected by a fall in the dependency rate expected over the 1990s–2010s along the Asia–Pacific Rim, then the rate of accumulation will also be unaffected, allowing the rate of capital deepening to accelerate if labour force growth rates eventually decline following the decline in dependency rates. That the effect of the dependency rate on savings is weak does not necessarily imply that the impact on the rate of capital deepening is weak; it is the latter that matters. A lot more needs to be learnt about those responses for countries along the Asia–Pacific Rim.

It seems to this writer that the literature has not spent enough time asking why it is that macro-estimates of the savings–dependency relationship are typically 'weak' when our Coale and Hoover priors had been so strong. An answer was offered by this writer when serving as a discussant for Kelley's paper on this topic presented at a Nairobi conference in 1986. It might be useful to repeat that answer by reference to Figure 4.2. High dependency rates and rapid population growth go together, and it seems highly plausible to expect that the latter will serve to augment investment demand, either by additional social overhead

## FIGURE 4.2
### Why the Dependency Rate Effect Might Be Estimated as 'Weak'

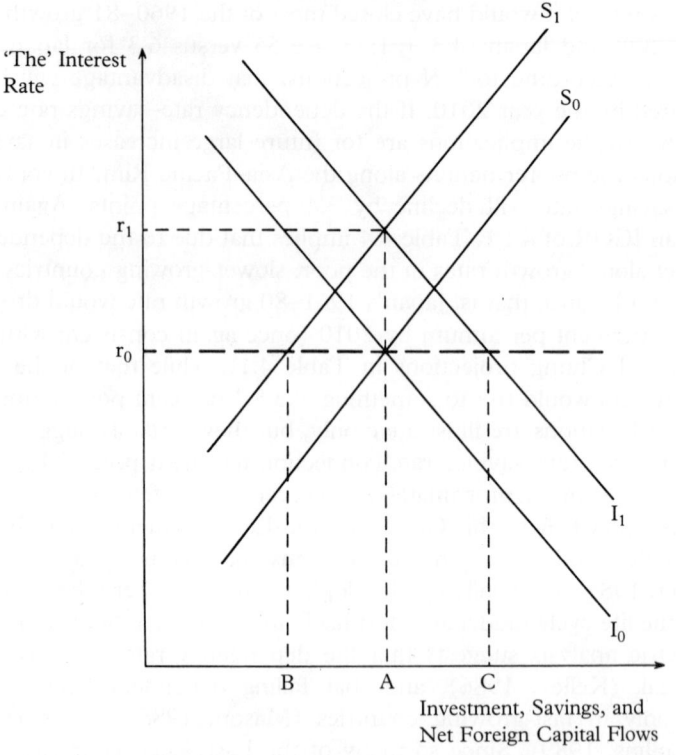

requirements or by encouraging firms to expand capacity given an augmented labour force. Thus, investment demand shifts outwards to the right. If Coale and Hoover are correct, the savings supply schedule shifts backwards to the left. Suppose, for the sake of argument, it shifted such as to reach a new equilibrium at a higher interest rate, $r_1$, but at the same level of savings and investment, A. This analysis assumes that the domestic economy is closed to foreign capital. If the assumption holds, then it would explain why savings rates and dependency rates often appear to be poorly correlated in conventional time series analysis. Suppose, instead, the economy is open to foreign capital inflows, and in fact takes the world interest rate as given, $r_0$, and can absorb as much at that rate as it wishes. In this case, domestic savings declines to B, investment expands to C, and net foreign capital inflows fill the gap, BC. Which of these two extreme assumptions about foreign capital inflows is most accurate?

Far more research needs to be done on the dependency rate–savings rate connection along the Asia–Pacific Rim. If such research were forthcoming, one of the first tasks would be to determine whether in fact these economies are savings-constrained. If they are not, then the dependency rate effect would simply translate into changes in net foreign capital inflows, not growth. But for many countries, like South Korea (Williamson, 1979a), a reduction in external capital dependence is an additional policy target, so even if these economies can be shown to be investment-driven, the dependency rate–savings rate connection still matters.

Finally, the literature on the dependency rate–savings rate connection has been much too narrow in the sense that it has ignored human capital responses, like schooling. Low dependency rates among the young imply sparsely populated cohorts among those of schooling age, placing weak demands on the schooling sector. The schooling sector is likely to respond either by crowding in some potential students who otherwise might not have attended or by raising the quality of the schooling of those who attend. Of course, low dependency rates among the young may also make it easier for parents to send their children to school. On the other hand, falling dependency rates in the future among the young are likely to coincide with rising dependency rates among the old and, as Kelley has pointed out, this may serve to deflect public resources from educating the young to supporting the old, especially among the more advanced countries in East Asia who have moved into more mature demographic stages. More needs to be learnt about the dependency rate–human capital connection, and later in this chapter some evidence will be offered which suggests that it matters a great deal.

## Mortality, Life Expectancy, and Human Capital Responses

The previous section focused on financial savings and conventional accumulation responses to changes in dependency rates. It also promised to offer some evidence on the dependency rate–human capital connection. But first, what about human capital accumulation responses to the rise in life expectancy?

Table 4.5 should serve to remind us just how impressive life

TABLE 4.5
Life Expectancy at Birth along the Asia–Pacific Rim, 1965 and 1985
(years)

| | Male | | | Female | | |
|---|---|---|---|---|---|---|
| Country | 1965 | 1985 | Change | 1965 | 1985 | Change |
| China | 54 | 68 | 14 | 55 | 70 | 15 |
| Japan | 68 | 75 | 7 | 73 | 80 | 7 |
| Hong Kong | 64 | 73 | 9 | 71 | 79 | 8 |
| South Korea | 55 | 65 | 10 | 58 | 72 | 14 |
| Indonesia | 43 | 53 | 10 | 45 | 57 | 12 |
| Malaysia | 56 | 66 | 10 | 60 | 70 | 10 |
| Philippines | 54 | 61 | 7 | 57 | 65 | 8 |
| Singapore | 64 | 70 | 6 | 68 | 75 | 7 |
| Thailand | 54 | 62 | 8 | 58 | 66 | 8 |

*Source*: World Bank (1987: 258–9, Table 29), *World Development Report*.

expectancy gains have been along the Asia–Pacific Rim. The most important mortality declines appear to have been experienced by the poorer countries along the Rim, that is, a rise in life expectancy from 43 to 53 in Indonesia is likely to have a bigger impact on accumulation behaviour than a rise from 68 to 75 in Japan. This is so for three reasons: it is a bigger absolute rise, 10 versus 7 years; it is an even bigger percentage rise, 23 versus 10 per cent; and it is at a more critical stage of the life cycle where the payoff to investment in human capital should matter most.

Ram and Schultz (1979) have argued that longer life expectancy leads to greater incentives for human capital deepening, and human capital even in India is large enough to matter. Their estimates from India suggest that total expenditures on human capital investment are about 55 per cent of conventional investment. This writer suspects that the figure is higher in South Korea and far higher in Japan since, based on twentieth-century European and American experience, the total capital stock tends to shift out of physical and into human capital as modern industrialization ensues. Indeed, Jorgenson and Fraumeni (1988: Table 31) have estimated the share of human wealth in total wealth in the United States in 1982 to be about 92 per cent! In any case, if Ram and Schultz are correct, then there is reason to suspect that the rise in life expectancy should have an even greater impact along the Asia–Pacific Rim where human capital investments presumably loom larger in total investments than in India. On the other hand, the life expectancy gains summarized in Table 4.5 exaggerate the likely impact on human capital accumulation responses since it is the rise in expected life-span from age 5 or 10 that matters to human capital investments, and they have increased much less than life expectancies at birth. From the scraps of data that could be collected from the United Nations, it appears that improvements in life expectancy at age 10 along the Asia–Pacific Rim (Hong Kong, Japan, South Korea, Malaysia, Taiwan, and Thailand) have been from one-third to one-half of those in India. None the less, they are large enough to warrant our attention.

Given the enormous size of the rise in life expectancies along the Asia–Pacific Rim, since 1950, far more needs to be known about the response of investments in nutrition, education, on-the-job training, and migration. This includes learning where in the life cycle changes in mortality experience are taking place, and what forms of human capital investment are most responsive to those age-specific mortality declines. Very little is known about these potentially important empirical issues for most of the countries along the Asia–Pacific Rim.

It could be argued, of course, that these postulated but unmeasured human capital responses are unlikely to matter in those economies where life expectancies at age 10 already stretch into retirement years. The only countries along the Asia–Pacific Rim where life expectancies at age 10 fall below 65 appear to be Indonesia, most of Malaysia, and Thailand. Even so, the distribution of life expectancies and their change over time may matter more than the average life expectancy experience. Who has gained most from life expectancy improvements in Asia? Have these gains centred on the poor who begin with very low life expectancies? This writer is not aware of any research which has focused on this potentially important problem. Far more needs to be learnt about the Ram–Schultz assertion and its likely influence on growth performance along the Asia–Pacific Rim over the next few decades.

While the Ram–Schultz hypothesis focuses solely on human capital accumulation responses to the rise in life expectancy, it may also have a profound effect on financial savings since young adults need to ponder more seriously the adequacy of their resources for retirement than did their parents who might well have expected brief retirement or no retirement at all.

## The Inequality Connection

The classical economists developed their models of growth and development during the British Industrial Revolution when economic life was relatively simple. They could talk about three inputs—labour, land, and physical capital—and about three social classes—labourers, landlords, and capitalists. When dealing with the sources of growth, they could discuss physical capital accumulation, while ignoring human capital accumulation. When dealing with inequality, they could reduce the problem to the functional share trilogy—wages, rents, and profits—while ignoring the distribution of human capital. And when dealing with the Smithian trade-off, they could restrict their focus to the impact of redistribution on conventional savings, ignoring investment in schooling, health, housing, nutrition, and migration. Twentieth-century economic life is more complex. Human capital matters to a far greater extent. This simple point is central to the trade-off debate and deserves amplification.

Support for the growth and equality trade-off has always rested on the belief that redistribution from the poor to the rich augments the supply of private savings and thus raises the rate of accumulation.[1] Not only was this belief central to nineteenth-century models of growth and distribution developed by British economists to explain their industrial revolution, but it is also central to Lewis's (1954) labour-surplus model and to recent debates over productivity slow-down in the advanced countries. In such models, the trade-off works through marginal propensities to save (mps). Any force redistributing income may raise aggregate savings and accumulation if those benefiting have a higher mps than the rest of society. Since higher income classes were always thought to have a higher mps, it would seem natural to conclude that any redistribution towards the rich would raise savings and capital accumulation. This argument should apply equally to eighteenth- or nineteenth-century redistributions through market forces and to twentieth-century redistributions through government action.

While intuitively plausible and a staple in political economy since

Adam Smith, redistribution has had little quantitative impact, in fact, on the aggregate savings rate. True, even in Asia, distribution variables help explain aggregate savings rates (Williamson, 1968). But when more sophisticated tools are applied, the trade-off seems modest. So say studies on aggregate United States data (Husby, 1971; Blinder, 1975), on Latin American data (Cline, 1972), and on international cross-sections (Della Valle and Oguchi, 1976; Musgrove, 1980). Rough calculations for nineteenth-century America (Williamson, 1979b) and nineteenth-century Britain (Williamson, 1985) say the same. (See the summary in Williamson, 1991: Lecture 3.)

With the spread of national independence, literacy, and suffrage in the Third World, rejection of the Smithian trade-off gained momentum under the leadership of McNamara and some World Bank economists (Chenery et al., 1974; Ahluwalia, 1976, 1980). Their competing view was that the Third World overlooked a vast range of policy options that would enhance growth by raising the value of the poor's assets: investment in public health, mass education, and rural infrastructure.

Indeed, these are exactly the prescriptions which appear to be backed by so much of twentieth-century Asian experience, that is, the economic history of the Asia–Pacific Rim appears to offer evidence which not only rejects the trade-off, but appears to offer some tentative support for the view that equality may foster growth. Consider the kind of evidence which encourages this revisionist position.

Table 4.6 augments Ahluwalia's (1976) data with more recent country estimates from the World Bank, cross-sectional information which Ahluwalia used to establish the Kuznets Curve. Kuznets (1955) hypothesized that inequality should rise with early development, falling as countries pass from NIEs to advanced development stages. However, the upswing of the hypothesized Kuznets Curve has generated the most active debate. After all, the variance around any estimated Kuznets Curve is always greatest from low to middle levels of development. Thus, inequality does not rise systematically across a pooled cross-section of early industrial revolutions. Even if many countries undergo increasing inequality during early modern economic growth, such correlations are bound to be poor since history has given less developed countries very different starting points.

Expansion on this point is called for. Production in traditional agrarian economies tends to be driven by two inputs, land and unskilled labour. In some traditional agrarian economies, like the European Old World and the Latin American New World, the holdings of the asset which matters, land, was highly concentrated, much more highly concentrated than was human or physical capital in urban sectors (Griffin, 1976; Hirashima, 1978). The forces of inequality driven by industrialization must push hard to increase aggregate inequality in such economies where the sector in which assets and incomes are most unequally distributed declines in relative importance. Such economies will have higher inequality in early stages of development, but they may

TABLE 4.6
The Kuznets Curve and the Virtuous Asians

| | Dependent Variable | | | | | | | |
|---|---|---|---|---|---|---|---|---|
| | Share of Bottom 20% | | | | Share of Top 20% | | | |
| Variable | (1) | (2) | (3) | (4) | (5) | (6) | (7) | (8) |
| Constant | 26.16 | 23.81 | 26.90 | 28.78 | −51.66 | −39.67 | −54.64 | −62.26 |
| | (4.32) | (4.30) | (4.62) | (4.95) | (1.84) | (1.47) | (2.00) | (2.23) |
| ln (GNP/POP) | −6.95 | −6.35 | −7.26 | −7.67 | 36.96 | 33.92 | 38.22 | 40.55 |
| | (3.60) | (3.39) | (3.91) | (4.21) | (4.14) | (3.96) | (4.39) | (4.89) |
| [ln (GNP/POP)]$^2$ | 0.54 | 0.50 | 0.57 | 0.60 | −3.13 | −2.93 | −3.24 | −3.41 |
| | (3.61) | (3.46) | (3.93) | (4.22) | (4.52) | (4.43) | (4.79) | (5.30) |
| ASIA dummy | | 1.15 | | | | −5.90 | | |
| | | (2.33) | | | | (2.60) | | |
| PACIFIC RIM dummy | | | 1.29 | | | | −5.17 | |
| | | | (2.35) | | | | (2.02) | |
| BIG 3 dummy | | | | 2.54 | | | | −12.27 |
| | | | | (2.95) | | | | (3.24) |
| $\bar{R}^2$ | 0.17 | 0.23 | 0.23 | 0.27 | 0.39 | 0.45 | 0.43 | 0.49 |
| F-stat | 6.52 | 6.52 | 6.56 | 7.88 | 18.80 | 16.15 | 14.65 | 18.28 |

*Sources*: Ahluwalia (1976: 340–1); World Bank (1987: 252–3), *World Development Report*, World Bank. BIG 3 = Japan, Taiwan, and Korea; PACIFIC RIM = BIG 3 plus Thailand, the Philippines, Malaysia, Hong Kong, and Indonesia; ASIA = PACIFIC RIM plus Pakistan, Sri Lanka, and India. The total sample includes 56 countries.

*Notes*: Figures in parentheses are t-statistics. The underlying data are taken from Ahluwalia (1976), excluding the socialist countries, and augmented by Hong Kong and Indonesia in the *World Development Report*, World Bank.

exhibit less steep upswings on the Kuznets Curve. In contrast, other traditional agrarian economies, like East Asia, Africa, and the American North, had less concentrated land holdings and more equal agrarian income distributions. Such economies are likely to exhibit lower inequality in early stages of development, but they may exhibit more steep upswings on the Kuznets Curve, *ceteris paribus*. The *ceteris paribus* is important, since the initial Latin American inequality may create a path dependent inegalitarian policy regime throughout the Latin American industrial revolution, just as the initial East Asian equality may create a path dependent egalitarian policy regime throughout the East Asian industrial revolution. These issues of initial conditions and path dependence are important, and will be returned to later in this chapter. They suggest that economic history is important to understanding contemporary events along the Asia–Pacific Rim.

More to the point of this symposium, however, Table 4.6 shows unambiguously that, after controlling for level of development, the Asian nations tend to have more egalitarian distributions. Thus, the coefficient of the dummy variable ASIA indicates that the 11 Asian countries in the sample (Hong Kong, Indonesia, Pakistan, Sri Lanka, India, Thailand, the Philippines, South Korea, Taiwan, Malaysia, and Japan) are significantly more egalitarian than the rest, and the differences are large. More or less the same results are forthcoming when only the Asia–Pacific Rim countries are included (dummy variable PACIFIC RIM). When only Japan, Taiwan, and Korea are included (dummy variable BIG 3), the results are even more striking: on average, the top 20 per cent claimed 12 per cent less of total income compared with other countries at comparable stages of development.

These differences warrant explanations. More also needs to be known about what contribution, if any, the more egalitarian distributions have made to impressive growth along the Asia–Pacific Rim.

Not only are Asian nations more egalitarian, but the more egalitarian among them seem to have grown fastest during the post-World War II decades. Table 4.7 offers some World Bank data for 16 nations, eight Asian along the Pacific Rim and eight Latin American. While the correlation between growth and equality is hardly perfect, the evidence not only rejects the Smithian trade-off postulate but suggests that equality may contribute to fast growth. That is, the four fast growers in East Asia had half the inequality of the four slow growers in East Asia, and all eight of these East Asian countries had less than half the inequality of the eight much slower-growing Latin American countries.

What might account for this pattern? There are four connections well worth pursuing, since they may have important implications for understanding dynamic growth along the Asia–Pacific Rim. First, more egalitarian societies may find it easier to pursue pro-growth government policies. Second, more egalitarian societies may find it easier to accumulate human capital. Third, demographic forces—a glut in the young age-groups—may have contributed both to slow growth (via dependency rate effects and low savings) and inequality (Paglin, 1975; Kuznets, 1976; Morley, 1981). Fourth, interest rate policies may have an impact

TABLE 4.7
Inequality and Growth: Which Drives Which?

| Country | GNP Per Capita Growth per Annum (1960–81) | Income Share of Bottom 20% | Income Share of Top 20% | Ratio, Top to Bottom |
|---|---|---|---|---|
| **Virtuous Asians** | | | | |
| *Fast growers* | | | | |
| South Korea (1976) | 6.9 | 5.7 | 45.3 | 7.95 |
| Hong Kong (1980) | 6.9 | 5.4 | 47.0 | 8.70 |
| Japan (1979) | 6.3 | 8.7 | 37.5 | 4.31 |
| Taiwan (1976) | 6.6 | 9.5 | 35.0 | 3.68 |
| Unweighted average | 6.7 | 7.3 | 41.2 | 5.64 |
| *Slower growers* | | | | |
| Indonesia (1976) | 4.1 | 6.6 | 49.4 | 7.48 |
| Philippines (1985) | 2.8 | 5.2 | 52.5 | 10.10 |
| Thailand (1975–6) | 4.6 | 5.6 | 49.8 | 8.89 |
| Malaysia (1973) | 4.3 | 3.5 | 56.1 | 16.03 |
| Unweighted average | 4.0 | 5.2 | 52.0 | 10.00 |
| **Bad Latins** | | | | |
| El Salvador (1976–7) | 1.5 | 5.5 | 47.3 | 8.60 |
| Peru (1972) | 1.0 | 1.9 | 61.0 | 32.11 |
| Costa Rica (1971) | 3.0 | 3.3 | 54.8 | 16.61 |
| Brazil (1972) | 5.1 | 2.0 | 66.6 | 33.30 |
| Mexico (1977) | 3.8 | 2.9 | 57.7 | 19.90 |
| Panama (1973) | 3.1 | 2.0 | 61.8 | 30.90 |
| Argentina (1970) | 1.9 | 4.4 | 50.3 | 11.43 |
| Venezuela (1970) | 2.4 | 3.0 | 54.0 | 18.00 |
| Unweighted average | 2.7 | 3.1 | 56.7 | 18.29 |

*Sources*: Inequality: World Bank (1987: 252–3, Table 26), *World Development Report*, and for Taiwan, (Myers, 1986: 24). Growth rates: World Bank (1983: 148–9, Table 1), *World Development Report*, and for Taiwan (1960–78), World Bank (1980: 111, Table 1), *World Development Report*.

on accumulation and inequality. As Scitovsky (1985) has stressed, Taiwan has pursued a high interest rate policy since the early 1950s. Not only has such a policy encouraged a labour-intensive growth path (with egalitarian implications), but it also appears to have contributed to a high domestic personal savings rate (although some might doubt the interest-elasticity optimism implied by that conclusion). Furthermore, the high interest rate policy implies a transfer from large firms' profits to small savers. Other countries along the Asia–Pacific Rim have pursued more conventional low interest rate policies combined with credit rationing, as in South Korea's case (Williamson, 1979a).

Sachs (1987) drew attention to the potential inequality–growth connections which have been cited in East Asian literature, and it may be useful to repeat these arguments.[2] Sachs and others have argued that by historical accident, Japan, South Korea, and Taiwan were all forced to introduce fundamental land reforms in the late 1940s and early 1950s.[3] The conditions making the land reforms possible were, of course, unique, but in all three cases land reform virtually eliminated farm tenancy. In fact, it could be argued that these land reforms were among the greatest in modern history (Fei et al., 1979; Mason et al., 1980; Oshima, 1988: S111; Kuznets, 1988: S15). Not only was land redistributed, raising incomes of the poor at the bottom of the distribution, but those with middle incomes did not have to pay much for the redistribution (through taxes) since the value of government bonds used to compensate the landlords at the top of the distribution were eroded away by rapid inflation. There was another force at work to redistribute wealth and income in these three economies—the destruction of wealth by war and inflation. Between 1935 and 1955, the wealth–income ratio in Japan declined precipitously from 4.15 to 2.20 (Egan, 1985: 63). This massive decline in the wealth–income ratio had two effects: (i) it tended to equalize incomes, since the rich held most of the physical and financial assets destroyed; and (ii) it must have contributed to the impressive rise in the savings rate which was characteristic of Japan's dynamic post-war development, as individuals tried to restore the pre-war wealth–income ratio.

While there is not similar evidence for Taiwan and South Korea, some observers feel that the same forces may well have been at work there too, at least in South Korea (Koo, 1984; Oshima, 1988: S116). This may offer one explanation for the rapid growth in South Korea, Taiwan, and Japan relative to other nations along the Asia–Pacific Rim.

These land reform explanations make much of historical accident in accounting for equality in South Korea, Taiwan, and Japan (and China, of course: Perkins and Yusuf, 1984: 105–30). What about the other eight countries underlying the ASIA dummy in Table 4.6? Here it might be helpful to stress comparative advantage and argicultural technologies Rice culture is small-scale, encouraging family farms, labour-intensive technology, and more egalitarian ownership. Sugar-cane, coffee, and other export crops typical of nineteenth- and twentieth-century Latin America are large-scale, encouraging commercial farms, inegalitarian ownership, and what Marx and British economic historians call a proletarianized agricultural labour market. This early specialization in different agricultural technologies is likely to have launched East Asia and Latin America on two quite different development paths.

So it is that Sachs and others argue that this inequality experience may have had important effects on post-war growth experience in these three dynamic economies. First, by replacing a tiny class of contentious landlords with a large class of contented peasants, the resulting political stability meant that government policy could focus attention on growth rather than rent-seeking. Second, the egalitarian revolution served to contribute to a minimum of labour unrest in the cities. Third, a dynamic agricultural sector was supported by protection and investment in rural infrastructure. As a result, a nation-wide egalitarian distribution was reinforced by egalitarian agriculture, and by small and declining income gaps between rural and urban areas. The agricultural sector is now, of course, very small in Japan, South Korea, and Taiwan, but it is still very large in the developing countries in the south of the Asia–Pacific Rim. Another item can be added to Sachs's list. To repeat, a more egalitarian distribution may have served to foster a rapid rate of human capital accumulation as the liquidity-constrained poor—facing imperfect capital markets—were better able to finance such investments from their own resources. Surely these facts of history made it easier for the poor in Asia to invest in human capital than was true of their counterparts in Latin America or even in eighteenth-century Britain. And surely these facts of history were translated into more interventionist government policies which favoured mass education in East Asia (Oshima, 1988: S109; 1987: 301–13) while suppressing it in Latin America and eighteenth-century Britain.

Far more research is needed on this inequality connection. How much of the economic dynamism along the Asia–Pacific Rim can be attributed to egalitarian distributions? If so, what were the strongest links? The pro-growth policy path outlined by Sachs? Human capital accumulation responses at the household level as the bottom income classes were better able to finance improved nutrition, education, migration, and other forms of human capital creation? Human capital responses accommodated by an interventionist government heavily committed to mass education and sensitive to strong peasant lobbying interests? A contented and stable labour force which encouraged firms to invest in firm-specific training? And how much of the inequality in the slower-growing nations can be attributed to demographic forces? This list of questions is much too ambitious to attempt an answer here, but this writer will try to shed some flickering light on one important part of the list—the schooling–inequality connection.

## A Brief Glance at Some Historical Experience with Schooling

That there has been a revolutionary increase in human capital deepening since the late 1800s is well known, at least as it is reflected in formal schooling. It is seen in enrolment rates (an investment flow per capita) and in schooling achievement (a stock per capita). Schultz (1987) documented the revolutionary magnitude of this schooling experience between 1960 and 1981, and this is reproduced in Table 4.8.

The rise in the schooling indicators has been truly spectacular. Even more striking is the fact that the percentage gains in schooling were greatest among the poor countries who had lower educational levels in 1960. The gap between rich and poor countries in what Schultz calls the 'expected years of schooling' collapsed dramatically over those two decades. While such evidence might suggest to some that this catching up by the poor countries is a recent phenomenon, Easterlin (1981) has shown that it has had a much longer history. The sharp rise in enrolment rates in much of the Third World can be dated back to at least 1920, and in a few cases even to the late nineteenth century.

TABLE 4.8
Growth in Educational Enrolment by School Level and Countries by Income Class, 1960–1981

| World Bank Country Class (number) | Primary Education (6–11) 1960 (1) | Primary Education (6–11) 1981 (2) | Secondary Education (12–17) 1960 (3) | Secondary Education (12–17) 1981 (4) | Higher Education (20–24) 1960 (5) | Higher Education (20–24) 1981 (6) | Expected Years of Schooling 1960 (7) | Expected Years of Schooling 1981 (8) | Percentage Increase in Enrolment Ratios (1960–81) Primary (9) | Secondary (10) | Higher (11) | Expected (12) |
|---|---|---|---|---|---|---|---|---|---|---|---|---|
| Low income (34) Excluding China and India | 0.80 | 0.94 | 0.18 | 0.34 | 0.02 | 0.04 | 5.98 | 7.88 | 18 | 89 | 100 | 32 |
|  | 0.38 | 0.72 | 0.07 | 0.19 | 0.01 | 0.02 | 2.75 | 5.56 | 89 | 171 | 100 | 102 |
| Middle income (38) Oil exporters | 0.64 | 1.06 | 0.09 | 0.37 | 0.02 | 0.08 | 4.48 | 8.98 | 66 | 311 | 300 | 100 |
| Oil importers | 0.84 | 0.99 | 0.18 | 0.44 | 0.04 | 0.13 | 6.32 | 9.23 | 18 | 144 | 225 | 46 |
| Upper-middle income (22) | 0.88 | 1.04 | 0.20 | 0.51 | 0.04 | 0.14 | 6.68 | 10.00 | 18 | 155 | 250 | 50 |
| High-income Oil exporters (5) | 0.29 | 0.83 | 0.05 | 0.43 | 0.01 | 0.08 | 2.09 | 7.96 | 186 | 760 | 700 | 281 |
| Industrial market (18) | 1.14 | 1.01 | 0.64 | 0.90 | 0.16 | 0.37 | 11.5 | 13.30 | −11 | 41 | 131 | 16 |
| East European non-market (8) | 1.01 | 1.05 | 0.45 | 0.88 | 0.11 | 0.20 | 9.31 | 12.60 | 4 | 96 | 82 | 35 |

*Source:* Schultz (1987: 417, Table 1).

HUMAN CAPITAL DEEPENING AND INEQUALITY        149

Furthermore, Figure 4.3 suggests that these Third World countries were also closing the gap with the American and European leaders long before 1960. The only event that made the 1960–80 period truly unique is the number of poor countries that had joined the 'catching up club'.

While there is evidence that the poor countries have been catching up with the rich in schooling investment rates, there is considerable variance in performance none the less. In the nineteenth century, America and Germany had far higher educational commitments than did France and the United Kingdom, suggesting quite different education accumulation regimes. Furthermore, conditions along the Asia–Pacific Rim since the late nineteenth century look different. In 1900, the primary school enrolment rates were higher in Japan than they were in 1840 among all the European industrial leaders (with the exception of Germany), and all of these countries were at comparable stages in their industrial revolutions. In addition, Figure 4.3 shows that Japan, the Philippines, Thailand, South Korea, and China all underwent far steeper increases in their commitment to educational investment after 1900 than

FIGURE 4.3
Primary School Enrolment Rates, 1830–1975 (per 10,000 population)

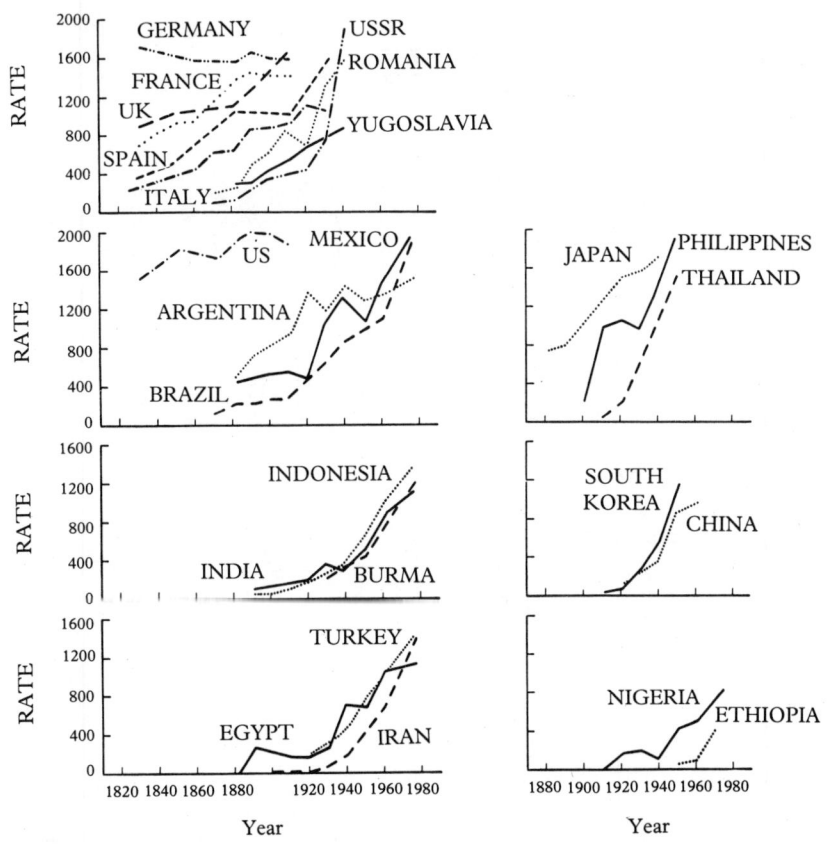

*Source*: Easterlin (1981: 8, Fig. 1).

TABLE 4.9
Has East Asia Always Invested More in Schooling? Twentieth-century Secondary School Enrolment Ratio
(Dependent Variable = Log of Secondary Enrolment Ratio)

| Equation | Time Period (Sample Size) | $R^2$ | Constant | Log GNP or GDP Per Capita | Latin America Dummy | East Asia Dummy | South Korea/ Japan/ Taiwan Dummy | Other East Asia Dummy |
|---|---|---|---|---|---|---|---|---|
| (1) | Pre-1950 (315) | 0.739 | −2.517 (76.240) | 0.904 (15.327) | −0.746 (8.997) | 1.966 (19.338) | — | — |
| (2) | 1950–9 (482) | 0.486 | −2.005 (44.205) | 0.879 (18.629) | −0.474 (6.091) | 1.254 (9.963) | — | — |
| (3) | 1950–9 (482) | 0.495 | −2.006 (44.573) | 0.873 (18.610) | −0.475 (6.148) | — | 1.539 (9.662) | 0.887 (4.974) |
| (4) | 1960–9 (732) | 0.574 | −1.801 (56.872) | 0.860 (29.164) | −0.134 (2.193) | 1.039 (11.220) | — | — |
| (5) | 1960–9 (732) | 0.577 | −1.802 (57.029) | 0.891 (30.790) | −0.134 (2.191) | — | 1.220 (9.739) | 0.845 (6.528) |
| (6) | 1970–9 (449) | 0.561 | −1.568 (46.338) | 0.685 (22.247) | 0.037 (0.540) | 0.675 (6.477) | — | — |
| (7) | 1970–9 (449) | 0.565 | −1.569 (46.538) | 0.654 (22.171) | 0.038 (0.558) | — | 0.884 (6.169) | 0.496 (3.286) |
| (8) | Total 20th Century (1,978) | 0.486 | −1.916 (90.755) | 0.816 (39.207) | −0.280 (6.847) | 1.135 (18.383) | — | — |
| (9) | Total 20th Century (1,978) | 0.490 | −1.916 (91.120) | 0.814 (39.211) | −0.280 (6.870) | — | 1.319 (17.109) | 0.849 (8.958) |

*Notes*: For the pre-1950 period in equation [1], the East Asian sample is limited to Japan. The dependent variable is the log ratio of those in secondary school to secondary school age population.

did all the nineteenth-century industrial nations and almost all of the precocious developers in the twentieth-century Third World. The latter suggests that whatever the source of the heavy commitment to human capital accumulation along the Rim, it has its roots way back in history.

A better picture than the evidence presented in Figure 4.3 can be obtained. After all, the East Asian countries may have been able to raise their commitment to educational investment more rapidly from the late nineteenth century onwards simply because they may have enjoyed more rapid income growth for other reasons. Table 4.9 controls for that fact and also expands the sample of countries (to 85 in the 1970s). However, the dependent variable is limited to the secondary school enrolment ratio, since that will be the focus in the next section. Equations (8) and (9) in the table include the full twentieth-century sample, including all countries as far back in time as the data make possible. Once again, considerable variety in country experience is documented—the Latin American countries always having invested less in secondary education, the East Asian countries always having invested more, and of the latter, South Korea, Japan, and Taiwan always having invested far more. Furthermore, these regional differences were more pronounced the further back in history, that is, the East Asian dummy has its highest coefficient in the pre-1950 period, falling somewhat in the 1950s, falling again in the 1960s, and falling still more in the 1970s. The same trend is apparent for South Korea, Japan, and Taiwan. Furthermore, Figure 4.4 shows that while Japan since 1930 has had higher secondary enrolment

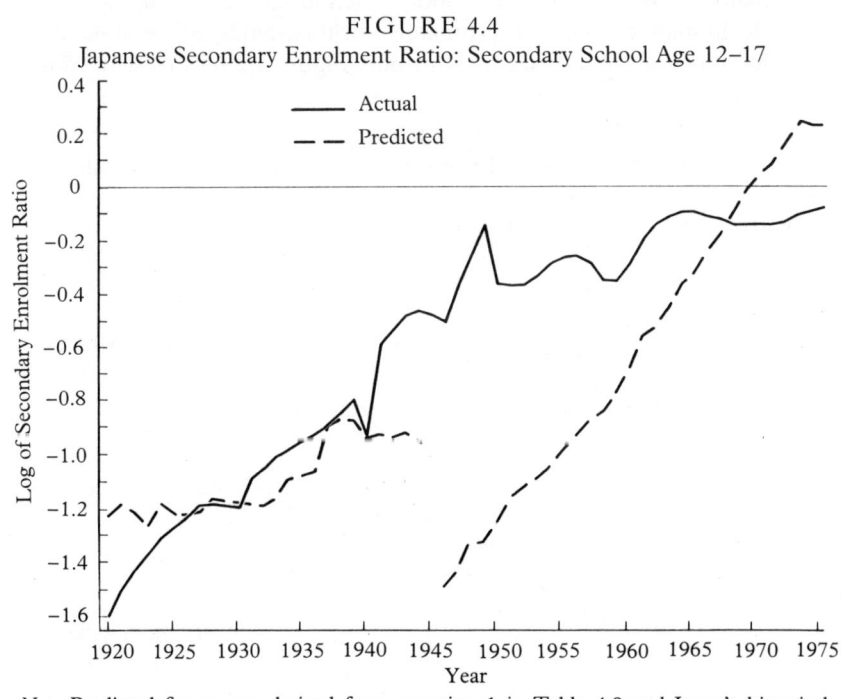

FIGURE 4.4
Japanese Secondary Enrolment Ratio: Secondary School Age 12–17

*Note*: Predicted figures are derived from equation 1 in Table 4.9 and Japan's historical GNP per capita estimates.

rates than would be predicted from equation (1) in Table 4.9, the biggest gap between actual and predicted ratios occurred in the 1940s and 1950s, a gap that disappeared by the 1970s. Thus, while East Asia has always invested more in secondary schooling compared with other nations at comparable stages of development, that edge has diminished over time. Whatever the forces which have produced the heavy commitment to educational investment along the Asia-Pacific Rim, they are rooted deeply in the past, but have weakened over time. The same has been true of Latin America. While Latin America has always under-invested in secondary education, the historical forces that account for that result appear to have weakened over time as the negative coefficient on the Latin American dummy declines systematically from the pre-1950 period to the 1970s.

Why does history show so much variance between countries in the commitment to schooling? Why is it that East Asia seems to have made the bigger commitment and Latin America the smaller commitment, patterns that clearly emerge in the residuals from Schultz's model (1987: 447)? Why have these regional differences diminished over time?

## Schooling, Inequality, Dependency Rates, and Culture

If the argument emerging is plausible, then a negative correlation between inequality and the commitment to education investment should be seen, that is, historical evidence should be found that rejects the Smithian trade-off even more soundly when investment is augmented to include human capital. Unfortunately, history tends to be unkind to simple mono-causal theories like this one. Figure 4.5 tells us why. While

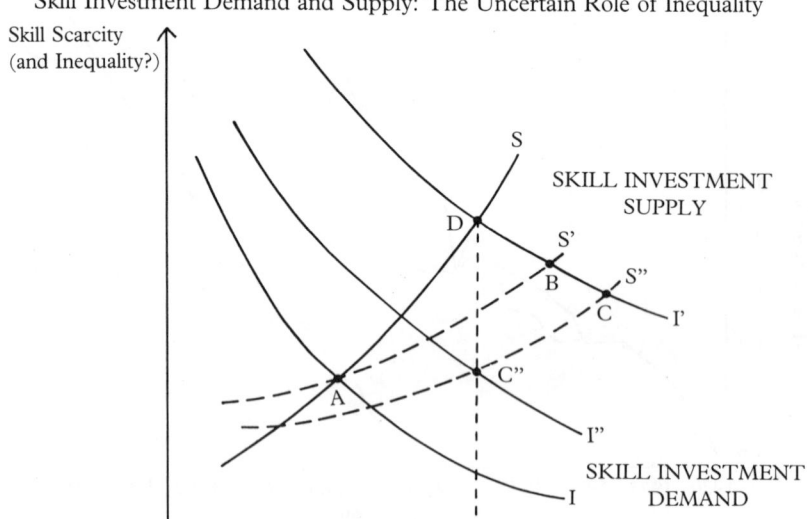

FIGURE 4.5
Skill Investment Demand and Supply: The Uncertain Role of Inequality

changes in income and earnings inequality are highly correlated—a proposition which has been confirmed at least by the economic histories of Britain and America (Williamson, 1991: Lect. 1)—levels of earnings and income inequality need not be. Thus, while both skill scarcity and earnings inequality can be put on the vertical axis, it must be remembered that different economies with the same earnings inequality may have different income inequality due to the initial distribution of land and other factors like those listed above for East Asia. Along the horizontal axis there is what might be called skill saving and investment, like school enrolment rates. Let some revolutionary industrial event create a boom in skill investment demand, written here as a shift to I'. Left solely to private sector responses, one economy with more inequality and lower incomes for the poor might exhibit an inelastic response to the skill scarcity starting at A and ending at D. Another more egalitarian economy is likely to find its poor better able to respond to skill scarcity ending up at B. This more egalitarian economy is also likely to set in motion political forces to increase the commitment to public education, perhaps shifting the skill investment supply function to the right, generating a new equilibrium at C. Were that all there was to the story, the expected historical correlation would be obtained: equality associated with high investment in skills and a rejection of the trade-off. However, there is no reason to expect that all countries will be faced with the same demand forces. Suppose the more egalitarian economy pursues a more unskilled labour-intensive growth regime so that the boom in skill investment demand is muted, say to I". The new equilibrium for the more egalitarian economy is now at C". What will history now reveal? No correlation at all between inequality and skill investment since D and C" imply the same commitment to human capital accumulation.

Can the influence of growth regime be unravelled from skill supply response when assessing the trade-off? Which has dominated in the past? Nineteenth-century Britain clearly represents the inequality-regime scenario which moves along the path from A to D (Williamson, 1985: Chap. 7), much like contemporary Brazil, while East Asia looks more like the egalitarian-regime scenario which moves along the path from A to C or C". But more evidence is needed and for this the writer turns once more to Schultz's 1987 paper.

Using a price dual of the production of school services and an aggregate demand for school services, Schultz estimated a reduced-form equation for school expenditures per child and enrolment rates, based on a large world cross-section of countries. While Schultz includes a wide range of explanatory variables, three account for the vast majority of the variance: income, or GNP per adult; the relative price of teachers, or teacher cost relative to GNP per adult; and relative cohort size, or share of population school aged. What is missing from the model, however, is an explicit statement of the market forces generating different investment demand for education, or of the income distributional forces influencing educational supply responses. This writer has been able to add the latter to his model, but, alas, not the former.

Table 4.10 presents the results for a somewhat smaller sample than Schultz's, since income distributional evidence is available for fewer countries (but the sample does include the following along the Rim: Japan, South Korea, Hong Kong, Malaysia, the Philippines, and Thailand). Only two dependent variables (all in logs) are reported in the table: the enrolment ratio and expenditure per school age child. Furthermore, the analysis is limited to secondary education where the variance across countries is greatest. The explanatory variables include four of Schultz's—income, the relative price of teachers, percentage urban, and the share of the population of secondary school age, plus the added distributional variable. To repeat, the expectations here are: given GNP per adult, the country with the more equal income distribution is likely to have the stronger schooling demands, and thus the higher enrolment rates. This writer is motivated by the suspicion that this is the reason Schultz finds positive residuals for East Asia where, as has been seen, incomes have been far more equally distributed in the post-war period. Any extension of Schultz's analysis to the Asia–Pacific Rim should pursue this connection between inequality and schooling. While all are aware of the impressive schooling commitment along the Asia–Pacific Rim, the reason needs to be pinpointed. Can it be explained in part by income inequality patterns, or is the explanation wholly cultural?

TABLE 4.10
Estimates of Secondary School Expenditure and Components, with the Price of Teachers Exogenous: 35 Countries, 1960–1980

|  | Dependent Variable in Logarithms | |
| --- | --- | --- |
| Explanatory Variable | Enrolment Ratio | Total Expenditure per Secondary School Age Child |
| GNP per adult in 1970 (log) | 0.313 | 1.330 |
|  | (2.379) | (10.931) |
| Relative price of teachers (log) | −0.457 | 0.629 |
|  | (5.272) | (7.839) |
| Proportion of population urban | 0.346 | 0.644 |
|  | (0.608) | (1.222) |
| Proportion of population of secondary school age | −1.860 | −6.261 |
|  | (0.809) | (2.944) |
| National household income distribution (bottom 40%/top 20%) | 0.796 | 0.956 |
|  | (1.234) | (1.603) |
| Intercept | −3.045 | −5.638 |
|  | (4.410) | (8.820) |
| $R^2$ | 0.831 | 0.956 |

*Notes*: Relative price of teachers is treated as exogenous and estimated with ordinary least squares. Absolute values of t-ratio are reported in parentheses beneath regression coefficients.

The estimated parameters on Schultz's variables more or less reproduce his results. First, educational commitment rises with income (GNP per adult), and the elasticity on total expenditures is high enough, about 1.3, so that the schooling investment share rises with development. Second, urbanization has no significant impact on educational commitment. Third, the relative price of teachers matters. Expenditures on teachers are by far the biggest component of direct schooling costs, and the relative price of teachers reflects how well the schooling sector is doing in keeping up with the growth in demand. When teacher prices rise, schooling costs per child rise, and the quantity of schooling may be choked off as a consequence. If the demand for schooling is price inelastic, total expenditures on schooling may, of course, rise, but enrolment rates—the critical proxy for human capital deepening—will decline. In short, where the relative price of teachers is high (that is, where schooling-capital goods are expensive), fewer children are educated (the enrolment rates are low). This is exactly what is found in Table 4.10. And the demand for schooling is price inelastic (about $-0.5$), so that expenditure rates are swollen where the relative price of teachers is high. This is an important finding which deserves emphasis. Given the quality of education, it is the quantity of schooling (enrolment rates) that matters to future economy-wide productivity growth, not the expenditures committed to schooling. In looking for evidence of human capital deepening, (quality-adjusted) enrolment rates and levels of educational attainment need to be examined, not the dollars committed to schooling. Furthermore, and to restate the obvious, the finding that the relative price of teachers matters suggests that current schooling performance will be conditioned by previous commitments to schooling. The heavy commitments to schooling along the Rim in the 1960s and 1970s would have been much harder to achieve without the heavy commitments to schooling in the 1940s and 1950s.

Fourth, there is strong evidence supporting the Coale and Hoover dependency rate effect. Cohort size effects are, of course, closely tied to the dependency rate effects discussed at length in the second section of this chapter. Any increase in the relative size of the school age population will put pressure on the educational system, the latter accommodating the pressure by spreading resources more thinly across the school population and lowering schooling quality. That is, and according to Table 4.10, a Malthusian glut of school age children tends to only weakly crowd children out of the schools (the t-statistic on the enrolment ratio is small), but it has a very powerful negative effect on expenditures per school age child. The elasticity here is very high, $-6.261$, and, given the weak impact on the number of children in school, it implies that the expenditure commitment per enrolled child declines as human capital widening diverts resources from human capital deepening. In short, the quality of education in the secondary schools must be very sensitive to the size of the school age cohort. One can only conclude that the high dependency rates in 1980 among the poorer countries to the south along the Rim has inhibited their human capital accumulation and contributed to their slower growth compared with those to the north where the Malthusian forces are far less pronounced. One must also conclude that the enormous projected decline in the dependency rates up to the year 2010 along the Rim (see Table 4.2) will have a big positive impact on growth potential if the quality of schooling matters as it is thought to do.

Finally, income distribution has the predicted effect: more egalitarian societies (where the bottom 40 per cent have high income shares relative to the top 20 per cent) make a greater commitment to education—they have higher enrolment rates and they commit more resources to each child enrolled. However, the t-statistics are lower than conventionally accepted. There is no evidence here which supports the Smithian trade-off, but there is also only weak evidence which confirms the contrary view. This writer suspects the reason for those small t-statistics on the income distribution variable in Table 4.10 can be found in Figure 4.5: societies with high inequality also pursue growth regimes that generate big booms in skill investment demand like that at I', while the opposite is true of more egalitarian societies. This assertion is not unambiguously proven and it seems to have high research priority.

What about the role of culture? In Oshima's words (1988: S108), 'besides asserting the importance of the rise of Protestant ethics in the emergence of capitalism in the West, ... Max Weber thought that Confucianism and Mahayana Buddhism of the East Asians were more favourable to the development of a capitalist society' than was Catholicism. Can evidence be found in support of this proposition in attitudes towards schooling in the 1970s? Schultz found some evidence to support that view in his secondary education regressions (Schultz, 1987: 449, Table 14), but his negative residuals for Latin America were far larger than his positive residuals for East Asia. For the smaller sample, Table 4.11 suggests much the same, although here a PACIFIC RIM dummy plays no significant role at all, while the LATIN AMERICA dummy is negative and highly significant. Since income inequality is so highly correlated with region—low in East Asia and high in Latin America—inequality and the regional dummies cannot be included in the same regression. What can be done, however, is to explore the determinants of the differences in secondary school enrolment rates in East Asia and Latin America by using the estimated equation in Table 4.10. What do the residuals look like? Did 'culture' matter?

Some startling answers are offered in Table 4.12 where two representative countries, South Korea and Brazil, are compared. The secondary school enrolment rate in the early 1970s was far higher in South Korea than Brazil, +0.271 higher. It turns out, however, that none of that difference can be explained by GNP per adult (which, after all, was lower in South Korea), by cheaper teachers (they were cheaper in Brazil), or by higher urbanization rates (the urban ratio was lower in South Korea). A modest share can be explained by the larger school age cohort glut in Brazil, but the demographic differences were too small to explain very much of the wide enrolment rate differential. Almost all of

## TABLE 4.11
### The Determinants of Secondary School Enrolment and Expenditure with Regional Dummies: 35 Countries, 1960–1980

|  | *Dependent Variable in Logarithms* | |
|---|---|---|
| *Explanatory Variable* | Enrolment Ratio | Total Expenditure per Secondary School Age Child |
| GNP per adult in 1970 (log) | 0.207 (1.782) | 1.289 (10.808) |
| Relative price of teachers (log) | −0.549 (6.098) | 0.530 (5.744) |
| Proportion of population urban | 0.874 (1.652) | 0.872 (1.609) |
| Proportion of population of secondary school age | −2.374 (1.226) | −6.821 (3.438) |
| LATIN AMERICA dummy | −0.589 (3.136) | −0.436 (2.265) |
| PACIFIC RIM dummy | −0.074 (0.383) | −0.232 (1.177) |
| Intercept | −1.998 (2.726) | −4.836 (6.437) |
| R-squared | 0.873 | 0.964 |

*Notes*: Price is treated as exogenous and estimated with ordinary least squares. Absolute values of t-ratio are reported in parentheses beneath regression coefficients.

the difference in secondary enrolment rates between South Korea and Brazil, therefore, can be attributed to two forces—far greater inequality in Brazil and a 'cultural bias' against education in Brazil. Culture does matter, but it has more to do with Latin America than East Asia, a finding at least partially consistent with that of Leff and Sato (1988) on

## TABLE 4.12
### Why Were Commitments to Secondary Education So Different in South Korea and Brazil in the Early 1970s?

| Variable | South Korea | Brazil | Difference (Δ) | $\hat{\beta}_{xj}\Delta X_j$ |
|---|---|---|---|---|
| Enrolment Ratio | 0.620 | 0.349 | +0.271 | |
| Dependent Variable ($X_j$): | | | | |
| Log GNP per adult | 6.800 | 6.904 | −0.104 | −0.033 |
| Log relative price teachers | 0.360 | −0.538 | +0.898 | −0.410 |
| Urban ratio | 0.494 | 0.582 | −0.088 | −0.030 |
| School age population ratio | 0.149 | 0.159 | −0.010 | +0.019 |
| Bottom 40%/Top 20% | 0.373 | 0.105 | +0.268 | +0.213 |
| 'Culture' = Residual | | | | +0.512 |

*Notes*: The dependent variable estimates underlie the regression reported in Table 4.10, and the $\hat{\beta}_{xj}$ are also reported in col. 1 of Table 4.10.

savings and investment behaviour in these two regions. In any case, it appears that education models like Schultz's are likely to be far more effective in understanding differences in human capital deepening along the Asia–Pacific Rim than between it and the rest of the world, such as Latin America.

## A Concluding Remark

There is certainly no shortage of research tasks still left undone regarding the contribution of human capital deepening to economic dynamism along the Asia–Pacific Rim. A systematic comparative assessment of the recent economic histories along the Rim will reveal a great deal about that contribution. Indeed, this symposium has already gone a long way towards launching that effort.

1. The next four paragraphs draw heavily from Lindert and Williamson (1985: 342–59).

2. Professor Sachs's paper has been liberally drawn on for the remainder of this paragraph (Sachs, 1987: 12–15).

3. Sachs overdraws the case in three ways. He ignores, first, the fact that Japan underwent important land reforms early in the Meiji Restoration; second, the fact that the poor in all three countries had relatively high levels of literacy and access to public health long before the late 1940s; and third, the fact that, compared with Latin America, land was also more equally distributed in much of South-East Asia (the Philippines being an obvious exception).

# 5
# Economic Growth Performance of Indonesia, the Philippines, and Thailand: The Human Resource Dimension

Ernesto M. Pernia

**Introduction**

THE shift in development thinking from physical capital to human capital in discussions about economic growth occurred in the early 1960s in the developed countries. This trend was soon picked up by those dealing with the problems of developing countries (Arndt, 1987). Despite some controversy regarding measurement of the contribution of human capital to economic growth, virtual unanimity has emerged about its crucial role.

Essentially, the literature on human capital concludes that investment in human resources raises labour productivity and entrepreneurial skills.[1] At the same time, the higher the general levels of education and health of a population, the faster is the advancement in production and consumption activities as scientific and technological innovations are more readily understood and accepted.[2] Given these premises, research has preoccupied itself with putting together better and more up-to-date empirical data in an attempt to figure out the relative contribution of human resource development to economic dynamism of countries.

Perhaps, in no other group of developing countries is the important role of human capital enhancement in economic growth better exemplified than in the Asian NIEs, namely Hong Kong, Singapore, Taiwan, and South Korea. Although these countries are probably better known for their outward-looking, market-oriented policies, it is no coincidence that they, too, have had solid and fast-deepening human capital bases to support their long-run economic growth. This is not to say that the availability of physical capital and technology and the adoption of appropriate macroeconomic policies have been less important. Indeed, the key seems to be the manner in which human and physical capital and technology are organized, and orchestrated with sound macroeconomic policies. Thus, while several factors must be involved, human capital represents one of the essential underpinnings for the growth process.

This chapter examines the economic growth performance of Indonesia, the Philippines, and Thailand during the post-war years, giving special attention to the underlying human resource factor. Although each country is undoubtedly *sui generis*, there is some basis for a comparative analysis. All three countries belong to the ASEAN group, their per capita incomes are roughly in the $500–1,000 range, and they are now reputed to be the next NIEs (not to mention Malaysia, of course); they adopted similar economic policies at one time or another in the past, and they have undertaken similar policy reforms more recently in the mid-1980s.

The chapter first takes an overview of macroeconomic performance from the 1950s to 1980s, highlighting the differences between the three countries. It then focuses on human resource developments in the three countries in order to better understand their links to economic growth. The penultimate section presents an econometric analysis using data on several Asian developing countries to lend further support to the central thesis of the chapter. The concluding section summarizes the main points of the chapter.

## Macroeconomic Performance

A common perception among development observers has been that the disparities in economic performance among Indonesia, the Philippines, and Thailand are of recent origin, say, in the late 1970s to early 1980s. Thailand and Indonesia are seen to have performed strongly or relatively well in recent years even as the Philippines was slipping into economic stagnation. This has resulted in Thailand surpassing, and Indonesia closing in on, the Philippines in terms of per capita income.

A review of early post-war data shows that the Philippines was way ahead of both Thailand and Indonesia in 1950. The Philippines then had a GNP per capita of $150 which was close to double that of Thailand (Table 5.1). During the 1950s it also exhibited the fastest GDP growth in real terms of 6.4 per cent per annum compared with Thailand's 5.7 per cent and Indonesia's 3.8 per cent (Table 5.2). In subsequent periods, however, the Philippines experienced a gradual slow-down in economic growth, culminating in negative growth rates during 1984–5. It thus appears that the 1950s were the most buoyant years of the post-war Philippine economy, with the stimulus largely coming from reconstruction activity.

The disparities in economic growth in favour of Thailand and Indonesia over the Philippines began in the 1960s and 1970s respectively. In the 1960s, Thailand's economic growth accelerated markedly to 7.8 per cent, while the Philippine economy slowed down to 5.4 per cent. Indonesia's growth rate also picked up to 4.6 per cent during this period. The 1970s saw the best economic performance for Indonesia, both

TABLE 5.1
GNP Per Capita (dollars, current prices)

|  | Indonesia | Philippines | Thailand |
| --- | --- | --- | --- |
| 1950 | – | 150 | 80 |
| 1967 | 50 | 210 | 170 |
| 1970 | 90 | 230 | 210 |
| 1980 | 480 | 680 | 670 |
| 1987[a] | 450 | 590 | 840 |
| 1988 | 430 | 630 | 1,000 |

Sources: World Bank, *World Tables 1988–9* and *Social Indicators of Development 1989*, except for 1950 data which are from Oshima (1987: 75).
[a]Estimate.

historically and in comparison with the Philippines and Thailand. Indonesia had a GDP growth of 8.0 per cent, while the Philippines had a 5.9 per cent and Thailand a 6.6 per cent growth rate.

During the first half of the 1980s, Thailand once again showed the best economic performance among the three countries, although its GDP growth rate this time was lower than in the 1960s and 1970s (see Table 5.2).

For the Philippine economy, the early 1980s was the worst chapter in its post-war history as it suffered a cumulative decline of about 11 per cent in 1984–5, triggered by a major political crisis. Indonesia, on the other hand, was badly hit by the world-wide recession which was exacerbated by a drastic fall in the price of oil, resulting in a halving of its average growth rate to about 4.0 per cent for the 1980–5 period. Thus, it was Thailand that weathered the hard times of the early 1980s relatively well. This was made possible by timely structural adjustments and policy reforms initiated in response to an unfavourable external economic environment (see Campbell, Chap. 3 in this volume).

TABLE 5.2
Real GDP Growth Rates (average percentage per annum)

|  | Indonesia | Philippines | Thailand |
| --- | --- | --- | --- |
| 1950–60 | 3.8 | 6.4 | 5.7 |
| 1960–73 | 4.6 | 5.4 | 7.8 |
| 1970–80 | 8.0 | 5.9 | 6.6 |
| 1980–5 | 4.1[a] | −0.3 | 5.7 |
| 1985–7 | 3.7[a] | 2.1 | 5.0 |
| 1988 | 5.7 | 6.7 | 11.0 |
| 1989 | 6.5 | 6.0 | 10.5 |

Sources: World Bank, *World Tables 1976* and *1988–9*; Asian Development Bank, *Asian Development Outlook 1989*, for 1988 figures.
[a]GNP growth rate.

After 1985, with an improving political climate complemented by some major economic reforms, the Philippines has shown some economic recovery. GDP growth averaged more than 2.0 per cent in 1985–7, was recorded at 6.7 per cent in 1988, and 6.0 per cent in 1989. The Indonesian economy also rebounded with accelerating growth rate of under 4.0 per cent in 1985–7, 5.7 per cent in 1988, and 6.5 per cent in 1989.[3] This economic rebound has been spurred by significant reforms in the trade, industrial, and financial sectors, which have resulted in, among other things, a lowering of Indonesia's dependence on oil exports. Meanwhile, Thailand, having had a head start on structural and economic reforms, has continued on a fast track with a record export-led economic growth of 11.0 per cent in 1988 and 10.5 per cent in 1989. As of 1988, per capita incomes were reported to be $1,000 in Thailand, $630 in the Philippines, and $430 in Indonesia.

Short-term forecasts suggest a probable deceleration of GDP growth rate for Thailand owing to infrastructural constraints and some slow-down in OECD countries. Indonesia is expected to maintain steady growth as the potential of restructuring and export diversification has not yet been exhausted. At the same time, the Philippine economy is likely to experience a more marked slow-down on account of its external

TABLE 5.3
Sectoral Distribution of GDP[a] (percentage shares)

|  | Agriculture | Industry | (Manufacturing)[b] | Services |
|---|---|---|---|---|
| Indonesia |  |  |  |  |
| 1958 | 51.0 | 17.0 | (12.0) | 32.0 |
| 1960 | 54.0 | 14.0 | (8.0) | 32.0 |
| 1970 | 45.0 | 19.0 | (10.3) | 36.0 |
| 1980 | 26.0 | 42.0 | (9.0) | 32.0 |
| 1987 | 26.0 | 33.0 | (14.0) | 41.0 |
| Philippines |  |  |  |  |
| 1948 | 39.4 | 20.3 | (12.3) | 40.3 |
| 1960 | 26.0 | 28.0 | (20.0) | 46.0 |
| 1970 | 28.3 | 25.3 | (16.0) | 46.4 |
| 1980 | 23.0 | 37.0 | (26.0) | 40.0 |
| 1987 | 24.0 | 33.0 | (25.0) | 43.0 |
| Thailand |  |  |  |  |
| 1950 | 57.8 | 16.0 | (10.5) | 26.2 |
| 1960 | 41.0 | 18.0 | (11.0) | 41.0 |
| 1970 | 28.3 | 25.3 | (16.0) | 46.4 |
| 1980 | 25.0 | 29.0 | (20.0) | 46.0 |
| 1987 | 16.0 | 35.0 | (24.0) | 49.0 |

Sources: World Bank, *World Tables 1971*, and *World Development Report* (various issues).
[a]In terms of purchaser values.
[b]Included in industry; in addition, industry comprises value added in mining, construction, electricity, water, and gas.

sector and fiscal deficits and given that domestic demand has weakened after its buoyancy in 1987–8 (Asian Development Bank, *Asian Development Outlook*, 1989).

Apart from differential macroeconomic performance, the corresponding pattern of agro-industrial transition in the three countries is also instructive. While the Philippines appeared to be the least agricultural (or most industrialized) in the early post-war years in terms of the relative shares of GDP and labour force accounted for by agriculture, the reductions in these shares over time were relatively negligible. In 1960, agriculture's share in total production in the Philippines was 26 per cent, declining to only 24 per cent by 1987 (Table 5.3). The corresponding decreases in agricultural product shares were far more dramatic in Indonesia (from 54 to 26 per cent) and in Thailand (from 41 to 16 per cent).

Similar intercountry differentials can be noted in the industrial (and manufacturing) shares of GDP in terms of their increases over time. As to sectoral distribution of labour force, the movement out of agriculture was also comparatively slow for the Philippines, with agriculture's share falling from 61 to 52 per cent over two full decades, 1960–80. In Indonesia and Thailand, the corresponding transitions (declines) were faster: 75–57 per cent and 84–71 per cent, respectively, over the same period (Table 5.4).

Statistical analysis indicates a significant positive relationship between agricultural growth and overall economic growth. The correlation coefficient between growth rates of the Philippines' agricultural output and real GDP was calculated to be 0.67 over 1950–85 and 0.78 over

TABLE 5.4
Sectoral Distribution of Labour Force (percentage shares)

|  | *Agriculture* | *Industry* | *Services* |
|---|---|---|---|
| Indonesia |  |  |  |
| 1960 | 75.0 | 8.0 | 17.0 |
| 1970 | 66.3 | – | – |
| 1980 | 57.0 | 13.0 | 30.0 |
| Philippines |  |  |  |
| 1950 | 66.0 | 8.0 | 26.0 |
| 1960 | 61.0 | 15.0 | 24.0 |
| 1970 | 59.0 | 18.0 | 23.0 |
| 1980 | 52.0 | 16.0 | 33.0 |
| Thailand |  |  |  |
| 1950 | 88.0 | 2.0 | 10.0 |
| 1960 | 84.0 | 4.0 | 12.0 |
| 1970 | 79.0 | 6.0 | 15.0 |
| 1980 | 71.0 | 10.0 | 19.0 |

*Source*: International Labour Office (1986).

1970–85 (Bautista, 1987). Moreover, regression analysis of 1983–4 data for 48 developing countries reveals that a 10 per cent increase in per capita agricultural output was associated with a 9–10 per cent rise in per capita GDP; in comparison a 10 per cent increase in per capita manufacturing output was associated with a mere 1.5–2.6 per cent rise in per capita GDP (Houck, 1986 as cited in Bautista, 1988: 12). These findings underscore the important role of agriculture in overall economic growth in developing countries with a large agricultural share in total production.

In summary, of the three countries, the Philippines had the highest per capita income in the early post-war years and was the most buoyant economy in the 1950s, but this comparative buoyancy was not to be sustained. As early as in the 1960s Thailand had already begun to outdo the Philippines. In the 1970s the Indonesian economy proved to be the fastest-growing, but in the 1980s the Thai economy stood out once again as the most steady, exhibiting singular performance in 1988 and 1989. Besides macroeconomic performance, the Philippines was the most industrialized (lowest share of agricultural output in GDP and lowest share of agricultural labour force in total labour force), to begin with, but its further agro-industrial transition in subsequent decades was the most sluggish.

What accounts for the differential economic performance among the three countries? Some have traced it back to historical factors— differences in initial conditions, so to speak. Oshima (1987), for example, has underscored the point about the concentration of land holdings and political power being much more pronounced during the pre-war years in the Philippines than in Thailand and Indonesia. Such concentration has been perceived as inimical to post-war long-run economic development (see also Williamson's Chap. 4 in this volume). Differences in cultural values and socio-political institutions have also been advanced as a major factor. Political stability in the NIEs, for example, has been regarded as a *sine qua non* (Gold, 1986; James, Naya, and Meier, 1989). This is probably also one reason why uninterrupted rapid growth occurred earlier in East Asia.

Many have also explained differential economic performance among countries on the basis of economic policies (James, Naya, and Meier, 1989). Although the three countries adopted similar policies in the post-war years, such as import-substitution industrialization, the Philippines appeared to have been stuck with inappropriate policies longer than Thailand or Indonesia. The Philippines pursued inefficient import-substitution industrialization over a long period when the more prudent approach, given the country's resource endowments and comparative advantage, would have been agricultural development first and then promotion of small-scale industries producing labour-intensive manufactures for export. Import substitution entailed the maintenance of unrealistic exchange rates, bias for capital-intensive technologies, and protection of inefficient industries at the expense of agriculture and small industries (Bautista, Power, and Associates, 1979).

Thailand appears to have paid greater attention to agricultural development and was quicker to adjust to changing external circumstances. For instance, the baht devaluation in 1984 has been seen as a timely trigger for its export drive. Indonesia's relative economic boom in the 1970s was fuelled largely by windfall gains from its oil wealth. After it was badly hit by the unfavourable price of oil in the early 1980s, it began to institute wide-ranging economic reforms in the trade, monetary, and financial sectors. The Philippines implemented structural reforms beginning with the new government in 1986 and these have been instrumental in the recovery process, but restructuring has been largely a stop-and-go process. It appears that in terms of swiftness in responding to changing parameters on the domestic front but more critically on the international front, Thailand acted first, followed by Indonesia, and then the Philippines. Compounding the Philippines' structural problems have been its external debt burden and political instability.

## The Human Resource Dimension

In the array of possible factors accounting for differential growth performance, one cannot overlook the human resource dimension. The Philippines began the post-war era with a clear edge in terms of human capital stock, which had been built up from earlier educational investment during the American colonial period. In 1948, adult literacy rate was already 60 per cent in the Philippines compared with 39 per cent in Indonesia in 1960; in Thailand adult literacy rate was 68 per cent in 1960 when it was 72 per cent in the Philippines (Table 5.5). As much as three-quarters of primary school age children were enrolled in the Philippines in 1950, compared with slightly over one-half in Thailand and 29 per cent in Indonesia in the same year. By the late 1960s, the Philippines had practically achieved universal primary education, while Thailand and Indonesia did not achieve universal primary education until about the late 1970s.

At the secondary level, school participation rate in 1950 was 22 per cent for the Philippines, 7 per cent for Thailand, and only 3 per cent for Indonesia. Over the period of three and one-half decades, secondary school participation rate tripled in the Philippines (to 68 per cent by 1986), while Thailand, starting from a lower base, quadrupled its secondary school attendance rate to 29 per cent in 1986. More remarkable still was the educational progress made by Indonesia where the enrolment rate in secondary schools surged more than thirteenfold—to 41 per cent by 1986. This educational stride has greatly helped in the growth and gradual modernization of the Indonesian economy (ILO/UNDP, 1988; Pernia and Wilson, 1989). The same can be said about Thailand's educational advancement relative to its economic development, although the relatively slow progress at the secondary education level now appears to be posing a constraint on the Thai economy's further industrialization (Sussangkarn, 1989).

## TABLE 5.5
### Adult Literacy Rates and Gross Enrolment Ratios (percentage)

|  | Indonesia | Philippines | Thailand |
| --- | --- | --- | --- |
| Adult literacy |  |  |  |
| 1948 | – | 60.0 | – |
| 1960 | 39.0 | 71.9 | 68.0 |
| 1970 | 57.0 | 82.6 | 79.0 |
| 1980 | 67.3 | 87.0 | 88.0 |
| Primary |  |  |  |
| 1950 | 29 | 74 | 52 |
| 1960 | 67 | 95 | 83 |
| 1970 | 75 | 114 | 81 |
| 1980 | 107 | 114 | 99 |
| 1986 | 118 | 106 | 99 |
| Secondary |  |  |  |
| 1950 | 3 | 22 | 7 |
| 1960 | 6 | 26 | 12 |
| 1970 | 15 | 50 | 18 |
| 1980 | 29 | 62 | 29 |
| 1986 | 41 | 68 | 29 |
| Tertiary |  |  |  |
| 1960 | 1 | 13 | 2 |
| 1977 | 2 | 24 | 5 |
| 1986 | 7 | 38 | 20 |

*Sources*: UNESCO (various years); World Bank, *World Development Report* (various years).

At the tertiary level, the Philippines was also far ahead of the other two countries in the early post-war years. About 13 per cent of college age youth were enrolled in tertiary schools in the Philippines in 1960, compared with 2 per cent in Thailand and 1 per cent in Indonesia. But Thailand made substantial progress in the subsequent two and one-half decades; Indonesia made some progress, too, but to a lesser extent. By 1986, Indonesia had a tertiary enrolment rate of only 7 per cent, while Thailand had 20 per cent and the Philippines 38 per cent.

The relationship between education (or mean years of schooling of the labour force) and economic growth is depicted by the scatter plot in Figure 5.1. The plot suggests that, in general, lower levels of schooling up to, say, junior secondary education are more critical than higher levels, or that higher levels of education have a lesser role in the lower to middle stages of economic growth. This is consistent with results of studies on rates of returns to education. The outliers in the scatter diagram are the Philippines and Sri Lanka. Both countries experienced lower GNP per capita growth rates than could be predicted from their educational levels. In the case of the Philippines, the policy environment,

FIGURE 5.1
Schooling and Economic Performance

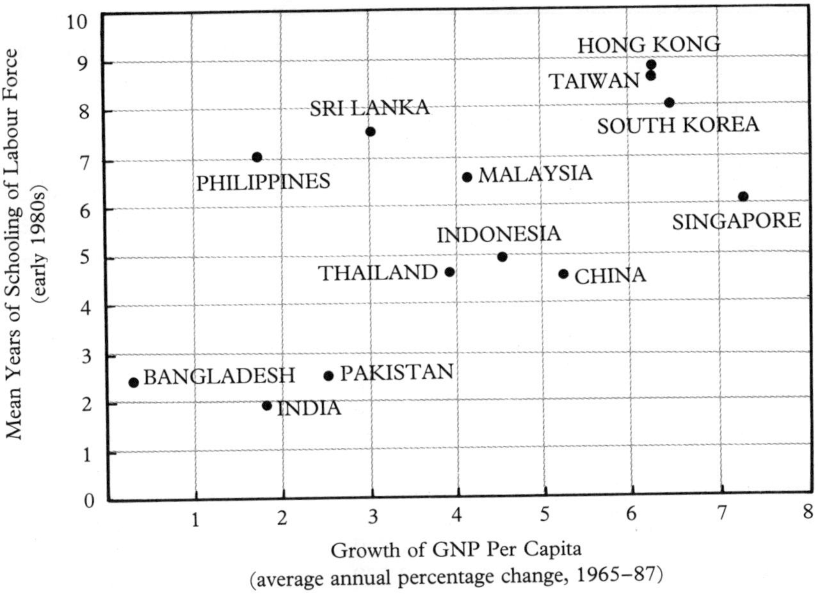

[Scatter plot: Mean Years of Schooling of Labour Force (early 1980s) on y-axis (0–10) vs. Growth of GNP Per Capita (average annual percentage change, 1965–87) on x-axis (1–8). Data points: Hong Kong (~6, 9); Taiwan (~6, 8.8); South Korea (~6.5, 8); Sri Lanka (~3.5, 7.7); Philippines (~2, 7); Malaysia (~4.5, 7); Singapore (~7.5, 6); Indonesia (~4.5, 5.2); Thailand (~3.5, 5); China (~5, 5); Bangladesh (~1.3, 2.5); Pakistan (~2.5, 2.5); India (~2, 2).]

*Sources*: World Bank, *World Development Report 1989*; Psacharopoulos and Arriagada (1986, Table 1).

as already mentioned, may have been less favourable to economic growth than in the other South-East Asian countries. This is in addition to its relatively rapid population growth and the fact that it suffered a serious economic recession in the first half of the 1980s triggered by its worst post-war political crisis. In the case of Sri Lanka, its welfare-oriented policies probably curtailed the economy's capacity to grow more rapidly despite its highly educated labour force. Of course, excessive dependence on primary commodities along with the deterioration in terms of trade also rendered the Sri Lankan economy vulnerable.

In the area of health, Thailand and the Philippines were at similar initial levels, with Indonesia lagging behind. Life expectancy at birth was 51 years in 1960 for both Thailand and the Philippines, and 41 years for Indonesia (Table 5.6). By 1987, life expectancy at birth had risen to 60 years for Indonesia and to about 64 years for the Philippines and Thailand. In terms of the infant mortality indicator (IMR), Thailand had the lowest (103) in 1960 and this fell sharply over time to 39 by 1987.

The comparatively advantageous health trend in Thailand was supported by favourable nutrition (Tsuya et al. in Chap. 12 of this volume) as reflected in relatively high daily calorie supply per capita of 2,101 in 1965 which rose further to 2,331 in 1986 (Table 5.6). Moreover, although health personnel availability was highest for the Philippines in the early post-war years, such an advantage was rapidly dissipated through the overseas 'brain drain'. By the mid-1980s, Thailand had the

## TABLE 5.6
Health, Nutrition, and Fertility Indicators

|  | Indonesia | Philippines | Thailand |
|---|---|---|---|
| Life expectancy at birth (years) | | | |
| 1960 | 41.0 | 51.0 | 51.0 |
| 1970 | 47.4 | 57.2 | 58.4 |
| 1980 | 52.7 | 61.0 | 62.2 |
| 1987 | 60.0 | 63.9 | 64.4 |
| Infant mortality rate (per 1,000 live births) | | | |
| 1960 | 150.0 | 106.0 | 103.0 |
| 1970 | 120.6 | 66.4 | 72.6 |
| 1980 | 105.0 | 52.2 | 51.2 |
| 1987 | 71.0 | 45.0 | 39.0 |
| Daily calorie supply per capita | | | |
| 1965 | 1,800 | 1,924 | 2,101 |
| 1986 | 2,579 | 2,372 | 2,331 |
| Population–physician ratio | | | |
| 1960 | 41,000 | 1,600 | 7,800 |
| 1970 | 26,510 | 9,100 | 8,430 |
| 1984 | 9,460 | 6,700 | 6,290 |
| Population–nursing person ratio | | | |
| 1960 | 4,510 | 1,590 | 4,900 |
| 1974 | 8,630 | – | 4,330 |
| 1984 | 1,260 | 2,740 | 930 |
| Total fertility rate (children per woman) | | | |
| 1965 | 5.5 | 6.8 | 6.3 |
| 1987 | 3.5 | 3.9 | 2.8 |

*Sources*: World Bank, *World Tables*, various issues, and *World Development Report*, various issues; Asian Development Bank (1989), *Key Indicators of Developing Member Countries of ADB*.

most favourable health personnel supply in terms of physicians and nursing persons. And although the Philippines still had a lower population–physician ratio than Indonesia in 1984, Indonesia had become better off in terms of the availability of nursing persons.[4]

The correlation between health (male life expectancy at birth) and economic growth is plotted in Figure 5.2. The relationship implies that basic health care that extends life through at least the working years is critical to a country's economic performance. As suggested in Figure 5.2,

## FIGURE 5.2
### Health and Economic Performance

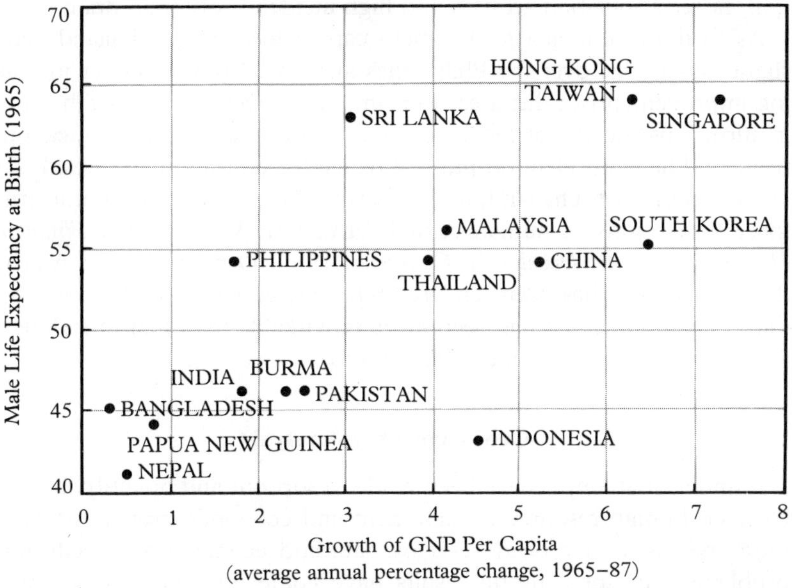

```
Male Life Expectancy at Birth (1965)

70 |
    |                              HONG KONG
65 |                               TAIWAN •       •
    |            • SRI LANKA                   SINGAPORE
60 |
    |                      • MALAYSIA   SOUTH KOREA
55 |          • PHILIPPINES    •       • CHINA       •
    |                      THAILAND
50 |
    |       INDIA  BURMA
45 |     • BANGLADESH • • PAKISTAN
    |     •
    |      PAPUA NEW GUINEA        • INDONESIA
40 |    • NEPAL
    +---+---+---+---+---+---+---+---+
    0   1   2   3   4   5   6   7   8
         Growth of GNP Per Capita
         (average annual percentage change, 1965–87)
```

*Sources*: World Bank, *World Development Report 1989*; People's Republic of China (1987); United Nations (1988c).

countries that had a high health status to begin with (in 1965) were the ones that grew fastest in the subsequent period (1965–87).

A critical area in which the Philippines has done particularly poorly is fertility reduction (see Table 5.6). While over the period 1965–87 Thailand had succeeded in bringing down its total fertility rate (TFR) from 6.3 (children per woman) to 2.8, and Indonesia from 5.5 to 3.5, TFR in the Philippines has remained relatively high at 3.9 as of 1987. This differential in fertility transition is no doubt partly attributable to differences in relative strengths of family planning programmes in the three countries. It would seem that the slower fertility transition in the Philippines has contributed to a gradual erosion of its lead in human capital formation. With slower economic growth and faster population growth, it has been difficult to expand educational and health services, let alone improve their quality which appears to have also fallen behind those in Thailand and Indonesia.

In sum, the Philippines began post-war economic development with a substantial educational advantage over Thailand and Indonesia. While in terms of primary education, the three countries are now roughly on par, the Philippines has maintained the edge in secondary and tertiary education.[5] None the less, the pace of improvement at the secondary and tertiary levels has been faster in both Thailand and Indonesia—especially secondary schooling for Indonesia and tertiary education for Thailand. This implies that there has been a steady erosion of the educational advantage the Philippines had in the initial post-war years. This erosion has been brought about by relatively low rates of investment in education, faster population growth, and high incidence of 'brain drain'.

As to the health aspect of human capital formation, Thailand had a slight initial edge over the Philippines and has also done better in making improvements in this area over time. Improvements in health status, in turn, have no doubt facilitated the advancement on the educational front in Thailand. Data on public finance for education and health services suggest that Thailand, too, has exerted the most effort in nurturing these dimensions of human capital formation (World Bank, *Financing Health Services in Developing Countries*, 1987; Oshima, 1987). And no doubt this effort has been rendered relatively easier with Thailand's fertility transition, which has been more remarkable than that in Indonesia and even more so than in the Philippines.

## Cross-country Analysis

A number of attempts have been made to sort out and quantify the links between human resource development and economic growth. Many of these exercises have been beset by data and econometric specification problems, but some useful results have come out in any case. As in many other studies on different topics, the findings may be considered more indicative than conclusive. What is encouraging, none the less, is that the results have consistently borne out the hypothesized strong positive relationship between human resource variables, on the one hand, and economic growth, on the other. Moreover, these results lend quantitative, if partial, support to the descriptive analysis of cross-country data presented above.

In a cross-section analysis of 83 developing countries, Hicks (1980) found that the 12 fastest-growing countries during the period 1960–77 also had literacy and life expectancy levels well above average at the beginning of the period. This association using simple statistical tools was substantiated by multiple regression analysis, wherein growth of per capita GDP was postulated to be influenced by the initial level of human resource development (literacy and life expectancy), the rate of investment, and the growth rate of imports. The results were found to be statistically significant. For instance, an increase in life expectancy of 10 years would result in a 0.7 percentage point additional growth rate in per capita GDP; likewise, a 20 percentage point rise in literacy rates would foster a 0.5 percentage point increase in economic growth.

A more rigorous analysis was undertaken by Wheeler (1980) using simultaneous equations techniques to identify cause and effect relationships and interactions over time. His results confirm those of Hicks's. As would be expected, changes in per capita income affect changes in literacy and life expectancy across countries. However, it is also apparent that human resource development (levels of literacy, life expectancy, and nutrition) has a significant impact on growth in per capita incomes.

Moreover, Wheeler finds a positive link between level of investment and export performance, on the one hand, and human resource development indicators, on the other. This suggests that the economic performance of countries in terms of exports and investment may not have been possible without the requisite human capital formation.

In the present study, the analysis by Hicks is extended to more recent data on Asian developing countries.[6] The basic regression equation applied to pooled cross-section and time series data (1970–80 and 1980–5) is of the following form:

$$GRYPC_{t,t+n} = a + b_1 YPC_t + b_2 HRD_t + b_3 GRIMP_{t,t+n} \qquad (1)$$

where
$GRYPC_{t,t+n}$ = average annual growth rate of real per capita GDP over time,
$YPC_t$ = level of real per capita GDP at time t,[7]
$HRD_t$ = human resource development indicator at t,
$GRIMP_{t,t+n}$ = average annual growth rate of imports over time,
and $a$ is a constant and $b_i$ are coefficients to be estimated.

$HRD_t$ is alternately indicated by literacy rate ($LIT_t$) and life expectancy at birth ($EXP_t$). Both are specified as stock variables to conform with the assumption that the initial condition of $HRD$ will have a bearing on economic growth performance over the subsequent interval.

Using $LIT_t$ as an indicator for $HRD_t$ gives the following results (subscripts omitted for convenience):

$$GRYPC = 1.351 - 0.001\ YPC + 0.082\ LIT + 0.661\ GRIMP \qquad (2)$$
$$(1.079) \qquad (2.235) \qquad (4.105)$$
$$\bar{R}^2 = 0.404 \qquad F = 7.107 \qquad n = 28$$

Equation (2) shows that both literacy (at the beginning of the period) and growth rate of imports (over the period) are significant variables in explaining variations in growth rate of output, but initial level of per capita income is not.[8] Among the explanatory variables included in the equation, growth rate of imports (*GRIMP*) appears to be the dominant one, implying the dependence of economic growth on imports of capital goods, intermediate products, and raw materials.

Alternatively, having $EXP_t$ (life expectancy at the start of the period) in the equation as a measure of $HRD_t$ yields the following estimates:

$$GRYPC = -6.531 - 0.001\ YPC + 0.228\ EXP + 0.656\ GRIMP \qquad (3)$$
$$(1.337) \qquad (1.907) \qquad (3.984)$$
$$\bar{R}^2 = 0.375 \qquad F = 6.399 \qquad n = 28$$

The results in equation (3) are quite similar to those in equation (2), although the overall explanatory power is less and the t-values are somewhat lower for the significant coefficients. The significant explanatory variables are life expectancy (*EXP*—here specified also to denote health 'stock' at the start of the period) and growth rate of imports (*GRIMP*).

Because the above regression estimates are probably affected by simultaneity bias, a two-stage procedure was introduced whereby $HRD_t$ was first related to $YPC_t$ using a quadratic specification. Hence,

$$\hat{HRD} = a + b_1\ YPC + b_2\ YPC^2 \qquad (4)$$

where a hat (^) denotes expected value and the deviation from this expected value is defined as $DHRD = HRD - \hat{HRD}$. Substituting $DHRD$ for $HRD$ (that is, $DLIT$ for $LIT$ and $DEXP$ for $EXP$) in equation (1) produces the following results, which are parallel to equations (2) and (3):

$$GRYPC = 5.851 - 0.000\ YPC + 0.097\ DLIT + 0.648\ GRIMP \qquad (5)$$
$$\phantom{GRYPC = 5.851\ }(0.090) \phantom{YPC + }(2.473) \phantom{DLIT + }(4.107)$$
$$\bar{R}^2 = 0.426 \qquad F = 7.690 \qquad n = 28$$

$$GRYPC = 5.902 - 0.000\ YPC + 0.338\ DEXP + 0.637\ GRIMP \qquad (6)$$
$$\phantom{GRYPC = 5.902\ }(0.088) \phantom{YPC + }(2.417) \phantom{DEXP + }(4.013)$$
$$\bar{R}^2 = 0.421 \qquad F = 7.547 \qquad n = 28$$

The results are virtually the same as in the previous formulations although the performance of the life expectancy variable is appreciably better in equation (6). Thus, equations (5) and (6) may be considered as serving to reinforce confidence in the hypothesized role of $HRD$ in economic growth.

The results thus far show that both indicators of $HRD$—literacy and life expectancy—are important factors in economic growth, with life expectancy apparently somewhat more so than literacy. However, the two variables are known to be highly correlated. Some studies suggest that the causality runs from literacy (or education) to life expectancy or health in general (Cochrane, O'Hara, and Leslie, 1980). Higher literacy tends to improve understanding of the need for hygiene, proper nutrition, and health care. This relationship between literacy and life expectancy is borne out by the following estimated equation:

$$EXP = 39.936 + 0.225\ LIT + 0.010\ YPC - 0.0002\ YPC^2 \qquad (7)$$
$$\phantom{EXP = 39.936\ }(6.547) \phantom{LIT + }(3.745) \phantom{YPC - }(2.681)$$
$$\bar{R}^2 = 0.848 \qquad F = 51.261 \qquad n = 28$$

Equation (7) shows literacy to be a highly significant variable in explaining variations in life expectancy. Accordingly, the estimated effect of life expectancy itself on income growth may be overstated to the extent that literacy is the more basic factor. Equation (7) also shows the non-linear relationship between income and life expectancy. Overall, the equation explains about 85 per cent of the total variance in life expectancies.

The above results are generally consistent with the earlier findings of Hicks (1980). Although both sets of results have to be interpreted with judicious caution considering the known pitfalls of cross-section analysis, they are supportive of the thesis that human resource variables (for example, education and health) make an important contribution to economic growth.

## Conclusion

The purpose of this chapter has been to highlight the role of the human resource factor in economic growth by taking a comparative view of the experiences of Indonesia, the Philippines, and Thailand. Although there has clearly been a host of factors involved in the growth process, such as historical background, cultural values, socio-political institutions, political stability, and economic policies and their timing, human capital formation has been one of the key underlying forces. The results of a comparative analysis of the historical experiences of the three countries are supported by a cross-sectional examination of data on several Asian countries.

Much of the economic head start the Philippines had in the early post-war years can be attributed to its considerable educational advantage over Thailand and Indonesia. This economic lead, however, steadily diminished over the next three decades as the Philippines' educational edge also narrowed. This implies that the Philippines did not adequately maintain and replenish its educational stock while Thailand and Indonesia were making steady progress in human capital formation (including investment in education, health, and fertility reduction). Contributing to the virtually continuous slow-down in growth of the Philippine economy were inappropriate economic policies which appeared to have been carried on longer than in Thailand and Indonesia. With economic mismanagement followed by a serious political crisis, this slow-down culminated in the economic retrogression of the early 1980s.

An inference that can be made from this comparative analysis is that without a relatively strong human capital base, the performance of the Philippine economy could in all likelihood have been worse. This human capital base sustained the Philippine economy and allowed for reasonable growth despite inappropriate policies and economic mismanagement. Notwithstanding its secular erosion (in terms of both quantity and quality), human capital remains a major plus factor for the Philippines. It will be this factor that will continue to help sustain the Philippine economy in the future—but first its depletion must be reversed—along with better economic management and infrastructure, among other requisites, of course. Given demographic momentum, the provision of basic education and health services needs to be expanded, and their quality improved. At the same time, an effective population programme must be in place and sustained. Moreover, vocational/technical education needs to be re-attuned to changing requirements, and stricter quality control exercised at the other higher education levels. Further, the 'brain drain' should be stemmed by improving the incentive system and providing an attractive professional environment.

Both Indonesia and Thailand appreciate the importance of human capital build-up in their drive towards industrialization and development. Policy prescriptions for the Philippines may be similarly applicable to Indonesia, except for the fact that its population programme (as also in Thailand) has been working well.[9] Its current Five-Year Development Plan (Repelita V) places great emphasis on human resource development. The aim is to raise compulsory basic education up to junior secondary schooling as well as to improve the quality in the education system in general. Meanwhile, because of a more dramatic fertility transition, Thailand can now focus its attention and resources on expanding and improving the quality of secondary and tertiary education. Finally, in the long-term view, all three countries would profit from greater attention paid to science and technology.

1. The expressions 'investment in human resources' and 'investment in human capital' are often used interchangeably. Such investment is usually in terms of spending for education and training, health, nutrition, and fertility (birth) regulation as fewer children often mean better-quality children. In turn, investment in human capital leads to human resource development.

2. Other benefits supposed to emanate from investment in human capital include, *inter alia*, positive income distribution effects and greater participation of people in the development process (Blaug, 1985).

3. The growth rate of 5.7 per cent in 1988 is the updated figure given by President Suharto in his recent Independence Day speech. This figure is well above previous official and private estimates (*The Asian Wall Street Journal*, 17 August 1989: 1, 8).

4. For more detailed analyses of health care trends in Indonesia, the Philippines, and Thailand, see Wirakartakusumah (1990), Herrin (1990), and Institute of Population Studies (1989), respectively.

5. The mean educational attainment of the labour force in 1980 was 7.0 years, 4.9 years, and 4.6 years for the Philippines, Indonesia, and Thailand, respectively (Psacharopoulos and Arriagada, 1986).

6. Countries included on the basis of complete data are: Bangladesh, Burma, India, Nepal, Pakistan, Sri Lanka, Indonesia, Malaysia, the Philippines, Thailand, Hong Kong, South Korea, Singapore, and Taiwan. Data sources include World Bank, *World Tables* and *World Development Report*, various issues; Asian Development Bank, *Key Indicators of Developing Member Countries of ADB*, various issues; and UNESCO, *Statistical Yearbook*, various issues.

7. This variable is included on the RHS of the equation principally as a control variable. Although this procedure appears econometrically awkward as the control variable is a part of the dependent variable on the LHS, it is often adopted in analysis of cross-country data for practical reasons.

8. Substituting investment ratio ($INVR_t$) for $YPC_t$ results in a lower t-value for $INVR_t$ as well as for $LIT_t$ and $GRIMP_{t,t+n}$.

9. Indonesia and Thailand (to a larger extent) have been benefiting from an effective population policy, and they now have a clear edge over the Philippines in this regard (for example, lower dependency burden).

# 6
# The Feminization of Labour in the Asia–Pacific Rim Countries: From Contributing to Economic Dynamism to Bearing the Brunt of Structural Adjustments

Lin Lean Lim

## Introduction

THIS chapter examines changing labour force participation of women in the growth and adjustment processes in the ASEAN and East Asian countries in the 1960s–1980s. It analyses the extent to which and the conditions under which the female gender has influenced and been influenced by the economic performance in these countries. While female participation made available not only elastic labour supply at low cost, but also the unique human resource qualities that fuelled the economic spurt of these countries in the 1960s and 1970s, women appear to have borne the brunt of the economic reversal and structural adjustments of the 1980s. Stabilization and adjustment processes in the Asia–Pacific Rim countries have been sex-asymmetric in so far as they have exposed women more than men to greater economic and social vulnerability, even as there has been increasing feminization of labour.

## Trends in Female Labour Force Participation

The feminization of labour can be examined in relation to three economic phases: the boom years of the 1960s and 1970s, the world recession and debt crisis of the early 1980s, and the structural adjustments since.

### Economic Growth and Female Labour Force Participation

In the 1960s and early 1970s, not only did the Asia–Pacific Rim countries grow faster than most other regions of the world (Table 6.1), they also experienced rapid mobilization of female labour (Table 6.2). A striking feature was that the sectors that were the engines of growth in

TABLE 6.1
GNP Per Capita and GDP Growth Rates in
Selected Asia–Pacific Countries

| Country | GNP Per Capita (dollars) 1980 | 1987 | GDP Annual Growth Rates (per cent) 1960–70 | 1970–80 | 1980–7 |
|---|---|---|---|---|---|
| Japan | 9,890 | 15,760 | 10.9 | 5.0 | 3.8 |
| Singapore | 4,430 | 7,940 | 8.8 | 8.5 | 5.4 |
| Hong Kong | 4,240 | 8,070 | 10.0 | 9.3 | 5.8 |
| South Korea | 1,520 | 2,690 | 8.6 | 9.5 | 8.6 |
| Malaysia | 1,620 | 1,810 | 6.5 | 7.8 | 4.5 |
| Philippines | 690 | 590 | 5.1 | 6.3 | −0.5 |
| Thailand | 670 | 850 | 8.4 | 7.2 | 5.6 |
| Indonesia | 430 | 450 | 3.9 | 7.6 | 3.6 |
| Pakistan | 300 | 350 | 6.7 | 4.7 | 6.6 |
| China | 290 | 290 | 5.2 | 5.8 | 10.4 |
| Sri Lanka | 270 | 400 | 4.6 | 4.1 | 4.6 |
| India | 240 | 300 | 3.4 | 3.6 | 4.6 |
| Nepal | 140 | 160 | 2.5 | 2.5 | 4.7 |

*Source*: World Bank, *World Development Report*, various issues.

these countries were also the sectors that tended to have female-dominated work-forces, with female employment growing faster than that of males. Although there may be problems of reliability and comparability (since the data were compiled from a number of different original sources), the magnitudes are sufficiently large in most countries listed in Table 6.2 to confirm the growing importance of female workers. The increase in female labour force participation was mainly in the non-agricultural sector; the agricultural sector accounted for a declining share of both female and male total employment. Since the most dynamic economic sectors were manufacturing, services, and trade, changes in female participation in these sectors, as shown in Table 6.3, can be examined.

The countries with the fastest rates of economic growth were also the ones with the most rapid industrial growth, and it was in export-oriented, labour-intensive, light, foreign investment-dominated manufacturing that female employment expanded fastest. The female proportion of productive low-wage workers rose significantly in those countries that set up large export processing zones—Singapore, Hong Kong, South Korea, Taiwan, Malaysia, the Philippines, and Thailand (Anker and Hein, 1986: 95). The share of women in manufacturing employment in the industrial export zones was known to exceed 80 per cent (Robert, 1983). 'For wages barely covering the basic cost of living, and often in very hard working conditions, both in the export processing zones and outside, women have contributed a great deal to the industrial

## TABLE 6.2
Labour Force Participation Rates: Male and Female[a]

| Country | Year | Male Participation Rate | Female Participation Rate |
|---|---|---|---|
| Hong Kong | 1966 | 86.1 | 41.0 |
|  | 1971 | 84.7 | 42.8 |
|  | 1980 | 80.9 | 45.7 |
|  | 1987 | 80.2 | 48.6 |
| Indonesia | 1961 | 88.9 | 31.2 |
|  | 1971 | 80.4 | 35.6 |
|  | 1980 | 80.4 | 37.1 |
|  | 1986 | 82.8 | 50.9 |
| Japan | 1970 | 84.3 | 50.9 |
|  | 1980 | 82.0 | 46.7 |
|  | 1985 | 80.3 | 47.7 |
|  | 1987 | 77.3 | 48.6 |
| South Korea | 1966 | 72.6 | 31.4 |
|  | 1970 | 74.8 | 38.4 |
|  | 1987 | 68.1 | 44.9 |
| Peninsular Malaysia | 1957 | 87.3 | 29.9 |
|  | 1970 | 78.9 | 35.6 |
|  | 1980 | 81.8 | 39.3 |
| Philippines | 1960 | 82.4 | 27.2 |
|  | 1970 | 78.3 | 34.1 |
|  | 1987 | 66.7 | 20.0 |
| Singapore | 1957 | 87.7 | 21.6 |
|  | 1970 | 82.3 | 43.8 |
|  | 1980 | 80.9 | 44.3 |
|  | 1987 | 78.6 | 47.0 |
| Thailand | 1960 | 89.5 | 81.4 |
|  | 1970 | 87.6 | 73.2 |
|  | 1980 | 83.3 | 62.3 |
|  | 1984 | 87.8 | 76.3 |

Source: International Labour Office, *Yearbook of Labour Statistics*, Table 1 (various years).
[a]Participation rates for those aged 15 and above.

take-off in their countries' (United Nations, 1986: 79). Rapid industrialization pushing these countries to newly industrialized and newly industrializing status was as much female-led as export-led.

Table 6.3 shows that in the 1970s, female employment in manufacturing grew substantially faster than that of males in all the countries of the region, except the Philippines. (In Indonesia and South Korea, female employment grew at about the same rate as male employment.) Various studies have also confirmed that female participation in the manufacturing sector was higher in East and South-East Asia than anywhere else in the world, with the exception of the planned economies of

TABLE 6.3
Relative Growth of Male and Female Employment in Manufacturing, Trade, and Services, 1970s

| Country | Manufacturing Average Annual Employment Growth Male | Manufacturing Average Annual Employment Growth Female | Manufacturing Ratio of Female–Male Employment Growth | Manufacturing Percentage of Female Employment in Nonagriculture | Trade Average Annual Employment Growth Male | Trade Average Annual Employment Growth Female | Trade Ratio of Female–Male Employment Growth | Trade Percentage of Female Employment in Nonagriculture | Services Average Annual Employment Growth Male | Services Average Annual Employment Growth Female | Services Ratio of Female–Male Employment Growth | Services Percentage of Female Employment in Nonagriculture |
|---|---|---|---|---|---|---|---|---|---|---|---|---|
| South Korea (1970–80) | 6.8 | 6.9 | 1.0 | 40.8 | 4.3 | 5.7 | 1.3 | 34.4 | 1.3 | 1.6 | 1.2 | 16.6 |
| Taiwan (1970–80) | 9.9 | 16.2 | 1.6 | 48.1 | 4.6 | 13.6 | 2.9 | 19.0 | 1.5 | 8.2 | 5.3 | 27.3 |
| Hong Kong (1971–81) | 3.2 | 4.4 | 1.4 | 54.1 | 9.3 | 13.7 | 1.5 | 22.4 | 1.1 | 2.6 | 2.4 | 18.1 |
| Singapore (1970–80) | 6.1 | 11.4 | 1.9 | 40.8 | 2.0 | 10.0 | 5.0 | 21.4 | 3.4 | 5.7 | 1.7 | 30.9 |
| Malaysia (1970–9) | 11.0 | 16.6 | 1.5 | 35.4 | 7.3 | 14.5 | 2.0 | 20.6 | 3.3 | 9.6 | 2.9 | 39.1 |
| Thailand (1970–6) | 10.9 | 16.0 | 1.5 | 35.2 | 8.3 | 7.0 | 0.8 | 33.4 | 2.5 | 5.1 | 2.0 | 27.1 |
| Philippines (1970–80) | 2.8 | −2.8 | — | 21.2 | 2.4 | 0.9 | 0.4 | 19.3 | 4.6 | 3.7 | 0.8 | 57.4 |
| Indonesia (1971–1980) | 5.5 | 5.3 | 1.0 | 24.1 | 4.1 | 5.8 | 1.4 | 41.1 | 6.4 | 8.7 | 1.4 | 32.2 |

*Source:* Jones (1984: 45).

Eastern Europe (Jones, 1984: 42–3; Khoo, 1987: 30; United Nations, 1986: 70, 1989a: 129).

What is significant, however, is not that rapid economic growth based on dynamic export-oriented industrialization led to large increases in female participation, but rather how female participation contributed to the successful industrialization and growth efforts (Lin Lean Lim, 1988b). It was the ready and seemingly endless supply of young, malleable, and cheap female labour that was (and still is) the cornerstone of industrial success and the magnet for foreign investments. For the type of industrialization pursued by these countries, female labour represented:

1. The necessary supply that could not be met by male workers only, especially where male participation rates were already high in the early stages of development.
2. Not only the necessary supply but also supply at relatively low and stable wages. Labour-intensive production intended for world markets has to depend on low-wage labour to be profitable and competitive, especially as labour tends to represent the single largest cost of production (Anker and Hein, 1985: 46). Young women, particularly in the Asian NIEs, have been socially and economically oppressed for so long that they have low 'aspiration wages' and low 'efficiency wages' (Standing, 1989: 5). Their wages were lower than those of equivalent male workers although their productivity tended to be as high (Lele, 1986: 209).
3. Supply of the type particularly attractive to multinationals: 'It is their very vulnerability that is one of their main attractions on the labour market' (United Nations, 1986: 21). The 'feminine' qualities that employers have been able to exploit have been their greater docility relative to men, manual dexterity, deference to command, willingness to subject themselves to the rigid discipline and tedious monotony of the assembly line, and very important, their lower likelihood to join or form unions (Eisold, 1984; L. Y. C. Lim, 1978; Lin Lean Lim, 1984).

The feminization of labour in the manufacturing sector was, however, confined to a limited range of industries—electronics, textiles, garments, food processing, footwear, chemicals, and rubber and plastic products—and within these industries, women have been bunched into menial 'dead end' jobs that 'are ill-paid and repetitive and that have poor career prospects' (United Nations, 1989a: 130). They have been severely underrepresented in the high-level managerial and supervisory positions but overrepresented in the lower end of the occupational hierarchy; and even within the group of production workers, men have dominated as production supervisors and foremen, while women have been the production operators.

Other than manufacturing, the services sector was also a major source of GDP growth. Here again, the growth of female employment tended to outstrip that of males in all the countries (Table 6.3), except the Philippines. Table 6.4 also shows that for both 1970 and 1980, the

TABLE 6.4

Structure of the Economically Active Population by Major Occupational Groups and Sex, 1970 and 1980

|  | Professional, Technical, and Related | | Administrative and Managerial | | Clerical Workers | | Sales Workers | | Service Workers | | Agricultural Workers | | Production and Related | |
|---|---|---|---|---|---|---|---|---|---|---|---|---|---|---|
|  | 1970 | 1980 | 1970 | 1980 | 1970 | 1980 | 1970 | 1980 | 1970 | 1980 | 1970 | 1980 | 1970 | 1980 |
| Indonesia | | | | | | | | | | | | | | |
| Male | 2.3 | 3.8 | 4.2 | 0.1 | 4.2 | 4.5 | 8.8 | 10.0 | 3.3 | 3.1 | 61.0 | 57.1 | 12.3 | 21.0 |
| Female | 2.1 | 3.3 | 2.0 | – | 1.1 | 1.4 | 13.5 | 18.5 | 4.9 | 6.7 | 58.6 | 53.3 | 11.3 | 15.0 |
| Japan | | | | | | | | | | | | | | |
| Male | 7.2 | 7.7 | 6.1 | 7.0 | 12.2 | 12.1 | 11.1 | 14.3 | 5.8 | 6.1 | 14.7 | 9.2 | 43.0 | 43.6 |
| Female | 6.2 | 10.1 | 0.5 | 0.9 | 18.8 | 23.6 | 12.6 | 15.0 | 11.6 | 12.0 | 26.1 | 13.6 | 24.3 | 24.7 |
| South Korea | | | | | | | | | | | | | | |
| Male | 3.8 | 5.2 | 1.4 | 1.6 | 7.5 | 10.0 | 10.4 | 12.3 | 4.5 | 5.4 | 45.8 | 32.5 | 25.4 | 32.9 |
| Female | 2.1 | 3.5 | 0.1 | – | 2.8 | 8.6 | 9.6 | 11.6 | 10.8 | 9.9 | 59.7 | 46.9 | 19.7 | 19.9 |

| | | | | | | | | | | | | | |
|---|---|---|---|---|---|---|---|---|---|---|---|---|---|
| Peninsular Malaysia | | | | | | | | | | | | | |
| Male | 4.5 | 5.2 | 1.0 | 1.4 | 5.3 | 6.7 | 10.3 | 10.5 | 8.1 | 8.8 | 43.9 | 30.8 | 23.9 | 29.8 |
| Female | 5.2 | 3.3 | 0.1 | 0.3 | 3.9 | 10.9 | 4.9 | 7.1 | 8.6 | 8.6 | 50.0 | 38.0 | 11.0 | 18.6 |
| Philippines | | | | | | | | | | | | | |
| Male | 3.5 | 3.5 | 1.2 | 1.4 | 2.9 | 3.6 | 4.2 | 5.7 | 3.7 | 4.9 | 61.6 | 59.5 | 18.6 | 21.2 |
| Female | 10.5 | 9.6 | 1.1 | 0.5 | 4.0 | 4.7 | 16.3[a] | – | 12.5 | – | 33.9 | 38.6 | 20.3 | 24.7 |
| Singapore | | | | | | | | | | | | | |
| Male | 6.8 | 8.1 | 2.2 | 6.3 | 11.7 | 8.4 | 17.9 | 15.7 | 10.6 | 9.2 | 4.4 | 3.1 | 41.8 | 40.4 |
| Female | 14.2 | 9.8 | 0.4 | 0.2 | 16.9 | 16.8 | 10.7 | 12.3 | 23.3 | 13.6 | 3.2 | 1.2 | 30.8 | 30.5 |
| Thailand | | | | | | | | | | | | | |
| Male | 1.9 | 2.5 | 2.6 | 2.0 | 1.5 | 1.9 | 4.2 | 6.4 | 2.8 | 2.5 | 75.6 | 67.9 | 11.2 | 16.8 |
| Female | 1.5 | 2.5 | 0.2 | 0.5 | 0.8 | 1.6 | 5.9 | 10.5 | 2.9 | 2.8 | 83.5 | 74.2 | 5.0 | 7.9 |

*Sources:* International Labour Office (1985: 104); ESCAP (1987: 186).
[a] No breakdown available for sales and service workers.

proportion of women concentrated in the services sector was greater than that of men in all the countries (International Labour Office, 1985: 105).

Within the services sector, women have been disproportionately concentrated in community services (health, education, and social welfare). Their participation as nurses, teachers, and social workers—or what have been segregated as the 'feminized' occupations—has often been explained as an extension of women's nurturing role into the public domain. It has also been observed that there was a tendency for such occupations to become more sex segregated in the process of economic development (L. Y. C. Lim, 1986: 16). Especially as the public sector in these countries expanded in the 1970s, so women's employment grew not only in these community service occupations but also in clerical work. The female share of public sector employment expanded significantly in the 1970s (Standing, 1989: 26–7). In Malaysia, for example, the government sector was the second most important sector for the growth of female employment (after manufacturing) (Lin Lean Lim, 1989a: 101). But in the public sector too, women were at the lower end of the job scale; they were far more important as nurses and paramedics than as doctors, they were clerical workers rather than managers, telephone operators rather than telephone engineers, and so on.

That women have been the mainstay of the worst paid jobs in the services sector is normally due to their concentration in domestic service and the retail trade (Joekes, 1987: 109). During this period of rapid growth, however, domestic service in the Asia–Pacific Rim countries was not as important a source of female employment in internal labour markets as in Latin America. In Singapore, South Korea, and Taiwan, domestic service declined rapidly in importance as a major occupation for local women. As alternative employment opportunities opened up in the industrial sector and as wage levels improved, female participation in paid domestic service fell. But the role of local women in domestic service has been substituted by international female migrants from the less developed countries such as the Philippines, Thailand, and Indonesia. Foreign domestic maids in Singapore, Hong Kong, and Malaysia have had some effects on 'releasing' local women for other types of occupational mobility.

From Table 6.3, it would also appear that, except in Thailand and the Philippines, women's involvement in trading expanded much faster than that of men in the 1970s (although, of course, part of this increase could have been due to shifts to forms of employment that were reflected in the data). Women in the ASEAN countries have traditionally featured prominently in petty trading, brokering, shopkeeping, and other small-scale enterprises; their contribution was in 'lubricating' the budding commercial market economy especially in the early stages of development. While they traditionally operated on an independent basis as entrepreneurs, own-account traders or unpaid family workers, with urbanization and modernization, more women in the trade sector moved into the employee category working in sales positions in the large department stores and shopping complexes in the region's main cities.

*The World Recessions and Female Unemployment*

The first oil shock and the recession of 1974–5 did not hit the ASEAN and East Asian countries as seriously as they did other developing countries or as compared to the global slow-down of the early 1980s. But the available evidence does suggest that in both world recessions, women in the ASEAN and East Asian countries bore the brunt of labour lay-offs in that they were more vulnerable than men in terms of being more likely to lose their jobs. Although in several parts of the developing world there was a higher increase in the number of men unemployed (United Nations, 1989a: 55), this could have been due partly to the fact that the employed population is predominantly male. A better indicator is the unemployment rate by sex (Table 6.5), which is determined by the sectors affected by the recession and the proportion of women in them.

Women in these countries were seriously affected not only because of their concentration in those sectors most sensitive to international demand conditions, but also because they were mainly in direct production jobs which fluctuated more closely with the actual level of the firm's

TABLE 6.5
Unemployment Rates by Sex, 1975, 1980–1987 (percentage)

|  | 1975 | 1980 | 1981 | 1982 | 1983 | 1984 | 1985 | 1986 | 1987 |
|---|---|---|---|---|---|---|---|---|---|
| Hong Kong | 9.1 | 3.8 | 3.6 | 3.6 | 4.5 | 3.9 | 3.2 | 2.8 | 1.7 |
| Male | 9.2 | 3.9 | 3.8 | 4.0 | 5.0 | 4.2 | 3.5 | 3.0 | 1.7 |
| Female | 9.0 | 3.4 | 3.1 | 3.1 | 3.5 | 3.4 | 2.6 | 2.5 | 1.8 |
| Japan | 1.9 | 2.0 | 2.2 | 2.4 | 2.6 | 2.7 | 2.6 | 2.8 | 2.8 |
| Male | 2.0 | 2.0 | 2.3 | 2.4 | 2.7 | 2.7 | 2.6 | 2.7 | 2.8 |
| Female | 1.7 | 2.0 | 2.1 | 2.3 | 2.6 | 2.8 | 2.7 | 2.8 | 2.8 |
| South Korea | 4.1 | 5.2 | 4.5 | 4.4 | 4.1 | 3.8 | 4.0 | 3.8 | 3.1 |
| Male | 5.0 | 6.2 | 5.7 | 5.5 | 5.2 | 4.8 | 5.0 | 4.9 | 3.9 |
| Female | 2.6 | 3.5 | 2.4 | 2.5 | 2.2 | 2.2 | 2.4 | 2.1 | 1.8 |
| Philippines | 3.9 | 4.8 | 5.4 | 5.5 | 4.9 | 7.0 | 6.1 | 6.4 | 9.1 |
| Male | 3.6 | 3.2 | 3.5 | 3.6 | 3.7 | 5.2 | 4.8 | 4.9 | 8.1 |
| Female | 4.5 | 7.5 | 8.6 | 6.7 | 6.7 | 10.0 | 8.2 | 8.9 | 10.9 |
| Singapore | 4.5 | 3.0 | 2.9 | 2.6 | 3.2 | 2.7 | 4.1 | 6.5 | 4.7 |
| Male | – | 2.9 | 2.8 | 2.4 | 3.2 | 2.6 | 4.2 | 7.0 | 5.1 |
| Female | – | 3.4 | 3.4 | 2.9 | 3.2 | 2.8 | 4.1 | 5.5 | 4.0 |
| Thailand | 0.4 | 0.8 | 1.3 | 2.8 | 2.9 | 2.9 | 2.6 | – | – |
| Male | – | 1.0 | 1.5 | 2.4 | 2.6 | 2.5 | 2.3 | – | – |
| Female | – | 0.7 | 1.1 | 3.1 | 3.3 | 3.4 | 2.9 | – | – |

*Source*: International Labour Office, *Yearbook of Labour Statistics* (various years).

operations than other types of jobs (such as design, supervision, or maintenance). Women in the new international division of labour were more vulnerable because the branch establishments of their multinational employers were expected to rapidly adjust their production levels in response to highly interdependent global requirements; there tended to be sudden redundancies, just as there could also be rapid or 'forced' increases of overtime (Eisold, 1984).

Women were also more likely than men to lose their jobs because of the prevailing concept of men as the breadwinners and women as the secondary workers who are therefore dispensable in tight employment situations. The age factor also worked more against women than men; there is considerable evidence to show that employers were much more likely to retrench 'older' women above 25 years of age as a cost reduction strategy as they tended to have accumulated seniority and to be earning higher wages. On the other hand, young women under 25 faced particularly serious problems of finding employment (Table 6.6). Data for Taiwan reinforce the point that in times of economic reversal it is the women who were worse hit by retrenchments. In the 1974–5 recession, women's employment fell by 14 per cent compared to 8 per cent among men. The export industries in Taiwan which were also the most 'feminized' (leather goods, toys, electricals and electronics, plastics, and clothing) were the most badly affected by the recession. In most other industries too, even where women were not particularly important in the industrial labour force, job loss was felt disproportionately among them. It was an across-the-board bias against female workers when jobs suddenly became scarcer (Joekes, 1987: 96–7).

In Malaysia too, annual data from the Ministry of Labour showed that more than half the total number retrenched between 1983 and 1985 were from manufacturing, with the largest proportion from electronics, followed by textiles—the two most feminized industries. Contrary to the dictum 'first in, last out' multinational firms retrenched older women who were earning higher wages (Ariffin, 1985). There was also a huge cut-back of clerks, another clearly feminized work category. In fact, there was a larger number of unemployed clerks from both the private and public sectors than even production workers (Lin Lean Lim, 1989b: 71–2).

Detailed studies in Malaysia show that in almost all cases, the impact of the loss of employment income was severe 'as these women's income can no longer be lightly dismissed as secondary' (Young and Salih, 1986: 45). The dependence of rural families of young female factory workers on their income from manufacturing employment both for necessities and extras had grown because of the regularity of income from factory work as compared to agricultural income. Retrenchment meant that these girls could no longer help out with family finances. But where older women were laid off work, their loss of jobs meant serious cut-backs in expenditures, particularly on food and education for their children. Older women also had to wait up to a year to secure another job and not at the same pay since they had to start at the bottom of the

## TABLE 6.6
### Unemployment Rates by Sex and Age-group

|  | \_ | Early 1980s | \_ | \_ | \_ | Mid-1980s | \_ | \_ |
|---|---|---|---|---|---|---|---|---|
|  | *Total* | *< 20* | *20–24* | *> 24* | *Total* | *< 20* | *20–24* | *> 24* |
| **Hong Kong** |  | 1982 |  |  |  | 1984 |  |  |
| Total | 4.3 | 12.1 | 5.6 | 3.0 | 3.6 | 13.3 | 5.7 | 2.4 |
| Male | 4.3 | 13.3 | 6.0 | 3.2 | 3.8 | 11.8 | 6.4 | 2.8 |
| Female | 4.1 | 10.8 | 5.2 | 2.6 | 3.3 | 14.8 | 4.7 | 1.4 |
| **Indonesia** |  | 1982 |  |  |  |  |  |  |
| Total | 3.0 | 8.5 | 8.4 | 1.0 |  |  |  |  |
| Male | 2.7 | 8.0 | 8.2 | 0.8 |  |  |  |  |
| Female | 3.6 | 9.1 | 8.8 | 1.3 |  |  |  |  |
| **South Korea** |  | 1982 |  |  |  | 1985 |  |  |
| Total | 4.4 | 12.5 | 8.9 | 2.9 | 4.0 | 10.9 | 9.7 | 2.8 |
| Male | 5.5 | 14.5 | 11.9 | 4.1 | 5.0 | 12.2 | 13.8 | 3.9 |
| Female | 2.5 | 10.5 | 6.0 | 0.7 | 2.4 | 9.9 | 6.3 | 0.8 |
| **Philippines** |  | 1983 |  |  |  | 1984 |  |  |
| Total | 4.1 | 7.2 | 9.8 | 2.5 | 6.1 | 9.7 | 14.5 | 3.9 |
| Male | 3.4 | 5.6 | 8.3 | 2.1 | 4.8 | 8.1 | 11.2 | 3.0 |
| Female | 5.3 | 9.6 | 12.2 | 3.1 | 8.2 | 12.2 | 19.9 | 5.4 |
| **Singapore** |  | 1982 |  |  |  | 1985 |  |  |
| Total | 2.6 | 6.3 | 3.7 | 1.6 | 4.1 | 7.9 | 6.6 | 3.1 |
| Male | 2.4 | 5.3 | 4.1 | 1.7 | 4.2 | 4.9 | 7.2 | 3.4 |
| Female | 2.9 | 7.3 | 3.2 | 1.5 | 4.1 | 11.0 | 5.9 | 2.3 |
| **Thailand** |  | 1982 |  |  |  | 1984 |  |  |
| Total | 3.6 | 4.3 | 5.2 | 2.9 | 2.3 | 2.6 | 4.9 | 1.5 |
| Male | 2.7 | 4.0 | 4.3 | 1.9 | 2.0 | 3.0 | 4.6 | 1.0 |
| Female | 4.6 | 4.6 | 6.1 | 4.1 | 2.6 | 2.2 | 5.3 | 2.1 |

*Source*: United Nations (1989a: 164).

salary scale again. There was also evidence of a process of 'informalization', with shifts from wage employment to self-employment in the informal sector (Young and Salih, 1986: 8). There may also have been a slide into prostitution among those faced with serious financial pressures.

Table 6.5 shows open unemployment to be higher among women than men in the Philippines (where female unemployment rates were more than double the rates for males in several years of the series), Singapore (from 1978 to 1984), and Thailand (since 1982). In Japan and Hong Kong, differentials between male and female unemployment rates were minimal, and it was only in South Korea that female unemployment rates have been consistently and significantly lower than those of males.

The effects of the recession cannot, however, be traced only through changes in unemployment. The data on open unemployment do not indicate the differences between rural and urban locations. More important, both the 'discouraged' and 'added' worker effects tend to be stronger among women than among men. Women, especially those with no previous work experience, are much less likely to actively seek work when the job market is tight. In Malaysia, for instance, data from the 1980 Population Census showed the passive unemployment rate as more than twice as high among females than males, although the active unemployment rate was higher for males.

On the other hand, women may have been forced to join the labour market to maintain household living standards, especially when the menfolk become unemployed. The additional worker effect reflects the response of some women to the recession. In terms of entering the labour force, then, the typical woman is not a victim, passively suffering the effects of the economic shocks, but a major agent, adapting her behaviour to the new economic environment and providing what the United Nations Children's Fund has called the 'invisible adjustment' (UNICEF, 1987). Their entry into the labour force may not, however, show in terms of higher formal activity rates, since most may have been forced into the informal sector.

*Structural Adjustments and the Feminization of Labour*

The structural adjustment policy packages that the Asia–Pacific Rim countries adopted in the 1980s in the wake of the world recession and the international debt crisis led to a renewed surge of feminization of labour, but on increasingly disadvantaged terms for women. Though differing in combination and strength from one country to another, the main components of these policy packages have been supply-side policies, demand-side policies, and policies to improve international competitiveness. Supply-side economics has introduced a reliance on economic liberalism and market mechanisms involving labour market deregulation and flexible job structures. Outward-looking strategies for open economies have emphasized cost competitiveness and the production of tradables, with a bias against non-tradables, such as food production. Demand-reducing policies, in particular traditional stabilization policies, have focused on efforts to reduce public budget deficits through a 'rolling back' of the state and privatization through hiving off of public enterprises to the private sector.

In the structural adjustment milieu, new job creation, although well below previous levels, has tended to favour women more than men (Table 6.7). Especially in the non-agricultural sector, the average annual rate of employment growth in the 1980s has been definitely faster for females than for males (Table 6.8). In Thailand, the absolute drop in female (and to a lesser extent, male) employment in the early 1980s, shown in Table 6.7, was mainly in the agricultural sector since Table 6.8 shows female non-agricultural employment expanding faster than for

## TABLE 6.7
### Growth Indices of Male and Female Total Employment (1980 = 100)

|  | 1981 | 1982 | 1983 | 1984 | 1985 | 1986 | 1987 |
|---|---|---|---|---|---|---|---|
| **Hong Kong** | | | | | | | |
| Male | 105.9 | 105.4 | 105.8 | 108.2 | 110.6 | 114.1 | 116.8 |
| Female | 111.1 | 111.6 | 113.4 | 118.9 | 119.3 | 123.3 | 126.4 |
| **Indonesia**[a] | | | | | | | |
| Male | – | 110.7 | – | – | 119.3 | 123.7 | – |
| Female | – | 118.4 | – | – | 128.5 | 152.6 | – |
| **Japan** | | | | | | | |
| Male | 106.7 | 101.3 | 102.2 | 102.7 | 103.2 | 103.9 | 104.6 |
| Female | 100.9 | 102.7 | 105.6 | 106.5 | 107.6 | 108.6 | 110.2 |
| **South Korea** | | | | | | | |
| Male | 102.6 | 103.5 | 104.2 | 105.1 | 108.0 | 110.4 | 115.1 |
| Female | 102.4 | 107.7 | 108.9 | 106.0 | 111.7 | 118.1 | 126.6 |
| **Malaysia** | | | | | | | |
| Male | 105.7 | 108.8 | 112.1 | 115.0 | 116.2 | 117.8 | – |
| Female | 106.1 | 111.4 | 117.8 | 118.9 | 121.9 | 125.3 | – |
| **Philippines** | | | | | | | |
| Male | 103.7 | 105.7 | 107.9 | 110.9 | 115.1 | 119.0 | 119.6 |
| Female | 104.1 | 113.7 | 122.0 | 116.6 | 124.7 | 127.5 | 124.3 |
| **Singapore** | | | | | | | |
| Male | 103.3 | 105.7 | 108.3 | 107.6 | 105.7 | 103.4 | 106.4 |
| Female | 105.6 | 108.6 | 111.0 | 114.1 | 112.3 | 115.0 | 121.3 |
| **Thailand** | | | | | | | |
| Male | 95.4 | 99.0 | 107.2 | 111.4 | 113.6 | 117.4 | – |
| Female | 89.7 | 92.6 | 95.6 | 99.4 | 100.9 | 105.9 | – |

Source: Computed from International Labour Office, *Yearbook of Labour Statistics*, Table 3A (various years).
[a] 1979 = 100.

males. The growing feminization of the labour force is, however, probably inadequately represented in these two tables in so far as they would not have captured entry of women into the informal sector nor their increasing participation in overseas contract labour markets which were previously male-dominated.

In addition to worsening employment and income distribution which affect women and men, stabilization policies have had sectoral implications that are particularly relevant for women, although some of these implications do not normally appear in aggregate employment statistics, which are concerned mainly with the formal sector. First, the tertiary sector has expanded, compared with other sectors, mainly in response to supply pressures. Growth has been particularly significant in the informal activities of the tertiary sector. Secondly, export-oriented industries have also grown.... Thirdly, there has been a contraction in the productive sectors, mainly in agriculture and industry producing for the national market; and a contraction or at least a significant change in the infrastructural sector. Fourthly, the public sector has tended to contract (United Nations, 1986: 132).

Table 6.9 confirms that, except for a few exceptional cases, in line with these sectoral shifts, there has been a definite labour feminization trend in community and personal services and especially in trade and tourism and, to a lesser extent, in manufacturing in the 1980s.

In terms of the employment of females in the manufacturing sector, it was only in Hong Kong that there was an absolute decline, but this was because the manufacturing sector as a whole has contracted since 1980. Changes in female employment in the manufacturing sector (and also the services sector) in Indonesia are not adequately reflected in Table 6.9 because of the significance of the informal, as compared to the formal, sector. The Indonesian experience has been relatively unusual in that growth of the manufacturing sector has been mainly in unregistered enterprises with no formal structures in terms of organization and operation (Evers, 1989). A case-study on Indonesia revealed a shift in the female labour force away from the categories of own-account workers and employees and towards the category of unpaid family workers (the share of the female work-force in unpaid family employment rose from 30 per cent in 1980 to 43 per cent in 1985, after having declined between 1971 and 1980) (United Nations, 1989a: 54).

But in Malaysia and Singapore, the increase in manufacturing

TABLE 6.8
Female Share of Paid Employment in Non-agricultural Employment and Average Annual Growth Rate of Female and Male Non-agricultural Employment, 1980–1986/7.

| Country | Female Share of Non-agricultural Employment 1980 | 1986/7 | Average Annual Growth Rate of Non-agricultural Employment 1980–1986/7 (per cent) Female | Male |
|---|---|---|---|---|
| Hong Kong | 34.8 | 36.8 | 3.4 | 2.2 |
| Indonesia | 39.1 | 38.8 | 7.5 | 7.7 |
| Japan | 37.5 | 39.2 | 1.9 | 0.9 |
| South Korea | 35.3 | 39.2 | 6.7 | 4.2 |
| Malaysia | 29.9 | 33.9 | 6.0 | 3.3 |
| Philippines | 46.1 | 46.8 | 4.2 | 3.8 |
| Singapore | 37.3 | 40.4 | 2.6 | 0.7 |
| Thailand | 42.0 | 43.5 | 6.3 | 5.2 |

*Source*: Computed from International Labour Office, *Yearbook of Labour Statistics*, Table 4 (various years).

## TABLE 6.9
Female Share of Employment and New Job Creation in Manufacturing, Services, and Trade, Restaurants and Hotels, 1980–1986/7

| Country | Female Share of Employment 1980 | Female Share of Employment 1986/7 | Female Share of New Job Creation 1980–86/7 |
|---|---|---|---|
| *Manufacturing* | | | |
| Hong Kong   | 50.2 | 45.6 | −32.2 |
| Indonesia   | 45.4 | 44.8 | 41.7 |
| Japan       | 38.6 | 39.2 | 55.2 |
| South Korea | 39.1 | 42.0 | 47.8 |
| Malaysia    | 38.3 | 45.1 | 95.1 |
| Philippines | 47.1 | 46.1 | 37.8 |
| Singapore   | 46.0 | 47.2 | 106.3 |
| Thailand    | 42.1 | 45.2 | 56.1 |
| *Services* | | | |
| Hong Kong   | 40.5 | 46.6 | 69.8 |
| Indonesia   | 31.0 | 26.3 | 14.4 |
| Japan       | 46.0 | 46.8 | 52.0 |
| South Korea | 34.3 | 41.3 | 56.8 |
| Malaysia    | 39.1 | 38.1 | 33.5 |
| Philippines | 56.3 | 56.2 | 55.9 |
| Singapore   | 34.0 | 42.9 | 101.2 |
| Thailand    | 46.1 | 49.3 | 56.8 |
| *Trade, Restaurants and Hotels* | | | |
| Hong Kong   | 28.8 | 36.1 | 54.2 |
| Indonesia   | 48.0 | 51.7 | 60.0 |
| Japan       | 46.2 | 47.8 | 65.3 |
| South Korea | 48.6 | 52.1 | 61.7 |
| Malaysia    | 27.9 | 37.3 | 56.5 |
| Philippines | 66.5 | 65.2 | 52.9 |
| Singapore   | 35.2 | 38.4 | 60.8 |
| Thailand    | 54.0 | 53.6 | 52.7 |

*Source*: Computed from International Labour Office, *Yearbook of Labour Statistics*, Table 3B (various years).

employment in the 1980s went almost exclusively to women. In Singapore, there was in fact an actual substitution of female labour for male labour which fell in absolute numbers, not only in manufacturing but also in services. In Japan and Thailand too, more than half of total jobs created in manufacturing went to women workers.

In the service sector, although the data are unfortunately not available, it is most likely that the personal services component has been expanding while public sector employment in community services has shrunk or at best remained stagnant, in line with the government austerity drives in countries such as Malaysia, Indonesia, and Thailand. In Malaysia, for example, unpublished information provided by the Ministry of Labour show that retrenchments from the community and social services sector of the government totalled almost 20,000 between 1983 and 1988. This might account for the relatively lower share of females in employment creation in the services sector in Malaysia, as compared to the other countries in Table 6.9. On the other hand, personal service jobs, such as catering, cleaning, the care of children and the aged, and domestic work increased for women because they require little extra-domestic specialization or training.

Table 6.9 also shows that in commerce, tourism and entertainment, more than half of all new jobs in all the countries went to women. The types of trading activities in these countries allow women relative flexibility of work organization and hours and, like other parts of the informal sector, have been relatively open to women 'creating' their own opportunities especially in times of economic need. A striking example is the spread of the night markets/bazaars or *pasar malam* in the ASEAN countries in the second half of the 1980s—markets in which women predominate and which were initially a response to the situation or safety valve for the jobless and underemployed during the recession but which now appear to have assumed a vibrancy and integral role in the economic structures of these countries. Recognition of the employment and income-generating potentials of these 'mobile' markets has led many governments to allocate sites, provide infrastructure, and simplify licensing procedures.

Tourism has been among the fastest-growing sectors in the 1980s, in part due to aggressive promotion by governments as a strategy for earning sorely needed foreign exchange. Tourism has been and is likely to continue to be an important absorber of female labour, in part because productivity growth in this sector tends to be slower than in industry (thereby requiring more workers). There has been striking growth of female employment not only in hotels and restaurants but also in a number of hospitality services which, apart from prostitution, include barber-shop girls, massage girls, hostesses in Japanese lounges or *karaoke* bars, escort services, etc. The demand for female labour in tourism has been based not only on their relative cheapness. The tourist industry in these countries has also thrived on the image that their women, as compared to Western women, are more subservient and ready to serve.

Another important aspect of the impact of the structural adjustment has been a shift in female employment status from wage and salary employment in the formal sector to self-employment in the informal sector or to wage employment within unorganized labour markets. The data in Table 6.10 confirm a growing trend of self-employment. Other available data also reveal a high proportion of female own-account workers in the manufacturing sector who are, in fact, contract workers, working either at home or in various workshops on a more or less casual basis. These workers do not enjoy any of the protection of labour legis-

TABLE 6.10
Female Share of Self-employment in Non-agriculture

| Country | Source | Year | Per Cent |
|---|---|---|---|
| Hong Kong | C | 1966 | 13.9 |
|  | Cs | 1976 | 15.8 |
|  | C | 1986 | 19.9 |
| Indonesia[a] | C | 1971 | 24.4 |
|  | HS | 1985 | 41.1 |
| South Korea | C | 1975 | 28.8 |
|  | LFSS | 1987 | 35.2 |
| Peninsular Malaysia[a] | C | 1970 | 23.4 |
|  | C | 1980 | 28.8 |
| Singapore | C | 1970 | 12.5 |
|  | LFSS | 1987 | 19.2 |
| Thailand | LFSS | 1970 | 39.8 |
|  | LFSS | 1980 | 43.6 |

*Source*: Standing (1989: 29–30).
*Notes*: C = Census.
Cs = Census, sample tabulation, size not specified.
HS = Household Survey.
LFSS = Labour Force Sample Survey.
[a]Includes agriculture.

lation that applies to employees in the formal sector, and their earnings are much lower (United Nations, 1989a: 152).

Another important element of the structural adjustment process that has significant implications for women is the emergence of new industrial technology and changing comparative advantage between industrialized and industrializing countries. Technological developments in the world economy, such as computer-aided design, numeric-controlled machines, and robotics, have tended to operate in the direction of reducing the labour cost advantage of assembly-line manufacturing which most of the Asia–Pacific Rim countries were enjoying (Lee, 1986; Nilsen, 1980). One development is that some of the technically more demanding and capital-intensive production processes have moved to the countries of the region with the highest efficiency, while simpler operations have shifted to less 'experienced' countries. Since Singapore embarked on its high-technology, high-skill, high-productivity, high-wage, wholly Singaporean policy in 1978, previous labour-intensive industries that relied on imported female labour have shifted to Malaysia and Thailand (Sieh Lee, 1988). Another trend is the reverse flow of previously relocated industries back to the industrialized countries where they have been able to regain their competitiveness through the use of micro-electronics and other information processing technologies (Rada, 1980). Another consequence of the technological rationalization is that there has been a 'deskilling' of the labour force in the sense of making their present skills irrelevant or ill-adapted to the needs of new production techniques.

A striking feature in the 1980s has been the growing reliance in the Asia–Pacific region on international flows of labour and the emerging feminization of these flows. For the sending countries, a major form of structural adjustment and source of foreign exchange has been the export of labour; they have come to rely increasingly on the 'comparative advantage of women's disadvantages' (Charlton, 1984). Remittances from contract migrants represent the single largest source of foreign exchange earnings in the Philippines, amounting to $792 million in 1987 (figure from the Philippine Overseas Employment Administration). The share of Filipina contract workers was estimated at about 30 per cent of the total remittances from the Middle East and about 89 per cent from Asian destinations (Cajuguiran-Quiray, 1989: 83). For the receiving countries, the entry of foreign female workers represents not only a new source of cheap labour supply but often also an alternative supply for jobs no longer wanted by locals.

Sex selectivity of the international migration flows can be examined for some of the countries in the region for which data are available. The Philippines is by far the largest exporter of female labour in the world. The sex ratio of all Filipino overseas contract workers in 1987 was 112 males per 100 females, but the feminized occupations—domestic helpers, entertainers, and nurses—were overwhelmingly female. Information provided by the Philippine Overseas Employment Administration shows that the number migrating as entertainers had risen from less than 2,000 in 1975 to 38,000 by 1987, while the increase in domestic and community service workers for the same period was from less than 3,000 to more than 106,000. These figures, of course, do not include the reputedly large numbers of illegal or clandestine migrants. The main destinations for Filipina migrants have been the Middle East and the richer Asian countries (Brunei, Japan, Hong Kong, Singapore, and Malaysia). But whereas they accounted for less than one-third of the total Filipino migrants in the Middle East, female migrants outnumbered males by 12 to 1 within Asian destinations. While there are many well-qualified professional Filipino women working overseas as nurses, midwives, secretaries, and teachers, the main markets for their labour have been in domestic service and entertainment (more often than not a euphemism for prostitution).

The female selectivity of Indonesian contract migration has also risen significantly over the years; in 1983 males outnumbered females by 1.4 to 1, by 1988 there were 3.4 female migrants for every male migrant (figures from the Department of Manpower, Indonesia). But unlike the Filipina migrants, Indonesian women have a much narrower range of overseas employment opportunities; more than 95 per cent were in domestic service mainly in Saudi Arabia, with much smaller numbers in neighbouring Malaysia, Singapore, and Brunei. Although Thai overseas labour migration is still heavily male-dominated, the number of Thai women seeking overseas work more than doubled between 1986 and 1988 to over 15,000 (figures from the Thai Overseas Employment Administration, Department of Labour). Since 1984 when the Thai government lifted a ban on female workers going to the Middle East, a major destination has been Saudi Arabia, but there are also large numbers in Hong Kong, Singapore, Brunei, and Japan.

Of the receiving countries within the region, Singapore has traditionally been a major importer of both male and female labour. Malaysian women, particularly from the southern state of Johore, have filled the needs of labour-short Singapore in the manufacturing and retail sectors, while Malaysian men have gone mainly into construction and shipbuilding. Since 1978 the Singapore government has also recruited from 'non-traditional' sources such as Sri Lanka, Thailand, and the Philippines, not only for the economic sectors but also for domestic work. Although Singapore has announced its plan of restructuring the economy to achieve a wholly Singaporean work-force by 1992, migrant labour has undoubtedly played an indispensable role in the Singapore 'success story'. While Malaysia has been exporting mainly semi-skilled female workers to Singapore and the Middle East and more recently to Taiwan, the entry of female guest workers into Malaysia has been into the domestic service, restaurant, and entertainment sectors. It is interesting that the largest occupational group of female immigrants into East Malaysia has been singers and entertainers from Taiwan and South Korea (Lin Lean Lim, 1989c: 150). With a foreign supply easily accessible, Hong Kong has also been importing large numbers of domestic maids mainly from the Philippines and Thailand. Taiwan too has emerged as an important importer of labour to meet the needs of its booming economy. Even Chinese Malaysian women are now looking to Taiwan for high-wage employment in factories (where salaries are reportedly at least three times higher than in Malaysia).

But it is the emergence of Japan as a major labour importer that represents the most dramatic structural change. Increasingly acute labour shortages in the 1980s in Asia's wealthiest country have attracted a flood of immigrants (mostly illegal) and in June 1990 motivated revisions in its Immigration Control Law of 1951 which previously banned the entry of foreign manual workers. However, the female immigrants do not appear to be going into the directly productive sectors (except for the relatively small but growing numbers of factory trainees); they are mainly headed for illegal work in bars, clubs, and cabarets as singers, dancers, and hostesses. In 1985 alone, of the 5,269 foreigners prosecuted for working illegally in Japan, 88 per cent were women (*Asia Magazine*, 20 September 1987: 18).

## The Supply Responses of Women

Economic trends in the Asia–Pacific Rim countries have clearly feminized labour use in the 1960s–1980s, due not only to increases in labour demand but also to labour supply. This section shows how the supply responses of female labour contributed to the economic dynamism of the 1960s and 1970s and, since then, how they have been behind the invisible adjustments of the 1980s.

To meet the specific demand for female workers created by the labour-intensive industrialization strategy pursued in the 1960s and 1970s, the supply of labour had to be able to adjust itself smoothly. Several writers (Chen, 1976; Jones, 1984; Eisold, 1984; Khoo, 1987) have implied that the Asia–Pacific Rim experience was unusual in that compared to other regions, there was a lack of institutional and socio-cultural barriers to female labour force participation, while educational and demographic patterns ensured that the supply factors were able to adjust smoothly to the growing demand for labour in the industrial sector.

This occurred either through the transfer of female labour from the subsistence sector (which could be either agriculture or traditional handicrafts and services) to the modern sector (with some implications for a shift from 'invisible' to more 'visible' forms of work for women), or through first-time entries of women into the labour force. In so far as the labour supply needed for modern sector development had to come from the subsistence sector and a very large proportion of the surplus labour was female, women played an important part in the reallocation of human resources. Where the male participation rate was already high in the early stages of development, it was the women whose economic involvement was initially low that had the potential for ensuring a perfectly elastic supply of labour at relatively low and stable wages: 'Thus if the supply factors of female labour participation can adjust themselves smoothly to the increasing demand for labour in the industrial sector, women workers constitute an important and very often the only available source of unlimited supply of labour in the process of rapid industrialization' (Chen, 1976: 140).

Part of the logic behind the export-led development strategies of these countries was the existence of large labour reserves. In the Asia–Pacific Rim countries, as in many other areas of the developing world, this surplus was generated by a decrease in employment opportunities in many traditional activities. Population growth as a result of high fertility rates in the immediate post-war period also added to the labour reserve. In many developing countries, the decline in traditional activities was not always compensated by an increase in modern sector job opportunities. But in the countries in question, demand in the modern sector was so great that women not only moved (and, just as important, were able to move) out of agriculture and other traditional activities but also increased their participation.

In the city-states of Hong Kong and Singapore where the amount of surplus labour available was limited because of the small size of the agricultural sector, increases in both the quantity and quality of female labour force participation were vital in their achievement of newly industrialized country (NIC) status. An important factor behind the supply response of the female labour force was education. Educational levels of women have risen significantly, and not only in these city-states. The younger female population in the Asia–Pacific Rim countries have typically achieved at least a lower secondary level of education. Unfortunately, although their educational attainments extended the horizons of these girls beyond farm work or housework, and proved an asset to the industrialization efforts, they were insufficient to get the female workers beyond low-status, low-paying jobs.

In the 1960s and early 1970s, the increases in labour supply were largely through the entry into the labour force of young girls taking up wage employment for the first time, where before they tended to remain at home or on the farm, after completing their education, and were waiting to get married and have children. In response to the unprecedented growth of employment opportunities in the dynamic manufacturing sector, autonomous female migration, especially of young single girls, from rural areas or small towns to the big urban centres and export processing zones was an important feature of the structural transformation in these societies.

In Table 6.11, whereas net rural–urban migration was male-oriented in the predominantly Muslim countries (Bangladesh, Iran, Iraq, Syria, and Turkey) which tended to have low rates of female labour force participation, in the ASEAN countries, many migration streams to the urban centres were strongly female selective. The Philippines stands out with the highest level of female participation in migration to urban and metropolitan areas (Fawcett, Khoo, and Smith, 1984). In the Indonesian capital of Jakarta, the overall sex ratio was 95.6 male migrants to

TABLE 6.11
Average Annual Rates of Net Rural Out-migration
and Net Urban In-migration by Sex (per 1,000 inhabitants)

| Country | Period | Net Rural Out-migration Male | Net Rural Out-migration Female | Net Urban In-migration Male | Net Urban In-migration Female | Sex Ratio of Net Rural–Urban Migration |
|---|---|---|---|---|---|---|
| Bangladesh | 1964–74 | 3.6 | 2.9 | 40.1 | 40.1 | 132.9 |
| India | 1961–71 | 2.7 | 2.4 | 10.9 | 10.9 | 116.7 |
| Indonesia | 1970–80 | 6.7 | 6.9 | 26.8 | 27.9 | 95.9 |
| Iran | 1966–76 | 18.5 | 15.3 | 23.5 | 20.1 | 127.3 |
| Iraq | 1967–77 | 27.5 | 24.9 | 18.2 | 17.5 | 112.5 |
| Philippines | 1970–80 | 8.6 | 10.9 | 16.6 | 19.5 | 80.8 |
| South Korea | 1970–80 | 28.0 | 30.6 | 28.2 | 30.6 | 92.4 |
| Sri Lanka | 1971–81 | −0.5 | −0.1 | −1.6 | −0.2 | 856.3 |
| Syria | 1972–82 | 6.9 | 6.5 | 8.0 | 7.8 | 109.6 |
| Thailand | 1970–80 | 5.5 | 6.0 | 30.4 | 32.6 | 90.4 |
| Turkey | 1960–70 | 17.6 | 14.7 | 34.9 | 34.9 | 116.3 |
| Fiji | 1966–76 | 5.1 | 7.0 | 9.4 | 12.5 | 76.5 |

*Source*: United Nations (1988b: 193).

100 female migrants and females predominated especially in the 15–19 and 45–plus age cohorts, reflecting the importance of migration of single and unaccompanied women to take up work as domestic servants and in other service occupations, as well as women accompanying their slightly older husbands and the movement of widowed women (Hugo et al., 1987: 215). In Malaysia, females outnumbered males in shorter distance, intra-state moves, and even in interstate moves female migration increased faster than male migration in the period 1970–80 (Lin Lean Lim, 1989b). In Thailand too, the proportion of women among migrants to the cities has been consistently rising over the years (Khoo, Smith, and Fawcett, 1984). South Korea had greater participation of women in migration to cities than the other countries of East Asia; females predominated especially in migration to Seoul and at the peak ages of 15–24 years (Khoo, Smith, and Fawcett, 1984: 1253). In Taiwan, female migrants exceeded males only in the age-group 15–19 years, while in Japan migration to cities tended to be highly male selective.

The age profiles of participation also confirm that the participation of young single girls, rather than other age-groups or marital status groups, was prominent—tailored to the specific needs of the development strategy of these countries. The sharp early peak found in age-specific female participation rates in the rapidly industrializing countries in Figure 6.1 and also in Malaysia in Figure 6.2 reflected the demand for young female labour who were more likely (compared to other segments of the labour force) to have the education, physical mobility, freedom from marital and childcare responsibilities, and other 'feminine' qualities required by the rapidly expanding export-oriented industries. The sharp decline in age-specific female labour force participation after the early peak in these countries can be explained partly by the Chinese–Confucianist cultural belief that married women should attend to the needs of their husbands and children, especially since extended family supports have been eroded and domestic help has become more expensive. Also, and just as importantly, many factories had a policy of not hiring married women.

In the less developed economies of the Philippines, Thailand, and Indonesia, the plateau-like pattern in Figure 6.2 is indicative of the less age-selective nature of female employment in agriculture, domestic service, petty trade, or handicrafts where the combination of childcare and work was possible and where experience of older women was a more valued characteristic. The levels of the plateaux in Figure 6.2 are, however, higher than those in Figure 6.3 for the South Asian countries, partly because there were no strong cultural sanctions against married women participating in the work-force in the ASEAN countries compared to the South Asian ones.

In the context of the economic crisis, although open unemployment rates increased, women were not merely passive victims. In many situations, women have been the agents of the 'invisible adjustment'. More women may have entered or stayed in the labour market and fewer may have left it, although the nature of their participation may have changed

THE FEMINIZATION OF LABOUR 197

FIGURE 6.1
Female Labour Force Participation Rate by Age in
Selected Industrialized or Newly Industrializing Asian Economies, 1982

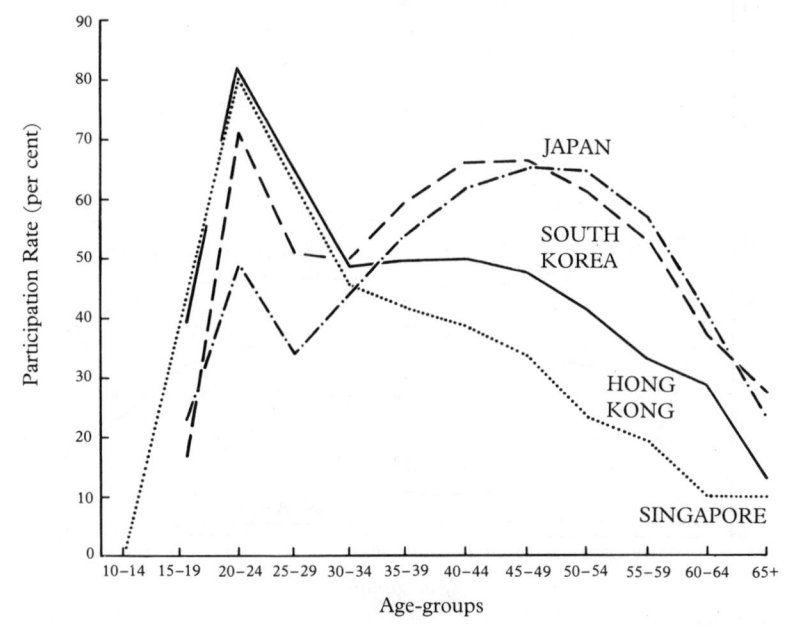

*Source*: International Labour Office, *Yearbook of Labour Statistics, 1983*.

FIGURE 6.2
Female Labour Force Participation Rate by Age in
Selected South-East Asian Countries

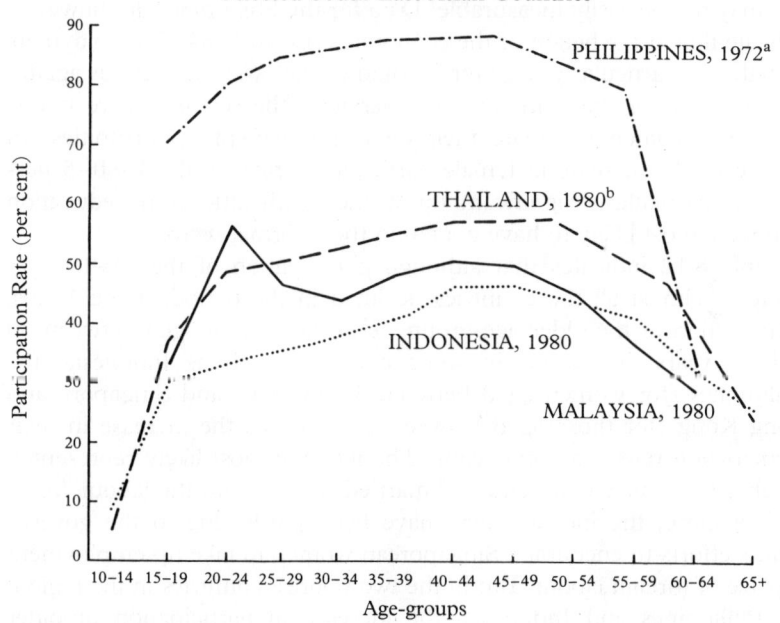

*Sources*: International Labour Office, *Yearbook of Labour Statistics, 1983* and *1984*.
[a]10-year age classification from 25 years.
[b]10-year age classification from 30 years.

## FIGURE 6.3
### Female Labour Force Participation Rate by Age in Selected South Asian Countries

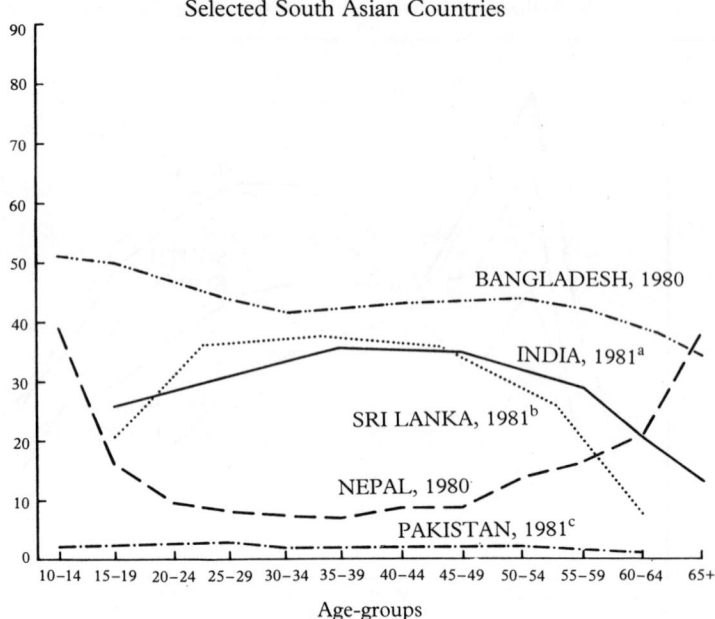

[Graph showing female labour force participation rates by age-group (10-14 through 65+) for Bangladesh 1980, India 1981[a], Sri Lanka 1981[b], Nepal 1980, and Pakistan 1981[c].]

Age-groups

*Sources:* As for Figure 6.2.
[a] 10-year age classification from 20 years.
[b] 10-year age classification from 45 years.
[c] 10-year age classification between 45 and 55 years.

and may not be easily measurable. Data for the Philippines do, however, indicate that at the height of the economic crisis in 1984–5, employment growth was particularly large for Filipino women (6.9 per cent as against 3.8 per cent for men) in sales and services, the sectors where it was easier for women to create their own employment opportunities. In Indonesia, the increase in female participation rates in the 1980–5 period was particularly significant for women with little or no education who were most likely to have gone into the informal sector.

Table 6.12 indicates that although participation of the 15–19 age-group in almost all the countries declined in the period of the 1980s, participation of the older age-groups, especially those aged between 30 and 44 years, increased. In some countries such as Indonesia, the Philippines (for women aged between 35 and 64), and Singapore and Hong Kong (for those aged between 25 and 44), the increase in their participation rates was significant. The increase most likely represented the first time entry or re-entry of married women into the labour force. In Singapore, the increase may have been partly due to the government's efforts to encourage Singaporean women to take up employment in place of foreign labour. But in the two poorest countries in the region, the Philippines and Indonesia, the increase in participation of older women was probably related to the additional worker effect in response to the economic crisis.

## TABLE 6.12
Female Labour Force Participation Rates by Age-groups

| Country | 15–19 | 20–24 | 25–29 | 30–34 | 35–39 | 40–44 | 45–64 | 65+ | Total |
|---|---|---|---|---|---|---|---|---|---|
| **Hong Kong** | | | | | | | | | |
| 1982 | 38.4 | 81.6 | 62.6 | 47.8 | 49.4 | 49.1 | 48.2 | 11.8 | 35.7 |
| 1987 | 29.4 | 84.5 | 73.1 | 53.9 | 53.0 | 55.9 | 36.5 | 9.9 | 37.8 |
| **Indonesia** | | | | | | | | | |
| 1978 | 36.2 | 38.3 | 44.4 | — | 52.6 | — | 52.2 | 27.0 | 28.4 |
| 1986 | 36.3 | 49.7 | 53.5 | 57.1 | 60.1 | 63.2 | 56.7 | 22.9 | 32.6 |
| **Japan** | | | | | | | | | |
| 1982 | 17.2 | 71.1 | 51.0 | 49.5 | 59.7 | 65.7 | 55.2 | 16.0 | 37.4 |
| 1987 | 16.6 | 73.6 | 56.9 | 50.5 | 61.3 | 68.4 | 56.1 | 15.4 | 39.1 |
| **South Korea** | | | | | | | | | |
| 1982 | 22.9 | 49.1 | 34.1 | 46.1 | 55.5 | 62.0 | 58.1 | 11.7 | 29.7 |
| 1987 | 19.3 | 54.3 | 39.7 | 47.1 | 59.8 | 61.4 | 56.6 | 17.6 | 32.3 |
| **Philippines** | | | | | | | | | |
| 1978 | 37.3 | 48.9 | — 51.5 — | | — 52.5 — | | 49.6 | 27.9 | 27.5 |
| 1987 | 33.3 | 50.7 | — 51.6 — | | — 57.3 — | | 55.8 | 28.8 | 20.0 |
| **Singapore** | | | | | | | | | |
| 1982 | 43.9 | 79.4 | 62.6 | 46.7 | 41.4 | 38.5 | 23.1 | 6.7 | 34.2 |
| 1987 | 27.0 | 79.9 | 71.2 | 56.3 | 50.2 | 45.5 | 26.7 | 5.5 | 36.3 |
| **Thailand** | | | | | | | | | |
| 1980 | 71.0 | 80.3 | 84.7 | — 86.8 — | | — 83.8[a] — | | 31.4[b] | 45.7 |
| 1984 | 70.7 | 81.0 | 84.5 | — 87.2 — | | — 83.4[a] — | | 26.4[b] | 50.1 |

*Sources*: International Labour Office, *Yearbook of Labour Statistics, 1983* and *1988*.
[a] Participation rate for age-group 40–60.
[b] Participation rate for age-group 60+.

Since the economic crisis would have forced many women to find jobs in the informal sector, the female supply responses may not have been fully translated into an increase in women's formal activity rates. Studies have shown that in the Western developed countries, one type of female-specific response to the economic crisis was to withdraw from the labour force (United Nations, 1989a: 49). But in the ASEAN countries, the discouraged worker effect was more likely in terms of relying on the informal, instead of the formal, sector, rather than completely giving up working. The informal sector can be broadly defined to include all non-contractual, casualized jobs from out-putting systems to low-level service jobs, domestic work, street vending, hawking, food catering, to prostitution. The informal sector also includes the invisible, hidden, or unregistered workers in manufacturing who provide vital labour for international as well as national markets, and women who play a far more important quantitative role than men (United Nations,

1989a: 129). For example, the Labour Force Surveys in Bangkok reveal that the number of women in the informal sector grew from approximately 597,000 in 1984 to 851,500 in 1987 or about 70 per cent of the total female labour force in the city. Most of the women in the informal sector were working as hawkers, vendors, labourers, and service workers. The men in the informal sector were mainly production process workers and labourers (Piampiti, 1990).

Movement of women into the informal sector, perhaps working outside their homes for the first time, in the 1980s can be explained by several factors. The economic crisis and adjustment have made poor families more dependent on the women's contributions. Especially when the jobs and incomes of their menfolk have been adversely affected, women have responded to help maintain the family's standard of living, as is confirmed by evidence from Malaysia (L. Y. C. Lim, 1978). There is also evidence of an increase in single-parent households, most of which are headed by women, related in part to the increasing migration of males in search of work and higher levels of divorce and separation, perhaps triggered by the stresses of the economic crisis (United Nations, 1989a: 46). The additional worker effect comes into play with women having to find jobs in the typically female occupations. The informal sector offers women a flexible solution to the need to balance employment with domestic and childcare responsibilities. There is greater flexibility of working hours, and part-time labour does not become an obstacle to the organization of work.

The other major form of supply response of women to the economic crisis is their entry into international labour markets for contract labour. The migration of women in search of employment has extended from internal to international labour markets. As remunerative employment opportunities for women have opened up in overseas labour markets with attractive income differentials compared to local jobs, and as demand for male guest workers slackened with the downturn of the construction industry, women have been the ones giving up family and hearth for work overseas. Participation of women in international labour migration can be seen as a family adaptation or survival strategy not only to maximize earnings of the family but also to minimize risks associated with ties to the local economy (Massey, 1988; Katz and Stark, 1986).

As a family survival strategy, the participation of young, single women in international labour migration is partly motivated by the belief, especially where cultural values are strong, that daughters are more willing than sons to fulfil family obligations (Trager, 1984: 1274). The migration of daughters is viewed as a temporary sojourn with the main aim of sending remittances home to maintain their families as a unit. Where married women have become international labour migrants, there are role reversals between wives and husbands (with the wives becoming the breadwinners and the husbands staying home) and some substitution among female members of the family (with grandmothers and older daughters taking over domestic and childcare responsibilities).

The implications of the changing labour force participation of women on the fertility transition in these countries cannot be ignored. Ogawa and Tsuya (Chap. 2 in this volume) show that from the 1960s to 1980s, the total fertility rate (TFR) declined by 57 per cent in East Asia and 39 per cent in South-East Asia, compared to 35 per cent in Oceania and 22 per cent in South Asia. The fertility transition of the East and South-East Asian countries has been substantially shorter than that in the developed countries and has occurred at considerably lower levels of economic development, compared with that for industrialized nations.

Although Ogawa and Tsuya identify strong political commitment and aggressive national family planning programmes as important factors behind the rapid fertility transition in these countries, it cannot be denied that the entry of young women into the labour force on a scale unprecedented in other regions of the world also exerted a crucial influence. This influence has operated in several ways. Age at first marriage has been rising significantly, not only because of rising levels of female education and the desire among young women to earn their own incomes and have a taste of independence, but also because with their daughters earning incomes, parents too have been less anxious or willing to marry them off at young ages. Poor families in particular have had greater reason to perceive their daughters as economic assets and to be more willing to invest in their human capital in terms of giving them better education and nutrition and postponing marrying them off. The autonomous migration experience and exposure to modern work and living conditions in urban areas have also affected attitudes of women towards family formation. Evidence from Malaysia also shows that women working in the heavily female-dominated export processing zones may have faced some shortage of suitable male partners, leading to a postponement in marriage. The large numbers of women employed in the informal sector might have reduced the relevance of the role-incompatibility hypothesis in these economies. But the more important countervailing factor would have been the rising costs of having children. In the adjustment context with governments cutting down on public expenditures and social subsidies, poor working women have been increasingly confronted with the rising costs of bringing up children. Those in the informal sector have also not been able to rely on private employers to help out with some of the social costs, such as medical, health, and educational benefits for children.

## Growing Labour Feminization and Growing Vulnerability

Growing labour feminization in the Asia–Pacific Rim countries has tended to be linked with greater vulnerability to exploitative conditions. In general, while women have moved into more economic sectors, they tend to be still confined to a limited range of lower rank occupations. The terms on which women have been employed have rested widely on

TABLE 6.13
Wage Rates and Earnings for Male and Female Manufacturing Workers, 1980 and 1985

| Country | Currency | Rate | 1980 Male | 1980 Female | 1980 Ratio of Female to Male (%) | 1985 Male | 1985 Female | 1985 Ratio of Female to Male (%) |
|---|---|---|---|---|---|---|---|---|
| Hong Kong | dollar | RT/d | 85.70[a] | 66.60[a] | 77.7 | 115.10 | 91.20 | 79.2 |
| Japan | yen | EG/m | 295,786 | 128,995 | 43.6 | 367,187 | 154,571 | 42.1 |
| South Korea | won | EG/m | 196,231 | 88,456 | 45.1 | 346,852 | 162,705 | 46.9 |
| Singapore | dollar | EG/h | 2.70 | 1.66 | 61.5 | 4.32 | 2.74 | 63.4 |

*Source*: International Labour Office, *Yearbook of Labour Statistics, 1986*, Table 17.
*Note*: EG = earnings; RT = rate; /m = per month; /d = per day; /h = per hour.
[a]Figures for 1982.

an implicit elasticity of their labour supply and an explicit inferiority of treatment of female relative to male labour. The reasons for the increasing feminization of labour tend to be founded on cost-cutting concerns and women's relatively weaker labour market position (which is itself a function of gender relations in society and also stereotyped assumptions about the secondary role of women). Pre-existing inequalities—in levels of literacy and training, health and nutrition, participation in decision-making at all levels—between women and men have tended to be exacerbated both by the economic crises themselves and by the policies adopted to cope with them.

The forms and seriousness of vulnerability differ, however, according to the sectors where women work. For the still significant numbers of women in the agricultural sector, apart from being adversely affected by (or at least not benefiting equally from) mechanization and technological innovations, their increasing vulnerability can be traced to the policy bias against agriculture, especially domestic food production (which is mainly the domain of women). A strategy that has been used by many of the countries to favour export-oriented manufacturing has been to keep the intersectoral terms of trade against agriculture (through pricing, marketing, subsidy policies, etc.) thus ensuring a low product wage and cheap shifts of labour to manufacturing.

In the manufacturing sector, the increasing vulnerability of female workers in the structural adjustment context can be traced to the pressures on enterprises to enhance international competitiveness through various cost-cutting measures, including the use of a more flexible or disposable labour force with lower fixed costs. Since the Asia–Pacific Rim countries were in the forefront of the outward-looking strategies and relied so heavily in the past on exports, their incentive for maintaining their competitive position can be expected to be especially great. Lower growth rates since the 1980s, greater difficulty of access to developed country markets, and eroding comparative advantage have combined to set a new premium on international competitiveness for these countries.

The limited available wage data (Table 6.13) do not reveal any discernible deterioration; there have, in fact, been improvements, but women continue to earn on average far less than men. What must be noted, however, is that the statistics on wage rates which have been gleaned normally from wage-setting decisions or the statistics on earnings from payrolls of establishments would not cover the situation of women in the informal sector and casualized employment. These women would have been most vulnerable to a decline in incomes, even as they have had to work harder. Also, changes in wages alone cannot indicate the quality of women's work life—other aspects, as discussed below, may have become more onerous or exploitative.

Even before the economic crisis, jobs in multinational factories had been highly insecure and unstable because of the common practice of labour shedding.

Labour shedding is related to the productivity of the companies. They do not want to keep girls after a few years because their wages would have risen, and this increase means that the companies are paying more for the same amount of work. After all, the actual work of the semi-skilled operators is easily learnt. The older workers can be replaced by cheaper workers. Besides, older workers are potential 'trouble makers' because they begin to understand the system. A more cynical reason is that the actual productivity of these girls declines with increasing years; usually due to declining stamina, health and eye sight (Salih et al., 1985: 72).

Female workers in manufacturing have therefore been vulnerable to advancing age rather earlier than most people. Marital status has also been a disadvantage as married women are encouraged by the firms to quit to ensure rapid worker turnover and lower costs. Those who lose their jobs have little mobility into other formal sector jobs because they have hardly picked up transferable skills in their assembly-type jobs.

As part of the adjustment policies involving economic liberalism, many governments reduced legal protection for women workers and took steps to make it easier for employers to have flexible work arrangements and easily disposable work-forces. The deregulation moves have implicitly exposed women to poorer working conditions and in some cases to a loss of fringe benefits that were previously guaranteed through legislation. In Malaysia, the government exempted industries operating in the export processing zones from observing the regulations on night shifts for women; while, on the other hand, it barred workers in electronics, who are mainly women, from forming a national union. Attempts by the workers to organize have been met by various forms of harassment and threats from the multinationals that they would shift their operations to other countries (*Asian Women Workers Newsletter*, 8(3), September 1989).

Job enlargement has been an important cost-cutting measure adopted by enterprises. Women have had to do more work or a greater variety of jobs for the same wages (Young, 1987: 30). For instance, many middle-management functions have been delegated to either clerical workers or to production workers who are usually women. Data from various issues of ILO *Yearbook of Labour Statistics* show that in South Korea the intensity of work in manufacturing, as measured by the average number of hours worked by women, has increased (from 52.6 hours per week in 1976 to 54.2 hours in 1985), and that women work longer hours than men (53.5 hours per week in 1985).

The most important means of reducing the fixed costs of labour have, however, been to substitute full-time wage and salary workers earning fixed wages and various fringe benefits by casual, temporary, or part-time workers and to increasingly resort to subcontracting or 'putting out' systems to home workers or small informal enterprises not covered by labour regulations. Many factories which do not rely on physically integrated production lines, high quality control standards, or constant technological monitoring have resorted to utilizing outworkers for piecework operations, instead of rehiring retrenched workers when production picked up.

Subcontracting by firms 'helps them to avoid complying with labour standards, to pay wages below the legal minimum, to deny social security and maternal benefits and so on. It also eliminates the risk of unionization, since the women are dispersed and disunited. Firms are not obliged to provide satisfactory working premises and a good working environment or to take responsibility for occupational safety and health. And in times of recession firms can easily do away with sub-contracted workers, and this provides an element of flexibility in management' (United Nations, 1986: 133). Subcontracting is particularly widespread in the 'feminized' industries—clothing, footwear, and electronics. Women therefore make up the bulk of domestic outworkers. 'Domestic outwork has the worst conditions in the industrial sector; it is essentially insecure, with the lowest piece-rate wages and without any of the non-output-related benefits that are to a greater or lesser extent the due of women in factory employment (though of course more routinely attainable by men)' (Joekes, 1987: 101). The strategy of bringing the production process into individual households has enabled capitalists to exploit situations of information asymmetry—unorganized women outworkers in individual households are entirely dependent on the producer or middlemen for market information.

The informal sector, whether as a safety valve to compensate for the blocked entries into other sectors or as a catch-all sector where pressures have been building up or as an informal survival strategy for poor households, does not tend to have the same implications for men and women. For men, an informal sector job may merely be a stopgap measure until employment conditions in the formal labour market improve and they also have opportunities for lucrative activities within the informal structure. The average income of male service workers in the informal sector in Bangkok was 2,883 bahts per month compared to 1,303 bahts for women (Piampiti, 1990: 17–18). For women, mobility is highly unlikely once they are in the informal sector, either because age works more against them, or because they face greater problems of access to credit, raw materials, skill training, control over output, or because they are less able to deal with harassment from the authorities (normally petty officials looking for bribes).

The informal sector also involves the rampant 'commoditization' of women in the flesh trade. Although prostitution-related occupations have always provided a substantial, if not major, share of female employment in the cities of many of these countries (Jones, 1984: 57; Phongpaichit, 1982), more may have been forced or lured into such occupations as a consequence of developments in the 1980s. The fact that earnings from such services tend to be much higher than the meagre wages from other sectors open to women has also been important.

For women in services, their vulnerability may be traced to different sources. Their concentration in the public sector has been one factor. Public sector retrenchments and the move towards privatization in the 1980s have hit women especially hard not only because the government has been a major employer of women in most of these countries but also because women's wages and employment conditions are better on average in the public sector than in private wage employment and wage sex differentials tend to be smaller or non-existent in the public sector (Standing, 1989: 25). The programmes of privatization of public enterprises (many of which were previously overmanned) that have been the order of the day in several countries have created a special case of redundancies (Lee, 1986: 7). Although documentation is lacking, the effects of privatization are likely to have been sex-asymmetric against women in so far as their reliance on the public sector has been greater than that of men and they are in clerical and administrative jobs which have been the targets of efficiency reorganization measures.

It is the women who have been drawn into domestic service and entertainment services overseas that have been particularly exposed to exploitative conditions. The weight of evidence suggests that females engaged in such international labour migration have been even more vulnerable than other groups of women, and certainly more than male workers. Higher wages abroad do not necessarily compensate for the malpractices they are exposed to in both sending and receiving countries.

Attention has been increasingly drawn to the fact that female (and male) migrants have been victims of the intermediation process. In spite of attempts by sending country governments to control the activities of the commercial recruiters and to regulate the fees they charge, the cost of getting a job abroad is alarmingly high and rising, though there are significant variations among the sending countries. In the Philippines, the average expenditure is about $400, but in Thailand, it is about $1,200 (Abella, 1989: 2). It has even been reported that Thai women wishing to work in Japan may have to pay as much as $6,000 to the agent because of the difficulties involved in arranging their illegal stays (Wyngaarde Mahajan, 1989: 19). This means that initial wages or savings from overseas jobs, if any, go into paying for the cost of movement or to service loans taken to finance the move. The resulting financial situation makes women even more prone to exploitation and fraud. Due to their relative lack of education and access to information compared to men, women are also more likely to be duped by unscrupulous agents who arrange non-existent jobs and promise wages that are never paid.

In the receiving countries, the marginalized situation of immigrant female workers in segmented or dualistic labour markets and the double, triple, or quadruple discrimination that they experience by virtue of their sex, birthplace and/or class structure, and their acceptance of their subordination as natural or inevitable are well known. But for the women from the ASEAN countries working as domestics and entertainers, their vulnerability is extreme (Lin Lean Lim, 1989d). Reports abound of these women experiencing severe hardships, including sexual harassment, very long hours of work, withholding of earned wages, and physical assault from either employers or recruitment agents or both. The women generally lack the means or ability to protect themselves. Their passports or other documents are often kept by the agents or employers, forcing them to submit to the exploitation. A major reason why female migrant workers tend to be more vulnerable than men is that they go into individualized situations (as maids in households) where there is greater isolation and lower likelihood of establishing networks of information and support compared to men working in groups (such as on construction sites). For women working in the Middle East, the situation tends to be even worse due in part to the strong traditions of female subordination, the social taboos on the free movement of young women, and the virtual isolation of these women from the rest of the national community, including friends and compatriots.

## The Policy Implications

This study has shown the responsiveness, contributions, and vulnerability of the female labour force in the Asia–Pacific Rim countries to economic cycles. While the overview nature of the study does not lend itself to detailed policy suggestions, certain implications emerge. Although increasing feminization of labour may connote economic gains to women, the crucial consideration is that their participation extended beyond national boundaries is not necessarily a liberating experience. Women have been drawn into insecure forms of economic activity that tend to rely heavily on their 'feminine' qualities and their assumed elasticity of supply, rather than their productive human resource potentials; and the conditions of their work are often retrogressive.

What is required are 'wide ranging policies to consolidate women's positions where advances have already been made, to reverse the harmful effects of international influences, and to attack conditions that perpetuate women's inferior position to men once they are in paid employment' (Joekes, 1987: 141). Before anything concrete can be done, though, the 'visibility' of women's positions will have to be improved. Standing (1989: 28), for instance, recommends that data be collected on women's different forms of control—over their own labour power, labour time, means of production, raw materials, output, proceeds of output, and labour reproduction or working capacity—to determine whether, in the labour feminization process, women themselves are gaining control or are subject to growing forms of control.

It may not be so much an issue of entry to jobs (in so far as there have been increasing opportunities for employment, although occupational segregation has not decreased significantly), but the conditions of women's work that will need close monitoring. Even as job opportunities have opened up for women, the pervasiveness of norms of sexual roles and hence status differentials between women and men have meant that women's economic roles remain devalued. It is discriminatory social gender relations rather than actual skill differentials that account for persistent wage differentials by sex. It appears that employers are able to pay women a going 'female' wage rate and then determine the nominal skill level or scope of functions of the job in conformity with that lower wage. It is partly in this connection that efforts to integrate women in development need to look beyond labour force participation of women to issues of empowerment for women and changing social gender relations.

Women because of their inherently weak position in society have had to rely on the intervention of the state for their protection and upliftment in many circumstances. Most countries have adopted various laws and ratified international instruments with a view to creating a legal basis for equality of opportunity and treatment in employment between the sexes. But without adequate and efficient administrative mechanisms capable of effectively promoting and monitoring the implementation of formal provisions and translating policies into positive or affirmative action programmes for women, the impact has tended to remain below the desired level (United Nations, 1989a: 262). The national machineries for promoting *de jure* and *de facto* equality of opportunity and treatment for women workers need to be strengthened. Both formal provisions for equality and protective measures should be constantly reviewed to accommodate the changing nature of women's economic participation. For instance, in so far as there has been a shift in women's labour status from wage employment to self-employment and discontinuous contract work in internal and international labour markets, traditional labour regulations that rely on enforcement in the formal workplace may need to be substituted by new arrangements to ensure, for example, that women are not discriminated against in terms of access to credit, skill development training, allocation of hawking sites, subsidies, etc. and to provide protection for women in individualized work relationships. A crucial requirement is that new forms of social security whether for work-related accidents, old-age insurance, or business fluctuations will have to be devised to substitute for employer obligations. In times of economic crises, it is also important to ensure that the same criteria are applied to all workers in case of redundancy or dismissal, without distinction based on sex, marital status, or age.

As the swing towards economic liberalism and deregulation, together with flexible work arrangements, leave women exposed, are there alternative measures of protection? Certainly, if the state is reducing its own direct role, it should assist women (or at least not put up barriers) to organize whether in the form of unions, co-operatives, consciousness-raising, or other self-help groups. Potentially important steps have been taken by women themselves to overcome precarious, individualized labour relationships. For example, self-employed women in India have organized to promote information networking and to provide group guarantees for credit and other forms of self-assistance; and female international migrants working as domestic maids have formed unions and support groups in places such as Hong Kong and Rome. But for clearly vulnerable groups of women—elderly women, female heads of households, autonomous young single migrants, international female migrants in irregular situations—the state cannot abdicate its responsibilities.

Another obvious requirement is that structural adjustment policy packages designed to lift countries out of economic crises must take the gender dimension into account and explicitly consider their impact on women as distinct from men or human resources in general. Certainly, there should not be an overemphasis on cost-cutting measures which disproportionately affect women. It would indeed be short-sighted to reduce labour protection or fringe benefits to workers merely to reduce current costs to the detriment of the long-term productivity of female human resources. Rather, the search should be for more innovative ways of increasing productivity within the workplace and promoting among workers a sense of having a stake in the performance of the industry.

The implications for education and training are always important, especially for women who, to date, have had unequal access to them relative to men. But what is needed is probably a much more realistic approach of recognizing, for instance, that formal education alone is not a ticket to a fulfilling job, and that there may be a need for periodic 'reskilling' in the light of technological and organizational rationalizations that are part of the adjustment process. For example, entrepreneurial skills, market sourcing techniques, and group management skills for women in subcontracting and out-putting systems would be useful. Skill training is particularly important because of the uncertain future of low-skilled, repetitive jobs in the export processing industries. Industrial restructuring trends and new technologies have whittled away the comparative advantage of endless supplies of cheap unskilled labour. 'In the coming years, the quality of skills and training will determine the quantity of jobs created in the export processing zones of the developing countries' (United Nations, 1989a: 149).

Finally, it should be emphasized that it is the combination of women's roles in economic production, human reproduction, and nurturing of children that is pivotal in human resource development; and policies should aim to support women in all their interrelated roles. While it is clear that there has been an increase in female labour force participation, what is not clear is how their functions in the home as wives, mothers, and homemakers have been affected. Attention should be devoted to making sure that participation in economic activities does not serve only to double or triple women's workload without enhancing their status or jeopardizing their nurturing role in the family.

# 7
# Labour Force Developments and Emerging Human Resource Policies in Japan

Kenichi Furuya and Robert L. Clark

## Introduction

AT the conclusion of World War II, the Japanese economy was devastated and its industrial potential severely damaged. In less than 15 years after the war, the economy had recovered to its pre-war levels. During the 1960s, the Japanese economy grew at an average annual rate of 11 per cent. The oil crisis of 1973 sharply reduced the rate of economic growth and led to considerable restructuring of the economy. The economy quickly recovered from the shock of higher oil prices and adjusted to these new economic conditions. Japan's average annual growth rate of real GNP was over 4 per cent between 1980 and 1988, much higher than in most other developed countries.

The existence of a high-quality labour force was a key factor in the post-war recovery of the Japanese economy. Governmental economic policies and the human resource policies of firms were also important components in producing the sustained economic growth. This chapter reviews important demographic and human resource changes in the Japanese labour force during the 1950s to 1980s. The importance of these changes in influencing past economic growth is assessed and the prospects for the future are explored given the current trends in the labour force.

## Education and the Quality of the Labour Force

The productive potential of an economy is determined by the size and quality of its natural resources, its human resources, its capital stock, and the existing technological base. Domestic natural resources available to Japanese industries are relatively scarce; over 90 per cent of energy requirements and 80 per cent of raw materials must be imported. Offsetting the lack of natural resources has been an energetic and high-quality labour force. Considerable resources have been devoted to improving the productive potential of the population. Investments in education and on-the-job training have continued to improve the stock of human capital per worker. This is reflected in the rising level of educational attainment of workers and increased job tenure along with greater firm investment in their workers.

A common characteristic among the economically successful nations in the Asia–Pacific region is a lack of natural resources. To counteract this limitation, these countries have made major investments in education and training. Their economic growth is based on the relatively large and rising stock of human capital per worker. In contrast, countries in Asia that have achieved much less economic success have been slow to improve the quality of their human resources (Ogawa and Tsuya in Chap. 2 of this volume).[1]

Japan has been the leader among the successful Asian countries in its long-term economic growth and increased investment in human resources. However, Taiwan, Singapore, South Korea, and Hong Kong have experienced rapid economic growth, rising educational attainment, and slowing population growth in the 1980s.

*Rising Educational Attainment*

Increases in educational attainment of workers have accompanied the rapid economic growth in Japan. Greater investment in human capital is both a cause and consequence of economic development; demand for a higher skilled work-force induces greater educational attainment while an increase in human capital further stimulates economic growth. The percentage of Japanese men who continued on into high school after completing compulsory education increased from 60 per cent in 1960 to 93 per cent in 1986. The proportion who entered universities increased from 20 to 26 per cent during this interval. The increases in educational attainment were even larger for women. The percentage of those continuing on to high school rose from 56 to 95 per cent and the percentage continuing on to college increased from 14 to 34 per cent (Japanese Institute of Labor, 1988).

The rising enrolments have led to a better educated labour force. Table 7.1 shows the change in the educational level of the labour force since 1970 for men and women. In 1970, 47 per cent of the male labour force had only a junior high school education, 39 per cent had achieved a high school degree, and 14 per cent had earned a college or university degree. By 1988, the proportion of the male labour force with only a junior high school education had fallen to 23 per cent while the proportion with a college or university degree had risen to 26 per cent. Similar increases in educational attainment are observed for women as the proportion with only a junior high school education fell from 42 per cent in 1975 to 22 per cent in 1988 and the proportion with a college or university degree increased from 6 to 16 per cent.

TABLE 7.1
Distribution of Labour Force by Highest Level of Educational Attainment[a] (per cent)

|      | Male | | | Female | | |
| --- | --- | --- | --- | --- | --- | --- |
| Year | Junior High School | High School | College or University | Junior High School | High School | College or University |
| 1970 | 46.9 | 39.4 | 13.7 | | | |
| 1975 | 39.9 | 43.1 | 17.1 | 42.1 | 51.8 | 6.1 |
| 1980 | 33.7 | 46.0 | 20.4 | 35.1 | 55.6 | 9.4 |
| 1985 | 26.7 | 49.4 | 23.9 | 27.4 | 58.9 | 13.7 |
| 1988 | 22.9 | 51.1 | 26.0 | 22.4 | 61.7 | 15.9 |

Source: Japanese Institute of Labor, *Basic Survey on Wage Structure*, various issues.
[a] Services sector is excluded from this analysis.

The rapid increase in the educational level of the Japanese labour force has steadily improved the quality of workers. More highly educated workers in conjunction with effective management techniques have enabled Japanese firms to rapidly introduce new production methods. The rate of introduction of robotics and micro-electronics that has occurred in the 1970s and 1980s could not have been achieved without a high-quality labour force.

The Japanese system of industrial relations promotes teamwork and emphasizes the success of the firm. This team orientation and the related personnel policies that have been adopted have made Japanese firms more flexible in their response to technological innovations and changing economic conditions.

*Increasing Job Tenure*

During this period, labour turnover declined and average job tenure of the labour force increased. Table 7.2 indicates that the average length of time that a male worker had been in his current job increased from 8.8 years in 1970 to 12.8 years in 1988. The increase in average job tenure is partly a function of the ageing of the labour force; older workers generally have greater tenure than younger workers. However, age-specific tenure data reveal that average tenure increased for all age-groups of men aged 30 and older. For example, tenure for men aged 50–59 increased from 15.2 years in 1970 to 20.3 years in 1988 and for men aged 40–49 tenure increased from 15.4 to 17.9 years. Tenure for men less than 30 years of age declined between 1970 and 1988 primarily because of the increase in years spent in schooling, thus reducing the available working years for these men.

As in most countries, women have much lower labour force participation rates and are much more likely to leave the labour force after marriage or the birth of children. Female workers in Japan are more likely to

## TABLE 7.2
Job Tenure by Sex and Firm Size

| Year | Male | Female | Total | Firm Size[a] 10–99 | 100–999 | 1,000 or more |
|---|---|---|---|---|---|---|
| 1970 | 8.8 | 4.5 | 7.7 | 5.8 | 6.3 | 10.2 |
| 1975 | 10.0 | 5.4 | 8.9 | 6.9 | 7.7 | 11.7 |
| 1980 | 11.6 | 6.4 | 10.4 | 8.2 | 9.4 | 12.5 |
| 1985 | 12.5 | 7.0 | 10.8 | 8.6 | 10.0 | 13.6 |
| 1988 | 12.8 | 7.3 | 11.0 | 8.9 | 10.5 | 13.7 |

*Source*: As for Table 7.1.
[a]Values are for both sexes.

be part-time or temporary workers and are thus subject to a greater probability of lay-off as firms attempt to adjust their levels of employment. However, during the 1970s and 1980s women have become a more integral part of the Japanese labour force. The greater commitment to the work-force by women has coincided with the decline in fertility.

Average tenure for all women increased from 4.5 years in 1970 to 7.3 years in 1988 (see Table 7.2). The increase in tenure for women is observed for all age categories 25 and over. For women aged 50–59, tenure increased from 8.1 years in 1970 to 12.9 years in 1988 and for women aged 40–49 tenure increased from 7.4 years in 1970 to 9.8 years in 1988.

Job tenure is much higher in large firms than in smaller firms (see Table 7.2). In 1988, average tenure for all workers in firms with 1,000 or more employees was 13.7 years. This compares to 10.5 years in firms with 100–999 employees and 8.9 years for firms with 10–99 employees. Tenure increased by 3–4 years in each of these firm size categories. Tenure also varies substantially by industry with average tenure for all workers being greatest in the utilities sector (17.1 years in 1988). In 1988, average job tenure ranged between 11.5 and 12.6 years in mining, manufacturing, and transportation while tenure was between 7.6 and 9.4 years in the real estate, services, and wholesale trade sectors.[2]

Human capital theory predicts that increased investment in human capital specific to the firm leads to reduced turnover and greater job tenure. Firms and workers will be more willing to make investments that increase the worker's productivity only to the current firm if longer job tenure is anticipated. Large investments in specific human capital will also result in lower turnover rates.

Mincer and Higuchi (1988) and Hashimoto (1979) conclude that investment in specific human capital is much greater in Japan than in the United States. They argue that this explains the greater increase in earnings with an additional year of job tenure in Japan compared to the

United States and the greater employment stability of the Japanese labour force.

A competing hypothesis explaining the greater job tenure and steeper age–earnings profile in Japan is the theory of long-term employment contracts. In this model, firms are viewed as being concerned about the high cost of worker turnover. To reduce quit incentives, workers are paid less than their productivity early in their work life and then paid more than their productivity late in their careers (Lazear, 1979). This model also predicts a rising tenure–earnings relationship and also explains the need for mandatory retirement policies; since workers are paid in excess of their productivity late in their careers the firm must establish a formal end to the contract.

Examining earnings data between 1971 and 1986, Clark and Ogawa (1992a) find that the earnings profile for workers is less steep when the mandatory retirement age is higher. This finding is consistent with the long-term employment contracting explanation of the Japanese labour market. The existence of mandatory retirement and re-employment after compulsory retirement but only at lower salaries is also consistent with the contracting model. These policies are counter to predictions of a labour market based on large investments in specific human capital.

## Ageing of the Labour Force

Growth in the number of people in the Japanese labour force has been dominated by fluctuating trends in fertility. The post-war baby boom in Japan lasted only three years from 1947 to 1949. The large number of births in these years is reflected in the high rate of labour force growth between 1965 and 1970 when this cohort began entering the labour force. Table 7.3 shows the trend in labour force growth by sex during the 1960s to 1980s. The rate of growth of males in the labour force has declined continuously since 1965–70 when the male labour force was increasing by 1.64 per cent per year to only 0.67 per cent per year between 1985 and 1988.

TABLE 7.3
Labour Force Growth Rates (per cent)

| Period | Total | Male | Female |
|---|---|---|---|
| 1960–5 | 1.19 | 1.53 | 0.70 |
| 1965–70 | 1.48 | 1.64 | 1.24 |
| 1970–5 | 0.65 | 1.29 | −0.37 |
| 1975–80 | 1.20 | 0.76 | 1.92 |
| 1980–5 | 1.08 | 0.74 | 1.61 |
| 1985–8 | 0.84 | 0.67 | 1.10 |

Source: Japanese Statistics Bureau, Management and Coordination Agency, *Annual Report on the Labour Force Survey*, various issues.

The rate of increase in the female labour force has been more volatile, and reached particularly high levels in the late 1970s. Since then, the growth rate has declined. Since 1975, the growth of the female labour force has been more than or almost twice that of the male labour force. Thus to a considerable degree, the increasing number of female workers has been substituting for the low rate of growth in male workers. However, the continuing marginal nature of female employment is reflected in the decline in the female labour force between 1970 and 1975 when economic growth was sharply curtailed. Reduced employment demand was accomplished by decreasing the number of female workers.

The growth rate of the labour force has been shaped by trends in population growth and these demographic changes have influenced the pace of economic growth in Japan. The ending of the Japanese baby boom led to a sharp reduction in the rate of population growth. From 1955 to 1985, the total population increased by 30 million or at an annual rate of less than 1 per cent; however, the population aged 25–59 continued to grow more rapidly based on past fertility experience. Between 1955 and 1975, this working-age population increased from 42.5 million to 67.2 million. The increase in the working-age population was 58 per cent or an annual rate of increase of approximately 2 per cent. After 1975, the rate of growth of this population also began to decline reflecting the ending of the baby boom that occurred twenty-five years earlier. This decline in the population in the prime working ages is the primary reason for the decline in the rate of growth of the labour force.

Slowing population growth and the related decline in the growth of the labour force has produced an ageing of the labour force. The ratio of labour force participants aged 20–24 to those aged 40–59 by sex is shown in Table 7.4. In 1970, this ratio for males was 0.66 implying that there were two persons aged 20–24 for every three persons aged 40–59. This high ratio reflects the entry of the baby boom cohort into the

TABLE 7.4
Ageing of the Japanese Labour Force[a]

| Year | Male 20–24/(40–59) | Mean Age | Female 20–24/(40–59) | Mean Age |
|---|---|---|---|---|
| 1970 | 0.66 | 34.5 | | |
| 1975 | 0.42 | 36.1 | 1.00 | 32.9 |
| 1980 | 0.26 | 37.7 | 0.74 | 34.6 |
| 1985 | 0.24 | 38.6 | 0.72 | 35.2 |
| 1988 | 0.23 | 39.0 | 0.71 | 35.4 |

Source: As for Table 7.1.
[a]Services sector is excluded from this analysis.

labour force. In 1988, this ratio had fallen to 0.23 or about one person aged 20–24 for every four persons aged 40–59. The ageing of the labour force is also reflected in the increase in the mean age of male labour force participants from 34.5 years in 1970 to 39.0 in 1988. The ageing of the female labour force has been moderated somewhat by increases in the labour force participation rates among younger women. However, the mean age still rose by 2.5 years between 1975 and 1988.

The ageing of the labour force is more completely shown in Table 7.5 which reports the age distribution of the labour force between 1950 and 1985. In 1950 and 1960, the proportion of the labour force aged 40 and over was 38 per cent while the proportion of the labour force aged 15–24 ranged between 25 and 30 per cent. The substantial ageing of the labour force is shown in the data for 1985 when 52 per cent of the labour force was aged 40 and over and only 12 per cent was aged between 15 and 24.

Projections of the population and labour force indicate a further ageing of the Japanese labour force. Continued low fertility and reductions in mortality at older ages is projected to increase the proportion of the population aged 65 and over from 11.9 per cent in 1990 to 24.6 per cent in 2020.[3] The ratio of the population aged 20–24 to those aged 20–64 will decline from 11.8 per cent in 1990 to 9.0 per cent in 2010 before beginning to increase slightly.

In summary, the rapid economic growth of the latter half of the 1950s and through the 1960s occurred during a period of time when the labour force was relatively young and rapidly growing. The lower wages of younger workers and the new human capital associated with more recent education helped to facilitate a high level of economic growth. In the 1990s and beyond, the labour force will grow only slowly and the labour force will continue to age. Given the seniority-based wage system that prevails in Japan, the ageing of the labour force is likely to lead to increases in labour costs and perhaps retard the rate of economic growth. In response to the ageing of the population, the Japanese government has been encouraging firms to raise their ages of mandatory

TABLE 7.5
Age Distribution of Employed Persons

| Year | Total Employment (millions) | Percentage in Age-group |||||
|---|---|---|---|---|---|---|
| | | 15–19 | 20–24 | 25–39 | 40–54 | 60+ |
| 1950 | 35.6 | 14.0 | 16.3 | 32.2 | 29.6 | 7.9 |
| 1960 | 43.7 | 10.5 | 14.7 | 36.7 | 29.6 | 8.4 |
| 1970 | 52.2 | 6.1 | 15.4 | 35.9 | 33.3 | 9.3 |
| 1980 | 55.8 | 2.7 | 9.9 | 37.8 | 39.9 | 9.7 |
| 1985 | 58.2 | 2.6 | 9.9 | 35.1 | 42.4 | 10.0 |

Source: Japanese Statistics Bureau, Management and Coordination Agency, *Population Census of Japan*, various issues.

retirement. This policy exacerbates the ageing of firm labour forces. Many companies are now considering new personnel policies to offset the higher labour costs associated with an ageing labour force.

## Labour Force Composition

Economic development, changes in household composition, and maturing social welfare and education systems have substantially altered the composition of the Japanese labour force. Labour force participation rates have declined for young and old men and women while participation rates for women aged 25–54 have increased somewhat. There has been a steady decline in employment in the primary sector and accompanying this restructuring of the economy has been a decline in the proportion of the labour force who are self-employed or unpaid family workers. These changes have been an important part of the evolution of the Japanese labour force.

*Shifting Patterns of Labour Force Participation*

Labour force participation rates of men have fallen over time in most developed countries. In general, these declines have occurred primarily among men aged 15–24 and those aged 55 and over. Japan conforms to this basic pattern. However, the decline in the proportion of older men who remain in the labour force has been much smaller than in the other developed countries. In contrast, participation rates of women in developed countries have tended to increase for women aged 25–54; however, the rise in female participation rates in Japan has tended to be lower than in other developed countries.

The proportion of men aged 15 and over who were in the labour force declined from 84.8 per cent in 1960 to 77.1 per cent in 1988 (Table 7.6). The labour force participation rates of men aged 25–54 remain between 96 and 98 per cent and were actually slightly higher in 1988 than in 1960. In contrast, there were sharp declines in the participation rates of the youngest and oldest segment of the male labour force. Consistent with the increased enrolment rates in educational institutions, the participation rate for men aged 15–19 declined sharply from 52.7 per cent in 1960 to only 17.2 per cent in 1988 while the proportion of men aged 20–24 who were in the labour force fell from 87.8 to 71.0 per cent.

The participation rates of Japanese men (see Table 7.6) can be compared to the rates for the other newly industrialized countries in Asia along with China (Table 7.7). In general, the participation rates of men aged 15–24 in these countries are higher than the Japanese rates; the exception is South Korea. Higher participation rates of men in these ages is consistent with less time spent in schooling.

Surprisingly, a larger proportion of older Japanese males remain in the labour force than older men in these Asian countries. This occurs

## TABLE 7.6
### Labour Force Participation Rates

|  | Male |  |  |  | Female |  |  |  |
|---|---|---|---|---|---|---|---|---|
| Age-group | 1960 | 1970 | 1980 | 1988 | 1960 | 1970 | 1980 | 1988 |
| Total (15–65+) | 84.8 | 81.8 | 79.8 | 77.1 | 54.5 | 49.9 | 47.6 | 48.9 |
| 15–19 | 52.7 | 31.4 | 17.4 | 17.2 | 49.0 | 33.6 | 18.5 | 16.5 |
| 20–24 | 87.8 | 80.5 | 69.6 | 71.0 | 70.8 | 70.5 | 70.0 | 73.7 |
| 25–29 | 95.5 | 97.2 | 96.3 | 96.2 | 54.5 | 45.6 | 49.2 | 58.2 |
| 30–34 | 96.6 | 98.0 | 97.6 | 97.0 | 56.5 | 48.2 | 48.2 | 50.9 |
| 35–39 | 96.2 | 97.7 | 97.6 | 97.5 | 59.0 | 57.5 | 58.0 | 61.3 |
| 40–44 | 96.8 | 97.5 | 97.6 | 97.5 | 60.9 | 63.0 | 64.1 | 68.1 |
| 45–49 | 95.9 | 97.1 | 96.5 | 97.2 | 60.7 | 63.0 | 64.4 | 69.3 |
| 50–54 | 94.9 | 96.0 | 96.0 | 96.0 | 54.9 | 58.6 | 59.3 | 63.3 |
| 55–59 | 88.9 | 91.4 | 91.2 | 91.3 | 49.7 | 48.8 | 50.5 | 50.9 |
| 60–64 | 81.4 | 81.4 | 77.8 | 71.1 | 43.0 | 39.1 | 38.8 | 38.6 |
| 65+ | 56.9 | 49.4 | 41.0 | 35.8 | 25.6 | 18.0 | 15.5 | 15.7 |

*Source*: As for Table 7.3.

despite the much higher per capita income and more developed pension systems in Japan.

Participation rates for men aged 65 and older in developed countries have steadily declined. Table 7.8 shows these declines for selected developed countries. Comparing these data to those for Japanese men aged 65 and older (see Table 7.6) shows that the Japanese rates are much higher and have declined much less than those in the other developed

## TABLE 7.7
### Male Labour Force Participation Rates: Selected Asian Countries

| Age-group | China 1982 | Hong Kong 1986 | South Korea 1986 | Malaysia 1980 | Singapore 1986 |
|---|---|---|---|---|---|
| 15–19 | 72.5 | 37.9 | 13.1 | 50.1 | 29.3 |
| 20–24 | 96.8 | 88.3 | 37.9 | 92.2 | 88.5 |
| 25–29 | 98.7 | 97.3 | 87.1 | 97.7 | 97.2 |
| 30–34 | 98.9 | 97.9 | 91.9 | 98.3 | 98.3 |
| 35–39 | 98.9 | 97.7 | 95.3 | 97.8 | 98.6 |
| 40–44 | 98.7 | 97.6 | 93.5 | 98.3 | 98.0 |
| 45–49 | 97.5 | 96.2 | 94.2 | 97.6 | 96.6 |
| 50–54 | 91.4 | 92.1 | 94.9 | 94.6 | 90.5 |
| 55–59 | 83.0 | 80.4 | 78.4 | 79.9 | 68.7 |
| 60–64 | 63.7 | 59.2 | 66.4 | 70.5 | 47.3 |
| 65+ | 30.1 | 29.7 | 36.5 | n.a. | n.a. |

*Source*: International Labour Office, *Yearbook of Labour Statistics*, 1987.
n.a. = Not available.

TABLE 7.8
Labour Force Participation Rates for Men Aged 65 and Over:
Selected Developed Countries

| Country | 1950 | 1960 | 1970 | 1980 | 1985 |
|---|---|---|---|---|---|
| Australia | 32.7 | 28.2 | 21.8 | 13.5 | 12.7 |
| Belgium | 19.4 | 9.4 | 6.2 | 4.6 | 4.4 |
| Canada | 40.9 | 30.4 | 21.7 | 14.6 | 13.8 |
| Denmark | 38.0 | 32.4 | 26.9 | 15.3 | 14.2 |
| France | 37.2 | 26.1 | 15.0 | 6.0 | 5.6 |
| Germany | 27.5 | 21.4 | 16.7 | 4.9 | 4.7 |
| Italy | 46.6 | 27.5 | 14.5 | 7.5 | 6.8 |
| Netherlands | 31.5 | 20.4 | 11.4 | 4.5 | 4.2 |
| Sweden | 36.4 | 27.7 | 19.0 | 10.3 | 9.7 |
| United Kingdom | 34.4 | 26.6 | 18.8 | 11.0 | 10.6 |
| United States | 45.0 | 33.9 | 25.5 | 19.1 | 18.2 |

*Source*: United Nations (1988d).

countries. The higher levels of participation by older Japanese males do not appear to be caused by low real income or the lack of pension and social security coverage (Clark, 1991).

The labour force participation rate for females aged 15 and over declined slightly from 54.5 per cent in 1960 to 48.9 per cent in 1988. This is primarily attributable to the sharp drop in the participation rate for women aged 15–19 (see Table 7.6). The rates for women aged 20–59 are generally somewhat higher, though the increase in the proportion of women in the labour force in Japan is considerably below the

TABLE 7.9
Female Labour Force Participation Rates: Selected Asian Countries

| Age-group | China 1982 | Hong Kong 1986 | South Korea 1986 | Malaysia 1980 | Singapore 1986 |
|---|---|---|---|---|---|
| 15–19 | 80.1 | 33.6 | 18.1 | 33.7 | 28.8 |
| 20–24 | 91.1 | 83.7 | 53.3 | 56.7 | 80.0 |
| 25–29 | 89.0 | 70.8 | 36.7 | 46.5 | 69.8 |
| 30–34 | 88.9 | 57.4 | 45.4 | 41.3 | 52.3 |
| 35–39 | 88.5 | 57.0 | 56.4 | 48.2 | 46.8 |
| 40–44 | 83.4 | 59.5 | 59.5 | 50.2 | 44.6 |
| 45–49 | 70.6 | 54.8 | 63.2 | 49.4 | 36.6 |
| 50–54 | 50.9 | 43.7 | 57.0 | 44.1 | 28.0 |
| 55–59 | 32.9 | 34.3 | 51.1 | 35.4 | 17.4 |
| 60–64 | 16.9 | 25.9 | 41.1 | 27.9 | 10.3 |
| 65+ | 4.7 | 12.1 | 14.6 | n.a. | n.a. |

*Source*: As for Table 7.7.
n.a. = Not available.

increase that has been experienced in other developed countries. The age-specific participation rates of Japanese women are slightly higher than those in the newly developed countries of Asia but much lower than similar rates in China (Table 7.9). The Chinese rates indicate a heavy reliance on female labour in that country.

*Decline in Self-employed Workers*

Structural changes in the economy have caused a substantial reallocation of workers from being self-employed and family workers towards being paid employees. Table 7.10 shows that for males the proportion of the labour force who were self-employed declined from 26.7 per cent in 1962 to 17.4 per cent in 1988, while the proportion who were family workers declined from 10.8 to 2.7 per cent. As a result, the proportion who were paid employees increased from 66.6 to 79.9 per cent.

Women are much more likely to be categorized as family workers. However, the proportion of women in this category declined from 43.5 per cent in 1962 to 18.7 per cent in 1988. In addition, there was a slight decline in the percentage of female workers who were self-employed. The proportion who were paid employees increased from 42.7 to 69.5 per cent. These changes reflect the shift away from employment in the primary sector towards employment in secondary and tertiary sectors.

The decline in the share of the self-employed and family workers is consistent with the changes accompanying economic development and the decline in employment in the agricultural sector in other countries. This generally takes the form of fewer young workers entering the primary sector as well as younger, mobile workers leaving agricultural employment. As a result, the labour force in the agricultural sector has been ageing more rapidly than the total labour force.

TABLE 7.10
Distribution of Labour Force by Type of Worker (per cent)

|      | Male | | | Female | | |
|---|---|---|---|---|---|---|
| Year | Self-employed | Family Worker | Paid Employee | Self-employed | Family Worker | Paid Employee |
| 1962 | 26.7 | 10.8 | 66.6 | 13.8 | 43.5 | 42.7 |
| 1965 | 24.7 | 8.7 | 66.7 | 14.1 | 39.5 | 46.4 |
| 1970 | 22.4 | 6.0 | 71.6 | 14.3 | 30.9 | 54.9 |
| 1975 | 20.2 | 3.9 | 76.0 | 14.2 | 25.8 | 60.0 |
| 1980 | 19.5 | 3.3 | 77.3 | 13.7 | 23.0 | 63.3 |
| 1985 | 18.0 | 2.8 | 79.2 | 12.5 | 20.0 | 67.5 |
| 1988 | 17.4 | 2.7 | 79.9 | 11.8 | 18.7 | 69.5 |

*Source*: As for Table 7.3.

*Redistribution of Employment by Industries*

The intertemporal changes in employment status, described above, have been closely tied to the shifts in manpower requirements by industry. In 1960, 37.5 per cent of the labour force was in the primary sector composed of agriculture, forestry, and fisheries and 24.4 per cent in the secondary sector composed of mining, manufacturing, and construction. The remaining 38.1 per cent of the labour force was employed in the tertiary sector of the economy. By 1986, considerable reallocation of the work-force had occurred. Only 8.5 per cent of the labour force was employed in the primary sector. Employment in the secondary sector had increased to 33.9 per cent of the total labour force and 57.2 per cent of the work-force was in the tertiary sector (Japanese Institute of Labor, 1988).

These changes in the interindustry distribution of employment indicate a rapid shift of workers from the primary sector to the tertiary industries of trade, finance, and the services. The dramatic redistribution of the Japanese labour force can be attributed to labour surpluses in rural agricultural areas in the 1960s which encouraged younger persons to leave these areas. In addition, the rapid growth of the urban industrial sector resulted in an increase in the relative demand for labour in the urban areas which provided an inducement for rural workers to move to the urban labour markets. These economic conditions produced increases in rural–urban migration rates. After 1970, rural–urban migration slowed in conjunction with slower economic growth in the urban areas and the decline in population growth in the rural areas. Past migration and lower fertility had depleted the excess supply of rural workers. As a result, employment and wage trends in the urban labour markets are increasingly determined by the native urban labour force.

*Capital Accumulation and Rate of Technological Innovation*

The capital stock of Japanese industries has increased rapidly, spurred along by a high national savings rate. The rapid increase in capital has facilitated the introduction of new technologies and production processes. The capital stock for all industries has more than doubled every ten years since 1955. This increase has been largest in the secondary and tertiary sectors of the economy.

The introduction of new technologies was facilitated by a growing labour force with a large number of entry-level workers who were more highly educated than the older workers. The rapid introduction of new technologies and the increase in available capital per worker shifted labour demand in favour of more highly educated workers. Thus, changes in production technology provided greater incentives for increased investment in human capital.

Accompanying these changes were a shift in the occupational distribution of the labour force. The percentage of workers who were professional, technical, and managerial workers increased from 7.1 per cent in 1960 to 12.9 per cent in 1986. Increases were also observed in the proportion of the labour force who were clerical, sales, and service workers. Increases in the share of total employment in these occupations were accomplished by the large decline in the proportion of the labour force who had been agricultural, forestry, and fisheries workers. The changing occupational mix of the labour force reflects the increased educational attainment of new entrants into the labour force.

## Employment Contracts and Compensation Policy

Over the past 50 years, the Japanese labour market has evolved into a system of long-term employment contracts for full-time workers. These contracts typically involve the promise of long-term employment that is terminated by mandatory retirement. While employed, the worker is largely protected from economic fluctuations. The worker receives regular cash compensation, a comprehensive set of employee benefits, and semi-annual bonuses.

For regular workers, cash earnings grow with seniority and the level of pay is often tied more to years of service than to performance. While workers are provided with considerable protection against lay-offs, the firm retains the right to move workers across many different jobs within the firm. Pay is unaffected by this flexibility of job assignment.

Semi-annual bonuses are paid to most workers. They are typically paid during the summer and at the end of the year. Bonuses may vary with the profitability of the firm; however, in the 1980s, they apparently have almost become a fixed percentage of compensation. Table 7.11 shows annual bonuses divided by monthly earnings for selected years. For most years, bonuses have ranged between 2.5 and 3.5 months of compensation. In the 1980s, the variation in the annual bonus has been much smaller ranging between 3.29 and 3.38 months of pay for men and between 2.91 and 2.98 months of pay for women.

In principle, the bonus system provides employers the opportunity to reduce total compensation during periods of low profitability. Thus, compensation is reduced instead of reducing employment. The lack of flexibility in the annual bonus during the 1980s suggests that this is no longer true as bonuses have become a quasi-fixed component of compensation.

Bonuses are a larger fraction of total compensation in larger firms. Table 7.11 shows that bonuses typically represent four months of earnings for workers in firms with 1,000 or more employees but only around two months for workers in firms with 10–99 workers. The lower bonuses for women than for men are primarily a reflection of the employment distribution of women compared to men. Within a firm, benefits and bonuses are typically determined by using the same formula for all permanent workers.

Female workers tend to have fewer years of job tenure and lower salaries than male workers. Their intermittent pattern of labour supply

TABLE 7.11
Annual Bonus Divided by Monthly Earnings (months)

|  |  |  |  | Firm Size |  |  |
|---|---|---|---|---|---|---|
| Year | Male | Female | Total | 10–99 | 100–999 | 1,000 or more |
| 1970 | 2.89 | 2.53 | 2.81 | 1.98 | 2.71 | 3.37 |
| 1975 | 3.63 | 3.09 | 3.52 | 2.57 | 3.49 | 4.16 |
| 1980 | 3.30 | 2.95 | 3.24 | 2.27 | 3.17 | 3.96 |
| 1985 | 3.32 | 2.99 | 3.26 | 2.19 | 3.20 | 4.02 |
| 1988 | 3.38 | 2.94 | 3.29 | 2.31 | 3.20 | 3.96 |

*Source*: As for Table 7.1.

associated with marriage and childbearing differs sharply from the long-term employment relationship of men with a single company. They are more often part-time or temporary workers. Part-time employees have higher turnover rates than permanent workers and are often excluded from many employee benefits. The proportion of employees who are part-time workers has increased from 2.9 per cent in 1975 to 8.6 per cent in 1985. Smaller firms have a higher percentage of part-time workers than larger firms; however, firms of all sizes have increased their utilization of part-time employees (Table 7.12).

Virtually all Japanese firms specify an age at which workers must retire. In 1988, 88 per cent of all firms with 30 or more employees enforced a mandatory retirement policy. The proportion of firms with such policies has increased steadily since 1973 when only two-thirds of firms had such policies. Large firms are more likely to have mandatory retirement policies than small firms. In addition, small firms are less likely to rigidly enforce mandatory rules.

The traditional age for mandatory retirement was 55; however, the age of mandatory retirement has been increasing over time. In 1967, 63 per cent of all firms imposed mandatory retirement at age 55. By 1989, the proportion of firms using age 55 had declined to 20.7 per cent

TABLE 7.12
Proportion of Employees Who Are Part-time Workers (per cent)

| Firm Size | 1975 | 1978 | 1979 | 1980 | 1984 | 1985 |
|---|---|---|---|---|---|---|
| Total | 2.9 | 4.7 | 6.0 | 5.8 | 7.6 | 8.6 |
| 5–29 | 5.4 | 7.0 | 9.8 | 7.9 | 10.0 | 11.4 |
| 30–99 | 3.2 | 5.4 | 7.3 | 6.7 | 11.2 | 11.2 |
| 100–299 | 2.9 | 5.1 | 6.0 | 6.8 | 6.9 | 8.9 |
| 300–999 | 1.6 | 3.5 | 4.8 | 6.3 | 6.0 | 7.3 |
| 1,000 or more | 1.4 | 3.1 | 2.9 | 3.8 | 5.3 | 5.7 |

*Source*: Japanese Institute of Labor (1987: 72).

TABLE 7.13
Mandatory Retirement Age by Size of Firm, 1989

| Firm Size | 54 or Lower | 55 | 56–59 | 60 | 61–64 | 65 | 66 or Older |
|---|---|---|---|---|---|---|---|
| All firms | 0.5 | 20.7 | 17.0 | 57.6 | 1.1 | 2.9 | 0.3 |
| 30–99 | 0.7 | 21.8 | 16.3 | 56.4 | 1.1 | 3.4 | 0.3 |
| 100–299 | 0.2 | 20.0 | 18.5 | 57.9 | 1.0 | 2.2 | 0.2 |
| 300–999 | 0.0 | 15.6 | 19.0 | 62.8 | 1.8 | 0.8 | 0.0 |
| 1,000–4,999 | 0.0 | 10.4 | 14.5 | 74.0 | 0.7 | 0.4 | 0.0 |
| 5,000 and over | 0.0 | 4.9 | 8.7 | 86.4 | 0.0 | 0.0 | 0.0 |

*Source*: Murakami (1991: 133).

while 57.6 per cent used age 60. Table 7.13 shows the distribution of mandatory retirement ages in 1989 by firm size. Large firms are much more likely to establish age 60 as the mandatory retirement age.

The government has been promoting the raising of the age of mandatory retirement as a social requirement of an ageing society. Since the government has been unable or unwilling to require firms to raise the age of retirement, the introduction has not been smoothly accomplished. One of the primary deterrents to raising the mandatory retirement age is the seniority-oriented wage system under which the postponement of retirement age leads to larger wage bills and tends to retard promotional prospects and reduce the rate of hiring of new workers.

With the increase in the mandatory retirement age, companies have begun to re-examine the seniority-based wage system and the related retirement benefits which are based on years of service and final earnings. Firms, particularly large firms, have started to modify the compensation system by basing a larger portion of pay on ability and slowing down the rate of increase associated with age or tenure. Martin and Ogawa (1988) and Clark and Ogawa (1992b) have found that the gain in earnings from remaining on the job has been modified over time. Pay increase based on seniority is affected by the age structure of the labour force and the rate of economic growth.

## Conclusion

One of the primary determinants of the rapid growth of the Japanese economy has been the quality of its labour force. During the 1950s and 1960s, low rates of fertility following the post-war baby boom meant that the labour force grew at a more rapid rate than the population. The existence of a relatively large stock of younger workers kept labour costs low given the prevailing seniority-based wage system. Thus, the increase in labour demand did not result in large increases in labour costs.

In the 1970s and 1980s, the growth of the labour force has slowed reflecting past fertility experience; however, the quality of the labour force has continued to improve. Educational attainment has risen sharply and investment in human capital by firms has increased the stock of human capital in Japan.

The Japanese population and labour force are now ageing rapidly. The challenge facing firms during the years 1990–2010 will be to manage an ageing labour force. Instead of having large entry-level cohorts who have relatively low wages, who bring the latest training from the educational system, and are more flexible in their job assignments, firms now face the prospect of dealing with relatively smaller entry-level cohorts and a larger number of older, relatively high-priced workers.

Industrial and governmental leaders are concerned about the economic effects of an ageing population and labour force. In order to stabilize social security and medical costs, the government is attempting to encourage later retirement. The government has attempted to raise the age of eligibility for Employees' Pension Insurance (the social security for paid employees) from 60 to 65 and to induce firms to raise their mandatory retirement ages to 65. To date these efforts have had only limited success but they are a clear signal for future government policy.

An increased age of retirement exacerbates the problems of an ageing labour force for individual firms. As a result, firms have responded by attempting to limit the rate of growth of pay for older workers and to reduce the value of continued employment on the accumulation of retirement benefits. These are attempts to lower the cost of older workers.

To a considerable degree, the future economic success of Japan will depend on its ability to adapt to an ageing labour force. The days of a young, growing labour force in which educational attainment was increasing rapidly are over. Labour productivity and labour costs of production will depend on the effective management of an ageing labour force.

---

1. The Philippines is an exception to this conclusion. Relatively high literacy rates have been achieved together with high levels of educational attainment; however, the rate of economic growth has remained relatively low.

2. All tenure data are based on findings from *Basic Survey on Wage Structure*, Japanese Institute of Labor.

3. These projections are from the macro-demographic model built by the Nihon University Population Research Institute.

# PART III
# EDUCATION IN DEVELOPMENT: CASE-STUDIES

# 8
# Dilemmas in Expanding Education for Faster Economic Growth: Indonesia, Malaysia, and Thailand*

Gavin W. Jones

## Introduction

INDONESIA, Malaysia, and Thailand have achieved sustained economic development over the 1970s and 1980s. It is difficult to determine to what extent the rapid expansion of their education systems has contributed to this rapid economic growth, and to what extent the expansion of education followed from this economic growth in the sense that the latter made it easier to finance the enlargement of the former. In any event, the enlargement of education systems has not yet run its course and crucial decisions remain about appropriate rates of expansion and appropriate educational structures. This chapter will address certain issues regarding the employment of the better educated which are occupying the minds of politicians and planners throughout the region.

## Trends in Labour Supply, Employment, and Education from the 1970s to 1990s

*Labour Supply*

Planners in South-East Asia are so used to dealing with the problems of a massive growth in the labour force that the changing demographic dynamics—which will interact with changing educational dynamics to lead to both a sharp decline in growth rates of the labour force and a dramatically different age–education profile—need to be emphasized.

The example of Indonesia will illustrate the point. During the 1970s the labour force was growing at about 2.7 per cent per annum and in the early 1980s by about 3 per cent per annum[1] as successively larger cohorts, born in the 1950s and 1960s, reached working age. However, with the onset of fertility decline in the 1970s, growth of the child population has decelerated. This deceleration was noted at primary school

*The author wishes to acknowledge the valuable research assistance provided by Pat Quiggin and Josefina Cabigon in the preparation of this chapter.

level from the early 1980s and has in the late 1980s begun to affect secondary school ages as well. The age-group 5–14 is expected to grow by only 0.5 per cent per annum in the Fifth Plan period, 1988–93 (Booth, 1989: Table 8). By the mid-1990s, the growth of the youngest segment of the labour force will have almost ceased, with actual declines in the number of labour force entrants in the provinces with the sharpest declines in birth rates (for example, East Java, Bali, and North Sulawesi).

These trends will take a long time to halt the growth of Indonesia's labour force because the older segments of the labour force are continuing to grow (Table 8.1). Moreover, even with the deceleration in growth of the number of work-force entrants, the ratio of entrants to leavers will be about four to one up to the end of the twentieth century (Keyfitz, 1989). Total labour force growth will, however, steadily decelerate. The 1990s will be the last decade in which the rapid overall growth of the labour force will constitute a major problem, but the problem will be exacerbated in its labour market impact by the additional problem of absorbing rapidly growing numbers of educated workers. The age–education profile of the labour force will change dramatically because the young labour force entrants will be progressively better educated, and the uneducated will be confined increasingly to progressively older segments of the work-force. Each person leaving the work-force is likely to be illiterate; three of the four persons replacing him will normally have a high school education.

Indonesian demographic trends will be a replay of those in Thailand, delayed by five or ten years. After 1990, the number at age 20–24 will cease to increase in Thailand, and after 1995, there will be no further growth in number at age 25–29 (Jones, 1988b: Table 8). But the older segments of the work-force will continue to grow rapidly well into the twenty-first century, leading to a significant ageing of the work-force. In Malaysia, the same trends will be in evidence, but in a more muted form, due to the deceleration in fertility decline after 1978.

TABLE 8.1
Indonesia: Index of Growth of Labour Force Age-groups, 1985–2000

|  | 1985 | 1990 | 1995 | 2000 |
|---|---|---|---|---|
| All ages 15–64 | 100 | 114 | 126 | 141 |
| 15–19 | 100 | 112 | 113 | 116 |
| 20–24 | 100 | 116 | 130 | 132 |
| 25–29 | 100 | 110 | 127 | 144 |
| 30–34 | 100 | 122 | 135 | 157 |
| 35–44 | 100 | 114 | 141 | 164 |
| 45–64 | 100 | 113 | 119 | 140 |
| Ratio, population 30–64/15–29 | 1.039 | 1.066 | 1.098 | 1.220 |

*Source*: Calculated from projections of the United Nations (1988d).

## Employment

Primary industry still dominates the employment structure in all three countries, but its dominance is declining fairly rapidly. Between 1965 and 1985, the percentage share of agriculture in total employment decreased in Indonesia from 71 to 55 per cent, in Malaysia from 59 to 30 per cent, and in Thailand from 82 to 68 per cent.

These figures can give only a rough indication, particularly for intercountry but also for intertemporal comparisons, because of the different approaches to counting people (especially women and unpaid family workers) as employed. However, the relative movement out of agriculture is clear and in Malaysia the point appears to have been reached where absolute numbers in agriculture are declining. Economic trends in Thailand since the mid-1980s have almost certainly meant that the surprisingly slow decline in agriculture's share of employment (Sussangkarn, 1988) is now a thing of the past.

The prospects are for a continued shift out of agriculture, probably at an accelerated pace (South Korea, after all, showed the way with a decline in agriculture's share from 55 to 36 per cent in just 15 years after 1965, a performance almost exactly paralleled, with a slight lag, by Malaysia). This will be associated with both increased urbanization and with a growing share of non-agricultural employment in rural areas (Anderson and Leiserson, 1980), some of which will be associated with the development of zones of intense urban–rural interaction (McGee, 1988).

Associated with these trends will be a rise in the share of professional, managerial, and clerical occupations (P, M, and C) in total employment. This has been the trend in recent years: the share of these occupations in total employment rose, between 1970 and 1985, from 4 to 7 per cent in Thailand, from 11 to 20 per cent in Malaysia, and from 6 to 8 per cent in Indonesia. Just how rapidly this share will increase in future will have a crucial bearing on employment prospects for the educated, because in 1985 this group of occupations provided between 55 and 66 per cent of total employment for those with senior high school education and above in the three countries under discussion.

As shown in Table 8.2, growth of employment in the P, M, and C occupations combined was 75 per cent faster than that of employment as a whole in Indonesia, and in Thailand and Malaysia more than three times as rapid. However, because of the small employment base in these occupations, the P, M, and C occupations provided only 11 per cent and 14 per cent of total employment growth in Indonesia and Thailand respectively over the 1970–85 period, though in Malaysia their share of employment growth was higher at 32 per cent.

The much higher share of P, M, and C occupations in total employment in Malaysia than in Indonesia or Thailand is because of its more advanced economy. In the simplest of terms, the share is high in Malaysia mainly because the share of agriculture in total employment is much lower there than in the other countries. But even if agriculture is

TABLE 8.2
Indonesia, Thailand, and Malaysia: Change in Employment by Occupation, 1970–1985

|  | Indonesia |  |  | Thailand |  |  | Malaysia |  |  |
|---|---|---|---|---|---|---|---|---|---|
|  | (thousands) |  | Percentage Increase | (thousands) |  | Percentage Increase | (thousands) |  | Percentage Increase |
|  | 1971 | 1985 | 1971–85 | 1970 | 1985 | 1970–85 | 1970 | 1985 | 1970–85 |
| Professional, technical, and related | 919 | 2,174 | 137 | 284 | 789 | 178 | 157 | 427 | 172 |
| Managerial and administrative | 206 | 99 | −52 | 247 | 402 | 63 | 25 | 129 | 416 |
| Clerical and related | 1,386 | 2,464 | 78 | 190 | 588 | 209 | 163 | 551 | 238 |
| Total P, M, and C | 2,511 | 4,737 | 89 | 721 | 1,779 | 147 | 345 | 1,107 | 221 |
| Sales | 4,565 | 9,276 | 103 | 833 | 2,447 | 194 | 272 | 626 | 130 |
| Service | 1,715 | 2,324 | 36 | 472 | 888 | 88 | 270 | 643 | 138 |
| Agricultural and farming | 27,407 | 34,555 | 26 | 13,217 | 15,340 | 16 | 1,750 | 1,720 | −2 |
| Production and related | 5,063 | 11,565 | 128 | 1,378 | 3,857 | 180 | 640 | 1,557 | 173 |
| Total | 41,261 | 62,457 | 51 | 16,652 | 24,220 | 45 | 3,287 | 5,653 | 72 |

*Percentage Distribution*

|  | Indonesia 1971 | Indonesia 1985 | Thailand 1970 | Thailand 1985 | Malaysia 1970 | Malaysia 1985 |
|---|---|---|---|---|---|---|
| Professional, technical, and related | 2.2 | 3.5 | 1.7 | 3.3 | 4.8 | 7.6 |
| Managerial and administrative | 0.5 | 0.2 | 1.5 | 1.7 | 0.8 | 2.3 |
| Clerical and related | 3.3 | 3.9 | 1.1 | 2.4 | 5.0 | 9.7 |
| Total P, M, and C | 6.0 | 7.6 | 4.3 | 7.4 | 10.6 | 19.6 |
| Sales | 11.1 | 14.9 | 5.0 | 10.0 | 8.3 | 11.1 |
| Service | 4.2 | 3.7 | 2.8 | 3.7 | 8.2 | 11.4 |
| Agricultural and Farming | 66.4 | 55.3 | 49.4 | 63.1 | 53.5 | 30.4 |
| Production and related | 12.3 | 18.5 | 8.3 | 15.8 | 19.4 | 27.5 |
| Total | 100.0 | 100.0 | 100.0 | 100.0 | 100.0 | 100.0 |

*Sources*: Indonesia: 1971 Population Census; 1985 Intercensal Survey (SUPAS); Thailand: 1970 Population Census; 1985 Labour Force Surveys; Malaysia: 1970 Population Census; 1985–6 Labour Force Survey.

*Notes*: For Thailand, figures for the two years are not strictly comparable. The figure used for 1970 is the economically active population which comprises those employed on the census date, or who had worked on any day during the seven days preceding the census date, as well as experienced workers who were looking for work and those waiting for the farming season. For 1985, the figures are the employed population averaged over the three rounds of the Labour Force Survey. For Indonesia in 1971 and for Malaysia in 1970, the groups 'others and unknown' (Indonesia) and 'occupation not adequately described' (Malaysia) was distributed pro rata across the occupational groups.

excluded, the share of P, M, and C employment in total non-agricultural employment is also higher in Malaysia than in Indonesia or Thailand (28 per cent as against 17 per cent and 20 per cent, respectively). In both Indonesia and Thailand, the share of P, M, and C employment in total non-agricultural employment actually fell slightly between 1970 and 1985, whereas in Malaysia it increased substantially.

The rise in the share of P, M, and C employment in total employment in these three countries can be expected to continue, if the experience of three advanced countries—Japan, the United States, and Australia—is any guide. Figure 8.1 shows the share of P, M, and C employment in these three countries from 1960 to 1988, compared with the South-East Asian countries under discussion. The relevance of the comparison is increased by linking the employment share with the level of per capita income at the time of the different observations (Figure 8.2), on the assumption that the pattern followed in the developed countries may be followed in other countries as they develop.[2]

The comparison shows that even in Malaysia, the share of P, M, and C employment can be expected to go higher than the 20 per cent already reached in 1984. In Japan, P, M, and C employment had reached 24 per cent of total employment by 1968, and by 1987 had risen further to almost 33 per cent. In the United States, the 33 per cent figure had already been reached in 1960, and in Australia before 1976.

FIGURE 8.1
Trends in Share of Professional, Managerial, and Clerical Employment Over Time: Selected Countries

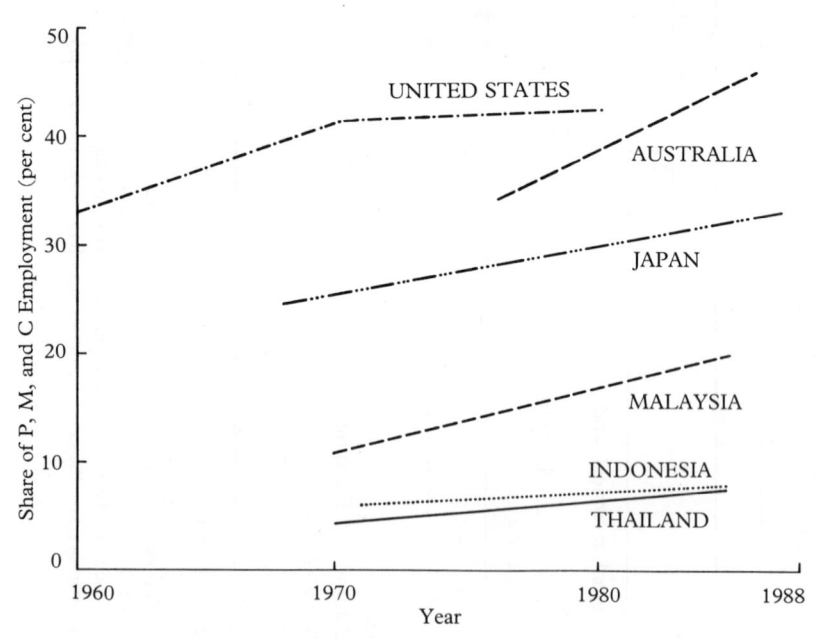

*Sources*: Based on census data in each country.

FIGURE 8.2
Share of Professional, Managerial, and Clerical Employment by Level of GNP Per Capita: Selected Countries

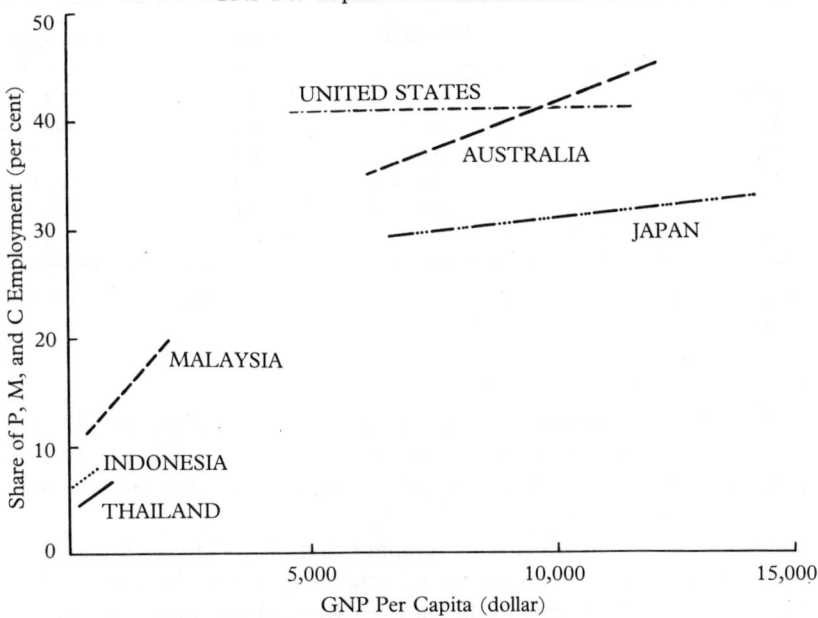

*Sources*: Based on census data in each country; GNP per capita data are from World Bank, *World Development Report 1990*.

In the United States, it had risen to 45 per cent in 1980, and to 46 per cent in Australia before 1986.

One might argue that the rise in the share of P, M, and C employment would tend to be slower if the labour force and total employment was growing rapidly, because there is likely to be a limit to the growth rates that could be achieved in P, M, and C employment. It is true that the growth rate of total employment in Japan, Australia, and the United States over the period being considered was only modest: not much over 1 per cent per annum in Japan, and about 1.5 per cent in Australia and the United States. By contrast, total employment in the three South-East Asian countries has grown much faster: by about 3 per cent per annum in Indonesia, 2.5 per cent in Thailand, and 3.7 per cent in Malaysia. These rapid growth rates will continue into the 1990s, though the rates will be slowing, most markedly in Thailand, as a result of a deceleration in growth of the labour force due to earlier fertility declines.

*Education*

A useful summary measure of the educational composition of the labour force is its mean years of schooling (Psacharopoulos and Arriagada, 1986). Table 8.3 shows how the mean years of schooling of the labour force in Malaysia, Thailand, and Indonesia have increased over time.

TABLE 8.3
Trends in Mean Years of Schooling of the Labour Force

|      | Malaysia | Thailand | Indonesia |
|------|----------|----------|-----------|
| 1960 | n.a.     | 3.3      | n.a.      |
| 1967 | 5.0      | n.a.     | n.a.      |
| 1971 | n.a.     | n.a.     | 2.8       |
| 1974 | n.a.     | 4.1      | n.a.      |
| 1980 | 6.5      | 4.6      | 3.6       |
| 1985 | 7.4      | 4.7      | 4.6       |

*Source*: Psacharopoulos and Arriagada (1986: Table 2); writer's calculations for Indonesia and for the other countries in 1985, using the same formula.
n.a. = Not available.

Although the schooling level has increased substantially in all cases, Thailand and Indonesia remain well below the level for Latin America and the Caribbean (5.8 years) and especially the developed market economies (10 years).

These changes in educational composition of the labour force reflect prior changes in the provision of schooling. Over the 1960s–1980s Indonesia, Thailand, and Malaysia have stressed the attainment of universal primary education. The limited evidence from rates-of-returns studies, not to mention the broader benefits of a literate population, suggests that this was an appropriate emphasis (Jones, 1988b). There is still some way to go in reaching universal primary education in Indonesia and Thailand, particularly if 'universal' means the elimination of 'drop out' before the completion of primary school. But the task remaining at the primary level is fairly straightforward, particularly in view of the slow growth of potential student numbers due to the sharp fertility declines in these three countries.

By the late 1980s, then, the emphasis has shifted to the expansion of secondary and tertiary education. Here the task is not so easy, both because of the higher costs per student and also because the secondary education base is still surprisingly small, particularly in Indonesia and Thailand (Table 8.4). Steady progress has been made over the 1970s and 1980s in raising secondary and tertiary enrolment rates in all three countries (though since the mid-1970s progress has been much slower in Thailand than in the other two countries), and there is no doubt that the rapid expansion of secondary education will be a major preoccupation of all three countries over the first half of the 1990s.

Secondary education in Thailand has been underdeveloped for a country at its stage of economic growth (Sussangkarn, 1988: 24). This can be partly explained by the underdevelopment, until recently, of the upper grades of primary education (Jones, 1975; Knodel and Wongsith, 1989b) as well as by the low returns to post-primary education in the dominant agriculture sector (Sussangkarn, 1988: 24–31). However, the

TABLE 8.4
Proportion of Age-group Enrolled in Secondary and Higher Education:
Comparison of ASEAN Countries with South Korea and Japan (per cent)

| Country | Secondary Education 1965 | Secondary Education 1987 | Higher Education 1965 | Higher Education 1987 |
|---|---|---|---|---|
| Indonesia | 12 | 46 | 1 | 7 |
| Philippines | 41 | 68 | 19 | 38 |
| Thailand | 14 | 28 | 2 | 20 |
| Malaysia | 28 | 59 | 2 | 7 |
| Singapore | 45 | 71 | 10 | 12 |
| South Korea | 35 | 88 | 6 | 36 |
| Japan | 82 | 96 | 13 | 28 |

*Source*: World Bank, *World Development Report 1989* and *1990*, Table 29.

*Note*: Secondary school age range depends on national definitions. It is most commonly considered to be 12–17 years. The age range for higher education is taken to be 20–24 years.

current rapid evolution of the Thai economy indicates the urgent need to increase the supply of middle-level manpower. This will require a rapid rise in the transition rate from primary to secondary education, which is currently less than 50 per cent. The need is particularly acute in view of the expected absolute decline in the primary school age population, the source of future secondary school enrolments (Sussangkarn and Chalamwong, 1989).

Peninsular Malaysia has made impressive gains in enrolments at the secondary school level since about 1960, and the gains have been particularly impressive for girls and for ethnic Malays of both sexes. The social change engendered by these trends would be hard to exaggerate. One can imagine the implications, for example, of the shift in the modal level of educational attainment of women as revealed by the 1980 census from no education for women in their 50s to primary education for those in their 30s and secondary education for those in their teens.

As successively better educated cohorts of young people enter the labour force, the average educational level of the labour force in these three countries will continue to rise. The remainder of this chapter will discuss some of the implications of this rise in educational levels.

## What Is the Appropriate Rate of Expansion of Secondary and Higher Education?

At certain periods in the economic development of most countries there is a need for rapid growth in the number of educated workers. Such periods may have to do with the replacement of expatriate administrators at the time of independence, or with periods of particularly rapid economic growth and structural change. Two related rigidities tend to

TABLE 8.5
Percentage Distribution of Occupations of Employed Population at Each Educational Level: Indonesia, Thailand, and Malaysia, 1985

| Main Occupation | No Schooling | Incomplete Primary | Primary School | General High School Junior | General High School Senior | Vocational High School | Academy | University | Total |
|---|---|---|---|---|---|---|---|---|---|
| **Indonesia** | | | | | | | | | |
| Professional | 0.1 | 0.1 | 0.5 | 2.4 | 10.8 | 36.7 | 51.8 | 51.3 | 3.4 |
| Managerial | 0.0 | 0.0 | 0.0 | 0.2 | 1.4 | 0.3 | 3.8 | 5.3 | 0.2 |
| Clerical | 0.1 | 0.5 | 2.1 | 10.0 | 35.7 | 17.3 | 31.1 | 34.4 | 3.9 |
| Sales | 13.9 | 13.8 | 16.4 | 22.5 | 18.3 | 9.4 | 3.5 | 2.5 | 14.8 |
| Service | 3.4 | 3.2 | 4.3 | 5.7 | 4.5 | 3.5 | 1.2 | 0.8 | 3.4 |
| Agriculture | 70.8 | 64.3 | 53.0 | 30.8 | 9.8 | 11.2 | 2.3 | 2.0 | 55.1 |
| Construction | — | — | — | — | — | — | — | — | — |
| Production | 11.2 | 17.4 | 23.2 | 28.4 | 19.5 | 21.6 | 6.3 | 3.7 | 18.4 |
| Total | 100.0 | 100.0 | 100.0 | 100.0 | 100.0 | 100.0 | 100.0 | 100.0 | 100.0 |
| Numbers ('000) | 13,562 | 21,489 | 17,233 | 3,525 | 2,194 | 3,658 | 471 | 326 | 62,457 |
| **Thailand**[a] | | | | | | | | | |
| Professional | 0.2 | 0.2 | 0.2 | 2.7 | 7.4 | 13.8 | 68.2 | 51.8 | 3.4 |
| Managerial | 0.5 | 0.6 | 0.5 | 3.5 | 5.5 | 6.9 | 4.1 | 24.5 | 1.4 |
| Clerical | 0.2 | 0.4 | 0.6 | 10.6 | 18.5 | 36.1 | 9.5 | 8.9 | 2.3 |
| Sales | 12.0 | 9.1 | 7.9 | 17.4 | 17.1 | 13.4 | 4.7 | 6.8 | 9.6 |
| Service | 2.0 | 3.2 | 9.9 | 12.3 | 10.5 | 2.2 | 1.7 | 4.4 | 4.7 |

|  |  |  |  |  |  |  |  |  |
|---|---|---|---|---|---|---|---|---|
| Agriculture | 75.6 | 70.8 | 66.5 | 29.1 | 24.0 | 8.6 | 6.0 | 1.2 | 63.5 |
| Construction | 0.6 | 2.8 | 2.0 | 6.2 | 4.2 | 3.6 | 0.9 | 0.6 | 2.6 |
| Production | 8.9 | 12.9 | 12.4 | 18.2 | 12.8 | 15.4 | 4.9 | 1.8 | 12.5 |
| Total | 100.0 | 100.0 | 100.0 | 100.0 | 100.0 | 100.0 | 100.0 | 100.0 | 100.0 |
| Numbers ('000) | 1,789 | 15,541 | 3,921 | 1,225 | 337 | 515 | 682 | 318 | 24,447 |
| Malaysia[b] |  |  |  |  |  |  |  |  |  |
| Professional | 0.4 | 1.2 |  | 3.2 | 14.8 | n.a. | 72.0 |  | 7.4 |
| Managerial | 0.2 | 0.9 |  | 1.3 | 3.8 | n.a. | 14.9 |  | 2.1 |
| Clerical | 0.3 | 1.5 |  | 9.0 | 33.9 | n.a. | 6.3 |  | 9.7 |
| Sales | 8.0 | 10.6 |  | 14.1 | 11.4 | n.a. | 3.0 |  | 10.8 |
| Service | 8.9 | 12.6 |  | 14.4 | 10.3 | n.a. | 1.0 |  | 11.5 |
| Agriculture | 66.5 | 39.6 |  | 16.6 | 6.6 | n.a. | 1.4 |  | 30.4 |
| Construction | – | – |  | – | – | – | – |  | – |
| Production | 15.7 | 33.6 |  | 41.4 | 19.2 | n.a. | 1.4 |  | 28.2 |
| Total | 100.0 | 100.0 |  | 100.0 | 100.0 | n.a. | 100.0 |  | 100.0 |
| Numbers ('000) | 822 | 2,220 |  | 1,138 | 1,145 | n.a. | 241 |  | 5,567 |

*Sources*: Indonesia: 1985 Intercensal Survey; Thailand: 1985 Labour Force Survey.

*Notes*: For all countries: 'Primary School' includes those with incomplete junior high school; 'Junior High School' includes those with incomplete senior high school. For Indonesia: 'Vocational High School' includes those with junior and senior vocational high school. For Thailand: 'Incomplete Primary' includes those with less than Pratom 4 and lower elementary; 'Academy' includes those with technical, vocational, and teacher training. Numbers and percentages may not total: Indonesia: occupation 'not stated' is excluded; Thailand: educational levels 'short course training', 'others', and 'unknown' are excluded.

[a] Data for Thailand are the averages of the February and August Rounds of the Labour Force Survey.

[b] Data for Malaysia refer to 1984; they are based on unpublished tabulations from the 1984 Labour Force Survey.

n.a. = Not available.

TABLE 8.6
Percentage Distribution of Educational Level of Employed Population in
Each Occupation Group: Indonesia, Thailand, and Malaysia, 1985

| | Professional | Managerial | Clerical | Sales | Service | Agriculture | Construction | Productions | Total |
|---|---|---|---|---|---|---|---|---|---|
| Indonesia | | | | | | | | | |
| No schooling | 0.7 | 1.0 | 0.5 | 20.5 | 19.9 | 28.1 | — | 13.3 | 21.7 |
| Incomplete primary | 1.3 | 4.3 | 4.1 | 32.2 | 29.7 | 40.4 | — | 32.7 | 34.4 |
| Primary school | 3.7 | 7.3 | 14.7 | 30.7 | 32.2 | 26.6 | — | 34.8 | 27.6 |
| Junior high school | 3.7 | 7.1 | 14.0 | 8.4 | 8.4 | 3.1 | — | 8.5 | 5.6 |
| Senior high school | 10.7 | 32.6 | 30.9 | 4.2 | 4.2 | 0.6 | — | 3.6 | 3.5 |
| Vocational high school | 61.2 | 12.8 | 25.5 | 3.7 | 5.3 | 1.2 | — | 20.2 | 5.9 |
| Academy | 11.0 | 17.7 | 5.8 | 0.2 | 0.2 | 0.0 | — | 0.2 | 0.8 |
| University | 7.7 | 17.2 | 4.5 | 0.1 | 0.1 | 0.0 | — | 0.1 | 0.5 |
| All education levels | 100.0 | 100.0 | 100.0 | 100.0 | 100.0 | 100.0 | — | 100.0 | 100.0 |
| Numbers ('000) | 2,151 | 98 | 2,439 | 9,180 | 2,300 | 34,198 | — | 11,445 | 62,457 |
| Thailand[a] | | | | | | | | | |
| No schooling | 0.5 | 2.5 | 0.6 | 9.1 | 3.2 | 8.7 | 1.8 | 5.2 | 7.3 |
| Incomplete primary | 4.7 | 28.6 | 11.5 | 60.1 | 42.8 | 70.8 | 67.5 | 65.7 | 63.6 |
| Primary school | 1.1 | 5.9 | 4.2 | 13.2 | 33.5 | 16.8 | 12.2 | 15.9 | 16.0 |
| Junior high school | 4.0 | 12.8 | 22.7 | 9.1 | 13.0 | 2.3 | 11.8 | 7.3 | 5.0 |
| Senior high school | 3.0 | 5.5 | 10.9 | 2.5 | 3.1 | 0.5 | 2.2 | 1.4 | 1.4 |

|  |  |  |  |  |  |  |  |  |
|---|---|---|---|---|---|---|---|---|
| Vocational high school | 8.7 | 10.6 | 32.5 | 3.0 | 1.0 | 0.3 | 2.9 | 2.6 | 2.1 |
| Academy | 57.0 | 8.4 | 11.3 | 1.4 | 1.0 | 0.3 | 1.0 | 1.1 | 2.8 |
| University | 20.2 | 23.3 | 5.0 | 0.9 | 1.2 | 0.0 | 0.3 | 0.2 | 1.3 |
| All education levels | 100.0 | 100.0 | 100.0 | 100.0 | 100.0 | 100.0 | 100.0 | 100.0 | 100.0 |
| Numbers ('000) | 817 | 336 | 573 | 2,341 | 1,153 | 15,527 | 645 | 3,054 | 24,446 |
| Malaysia[b] |  |  |  |  |  |  |  |  |  |
| No schooling | 0.9 | 1.6 | 0.4 | 11.0 | 11.5 | 32.3 | – | 8.2 | 14.8 |
| Incomplete primary | 6.7 | 16.8 | 6.4 | 39.2 | 43.8 | 51.9 | – | 47.5 | 39.0 |
| Primary school |  |  |  |  |  |  |  |  |  |
| Junior high school | 8.8 | 12.6 | 18.9 | 26.8 | 25.7 | 11.1 | – | 30.1 | 20.4 |
| Senior high school | 41.3 | 37.8 | 71.6 | 21.8 | 18.6 | 4.5 | – | 14.0 | 20.6 |
| Vocational high school | – | – | – | – | – | – | – | – | – |
| Tertiary | 42.3 | 31.2 | 2.7 | 1.2 | 0.4 | 0.2 | – | 0.2 | 4.3 |
| All education levels | 100.0 | 100.0 | 100.0 | 100.0 | 100.0 | 100.0 | – | 100.0 | 100.0 |
| Numbers ('000) | 410 | 115 | 541 | 600 | 638 | 1,694 | – | 1,568 | 5,667 |

*Sources*: As for Table 8.5.
*Notes*: As for Table 8.5.
[a]Data for Thailand are the averages of the February and August Rounds of the Labour Force Survey.
[b]Data for Malaysia refer to 1984; they are based on unpublished tabulations from the 1984 Labour Force Survey.

result, both of which are associated with the dynamics of labour force growth in youthful populations (that is, populations in which each successive age cohort is substantially larger than the cohort which precedes it). The first is that the better educated cohorts produced as a result of the initial increase in demand remain in the labour force for decades, long after the initial structural change has slowed down, and continue to raise its average educational level as they succeed older, more poorly educated cohorts. The second is that there is a 'ratchet effect' in the production of the educated: once an expansion of capacity has been achieved, there is a built-in tendency to utilize, and indeed to expand, that capacity, reinforced by: (i) the dynamics of the progression of cohorts of pupils through the school system and into higher education; and (ii) the non-labour market sources of demand for higher education.

Planners, then, cannot readily adjust the stream of educated young people entering the labour market to the perceived requirements of the labour market as if they were turning a tap. The tendency for the supply of educated individuals to outstrip the demand for them has long been noted in countries such as India and the Philippines. (The evidence is in the narrowing of wage differentials by education, and higher levels of unemployment among the educated.) Stewart (1987: 141) argues that this tendency 'is based on the historical observation that, in the long run, the income elasticity of demand for advanced education is higher than the income elasticity of demand for educated workers'.

In Indonesia, Malaysia, and Thailand, workers with secondary and tertiary education are heavily concentrated in three groups of occupations: professional, managerial, and clerical. In turn, a high proportion of jobs in these occupations are held by those with secondary and tertiary education (Tables 8.5 and 8.6). Whereas workers with a primary school education or less are heavily concentrated in agriculture, production, and sales occupations, for those with a high school education the balance shifts towards clerical and professional employment. Of those with senior high school education, one-third in Thailand and one-half in Indonesia and Malaysia are found in the occupational trio: professional, managerial, and clerical (P, M, and C).[3] At the top end of the educational range, among those with academy or university education, less than one-fifth are found outside the P, M, and C occupations, and more than half, indeed, 60 per cent in Thailand and 70 per cent in Malaysia are in the professions, including, of course, the teaching profession.

From the late 1970s to mid-1980s, the growth of employment in P, M, and C occupations appears to have been fast enough in Indonesia to maintain the proportions of the senior high school and college educated who find work in these occupations. But in Thailand, there is some evidence of slippage of the better educated into other, lower status occupations between 1977 and 1985 (Jones, 1988b: 24). This may have altered in the late 1980s with the high demand for educated workers resulting from double digit rates of annual economic growth.

As noted earlier, Thailand could face a shortage of middle-level (mainly high school educated) manpower. Paradoxically, however, it could simultaneously face an oversupply of university graduates in certain fields, particularly as a result of the rapid expansion of enrolments in open universities. In both Malaysia and Indonesia, the real testing period is yet to come because the numbers graduating from secondary and higher education and entering the labour market will increase rapidly.

To summarize, those with upper secondary and tertiary education are heavily concentrated in professional, managerial, and clerical occupations. This cluster of occupations has been growing quite rapidly, though probably not as fast as the numbers of the better educated. In future, the relative growth rates are likely to diverge much more dramatically, necessitating important rethinking of educational and employment policy.

**Likely Future Trends and Their Implications: Indonesia**

Two factors will lead to an inexorable momentum in the growing numbers of the better educated in Indonesia. The first factor is the much higher educational levels of each successive cohort entering the work-force since the 1950s. As these move up through the work-force and replace older cohorts, the average educational attainment of the work-force will continue to rise. The second factor is the official policies which ensure the further expansion of educational systems, in particular by increasing the transition rate from primary to secondary school. In Indonesia, the transition rate from primary to lower secondary school is targeted to rise from 68 to 85 per cent over the course of the Fifth Five-Year Plan period, and the lower secondary enrolment rate to rise from 53 to 67 per cent (Booth, 1989: 25). The aim is to achieve compulsory lower secondary education during the Sixth Plan period, that is, in the mid-1990s, and rapid expansion of upper secondary and tertiary education (Republik Indonesia, 1989: Chap. 20).

These two factors will ensure further rapid increases in the numbers of the better educated entering the work-force. Importantly, however, in the 1970s and 1980s the main source of pressure on the education system to expand—i.e. the ever increasing numbers moving through the primary school system where compulsory education policies were increasingly applied—had ceased to be operative in Thailand and Indonesia, because the near attainment of universal primary education has coincided with the attainment of near stationariness in the number of primary school age children. One implication is that the drive to achieve compulsory lower secondary education will be much more likely to succeed than if it had been attempted a decade earlier, around 1980.

In this section, some of the labour market issues arising in Indonesia as a result of these trends will be traced out. Can the economy absorb the rapidly growing numbers of high school and college educated in occupations where their education is appropriately utilized? It was noted earlier (in the first section) that on the basis of international comparisons, the share of P, M, and C employment should increase substantially as the Indonesian economy develops. A key issue for planners is whether this increase will come close to matching the increase in the numbers of better educated workers.

In examining this issue, the following steps will be taken: first, the growth of the better educated segment of the work-force will be projected; secondly, structural shift in employment based on projected rates of economic growth will be projected, that is, the projected growth in output and employment by industry in the Fifth Five-Year Plan (Repelita V) will be extrapolated up to the year 2000 for this purpose; thirdly, industry–occupation matrices will be used to project the growth of employment by occupational category in a number of different scenarios; and finally, based on occupation–education matrices as measured in the past, and observed trends in such matrices in more developed countries, trends in the allocation of better educated workers across occupational groups will be projected. The issues posed by these projections for educational and manpower planning will then be discussed.

*Educational Projections*

The following is the way in which the numbers in the work-force with junior high, senior high, and tertiary education were projected.

1. For the age-groups beyond school age in 1985, the educational attainment of each five-year cohort in 1985 was assumed to remain unchanged throughout the projection period, that is, there was assumed to be no mortality differential by education and no increase in education levels through adult education or other means.
2. For the age-groups within school age in 1985, the educational targets of the Fifth Five-Year Plan were used to project subsequent educational attainment, which again was assumed to remain constant once they had passed through the normal ages of high school and college education.
3. The projections were carried beyond the end of the Plan period (1993) to the year 2000 using assumptions about the likely increase in enrolment and graduates from the different levels of education, and the allocation of these graduates to appropriate age-groups.[4]

The results are summarized in Table 8.7, which shows that, given the above assumptions, the working-age population with high school or tertiary education will grow very rapidly up to the year 2000, leading to almost a trebling in these numbers in just 15 years. The growth will be most rapid at the tertiary level. In contrast, by the late 1990s, the numbers with no education or only primary school education will barely be growing. (In fact, the numbers with no education will be declining and the numbers with primary education continuing to increase.) The educational profile of potential workers will differ dramatically by age-group. Those aged above 40 will constitute almost half of the poorly educated groups (that is, with none or primary education), whereas

## TABLE 8.7
Summary Results of Educational Projections

### Average Annual Rates of Increase of 'Potential Work-force' (aged 20–64) by Education Level

| Level of Education | 1985 | 1990 | 1995 | 2000 | 1985–95 | 1995–2000 |
|---|---|---|---|---|---|---|
| None or primary | 62,651 | 67,586 | 70,729 | 73,036 | 1.2 | 0.6 |
| Lower secondary | 6,108 | 8,394 | 11,453 | 14,804 | 6.5 | 5.3 |
| Upper secondary | 7,826 | 11,329 | 16,138 | 22,107 | 7.5 | 6.5 |
| Tertiary | 750 | 1,412 | 2,678 | 4,410 | 13.6 | 10.5 |
| Total in secondary and tertiary | 14,684 | 21,135 | 30,269 | 41,321 | 7.5 | 6.4 |
| Total | 77,335 | 88,721 | 100,968 | 114,357 | 2.7 | 2.5 |

*Average Annual Rates of Increase (per cent)*

### Percentage Distribution of Potential Workers with Different Levels of Education by Age

| Age-group | None or Primary 1985 | 2000 | Lower Secondary 1985 | 2000 | Upper Secondary 1985 | 2000 | Tertiary 1985 | 2000 |
|---|---|---|---|---|---|---|---|---|
| 20–29 | 32 | 25 | 50 | 48 | 58 | 57 | 31 | 42 |
| 30–39 | 25 | 27 | 28 | 28 | 25 | 24 | 37 | 43 |
| 40–64 | 43 | 48 | 22 | 24 | 17 | 19 | 32 | 15 |
| All ages | 100 | 100 | 100 | 100 | 100 | 100 | 100 | 100 |

those in their 20s will constitute almost half of the secondary and tertiary educated.

### Structural Shift in Employment

The Fifth Five-Year Plan forecasts a 5 per cent average annual growth rate of GDP and a 3 per cent growth rate in employment. Agricultural employment is projected to grow at 2 per cent per annum and non-agricultural employment at 4.1 per cent per annum, with growth of

TABLE 8.8
Projection of Employment by Industry: Indonesia, 1985–2000

| Industry | Employment (thousands) 1985[a] | 1993[b] | 2000 | Percentage Increase 1985–2000 | Percentage Shares 1985 | 2000 |
|---|---|---|---|---|---|---|
| Agriculture and mining | 34,558 | 43,000 | 46,700 | 35 | 55.3 | 46.9 |
| Manufacturing | 5,796 | 8,300 | 12,100 | 109 | 9.3 | 12.2 |
| Electricity, gas, and water | 70 | 97 | 122 | 74 | 0.1 | 0.1 |
| Construction | 2,096 | 3,170 | 3,989 | 90 | 3.3 | 4.0 |
| Trade | 9,345 | 14,150 | 17,786 | 90 | 15.0 | 17.9 |
| Transport and communications | 1,958 | 2,924 | 3,663 | 87 | 3.1 | 3.7 |
| Finance, insurance, etc. | 250 | 346 | 448 | 79 | 0.4 | 0.5 |
| Public services | 8,317 | 11,725 | 14,733 | 77 | 13.3 | 14.8 |
| Total | 62,457 | 83,700 | 99,500 | 59 | 100 | 100 |

[a] Data are from the 1985 Intercensal Survey (SUPAS).
[b] End of Repelita V period.

manufacturing employment the fastest at 6.7 per cent per annum. The Plan implies the absorption of the growing labour force without increasing levels of unemployment. In the projections from 1993 to the year 2000, the writer used the same assumption.[5]

Employment was therefore projected to increase at 2.5 per cent per annum over this period, reflecting a decline in the growth of the work-force compared with the 1988–93 period. Agriculture was assumed to grow at 1.2 per cent per annum and non-agriculture at 3.8 per cent per annum. Detailed projections of employment by industry are shown in Table 8.8.

*The Industry–Occupation Matrix*

The next step is to convert these figures of employment by industry into estimates of employment by occupation, utilizing industry–occupation matrices. In general, the trends in industrial composition of employment could be expected to lead to a rise in the share of P, M, and C occupations, because the share of industries in which these occupations are underrepresented, especially agriculture, will fall. In addition to this, however, it is necessary to investigate whether industry–occupation matrices tend to remain constant over time, or whether experience in Indonesia as well as in other countries indicates the need to assume changes.

There are, in fact, enormous differences between the occupational composition of particular industries in Western countries and in a country such as Indonesia. For example, the P, M, and C occupations constitute 28 per cent of employment in the manufacturing sector in Australia (1986) but only 4 per cent in Indonesia (1985), reflecting the predominance of small-scale and cottage industries in Indonesia and of large and administratively more complex enterprises in Australia. Table 8.9 shows that the P, M, and C occupations tend to have a much larger share of employment within each industry in Australia compared with Indonesia. Over time, as the Indonesian economy gains in complexity, a rising share of P, M, and C employment within given industries could be expected.[6]

A shift–share analysis was conducted to test whether such a rise in the proportion of P, M, and C occupations in given industries has had a major part to play in the rising share of these occupations in total employment in Indonesia between 1971 and 1985. It revealed that of the total change in occupational structure, the industry shift effect accounted for 79 per cent, and the changing occupational composition of industries for the remainder of just over 20 per cent.[7] As shown in Table 8.10, much the same is true of P, M, and C occupations taken together: most of the net shift into these occupations is explained by

TABLE 8.9
Proportion of Employment in Professional, Managerial, and Clerical Occupations to Total Employment within Major Industries: Indonesia, Malaysia, and Australia (per cent)

|  | Indonesia 1985 | Malaysia 1984 | Australia 1986 |
|---|---|---|---|
| Agriculture | 0.0 | 0.9 | 73.0[b] |
| Mining and quarrying | 10.7 | 24.2 | 31.2 |
| Manufacturing | 4.0 | 13.0 | 28.1 |
| Electricity, gas, and water | 30.0 | 35.0 | 41.8 |
| Construction | 3.6 | 12.2 | 27.5 |
| Commerce and trade | 0.9 | 11.2 | 32.8 |
| Transport and communications | 10.2 | 28.1 | 29.7 |
| Finance and insurance | 61.6 | 77.4 | 71.6 |
| Community services[a] | 49.2 | 48.4 | 65.5 |
| All industries | 7.5 | 19.1 | 48.7 |

Sources: Indonesia: Supas, 1985; Malaysia: Unpublished tables from 1984 Labour Force Survey; Australia: 1986 Census, Cross Classified Characteristics of Persons and Dwellings, Table C41.

[a]Includes public administration and recreational services.
[b]The 'managerial' occupation appears to include all self-employed farmers. In earlier years, P, M, and C occupations contributed only about 2 per cent of total employment in agriculture. It should be noted that employment in agriculture constitutes only 6 per cent of total employment in Australia.

TABLE 8.10
Shift–Share Analysis of Change in Employment in Occupational Groups: Indonesia, 1971–1985

| Occupation | Number of Employees 1971 (1) | Number of Employees 1985 (2) | 1985 Total Weighted by 1971 Distribution Occupation (3) | 1985 Total Weighted by 1971 Distribution Occupation in Industry (4) | Actual Change (2) − (1) (5) | Expected Change (3) − (1) (6) | Net Shift (5) − (6) (7) | Components of (7) Industrial Shift (4) − (3) (8) | Components of (7) Occupation Shift (2) − (4) (9) | Percentage of Components to (1) Net Shift (7)/(1) (10) | Percentage of Components to (1) Industrial Shift (8)/(1) (11) | Percentage of Components to (1) Occupation Shift (9)/(1) (12) |
|---|---|---|---|---|---|---|---|---|---|---|---|---|
| Professional, technical, and related | 962,077 | 2,173,732 | 1,456,297 | 1,907,203 | 1,211,655 | 494,220 | 717,435 | 450,906 | 266,529 | 74.6 | 46.9 | 27.7 |
| Managerial and administrative | 206,309 | 98,569 | 312,290 | 420,137 | −107,740 | 105,981 | −213,721 | 107,847 | −321,568 | −103.6 | 52.3 | −155.9 |
| Clerical and related | 1,383,497 | 2,464,522 | 2,094,201 | 2,984,280 | 1,081,025 | 710,704 | 370,321 | 890,079 | −519,758 | 26.8 | 64.3 | −37.6 |
| Sales | 4,560,083 | 9,275,913 | 6,902,602 | 9,158,549 | 4,715,830 | 2,342,519 | 2,373,311 | 2,255,947 | 117,364 | 52.0 | 49.5 | 2.6 |
| Services | 1,712,795 | 2,323,803 | 2,592,659 | 3,461,051 | 611,008 | 879,864 | −268,856 | 868,392 | −1,137,248 | −15.7 | 50.7 | −66.4 |
| Agricultural and farming | 27,378,539 | 34,555,877 | 41,442,919 | 33,943,489 | 7,177,338 | 14,064,380 | −6,887,042 | −7,499,430 | 612,388 | −25.2 | −27.4 | 2.2 |
| Production and related | 5,057,915 | 11,564,722 | 7,656,170 | 10,582,429 | 6,506,807 | 2,598,255 | 3,908,522 | 2,926,259 | 982,293 | 77.3 | 57.9 | 19.4 |
| Total | 41,261,215 | 62,457,138 | 62,457,138 | 62,457,138 | 21,195,923 | 21,195,923 | 0 | 0 | 0 | | | |

changing industrial structure of employment. (The picture is somewhat blurred by the sharp decline in employment in managerial and administrative occupations, resulting from changes in definition.)

The fact that the compositional effect within industries explained little of the net shift in the occupational structure in Indonesia over this 14-year period does not necessarily mean that it will be unimportant in the future. As the Indonesian economy develops, it would be surprising if the occupational composition of employment within industries did not shift some way towards that prevailing in the industrialized countries. The difficulty is to find a basis on which to project this shift, particularly since it was not very important in this period of quite rapid economic development.

In the projections, three different scenarios are simply provided to test how much difference they would make. The first approach is to assume no compositional change within industries, so that any change in occupational structure is due entirely to the projected change in employment across industries. The second approach is to assume that the share of P, M, and C employment in each industry would shift one-half of the way towards its share in each industry in Malaysia in 1985. (This leaves the share well below that reached in industrialized countries; see Table 8.9 and Figure 8.2.) The third approach is to assume a shift towards Australian patterns of P, M, and C employment within industries. A shift sufficient to close one-third of the gap between these levels in Indonesia and Australia in 1985 is assumed; it would be unrealistic to expect that industrial country levels could be approached more rapidly than this rate in such a relatively short time period.

The growth of employment in different occupations according to these three different assumptions is shown in Table 8.11. The expected change in the industrial structure by itself would lead to a rise in the share of P, M, and C employment from 7.5 per cent in 1985 to 8.9 per cent in the year 2000. The additional occupational shift within industries implied by a halving of the gap between Indonesia and Malaysia would raise it further to 11.2 per cent, and finally a shift towards Australian levels would raise it to 13.4 per cent.

*The Occupation–Education Matrix*

The final step is to project the trend in employment for workers with different educational backgrounds, based on the most recent available occupation–education matrix (1985). Table 8.12 shows that if no change is hypothesized either in the industry–occupation matrix or the occupation–education matrix, there will be a substantial shortfall in jobs for the high school and tertiary educated; in fact, a dramatic shortfall in the case of the tertiary educated. In this case, changes in the employment of the better educated are due entirely to the shift in the industrial structure of employment. The assumption that the occupational structure within industries will shift towards Malaysian or Australian patterns, with a rising share of P, M, and C occupations, leads to a greater

TABLE 8.11
Projection of Employment by Occupation: Indonesia, 2000

| Occupation | Employment 1985 (1) | Employment in the Year 2000 under: ||||Percentage Increase in Employment 1985–2000 |||
|---|---|---|---|---|---|---|---|
| | | Assumption (1)[a] (2) | Assumption (2)[b] (3) | Assumption (3)[c] (4) | Assumption (1)[a] (5) | Assumption (2)[b] (6) | Assumption (3)[c] (7) |
| Professional, technical, and related | 2,289 | 4,051 | 4,427 | 5,091 | 77 | 93 | 122 |
| Managerial and administrative | 100 | 185 | 703 | 1,508 | 85 | 603 | 1,408 |
| Clerical and related | 2,562 | 4,593 | 5,995 | 6,748 | 79 | 134 | 163 |
| Total P, M, and C | 4,951 | 8,829 | 11,125 | 13,347 | 78 | 125 | 170 |
| Sales | 9,201 | 17,479 | n.a. | n.a. | 90 | n.a. | n.a. |
| Services | 2,431 | 4,323 | n.a. | n.a. | 78 | n.a. | n.a. |
| Agricultural and farming | 34,222 | 46,336 | n.a. | n.a. | 35 | n.a. | n.a. |
| Production and related | 11,653 | 22,574 | n.a. | n.a. | 94 | n.a. | n.a. |
| Total | 62,457 | 99,541 | 99,541 | 99,541 | 59 | 59 | 59 |

[a]Assumption (1): The 1985 industry-occupation matrix is unchanged in the year 2000.
[b]Assumption (2): Rise in P, M, and C share of employment in individual industries to close one-half of the gap between Indonesia and Malaysia in the share of these occupations. However, the share of clerical occupations was left unchanged in three industries: electricity, gas, and water; finance and insurance; and public services, because it was already slightly higher in Indonesia than in
[c]Assumption (3): Rise in P, M, and C share of employment in individual industries to close one-third of the gap between Indonesia and Australia in the share of these occupations. The one exception is agriculture, where the results of Assumption (2) were substituted.
n.a. = Not available.

absorption of the high school and tertiary educated, particularly if the share of the less educated in P, M, and C occupations is assumed to fall. But except in the case of a rapid shift toward Australian patterns, the growth rate of P, M, and C employment still lags behind the growth rate of the educated labour force, meaning that these occupations would not even be maintaining their share of the better educated work-force. The shortfall is particularly acute for the academy and university educated. The implication is that unemployment among the better educated would increase—and increase rapidly—unless the educated capture a higher share than before of employment, not only in P, M, and C occupations but in a wide range of other occupations as well.

What can be learned from more developed countries, which have a higher proportion of their labour force in the better educated groups, about likely trends in the educational mix in different occupations? International data available to the writer (for Malaysia, Taiwan, South Korea, Japan, Australia, and the United States) show that not only does the share of the better educated in P, M, and C occupations tend to rise over time but also their share in other occupations as well—for example, in sales, production, and services. This is what must happen in Indonesia as well unless unemployment of the educated is to rise.

Fortunately, there may be considerable change in the nature of jobs falling under the umbrella of the different broad occupational groups. (See Rumberger, 1981a for a study of such trends in the United States.) The nature of jobs in different broad occupational categories changes with development: for example, the locus of sales work tends to shift from market-selling and street-vending to that of sales assistants in shopping complexes and supermarkets; the locus of transport occupations from pedalling *becak* (pedicab) to driving taxis; and the locus of production work from home weaving of mats or production of batik to factory work. In contrast to traditional transport, sales, or production work, these newer occupations may be seen by the educated as providing them more palatable options, at least in the absence of really attractive work opportunities.

In summary, rising levels of unemployment for the better educated can only be avoided by a number of interrelated changes in the economic and employment structures. The assumptions underlying the projections in this section were: (i) total employment growth of 3 per cent, falling to 2.5 per cent; (ii) changes in the assumed growth rates of individual industries, in particular the faster growth of non-agricultural industries; (iii) fairly drastic changes in industry–occupation matrices, resulting in a rising share of P, M, and C employment; and (iv) changes in the occupation–education matrices, resulting in a rise in the employment share of the better educated in a wide range of occupations. The second of these assumptions only serves to increase the employment of the educated to the extent that the faster-growing industries are those with an occupational mix favouring the educated. The third and fourth assumptions provide scope for greater increases in absorption of the

TABLE 8.12
Trends in Absorption of Better Educated, 1985–200, Assuming No Change in Industry–Occupation Matrix
(that is, Assumption (1) in Table 8.11) or in Occupation–Education Matrix

|  | 1985[a] | | | 2000 | | |
|---|---|---|---|---|---|---|
|  | High School | Academy and University | Total | High School | Academy and University | Total |

1. Employment of better educated aged 20–64 in different occupation ('000)

| | | | | | | |
|---|---|---|---|---|---|---|
| Professional/technical | 1,562 | 409 | 1,971 | 2,740 | 716 | 3,456 |
| Managerial | 47 | 33 | 80 | 87 | 61 | 148 |
| Clerical | 1,627 | 252 | 1,879 | 2,892 | 447 | 3,339 |
| Professional, Managerial, and Clerical | 3,236 | 694 | 3,930 | 5,719 | 1,224 | 6,943 |
| Sales | 1,354 | 27 | 1,381 | 2,549 | 49 | 2,598 |
| Services | 393 | 7 | 400 | 693 | 12 | 705 |
| Farmers | 1,621 | 0 | 1,621 | 2,031 | 0 | 2,031 |
| Production | 1,986 | 33 | 2,019 | 3,817 | 65 | 3,882 |
| Total employed | 8,590 | 761 | 9,351 | 14,809 | 1,350 | 16,159 |
| Unemployed | 778 | 38 | 816 | | | |
| Total in Labour Force | 9,368 | 799 | 10,167 | | | |

|   |   |   |   |   |
|---|---|---|---|---|
| 2. Number of better educated aged 20–64 in the work-force ('000)[b] | 9,368 | 10,167 | 24,093 | 4,258 | 28,351 |
| 3. Average annual rate of increase in numbers of better educated in the work-force, 1985–2000 (per cent) | | 799 | 6.5 | 11.8 | 6.9 |
| 4. Average annual rate of increase in employment of better educated workers, 1985–2000 (per cent) | | | 3.7 | 3.9 | 3.7 |
| 5. Average annual shortfall in employment growth, 1985–2000 (per cent) | | | 2.8 | 7.9 | 3.2 |
| 6. Absolute shortfall[c] ('000) | | 7,938 | 2,840 | 10,778 |
| 7. Percentage shortfall | | 33 | 67 | 38 |

[a]Derived from 1985 SUPAS Report, Table 52.9, assuming that distribution of educated population aged 20–64 across industries was identical to that of the educated population aged 10–.

[b]Figures for 2000 based on projections of numbers of high school and tertiary educated shown in Table 8.7 and the assumption that work-force participation rate of high school and tertiary educated aged 20–64 remains unchanged after 1985, at 68.1 per cent for high school educated and 89.5 per cent for tertiary educated. There is a small discrepancy between the figures in Table 8.7 and the present table, due to the inclusion of 'Diploma I/II' in the tertiary educated in the present table.

[c]This shortfall is the net increase in the number of unemployed that will occur if 1985 unemployment rates for the secondary and tertiary educated remain constant.

educated, though much will depend on behavioural adaptation on the part of those seeking work.

The Indonesian government is well aware of the problem. The Fifth Five-Year Plan estimates that 500,000 graduates of tertiary institutions will have to find work in jobs that such graduates have not traditionally performed (Republik Indonesia, 1989: 6–22).[8] Given the still large share of agriculture in the Indonesian economy, a full absorption of the better educated into employment is unlikely unless quite substantial numbers of them enter this sector. The share of tertiary educated workers in agriculture in 1985 was miniscule (about 2 per cent), and a substantial increase is hard to visualize without major changes in the structure of Indonesian agriculture, bringing diversification beyond the present peasant farming–estate dichotomy and broadening the range of occupations and skills required in the agricultural sector.

## Conclusion

Concern over lack of suitable jobs for the rapidly growing number of the better educated has been felt in most countries during periods of rapid educational expansion. For example, in the United States, Harris (1949: 64) noted that 'college students within the next twenty years are doomed to disappointment after graduation, as the number of coveted openings will be substantially less than the numbers seeking them'. But the anticipated evidence for such oversupply of educated job seekers—a narrowing of income differentials between the better and lesser educated, along with rising levels of unemployment for the better educated—has not always eventuated. It has been noted in the United States that the options for young high school graduates tend to be worse than those for college graduates, because although many college graduates were forced to take jobs traditionally performed by high school graduates, unlike the latter, the former were not being 'squeezed from above' to any great extent by claimants on their traditional jobs (Howe, 1988: 6).

The projections in the previous section showed that in Indonesia the growth of positions traditionally filled by the better educated, and of P, M, and C employment in particular, is unlikely to match that of the better educated segment of the labour force, with the result that there will be a 'pushdown' effect on the occupational distribution of the better educated. The same is likely to be true of Malaysia as well. In both countries, the rapid increase in the number of the high school and university educated in the 1980s coincided with a freeze on government employment, the sector which provides a major proportion of jobs for such educated workers (Jones, 1988b: 28–9). It is true that in Malaysia and Thailand and to a lesser extent in Indonesia, very rapid economic growth and high levels of foreign investment from 1988 onwards led to higher rates of absorption of the highly educated than had been anticipated, and even to shortages in certain fields. But at the somewhat more modest rates of growth likely to be sustained throughout the 1990s, the issue of education–occupation 'mismatch' will not go away. A longer-term projection for Malaysia indicated that over a 40-year projection period, 60 per cent of better educated workers would have to accept occupations with a lower status than their education would lead them to expect in the mid-1980s, if unemployment rates for the educated were not to increase (Jones, 1988b: 30). The problem in Malaysia is further complicated by its ethnic dimension: by the late 1980s, Malay graduates, who had earlier come to expect ready access to good jobs due to expansion of the government sector and policies favouring them in a wide range of other fields, were entering the labour market in such numbers that the jobs they expected were just not there. Though estimates vary, perhaps 15–19 per cent of Malaysia's graduates are jobless, and almost 90 per cent of unemployed graduates are Malays (*Bangkok Post*, 8 July 1989).

P, M, and C employment should continue to grow more rapidly than employment as a whole, for two reasons: first, a shift in the industrial structure towards industries tending to employ a higher proportion of P, M, and C workers; and second, a shift towards a higher proportion of P, M, and C workers within industries. As noted earlier, the share of P, M, and C employment has risen steadily in a group of industrialized countries (see Figures 8.1 and 8.2). Moreover, at 30 or 40 per cent of total employment, P, M, and C employment in these countries is far above the level of about 20 per cent reached in Malaysia and even further ahead of the levels of below 10 per cent in Indonesia and Thailand. Even so, the rise in P, M, and C employment seems unlikely to be rapid enough to keep pace with the growth in the numbers of educated workers. Therefore large numbers of these workers will have to look to other occupations, some of which, happily, require more education than they formerly did because technological changes are altering the nature of the work performed.

Objective evidence for an oversupply of the educated would be a narrowing of income differentials between the better and lesser educated, perhaps along with rising levels of unemployment for the better educated. In Indonesia, unemployment rates for young secondary and tertiary graduates have been increasing in urban areas during the 1980s (Jones and Manning, 1992). Earnings differentials have also been narrowing. The ratio of average monthly earnings of tertiary graduates to those of employees with incomplete primary school fell from 8.99 in 1978 to 5.04 in 1982 and to 4.30 in 1986 (Keyfitz, 1989: Table 11).

These symptoms of oversupply of educated workers may in themselves contain the elements for a rectification of the situation. Evidence of high graduate unemployment and narrower wage differentials may discourage many young people from continuing their studies. A lessened wage premium on educated manpower should also foster structural changes in favour of sectors which utilize such manpower, for example, certain export-oriented industries. But it would be overly sanguine to

## FIGURE 8.3
### The Possible Effects of Overeducation in the Workplace

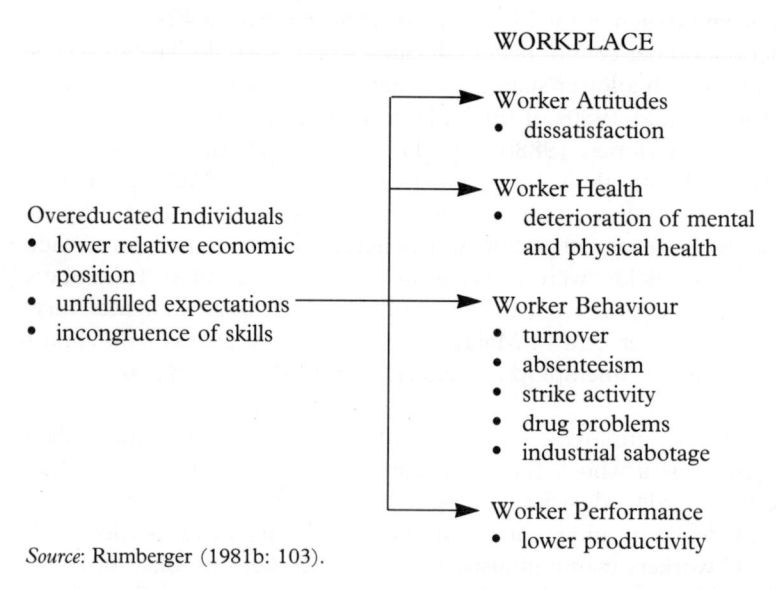

WORKPLACE

Overeducated Individuals
- lower relative economic position
- unfulfilled expectations
- incongruence of skills

→ Worker Attitudes
- dissatisfaction

→ Worker Health
- deterioration of mental and physical health

→ Worker Behaviour
- turnover
- absenteeism
- strike activity
- drug problems
- industrial sabotage

→ Worker Performance
- lower productivity

*Source*: Rumberger (1981b: 103).

assume that the market will take care of everything. For instance, institutional rigidities may be built in through the adoption of a minimum school-leaving age. Also, many potential adjustments take time and others may take socially perverse forms, such as the decision of the young educated, disappointed in their job prospects, to seek even higher levels of education in the hope that this will give them a competitive edge.

In a series of publications on skill requirements of jobs and 'surplus schooling' in the United States, Rumberger (1981a, 1981b, 1987) argued that, because opportunities for high-skilled employment had increased only modestly in the 1970s, during a period when the supply of skilled labour, especially college educated workers, grew substantially, a growing number of workers may hold jobs for which they are overqualified. He argued that the situation could have grave social consequences: promoting job dissatisfaction and adversely affecting productivity in the workplace (Rumberger, 1981b: Chap. 5). The concerns he expressed are reproduced in Figure 8.3, which although perhaps unduly pessimistic, will certainly have resonance with the concerns of South-East Asian planners.

But Rumberger's comments on the required skill levels for particular jobs and on the grave consequences of 'over-skilling' on worker attitudes and behaviour beg the question: 'May there be offsetting productivity benefits from having workers do jobs for which they are in some sense overqualified?' As Gannicott (1987: 65) notes:

The entire international experience is that educational expansion contributes to economic development by the diffusion throughout the occupational structure of better educated workers—and this process itself aids employment creation through raising labour productivity, through cost savings, through widening the range of techniques which can be adopted, through the better responsiveness of the labour force to entrepreneurial initiatives, and so on.

There is no doubt that dissatisfaction with the kinds of jobs available to high school graduates does lead to social problems in South-East Asian countries. Changes in perceptions of appropriate work for the better educated, though required by changing realities, may come only slowly and painfully. A village study from Trengganu state in Malaysia noted the problem of young men who had completed the third year high school examination, but not the fifth year.

... by 1979 there were half a dozen young men in the village who were highly discontented. They had envisioned themselves as government employees with regular salaries. They failed the examinations, and were confronted with the prospect of becoming village workers like their fathers. There may be other alternatives for them, but the young men have a limited perspective of the possibilities. They could be found together most evenings, just 'hanging out' and complaining, increasing each other's frustrations. Their parents and the parents of some younger boys worried about them and their influence. There was talk among adults about their use of marijuana, unknown in the village five years earlier. Generally, the group was perceived as a local problem for which no one had a solution (Strange, 1981: 95).

These are difficult problems, which will continue to occupy the minds of planners, but they cannot be allowed to dominate the debate on appropriate development of education, because education plays such diverse roles in the economy, society, and polity. Easterlin (1981) has made a case for giving the expansion of formal education systems a central place in explaining international differences in rates of economic growth. Haveman and Wolfe (1984), in a study which attempted to place a rough value on a range of non-economic effects of education, concluded that standard human capital estimates capture only about one-half of the total value of an additional year of schooling. Many studies in the region show that high school educated mothers have lower fertility and higher rates of child survival than do the lesser educated. Education may be seen as important for national cohesion.

As noted earlier, powerful built-in mechanisms will ensure that the numbers of better educated in South-East Asia will continue to grow rapidly. Continued rapid economic development is essential to employment growth, and the Philippines and Sri Lanka are object lessons in what to avoid in this respect. In addition, part of the educational process itself must include counselling of those going on to higher levels to appraise realistically their own future employment prospects.

1. The actual growth rate in the early 1980s is hard to determine because of the tendency of the 1985 Intercensal Survey (SUPAS) to record a much larger number of unpaid family workers than did the 1980 Census (Jones, 1987; Manning, 1988). The Fifth Five-Year Plan adopts a figure of 3 per cent for the annual growth of the labour force in the 1988–93 period.

2. The data in Figure 8.2 are only rough, because the dollar equivalents are in current values for the years concerned, and are not indexed to a given year's value of the dollar. Also, GNP per capita was only traced for the years 1972–86, excepting 1980–1, so any other years are interpolations or extrapolations.

3. The picture in Malaysia looks very different if the 1980 census data are used instead of the 1984 Labour Force Survey. According to the census, 60 per cent of all high school educated work in P, M, and C occupations, whereas according to the labour force survey, only 33 per cent of the high school educated work in these occupations. Only a small part of the difference could be due to real changes over time.

4. More details of methods used in the projections can be obtained from the writer.

5. Although the forecasts of the Five-Year Plan are used for the purposes of the projections, reservations can be held about a number of the assumptions, for example, it is debatable whether the labour force will grow as rapidly as assumed (a rise in female participation rates is assumed); whether agricultural employment will grow as rapidly as 2 per cent per annum; and whether manufacturing employment will grow as rapidly as assumed, in view of the great potential for large-scale capital-intensive industry to displace labour-intensive, small-scale, and cottage industries.

6. One factor likely to hold down the growth rate of P, M, and C occupations in the community service sector, and in the economy as a whole, is the projected deceleration in the growth of demand for teachers; even the rapid rise in enrolment ratios at secondary and tertiary levels will be considerably dampened in its effect on total teacher numbers, by the stabilization of numbers enrolled in primary school, and hence in the demand for primary school teachers. Thus teacher numbers are unlikely to increase as rapidly in the 1990s as they did in the 1970s and 1980s. The effect of this on total numbers employed in P, M, and C occupations will be extremely important, because in 1985 teachers constituted 79 per cent of all professional employment and 39 per cent of all P, M, and C employment, for those with secondary and tertiary education.

7. In a comparable study for the United States over the 1960–70 period, the industry shift effect accounted for about two-thirds of the change in occupational structure, changes in occupational composition within industries for one-third, and there was a slight interaction effect (Singelmann and Browning, 1980).

8. One adviser to the Indonesian government has recently published a paper on the issues involved (Keyfitz, 1989), though he uses what this writer considers to be an unrealistically high figure for the growth of demand for labour (5 per cent per annum), thus understating the scale of the problem.

# 9
# Demographic Change, Household Resources, and Schooling Decisions

Andrew Mason

## Introduction

ECONOMISTS and other social scientists concerned with social and economic development increasingly emphasize the role of human resources. In the Asia–Pacific Rim, the importance attached to education is cited as one of the critical factors that explain rapid economic growth in Japan, the NIEs, and the increasingly successful members of ASEAN. The World Bank has long been a major proponent of primary education as a fundamental vehicle for achieving economic development. Increased educational attainment of women is also widely believed to be a central element in reducing child mortality, successfully promoting family planning, and reducing rates of population growth. A consensus has clearly emerged among social scientists and development institutions that a strong human resource base is the key to social and economic development.

There is considerably less agreement among economists and other social scientists about the relative importance of different dimensions of human resources or about the reasons some countries are so successful at accumulating human resources and others are not.

Part of the problem that confounds students of human resources is the impossibility of measuring it. Health is so multidimensional and subjective in nature that the only widely accepted indicators are measures of mortality which only distinguish rather extreme states of healthfulness. Research on education has a slight advantage, relying on standard measures of educational attainment, for example, the years of schooling or the percentage completing secondary school. But even here there are enormous differences in quality that typically go undetected. And it requires only a moment's reflection to realize that years of schooling is actually a measure of the student's input, not the results of the educational process.

The research reported in this chapter suffers from the same constraints and limitations that have affected other studies. The emphasis is on only one aspect of human resources, education or, more broadly, intellectual development. In the absence of true measures of educational achievement, the analysis emphasizes differences in inputs. The focus is on a particular issue—the impact of fertility decline on the educational achievement of children.

Rather than present a comprehensive review of what is already known about the relationship between family size and human resource development, the research described below will be motivated by briefly presenting two influential studies on the topic. The first is a recent study of education based on cross-national data on school enrolment and educational inputs (Schultz, 1987). At the national level, slower population growth leads to a decline in the young dependency ratio or the number of school age children per adult (taxpayer). Schultz examines how the public sector has responded to the situation. Three possibilities exist: expenditures per taxpayer can be reduced, expenditures per student can be increased, and/or enrolment ratios can be increased. Although the choice may vary from country to country, Schultz finds that historically the response has been to increase expenditures per student, whereas the proportion enrolled has been unresponsive. These aggregate data indicate, then, that fertility decline has affected human resources through its impact on the quality, but not the quantity, of education.

A quite different approach to the link between fertility and human resources has focused on the relationship between the number and parity of children and intelligence or educational attainment using micro data. Figure 9.1 shows the results of Belmont and Marolla's 1973 study of the mental age of 386,000 Dutch males who reached the age of 19 between 1963 and 1966. There is a clear tendency for mental age to decline with birth order and with family size. For any family size, the last born is particularly disadvantaged.[1]

In this chapter, the approach taken in studying the link between fertility or family size and human resource development is quite similar to

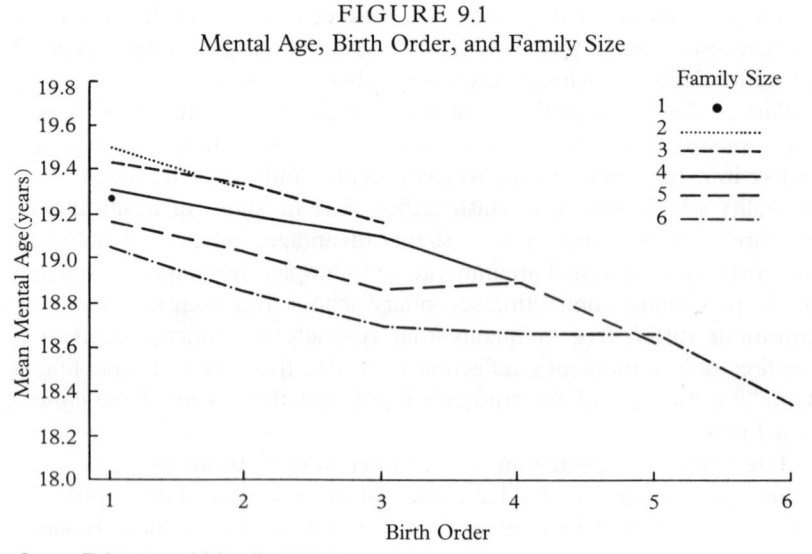

FIGURE 9.1
Mental Age, Birth Order, and Family Size

*Source*: Belmont and Marolla (1973).

those described above and others that have preceded it. First examined is the relationship between family size and the household's limited resources, both the time of the household members and the household's financial resources. Higher fertility dilutes those resources because they must be spread over additional children. Complicating matters is the fact that the household's total resources may be affected by fertility because children may become contributing, productive members of the household as they age and because their presence will influence the behaviour of other household members.

In both South Korea and Thailand, the number of adults per child in family households with school age children has risen substantially in the mid-1980s and will continue to do so as a consequence of fertility decline. With lower fertility, the average number of adults per household will decline somewhat because fewer adult children will be living at home. Moreover, increased labour force participation among women will reduce the average number of adults whose primary attachment is to the home. But these changes are not as significant as the change in the average number of children per household. Particularly in households with young children, the availability of adult time per child is increasing because mothers are less likely to work outside the home.

Analysis of disposable household income in South Korea and Thailand shows that the dilution effect, that is, the decline in per capita income that results from an increase in the denominator, dominates. In present-day South Korea, total disposable household income is almost completely independent of household size; in Thailand, household income is depressed by the presence of young members and enhanced modestly by the presence of teenagers.[2] But in both countries, an additional child of either sex and any age, depresses per capita disposable household income.

In the final parts of the chapter, the link between human resources and the number of children is more directly examined by presenting evidence regarding expenditures on education by the household and school enrolment by household members. In general, expenditures on education per school age child have increased in both South Korea and Thailand as a result of declines in the number of children in the typical household. Also, in present-day Thailand, school enrolment rises as a result of a decline in the number of children. In South Korea, school enrolment by the late 1980s was so high that demographic and other factors have no discernible effect, but analysis of 1970 census data shows that fertility decline in South Korea was partly responsible for the high rates of enrolment observed today.

The empirical findings reported here draw primarily on studies of South Korea (supported by the General Motors Research Laboratories and USAID), and Thailand (carried out in collaboration with the Asian Development Bank's Economics Office and Thailand's National Economic and Social Development Board and National Statistics Office). Both projects use the HOMES model, developed at the East–West Population Institute, Honolulu, to examine changes in the demographic character of the household and their impact on earnings, labour force participation, spending patterns, schooling decisions, and other dimensions of household behaviour.[3]

The HOMES model is a natural extension of earlier models that project the number of households using headship-based methodologies. HOMES also projects the number of households by the age and sex of the household head, but goes an important step further by projecting household membership, that is, the number of members by their age, sex, and relationship to the household head. The resulting demographic information is used for sectoral planning and macroeconomic forecasting based on empirical studies that rely on census and survey data. For example, forecasts of the supply of labour are based on micro-level estimates of the impact of the number of children, among other factors, on female labour force participation. The household projection model is combined with the micro-level analysis to forecast changes in participation and the supply of labour at the household level and to aggregate those changes up to the national level. In addition to applications to the labour supply and wages, the model is being used to forecast changes in savings, expenditure patterns, housing demand, health care utilization, school enrolment, and household income.

## Household Time

One of the most clear-cut and undeniable impacts of Asia's demographic change is its effect on the availability of household time. Surely, children with fewer siblings can expect to enjoy a greater number of hours of undivided attention from their mother and father, and, in extended households, from their grandparents and other adult relatives. In countries that have experienced such rapid fertility decline, for example, South Korea and Thailand, the decline in the number of children and the rise in the potential for more extensive interaction with adults is truly remarkable.

Figure 9.2 shows just how significant the impact of fertility decline in Thailand during the 1970s and 1980s on family size is likely to be. The average family size reported in Figure 9.2 refers to family households and excludes one-person households and households consisting of unrelated individuals because essentially all children live in family households. Special tabulations from the 1980 census of Thailand show that in 1980 average family size rose from about 3.2 members per household in which the head was 15–19 years of age to peak at over six members per household in which a head was at the peak of the childrearing years, 40–49. Thereafter, household size declines to a little below five members for households headed by an individual aged 65–69. The slight rise among older households reflects births to childbearing women living in three-generation households.

Primarily as a result of reduced rates of childbearing, average household size is forecast to decline by as much as two members, between 1980 and 2000, and by as much as an additional member by 2015.

## FIGURE 9.2
### Average Household Size: Thailand

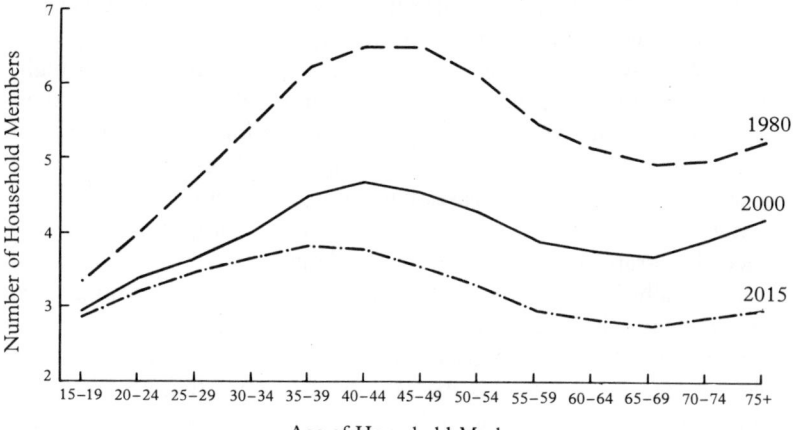

*Source*: HOMES Project, East–West Center, Honolulu.

Overall, average size is forecast to decline from 5.5 members in 1980 to 4.1 members in 2000 and to only 3.4 members in 2015. But what does this imply about the availability of the time of adult members?

A closer look at the issue reveals a number of factors that require consideration. First, within any family the supply of time to children will vary among the children and for any particular child will vary during his childhood. During the first few years of life, first-born children receive the undivided attention of their parents, or, at least, they need not compete with siblings. Higher parity children, on the other hand, must compete with siblings during their formative years but later in life, when older brothers and sister have left home, may look forward to more time inputs from their parents. Of course, a mother's time is undoubtedly more important to young children than to the older ones.[4] When fertility and the number of surviving children declines, the availability of time will increase by differing amounts depending upon a particular child's position in the family. This fact is also reflected in the aggregate data presented in Figure 9.2. Average household size declines by much less among young households because, irrespective of the number of children they might eventually bear, most of these households will have had the opportunity to bear no more than one, or at most, two children.

A second factor is important in many high-fertility societies where younger and older siblings may differ considerably in age. Rather than compete with younger brothers and sisters, older siblings often care for them. Of course, the quality of the care may be lower than that provided by a parent, but the supply of household time is diminished by the loss of services of older children.

A third factor is the role of grandparents as providers of care in many Asian families. During Asia's demographic transition, the supply of grandparents has risen for two reasons. First, with increased longevity, a great many parents are surviving long enough to enjoy the pleasures and responsibilities of grandparenthood. A second reason, and a probably more important one, is that in East and South-East Asia, the prevalence of the stem-type extended family means that, at any one time, grandparents will be living with only one married son or daughter. In a high-fertility society, then, the likelihood that children will be living with their grandparents will be diminished in direct proportion to the number of surviving aunts and/or uncles. And as fertility declines, the chances of living with a grandparent increases barring changes in the rules governing living arrangements. It is easy to overstate the importance of care provided by grandparents, because a relatively small percentage of children actually live with their grandparents. This is not because most elderly are living independently, but simple demographics—there are many more grandchildren than grandparents. For example, in Thailand in 1980, for family households the ratio of the population 65 and older to the population under 15 was only 0.08.

When each of these considerations is factored into the analysis, the demographic impact of fertility decline on the supply of adult time to children is considerable. In the case of Thailand, the number of adults (members aged 15 and older) per child (members under age 15) in households with children under age 5 is projected to increase from 1.3 adults per child in 1980, to 2.2 adults per child in 2000, and 2.7 adults per child in 2015.[5] Figure 9.3 decomposes the increase in adults per child into three age-groups. Adults aged 15–24 would include both older siblings and young parents; adults 25–64 is dominated by the parents of children aged 0–4; and adults aged 65 and older is composed almost entirely of grandparents. In both percentage and absolute terms, the biggest increase is in the number of adults aged 25–64, which rises by almost 150 per cent between 1980 and 2015. The number of elderly

FIGURE 9.3
Adults per Child in Thai Households with Members Aged 0–4

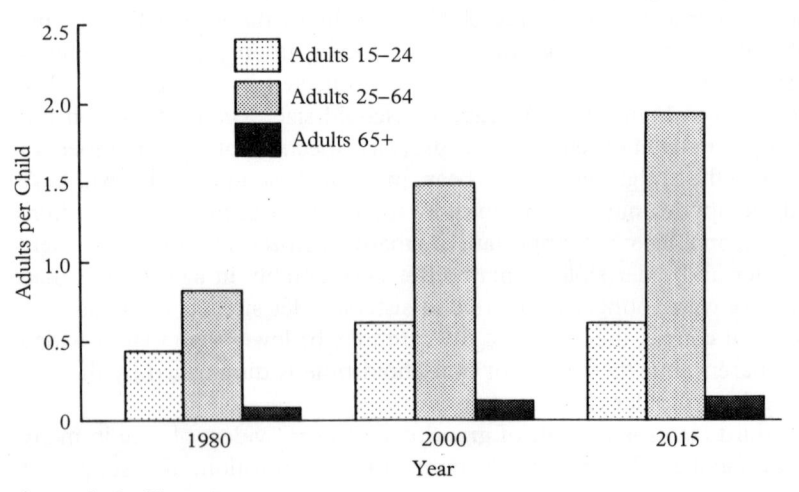

*Source*: As for Figure 9.2.

per child almost doubles during the same period, but, even so, by 2015 the projection is only 0.15 elderly per pre-school child. The slowest increase is in the number of young adults per pre-school child which rises by about 50 per cent. The reasons for the low increase are described above. The average number of children living in households with young parents will not decline to the extent that it will among older parents. Moreover, with lower fertility, pre-school children will have fewer siblings over the age of 15.

All qualifications and refinements aside, declining fertility and, to a much lesser extent, increased longevity have contributed to an increase in the potential availability of adult time to children. There are two other considerations which bear directly on the extent of time resources available to children to which the analysis now turns. The first is changes in living arrangements. The second is changes in labour force participation among women.

*Changes in Living Arrangements*

Projections of changes in the supply of adults in Thailand and similar results for other countries are obtained under the assumption that the rules governing living arrangements will not change during the projection period. Analysis of the situations in South Korea and Thailand in 1970 and 1980 reveal no important changes in living arrangements there. But a recently completed study of Japan reveals important changes during the 1970s and 1980s (Mason, Ogawa, and Fukui, 1992). Important changes that may bear directly on child welfare include the following: if the values or economic circumstances preserving the extended family erode over time, the elderly may live independently from their children reducing the time inputs of the elderly to young children.

Perhaps a more important and potentially damaging change would be a substantial increase in marital disruption due to divorce, widowhood, or separation for other reasons, for example, labour migration. The prevalence of divorce and widowhood varies among the countries of East and South-East Asia, but in such cases children cannot count on the presence of both parents. Table 9.1 shows the percentage of women towards the end of their childbearing years (40–44 and 45–49) and men in the same age categories who head family households with no spouse present. A few clear patterns are evident. Rates are generally much lower for men. They are less likely to be widowed than women because husbands are usually older than their wives and survival rates are generally higher for women. Moreover, men are much more likely to remarry in the event of divorce or death of a spouse than are women in most Asian countries. In the Philippines, where rates of single headship among women are relatively low and closer to those observed for men, remarriage is relatively more common.

The probability of being a single head of a family household also increases with age in nearly every instance because, with the passing of

## TABLE 9.1
Single Headship by Sex and Age-group among Selected Asian Countries

|  | Female | | Male | |
|---|---|---|---|---|
|  | *40–44* | *45–49* | *40–44* | *45–49* |
| Indonesia, 1976 | 13.4 | 16.6 | 2.2 | 3.1 |
| Indonesia, 1980 | 12.7 | 15.7 | 2.3 | 2.8 |
| Japan, 1970 | 7.1 | 10.5 | 1.6 | 2.0 |
| Japan, 1975 | 6.3 | 8.1 | 1.7 | 2.1 |
| Japan, 1980 | 6.3 | 8.0 | 2.0 | 2.3 |
| Japan, 1985 | 7.3 | 8.5 | 3.0 | 2.9 |
| South Korea, 1970 | 12.5 | 14.8 | 2.1 | 3.1 |
| South Korea, 1980 | 11.2 | 15.2 | 2.1 | 2.7 |
| Malaysia, 1980 | 12.0 | 16.3 | 3.4 | 4.1 |
| Philippines, 1975 | 6.4 | 9.1 | 4.3 | 5.6 |
| Thailand, 1970 | 10.5 | 15.7 | 2.7 | 3.9 |
| Thailand, 1980 | 10.0 | 14.2 | 2.7 | 4.2 |

*Sources:* Mason (1987b) and unpublished census tabulations.

time, husbands and wives are more likely to experience divorce or widowhood.

The secular trend in single headship is less clear cut. Examining the data for countries in which there are several observations, the likelihood that a woman will be a single head appears to be declining over time. But in Japan, for which there are the most extensive data, the trend has recently reversed itself and single headship rose substantially between 1980 and 1985 (Mason, Ogawa, and Fukui, 1992). The changes in Japan reflect the countervailing effects of changes in widowhood and divorce and an increased tendency for unmarried women to head their own households. Among females aged 45–49, the percentages widowed reported in successive censuses beginning in 1970 are 9.1, 6.3, 5.0, and 4.3 in 1985; the percentages divorced in each census are 4.3, 3.8, 3.7, and 4.5 in 1985. Until 1985, then, the decline in widowhood dominated, although even the percentage divorced declined until 1980. But between 1980 and 1985, the percentage divorced began to rise in Japan among women 45–49 and at other ages, as well. The rise in divorce in Japan since 1980 has been relatively large but only with respect to the very low rates of divorce prevailing in the past. It is difficult to foresee the extent to which divorce will increase in the future, but it is an obvious source of concern from the perspective of human resource development. At least in the early 1990s, with the possible exception of South Korea aside, the decline in widowhood appears to be dominating changes in divorce increasing the proportions of children living in households with both parents present.

The extent to which households headed by unmarried men and women translates into children living in such households depends on a number of factors especially the extent to which childbearing has been disrupted by marital separation or dissolution. Figures 9.4a and 9.4b display the proportions of children aged 0–4, 5–9, and 10–14 living in households with a 'single' male or female head.[6] Mostly, older children are somewhat more likely to live in these households and children are much more likely to live with their mothers than with their fathers. The highest values are in Thailand, where the percentage living in households with single heads rises from 8.8 for those aged 0–4, to 9.2 for those aged 5–9, and to 12.6 for those aged 10–14. The lowest values are in Japan where only 3.6 per cent of children aged 0–4, 5.5 per cent of those aged 5–9, and 8.3 per cent of those aged 10–14 live in households with a single head.

The impact of such living arrangements on the resources available to children will depend on a number of factors, including the response of other potential household members to marital disruption and the allocation of time by individuals who live in non-intact households. The evidence available suggests that the absence of a spouse does not reduce the number of adults in the household in a one-to-one manner. Adult children are likely to delay their departure or other adults may live in the household at earlier childrearing stages. For Thailand, there is a very consistent relationship that does not vary with the age of the household head—non-intact households headed by women have 0.75 fewer adult members than intact households. Because childbearing is depressed for women of childbearing age who are separated from their husbands, the number of adults per child in non-intact households headed by females

FIGURE 9.4a
Children Living in Non-intact Households: Households Headed by Females

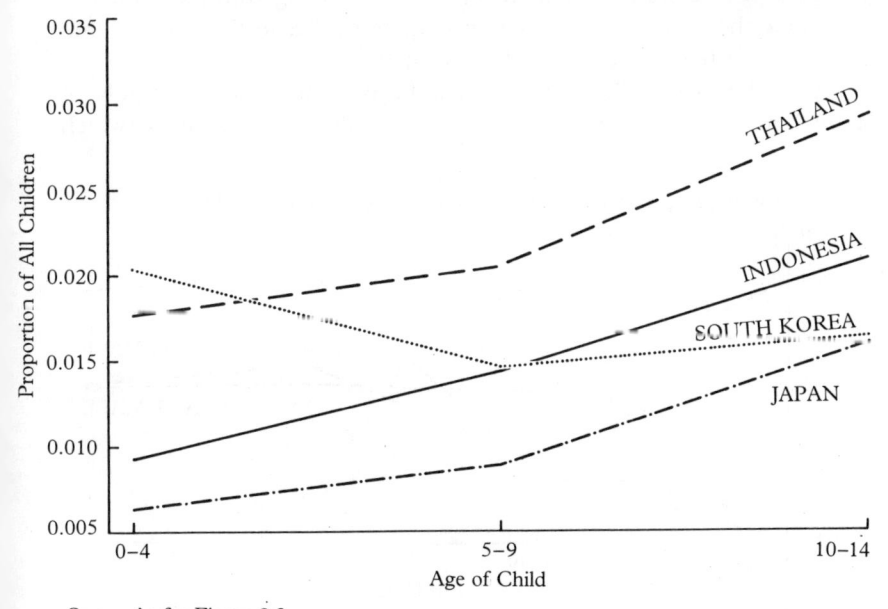

*Source*: As for Figure 9.2.

## FIGURE 9.4b
Children Living in Non-intact Households: Households With Female Heads

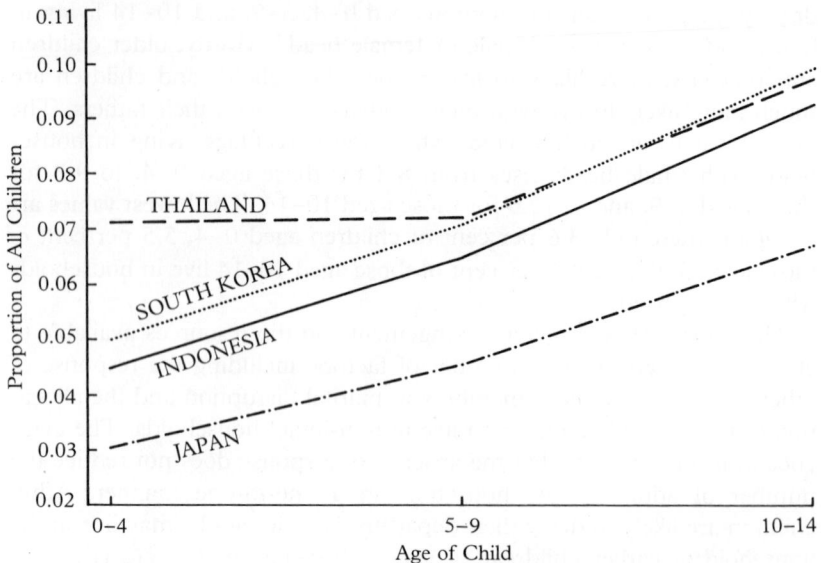

is similar to intact households with a head under age 50. But as Figure 9.5 shows, children living in households headed by older women are disadvantaged as compared with children living in intact households. The situation for the smaller numbers of children living in non-intact households headed by young males is considerably different. Non-intact households headed by young males generally have fewer children and the adults per child is very high. For children living with older men in non-intact households, the situation is quite similar to that for children in non-intact households headed by women.[7]

Up to this point, the discussion has been confined to the supply of adult household members with no concern about the extent to which

## FIGURE 9.5
Adults per Child in Intact and Non-intact Households: Thailand

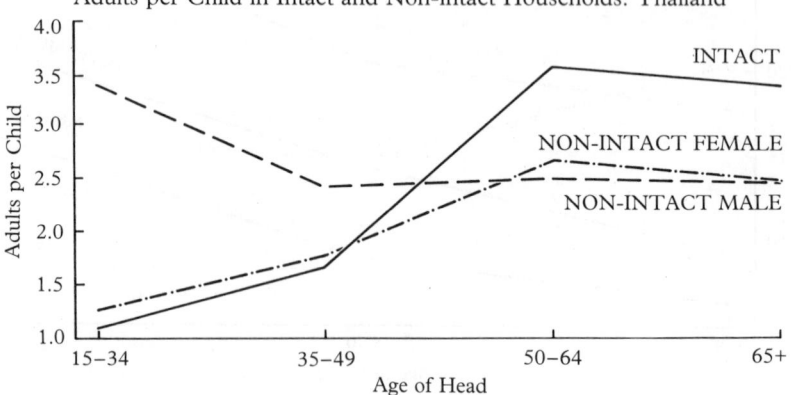

*Source*: As for Figure 9.2.

their time is devoted to childrearing as opposed to work, schooling, or other activities which are of no direct benefit to children. This issue is particularly salient for non-intact households headed by women, but is of general interest because of the widely noted changes in female labour force participation accompanying fertility decline. This issue is discussed in the next section.

*Labour Force Participation*[8]

The causal linkages between childrearing, labour force participation by women, and related factors, for example, increased educational attainment, are difficult to untangle. To some extent, increased economic opportunities have induced women to enter the labour force and, along with a shift in the locus of employment away from the home, have led women to bear fewer children. To some extent, family planning efforts have allowed women to reduce their childbearing to levels more consistent with their own desires and, with fewer obligations at home, to join the work-force.

Irrespective of the causality, the decline in fertility in Asia has been accompanied by a shift in activity away from the home, so that the increased supply of adult members highlighted above overstates the actual availability of time to children in lower fertility societies.

But analysis of labour force behaviour by women shows a clear effort on the part of women to tailor their employment so as to reduce its impact on the time available for childrearing. Analysis of the situation in Thailand, based on the 1984 Labour Force Survey conducted during the peak of the agricultural season, shows that mothers of pre-school children are considerably more likely to remain at home and refrain from participating in the labour force. The extent of the differences in participation depends on the age of the child and that of the mother, but participation by women with one pre-school child may be as much as 20 percentage points lower than participation by women with none (Bauer et al., 1988).

The choice between labour force participation and childrearing is no doubt a more difficult one for women who head their own households or women living in non-intact households. Table 9.2 compares estimated

TABLE 9.2
Labour Force Participation by South Korean Women, 1983
(per cent)

| Household Type | Number of Pre-school Children | |
| --- | --- | --- |
| | *None* | *One* |
| Intact | 0.30 | 0.27 |
| Non-intact | 0.84 | 0.60 |

*Source*: Bauer (1989).

TABLE 9.3
Working Status of Employed South Korean Women, 1983 (per cent)

| Status | Household Type | |
| --- | --- | --- |
|  | Intact | Non-intact |
| Employer | 2.0 | 2.1 |
| Self-employed | 17.2 | 32.5 |
| Family worker | 41.0 | 4.0 |
| Regular employee | 20.2 | 33.6 |
| Temporary employee | 11.3 | 17.9 |
| Daily worker | 8.4 | 9.9 |
| Total | 100.0 | 100.0 |

Source: Bauer (1989).

participation rates for South Korean women aged 25–34 based on the 1983 Economically Active Population Survey. Women in non-intact households are much more likely to work than are those in intact households, and although the presence of a pre-school child reduces participation considerably, well over half of all women with pre-school children are still in the labour force.[9]

One additional and important consideration is the incompatibility between work and childrearing. Many women work at home or in other situations which may accommodate childrearing. For women in non-intact households, finding compatible employment would be particularly attractive. Unfortunately, at least in South Korea, non-intact households are much less likely to operate family-owned, home-based businesses. Thus, women from non-intact households are much less likely to be family workers than are women from intact households. A higher percentage of such women are self-employed and, no doubt, many of these are home-based. But even considering this possibility, a higher percentage of working women from non-intact households are apparently working away from home (Table 9.3).

To the extent that women or men[10] increase their employment, the time available to the household for childrearing and other home activities is reduced, but financial and physical resources available to the household are increased. The supply of these resources is discussed in the next section.

*Household Income*

When a woman bears a child, per capita income declines because a given household income must be spread over more members. This is not to say that the parents or the siblings or other relatives of the new member are worse off. Members may experience a decline in their material standard of living but will enjoy the companionship and love of a new family member. Indeed, if the new child was 'wanted', those who chose to bear the child are unquestionably better off given any reasonable measure of welfare. But, it is not possible to demonstrate that siblings are better off and the material resources available to any one child will be reduced.

The impact of children on per capita income is complex because household income is influenced by the number of children. In many developing countries, children work at a relatively young age and may contribute directly to household income. To the extent that additional children dilute material resources, other household members may be encouraged to enter the labour force or work harder. On the other hand, children, and especially young children, are 'time intensive', in the parlance of the new home economics, and may induce lower labour force participation by those most directly responsible for childrearing, be they the child's mother, grandmother, or an older sibling.

There are two approaches that can be employed to estimate the impact of children on household earnings. Mueller (1976) or Lindert (1983) represents the detailed approach which estimates the earnings of individual family members and the variation of the earnings with age, gender, and, ideally, the composition of the household. A complete accounting of household income would also include interest and property income that can be calculated only by assessing the impact of children on household savings. Obviously, analysis that details each source of income separately is a major undertaking.

This research has taken a simpler, though not necessarily less reliable, regression approach that relies on statistical analysis of household income using the 1981 Socio-Economic Survey of Thailand and the 1984 Family Income and Expenditure Survey of South Korea. These data have been used to estimate the dependence of per capita disposable income on demographic characteristics of the household and other socio-economic variables that affect household income, for example, the age and the occupation of the household head.[11]

Because interest is focused only on the impact of fertility, Table 9.4

TABLE 9.4
Impact of Children on Per Capita Household Disposable Income
(per cent)

|  | South Korea | Thailand |
|---|---|---|
| Impact of an additional child |  |  |
| Male, 0–2 | −22.0 | −22.8 |
| Female, 0–2 | −22.6 | −21.6 |
| Male, 3–12 | −21.0 | −17.6 |
| Female, 3–12 | −21.0 | −16.9 |
| Male, 13–19 | −21.1 | −10.6 |
| Female, 13–19 | −14.1 | −9.2 |

*Sources*: Data for South Korea are from Koo and Mason (forthcoming); for Thailand, from Phananiramai and Mason (1987).

presents the estimated impact of additional children on per capita household disposable income obtained from a least squares regression equation of the following form:

$$\ln Y_d/N = \alpha_0 + \sum_{k=1}^{K} \alpha_k M_k + \ldots + \epsilon \qquad (1)$$

where $Y_d/N$ is per capita household disposable income and $M_k$ is the number of members in age and sex category $k$ living in the household.

Results from both South Korea and Thailand show, unsurprisingly, that an additional child depresses per capita household income. In South Korea, the results are remarkably independent of the age and gender of the child. Per capita household income is depressed by 21–23 per cent by the addition of any child except a teenage daughter. In the latter case, per capita household income is depressed by only 14 per cent, no doubt reflecting the daughter's direct contribution to household income. There is considerably more variation in the case of Thailand. The impact does not differ appreciably between boys and girls, but younger children have a much greater depressive impact on earnings than do older children. Infants depress household income by about 22 per cent (just as in South Korea), children depress income by about 17–18 per cent, and teenagers by about 10 per cent.

Figure 9.6 compares the estimated decline from one additional child with the expected decline if household income is independent of the number of children. In South Korea, average household size for the survey was between 4 and 5 members, so an additional child reduces per capita household income by about 20 per cent if household income is constant. The average Thai household had 5.6 members so the decline would be about 16 per cent.[12]

FIGURE 9.6
Percentage Decline in Per Capita Household Income:
Impact of an Additional Child

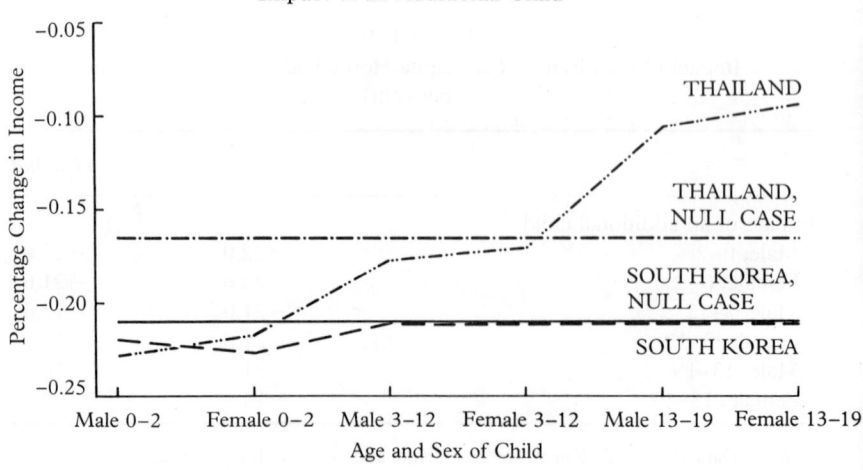

In South Korea, there is no appreciable difference between the null and the estimated impact except in the case of teenage girls who 'contribute' a 7 per cent increase in total household income. The Thai case is quite different. Infants depress per capita income by well more than might be expected, probably because they depress labour force participation by their mother. Both teenage girls and boys depress per capita income by considerably less than might be expected, probably because of direct contributions that amount to 6–7 per cent of household income.

The evidence concerning the impact of fertility decline on the resources available for human resource investment is quite clear. Smaller family size is associated with an increased availability of adult time per child and an increased level of per capita disposable income. The availability of resources does not mean that they are applied towards a particular end. Whether the greater availability of resources has translated into, first, additional expenditure on education and, second, higher rates of school enrolment in South Korea and Thailand is considered in the next section.

## Educational Expenditure

The determinants of educational expenditure by households are estimated using consumer expenditure surveys for South Korea and Thailand mentioned above. Statistical analysis followed standard procedures in that the share of the household budget devoted to education is regressed on independent variables, for example, per capita household disposable income, age of the head, demographic composition of the household, occupation, etc. (Deaton and Muellbauer, 1980). The portion of the share equation of interest here is:

$$s = \beta_0 + \beta_1 \ln Y_d/N + \beta_2 (\ln Y_d/N)^2 + \sum_{k=1}^{K} \alpha_k M_k + \ldots + \epsilon \quad (2)$$

where $s$ is the share of household disposable income spent on education, $Y_d/N$ is per capita disposable income, and $M_k$ is the number of household members in age and sex category $k$. Household members were divided into five age-groups, 0–2, 3–12, 13–19, 20–64, and 65 and over.

At the household level, per capita income affects educational expenditure for several reasons. To the extent that such expenditure represents investment, the returns to education will vary across individuals and may be systematically related to household income or its correlates. Moreover, constraints on borrowing may preclude low income households from spending as much on schooling as the returns warrant. To the extent that education represents consumption, high-income households may spend more on education than they would on any normal goods. The squared income term is included to allow for a flexible relationship between educational expenditure and the standard of living—more specifically, to allow the income elasticity to vary with per capita income.[13]

The impact of an increase in the number of children on expenditure will depend on the age and, perhaps, the sex of the child involved. In the simplest of all worlds, expenditure per school age child would not vary with the number of children and households with more school age children would devote a larger share of their budget to education so as to ensure that their children were not relatively disadvantaged. In reality, other considerations will intervene. First, because additional children constitute an economic burden for households, investment in education may suffer.[14] Second, older children represent an economic asset to the household and the value of their time, the opportunity cost of schooling, may depend on the number of other household members. The presence of a young child should generally increase the opportunity cost of school attendance by an older sibling and depress expenditure on education beyond the impact of a young child on the household's material standard of living. But the presence of an additional older child in the household should reduce the opportunity cost of schooling for other siblings, increase school attendance, and expenditure on education.

Statistical results from the analysis of educational expenditure in Thailand and South Korea are presented in Table 9.5. The coefficients are, in all cases, statistically significant and in accord with economic theory. Moreover, there is a surprising consistency between the results in South Korea and Thailand even though per capita income and the share devoted to education is considerably higher in South Korea. But as will become clearer below, the similarities are in important respects

TABLE 9.5
Expenditure on Education: Selected Results

| Variable | South Korea Coefficient | South Korea Standard Error | Thailand Coefficient | Thailand Standard Error |
|---|---|---|---|---|
| $lnY_d/N$ | 0.02407 | 0.00186 | 0.01941 | 0.00219 |
| $(lnY_d/N)^2$ | −0.00011 | 0.00080 | −0.00146 | 0.00017 |
| Male, 0–2 | −0.00354 | 0.00114 | −0.00345 | 0.00056 |
| Female, 0–2 | −0.00413 | 0.00119 | −0.00358 | 0.00053 |
| Male, 3–12 | 0.01000 | 0.00067 | 0.00180 | 0.00024 |
| Female, 3–12 | 0.00806 | 0.00059 | 0.00144 | 0.00025 |
| Male, 13–19 | 0.03946 | 0.00085 | 0.00281 | 0.00015 |
| Female, 13–19 | 0.03243 | 0.00081 | 0.00332 | 0.00015 |
| N | 44,540 | | 11,891 | |
| $\bar{R}^2$ | 0.144 | | 0.158 | |
| Budget share | 0.053 | | 0.011 | |
| $\eta$ | 1.4 | | 1.2 | |

Sources: As for Table 9.4.

superficial. There are important ways in which the responses in expenditure differ between Thailand and South Korea.

The estimated income elasticity at the mean per capita income is about 1.4 in South Korea and about 1.2 in Thailand. In both countries, the elasticity declines as per capita income increases but very slowly, particularly in South Korea. Despite the similarities in the income elasticities between the two countries, it should not be overlooked that per capita income in South Korea is considerably higher than in Thailand. One would expect a higher income elasticity in Thailand were the extent of privatization and the attitudes towards education similar in both countries.

The estimated coefficients for household membership variables are partial effects that do not include the impact of an additional member on per capita income. The direct impact of an additional infant on education is nearly identical in both countries. Although the coefficient may seem small in magnitude, it is not. An additional infant depresses educational expenditure by around 10 per cent. The presence of an additional school age member increases educational expenditure by a considerable amount in South Korea: expenditure increases by 20 per cent with the addition of a member aged 3–12 and by nearly 70 per cent with the addition of a teenager. But in Thailand, an additional child aged 3–12 increases expenditure by only 5 per cent and an additional teenager by only 9 per cent. These are small increases given that the additional child is of school age.

The estimated coefficients of the number of household members provides a partial picture of the impact of additional children because they take no account of the increased household size on per capita disposable income. Table 9.6 provides a more comprehensive assessment of the

TABLE 9.6
Impact of Children on Educational Expenditure by Households

|  | South Korea | | Thailand | |
| --- | --- | --- | --- | --- |
|  | Share | Expenditure per Child[a] | Share | Expenditure per Child[a] |
| Base values | 0.084 | 100.0 | 0.012 | 100.0 |
| Children halved | 0.060 | 141.9 | 0.009 | 149.1 |
| Children doubled | 0.137 | 81.3 | 0.018 | 73.7 |
| Impact of an additional child | | | | |
| Male, 0–2 | 0.077 | 91.2 | 0.008 | 70.3 |
| Female, 0–2 | 0.076 | 90.5 | 0.008 | 69.2 |
| Male, 3–12 | 0.090 | 77.1 | 0.014 | 81.9 |
| Female, 3–12 | 0.088 | 75.4 | 0.013 | 79.7 |
| Male, 13–19 | 0.120 | 102.2 | 0.015 | 88.0 |
| Female, 13–19 | 0.113 | 96.2 | 0.015 | 91.0 |

Sources: As for Table 9.4.
[a]Expenditures are divided by the number of school age children.

impact of the number of children by calculating shares and expenditure per child given different numbers of children, but holding total household income constant.[15] To facilitate comparisons, expenditures per school age child are expressed as a percentage of those calculated using observed means for households with a head aged 45–49.[16]

In South Korea, the households in question, that is, those with a head 45–49 years of age, averaged about 2.5 children under age 20, about half aged 3–12, and the other half were teenagers. Given the membership of the households, it is not surprising that 8.4 per cent of the budget was devoted to education compared with 5.3 per cent for households, in general. How will variation in household size affect educational expenditure? The rows marked 'halved' and 'doubled' consider two extremes in which the numbers in each sex and age-group under 20 are halved, in the first instance, or doubled, in the second. Halving the number of children, to 1.25, increases expenditure per school age child by nearly 50 per cent; doubling decreases expenditure per school age child by about 20 per cent.

The remaining rows in the table quantify the impact of an additional child in each of the age-groups and sex groups. An additional infant reduces expenditure per school age child by about 10 per cent. Although the South Korean household devotes a somewhat higher share of its budget to education with the addition of a child aged 3–12, expenditures per school age child declines by nearly 25 per cent. Somewhat puzzling, however, is the maintenance of expenditure per child with the addition of a teen. The explanation is probably that, on average, expenditures on a teen's education are considerably higher than those on younger children. With the addition of a teen, expenditure on both teens and younger children may decline, while average expenditure on the children combined increases. Unfortunately, the data do not allow tracking of expenditure on individual members.

The results from Thailand are intended to compare the responses of the two countries to similar changes in demographic circumstances. Thus, the Thai results use the Thai regression coefficients and per capita disposable income but the same demographic circumstances. Although the typical Thai household spends a much smaller share of its budget on education, the percentage responses to changing demographic features are quite similar. The major difference is that the percentage decline with the addition of an infant is much greater in Thailand. As in South Korea, the addition of a teen has a smaller depressive impact on educational expenditure, but in Thailand expenditure per school age member does decline by about 10 per cent.

The results are very much in accord with Schultz's findings with regard to public expenditure. It appears that the government and the private sector are acting in concert when it comes to spending on education. But what of school enrolment? Schultz finds no evidence at the aggregate level of an inverse relationship between school enrolment and fertility. Analysis of Thai data presented below indicates that the dilution of economic resources accompanying larger family size results in lower school enrolment. In South Korea, however, the evidence is more mixed and it is difficult to assess the extent to which rapid fertility decline contributed to the high levels of education attained there. A detailed look at this evidence is presented in the next section.

## School Enrolment

Statistical analysis of school enrolment in Thailand is based on three schooling age-groups: individuals aged 12–14, 15–17, and 18–24. Independent variables include the sex and age of the individual, the type of household and sex and age of the head, the educational attainment of the head, per capita income,[17] 12 socio-economic class dummy variables that are closely related to occupational status of the head, and the number of household members in 7 age categories: 0–2, 3–5, 6–11, 12–17, 18–24, 25–59, and 60 and over.

A proper interpretation of the direct impact of a change in the number of household members on school enrolment requires careful attention, because per capita income is held constant. Thus, any adverse impact of children on the material or financial resources available to each child is not captured by the household member variables. However, changes in the number of members does capture changes in the supply of time within the household. But how should school enrolment be influenced by the change in time? To understand the results presented below requires that the impacts of younger from older children be distinguished. Consider the situation of a teenager. One of the most important costs of continuing in school is the opportunity cost of the teenager's time. Research on the economics of education has focused on lost wages, but teenagers may make a more important contribution to the household through home production. This is particularly likely to be so in a high-fertility situation where teenagers provide childcare. Moreover, the opportunity cost should increase with the number of young children in the household, depressing school enrolment. But what if the same teenager has one or more brothers or sisters who are also teenagers or young adults, and net suppliers rather than net users of time? As in any production process, the value of the teenager's time in home production will be depressed and the opportunity cost of schooling will be lower. Thus, the presence of older brothers and sisters should lead to higher school enrolment given per capita income. There is one additional consideration. A teenager with several older siblings will have, on average, received less time inputs from adults when he or she was a child. To the extent that this has retarded human resource development, an earlier drop out age and lower school enrolment might be anticipated.

The direct impact of the number of household members on school enrolment estimated from the 1981 Socio-Economic Survey of Thailand is presented in Table 9.7. Although all of the effects are not individually statistically significant, a very clear pattern emerges. The presence of younger children in the household and, especially, pre-school children, depresses school enrolment among older siblings. But, the presence of

### TABLE 9.7
Impact of Children on School Enrolment: Thailand, 1981

|  | Age-group |  |  |
|---|---|---|---|
|  | 12–14 | 15–17 | 18–24 |
| Direct effect |  |  |  |
| Age 0–2 | −0.251[a] | −0.027 | −0.677[a] |
| Age 3–5 | −0.058 | −0.282[a] | −0.240 |
| Age 6–11 | −0.034 | −0.088 | −0.042 |
| Age 12–17 | 0.113[a] | 0.187[a] | 0.133[a] |
| Age 18–24 | 0.075 | 0.113[a] | 0.291[a] |
| Income effect | −0.012 | −0.221[a] | −0.342[a] |
| N | 4,070 | 3,712 | 6,875 |

*Note*: Based on logit analysis, coefficients are impact of an additional child on the log odds of enrolment.
[a]Statistically significant at 5 per cent level.

older children in the household increases the likelihood that older children will be enrolled.[18] This result is consistent with the view that enrolment is affected by the opportunity cost of schooling which depends, in turn, on the household's childrearing responsibilities. It is inconsistent, however, with the thesis that the dilution of time inputs of parents *per se*, associated with high rates of childbearing, retards school enrolment.

The second impact of children is that they dilute the household's financial resources. Statistical analysis found that lower per capita income reduced school enrolment in Thailand. The impact of an additional child through his or her impact on household income is evaluated at the means of the independent variables and reported in Table 9.7.[19] The direct and income effects are additive so that the total effect for any particular age-group is the sum of the age-specific direct effect and the age-independent income effect. The income and direct effects are reinforcing in the case of additional young household members, that is, school enrolment will be depressed among older siblings. Among older siblings the effects are partially offsetting. For students at lower secondary school age, neither effect dominates. But for students of upper secondary and tertiary school age, the income effect is generally stronger. Thus, additional older children in the household depresses school enrolment at these levels.

Are these results peculiar to Thailand or have advances in educational attainment been influenced in other Asian countries in similar fashion? Unfortunately, the data available to examine such issues in Thailand are considerably richer than data available in many other countries, so that a precise answer is not available. Analysis of school enrolment in South Korea (Koo and Mason, forthcoming) yields results that are broadly consistent with the Thai findings.

The South Korean analysis is based on two different data sources.

The 1986 Social Statistical Survey (SSS) is used to analyse the determinants of college enrolment among South Koreans aged 18–24. This survey could not be used to examine the determinants of secondary school enrolment because, in South Korea, secondary school enrolment was nearly universal by 1986. As a result, a 1/1,000 sample from the 1970 census was used to analyse school enrolment among Koreans aged 12–14, 15–17, and 18–24. Thus, the primary South Korean analysis looks at the conditions that led to rapid improvements in educational attainment at a critical moment in South Korea's economic and demographic development.

The results from the South Korean analysis are not directly comparable to the Thai analysis in two respects. First, neither household income nor expenditure data are available from either data source. Other variables, including housing characteristics, educational attainment of the head and spouse, and occupational status variables are used as imperfect controls for household income. But it is not possible to control for per capita household income. Thus, independent estimates of the direct and income effects of the number of children cannot be obtained. Rather, the analysis yields a combined estimate of the two effects which is roughly comparable to the combined effect for Thailand described above. Second, the 1986 SSS provides less detailed demographic information than the Thai SES or the South Korean census so that only the combined impact of additional members under age 15 on college enrolment in 1986 can be estimated. Despite these limitations, the results of the South Korean analysis are instructive.

Table 9.8 reports the regression coefficients from a least squares estimate of the impact of number of members on the proportion enrolled at each schooling level.[20] Results from the 1970 census are quite similar to the Thai results in two important respects. First, additional young girls or boys in the household discourages school enrolment among older siblings. Most coefficients are statistically significant and the effects are quite substantial. An additional child under age 6 is estimated to have reduced school enrolment at the middle schooling levels by 9–11 per cent. The absolute size of the effects are somewhat less at the higher schooling levels, but the proportion enrolled at these levels is also lower and the percentage impact on enrolment of an additional child is quite substantial.

The impact of the presence of older children in the household is quite interesting. The presence of older male children in the household had no consistent impact on school enrolment. As in Thailand, school enrolment is not depressed by the presence of older children to the extent that is true when younger children are present. In some cases, older male children may actually encourage school enrolment. On the other hand, the presence of older female children in the household has a very consistent positive impact on school enrolment. Does this reflect gender-based differences in the contribution of children to the household? It seems likely that older daughters contribute more to household production in South Korea than do sons. An additional older daughter reduces

## TABLE 9.8
Impact of Children on School Enrolment: South Korea

|  | 1970 Census | | | 1986 SSS |
|---|---|---|---|---|
|  | 12–14 | 15–17 | 18–24 | 18–24 |
| Males aged | | | | |
| 0–5 | −0.110[a] | −0.053[a] | −0.310[a] | |
| 6–11 | −0.020 | −0.058[a] | −0.026[a] | −0.032 |
| 12–14 | −0.080[a] | 0.057[a] | 0.017 | |
| 15–17 | −0.030 | 0.057 | 0.013 | −0.037 |
| 18–24 | 0.003 | −0.020 | 0.028 | 0.004 |
| Females aged | | | | |
| 0–5 | −0.090[a] | −0.044[a] | −0.000 | |
| 6–11 | 0.000 | −0.043[a] | −0.033[a] | −0.022 |
| 12–14 | −0.050 | 0.033 | 0.015 | |
| 15–17 | 0.065[a] | 0.034 | 0.031[a] | −0.017 |
| 18–24 | 0.054[a] | 0.018 | 0.029[a] | −0.008 |
| N | 1,206 | 964 | 1,101 | 2,302 |

[a]Statistically significant at 5 per cent level.

the opportunity costs of school attendance by other children, but an additional older son does not have a discernible impact.[21]

Results from the analysis of the 1986 SSS are not very enlightening. The estimated coefficients are not statistically significant. Although the estimated impact of young children is negative, the positive impact of older children has disappeared. It may be that the 1986 results represent a natural transition in the development process. With generally lower fertility and higher income, the presence of additional children may have much less impact on the demand for schooling in a society which places such a high value on education. Moreover, if the productive role of children also declines with development, the enhancing impact of older children on school enrolment among siblings might also be expected to disappear. Without further evidence, speculation prevails.

## Conclusion

South Korea's and Thailand's experience provides considerable, if not conclusive, support for the view that the fertility declines experienced there have increased the resources available for investment in the human resource development of children. Moreover, in both countries, households with fewer children have apparently been using the increased availability of resources to invest more in the schooling of their children. It is less clear whether the rapid rise in educational attainment in South Korea can be fairly attributed to a decline in average family size, but in Thailand couples with fewer children are opting for more education for their children.

Of course there are many important issues that are not adequately addressed in this chapter or elsewhere. Education is only one aspect of human resource development and others may be equally or even more important to some aspects of social and economic development. Even though attention has been confined to this single aspect of human resources, it has not really been demonstrated that additional expenditure on education or even additional school attendance leads to more human capital. But the greatest limitation of this and other studies is the unclear guidance provided for those attempting to develop and implement policy. Have family planning programmes led people to bear fewer children and, as a result, invest more in their education? If so, the value of family planning programmes are further buttressed. But, perhaps, changes in economic opportunities have led couples to want more education for their children and the increased cost of childrearing has led to lower rates of childbearing. No doubt there is an element of truth in both possibilities, but a clear resolution of policy issues will only be possible once the exact causal nature of family decision-making about childbearing and human resources is better understood.

1. These two studies are offered to illustrate the potential impact of fertility decline on human resources. They should not be accepted as conclusive. Indeed other studies have found no relationship between birth order and intelligence (Retherford and Sewell, 1991) and there is considerable disagreement about whether being reared in a large family actually causes intellectual development to suffer.
2. The causality here is not entirely clear. Per capita income of households with young children may be lower because low-income couples have higher fertility.
3. For a technical description of the HOMES model, see Mason et al. (1987).
4. The relationship between parity and household time will vary with the rules governing living arrangements. In traditional South Korean society, the eldest son remains at home after marriage and his younger brothers and sisters may benefit from his presence or suffer from the competition with their cousins. In Thailand, the youngest daughter traditionally remains at home after marriage. Thus, higher parity children are less likely to find themselves competing with cousins for the attention of their parents.
5. These estimates are obtained by taking weighted averages of the number of adults and children in family households with a head aged $a$ where the weights are the proportions of children aged 0–4 living in households with a head aged $a$.
6. The data on which these calculations are based do not report whether the head is the mother or father of the child or not. Some cases may be included in which the head is the child's grandparent and both parents are present in the household. To reduce this possibility, households with a head 60 or older were not included in the calculations.
7. This result could be misleading because the averages include non-intact households with no children. The adults per child for non-intact households with male heads which contain children will be lower and, possibly, by a considerable amount.
8. The material presented in this section is drawn from two studies: Bauer et al. (1988) and Bauer (forthcoming).
9. Women living in non-intact households also work more hours. Those in urban households average 2 hours more per week and those in rural households 4 more hours per week than working women in intact households.
10. Analysis of participation by South Korean men shows that their labour force participation increases slightly with the number of children in the household, but the changes are not statistically significant.
11. The major omission in this analysis is educational attainment variables. Although they are available in the Thai survey, they are not in the South Korean survey analysed.

To maintain comparability they were not included in the Thai analysis.

12. This procedure is approximate because the size of households with children of a given age will differ from the national average household size.

13. Income elasticity, $\eta$, is calculated as $1 + [\beta_1 + 2\beta_2 \ln Y_d/N]/s$.

14. The income effect will be captured by the per capita income terms to the extent that per capita income accurately measures the household's 'real' standard of living.

15. This ignores any impact of children on the earnings of other household members or any contribution that children may themselves make to household income.

16. This group was selected for analysis because, in South Korea, these households have the largest number of teenagers.

17. Per capita expenditures are used rather than per capita income so as to obtain a closer measure of permanent income. Both the natural log and its square were included to allow for a flexible relationship.

18. Additional prime age adults or elderly household members also increase the probability that a teenager or young adult is enrolled in school, providing further support for the opportunity cost argument.

19. These estimates do not take into account the impact of children on household income. There are some complexities involved in doing so because a child's contribution to household income will depend on whether or not the child is in school.

20. Logit analysis produced very similar results, but the least squares coefficients are easier to interpret.

21. An additional son may reduce the opportunity cost of school enrolment but not sufficiently to outweigh the negative income effect.

# 10
# Education, Earnings, and the Self-employment Choice: A Study of the Male Chinese in Peninsular Malaysia

David Demery and Andrew Chesher

**Introduction**

THE objectives in this chapter are twofold. The first is to estimate the private returns to schooling amongst Chinese males in Peninsular Malaysia in 1983-4. Secondly, it is to investigate the role of formal schooling in the choice between paid employment and self-employment.[1] The estimated returns are derived from Mincer earnings functions fitted to data from a household income and labour force survey undertaken by the Economic Planning Unit (EPU) and the Department of Statistics (DOS), Kuala Lumpur. However, our approach departs from and extends the familiar Mincer approach by investigating separately the returns to schooling to those in paid employment and those in self-employment. As shall be seen, this involves much more than deriving a set of earnings regressions for each category in turn.

Differential returns to schooling and work experience by employment status have been generally neglected in the empirical literature (for both developed and developing countries). According to Willis (1986), most studies of rates of return in the developing countries have relied on data on wage and salary workers. The quality of the reported income data for the self-employed is doubtless partly responsible for this but there are additional conceptual problems in the interpretation of such data.

The role of education in encouraging and promoting enterprise is clearly a central concern for policymakers yet there has been relatively little research on the role of education in employment choice. Limited but sketchy evidence is available for developed countries. For the United Kingdom, Boswell (1972) and Gudgin et al. (1979) present evidence that is not inconsistent with the view that those with more education are more likely to form their own businesses than those with less. Further support for this view is reported by Rees and Shah (1986) who find that education raises the probability of self-employment in the United Kingdom. However for the United States, Fuchs (1982) has found that education has little impact on the employment choice. For a key subgroup of workers in the sample—the sales and service workers—academic success does influence employment choice but years of schooling has only an indirect effect through its influence on relative earnings. Increased levels of schooling are associated with a lower probability of self-employment (for both the whole sample and for the sample of sales and service workers).

The chapter is organized as follows. First, a model of employment choice is presented, and second, models of earnings determination are discussed. Previous studies of returns to schooling in Malaysia are briefly previewed, followed by an overview of the data used in this study. Estimation techniques are then discussed and the results presented. Finally, a summary of the main findings is offered.

## A Model of Employment Choice

The choice between paid employment and self-employment is undoubtedly influenced by many observable and unobservable characteristics of individuals in the sample. Self-employment is generally regarded as being more risky than paid employment and this impression is confirmed in the Malaysian data described below. This implies that those characteristics affecting attitudes towards risk can be expected to influence the employment choice. Of course, non-monetary differences between paid employment and self-employment may also have a bearing on this choice. Flexibility of work arrangements and work satisfaction are attractive features of self-employment, but for many the greater degree of responsibility involved in self-employment may make paid employment more appealing.

Following Rees and Shah (1986), the choice problem confronting the worker is formalized by assuming he faces a utility function of the form $U(Y_{ji}, Q_{ji})$, where $Y_{ji}$ is the income earned by individual $i$ in employment category $j$ and $Q_{ji}$ is a hedonic index which places a value on the non-pecuniary job characteristics. A worker will choose self-employment if $U(Y_{si}, Q_{si})$ is greater than $U(Y_{pi}, Q_{pi})$ where the subscripts $s$ and $p$ refer to self-employment and paid employment respectively. This way of formalizing the employment choice clearly takes no explicit account of differences in the patterns of income over the life cycle. Now assume the utility function has the following explicit form:

$$U(Y_{ji}, Q_{ji}) = e^{\delta Q_{ji}} \frac{Y_{ji}^{(1-\alpha)}}{(1-\alpha)} \tag{1}$$

where $\delta$ is a constant and $\alpha$ is a measure of the degree of relative risk aversion. Rees and Shah show that if $Y_{ji}$ is lognormally distributed, maximization of the expected value of (1) is equivalent to the maximization of the following utility index:

$$V(\bar{Y}_{ji}, c_{ji}, Q_{ji}) = \log \bar{Y}_{ji} - \frac{\alpha}{2} \log(1 + c_{ji}^2) + \frac{\delta Q_{ji}}{(1 - \alpha)} \quad (2)$$

where $\bar{Y}_{ji}$ is the mean of $Y_{ji}$ and $c_{ji}$ is its coefficient of variation. Self-employment will be chosen if $V(\bar{Y}_{si}, c_{si}, Q_{si}) \geq V(\bar{Y}_{pi}, c_{pi}, Q_{pi})$ and this implies:

$$\log \bar{Y}_{si} - \log \bar{Y}_{pi} \geq \frac{\alpha}{2} [\log(1 + c_{si}^2) - \log(1 + c_{pi}^2)]$$

$$- \frac{\delta}{(1 - \alpha)} [Q_{si} - Q_{pi}] \equiv R_i \quad (3)$$

The inequality states that the expected income advantage of self-employment over paid employment must compensate for the non-pecuniary disadvantage of being self-employed and the utility cost of the differences in income variability (the writers expect $\log(1+c_{si}) > \log(1+c_{pi})$). The effect of income variability on the choice depends on the degree of relative risk aversion (measured by $\alpha$). The aim in the empirical application of (3) is to find a vector of observable characteristics ($z_i$) to explain variations in $R_i$ across the individuals in the sample. Let $R_i = z_i'\gamma + \epsilon_i$ (where $\epsilon_i$ has mean zero and constant variance). Then (3) may be written:

$$\log \bar{Y}_{si} - \log \bar{Y}_{pi} \geq z_i'\gamma + \epsilon_i \quad (4)$$

This choice criterion for the $i$th individual may thus be written:

$$I_i^* = \log \bar{Y}_{si} - \log \bar{Y}_{pi} - z_i'\gamma - \epsilon_i \quad (5)$$

where the individual $i$ will choose to be self-employed if $I_i^* \geq 0$. Of course, $I_i^*$ is not observed, but a binary variable $I_i$ is observed with the following relationship with $I_i^*$:

$I_i = 1$ if $I_i^* \geq 0$
$I_i = 0$ if $I_i^* < 0$

Then clearly when $I_i = 1$ (that is, self-employment is selected), the observed income will equal income from self-employment (that is, $\bar{Y}_i = \bar{Y}_{si}$) and when $I_i = 0$ (paid employment is selected), the observed income will equal income from paid employment (that is, $\bar{Y}_i = \bar{Y}_{pi}$).

## A Model of Earnings

It now remains to specify a model for earnings in paid employment and self-employment. In general terms:

$$\log \overline{Y}_{si} = x'_1 \beta_s + \epsilon_{si}$$
$$\log \overline{Y}_{pi} = x'_1 \beta_p + \epsilon_{pi} \qquad (6)$$

The key elements of the vector $x_i$ are the human capital variables—formal schooling and work experience. Since their introduction by Mincer (1974) these variables have been widely used in the analysis of earnings differences in both developed and developing countries. (See Willis (1986) for a survey of the theoretical and econometric issues and Psacharopoulos (1985) for a review of the international evidence on returns to schooling.) Blaug (1972: 54) has argued that the universality of the positive association between earnings and education is 'one of the most striking findings of modern social science. It is indeed one of the few safe generalizations that one can make about labour markets in all countries, whether capitalist or communist.' Equally well documented is the non-linear relationship between work experience (often proxied by age) and earnings. These empirical regularities are not in question; their meanings and interpretations are.

Mincer's empirical earnings function may be written:

$$\log \overline{Y} = \beta_0 + \beta_1 S + \beta_2 E + \beta_3 E^2 + \epsilon \qquad (7)$$

where the subscripts have been dropped for convenience. $S$ is the number of years of schooling; $E$ is years of work experience, $Y$ is after-tax earnings; and $\epsilon$ is a random error term. Mincer's justification of equation (7) is 'a blend of theory and pragmatism' (Willis, 1986: 542). He interprets the coefficient $\beta_1$ as the average private rate of return to schooling—an interpretation based on the assumption that the only cost of schooling is forgone earnings. If private direct costs of schooling are covered by part-time work during schooling, the assumption may be a good approximation. In cases where formal schooling and work experience bestow 'general' (and therefore marketable) skills (rather than firm-specific ones), competition will force the worker (rather than the firm) to pay the costs and enjoy the return to the acquisition of these skills.

This interpretation of equation (7) has been criticized on several counts but two in particular have important implications for the analysis. First, there is an endogeneity problem. If individuals with greater ability receive more schooling than those with less ability, the coefficient $\beta_1$ will overstate the true rate of return to schooling if ability and earnings are correlated (Rosen, 1977; Willis and Rosen, 1979). When the data permit the inclusion of ability effects (through IQ scores or through studies of twins), they have been found to be quantitatively important. One way round this would be to find instrumental variables for $S$ and $S^2$ that are uncorrelated with ability but this is not possible given the data set.

A related but conceptually distinct criticism is the screening hypothesis. According to this view, education does not raise income through raising worker productivity, but because it 'signals ability' to prospective employers (Spence, 1974). If the costs of acquiring this signal are lower to the more able workers, then they will acquire more schooling. They will thus be observed to earn more than unschooled workers because of their superior ability rather than through the effect of education on productivity. The theory is not easily tested and the limited empirical literature on screening is inconclusive (although favourable evidence is presented by Riley, 1979). In the writer's own analysis of earnings from paid employment and self-employment, the screening hypothesis is more relevant to the former than to the latter. Wolpin (1977) has exploited this implication and by comparing the two groups concludes that the evidence does not support the screening hypothesis. This will be taken up again when the estimated returns to schooling are considered.

It is clear that the Mincer earnings function—equation (7)—is an approximation at best. Nevertheless, after reviewing the theoretical and empirical literature, Willis (1986: 590) concluded 'that the simple Mincer-type earnings function does a surprisingly good job of estimating the returns to education' and for this reason the Mincer earnings function will form the basis for the model of the earnings of those in paid and self-employment.

## Previous Studies

There have been a number of studies of the returns to schooling in Malaysia. Anand (1983) estimated equation (7) using a sample of 8,263 urban individuals from the 1970 Census Post-Enumeration Survey. The data were further analysed by occupation category and by ethnicity. For the full sample, Anand found a return of 14.77 per cent and schooling, experience, and experience squared explained 48.5 per cent of the inequality in urban incomes. The rate of return to schooling for the urban Chinese was estimated to be 13.87 per cent.

Using data from the same survey together with data from the Migration and Employment Survey of 1975, Mazumdar (1981) found that the rate of return to schooling increased with the level of schooling. According to Psacharopoulos (1985), the private rate of return to education in developing countries is generally highest at the primary level (31 per cent for Asia) and lower at secondary and tertiary levels (the Asian figures being 15 per cent and 18 per cent respectively). But Mazumdar finds the return to schooling rises from 8.6 per cent and 8.2 per cent for those completing primary and lower secondary schooling respectively to 14.2 per cent for those finishing upper secondary schooling.

Finally, Grootaert (1986) analysed the Rand Corporation Family Life survey of 1,064 households in 1976–7. Although the sample used had important deficiencies for the questions being considered, Grootaert confirmed Mazumdar's finding of increasing returns. The returns to schooling were estimated to rise from 6 per cent at primary to 17 per cent at secondary and 21 per cent at tertiary levels. In the application of equation (7) to the Malaysian case, it will be necessary to allow the rate of return to depend on the level of schooling itself.

## EPU–DOS Household Income Survey

In this chapter, the focus is specifically on Chinese males of 25 years of age or over. The reasons for selecting this sub-sample are as follows. First, those under 25 years were excluded to ensure a sample of only those who had actually completed their formal schooling. Secondly, to analyse the choice between paid and self-employment, the analysis was limited to the ethnic community traditionally associated with self-employment in Malaysia—the Chinese. Finally, the analysis is limited to males simply to avoid the implications of allowing for the decision to participate in the work-force. The analysis was made possible by the provision by EPU of the appropriate records from the 1984 EPU–DOS Household Income Survey. However, the implications of unemployment are not examined in the analysis. In addition, retained in the sample are only those individuals whose 'usual' occupational category is known. As a result of the application of these filters, the final sample consisted of 12,720 individuals.

The sample was then divided into those in paid employment and those in self-employment. In most cases, the classification was straightforward as only one income source was identified. However, for around 8 per cent of the sample, income was received from both paid employment and self-employment. In these cases, individuals were identified as in paid employment if income from paid employment accounted for at least half of their total income. The remainder were treated as self-employed. Of the 12,720 in the sample, 8,606 are in paid employment and 4,114 are classified as self-employed. As the aim is to estimate the private rate of return to schooling, tax paid from gross income was deducted (measured in Malaysian ringgit per annum at 1983 prices).[2]

Of course, income from self-employment is conceptually different from that in paid employment, for the former includes an element of capital income (in the form of a return to the capital owned by the proprietor) as well as labour income. The measure of labour income from self-employment will be contaminated by elements of capital income. This raises no econometric problems though the variance of income from self-employment can be expected to exceed that from paid employment even if the labour income component of the former behaved identically to the latter. Moreover, if the expected return on capital is positive, mean incomes from self-employment will be greater than those from paid employment.

Descriptive statistics for selected variables are set out in Table 10.1. These figures are presented first for the entire sample and then for those working in sales and services for reasons explained below. Over the

## TABLE 10.1
Descriptive Statistics

| Variable | Mean | Standard Deviation |
|---|---|---|
| *All Occupations* | | |
| *All Workers* | | |
| Annual income (ringgit) | 11,935 | 16,563 |
| Years of schooling | 7.490 | 3.960 |
| Work experience (years) | 25.097 | 11.674 |
| *Paid Employees Only* | | |
| Annual income (ringgit) | 11,268 | 10,162 |
| Years of schooling | 8.104 | 4.106 |
| Work experience (years) | 23.017 | 11.177 |
| *Self-employed Only* | | |
| Annual income (ringgit) | 13,329 | 25,089 |
| Years of schooling | 6.204 | 3.280 |
| Work experience (years) | 29.447 | 11.491 |
| *Sales and Service Workers* | | |
| *All Workers* | | |
| Annual income (ringgit) | 12,217 | 14,622 |
| Years of schooling | 7.226 | 3.411 |
| Work experience (years) | 26.277 | 12.020 |
| *Paid Employees Only* | | |
| Annual income (ringgit) | 10,529 | 8,787 |
| Years of schooling | 8.210 | 3.396 |
| Work experience (years) | 22.326 | 11.292 |
| *Self-employed Only* | | |
| Log income | 13,708 | 18,160 |
| Years of schooling | 6.358 | 3.182 |
| Work experience (years) | 29.765 | 11.566 |

entire sample, the mean income of the self-employed is greater than that for paid employees (about 18 per cent higher), but its variance is also appreciably greater. Workers in paid employment have experienced more years of schooling than those in self-employment (a mean level of around 8 years compared with around 6 years) and the self-employed have generally had more years of work experience (6 years more on average). Taken together these imply that the self-employed sample is older on average.

Of the total sample, 29 per cent (that is, 3,700 individuals) are classified as sales and service workers. This group covers shop workers, salesmen, restaurateurs, etc. For these workers, the mean income from self-employment is 30 per cent higher than from paid employment though its standard deviation is again appreciably higher. The mean levels of schooling and work experience are almost identical to those of the entire sample.

The relationships between earnings, schooling, and age are set out graphically in Figures 10.1–10.4. Figure 10.1 presents the earnings–age profiles for each of four levels of schooling: 1–6 years (primary), 7–9 years (lower secondary), 10–13 years (upper secondary), and 14 years and over (tertiary). Each plot is derived by smoothing the raw data using a non-parametric procedure.[3] The familiar inverse-U age pattern is clearly in evidence, particularly for workers possessing tertiary schooling. The earnings profiles are displaced vertically with progressively higher levels of schooling; the vertical displacement being greater, the higher the level of schooling.

The profiles drawn separately for the paid employed and the self-employed are set out in Figure 10.2. The profiles for the paid employed show similar patterns to those in Figure 10.1, but the patterns for the self-employed are distinctly different. The concavity of the age profiles is less pronounced (especially for upper secondary and tertiary workers) and for tertiary workers there is no decline in later life. There are relatively few self-employed with tertiary education in the sample, so inference for this group is difficult.

The earnings–age profiles for selected occupational categories are set out in Figures 10.3 and 10.4. For professional, technical, administrative, and managerial workers (professionals and managers), the profile for

FIGURE 10.1
Earnings–Age Profiles by Years of Education

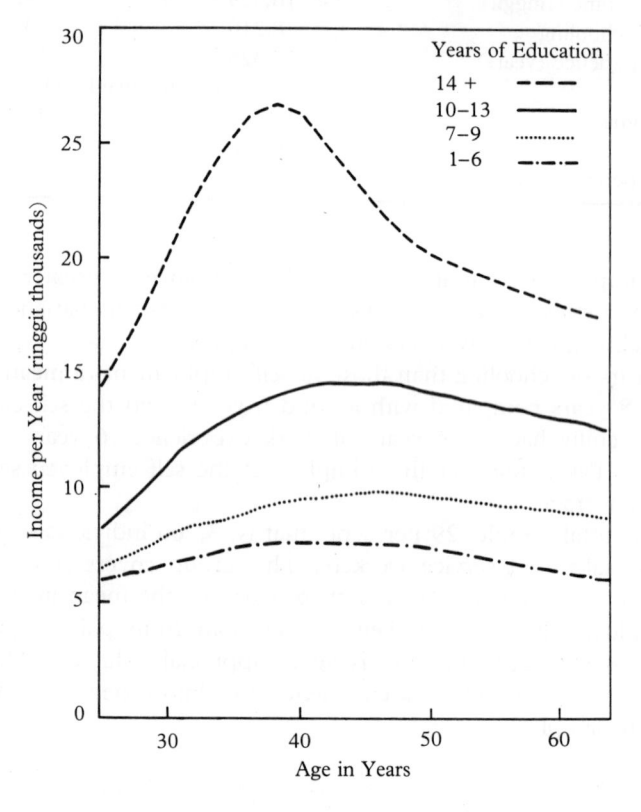

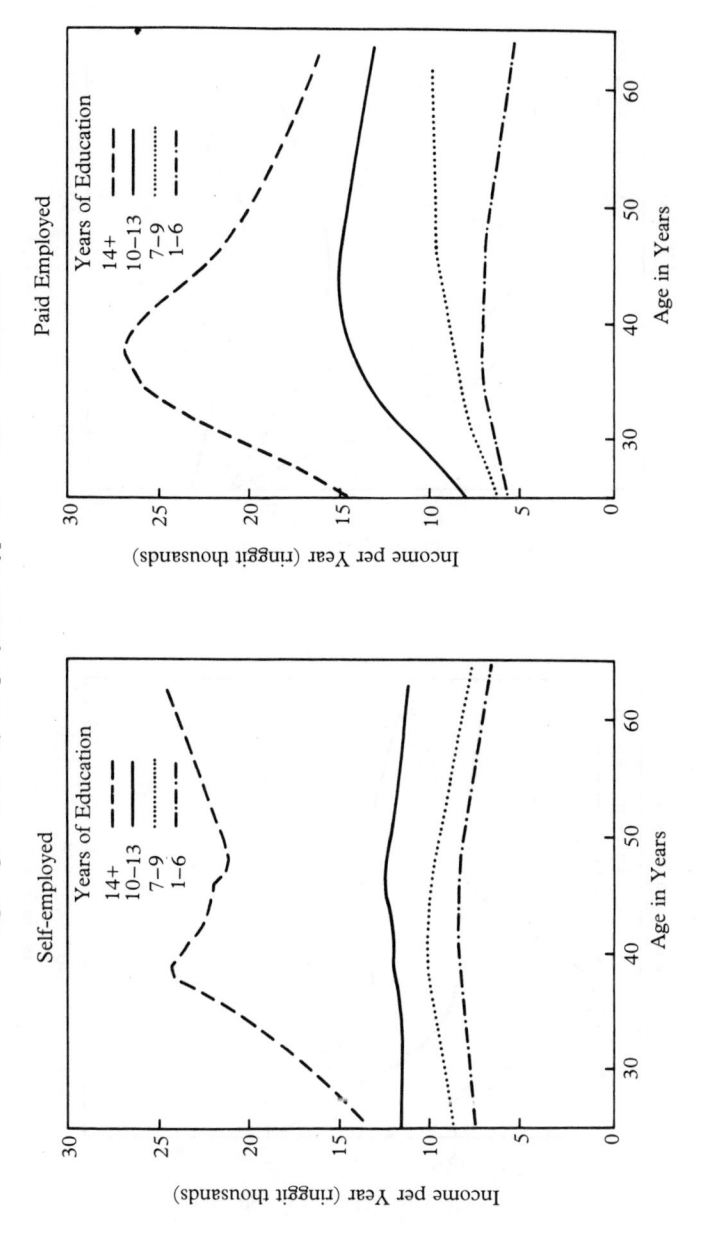

FIGURE 10.2
Earnings–Age Profiles by Employment Type and Years of Education

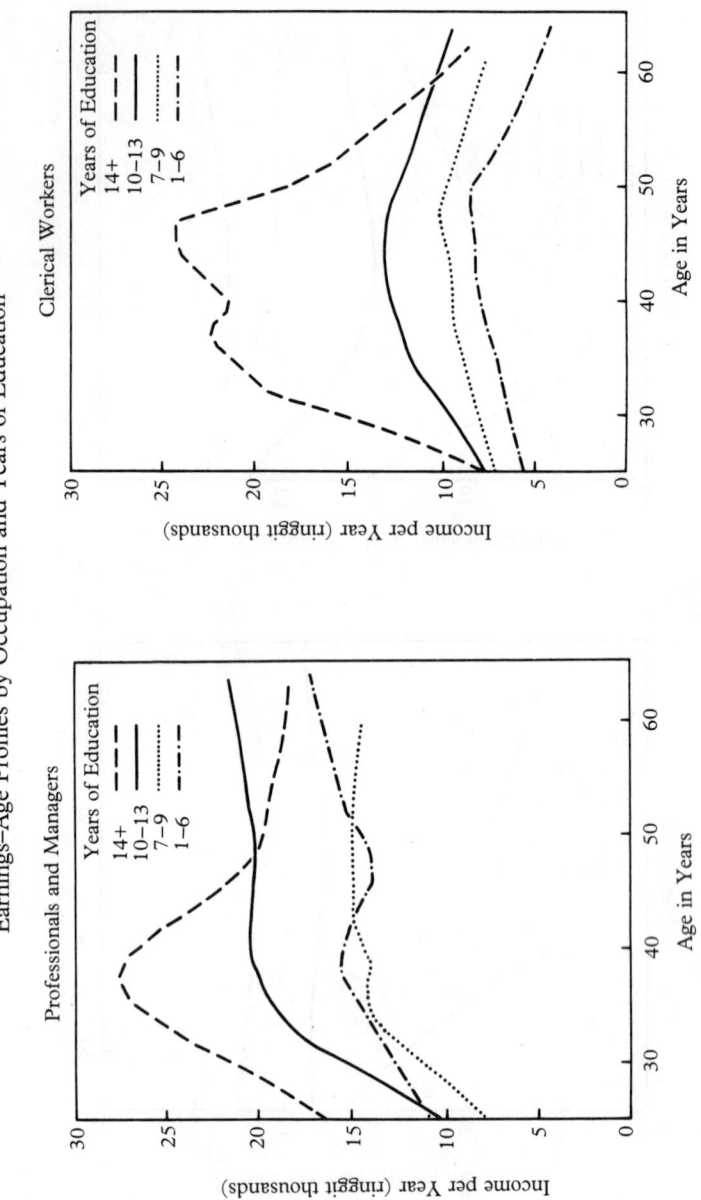

FIGURE 10.3
Earnings–Age Profiles by Occupation and Years of Education

FIGURE 10.4
Earnings–Age Profiles by Occupation and Years of Education

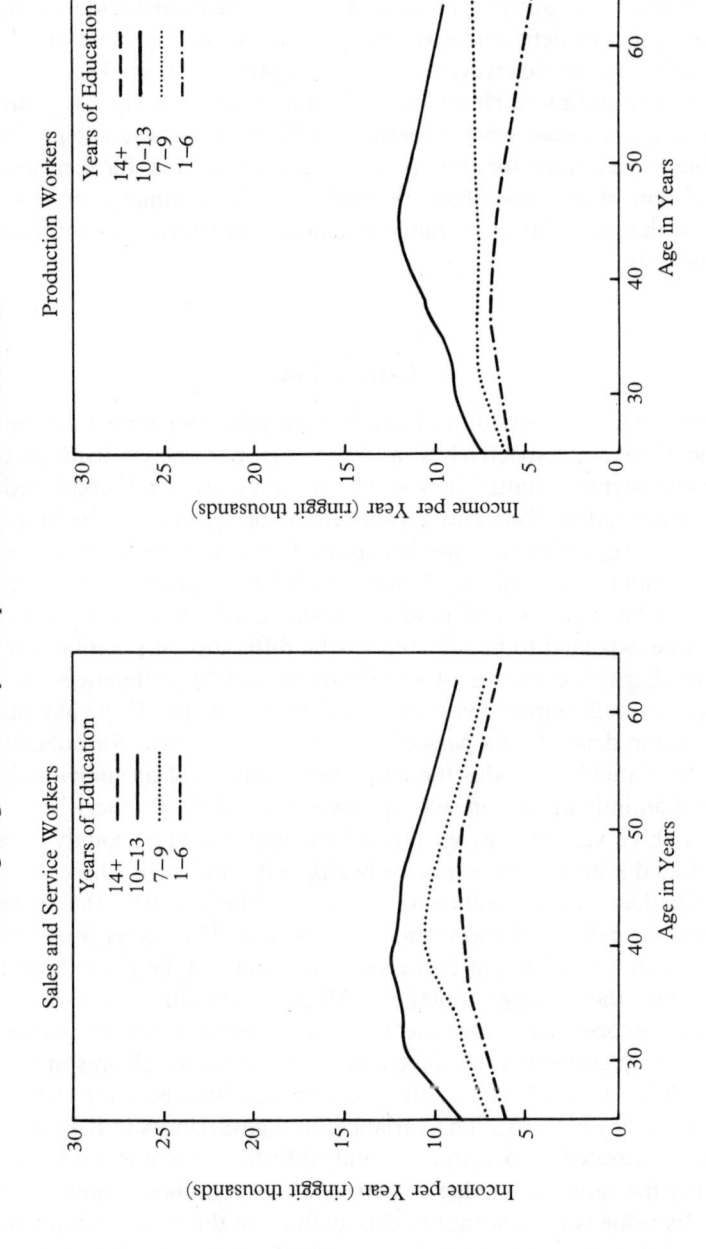

workers with primary schooling shows an erratic age pattern, but the profiles for lower and upper secondary workers display a more regular inverse-U pattern. Of course, the patterns observed in the figure may reflect cohort (that is, year of birth) effects rather than life cycle phenomena. The profiles for clerical workers are more regular, with substantial gains evident for those with tertiary schooling. The profiles for both sales and service workers and for all production workers are somewhat flatter and more closely spaced, indicating relatively low returns to schooling and weak work experience effects. For these categories, the sample observations for tertiary workers were too few for a meaningful application of the smoothing method used. In summary, these figures suggest that the Mincer earnings functions will provide a good basis for the analysis.

## Estimation

Suppose that the logarithm of earnings in self-employment and in paid employment are respectively $y_s$ and $y_p$ ringgit per year. Individuals reveal their employment status, that is whether they are a self-employed or a paid employed worker, and a value for $y_s$ or $y_p$, but not for both. The choice of employment status is captured by a variable $I^*$ which ranges over positive and negative values, with an individual choosing self-employment if $I^* \geq 0$ and paid employment otherwise. The value of $I^*$ would be expected to be affected by the difference in potential earnings in the alternative modes of employment and by differences in other aspects of self-employment and paid employment. $I^*$ would also be expected to depend on a person's attitude to risk. In the formulae below, a binary variable, $I$, codes the employment status of an individual, with $I = 1$ if an individual is in self-employment, and $I = 0$ otherwise.

The three variables $y_s$, $y_p$, and $I^*$ are assumed to be jointly normally distributed with means respectively $x'\beta_s$, $x'\beta_p$, and $x'\beta_I$. These are linear combinations of the elements of a vector $x$ which records the characteristics of an individual and of his environment. The vector $x$ is common to the three variables, but exclusion restrictions on the $\beta$ coefficients are possible in the earnings functions. All arguments in the earnings functions are expected to enter the $I^*$ equation because relative earnings is one of its determinants. However, there may be determinants of employment choice which have no effect on earnings (that is, some elements of $\beta_s$ and $\beta_p$ may be zero). The variances and covariances of the three variables are denoted by $\sigma_{pp}$, $\sigma_{ps}$, $\sigma_{pI}$, and so forth. Since it is not possible to observe the numerical values taken by $I^*$, its variance cannot be estimated. Its value is not relevant to this analysis so this is of no concern. For convenience, $\sigma_{II}$ is set equal to one in the formulae which follow.

In this model, the binary data, $I$, are generated by a probit model with:

$$P[I = 1 | x] = \phi(x'\beta_I)$$

which is the standard normal distribution function evaluated at $x'\beta_I$. Data recording $I$ and $x$ can be used to estimate $\beta_I$ by maximizing a log likelihood function, a typical contribution to which is:

$$L = I \log\{\phi(x'\beta_I)\} + (1 - I) \log\{\phi(-x'\beta_I)\}$$

If everyone revealed data on their earnings in self-employment and paid employment, then a simple least squares regression would produce usable estimates of $\beta_s$ and $\beta_p$. In fact, only those in self-employment reveal $y_s$ and only those in paid employment reveal $y_p$. In this circumstance, simple least squares regressions of $y_s$ and $y_p$ on $x$ will generally produce biased estimates of $\beta_s$ and $\beta_p$. This is because among those who select self-employment, the expected value of log earnings is:

$$E(y_s) = x'\beta_s + \rho_{sI} h(-x'\beta_I)/\sigma_{ss}^{-1/2} \tag{8}$$

and among those choosing paid employment, the expected value of log earnings is:

$$E(y_p) = x'\beta_p - \rho_{pI} h(x'\beta_I)/\sigma_{pp}^{-1/2} \tag{9}$$

Here, $\rho_{sI}$ and $\rho_{pI}$ are the correlations between $y_s$ and $I^*$ and between $y_p$ and $I^*$. The function $h(w)$ is the standard normal hazard function, the ratio of the standard normal probability density function to one minus the standard normal distribution function. This function is convex and increasing. For large negative values of $w$, $h(w)$ is close to zero. For large positive values, $h(w)$ is close to but above $w$. It is the non-linear terms in equations (8) and (9) involving the standard normal hazard function which cause simple least squares estimators to be biased.

Consider equation (8). Individuals whose characteristics are such that they are very likely to enter self-employment and who do in fact enter self-employment will have expected log earnings close to $x'\beta_s$. This is because such people will have large positive values of $x'\beta_I$, so $h(-x'\beta_I)$ will be close to zero. Individuals whose characteristics are such that they are very unlikely to enter self-employment but who are nevertheless found in self-employment will have expected log earnings deviating greatly from $x'\beta_s$ unless the correlation $\rho_{sI}$ is zero. This is because such people will have large negative values of $x'\beta_I$, so $h(-x'\beta_I)$ will be far from zero. The deviation from $x'\beta_s$ will be upwards if $\rho_{sI}$ is positive and downwards if it is negative.

It is not possible to sign the correlations $\rho_{sI}$ and $\rho_{pI}$ a priori. One might expect to find $\rho_{sI}$ positive and $\rho_{pI}$ negative so that people found in each employment mode would tend to have earnings above the average for earnings in each mode calculated over the whole population. But suppose that there is some unobservable variable omitted from the model which tends to depress earnings in both modes of employment and which also tends to predispose people away from paid employment—'unreliability' is perhaps a good example. Then both $\rho_{sI}$ and $\rho_{pI}$ will be negative, and those unusual people found in self-employment when their observable characteristics would lead us to expect them to be in paid employment will have earnings below the average of potential earnings in self-employment calculated over the whole population.

It is possible to estimate the parameters of this model by applying a least squares procedure to these equations, replacing the unknown $\beta_I$ by an estimate obtained in an initial probit analysis. This two-step procedure is described in Heckman (1979). Estimates produced in this way can be somewhat unreliable (Greene, 1985) and they are inefficient, but they have been widely used.[4] Here maximum likelihood estimates are reported. They are obtained from a log likelihood function based on the information embodied in $I$ and in the revealed values of $y_p$ and $y_s$. The log likelihood function has the following typical contributions (excluding inessential constants):

$$L = I \left\{ -0.5 \log(\sigma_{ss}) - \frac{0.5}{\sigma_{ss}} (y_s - x'\beta_s)^2 \right.$$

$$+ \log \phi \left[ \frac{x'\beta_I + \rho_{sI} (y_s - x'\beta_s)/\sqrt{\sigma_{ss}}}{(1 - \rho_{sI}^2)^{1/2}} \right] \right\}$$

$$+ (1 - I) \left\{ -0.5 \log(\sigma_{pp}) - \frac{0.5}{\sigma_{pp}} (y_p - x'\beta_p)^2 \right.$$

$$+ \log \phi \left[ -\frac{x'\beta_I + \rho_{pI} (y_p - x'\beta_p)/\sqrt{\sigma_{pp}}}{(1 - \rho_{pI}^2)^{1/2}} \right] \right\}$$

Estimates were obtained using the quasi-Newton procedure described in Berndt et al. (1974).

It is straightforward to constrain maximum likelihood estimates to satisfy restrictions which flow from the economic theory sketched above. For example, suppose one believes that a subset of variables influence $I^*$ only because of their effect on relative potential earnings under the two modes of employment. Let the other variables affecting $I^*$ be denoted by $x_o$. Then the expected value of $I^*$ can be written as:

$$E(I^*|x) = x'\beta_I = \delta(x'\beta_s - x'\beta_p) + x'_o \beta_{Io} \tag{10}$$

and the likelihood function maximized with respect to $\beta_s$, $\beta_p$, $\beta_{Io}$, $\delta$, and the variance and covariance parameters. When more than one element of $x$ is excluded from $x_o$ this constitutes a restriction on the model. Of course, $\delta$ would be expected to be positive.

## Results

*Ordinary Least Squares*

Before the maximum likelihood results are examined, first consider the estimated returns to schooling obtained using ordinary least squares (OLS). In Table 10.4, the results of applying OLS to the entire sample of 12,720 observations in the data set are presented. In column (1), the results obtained by a regression of log earnings on the number of years of schooling (S) are reported (divided by 10 for reasons of presentation). The private rate of return to schooling is estimated to be around 8 per cent and the equation explains 17 per cent of the variance in log earnings. It is well known that this estimate is biased downwards.

The model is further extended in column (2). First, increasing returns to schooling are allowed for by adding schooling squared (divided by 100). Secondly, experience (E, divided by 10) and experience squared (divided by 1,000) are included. Separate information on work experience is not given in the data used so work experience is defined as age minus years of schooling minus six years. This procedure—though widely used in the literature—means that the separate influences on earnings of cohort and experience cannot be identified. Some of the unusual features of the earnings–age profiles set out graphically above may be due to cohort rather than experience (or human capital).[5]

The extended model explains around 21 per cent of the variance of log earnings. The schooling and experience terms have the expected signs and are all highly significant. Moreover, the results confirm the presence of increasing returns (the quadratic term in schooling carries a positive coefficient). The marginal returns to schooling can be computed by noting that:

$$\hat{r}(S) = \frac{d(\log Y)}{dS} = \hat{\beta}_1 + 2\hat{\beta}_2 S \qquad (11)$$

where $\hat{r}(S)$ is the estimated marginal return to schooling at level $S$; $\hat{\beta}_1$ is the estimated coefficient of $S$ and $\hat{\beta}_2$ is the estimated coefficient of $S^2$ (Willis, 1986: 532). The estimated marginal returns (per cent) for primary ($\hat{r}_p$), lower secondary ($\hat{r}_{ls}$), upper secondary ($\hat{r}_{us}$), and tertiary ($\hat{r}_t$) levels of schooling are also presented in Table 10.4. For the model estimated in column (2), the returns rise from just over 7 per cent at primary level (or six years of schooling) to over 18 per cent at tertiary level. (It is assumed that tertiary schooling implies 17 years of schooling, since the precise number of years of schooling for this group were not coded in the data.)

In column (3), the model is again extended by the addition of further regressors. The means and standard deviations for these variables are set out in Table 10.2 for the whole sample and in Table 10.3 for those in sales and services. The first four variables are location dummies: 'KL'

### TABLE 10.2
Exogenous Variables: Descriptive Statistics for All Occupations

| Variable | Mean | Standard Deviation |
|---|---|---|
| *All Workers* | | |
| KL | 0.199 | 0.399 |
| Metro | 0.560 | 0.496 |
| Urbl | 0.183 | 0.387 |
| Urbs | 0.090 | 0.287 |
| Fail | 0.195 | 0.396 |
| Mar | 0.800 | 0.399 |
| Wid | 0.010 | 0.099 |
| Div | 0.005 | 0.072 |
| Head | 0.698 | 0.459 |
| *Paid Employees Only* | | |
| KL | 0.216 | 0.412 |
| Metro | 0.600 | 0.489 |
| Urbl | 0.175 | 0.380 |
| Urbs | 0.072 | 0.259 |
| Fail | 0.222 | 0.415 |
| Mar | 0.754 | 0.430 |
| Wid | 0.008 | 0.089 |
| Div | 0.005 | 0.072 |
| Head | 0.653 | 0.475 |
| *Self-employed Only* | | |
| KL | 0.161 | 0.367 |
| Metro | 0.476 | 0.499 |
| Urbl | 0.200 | 0.400 |
| Urbs | 0.128 | 0.334 |
| Fail | 0.139 | 0.346 |
| Mar | 0.896 | 0.305 |
| Wid | 0.014 | 0.118 |
| Div | 0.005 | 0.071 |
| Head | 0.791 | 0.405 |

refers to residence in Kuala Lumpur, 'Metro' to metropolitan residence, and 'Urbl' and 'Urbs' to large and small urban locations respectively. The location reference group is rural. Of the sample, 56 per cent live in metropolitan districts and 20 per cent in Kuala Lumpur, while 18 and 9 per cent reside in large and small urban locations, respectively. The remainder (17 per cent) are rural. Differences between the paid employed and self-employed are not great: 15.3 per cent of paid employees and 18.6 per cent of the self-employed are rural. The location patterns for sales and service workers are similar to those in Table 10.2. In the earnings equations, these dummy variables may capture non-pecuniary advantages (and disadvantages) associated with location (workers may like city life and will be prepared to accept lower pay to secure employment there), or they may be associated with different costs of living between rural and urban locations.

EDUCATION, EARNINGS, SELF-EMPLOYMENT CHOICE

TABLE 10.3
Exogenous Variables: Descriptive Statistics for Sales and Service Workers

| Variable | Mean | Standard Deviation |
|---|---|---|
| *All Workers* | | |
| KL | 0.209 | 0.406 |
| Metro | 0.593 | 0.491 |
| Urbl | 0.207 | 0.405 |
| Urbs | 0.085 | 0.279 |
| Fail | 0.181 | 0.385 |
| Mar | 0.810 | 0.392 |
| Wid | 0.011 | 0.107 |
| Div | 0.006 | 0.078 |
| Head | 0.712 | 0.452 |
| *Paid Employees Only* | | |
| KL | 0.242 | 0.428 |
| Metro | 0.670 | 0.470 |
| Urbl | 0.179 | 0.384 |
| Urbs | 0.061 | 0.239 |
| Fail | 0.221 | 0.415 |
| Mar | 0.709 | 0.454 |
| Wid | 0.009 | 0.095 |
| Div | 0.007 | 0.086 |
| Head | 0.606 | 0.488 |
| *Self-employed Only* | | |
| KL | 0.180 | 0.384 |
| Metro | 0.525 | 0.499 |
| Urbl | 0.232 | 0.422 |
| Urbs | 0.106 | 0.308 |
| Fail | 0.147 | 0.354 |
| Mar | 0.898 | 0.301 |
| Wid | 0.013 | 0.116 |
| Div | 0.005 | 0.071 |
| Head | 0.807 | 0.394 |

'Fail' is a dummy variable which takes the value one if the individual did not obtain the formal academic qualifications appropriate to his level of schooling. From Table 10.2, it can be seen that about 20 per cent of the total sample did not achieve academic success in this sense. Note that this proportion is lower for the self-employed. (The corresponding figures for sales and service workers are not too dissimilar.)

The remaining variables in Tables 10.2 and 10.3 are marital status and household head dummies. These are assumed to influence employment choice but not earnings. Of the total sample, 80 per cent are married (Mar), 1 per cent are widowed (Wid), and apart from a few divorced individuals (Div), the remainder are single; while 70 per cent of the sample are heads of household (Head). The figures in Table 10.3 for sales and service workers are again not dissimilar.

Returning to the extended OLS results reported in Table 10.4, the

## TABLE 10.4
### OLS Earnings Regressions, Paid Employed Dependent Variable: Log of Post-tax Annual Earnings

|  | (1) | (2) | (3) | (4) |
|---|---|---|---|---|
| $S/10$ | 0.778 | 0.117 | 0.041 | – |
|  | (0.015) | (0.052) | (0.052) |  |
| $S^2/100$ | – | 0.508 | 0.575 | – |
|  |  | (0.028) | (0.028) |  |
| $E/10$ | – | 0.487 | 0.487 | 0.476 |
|  |  | (0.024) | (0.024) | (0.024) |
| $E^2/1000$ | – | −0.717 | −0.723 | −0.736 |
|  |  | (0.041) | (0.041) | (0.041) |
| Fail | – | – | −0.156 | −0.088 |
|  |  |  | (0.018) | (0.020) |
| Metro | – | – | 0.151 | 0.155 |
|  |  |  | (0.017) | (0.017) |
| Urbl | – | – | 0.055 | 0.056 |
|  |  |  | (0.020) | (0.020) |
| Urbs | – | – | −0.049 | −0.047 |
|  |  |  | (0.023) | (0.024) |
| KL | – | – | 0.159 | 0.164 |
|  |  |  | (0.016) | (0.016) |
| $D_p$ | – | – | – | 0.139 |
|  |  |  |  | (0.026) |
| $D_{ls}$ | – | – | – | 0.366 |
|  |  |  |  | (0.031) |
| $D_{us}$ | – | – | – | 0.740 |
|  |  |  |  | (0.031) |
| $D_t$ | – | – | – | 1.550 |
|  |  |  |  | (0.042) |
| Constant | 8.492 | 7.950 | 7.871 | 7.949 |
|  | (0.012) | (0.042) | (0.043) | (0.043) |
| $\hat{r}_p$ | – | 7.268 | 7.309 | 2.312 |
|  |  | (0.246) | (0.252) |  |
| $\hat{r}_{ls}$ | – | 10.316 | 10.758 | 7.577 |
|  |  | (0.195) | (0.221) |  |
| $\hat{r}_{us}$ | – | 14.380 | 15.358 | 9.337 |
|  |  | (0.311) | (0.345) |  |
| $\hat{r}_t$ | – | 18.444 | 19.957 | 20.250 |
|  |  | (0.506) | (0.540) |  |
| $R^2$ | 0.170 | 0.214 | 0.243 | 0.236 |
| $\hat{\sigma}$ | 0.679 | 0.661 | 0.649 | 0.652 |
| $N$ | 12,720 | 12,720 | 12,720 | 12,720 |

*Note*: Numbers in parentheses are estimated standard errors.

## TABLE 10.5
OLS Earnings Regression; Paid Employed Dependent Variable: Log of Post-tax Annual Earnings

|  | (1) | (2) | (3) |
|---|---|---|---|
| $S/10$ | 0.897 | 0.239 | 0.113 |
|  | (0.015) | (0.055) | (0.054) |
| $S^2/100$ | – | 0.487 | 0.585 |
|  |  | (0.028) | (0.028) |
| $E/10$ | – | 0.545 | 0.544 |
|  |  | (0.029) | (0.024) |
| $E^2/1000$ | – | −0.830 | −0.843 |
|  |  | (0.044) | (0.044) |
| Fail | – | – | −0.186 |
|  |  |  | (0.018) |
| Metro | – | – | 0.154 |
|  |  |  | (0.018) |
| Urbl | – | – | −0.006 |
|  |  |  | (0.026) |
| Urbs | – | – | −0.082 |
|  |  |  | (0.026) |
| KL | – | – | 0.081 |
|  |  |  | (0.016) |
| Constant | 8.348 | 7.768 | 7.739 |
|  | (0.014) | (0.042) | (0.042) |
| $\hat{r}_p$ | – | 8.227 | 8.150 |
|  |  | (0.258) | (0.261) |
| $\hat{r}_{ls}$ | – | 11.148 | 11.662 |
|  |  | (0.187) | (0.211) |
| $\hat{r}_{us}$ | – | 15.042 | 16.345 |
|  |  | (0.284) | (0.319) |
| $\hat{r}_t$ | – | 18.936 | 21.027 |
|  |  | (0.476) | (0.512) |
| $R^2$ | 0.286 | 0.347 | 0.379 |
| $\hat{\sigma}$ | 0.582 | 0.557 | 0.543 |
| $N$ | 8,606 | 8,606 | 8,606 |

*Note*: Numbers in parentheses are estimated standard errors.

addition of these extra terms raises the proportion of the variance explained to 24 per cent but the estimated returns to schooling are largely unaffected. The coefficient of the 'Fail' dummy variable is significantly less than zero. Failure to achieve the appropriate academic qualifications at the end of schooling experience lowers income substantially (by some 15 per cent). This result is consistent with the view that 'screening' is an important factor behind the role of schooling in Malaysia.

Workers in metropolitan and large urban settings earn more than those in rural areas, but those in small urban locations do not. Workers in the Kuala Lumpur area earn more than those from other metropolitan areas.

In the final column, schooling effects on earnings are allowed for through the inclusion of four dummy variables: $D_p$ is 1 for individuals who have received 1–6 years of schooling and 0 otherwise (primary schooling); $D_{ls}$ is 1 for those with 7–9 years of schooling (lower secondary); $D_{us}$ is 1 for those with 10–13 years of schooling (upper secondary); and $D_t$ is the dummy variable for those with 14 years of schooling or more. The estimated returns to schooling again reveal increasing returns, but the return to primary schooling is far lower than that derived from the quadratic specification. This may be due to the

TABLE 10.6
OLS Earnings Regressions, Self-employed Dependent Variable:
Log of Post-tax Annual Earnings

|  | (1) | (2) | (3) |
|---|---|---|---|
| $S/10$ | 0.556 | −0.014 | 0.010 |
|  | (0.040) | (0.120) | (0.117) |
| $S^2/100$ | – | 0.444 | 0.438 |
|  |  | (0.079) | (0.079) |
| $E/10$ | – | 0.289 | 0.270 |
|  |  | (0.062) | (0.061) |
| $E^2/1000$ | – | −0.459 | −0.426 |
|  |  | (0.096) | (0.094) |
| Fail | – | – | −0.113 |
|  |  |  | (0.044) |
| Metro | – | – | 0.151 |
|  |  |  | (0.037) |
| Urbl | – | – | 0.184 |
|  |  |  | (0.040) |
| Urbs | – | – | −0.014 |
|  |  |  | (0.045) |
| KL | – | – | 0.378 |
|  |  |  | (0.039) |
| Constant | 8.726 | 8.468 | 8.327 |
|  | (0.278) | (0.108) | (0.107) |
| $\hat{r}_p$ | – | 5.191 | 5.365 |
|  |  | (0.533) | (0.560) |
| $\hat{r}_{ls}$ | – | 7.855 | 7.996 |
|  |  | (0.620) | (0.679) |
| $\hat{r}_{us}$ | – | 11.407 | 11.504 |
|  |  | (1.103) | (1.165) |
| $\hat{r}_t$ | – | 14.959 | 15.012 |
|  |  | (1.687) | (1.748) |
| $R^2$ | 0.046 | 0.056 | 0.100 |
| $\hat{\sigma}$ | 0.832 | 0.828 | 0.809 |
| $N$ | 4,114 | 4,114 | 4,114 |

Note: Numbers in parentheses are estimated standard errors.

fact that in computing returns to schooling it is assumed that within each of the four groups individuals have experienced the same amount of schooling. This is likely to produce downward bias in the estimate of the returns to primary schooling. However, given the intention to derive maximum likelihood estimates and given the size of the data set being analysed, it will be important to adopt a parsimonious parameterization of the model, so the quadratic specification holds in what follows.

In Tables 10.5 and 10.6, OLS results are reported for the paid employed and self-employed respectively. A number of features stand out from these tables. First, increasing returns are characteristic features of the results for both sets of workers. Secondly, the returns to schooling

TABLE 10.7
OLS Earnings Regressions, Sales and Service Workers Dependent Variable: Log of Post-tax Annual Earnings

|  | All Workers | Paid Employed | Self-employed |
|---|---|---|---|
| $S/10$ | 0.127 | 0.474 | 0.161 |
|  | (0.122) | (0.155) | (0.181) |
| $S^2/100$ | 0.465 | 0.455 | 0.238 |
|  | (0.077) | (0.090) | (0.128) |
| $E/10$ | 0.462 | 0.577 | 0.197 |
|  | (0.051) | (0.061) | (0.087) |
| $E^2/1000$ | −0.657 | −0.861 | −0.314 |
|  | (0.084) | (0.107) | (0.133) |
| Fail | −0.148 | −0.151 | −0.642 |
|  | (0.035) | (0.039) | (0.060) |
| Metro | 0.064 | 0.151 | 0.035 |
|  | (0.041) | (0.054) | (0.058) |
| Urbl | 0.072 | 0.072 | 0.110 |
|  | (0.044) | (0.059) | (0.061) |
| Urbs | −0.044 | −0.089 | −0.029 |
|  | (0.054) | (0.076) | (0.073) |
| KL | 0.207 | 0.067 | 0.365 |
|  | (0.033) | (0.037) | (0.052) |
| Constant | 7.971 | 7.428 | 8.585 |
|  | (0.094) | (0.112) | (0.155) |
| $\hat{r}_p$ | 6.847 | 10.204 | 4.458 |
|  | (0.542) | (0.688) | (0.818) |
| $\hat{r}_{ls}$ | 9.635 | 12.936 | 5.883 |
|  | (0.582) | (0.618) | (1.062) |
| $\hat{r}_{us}$ | 13.353 | 16.578 | 7.784 |
|  | (1.031) | (1.081) | (1.891) |
| $\hat{r}_t$ | 17.071 | 20.220 | 9.685 |
|  | (1.595) | (1.730) | (2.850) |
| $R^2$ | 0.104 | 0.264 | 0.060 |
| $\hat{\sigma}$ | 0.726 | 0.601 | 0.792 |
| $N$ | 3,700 | 1,735 | 1,965 |

*Note*: Numbers in parentheses are estimated standard errors.

are higher for paid employees, rising from around 8 per cent at the primary level to around 20 per cent at tertiary; whereas the corresponding figures for the self-employed are 5 and 15 per cent. Thirdly, as would be expected, the error variance is greater for the self-employed (with lower $R^2$ and higher standard error of the estimate, $\hat{\sigma}$). Finally, the failure dummy exerts a significant downward effect on log earnings for both sets of workers. Its effect is particularly pronounced for the paid employed.

As shall be argued later, it is informative to examine a more homogeneous subgroup of what is, in fact, a highly heterogeneous sample (from highly skilled professionals to unskilled production workers). In Table 10.7, some OLS results for sales and service workers are presented. The overall rates of return to schooling are estimated to be lower than those obtained from the whole sample. As before, the rates of return for the self-employed are both lower and 'flatter' than those for the paid employed. In summary, from the application of OLS to the data it can be concluded that the Mincer earnings function works satisfactorily on data for both paid employed and the self-employed, with the estimated return to schooling higher for the former.

*Maximum Likelihood*

Turning to the application of the maximum likelihood (ML) methods described above, the results for the entire sample are reported in Table 10.8. The results for the probit or indicator equation (I) are presented on the left and those for the two earnings functions on the right. The effect of schooling on employment choice is non-linear and the quadratic term is negative so that those with higher levels of schooling are less likely to be in self-employment. This point will be taken up again later. Work experience does not significantly affect employment choice. Those who fail to achieve the relevant academic qualifications are more likely to be in self-employment. Workers in metropolitan locations are more likely to be in paid employment than those in rural areas and those in small urban settings are more likely to be self-employed. Of course, location may influence employment choice in ways other than through earnings (for example, differential access to capital markets). The marital status variables are included to capture differential attitudes towards risk. The reference group is the single male: married (Mar) and widowed males (Wid) are more likely to be in paid employment than single males. Divorced males (Div) do not differ from single males in their employment choice. Finally, the likelihood of being in self-employment is higher for heads of household (Head).

The ML estimates for the earnings functions of the two groups are presented in the two right hand columns of Table 10.8. The estimated returns to schooling for paid employees are marginally higher than those from the OLS regressions. In both cases, the return at primary level is estimated to be around 8 per cent but the ML estimates rise to 23 per cent at tertiary level compared with around 20 per cent for OLS.

### TABLE 10.8
### Maximum Likelihood Estimation: All Occupations

|  | Indicator Variable | Log Earnings Paid Employment | Log Earnings Self-employment |  |
|---|---|---|---|---|
| S/10 | 0.624 | 0.016 | −0.257 | S/10 |
|  | (0.109) | (0.053) | (0.127) |  |
| $S^2/100$ | −0.820 | 0.675 | 0.790 | $S^2/100$ |
|  | (0.064) | (0.029) | (0.084) |  |
| E/10 | 0.005 | 0.477 | 0.073 | E/10 |
|  | (0.057) | (0.025) | (0.064) |  |
| $E^2/1000$ | 0.176 | −0.816 | −0.252 | $E^2/1000$ |
|  | (0.091) | (0.042) | (0.097) |  |
| Fail | 0.289 | −0.225 | −0.254 | Fail |
|  | (0.039) | (0.020) | (0.047) |  |
| Metro | −0.148 | 0.189 | 0.219 | Metro |
|  | (0.035) | (0.019) | (0.041) |  |
| Urbl | −0.029 | 0.012 | 0.190 | Urbl |
|  | (0.040) | (0.022) | (0.044) |  |
| Urbs | 0.187 | −0.109 | −0.092 | Urbs |
|  | (0.047) | (0.028) | (0.051) |  |
| KL | −0.017 | 0.090 | 0.398 | KL |
|  | (0.035) | (0.017) | (0.040) |  |
| Mar | 0.572 | 7.694 | 9.387 | Constant |
|  | (0.035) | (0.044) | (0.128) |  |
| Wid | 0.410 | 8.262 | 6.902 | $\tilde{r}_p$ |
|  | (0.118) | (0.260) | (0.610) |  |
| Div | 0.070 | 12.313 | 11.640 | $\tilde{r}_{ls}$ |
|  | (0.159) | (0.227) | (0.714) |  |
| Head | 0.321 | 17.713 | 17.958 | $\tilde{r}_{us}$ |
|  | (0.028) | (0.350) | (1.219) |  |
| Constant | −1.211 | 23.113 | 24.275 | $\tilde{r}_t$ |
|  | (0.095) | (0.548) | (1.835) |  |
| N | 12,720 | 8,606 | 4,114 | N |
|  |  | 0.594 | 0.975 | $\tilde{\sigma}$ |
|  |  | −0.605 | −0.691 | $\tilde{\rho}$ |

*Note*: Numbers in parentheses are estimated standard errors.

However, the ML estimates for the self-employed are distinctly different. Whilst the OLS results suggested far lower returns to schooling (5 per cent at primary level to around 15 per cent at tertiary), the ML estimates for the self-employed are closer to those of the paid employed (7 per cent for primary and rising to 24 per cent for tertiary). The correction for selectivity effects has led to pronounced differences, especially for the self-employed. Also note that the correlations of the errors of the earnings functions with those of the probit function (given as $\tilde{\rho}$ in Table 10.8) are both negative. This suggests that there may be some omitted variable that has a depressing effect on the earnings of both paid workers and the self-employed, but which predisposes workers to be self-employed. Finally, note that the estimated standard error of the earnings function for the self-employed is greater than that for paid workers ($\bar{\sigma}$), confirming our conjecture that income from self-employment is more volatile.

Obtaining estimates over the whole sample of observations in this fashion will be inappropriate if there are distinct structural models for each occupational group. For example, the influences on the choice between paid and self-employment (or the determinants of earnings) for professional and technical workers will be very different from those in clerical jobs or those engaged as production workers. Indeed, in some occupational categories, self-employment is almost non-existent (notably for professional and technical workers and especially for clerical workers, where only 2 per cent of the sample are self-employed). To be sure that true 'structural' parameter estimates are being obtained, it is desirable to estimate the model for a homogeneous subset of the sample. For this reason, workers engaged in sales and services are now examined. This sub-sample is perhaps the most homogeneous available and is one in which the choice between paid and self-employment is considered to be a real one.

The reduced form ML estimates for sales and service workers are presented in Table 10.9. For both paid employees and the self-employed, there are increasing returns to schooling and academic failure lowers earnings substantially. The estimated marginal returns to schooling are higher at each level for the paid employees. Work experience has no significant effect on the earnings of the self-employed but for the paid employees it follows the familiar pattern. The standard error for the earnings equation is, as expected, greater than that for the paid workers. As before, the correlation between errors in the earnings equation and the indicator equation is negative.

Schooling has a depressing effect on the probability of being self-employed. Again, academic failure tends to raise the probability of self-employment. Unlike the results for the full sample, work experience does influence employment status in a non-linear fashion. The relationship between the probability of being self-employed and experience is inverse-U shaped. These parameter estimates suggest that the probability of being self-employed rises with age up to around 45 years of work experience and then declines. The observed pattern is consistent with the view that many workers first enter into paid employment and are more likely to set up their own businesses as they acquire work experience. Only in old age are they likely to revert to paid employment (perhaps handing the business on), but of course the observed downturn in self-employment probability may be picking up cohort effects (older Chinese males may have been less inclined to self-employment than more recent cohorts).

Once again the estimated returns to schooling derived from the application of ML methods differ from those obtained using OLS. This is especially true of the returns estimated for the self-employed. For ex-

# TABLE 10.9
Maximum Likelihood Estimation, Sales and Service Workers: Reduced Form Results

|  | Indicator Variable | Log Earnings Paid Employment | Log Earnings Self-employment |  |
|---|---|---|---|---|
| S/10 | −0.010 | 0.483 | 0.151 | S/10 |
|  | (0.223) | (0.148) | (0.203) |  |
| $S^2/100$ | −0.490 | 0.493 | 0.384 | $S^2/100$ |
|  | (0.137) | (0.089) | (0.141) |  |
| E/10 | 0.319 | 0.336 | −0.058 | E/10 |
|  | (0.100) | (0.071) | (0.092) |  |
| $E^2/1000$ | −0.353 | −0.608 | 0.003 | $E^2/1000$ |
|  | (0.160) | (0.115) | (0.140) |  |
| Fail | 0.245 | −0.201 | −0.235 | Fail |
|  | (0.064) | (0.045) | (0.059) |  |
| Metro | −0.282 | 0.259 | 0.121 | Metro |
|  | (0.072) | (0.057) | (0.068) |  |
| Urbl | −0.143 | 0.124 | 0.143 | Urbl |
|  | (0.079) | (0.062) | (0.070) |  |
| Urbs | 0.042 | −0.094 | −0.037 | Urbs |
|  | (0.099) | (0.083) | (0.082) |  |
| KL | 0.0004 | 0.076 | 0.370 | KL |
|  | (0.060) | (0.041) | (0.054) |  |
| Mar | 0.639 | 7.350 | 9.244 | Constant |
|  | (0.060) | (0.120) | (0.177) |  |
| Wid | 0.301 | 10.751 | 6.114 | $\tilde{r}_p$ |
|  | (0.199) | (0.687) | (0.870) |  |
| Div | −0.130 | 13.709 | 8.415 | $\tilde{r}_{ls}$ |
|  | (0.334) | (0.684) | (1.120) |  |
| Head | 0.402 | 17.653 | 11.484 | $\tilde{r}_{us}$ |
|  | (0.050) | (1.163) | (2.032) |  |
| Constant | −0.805 | 21.597 | 14.552 | $\tilde{r}_t$ |
|  | (0.170) | (1.804) | (3.091) |  |
| N | 3,700 | 1,736 | 1,964 | N |
|  |  | 0.696 | 0.876 | $\tilde{\sigma}$ |
|  |  | −0.692 | −0.595 | $\tilde{\rho}$ |

*Note*: Numbers in parentheses are estimated standard errors.

ample, the returns at primary and tertiary levels from the OLS regressions for this group are 4.5 per cent and 9.7 per cent respectively. The ML estimates are 6.1 per cent and 14.6 per cent.

The main focus in this chapter is the influence of schooling and academic performance on earnings and employment choice. Therefore, a 'structural model' is estimated in which is imposed the restriction that $S$ and $S^2$ affect employment choice only through their influence on the earnings differential (that is, the remaining variables in the indicator equation are left unrestricted). In terms of equation (10) above, the effect of the earnings differential is identified by excluding these two schooling variables from the vector $x_o$. A likelihood ratio test of these restrictions yielded a test statistic of 1.43 which compares favourably with a critical value of 3.84 (with 1 degree of freedom).

The results obtained from this structural model are reported in Table 10.10. In general, the estimated parameters are close to those derived from the reduced form and nothing more shall be said about them. The estimate of $\delta^*$ $(= \delta/\sqrt{\sigma_{II}})$ is 1.544 and is statistically significant. Interestingly, of the other influences on the indicator $E$, $E^2$, Fail,

TABLE 10.10
Maximum Likelihood Estimation: Sales and Service Workers Structural Model

|  | Indicator Variable | Log Earnings Paid Employment | Log Earnings Self-employment |  |
|---|---|---|---|---|
| $\tilde{\delta}$ | 1.544 | 0.426 | 0.331 | $S/10$ |
|  | (0.390) | (0.148) | (0.112) |  |
| $E/10$ | 0.987 | 0.525 | 0.265 | $S^2/100$ |
|  | (0.224) | (0.089) | (0.087) |  |
| $E^2/1000$ | −1.423 | 0.340 | −0.080 | $E/10$ |
|  | (0.367) | (0.070) | (0.091) |  |
| Metro | −0.066 | −0.621 | 0.048 | $E^2/1000$ |
|  | (0.163) | (0.115) | (0.136) |  |
| Urbl | −0.166 | −0.203 | −0.232 | Fail |
|  | (0.155) | (0.045) | (0.059) |  |
| Urbs | −0.039 | 0.260 | 0.121 | Metro |
|  | (0.191) | (0.057) | (0.068) |  |
| KL | −0.461 | 0.126 | 0.142 | Urbl |
|  | (0.168) | (0.062) | (0.070) |  |
| Mar | 0.639 | −0.093 | −0.040 | Urbs |
|  | (0.060) | (0.083) | (0.082) |  |
| Wid | 0.300 | 0.076 | 0.373 | KL |
|  | (0.199) | (0.041) | (0.054) |  |
| Div | −0.145 | 7.367 | 9.209 | Constant |
|  | (0.337) | (0.121) | (0.171) |  |
| Head | 0.399 | 10.566 | 6.492 | $\tilde{r}_p$ |
|  | (0.049) | (0.687) | (0.809) |  |
| Fail | 0.289 | 13.717 | 8.081 | $\tilde{r}_{ls}$ |
|  | (0.135) | (0.685) | (1.084) |  |
| Constant | −3.624 | 17.919 | 10.200 | $\tilde{r}_{us}$ |
|  | (0.660) | (1.160) | (1.651) |  |
|  |  | 22.120 | 12.318 | $\tilde{r}_t$ |
|  |  | (1.797) | (2.292) |  |
| $N$ | 3,700 | 1,736 | 1,964 | $N$ |
|  |  | 0.486 | 0.767 | $\tilde{\sigma}$ |
|  |  | −0.694 | −0.595 | $\tilde{\rho}$ |

Note: Numbers in parentheses are estimated standard errors.

## TABLE 10.11
### Predicted Probabilities of Self-employment

|  | Reduced Form | | Structural Model |
|---|---|---|---|
|  | *All Workers* | *Sales and Service* | *Sales and Service* |
| | Successful Academic Record | | |
| Primary | 0.351 | 0.522 | 0.517 |
| Lower secondary | 0.287 | 0.433 | 0.427 |
| Upper secondary | 0.151 | 0.273 | 0.276 |
| Tertiary | 0.039 | 0.116 | 0.128 |
| | Unsuccessful Academic Record | | |
| Primary | 0.463 | 0.618 | 0.612 |
| Lower secondary | 0.392 | 0.531 | 0.524 |
| Upper secondary | 0.228 | 0.360 | 0.363 |
| Tertiary | 0.070 | 0.171 | 0.186 |

KL, Mar, and Head are all significant. The significance of Fail is particularly noteworthy. Academic failure is seen to lower the earnings of both the self-employed and paid employees. It also raises the probability of an individual choosing self-employment even when its effect through the earnings differential has been controlled for. This last feature is a further indication that screening may be an important feature of the Malaysian labour market.

To illustrate the effects of years of schooling and academic success on employment choice, the estimated probabilities of self-employment by schooling are presented in Table 10.11. In the top panel, it is assumed that schooling is successful in terms of academic qualifications obtained. The estimates are computed for a married man who is a head of household and living in Kuala Lumpur with 10 years of work experience. The probabilities are computed using the parameters obtained from the sample of all workers (reported in Table 10.8) and for the sales and service workers only (reported in Tables 10.9 and 10.10). In all cases, the probabilities decline with schooling. In the bottom panel, it is assumed that schooling is 'unsuccessful' (Fail = 1) and the effect on self-employment probability is pronounced. For example, an individual completing lower secondary schooling is predicted to have a probability of being self-employed in sales and service of 0.43 if he succeeds in gaining the relevant academic qualifications. If he fails, the probability rises by over 20 per cent to 0.52.

## Summary

The aim in this chapter has been to estimate the private returns to schooling amongst Chinese males in Peninsular Malaysia and to examine the impact of schooling and academic performance on the choice between paid employment and self-employment. To achieve these aims, earnings functions for self-employed and paid employees were estimated simultaneously using consistent and efficient statistical methods together with an indicator function determining the choice to be self-employed.

The writers' conclusions are briefly as follows:

1. The returns to schooling rise with the level of schooling and are highest for the tertiary level. This finding applied to the entire sample of individuals and to a subset of the sample engaged in sales and service. The returns at lower secondary level and above may be considered to be above the normal return to non-human capital.
2. The application of ordinary least squares produced lower estimated rates of the return to schooling for the self-employed compared with those derived using a maximum likelihood procedure in which allowance is made for the impact of self-selection into paid employment or self-employment.
3. Over the whole sample, the returns to schooling for the self-employed workers are the same as those for the paid employees. However, for the more homogeneous sub-sample of sales and service workers, the private returns to schooling are significantly higher for workers in paid employment. This may point to the importance of the screening hypothesis as an explanation for the observed effect of schooling on earnings.
4. In a structural model for the sales and service workers, proportionate difference between expected earnings in self-employment and earnings in paid employment significantly influences the decision to become self-employed.
5. Failure to obtain the academic qualifications appropriate to the level of schooling attained depresses earnings for both groups of workers and raises the probability that an individual will choose self-employment. These features again add support to the view that screening plays an important role in explaining the impact of schooling on earnings.

---

1. The choice between self-employment and paid employment shall henceforth be simply referred to as the 'employment choice'.

2. The EPU–DOS survey has information on the number of hours worked over the reference period but information is not available on the number of weeks worked in the year. For this reason the analysis is restricted to annual earnings.

3. The scatter plot smoothing technique used here is the procedure described in Cleveland (1979) as provided in the S Programming Environment (Becker, Chambers, and Wilks, 1988).

4. For an application of the two-step procedure to self-employment, see Rees and Shah (1986) and for a broader application to occupational choice, see Dolton, Makepeace, and Van der Klaauw (1989).

5. Mincer (1974) found that when work experience and age were separately identified, the experience term retained its significance.

# PART IV
# HEALTH AND AGEING

# 11
# Socio-economic Development, Child Health Care, and Infant Mortality Change in Thailand

Noriko O. Tsuya, Naohiro Ogawa,
Napaporn Chayovan, and Siriwan Siriboon

**Introduction**

INFANT mortality has been recognized as an important summary index of living standards and general health status of the population, closely related to overall socio-economic development of a society. Some have argued that the rapid mortality decline (including that of infant and child mortality) experienced by many developing countries during the decades immediately after World War II was not necessarily due to socio-economic development, but rather to a diffusion of health/medical technology and information 'imported' from the developed world (Arriaga, 1970; Stolnitz, 1965, 1975). This opinion that improvement in mortality (thus, by implication, in health) can be achieved by interventions dissociated from broader socio-economic development was based mainly on the remarkable success, from the late 1940s to the 1960s, of large-scale programmes in developing countries in controlling infectious diseases through immunization and therapy, aided by powerful insecticides, vaccines, and antibiotics brought from industrialized countries (Ruzicka and Hansluwka, 1982). Since then, however, the tempo of mortality decline has slowed in some of the developing countries, while in others, the decline has stagnated altogether (Sivamurthy, 1981; United Nations and World Health Organization, 1982); and studies have shown the limitations of public health programmes in the absence of social and economic development; thus emphasizing the importance of socio-economic improvement as a condition and correlate of mortality reduction (Hansluwka, 1973; Ruzicka and Hansluwka, 1982; World Health Organization, 1974; Yang and Pendleton, 1980). Moreover, recent evidence from multivariate analysis of determinants of infant and child mortality in the late 1980s suggests that social and economic development, reflected in such factors as parental (especially, mother's) education, urban–rural residence, living standards, and employment status, affect mortality significantly (DaVanzo and Habicht, 1986; Hobcraft et al., 1984; Martin et al., 1983; Palloni and Tienda, 1986; Pebley and Stupp, 1987; Vorapongsathorn et al., 1986).

To be sure, findings from these studies do not downplay the important role of health care in mortality reduction. Many health care factors, together with environmental and child's biological factors, are the variables directly affecting infant and child mortality (that is, proximate determinants of infant and child mortality) and some socio-economic variables can be considered as proxies of ability to utilize available health care effectively (Caldwell, 1979; Hobcraft et al., 1984). What is suggested here is that mortality (including infant and child mortality) decline was produced both by socio-economic development and by the diffusion of public health measures and preventive medicine, and that the mechanism determining mortality is not monolithic, but rather complicated and multidimensional.

Especially in individual countries, the roles of socio-economic and health care factors are difficult to separate due not only to the complexity of their interrelationship, but also to the fact that statistical data needed for such multivariate analysis are sadly inadequate or completely lacking (ESCAP, 1982; Ruzicka and Hansluwka, 1982). In this sense, the 1987 Thailand Demographic and Health Survey (TDHS) provides a unique opportunity to study the effects of demographic and socio-economic factors as well as utilization of health care on infant mortality in the 1970s and 1980s in a multivariate context. As in many other developing countries, previous studies on infant (and child) mortality in Thailand concentrated upon an investigation of levels, trends, and differentials and, although some multivariate studies were conducted (for example, Prasithrathsint et al., 1986; and Vorapongsathorn et al., 1986), to the writers' knowledge, there has not yet been a multivariate study on determinants of infant mortality utilizing micro-level data.

Specifically, this chapter first looks at trends in infant and child mortality levels during the 1970s and the 1980s, together with changes in GNP per capita and indices of expenditures on health services. An attempt is also made to explore sources of possible underreporting of infant and child deaths in the TDHS data. Secondly, it examines socio-economic and demographic differentials of infant and child mortality for births during 1977–87. Thirdly, in order to examine changes in a causal mechanism operating in infant mortality in Thailand, it first analyses changes in demographic and socio-economic covariates of infant mortality in Thailand from the early 1970s to the mid-1980s by comparing logistic regression results for births during 1970–4 and those of births during 1982–6. Then, again utilizing logistic regression analysis, it further examines demographic, socio-economic, and health care covariates of infant mortality in rural and urban Thailand during 1982–6. The chapter concludes with a discussion of the implications of the findings.

## Data and Methodology

The data used in this study are drawn mainly from the TDHS, but for analysis of changes in causal relationships between infant mortality and socio-economic and demographic factors between the early 1970s and the mid-1980s, data from the Survey of Fertility in Thailand (SOFT) are also employed. The TDHS was conducted from March to June 1987 as part of the International Demographic and Health Surveys project to collect nationally representative data on fertility, family planning, and child and maternal health. Utilizing a multi-stage stratified sampling design, a total of 9,045 households and 6,775 ever-married women aged 15–49 were interviewed. The TDHS sample was designed to provide independent estimates for each of the rural areas of the four major regions of Thailand (that is, central, north, north-east, and south), for the provincial urban areas, and for the Bangkok metropolis. Through appropriate weighting, nationally representative results can be obtained. (Details of the survey have been reported in Chayovan, Kamnuansilpa, and Knodel, 1988.)

The TDHS data on infant and child mortality are derived from its birth histories. For each live birth, information was collected concerning the date of birth, sex of child, and survival status, and for those who died, age at death in days, months, and years. To this basic infant/child data, information on demographic and socio-economic characteristics of mother and household, derived mainly from the household roster and the household background information in the TDHS, was added. Based on this information (and applying sample weights), life-table estimations of levels and differentials of infant, child, and under-five mortality are made for 7,884 births which occurred during 1977–87, the results of which will be presented and discussed in detail in the following sections.

Furthermore, in the TDHS, for all live births occurring since January 1982, questions were also asked concerning utilization of prenatal care, health care at birth, and breast-feeding practices and duration. The inclusion of these birth-interval-specific data on proximate determinants of fertility and on health care utilization is, along with the wealth of socio-economic information on households and individuals, probably the most significant contribution of the TDHS. Utilizing this data set with sample weights, the writers conducted a logit analysis of infant mortality.[1] To avoid complex calculations of exposure to risk, it was decided to exclude births that occurred less than 12 months before the date of interview (17.4 per cent of all births occurring since January 1982). Therefore, the sample selected from the TDHS for logit analyses is the 3,238 live births that occurred between January 1982 and June 1986 to ever-married women aged 15–49. Of the 3,238 births in this sample, 104 infant deaths (deaths within the age interval of 0–12 months) and 16 child deaths within the age interval of 1–5 years) were recorded.

As mentioned earlier, in order to examine changes in the causal mechanism for infant mortality, logistic regression analysis is also conducted for births occurring during 1970–4, utilizing the data drawn from the Survey of Fertility in Thailand (SOFT). SOFT was conducted from March to June 1975 as part of the World Fertility Survey to obtain internationally comparable data on fertility patterns and levels, and other fertility-related variables such as nuptiality, family planning, and fertility preferences. It consists of four sub-surveys: Household, Husband's, Fertility, and Community Surveys. Utilizing the multi-stage stratified sampling technique, a nationally representative sample of 4,465 households was first selected. Based on information from the Household Survey, the Fertility Survey was then conducted by selecting 4,002 'eligible' women (that is, ever-married women aged 15–49 who had slept in the household on the night prior to the interview date), and the Husband's Survey was also carried out for 3,438 males whose wives would be 'eligible' for the Fertility Survey. Conducted first independently, data from the Fertility and Husband's Surveys were then matched, resulting in a sample of 2,967 couples. (Details of SOFT are explained in Institute of Population Studies, Chulalongkorn University and Population Survey Division, National Statistical Office, 1977.)

Although SOFT was conducted primarily to collect data on fertility, as in the case of the TDHS, it is possible to extract information on infant and child deaths from birth histories (of the Fertility Survey). To this basic infant/child data, information on demographic and socio-economic characteristics of mother and household, derived from the Fertility, Husband, and Household Surveys, was added. Unlike the TDHS, however, no health care questions were asked for births in SOFT. Therefore, for 1970–4 births derived from SOFT data, no health care information could be added, except for breast-feeding practice for the two most recent births, questions on which were included in SOFT. In order to make the two different data sets comparable, analysis of SOFT data was limited to live births which occurred during the five years preceding the survey. Furthermore, also excluded were births that occurred less than twelve months before the date of interview (that is, 18.6 per cent of all live births occurring in the five years prior to the survey). Consequently, the sample selected from SOFT for logit analysis is the 3,170 live births that occurred between March 1970 and June 1974 to currently married Thai women aged 15–49.[2] Of the 3,170 births in this sample, 216 infant deaths (deaths within the age interval of 0–12 months) and 78 child deaths (deaths within the age interval of 1–5 years) were recorded. Since it is known that different sets of factors affect infant and child mortality[3] and because the number of child deaths compared to the number of births of the last 5 years for the TDHS and SOFT are too small, it has been chosen in this study to conduct logit analysis only for infant mortality.

In addition to the problem of relatively small numbers of infant and child deaths, which often occurs not only in data from developed countries, but also in data from developing countries (many of which have experienced declines in infant and child mortality in the post-war period), it has to be pointed out that there might be underreporting of events and misreporting of birth and death dates in the TDHS and SOFT because, like all the other surveys, the information on birth histories was collected through retrospective reports of women. Since this problem is usually expected to be less serious for time periods closer to the survey date, the time period for the logit analysis was limited to 5 years prior to the survey. Finally, the data also suffer from censoring because women past age 49 at the time of the survey were not interviewed. However, the effect of censoring may be expected to be minimal since the fertility (and thus, infant and child mortality) of Thai women aged 40 or above became very low during the 1970s and the early 1980s (Knodel and Debavalya, 1978; United Nations, 1988a: 593).

## Trends of Infant and Child Mortality Levels, 1972–1987

Table 11.1 presents life-table estimates of infant, child, and under-five mortality ($_1q_0$, $_4q_1$, and $_5q_0$) per 1,000 live births in Thailand for selected time periods during 1972–87. It can be seen from the table that Thailand has experienced considerable, if not dramatic, declines in infant and child mortality levels during those 15 years. Between the periods 1972–6 and 1982–7, infant mortality declined continuously (by around 36 per cent) while child mortality declined only between the last two five-year periods (by about 17 per cent). Moreover, the degree of decline was much higher for infant mortality than for child mortality during the 15-year period. Therefore, a major part of the decline in under-five mortality was due to infant mortality reduction.

It should be pointed out that although the downturn in infant (and

TABLE 11.1
Life-table Estimates of Infant, Child, and Under-five Mortality per 1,000 Live Births in Thailand for Selected Time Periods

|  | Infant Mortality ($_1q_0 \times 1,000$) | Child Mortality ($_4q_1 \times 1,000$) | Under-five Mortality ($_5q_0 \times 1,000$) |
|---|---|---|---|
| Time period |  |  |  |
| 1972–6 | 55 | 12 | 67 |
| 1977–81 | 41 | 12 | 53 |
| 1982–7[a] | 35 | 10 | 45 |
| Percentage change from |  |  |  |
| 1972–6 to 1977–81 | −25 | 0 | −21 |
| 1977–81 to 1982–7 | −15 | −17 | −16 |
| 1972–6 to 1982–7 | −36 | −17 | −33 |

Source: Chayovan, Kamnuansilpa, and Knodel (1988: 90).
[a] For 1987, only births occurring up to the calendar month preceding the survey are included.

child) mortality during the 1970s and the 1980s is also indicated by estimations based on other national survey data (Institute for Population and Social Research, 1985: 16; 1988: 92–4; Porapakkham, 1986: 18–21), the level of infant mortality for the period 1982–7 derived from the TDHS data is low in comparison to the level estimated by the 1985–6 Survey of Population Change (SPC). Specifically, the SPC found an infant mortality rate of 41 per 1,000 live births for the one-year period from mid-1985 to mid-1986 (National Statistical Office, 1989), while the TDHS estimate of infant mortality rate for the period 1982–7 is 35 per 1,000 live births. Since the TDHS estimate covers a longer period in the past over which infant mortality was declining, one would expect the TDHS estimate to be higher, instead of lower, than the SPC estimate.[4] If the SPC estimate is more accurate, it is then implied that there is a certain level of underreporting of infant deaths in the TDHS for this period.

In order to examine sources of this possible underreporting of infant deaths, sex-specific values of $l_x$ (cumulative proportion surviving at the beginning of interval) for the TDHS births during 1982–7 were first compared with those of this life-table function for Japanese males in 1955 and Japanese females in 1962 (chosen because the levels of male and female infant mortality for the TDHS births are approximately the level of Japanese male infant mortality in 1955 and that of Japanese female infant mortality in 1962 respectively) (Table 11.2). The Japanese life-table data are utilized for comparative purposes since their accuracy is known to be high and age intervals in months are available for mortality during infancy.

From the table, it can be seen that for males, even as the $l_x$ values for the TDHS births are always higher than those for Japan in 1955, the degree of discrepancy becomes especially pronounced after the first 12 months of life, indicating that proportions dying (life-table functions of $_nq_x$) for the intervals after infancy are proportionately 'too low' for the TDHS births. This in turn implies a possibility of underreporting of male child deaths after infancy in the TDHS. For females, the $l_x$ values for the TDHS births are higher than those for Japan in 1962 for the period after the first month to the second year, while the opposite is the case for the values thereafter, suggesting that proportions dying during the period from the second month to the second year of life are too low for the TDHS births. This implies a possible underreporting of post-neonatal and early childhood mortality of female births in the TDHS.

In order to further examine this possible underreporting of female deaths during the post-neonatal and early childhood periods, and of male child deaths after infancy, the Weibull model test was also conducted for possible inaccuracy of the life-tables of the TDHS births during 1982–7.[5] Specifically, utilizing a life-table function of $l_x$, $\ln(\ln(1/l_x))$ can be plotted against $\ln(x)$ values. If the plotted points form an approximately straight line, it can be considered that reported age-specific mortality rates are generally accurate. If not, however, local deficiency of the

TABLE 11.2
Cumulative Proportions Surviving at the Beginning of Interval ($l_x$):
Births in Thailand during 1982–1987 and in Japan in 1955 and 1962

| Beginning of Interval in Months | Male | | | Female | | |
|---|---|---|---|---|---|---|
| | TDHS[a] Births 1982–7 (1) | Japan[b] 1955 (2) | Difference (1) − (2) | TDHS[a] Births 1982–7 (4) | Japan[b] 1962 (5) | Difference (4) − (5) |
| 0  | 1.0000 | 1.0000 | 0.0000 | 1.0000 | 1.0000 | 0.0000 |
| 1  | 0.9765 | 0.9757 | 0.0008 | 0.9853 | 0.9862 | −0.0009 |
| 2  | 0.9729 | 0.9712 | 0.0017 | 0.9848 | 0.9838 | 0.0010 |
| 3  | 0.9709 | 0.9683 | 0.0026 | 0.9826 | 0.9822 | 0.0004 |
| 6  | 0.9650 | 0.9634 | 0.0016 | 0.9804 | 0.9793 | 0.0011 |
| 12 | 0.9628 | 0.9582 | 0.0046 | 0.9769 | 0.9762 | 0.0007 |
| 24 | 0.9614 | 0.9527 | 0.0087 | 0.9714 | 0.9735 | −0.0021 |
| 36 | 0.9598 | 0.9482 | 0.0116 | 0.9705 | 0.9719 | −0.0014 |
| 48 | 0.9586 | 0.9448 | 0.0138 | 0.9693 | 0.9706 | −0.0013 |
| 60 | 0.9567 | 0.9442 | 0.0145 | 0.9693 | 0.9696 | −0.0003 |

[a]TDHS refers to the 1987 Thailand Demographic and Health Survey.
[b]Japan 1955 and 1962 data are taken from the Japan Ministry of Health and Welfare, Statistics and Information Department's 1983 publication entitled *The 15th Life Table* (Tokyo: Kose. Tokei Kyokai).

observed age-specific mortality is implied. Figure 11.1 shows the plots of $\ln(\ln(1/l_x))$ against $\ln(x)$ for the life-tables of male and female births during 1982–7 in the TDHS. From the figure, although the evidence is not very clear, it can be seen that the values of the vertical axis for both females from the second month to the second year of birth and for males after the twelfth (or even sixth) month do not quite form a straight line.

From these albeit inconclusive findings, it can be considered that the TDHS might underreport male child deaths after infancy, and female deaths during the post-neonatal period and early childhood. If there is indeed a certain level of underreporting of infant deaths in the TDHS for the period 1982–7, then it is thought to be due, at least partly, to an underreporting of post-neonatal deaths of female infants. Reasonable explanations for this possible underreporting of female post-neonatal deaths, however, are difficult to find. Strong preference for a son, which is characteristic of many Asian populations, is not evident in Thailand (Kamnuansilpa et al., 1982; Knodel and Prachuabmoh, 1976; Porapakkham, 1986: 14; Prachuabmoh et al., 1974) and the analysis does not show any systematic evidence of sex-selective treatment and care of female children. Clearly, further examination of a possibility of underreporting of infant (and child) deaths is needed.

FIGURE 11.1
Test of the Weibull Model: Infant and Child Mortality in Thailand, 1982–1987

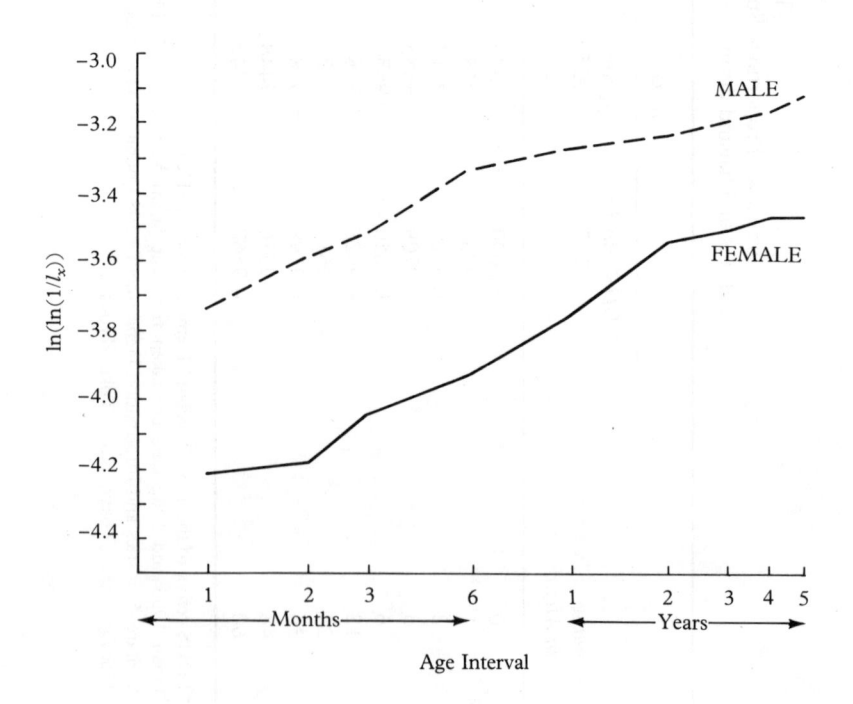

## Changes in Indices of Economic Development and Health Expenditures

Although estimates from different surveys do not agree on the levels of infant mortality in Thailand during the 1970s and 1980s, considerable declines in infant mortality during the period are supported by almost all the estimates and statistics (Institute for Population and Social Research, 1988: 92–4; Porapakkham, 1986: 18–21). The period prior to and during these mortality declines was also one of economic growth and health care development in Thailand. Although the writers do not attempt to examine the impacts of economic development on infant mortality declines in any systematic way here, some general comments on changes during the 1970s and the early 1980s in GNP per capita as well as in indices of (both government and private) per capita health expenditure are in order.

GNP per capita at constant (1972) prices increased steadily from 4,134 baht in 1970 to 6,882 baht in 1984, a growth of approximately

TABLE 11.3
GNP Per Capita and Indices of Health-related Government Expenditure Per Capita and Private Consumption Expenditure Per Capita at Constant (1972) Prices: Thailand, 1970–1984

|  | GNP Per Capita |  | Indices[a] |  |  |  |
| --- | --- | --- | --- | --- | --- | --- |
|  |  |  | Government Expenditure Per Capita |  | Private Consumption Expenditure Per Capita |  |
| Year | Amount (baht) | Index | Health Services | Others | Personal Care and Health | Food |
| 1970 | 4,134 | 100 | 100 | 100 | 100 | 100 |
| 1971 | 4,200 | 102 | 111 | 103 | 112 | 101 |
| 1972 | 4,282 | 104 | 105 | 93 | 109 | 95 |
| 1973 | 4,559 | 110 | 89 | 84 | 98 | 80 |
| 1974 | 4,698 | 114 | 74 | 69 | 85 | 68 |
| 1975 | 4,913 | 119 | 81 | 71 | 89 | 67 |
| 1976 | 5,191 | 126 | 91 | 76 | 94 | 67 |
| 1977 | 5,424 | 131 | 91 | 75 | 92 | 64 |
| 1978 | 5,781 | 140 | 99 | 78 | 89 | 59 |
| 1979 | 5,937 | 144 | 101 | 79 | 82 | 52 |
| 1980 | 6,125 | 148 | 95 | 68 | 76 | 45 |
| 1981 | 6,281 | 152 | 105 | 66 | 75 | 44 |
| 1982 | 6,375 | 154 | 100 | 65 | 79 | 42 |
| 1983 | 6,649 | 161 | 97 | 64 | 83 | 43 |
| 1984 | 6,882 | 166 | 109 | 64 | 85 | 43 |

Source: Porapakkham (1986: 53–5).
[a] 1970 = 100.

1.7 times (Table 11.3). Compared with this economic growth, government expenditure on health services at constant prices grew rapidly. Moreover, the tempo of increases in government health expenditure at 1972 constant prices is much quicker than that of economic growth and it becomes even more remarkable when the increases in health service expenditure are compared with those in other components of government expenditure per capita: the former increased by 3.3 times whereas the latter grew by 1.9 times during the period 1970–84. This rapid increase of government expenditure on health services provides evidence for the government's long-term commitment to the capital investment on health infrastructures and development of health manpower, aimed at in the Third (1972–6), Fourth (1976–81), and Fifth (1982–6) National Development Plans (Porapakkham, 1986: 53, 97–104).

In Thailand, the government has played a major role in providing health services, the only exception being the Bangkok metropolis where the private sector also plays an important role (Ogawa et al., 1988). Moreover, since the beginning of the Fifth National Development Plan in 1982, the allocative pattern of government expenditure (especially that of the Ministry of Public Health) has shifted from urban and hospital expenditure to rural and primary health care expenditure (Ogawa et al., 1988; Porapakkham, 1986: 101–4). From Table 11.3, it can also be noticed that, in addition to government health care expenditure, private expenditure per capita on personal care and health, and on food, also increased in real terms during this period. Especially substantial were the increases in expenditure on personal care and health: an increase of 2.6 times over the 15 years. Therefore, under the government's continuous emphasis on development of health care provision, the average amount that Thai people spend on health care and food increased steadily during 1970–84. Through logit analysis of determinants of infant mortality in 1982–6, the details of which will be presented later, the effects of utilization and provision of health care will be further examined in a multivariate context.

## Differentials of Infant and Child Mortality

Before conducting an analysis of the changing causal mechanism of infant mortality in Thailand, differentials of infant and child mortality for births occurring in the period 1977–87 were examined by selected demographic and socio-economic characteristics.[6] Table 11.4 presents life-table estimates of infant, child, and under-five mortality by such different characteristics as: sex of child, urban–rural residence, region, mother's age at birth, birth order, mother's education, and previous birth interval for births of order two or higher. As shown in the table, male children have considerably higher infant mortality than females while there is no sex differential in child mortality. This finding is in agreement with other studies which found that, in the absence of strong son preference, the sex of child is important during the first year of life,

TABLE 11.4
Life-table Estimates of Infant, Child, and Under-five Mortality by
Selected Characteristics: Births during 1977–1987, Thailand

| Characteristics | Infant Mortality | Child Mortality | Under-five Mortality |
|---|---|---|---|
| Total | 38 | 11 | 49 |
| Sex of child | | | |
| Male | 45 | 11 | 56 |
| Female | 31 | 11 | 42 |
| Urban–rural residence | | | |
| Urban | 27 | 8 | 35 |
| Rural | 41 | 12 | 52 |
| Region | | | |
| Bangkok | 20 | 8 | 28 |
| Central | 34 | 11 | 45 |
| North | 40 | 12 | 51 |
| North-east | 44 | 9 | 53 |
| South | 40 | 16 | 56 |
| Mother's age at birth | | | |
| Less than 20 | 40 | 14 | 53 |
| 20–29 | 33 | 9 | 42 |
| 30–34 | 37 | 10 | 47 |
| 35+ | 69 | 22 | 89 |
| Birth order | | | |
| One | 30 | 8 | 38 |
| Two to three | 36 | 10 | 46 |
| Four to six | 48 | 14 | 61 |
| Seven or higher | 74 | 24 | 96 |
| Previous birth interval[a] | | | |
| Less than 24 months | 58 | 19 | 76 |
| 24–47 months | 38 | 9 | 47 |
| 48 months or more | 32 | 11 | 42 |
| Mother's education | | | |
| No education | 54 | 22 | 74 |
| Primary | 39 | 10 | 49 |
| Secondary or higher | 19 | 2 | 21 |

*Source*: Chayovan, Kamnuansilpa, and Knodel (1988: 91–3).
[a]Based on births of order two or higher.

with males tending to have higher mortality, but unimportant after the first year (Mosley and Chen, 1984; Preston, 1985; Mensch et al., 1985; Pebley and Millman, 1986).

Rural areas have substantially higher infant and child mortality than their urban counterparts. In regional variations, Bangkok has the lowest infant and child mortality. The central region follows Bangkok in terms of infant mortality while the remaining three regions (north, south, and north-east) have infant mortality of 40 per 1,000 live births or higher.

The relationship between mother's age at birth and infant and child mortality is J-shaped: infant and child mortality is lowest for mothers aged 20–29 while that for younger or older mothers is higher and the rate for mothers aged 35 and above is more than twice the rate for mothers aged 20–29 (see Table 11.4).

On the other hand, child's birth order is positively related to infant and child mortality. Although the higher infant and child mortality of first-born children as compared to second- and third-born has been previously documented, the picture of relatively high first-born mortality is based largely upon data from developed countries with low fertility (Preston, 1985). The finding here is in accordance with many recent multivariate studies on infant and child mortality in developing countries that have also shown relatively normal or even exceptionally low mortality of first-born children (Martin et al., 1983; Preston, 1985; Trussell and Hammerslough, 1983; Tsuya and Choe, 1989).

The length of previous birth interval is negatively related to infant mortality, the rate for births occurring within 24 months after previous births being notably high. No systematic pattern is seen for child mortality, but child mortality for children born less than 24 months after previous births is considerably higher than the rate for other children with longer previous intervals. These findings therefore indicate that a very short previous birth interval (defined here as 24 months or less) is associated with higher infant and child mortality.

Both infant and child mortality are inversely related to mother's education. Mothers with higher education (secondary or above) are likely to have higher economic status, better access to health care, and an ability to utilize the care more effectively; this may account in part for the lower mortality rates of their children. In the following sections, an attempt is made to account for demographic, socio-economic, and health care determinants of infant mortality in a multivariate context.

### Logit Analysis of Changes in Demographic and Socio-economic Covariates of Infant Mortality

Through the life-table analysis presented in the previous section, it was found that there were considerable demographic and socio-economic differentials in infant mortality for births occurring during 1977–87 in Thailand. What kind of causal mechanisms are operating to produce these complicated patterns of infant survival? Are there any changes in causal mechanisms influencing the probability of infant survival? An attempt is made to answer these questions by investigating different covariates of infant mortality. In this section, utilizing logistic multiple regression analysis, demographic and socio-economic covariates of infant mortality for births during 1970–4 (from the SOFT sample) and those for births during 1982–6 (from the TDHS sample) are examined and then compared.

*Definitions of the Variables*

Definitions and descriptive statistics of the demographic and socio-economic covariates used in the logit analyses of infant mortality in Thailand for births during 1970–4 and those during 1982–6 are given in Tables 11.5 and 11.6, respectively. These variables are selected, within the constraints imposed by availability of data, as the most relevant covariates because in other studies they were found to significantly influence infant mortality and/or because they are thought to have theoretical and practical (policy) importance in explaining the mechanism of deaths of children during infancy (Choe, 1987; DaVanzo and Habicht, 1986; DaVanzo et al., 1983; Palloni and Tienda, 1986; Pebley and Millman, 1986; Preston, 1985; Retherford et al., 1989; Tsuya and Choe, 1989).

As mentioned before, births that occurred less than a year before the

TABLE 11.5
Definitions and Descriptive Statistics of Covariates Used in
Logit Analysis of Infant Mortality: Births during 1970–1974,[a] Thailand

| Covariates | Means | Standard Deviation |
|---|---|---|
| Demographic Variables | | |
| Sex of child (male = 1, female = 0) | 0.525 | 0.499 |
| Mother's age at birth | 27.264 | 6.887 |
| Birth order and previous birth interval | | |
| Birth order >1 and previous interval <24 months | 0.371 | 0.483 |
| Birth order >1 and previous interval ≥24 months | 0.539 | 0.499 |
| (Reference group is birth order = 1.) | | |
| Breast-feeding of child (yes = 1, no = 0) | 0.925 | 0.264 |
| Socio-economic Variables: | | |
| Rural–urban residence (rural = 1, urban = 0) | 0.895 | 0.306 |
| Region | | |
| Central | 0.197 | 0.397 |
| North | 0.186 | 0.389 |
| North-east | 0.440 | 0.496 |
| South | 0.116 | 0.320 |
| (Reference group is Bangkok.) | | |
| Women's education | | |
| No education | 0.177 | 0.382 |
| Primary education | 0.789 | 0.408 |
| (Reference group is secondary or higher.) | | |
| Women's non-agricultural employment (yes = 1, no = 0) | 0.274 | 0.446 |
| Economic status of household in 1975 (below average = 1, average or above = 0) | 0.559 | 0.497 |

[a] Including only last two births occurring during the five years prior to the survey, but excluding births that occurred less than a year before the date of interview.

TABLE 11.6
Definitions and Descriptive Statistics of Covariates Used in
Logit Analysis of Infant Mortality: Births during 1982–1986,[a] Thailand

| Covariates | Total Mean | Total Standard Deviation | Urban Mean | Urban Standard Deviation | Rural Mean | Rural Standard Deviation |
|---|---|---|---|---|---|---|
| **Demographic Variables:** | | | | | | |
| Sex of child (male = 1, female = 0) | 0.514 | 0.500 | 0.504 | 0.500 | 0.516 | 0.500 |
| Mother's age at birth | 25.956 | 6.087 | 25.886 | 5.575 | 25.970 | 6.184 |
| Birth order and previous birth interval | | | | | | |
| Birth order >1 and previous interval <24 months | 0.167 | 0.373 | 0.164 | 0.371 | 0.167 | 0.373 |
| Birth order >1 and previous interval ⩾24 months | 0.488 | 0.500 | 0.395 | 0.489 | 0.506 | 0.500 |
| (Reference group is birth order = 1.) | | | | | | |
| Breast-feeding of child (yes = 1, no = 0) | 0.937 | 0.243 | 0.871 | 0.336 | 0.950 | 0.218 |
| **Socio-economic Variables:** | | | | | | |
| Rural–urban residence (rural = 1, urban = 0) | 0.835 | 0.371 | — | — | — | — |
| Region | | | | | | |
| Central | 0.194 | 0.395 | 0.126 | 0.332 | 0.207 | 0.408 |
| North | 0.188 | 0.391 | 0.076 | 0.265 | 0.211 | 0.492 |
| North-east | 0.360 | 0.480 | 0.109 | 0.312 | 0.410 | 0.492 |
| South | 0.157 | 0.364 | 0.080 | 0.271 | 0.172 | 0.378 |
| (Reference group for the total and the urban is Bangkok; that for the rural is Central.) | | | | | | |
| Women's education (less than secondary = 1, secondary or higher = 0) | 0.881 | 0.324 | 0.649 | 0.478 | 0.926 | 0.261 |

| | | | | | |
|---|---|---|---|---|---|
| Women's employment in non-agriculture (yes = 1, no = 0) | 0.232 | 0.423 | 0.543 | 0.498 | 0.170 | 0.376 |
| Economic status of household in 1987 (below average = 1, average or above = 0) | 0.581 | 0.493 | 0.328 | 0.470 | 0.631 | 0.483 |
| **Health Care Variables** | | | | | | |
| Prenatal care from MD/nurse (yes = 1, no = 0) | 0.761 | 0.426 | 0.945 | 0.228 | 0.725 | 0.447 |
| Delivery attendance (MD/nurse/midwife = 1, otherwise = 0) | 0.636 | 0.481 | 0.955 | 0.207 | 0.573 | 0.495 |
| Population per hospital bed in the province of residence at the year of birth | 1036.1 | 523.92 | 536.58 | 378.31 | 1134.8 | 491.37 |
| Time (in minutes) to the nearest health centre/hospital | – | – | – | – | 13.741 | 17.168 |
| Quality of household drinking water (poor = 1, otherwise = 0) | 0.808 | 0.394 | 0.228 | 0.420 | 0.922 | 0.268 |

*Note*: Figures above are based on the full model, estimation results of which are presented in Table 11.8.
[a]Births that occurred less than a year before the date of interview were excluded.

date of interview are excluded, thus making the total sample sizes for the logit analyses: 3,170 births during 1970–4 and 3,238 births during 1982–6, respectively. Among the 3,170 SOFT births, 112 were excluded due to missing values of covariates, and among the remaining 3,058 births, 216 died within the first 12 months of birth. Among the 3,238 TDHS births, 75 were deleted due to missing values, and among the remaining 3,163 births, 94 died during infancy. Therefore, roughly speaking, the level of infant mortality in Thailand declined from a little over 70 per 1,000 births during the early 1970s to approximately 30 per 1,000 births during the mid-1980s.

In this study, the covariates of logit analysis can be divided into three general groups: demographic characteristics of mother and child; socio-economic characteristics of mother, her husband/household, and her community; and health care variables, including both care utilization by mother and provision of care in her community/province of residence. As mentioned earlier, however, since birth-interval-specific information on health care is not available in SOFT, only changes in socio-economic and demographic covariates of infant mortality can be analysed in this section. An explanation concerning the health care variables utilized in the model is given in the following section.

Demographic characteristics consist of such variables as: sex of child, mother's age at childbirth, birth order and interval from the previous birth to the birth of index child (that is, the previous birth interval), and breast-feeding of the index child. Socio-economic characteristics include: urban–rural residence, region, mother's education, mother's employment, and economic status of household in the year of survey.

Specifically, the variable of sex of child is dichotomous, male being coded as 1 and female as 0. As shown in Tables 11.5 and 11.6, around 52 per cent of the total births during 1970–4 are males; and the corresponding proportion for the total births during 1982–6 is 51 per cent. Previous studies found that most Thai couples prefer to have at least one child of each sex, and a strong son preference, which characterizes many Asian populations, is not evident in Thailand (Kamnuansilpa et al., 1982; Knodel and Prachuabmoh, 1976; Porapakkham, 1986: 14; Prachuabmoh et al., 1974).[7] In the absence of strong son preference, it is therefore hypothesized that male infants have higher mortality than females, thus this variable is positively related to infant mortality.

The tables show that mean age of mothers at birth was approximately 27 years for births during 1970–4 and it decreased to around 26 years for births during 1982–6, due probably to a shift in the age pattern of fertility from prolonged childbearing to curtailment of childbearing before the onset of natural sterility between the two time periods under consideration. This is a continuous variable and its square is also introduced into the model because of the curvilinear relationship between infant mortality and mother's age at birth found in the previous section.

The combined effects of birth order and previous birth interval were measured by two dummy variables, with birth order being one as a reference category. These covariates are included because the mortality effects of birth order and short preceding birth interval were found to be strong in many studies on populations of developing countries (Preston, 1985; Palloni and Tienda, 1986; Pebley and Stupp, 1987; Tsuya and Choe, 1989), and also because the life-table analysis of births during 1977–87 shown in the previous section indicated considerable differentials in infant mortality by birth order and, for births of order two or higher, by previous birth interval.[8] It is therefore expected that first-order births have lower infant mortality than births of higher order, and that among second- or higher-order births, short previous birth interval (defined as 24 months or shorter) is associated with higher infant mortality.

Breast-feeding is also an important variable affecting child survival in more than one way (Huffman and Lamphere, 1984).[9] Breast-milk is known to be more nutritious, more hygienic, and cheaper than bottle-feeding and, in addition, immunizes infants against common infections (Chayovan et al., 1989; Yamamoto, 1987). Moreover, breast-feeding is associated with longer birth spacing (this being especially true when contraception is not widely practised), which in turn promotes not only the health of the breast-fed child, but also of the next child. While breast-feeding is advantageous for births the world over, it is especially important in developing countries where families are, in general, economically deprived, health services less adequate, and the environment less sanitary.

The breast-feeding variable in the model is a dichotomous variable, indicating that 92 per cent of infants born during 1970–4 were breast-fed while the corresponding figures for infants born during 1982–6 was 94 per cent (see Tables 11.5 and 11.6), thus showing a slight increase in proportion of infants ever breast-fed between the two time periods under consideration.[10] The writers hypothesize that breast-feeding positively affects child survival, and is thus negatively associated with mortality.[11]

The tables show that approximately 89.5 per cent of the SOFT births considered here are rural while the corresponding proportion for the TDHS births is 83.5 per cent, indicating that urbanization in Thailand is under way, though at a relatively slow tempo. Based on the result of life-table analysis of infant mortality by urban–rural residence presented in the previous section, the writers hypothesize that rural births have higher infant mortality than their urban counterparts.

In addition to the urban–rural differential, the model also includes dummy variables that account for the four major regions of central, north, north-east, and south, with Bangkok region as the reference category.[12] According to the regional differentials in life-table estimates presented in the previous section, the north, north-east, and south regions had higher infant mortality. A multivariate study utilizing aggregate data from the 1980 census in Thailand found considerably higher infant mortality in the north and north-east regions

(Vorapongsathorn et al., 1986) and indirect estimates of infant mortality by region also indicated higher mortality in the north and north-east regions during the 1970s (Institute for Population and Social Research, 1985: 18). These findings by previous studies are understandable since the north-east and north regions are the poorest and the second poorest regions with respect to most socio-economic development indicators (Chayovan, Kamnuansilpa, and Knodel, 1988: 5). Thus, positive effects of the two regional variables of the north and north-east are expected.

Another important socio-economic covariate of infant mortality is mother's education. Education of parents, especially of the mother, has been found in a number of studies to significantly influence infant and child mortality (Cochrane et al., 1980; DaVanzo and Habicht, 1986; DaVanzo et al., 1983; Martin et al., 1983; Pebley and Stupp, 1987; Preston, 1985; Trussell and Hammerslough, 1983). It was even suggested that higher education enables mothers to have the skills and resources to overcome some of the risks associated with very young and old maternal age at birth and short birth intervals (Pebley and Stupp, 1987). For births during 1970–4 (drawn from the SOFT sample), the effect of mother's education is measured by two dummy variables that account for no education (that is, zero years of schooling) and primary education (defined as 1–4 years of schooling) with the highest level, secondary or higher, as the reference category. A considerable proportion (approximately 18 per cent) of babies born during 1970–4 had mothers with no schooling and a very small proportion (around 3 per cent) had mothers with secondary or higher education (see Table 11.5). However, owing to rapid increases in female educational attainment in Thailand since the 1950s (Porapakkham, 1986: 6–10; Knodel and Wongsith, 1989a), the proportion of mothers with no education declined quickly to a very low level by the mid-1980s. Consequently, by grouping 'no education' and 'primary education' together, the variable of maternal education for births during 1982–6 is dichotomized: 1 if mother's education is lower than secondary (defined as 6 years of schooling or less), 0 if secondary or higher.[13] It is hypothesized that lower maternal education is positively associated (that is, higher maternal education is negatively associated) with infant mortality.

Women's employment at the time of the survey is also included in the model. This variable is again dichotomous: 1 if women's current employment is outside agriculture, 0 if otherwise. Although the possibility of reverse causation (that is, infant death occurring prior to the survey possibly affecting women's employment at the time of the survey) cannot be denied, it was decided to employ this variable because the employment status of mother can be an important determinant of infant mortality. Women's work, especially outside the home, may directly affect survival chances of infants by preventing mothers from fully caring for their children. This may also have substantial effects through a lack of proper feeding, particularly breast-feeding before weaning. At the same time, however, work in a non-traditional sector is likely to be associated with modernity and higher family income, both of which probably increase survival chances of infants. Therefore, there are no firm theoretical grounds for positing the direction of relationships between women's employment and infant mortality.

The model also includes economic status of households in the year of survey (1975 for SOFT and 1987 for the TDHS). In SOFT, an index of household economic status (household living standards) was constructed based on housing quality (for example, types of flooring and roofing, building materials used in construction of house, household water supply, and availability of electricity) and ownership of consumer durable goods. Since different classification schemes were used in SOFT for urban and rural areas, the covariate of household economic status for the model was constructed by employing separate criteria for dichotomizing an index of household economic status with a scale of 0 to 24: for rural areas, if the index score is less than 7, household economic status is considered 'below average' and the variable is therefore coded as 1, and 0 if otherwise; for urban areas, if the index score is less than 11, household economic status is considered 'below average', and the variable is thus coded as 1, and 0 if otherwise. On the other hand, in the TDHS, an index of household economic status was constructed based on information regarding: the type of vehicle possessed by the household, the type of flooring in the house, and the type of toilet facility. The survey also collected information on household possession of such electric appliances as television, radio, and refrigerator. However, these items require electricity, and thus their possession is dependent on the availability of electricity in the locality and may not reflect the household's ability to purchase them. Therefore, avoiding incorporation of items that are dependent on the availability of electricity into the index, the TDHS came up with the index of household economic status which has a scale of 0 to 17. In this study, the indexed variable of wealth level is dichotomized: 1 if household economic status is below average, 0 if average or above. The effect of this variable on infant mortality is expected to be positive.

*Results of Logit Analysis*

The results of logit analysis of infant mortality of births during 1970–4 and that of births during 1982–6 in Thailand are presented in Table 11.7. Coefficients indicate the effect of each variable on the log odds of infant death versus survival during infancy. As shown in the table, contrary to our expectation, sex of child being male is found to have an insignificant effect on infant mortality during 1970–4 as well as that during 1982–6. However, since it is also found that the effect of child's sex becomes significant once health care covariates are included in the model (see Table 11.8), it seems to be confirmed that, as proximate determinants, health care variables are intervening in the relationship between child's sex and infant mortality.

TABLE 11.7
Estimated Coefficients and Standard Errors from Logit Analyses of Infant Mortality
Utilizing the Model with Demographic and Socio-economic Covariates: Births during 1970–1974 and 1982–1986 in Thailand

| Covariates | 1970–4 Births Coefficient (α) | Standard Error | 1982–6 Births Coefficient (α) | Standard Error |
|---|---|---|---|---|
| Constant | −3.322[a] | 1.459 | −1.833 | 1.918 |
| Demographic Characteristics | | | | |
| Sex of child being male | 0.094 | 0.146 | 0.342 | 0.221 |
| Mother's age at birth | −0.170[a] | 0.081 | −0.202 | 0.124 |
| Mother's age at birth squared | 0.003 | 0.001 | 0.004 | 0.002 |
| Birth order >1 and previous interval <24 months | 2.396[b] | 0.594 | 1.026[b] | 0.323 |
| Birth order >1 and previous interval ≥24 months | 1.895[b] | 0.603 | 0.244 | 0.324 |
| Breast-feeding | −0.833[b] | 0.267 | −3.313[b] | 0.260 |
| Socio-economic Characteristics | | | | |
| Rural residence | 0.421 | 0.408 | 0.391 | 0.524 |
| Region | | | | |
| Central | 0.058 | 0.513 | −0.511 | 0.721 |
| North | 0.362 | 0.514 | 1.001 | 0.709 |
| North-east | 0.080 | 0.512 | 1.064 | 0.692 |
| South | −0.196 | 0.542 | 0.193 | 0.724 |

| Women's education | | | | |
|---|---|---|---|---|
| No education | 1.411[a] | 0.758 | | |
| Primary education | 1.029 | 0.743 | | |
| Less than secondary | | | 2.025[b] | 0.737 |
| Women's non-agricultural employment | −0.467[a] | 0.228 | 0.076 | 0.317 |
| Below average household living standard in the survey year | −0.008 | 0.163 | 0.191 | 0.261 |
| (N), sample size | (3,058) | | (3,163) | |
| Log-likelihood | −722.30 | | −354.83 | |

[a] Significantly different from zero at the 5 per cent level using a one-tail or two-tail test as appropriate to the hypothesis.
[b] Significantly different from zero at the 1 per cent level using a one-tail or two-tail test as appropriate to the hypothesis.

TABLE 11.8
Logit Analyses of Infant Mortality Utilizing the Full Model: Births during 1982–1986 in Thailand

| Covariates | Total Coefficient ($\alpha$) | Total Standard Error | Urban Coefficient ($\alpha$) | Urban Standard Error | Rural Coefficient ($\alpha$) | Rural Standard Error |
|---|---|---|---|---|---|---|
| Constant | −1.067 | 1.965 | 6.810 | 3.764 | −16.734 | 1,720.500 |
| Demographic Characteristics | | | | | | |
| Sex of child being male | 0.429[a] | 0.225 | 0.985[a] | 0.542 | 0.406 | 0.268 |
| Mother's age at birth | −0.152 | 0.126 | −0.570[a] | 0.250 | −0.074 | 0.157 |
| Mother's age at birth squared | 0.003 | 0.002 | 0.010[a] | 0.004 | 0.002 | 0.003 |
| Birth order >1 and previous birth interval <24 months | 0.756[a] | 0.334 | 1.204[a] | 0.701 | 0.698[a] | 0.402 |
| Birth order >1 and previous birth interval ⩾24 months | 0.101 | 0.331 | 0.554 | 0.756 | 0.025 | 0.395 |
| Breast-feeding | −3.531[b] | 0.280 | −3.472[b] | 0.604 | −3.611[b] | 0.335 |
| Socio-economic Characteristics | | | | | | |
| Rural residence | 0.212 | 0.583 | | | | |
| Region | | | | | | |
| Central | −0.284 | 0.727 | −2.539[a] | 1.281 | | |
| North | 1.240[a] | 0.728 | 1.276 | 1.124 | 1.338[b] | 0.534 |
| North-east | 1.829[a] | 0.797 | 1.875 | 1.474 | 1.999[b] | 0.622 |
| South | 0.258 | 0.743 | 0.399 | 0.989 | 0.347 | 0.561 |

| | | | | | | | |
|---|---|---|---|---|---|---|---|
| Women's education less than secondary | 1.912[b] | 0.748 | 0.411 | 0.663 | 17.114 | 0.413 | 1,720.500 |
| Women's employment in non-agriculture | 0.152 | 0.325 | −0.169 | 0.535 | 0.198 | 0.413 | |
| Below average household economic status in 1987 | 0.070 | 0.268 | 0.576 | 0.641 | 0.009 | 0.322 | |
| Health Care Characteristics | | | | | | | |
| Prenatal care from MD/nurse | −0.293 | 0.262 | −1.540[a] | 0.855 | −0.204 | 0.309 | |
| Delivered by trained professionals (MD/nurse/midwife) | −0.724[b] | 0.284 | −1.203 | 0.935 | −0.768[b] | 0.330 | |
| Population per hospital bed | −0.0008[a] | 0.0003 | −0.0009 | 0.001 | −0.0009[a] | 0.0004 | |
| Poor quality of drinking water | 0.133 | 0.440 | 0.456 | 0.616 | −0.226 | 0.557 | |
| Time to the nearest health centre/hospital | | | | | −0.0001 | 0.007 | |
| (N), sample size | (3,163) | | (1,046) | | (2,117) | | |
| Log-likehood | −346.50 | | −69.355 | | −244.95 | | |

[a]Significantly different from zero at the 5 per cent level using a one-tail or two-tail test as appropriate to the hypothesis.
[b]Significantly different from zero at the 1 per cent level using a one-tail or two-tail test as appropriate to the hypothesis.

Controlling for the effects of other demographic and socio-economic covariates, the J-shaped relationship between mother's age at childbirth and infant mortality remains significant for births during 1970–4 whereas the effect of mother's age at birth is statistically insignificant among births during 1982–6 (see Table 11.7). Hence, it can be thought that babies born from very young or older mothers (usually those younger than age 20 and those aged 35 or older) had significantly higher risks of infant deaths during the early 1970s, but these risks of higher infant mortality dependent upon mother's age at birth became insignificant by the mid-1980s, due probably to overall advancement of medical technology as well as to socio-economic development of Thailand between these two time periods. However, there is also a possibility that provision and utilization of health care at a more micro-level are intervening between mother's age at birth and infant mortality. Although this cannot be tested for births during 1970–4 (due to unavailability of data), such analysis can be conducted for births during 1982–6, the results of which are discussed in the following section.

For births occurring in the period 1970–4, second- and higher-order births have a significantly higher risk of infant deaths relative to first births (see Table 11.7). Among second- or higher-order births, the difference between the mortality effect of long (previous) birth interval and that of short birth interval is found to be statistically insignificant although short birth interval is associated with higher infant mortality risks than long birth interval. For births occurring in the period 1982–6, second- or higher-order births are also found to have a significantly higher risk of infant deaths than first births. Moreover, when previous birth interval (that is, the interval from previous to the index child) is long (defined as 24 months or longer), infant mortality differentials between first births and the higher-order births become insignificant, suggesting that having two children in a short interval strongly affects survival of infants, probably because the two small children have to compete for their parents' (especially the mother's) care and attention.

Breast-feeding has a significant negative effect on infant mortality for both time periods under consideration (see Table 11.7). It is therefore suggested that the effect of breast-feeding on infant survival remained significant under rapid socio-economic development and advancement of medicine and health care in Thailand during the 1970s and the early 1980s.

Turning to socio-economic covariates, contrary to expectation, rural residence does not have any statistically significant effect on infant mortality. Similarly, no significant regional effects on infant mortality can be detected (see Table 11.7). However, there seems to be a possibility that health care variables are influencing the relationship between regional variables and infant mortality because, for births during 1982–6, the north and north-east regions are found to suffer from significantly higher infant mortality than the Bangkok metropolis when the effects of health care covariates are controlled (see Table 11.8). Regional effects on infant mortality are examined in the following section.

Low maternal education is significantly associated with a higher probability of infant deaths. This finding supports our hypothesis and it is in agreement with findings of many other studies on infant mortality in developing countries (Cochrane et al., 1980; DaVanzo and Habicht, 1986; DaVanzo et al., 1983; Martin et al., 1983; Pebley and Stupp, 1987; Preston, 1985; Trussell and Hammerslough, 1983). Specifically, for births during 1970–4, 'no education' of a mother is found to have a significant positive effect on infant mortality; and for births during 1982–6, less than secondary maternal education is found to be significantly associated with higher infant mortality risks. Therefore, it is suggested that although a threshold for significant improvement in child survival changed from primary education to secondary education during the 1970s and the early 1980s due to rapid increases in female educational attainment, higher maternal education continues to be associated with lower infant mortality.

Women's non-agricultural employment is found to be associated significantly with lower infant mortality for births during 1970–4, implying that women's work in a non-traditional sector might be associated with modernity and ability to utilize health care services more effectively, both of which probably increase chances of infant survival. However, a significant effect of mother's employment outside agriculture on infant mortality disappeared by the mid-1980s (see Table 11.7). From these findings, it can therefore be considered that as the Thai society modernized and developed during the 1970s and the 1980s, unemployed mothers and mothers in agriculture came to have levels of modernity and access to health care that are not significantly different from those enjoyed by their counterparts in non-agricultural employment. To be sure, women's employment is measured at the time of the survey whereas infant deaths occurred sometime during the five years prior to the survey. However, because the degree of stability in women's employment status between infancy of the index child and the date of the survey is considered to be relatively high, interval-specific information on women's employment status may not produce very different results.

Finally, household economic status is found to have no significant effect on infant mortality for both of the two time periods under consideration. Similar to the case of women's employment status, this may be due to the fact that this covariate is measured at the time of the survey. This limitation, however, is thought to be a minor drawback because household economic status in the survey year is likely to be highly correlated with economic status during the five years preceding the survey. If this is the case, birth interval-specific information on household economic status is unlikely to yield substantially different results.

In summary, from the results of logit analyses of demographic and socio-economic covariates of infant mortality during 1970–4 and 1982–6, it was found that effects of such covariates as mother's age at childbirth and mother's employment status changed under overall socio-economic development, medical advances, and improvements in the health care system in Thailand during the 1970s and 1980s and despite these rapid societal changes, some covariates continue to have significant effects on infant mortality. They are breast-feeding, maternal education, birth order, and to a lesser extent, previous birth interval. In addition, it was also suggested that there is a possibility for health care variables to be intervening in the relationship between some demographic and socio-economic covariates and infant mortality. In the next section, causal mechanisms of infant mortality in the 1970s and 1980s are examined by including in the model not only demographic and socio-economic variables but also information on health care provision and utilization, with special attention paid to rural–urban differences in such mechanisms.

## Logit Analysis of Demographic, Socio-economic, and Health Care Determinants of Infant Mortality

The previous section examined changes in socio-economic and demographic covariates of infant mortality from the early 1970s and the mid-1980s. This section attempts to account more fully for a causal mechanism of recent infant mortality over the same period by adding to the model an important group of covariates—provision and utilization of health care. Since such a causal mechanism may vary from urban to rural areas, separate analyses for urban and rural births are conducted in addition to the logit analysis of total births occurring during 1982–6. Because health care variables are proximate determinants of infant mortality, directly influencing the probability of child survival, they are expected to increase our understanding concerning a complex causal structure that influences infant mortality.

### Definitions of the Variables

Since the dependent variable as well as the demographic and socio-economic covariates in the model are already explained in the previous section, only health care covariates are defined here.

Of the 3,238 TDHS births occurring during 1982–6, 1,064 were born to mothers residing in urban areas and 2,174 to mothers in rural areas. Of these, 18 and 57 were deleted respectively due to missing values of covariates, thus making the final urban and rural sample sizes 1,046 and 2,117 respectively. Among the remaining 1,046 urban births, 23 (approximately 22 per 1,000 births) died during infancy, while 71 infants (around 34 per 1,000 births) died among the remaining 2,117 rural births.[14]

In the full model (that is, the model that includes all demographic, socio-economic, and health care covariates shown in Table 11.6), there are four health care variables (five for rural births), all of which have important policy implications: prenatal care, delivery attendance, population per hospital bed in mother's residing province at the year of birth, quality of household drinking water, and, in addition, for rural births, time (in minutes) to the nearest health centre/hospital.[15] The first two variables are indicators of health care utilization while the remaining variables are indicators of health care provision.

Concerning prenatal, maternal, and child health care in Thailand, the Ministry of Public Health (MOPH) has a clear policy to provide good health service coverage to mothers and children. One of the primary emphases of the policy is to help ensure the health of children even before birth through a prenatal care programme. Specifically, the MOPH has designed a total programme of four prenatal examinations for each pregnant woman, with at least two examinations recommended for rural women. In the TDHS, however, a question was asked, not regarding frequency of prenatal care received, but whether a woman had had any check-up during each pregnancy (leading to a live birth) during the last five years, and if she had, from whom she received it.[16] In this study, the variable of prenatal care is again dichotomized: 1 if mother has received prenatal care from an MD or trained nurse/midwife, 0 if otherwise. This variable is expected to have a negative effect on infant mortality.

Care at birth (perinatal care) is another important determinant of infant mortality since the competence and skills of the attendant to help avoid complications at delivery influence chances of infants' survival. The TDHS provides information on the type of assistance available during delivery.[17] In the model, the variable of delivery attendance is dichotomous: 1 if delivered by MD/nurse/midwife, 0 if otherwise. Its relationship with infant mortality is expected to be negative.

In order to utilize health care, it first has to be available. In this sense, the 'supply-side' factors of health care are important determinants of child health and survival. In Thailand, increases in trained medical staff, number of hospital beds, and equipment have indeed been one of the main objectives since the beginning of the First National Development Plan in 1962 (Porapakkham, 1986: 96-104). Because the TDHS did not collect such information as the number of medical staff, hospital beds, and equipment for all communities/localities,[18] the writers separately obtained the unpublished data from the MOPH on several 'supply-side' variables (that is, population per hospital bed, per MD, per nurse, and per MD or nurse in each province) for the years under consideration (1982-6) and linked them with the child data from the TDHS.[19] Among these MOPH variables on health care provision, it was decided to include only the variable of population per hospital bed because all these variables are highly correlated one to another and the chosen variable has the smallest number of missing cases as well as the highest correlation with infant mortality. Because lower population per bed means higher provision of health care (facility), this variable may be positively associated with infant mortality. On the other hand, it is also possible that higher provision of health care can be negatively associated with infant death because the government may put more resources into areas/provinces which suffer from higher infant mortality. Therefore, there is no firm hypothesis concerning the sign of the mortality effect of this covariate.

Another variable of health care provision included in the model for rural births is the time (in minutes) from the community of mother's residence to the nearest health centre/hospital. The TDHS collected such community-based data on health care provision for rural areas as distance (in kilometres) to the nearest health centre, distance to the nearest hospital, time (in minutes) to the nearest health centre, and time to the nearest hospital. For urban communities, this information was not collected because they were all thought to have good access to medical facilities. Among these community-based variables, it was decided to construct, from the two time variables, a variable that measures the time to the nearest health centre or hospital (whichever is closer in terms of time) because it was thought that people are likely to go to the most accessible health care facility when the need arises, and also because time variables are better measures of accessibility than distance variables because accessibility is affected not only by distance but also by the means of transportation and the condition of the roads.[20] Since a health centre is closer than a hospital in a large majority of rural communities, this variable mostly measures accessibility to a health centre which is a locus of primary health care in rural areas. Because a shorter time to the nearest health centre or hospital means better access to the health care facility, it is hypothesized that the time to the nearest health centre/hospital is positively related to infant mortality.

Finally, quality of drinking water is also an important health care variable, for which improvement has been advocated ever since the First National Development Plan (1962–6) and has specifically been made an objective of the national health policy for the Fourth and Fifth Plans (1976–81 and 1982–6 respectively) (Porapakkham, 1986: 96–104). Although this variable could easily be considered a socio-economic variable because quality of drinking water can be an indicator of development of societal infrastructure, it was decided to classify this factor as a health care variable due to the policy emphasis put on it. The TDHS found that a vast majority of mothers in Thailand give their infants plain water while breast-feeding (Chayovan et al., 1989). In this sense, the poor quality of household drinking water can be a source of contaminants, and thus a determinant of infant mortality. In the model, the 'poor' quality of drinking water is defined as water from: a well or pond (both private and public); river, spring, and surface water; tanker truck or other vendor; and rain-water. On the other hand, the 'non-poor' (that is, good) quality of drinking water is defined as tap water (both public and private).

*Results of Logit Analysis*

The results of logit analysis of infant mortality of births during 1982–6 for total Thailand as well as for urban and rural areas separately, are presented in Table 11.8, utilizing the full model. From Tables 11.6 and

11.8, it can be noticed that once health care covariates are introduced into the model, sex of child being male comes to have a significant positive effect on infant mortality in total Thailand as well as in urban areas, as expected. On the other hand, in rural areas, sex differential in infant mortality is found to be still statistically insignificant although male infants still have a higher risk of mortality than female infants. This finding indicates that male children have significantly higher infant mortality than female children in urban areas and in Thailand as a whole while there is no significant sex differential in rural areas.

It is also found that controlling for the effects of other covariates, the effect of mother's age at birth is statistically insignificant in Thailand as a whole and in rural areas, while the J-shaped relationship between mother's age at childbirth and infant mortality appears for births in urban areas. It is unclear why the curvilinear relationship remains among urban births during 1982-6 after controlling for the effects of other covariates.[21]

Consistent with the model including only demographic and socio-economic covariates, second- and higher-order births that took place within 24 months after previous births have a significantly higher risk of deaths during infancy than do first births (see Table 11.8). However, when the interval from the previous to the index birth becomes 24 months or longer, infant mortality differentials between first births and higher-order births become statistically insignificant. This is the case not only for Thailand as a whole, but also for urban and rural areas separately, suggesting that having two children in a short interval significantly affects survival of infants.

Breast-feeding is found to have a strong negative effect on infant mortality also in the full model, as expected. In fact, this is the single most significant variable among all the covariates considered, and this is the case not only for total Thailand but also for urban and rural areas. This finding indicates the profound effect breast-feeding has had on infant survival and health in the 1970s and 1980s.

Turning to socio-economic covariates, it can be seen from Table 11.8 that inclusion of the health care variable does not alter estimation results concerning rural residence: it still does not have any significant effect on infant mortality. It can therefore be seen that once the effects of other socio-economic and demographic variables are taken into account, the urban–rural differential found in the previous life-table analysis disappears, probably because the urban–rural differential is associated with other variables in the model such as breast-feeding and mother's education.[22]

Concerning regional variations in infant mortality, it can be seen from Table 11.8 that inclusion of health care variables in the model produced the expected results. Specifically, it is found that, for Thailand as a whole, the north and north-east regions have significantly higher infant mortality than the Bangkok metropolis, while infant mortality in the central and south regions does not differ significantly from that of Bangkok. Considering urban and rural births separately, it is then seen that rural areas of the north and north-east regions suffer much higher infant mortality than rural areas of the central region, while no urban areas of the four major regions have significantly higher mortality than the Bangkok metropolis (rather, urban areas of the central region have significantly lower mortality than Bangkok). Therefore, the high infant mortality in the north and north-east regions in the 1970s and 1980s is considered to be due primarily to the still very high mortality in rural areas of these two regions over this period.

The significant negative effect of mother's low education (defined here as less than secondary) on infant mortality still persists after controlling for the effects of health care covariates for births during 1982–6 in Thailand as a whole (see Table 11.8), indicating that higher education indeed helps mothers lower risks of infant deaths. However, interestingly, once urban and rural areas are examined separately, the significant effect of maternal education disappears. This is thought to be due to the fact that because women with secondary or higher education are concentrated in urban areas while those with less than secondary education congregate in rural areas, the variability of the education variable is relatively limited within each sample, thus making maternal education insignificant when urban and rural births are examined separately.[23]

With regard to the remaining two socio-economic covariates (women's non-agricultural employment and household economic status in 1987), inclusion of health care covariates in the model did not alter the results: both still have no significant effects on recent infant mortality not only for Thailand as a whole but also for urban and rural areas separately, after controlling for the other demographic, socio-economic, and health care variables.

Of the four health care variables, two (delivery attendance being from medical and trained health professionals and population per hospital bed) are found to have significant negative effects on infant mortality for total Thailand and, to a stronger degree, for rural areas, implying that utilization of 'quality' health care at birth as well as provision of medical/health professionals and facilities are important factors influencing infant health and survival in Thailand, especially in rural areas. On the other hand, these two health care variables are found to be insignificant in urban areas possibly because of their wide prevalence in urban areas. Specifically, as shown in Table 11.8, almost all urban births are attended by medical and trained health professionals at their delivery while only around 60 per cent of rural and total births had such professional delivery attendance. In addition, the average population per hospital bed is much smaller in urban areas than the corresponding figures for total Thailand and rural areas, indicating that most urban areas enjoy relatively good provision of medical/health professionals and facilities while much needs to be improved in this respect in rural areas, where over 80 per cent of the population lives.

In contrast, the effect of prenatal care is found to be significant only for urban areas although the sign of the coefficient is also in the negative direction as expected for total Thailand and for rural areas. This finding is somewhat contrary to the writers' expectation in the sense that the variability of the covariate is much smaller for urban areas than those for total Thailand and rural areas (see Table 11.6).

One possible explanation, then, is that since the prenatal care variable in the model does not measure the quantity but measures whether mothers had prenatal care at least once, there may be greater urban–rural differentials in the actual quantity (and quality) of prenatal care than the levels indicated by the variable, that is, if a certain quantity of prenatal care is needed in order for it to be effective in reducing infant mortality (meaning, once or even twice is not effective enough), and if the frequency of check-ups for many rural mothers who had prenatal care was only once or twice while most of their urban counterparts had more frequent (and probably better quality) prenatal care, it means that only urban mothers could enjoy prenatal care that is effective enough to prevent infant deaths. If this is the case (and this may be likely because, while the generally designated frequency is four, the MOPH recommended at least two examinations for rural women), it is then implied that more frequent prenatal check-ups from trained health professionals is necessary for pregnant women in rural areas.

Additional 'supply-side' variable for rural areas, time to the nearest health centre or the nearest hospital (whichever is closer), is found to have no significant effect on infant mortality, and the result was the same even if one of the two original time variables was introduced in the model instead of this constructed time variable (figures not shown). This finding is somewhat puzzling because another variable of health care provision (population per hospital bed) turns out to be significant. One possible interpretation, then, is that since most of the rural communities under consideration appear to have good access to a health centre/hospital, accessibility to a health care facility (whether it is for primary out-patient care or for more complicated in-patient care) is no longer a problem in rural Thailand.[24] What matters, instead, is the quality of health care provided which may be captured by the variable of population per hospital bed.

Contrary to expectation, quality of household drinking water is found to lack any statistical significance in relation to infant mortality. This does not mean that quality of drinking water does not affect child health and mortality, but it suggests that in Thailand, tap water is of a quality not significantly different from well, pond, river, and other unsanitary sources of water. It may also be the case that because mothers are thought to boil water before feeding it to their infants, the water quality, even if it is poor, has relatively little effect on infant health and survival.

## Conclusions and Implications

Infant mortality in Thailand has declined considerably during the 1970s and 1980s although our estimate of the level in the 1980s does not correspond exactly with the estimate derived from the 1985–6 Survey of

Population Change. Examining the life-tables derived from the births during 1982–7 in the data through comparison with Japanese life-tables and through the Weibull model test, the writers found, though not conclusively, a possibility for underreporting of female deaths during the post-neonatal and early childhood periods, and of male child deaths after infancy. Further analyses are necessary to assess the accuracy level of infant mortality in Thailand in the 1980s.

Despite the improvements in chances of child survival during the 1970s and 1980s due to the steady socio-economic development and continuous government effort to improve the people's health status, the bulk of deaths in Thailand still occur among children under one year of age, and large socio-economic differentials in infant mortality still remain. What kind of socio-economic, demographic, and health care factors, then, affect infant mortality in Thailand? Was there any change in causal mechanisms determining patterns of infant mortality in the 1970s and 1980s?

The logit analyses of demographic and socio-economic covariates of infant mortality for births during 1970–4 and 1982–6 showed that infant mortality effects of mother's age at childbirth and mother's employment status changed significantly under the overall socio-economic development and improvements of health care system in Thailand during the 1970s and 1980s. It was also found that despite these rapid socio-economic changes, such covariates as breast-feeding, maternal education, and birth order continue to affect infant mortality significantly. In addition, there are also indications that health care variables intervene in the relationship between some demographic/socio-economic covariates and infant mortality.

Furthermore, the logit analysis of demographic, socio-economic, and health care covariates of infant mortality for births during 1982–6 revealed that factors significantly affecting recent infant mortality in Thailand as a whole are sex of child, previous birth interval, breast-feeding, and maternal education. It is also found that controlling for other demographic, socio-economic, and health care factors, the northeast and north regions suffer higher infant mortality, due probably to very high mortality in rural areas of these two regions. Care at birth (delivery attendance) and provision of 'quality' professionals and facilities for health care are also found to have significant effects on infant mortality in Thailand, especially for rural areas, whereas prenatal care is found to be significant only in urban areas.

What, then, are the implications of these findings for future national health policies in Thailand as well as those in other developing countries in Asia? The first and direct implication is the importance of breast-feeding for child health and survival. As discovered, breast-feeding continues to have a strong direct effect on the health and survival chances of the breast-fed child under rapidly changing social environments. Furthermore, breast-feeding is also a major determinant (especially in the absence of effective contraception) of birth intervals, which in turn significantly influences the health and survival chances of the next child.[25] Given these profound effects of breast-feeding on child health and survival, the practice of breast-feeding needs to be further encouraged.

Secondly, higher maternal education also continues to be important for reductions in infant mortality although a threshold of significant improvement in child health and survival seems to have changed during the 1970s and 1980s, owing probably to impressive increases in educational levels of Thai women during the period. The TDHS data, for example, indicated that a large majority of ever-married women aged 15-49 in 1987 had completed primary education (4-6 years of schooling). Nevertheless, the proportion of women with secondary or higher levels of education is still relatively small; further efforts should therefore be made to encourage women to go on to secondary or higher education. Although advancement of women's education would not immediately affect child health and survival (since its effects are rather long-term), the important effects of this aspect of human resource development on survival and health of children need to be understood by policymakers and by society as a whole.

Thirdly, since previous birth interval is a significant determinant of recent infant mortality not only in rural areas but also in urban areas, it is suggested that effective child spacing is important for child health and survival. Breast-feeding contributes, at least partly, to extending birth intervals. In addition, effective contraceptive practice is also necessary. Therefore, policy efforts also need to be orchestrated in many developing countries with high fertility to increase contraceptive prevalence among married women in reproductive ages, and also to help contracepting women learn to use contraception more effectively not only for fertility reduction but also for child survival and health.

Fourthly, our multivariate analysis of infant mortality in 1982-6 showed that rural areas of the two poorest regions of Thailand (that is, the north-east and north) still suffer significantly higher infant mortality than the other three regions. This seems to indicate the inefficiency and ineffectiveness of the health intervention measures in rural areas of the north-east and north regions, thus suggesting the need to distribute more resources and to concentrate more policy efforts to rural areas of these two regions.

Finally, care at birth, supply of 'high-quality' medical professionals and facilities, and frequent prenatal care appear to be important in improving child health and chances of child survival. Thailand's national policy continues to place great emphasis on prenatal, natal, and postnatal health care; improvements in the health status of children are thought to be due, at least partly, to effective health interventions by the government and other non-governmental agencies (Porapakkham, 1986). It is therefore important for developing countries with high infant and child mortality to make efforts to increase availability and utilization of medical (both governmental and non-governmental) services for child and maternal health.

All in all, there clearly is a need for more efforts to better understand various factors determining the risk of infant death, and to elucidate processes that link these factors to infant mortality. Findings of this study indicate some crucial factors affecting child health and survival. Direct health interventions in the absence of social and economic development have only limited potential. A more effective approach would be provided by a combination of both public health programmes and improved living standards.

1. For details on the logistic multiple regression model, see Aldrich and Nelson (1984), Maddala (1983), and Walker and Duncan (1967).
2. The writers had to restrict their analysis of SOFT data to births from currently married women, instead of ever-married women, because information concerning household economic status and occupation was available only in the Husband's Survey.
3. In general, infant mortality is affected more by biological factors while child mortality is influenced more by socio-economic and environmental factors. See Mensch et al. (1985), Mosley and Chen (1984), Preston (1985), and Tsuya and Choe (1989).
4. Interestingly, when infant mortality estimates from the TDHS for the period 1972–6 are compared with the estimate from the earlier SPC for the period from mid-1974 to mid-1976, the two estimates correspond quite nicely: 55 versus 52 per 1,000 live births for the TDHS and the SPC respectively. For details, see National Statistical Office (1978).
5. For details on the Weibull model test, see Choe (1981). An example of application of the test is given by Tsuya and Choe (1989).
6. Life-table estimates for socio-economic and demographic differentials of infant and child mortality for the SOFT sample (that is, live births during 1970–4) could not be computed because duration between birth and death for dead children was measured by an ordered categorical variable, instead of a continuous variable (in months), in SOFT.
7. For example, utilizing the data from the One-Per-Thousand National Fertility Survey, Arnold and Liu (1986) found that although there are considerable regional variations, some provinces of China have a strong son preference, the strongest being Jilin Province. An even stronger son preference was discovered by Park (1983) for South Korea. It is also indicated that where there is strong preference for sons, boys receive preferential treatment in feeding and medical care (Williamson, 1976), salient examples of which are found in India and Bangladesh (D'Souza and Chen, 1980; Ramanamma and Bambawale, 1980).
8. To be sure, infant death is likely to be correlated with a shorter subsequent birth interval (partly because women try to make up for the loss by quickly giving birth to another child, and partly because duration of post-partum amenorrhoea tends to be shortened by interruption of breast-feeding). However, the possibility for reverse causation between infant death and previous birth interval is nil because interval from birth of previous child to birth of index child cannot be a consequence of death of the index child.
9. Trends and patterns of breast-feeding practice in Thailand are discussed in Knodel and Debavalya (1980), Knodel et al. (1985), and Knodel et al. (1990). Details concerning findings on infant feeding practices in the TDHS are also given by Chayovan et al. (1989) and Knodel et al. (1990).
10. Both SOFT and the TDHS also include information on breast-feeding duration. However, it was decided not to employ this variable partly because, in the case of the infant's death, breast-feeding duration can be dependent on duration of infant survival, and also because it resulted in more missing cases (due to a higher number of 'no' responses in the duration variable). Nevertheless, for testing purposes, the writers also attempted to include in an earlier model this duration variable instead of the dichotomous variable indicating whether the index child has ever been breast-fed. This replacement did not, however, alter the outcome.

11. In an earlier model, contraceptive practice before the birth of index child was also included. Since this variable was found to be insignificant (probably because it is associated with the duration of previous birth interval), it was decided to exclude this variable from the final model.

12. In the next section, also analysed are demographic, socio-economic, and health care covariates of the TDHS births by urban–rural residence. The logistic regression model for rural births includes only three dummy variables with central region as the reference category because the Bangkok metropolis is totally urban. See Table 11.6 for descriptive statistics of this regional variable.

13. About 18 per cent of children born during 1982–6 have mothers with secondary or higher education while a majority (approximately 70 per cent) of the children under consideration have mothers with education of 4–6 years. In Thailand, the compulsory level of education changed in 1977 from 4 to 6 years. Consequently, older women in the TDHS sample will have finished their compulsory education with 4 years of schooling and younger women with 6 years of schooling. In the model for the TDHS births, initially included were two dummy variables of mother's education: 0–3 years (no schooling or those with some primary education), and 4–6 years (those who completed primary education), with secondary or higher as the reference category. However, since inclusion of these two dummy variables did not change the results of analysis, it was decided to group these two variables into one.

14. Logit analyses of SOFT births were also carried out separately for rural and urban births. However, due probably to the small number of cases, the model for urban births did not converge while the results from analysis of rural births were not different from those from analysis of total births. Therefore, only the results for total births are presented and compared with those for the TDHS births.

15. The TDHS also collected information on immunization. The proportion of children protected by immunization against potentially life threatening diseases is regarded as an important indicator of child health status in Thailand. Begun in 1977, Thailand's Expanded Programme of Immunization (EPI) seeks to immunize children against tuberculosis, diphtheria, pertussis, tetanus, polio, and measles. However, despite the importance of this variable as an indicator of health care utilization, it could not be included in the model, partly because Thai children are not expected to have completed the full schedules of immunization until the age of 12 months (Chayovan, Kamnuansilpa, and Knodel, 1988: 98–104; Pitaktepsombati et al., 1989). Therefore, immunization status can be, instead of a determinant of infant mortality, a dependent variable of infant survival. Another reason for the exclusion of this variable is the large number of missing cases, due probably to infant deaths before the completion of the full immunization schedule.

16. Earlier findings from the survey indicated that almost all of the women who had prenatal care received it from medical or trained health professionals (Chayovan, Kamnuansilpa, and Knodel, 1988: 94).

17. The TDHS also provides information on the place of delivery. However, it was decided to include in the model only the variable of the type of delivery attendance because delivery attendance and the place of delivery are closely related in the sense that a vast majority of deliveries assisted by medical or trained health professionals also occurred in hospitals and other health facilities. The correlation coefficient (r) between the two dichotomous variables is about 90.

18. The TDHS collected information on some 'supply-side' variables such as the number of medical staff and hospital beds for the reported nearest health outlet. However, since this information was available only for rural communities, it was decided to use the Ministry of Public Health (MOPH) data which cover both urban and rural provinces.

19. The data obtained from the MOPH are on the number of hospitals, hospital beds, patients, physicians, and nurses for each province during the fiscal years 1982–6. These data are compiled from government hospitals, state enterprise hospitals, municipality hospitals, and private hospitals.

20. Among the 209 rural communities studied by the TDHS, the data concerning time to the nearest hospital are available for all of them while the information on time to the nearest health centre is not reported for 7 communities (that is, 57 births). For the cases

without the information on time to health centre, the information on time to the nearest hospital was utilized. For the remaining cases that have both kinds of information, whichever was closer (in terms of time) was chosen. In most cases, health centres were closer than (or a similar distance from) hospitals.

21. As shown in Table 11.6, the mean age of mother at childbirth is very similar for urban and rural areas. In addition, there is little urban–rural differential in the range of mother's age at birth: 14–47 years old for urban areas and 13–46 years old for rural areas.

22. For details on urban–rural differentials in breast-feeding and education, see Chayovan, Kamnuansilpa, and Knodel (1988).

23. Specifically, of the 2,643 births whose mothers have less than secondary education, 74.5 per cent reside in rural areas; of the 520 births whose mothers have secondary or higher education, 71.5 per cent live in urban areas. Thus, urban areas have a large share of mothers with secondary or higher education whereas their rural counterparts more often have less than secondary education.

24. For around 97 per cent of the rural communities under consideration, it takes 30 minutes or less to go to the nearest health centre or hospital (whichever is closer). Since a health centre is closer than a hospital for most of the communities, it can be considered that most of them have a health centre within 30 minutes' distance. Considering the time to the nearest hospital only, for around 87 per cent of the communities, it takes 1 hour or less to reach the nearest hospital.

25. The duration of the period of post-partum infecundability (that is, infecundable state following childbirth) is largely a function of the duration and intensity of breast-feeding in the absence of contraception. For details on the fertility-inhibiting effect (and thus the birth-spacing effect) of breast-feeding, see Bongaarts (1978, 1980).

# 12
# Health Status of the Elderly and Their Labour Force Participation in the Developing Countries along the Asia–Pacific Rim

Naohiro Ogawa, Noriko O. Tsuya,
Malinee Wongsith, and Ehn-Hyun Choe

**Introduction**

UNTIL the early 1980s, many of the governments of developing countries in Asia perceived population ageing to be an issue among developed nations only. As a consequence of their rapid fertility declines since the mid-1960s, however, these Asian governments have become increasingly aware of various ageing problems in their own countries which require more focused attention in the formulation of their long-term development plans. It should be stressed that because the fertility transition in these developing countries in Asia has been substantially shorter than in the developed nations, the speed of population ageing in the former has been and will be considerably faster than that observed in the latter (Leete, 1987). Moreover, although in the late 1980s the mortality effect on population ageing was limited in most of these Asian developing countries, if the trends of the 1960s–1980s in remarkable mortality improvement continue, mortality at advanced ages will fall pronouncedly in the relatively near future, thus further contributing to population ageing (Myers, 1988).

Both fertility declines and mortality improvements affect not only the proportion of the elderly in the total population at the macro-level but also the elderly people's way of life at the micro-level. As a consequence of lowered fertility, each old person has fewer children to depend upon for old-age security (Martin and Culter, 1983). Due to the extension of longevity, old persons may need to modify their retirement plans (Livi-Bacci, 1982).

Besides the fertility and mortality changes, the urbanization process is likely to affect the welfare of the aged. Urbanization, which is both an antecedent and consequence of economic development (Hauser, 1982; Ogawa, 1985a), tends to lead to an increase in the number of nuclear families and to a decrease in the number of traditional extended families. It also brings about numerous lifestyle changes not only among the young but also among the aged. In parallel with such changes in family structure and lifestyles, economic development induces a rise in rural–urban mobility of the young, which in turn poses geographical obstacles to reciprocal family aid. Economic development also facilitates vertical mobility, which places parents and offspring in different social classes, consequently weakening the filial relationship (Davis and van den Oever, 1981).

As a consequence of these demographic changes coupled with economic development, the pattern of support for the elderly has been gradually shifting from informal family support to formal public support in a number of developing countries, particularly along the Asia–Pacific Rim (Martin, 1988). However, most of these countries are still at an early stage of this transition, and a considerably higher proportion of the elderly in the Asia–Pacific Rim area, compared with the aged in the developed region, are still in the work-force to support themselves as well as their families.

Although there are a host of factors affecting labour force participation among the elderly, a number of past studies (Boskin, 1977; Zabalza, Pissarides, and Barton, 1980) show that the health status of the aged plays an important role in determining whether or not they participate in the work-force. In virtually all populations, older age-groups experience more illness and need more health services than younger age-groups. Due to limited access to health care in both public and private sectors, however, the health condition of the elderly in the developing countries along the Rim is generally less favourable than those in developed nations (Ogawa, 1990). It should be stressed that health is not only a vital determinant of achieving and maintaining individual and societal well-being, but also a primary lever for initiating the development process (Maddox, 1982).

This chapter examines the relationships between two key factors in human resource development, that is, the work pattern of the elderly and its relationship with their health status. To achieve this objective, micro-level data gathered in Thailand and South Korea are heavily drawn upon.

To facilitate the statistical analysis which follows, the demographic profile of the aged population and their socio-economic status in developing countries along the Rim is first reviewed in the next section. Later in this chapter, an attempt is made to analyse the effect of a change in the health status of elderly persons upon their labour force participation in the two Asian countries at different stages of economic development.

## The Elderly in the Asia–Pacific Region: Demographic Profile and Socio-economic Status

*Demographic Status*

The population aged 65 and over in the three subregions of Asia (East, South-East, and South Asia) was estimated at 128.3 million in 1985 (United Nations, 1989c). These elderly persons correspond to 4.7 per cent of the total population living in the three subregions, which is considerably lower than that for the developed region (11.5 per cent), and slightly below that for the world total (6.0 per cent).

Table 12.1 compares the proportion of the population at ages 65 and over for selected countries along the Rim and Western countries in 1985. In the Asia–Pacific region, Japan's population is by far the most aged; 10.3 per cent of its population are aged 65 and over. Japan is followed by Hong Kong (7.6 per cent), China (5.3 per cent), and Singapore (5.2 per cent). Although Japan's population is pronouncedly aged among the countries in the Asia–Pacific region, it is still young relative to the populations of most Western industrialized countries.

All the populations along the Asia–Pacific Rim are projected to age substantially in the period to 2020 (United Nations, 1989c). As discussed elsewhere (Ogawa, 1988a), most of these populations are expected to show a marked increase in the proportion of old-old persons (75 years of age and over). Moreover, due to the difference in life expectancy at higher ages between males and females, each of these populations is projected to undergo a pronounced predominance of women among the elderly.

It should also be emphasized that the nexus between the development of an urban–industrial economy and population ageing observed in the

TABLE 12.1
International Comparison of the Proportion of the Population Aged 65 and Over, 1985 (per cent)

| Asian Countries | Proportion of Aged Population to Total Population | Western Countries | Proportion of Aged Population to Total Population |
|---|---|---|---|
| Japan | 10.3 | Australia | 10.1 |
| Philippines | 3.4 | New Zealand | 10.5 |
| Indonesia | 3.6 | United States | 11.9 |
| Thailand | 3.6 | France | 13.0 |
| Malaysia | 3.8 | Switzerland | 14.6 |
| South Korea | 4.3 | West Germany | 14.7 |
| Singapore | 5.2 | United Kingdom | 15.1 |
| China | 5.3 | Norway | 15.5 |
| Hong Kong | 7.6 | Sweden | 17.9 |

*Source*: United Nations (1989c).

present-day developed countries will not be as close in these Asia–Pacific countries (Jones, 1988a). Some Asian countries such as South Korea and Malaysia are likely to be as urbanized and industrialized as Western industrialized countries were when they became aged. In contrast, other Asian countries along the Rim, such as China and Thailand, will become aged societies at considerably lower levels of urbanization and agro-industrialization. Owing to this difference in population ageing in the context of development between Asia and the West, the applicability of the ageing policies formulated in the Western industrialized nations to these Asian countries seems to be rather limited.

More importantly, the speed of population ageing is likely to accelerate in some of the countries along the Rim in the early part of the twenty-first century. For instance, between the years 2000 and 2025, the aged population is expected to increase from 7.0 to 13.0 per cent in China, from 10.8 to 21.0 per cent in Hong Kong, from 6.3 to 13.9 per cent in South Korea, from 7.1 to 19.1 per cent in Singapore, and from 5.0 to 10.2 per cent in Thailand. These projected increases indicate that the tempo of population ageing in these Asian countries along the Rim is substantially faster, compared with that for the Western industrialized populations. For this reason, these Asian countries will go through an extremely compressed process of population–development interactions, and this is likely to lead to a host of difficult adjustment problems at various familial and societal levels.

*Socio-economic Status of the Elderly and Family Support*

This section discusses the more proximate demographic factors which may influence the degree of support across generations. In the 1980s, demographers have been increasingly referring to familial support ratios, to assess the availability of intergenerational family support for the elderly (Myers, 1988). These ratios, which relate the population at ages 45–49 to those aged 65–79, enable the number of adult children to be evaluated in terms of a single generation of parents who would have borne them at ages 15–34. Table 12.2 presents the familial support ratios for the nine countries along the Rim in 1985 and 2025. Over the 1990s–2020s, all the countries are expected to face a fast reduction in the demographic potential of adult children to support the elderly. Such declining trends are particularly pronounced in Japan, China, South Korea, Hong Kong, and Singapore. In these countries, manpower resources for the provision of home care will be increasingly scarce.

A more relevant measure for assessing the availability of family support is the living arrangements for the elderly which are often taken as a first indicator of family relations. One of the national sample surveys undertaken in South Korea in 1985 shows that 79 per cent of 1,856 respondents aged 60 and over were living with their children (Choi, 1985). A sample survey conducted in one of the provinces in

TABLE 12.2
Familial Support Ratios for Selected Asian Countries, 1985 and 2025[a]

| Country | 1985 | 2025 |
|---|---|---|
| Hong Kong | 0.74 | 0.37 |
| Japan | 0.80 | 0.38 |
| China | 0.95 | 0.56 |
| Singapore | 1.10 | 0.35 |
| Philippines | 1.21 | 1.01 |
| Malaysia | 1.24 | 0.80 |
| Thailand | 1.28 | 0.83 |
| Indonesia | 1.35 | 0.95 |
| South Korea | 1.38 | 0.59 |

*Source*: As for Table 12.1.
[a] Familial support ratio = (those aged 45–49)/(those aged 65–79).

northern China in 1983 found that 79 per cent of the rural elderly were living with their children (Qu, 1984). According to World Health Organization (WHO) surveys on the elderly conducted in the 1980s, 72 per cent of Malaysians aged 60 and over were living with their children, and the corresponding figure for their Philippine counterparts was 79 per cent (Andrews et al., 1986). Data gathered from the ASEAN ageing survey have yielded a highly comparable result; over 70 per cent of the elderly were living with their children in the four ASEAN countries (Singapore, Malaysia, the Philippines, and Indonesia) (Chen and Jones, 1989). Furthermore, a 1986 international comparative study covering five countries (Japanese Statistics Bureau, Management and Coordination Agency, 1987) indicated that in Thailand, 48.5 per cent of the elderly aged 60 and over were residing in a three-generation arrangement. In sharp contrast, only 0.2 per cent of the elderly aged 60 and over in Denmark, 0.5 per cent in the United States, and 14.1 per cent in Italy were living in a three-generation household.

The multigenerational living arrangements tend to facilitate intergenerational familial support, both economic and non-economic, from adult children to their elderly parents. This pattern of support for the elderly is documented by some of the micro-level survey findings. According to the WHO surveys on the elderly, in the case of South Korea, the sources of their income were from family (67 per cent), work (19 per cent), pensions (6 per cent), and others (8 per cent). For the Malaysian respondents, the percentage distribution of these responses was 62, 19, 14, and 5 per cent, respectively, while it was 54, 22, 13, and 11 per cent for the Philippine elderly. A similar pattern of main income sources for the elderly can be observed among other Asian countries (Singapore, Thailand, and Indonesia), as demonstrated by data gathered from ASEAN surveys on ageing in the 1980s (Chen and Jones, 1989). Taking Thailand for example, 53 per cent of the respondents stated that their main income source was their families, while 28 per cent cited work, and 2 per cent, pensions. It is also important to note that data from both WHO and ASEAN surveys show that these percentage distributions vary substantially with age and sex. For instance, older respondents and women were particularly likely to report dependence on the family as the main source of income. In the male population, decreasing involvement in the paid work-force is also associated with increased dependence on the family for financial support. In addition to this, pensions become an important source of income, particularly for men over 65 years.

It should be borne in mind, however, that although support for the elderly remains a family responsibility in most Asian societies, the extent to which family support is provided to old persons differs in urban and rural areas; the traditional family support system is more widely practised in rural than in urban areas (Gibson, 1988). Figure 12.1 illustrates the intercountry differences in the proportion of the elderly residing in rural areas in the early 1980s. From this figure, it can be observed that the majority of aged persons in the developing countries along the Asia–Pacific Rim are still living in rural areas.

Moreover, largely because the predominant portion of the elderly in these developing countries inhabit rural areas where poverty is prevalent, their labour force participation rates are rather high. Table 12.3 displays the age–sex labour force participation rates among the elderly for selected countries in both Asia and the West. The data reported in this

FIGURE 12.1
Proportion of the Population Aged 65 and Over Residing in Rural Areas in Selected Asian Countries in the Early 1980s

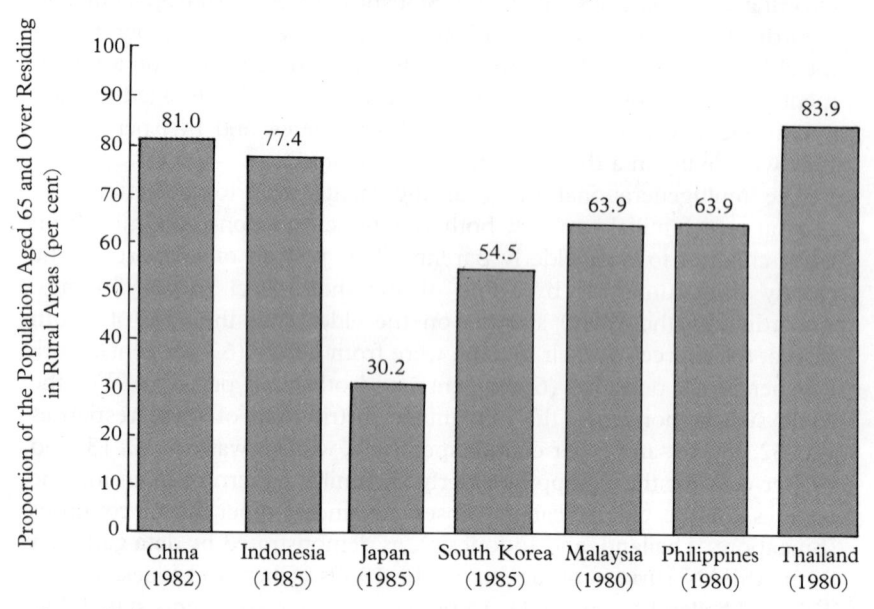

| Country | Year | Proportion (per cent) |
|---|---|---|
| China | (1982) | 81.0 |
| Indonesia | (1985) | 77.4 |
| Japan | (1985) | 30.2 |
| South Korea | (1985) | 54.5 |
| Malaysia | (1980) | 63.9 |
| Philippines | (1980) | 63.9 |
| Thailand | (1980) | 83.9 |

*Source*: United Nations (1989d).

TABLE 12.3
Labour Force Participation Rates for Males and Females Aged 60 and Over
in Selected Countries, c.1980 (per cent)

|  |  | Males | | Females | |
| --- | --- | --- | --- | --- | --- |
| Country | (Year) | 60–64 | 65 and Over | 60–64 | 65 and Over |
| Asian Countries | | | | | |
| China | (1982) | 63.7 | 30.1 | 16.9 | 4.7 |
| Hong Kong | (1986) | 59.2 | 29.7 | 25.9 | 12.1 |
| Indonesia | (1980) | 76.7 | 53.4 | 32.9 | 19.0 |
| Japan | (1985) | 78.3 | 41.6 | 37.9 | 15.2 |
| South Korea | (1980) | 68.8 | 40.6 | 31.3 | 13.0 |
| Malaysia | (1980) | 69.0 | 49.4 | 26.7 | 18.9 |
| Philippines | (1975) | 84.1 | 62.4 | 19.5 | 13.6 |
| Singapore | (1980) | 52.5 | 28.6 | 11.3 | 6.4 |
| Thailand | (1980) | 69.6 | 39.0 | 38.1 | 17.6 |
| Western Countries | | | | | |
| France | (1982) | 39.1 | 5.0 | 22.4 | 2.2 |
| Sweden | (1985) | 63.2 | 11.3 | 45.6 | 3.1 |
| United Kingdom | (1981) | 74.5 | 10.8 | 22.3 | 3.7 |
| United States | (1980) | 60.4 | 19.3 | 34.0 | 8.2 |

*Source*: International Labour Office (1988), *Yearbook of Labour Statistics*.

table show that there are substantial differences in the labour force participation rates between the two groups, particularly among those aged 65 and over, regardless of sex; the participation rates after age 65 decline more sharply in the Western than in the Asian countries. One can also note wide variations within the two groups of countries. Among the nine Asian countries included in this table, for instance, the male labour force participation rate of those aged 65 and over is the highest in the Philippines (62.4 per cent), while the corresponding figure for women is 19.0 per cent for Indonesia. In contrast, among the four selected Western nations, the United States has the highest labour force participation rates of those aged 65 and over, that is, 19.3 per cent for men and 8.2 per cent for women.

In a society where public income support is rarely provided to the elderly, the deterioration of their health conditions is often the onset of their retirement life (Petri, 1982). In the WHO surveys on ageing, each respondent was asked to evaluate their health. In South Korea, 54 per cent of the male respondents felt healthy, compared with 45 per cent of their female counterparts. In Malaysia, most people (72 per cent) reported that they felt healthy, and no sex difference was noted. In the Philippines, 84 per cent of the elderly responded positively to this question, but there was a small sex difference. The WHO data also show that contrary to the stereotyped view that the elderly are incapacitated and therefore unable to control their lives, most respondents in these Asian countries along the Rim were able without help to cope with almost all activities of daily living. Despite such high overall positive self-assessment of health, the data reveal that there was a general deterioration in reported health status with advancing age.

Comparable results emerged from data from the ASEAN ageing surveys which collected a range of information about the health and disability status of the aged. In Malaysia, the Philippines, and Thailand, from one-third to almost one-half of respondents reported a significant health impairment over the previous year prior to the survey, the figures being higher for women than for men and increasing with age. Moreover, data gathered in Thailand indicate that because of the high incidence of multigenerational living arrangements, spouse and children are the care-givers in the great majority of cases of illness among the elderly. Although the information is available only for Thailand, it is likely that the situation does not differ very much in the other ASEAN countries (Chen and Jones, 1989).

The foregoing discussions point to the demographic and socio-economic profile of the elderly in the developing region along the Rim as follows: the majority of the elderly are living with their children and in rural areas; families continue to provide most income, health, and supportive services required by older people; and more importantly, a substantial proportion of the elderly are healthy and engaged in economic activities.

*Availability of Public Support*

In the process of economic development, however, this general profile of the elderly in Asia has been gradually changing, partly in response to improved public support programmes. As suggested by the modernization hypothesis (Cowgill and Holmes, 1972), in parallel with socio-economic development, the responsibility for the provision of economic security for the dependent elderly tends to be shifted from the family to the state. A simple intercountry data analysis suggests the possibility that as the level of economic development is heightened, the pattern of allocation of support resources changes from informal to formal support (Ogawa, 1992).

In the Asia–Pacific Rim countries, however, the relative share of the social security expenditure in GDP is considerably lower than that of Western developed nations. In the early 1980s, for instance, it was 1.7 per cent for Malaysia, 0.6 per cent for the Philippines, 5.2 per cent for Singapore, and 0.2 per cent for Thailand (International Labour Office, 1988a). In Asia, Japan is an exception; 10.9 per cent of its GDP was allotted to the social security programme in 1982–3. In contrast, the corresponding figures for Western industrialized nations are much higher; it was 28.0 per cent for France, 32.6 per cent for Sweden, and 19.5 per cent for the United Kingdom.

In most countries along the Rim, public pensions, which are one of the core components of the public support system, are available to only a small proportion of the elderly—usually those living in urban areas. Singapore's Central Provident Fund, which was established in 1953, covered 36 per cent of 54-year-olds in 1983 (Chen and Jones, 1989). This system has been under operation with the principle of equity; each individual has his/her own account. Similarly, a number of developing Asian countries have instituted such provident fund schemes. In Malaysia, the provident fund, instituted in 1952, covered approximately 73 per cent of the work-force in 1981. In other countries along the Rim, provident funds are also in operation, but on a more limited scale—Indonesia serves as a case in point. In the Philippines, social insurance schemes are available, though they are not only at a premature stage but also limited in coverage (Jones, 1988a). In Thailand, the existing old-age pension plans cover government employees, state enterprise employees, and private enterprise employees (Kiranandana, Wongboonsin, and Kiranandana, 1988). In 1985, it was estimated that only 7 per cent of the elderly aged 60 and over received benefits from these highly urban-based pension plans. In China, in 1981, 45 per cent of urban retirees are pension recipients, as opposed to 1.5 per cent for rural retirees (Ogawa, 1988b). Because of such limited coverage in rural areas, the rural aged continue to work as long as their physical conditions permit.

In addition to public pensions, the government medical service programme is a major component of the social security system. Compared with pensions, health care is more widely available to the elderly of Asia. However, the adequacy and accessibility of health care differs from country to country as well as within each country. In China, for example, urban elderly retired from state-owned enterprises receive free medical care services, whereas the medical care costs of all other urban elderly are paid by municipal governments. In rural areas, most brigades have co-operative health plans (Yang, 1988). In Singapore, a part of each person's account in the Central Provident Fund has been used for the Medisave programme since 1984. In Malaysia, comprehensive health and medical services have been available to the general population, but not specifically for the elderly.

Moreover, data collected from the WHO surveys on ageing indicate that 9 per cent of Malaysians and 16 per cent of Filipinos felt that they needed more medical care than they were already obtaining. The desire for more medical services was distributed evenly across both sexes, all age-groups, and rural/urban boundaries. In South Korea, almost half believed that their medical care was inadequate. It is important to note that the WHO surveys show that the main reason for not having received medical services was that they could not afford it.

The above cursory overview of pension and medical programmes available for the elderly in the 1980s in the Asian developing countries along the Rim attests to the fact that both the scope and depth of social security provision is limited by their overall level of socio-economic resources and competing demands upon these resources by different social groups. Put differently, in the developing countries along the Asia–Pacific Rim, family members provide economic support to older relatives, as well as serving as front-line health caregivers, while the public sector plays a marginal role. In view of the recent demographic and socio-economic developments, however, many of the governments have been increasingly aware of the necessity of improving public support to needy older persons. In fact, the crucial question facing these governments is the extent to which they should assist the elderly and the level of resources to be allocated. There is little doubt, however, that such improved public support programmes will have an impact on the health status of the Asian elderly as well as their labour force participation, which is the main focus of the next section.

## Labour Force Participation and Health Status of the Aged: A Micro-level Analysis

As discussed earlier, a considerable number of significant cross-national surveys on ageing have been conducted in a number of developing nations along the Asia–Pacific Rim in the 1980s. Despite a variety of methodological and statistical shortcomings in them, valuable baseline data on the demographic and socio-economic status of the elderly have been obtained (Martin, 1989a). Because most of these sample surveys have been based upon a wide-ranging core questionnaire, some cross-national comparative analyses have been carried out in the late 1980s (Martin, 1989b; Manton, Myers, and Andrews, 1987; Chen and Jones, 1989).

Following along a similar line of research interest, an attempt is made to analyse the nexus between the labour force participation of the elderly and their health status, on the basis of micro-level data gathered from recent surveys undertaken in South Korea and Thailand. Data for South Korea were collected in 1988 as part of the ESCAP ageing survey project, while those for Thailand were gleaned from the national survey on the aged conducted in 1986 as part of the ASEAN ageing project.

These country data sets are considerably different from each other in terms of survey objectives, scope, coverage, sampling designs, and data collection methods. For instance, the South Korean survey covered elderly persons aged 60 and over (798 respondents) as well as their resident primary care providers (538 respondents). Although these respondents were selected from both rural and urban areas, information gathered was not expected to be nationally representative due to a lack of proper weights. In the case of the Thai survey, data were collected from 3,252 respondents aged 60 and over. Because a detailed description of each of these surveys has been made available elsewhere (Choe, 1988; Chayovan, Wongsith, and Saengtienchai, 1988), no further discussion on the nature and scope of each data set is made here. In addition, in view of the differing degree of the availability of information on the elderly between the two country surveys, the Thai data set is heavily drawn upon as a main source of information for analysis, and the South Korean data set is used for cross-national comparison to the maximum possible extent.

Table 12.4 compares labour force participation rates of the elderly in both Thailand and South Korea by respondents' characteristics. Although the computed rates are substantially higher in South Korea than in Thailand, both countries show a comparable pattern of labour force participation with respect to each selected characteristic. The labour force participation rates decline with an increase in age, and are higher among men than among women. Rural elderly persons show a higher participation rate than their urban counterparts.

More importantly, those who are healthy have a higher propensity to participate in the work-force than those with poor health status. Similar to many surveys such as the Retirement History Survey in the United States (Stern, 1989), information on the status of health is not physician-diagnosed but self-reported in both Thai and South Korean surveys. In the Thai survey, each respondent was asked to evaluate his/her own health status during the week prior to the survey, and to select one of the following response categories: (i) 'excellent', (ii) 'good', (iii) 'fair', and (iv) 'not healthy'. The percentage distribution of responses was 3.8, 31.4, 24.2, and 39.7, respectively. To compute the participation rates shown in Table 12.4, the first three categories have been combined into a new category of 'healthy'. In the South Korean

TABLE 12.4
Labour Force Participation Rate of the Elderly by Age, Sex, Urban–Rural Residence, and Health Status: Thailand in 1986 and South Korea in 1988 (per cent)

| Respondent's Characteristics | Thailand[a] | South Korea[b] |
|---|---|---|
| Age | | |
| 60–64 | 41.2 | 61.2 |
| 65–69 | 34.7 | 47.8 |
| 70 and over | 16.8 | 40.8 |
| Sex | | |
| Male | 39.5 | 61.3 |
| Female | 23.2 | 38.9 |
| Place of residence | | |
| Urban | 22.9 | 26.5 |
| Rural | 32.4 | 87.5 |
| Health status | | |
| Healthy | 34.2 | 55.9 |
| Not healthy | 23.6 | 37.8 |

[a]3,074 cases.
[b]797 cases.

case, each respondent was asked about his/her health status at the time of the survey, and the response categories were dichotomous; 'healthy' (59.1 per cent) and 'not healthy' (40.9 per cent). It should be noted that the percentage distribution of the 'healthy' versus 'not healthy' is highly comparable between the two surveys.

The foregoing tabular results indicate that the probability of older persons being in the labour force varies considerably with their demographic and socio-economic characteristics. In the rest of this section, the factors determining whether or not an elderly person stays in the labour force are identified. For this purpose, a logit analysis is conducted by introducing a variety of plausible explanatory variables into the participation equation. The dependent variable is dichotomous; it takes a value of 1 if an old person participates in the labour force, and 0 otherwise. Based upon a number of previous empirical analyses (Boskin, 1977; Zabalza, Pissarides, and Barton, 1980) and the discussion on the profile of the elderly earlier in this chapter, the explanatory variables have been chosen from both surveys. For the Thai case, these variables include: (i) sex (male, female*), (ii) age (60–64, 65–69, 70–74, 75 and over*), (iii) marital status (married, not married*), (iv) religion (Buddhist, non-Buddhist*), (v) educational attainment (no education*, grades 1–3, grade 4, grade 5 or higher, other education), (vi) current place of residence (urban, rural*), (vii) number of consumer durable goods available in each household, (viii) number of living children, (ix) whether or not the main income source is a pension, and (x) health status (healthy, not healthy*). In the foregoing description of the explanatory variables, some of them are of a classificatory nature and the omitted category has been indicated by an asterisk. Moreover, although information on household structure was gathered in the survey, due to the fact that it had not been coded at the time of the present analysis, the number of living children has been used as a proxy.

For the South Korean case, a comparable set of explanatory variables have been selected. It should be noted, however, that due to the unavailability of required data, the variable representing the number of consumer durables (or its proxy) has been excluded. In addition, a respondent's educational attainment is defined differently, that is, no education*, primary school, middle school, high school, or higher.

One of the key predictor variables is a respondent's health status. It is often considered that the health status variable is endogenous. Overlooking the endogeneity of this variable would tend to bias the impact of an old person's health condition upon his/her labour force participation. Unfortunately, due to the fact that the available data in both the Thai and South Korean surveys did not provide a sufficient number of good instruments to carry out estimation, no practical solution to this potential estimation problem is available in the present study. In addition, Stern (1989) has demonstrated, using two survey data sets for the United States, that there is only weak evidence of endogeneity of variables related to health status. Furthermore, a large number of earlier studies on health and labour force participation among the elderly have assumed that the causal relationship is predominantly one-way from the former to the latter (Boskin, 1977; Zabalza, Pissarides, and Barton, 1980). It is also important to note that in Stern's study, an elderly person's health status has proved to affect his/her participation non-linearly. For this reason, an alternative logit regression was run with a health status variable representing diminishing health from excellent to poor. It should be noted, however, that this alternative run is feasible only for the Thai case, due to the unavailability of necessary information in the South Korean data set.

A respondent's educational attainment, which represents a level of his/her human capital, is expected to be related to his/her labour force participation. The greater his/her human capital, the higher the probability of his/her participation in the work-force. It is also conceivable that the effect of educational attainment upon participation may be mediated through health status. As regards a respondent's marital status, the presence of his/her spouse is likely to motivate him/her to stay in the labour force to support the spouse. At the same time, it is plausible that the presence of the spouse will increase household income through his/her participation in the labour force (Boskin, 1977). The net effect of these two opposite forces is subject to empirical tests. The number of consumer durable goods is a proxy for income from assets; the greater the number of consumer durable goods, the less likely a respondent is to work. The number of living children, which is a proxy for the variable representing household structure, is expected to capture the effect of informal familial support for their aged parent upon his/her participation. Older persons who have a greater number of living children are less likely to encounter serious financial needs, thus reducing their probability of being in the work-force. A respondent's religion is introduced into the equation in hopes of capturing his/her values towards work, although the direction of its impact is ambiguous. The elderly who receive pensions are more inclined to withdraw from the work-force. It is more desirable to employ a variable to represent whether or not the elderly receive pensions; due to the limitation of data, however, a dummy-coded variable to indicate whether or not their main income source is a pension has been used as a proxy.

Table 12.5 presents the estimated results for the two different logit regressions for Thailand, that is, the base run with the dichotomous health status variable incorporated and the alternative run with the ordered health status variable used. Because these two regressions show highly comparable results, mainly the results for the base run are discussed. All the explanatory variables, except for religion, educational attainment, and the number of consumer durable goods, have estimated coefficients which are not only statistically significant but also consistent with theoretical predictions. (The means and standard deviations of the explanatory variables for the logit regressions are shown in Table 12.6).

TABLE 12.5
Logit Regressions Coefficients for Labour Force Participation of
Old Persons Aged 60 and Over: Thailand, 1986

|  | Parameter Estimates (t-statistics) | |
| --- | --- | --- |
| Explanatory Variable | Base | Alternative |
| Intercept | −2.1514 | −2.1131 |
|  | (−10.529) | (−10.294) |
| Male | 0.6856 | 0.6682 |
|  | (6.954) | (6.757) |
| Age-group |  |  |
| 60–64 | 1.4171 | 1.4095 |
|  | (9.724) | (9.644) |
| 65–69 | 1.0750 | 1.0653 |
|  | (7.377) | (7.298) |
| 70–74 | 0.3536 | 0.3582 |
|  | (2.177) | (2.203) |
| Currently married | 0.6383 | 0.6376 |
|  | (6.380) | (6.367) |
| Buddhist | −0.1445 | −0.1614 |
|  | (−0.988) | (−1.101) |
| Educational attainment |  |  |
| Grade 1–3 | −0.0816 | −0.0882 |
|  | (−0.595) | (−0.642) |
| Grade 4 | −0.1230 | −0.1185 |
|  | (−1.082) | (−1.041) |
| Grade 5 and over | 0.0748 | 0.0627 |
|  | (0.380) | (0.318) |
| Other education | 0.0221 | 0.0414 |
|  | (0.096) | (0.179) |
| Urban residence | −0.4495 | −0.4589 |
|  | (−3.828) | (−3.898) |
| Number of consumer durable goods | −1.0173 | −0.0185 |
|  | (−0.893) | (−0.953) |
| Number of living children | −0.0447 | −0.0455 |
|  | (−2.773) | (−2.819) |
| Pension as the main income source | −1.7490 | −1.7789 |
|  | (−4.999) | (−5.068) |
| Health status |  |  |
| Healthy | 0.4652 |  |
|  | (5.138) |  |
| Excellent |  | 0.8828 |
|  |  | (4.146) |
| Good |  | 0.4733 |
|  |  | (4.573) |
| Fair |  | 0.3858 |
|  |  | (3.435) |
| Log-likelihood | −1625.0 | −1622.4 |

Note: Sample size, $N = 2,999$.

TABLE 12.6

Means and Standard Deviations of Explanatory Variables Introduced into the Logit Regressions

| Explanatory Variable | Mean | Standard Deviation |
|---|---|---|
| Male | 0.4168 | 0.4931 |
| Age-group | | |
| 60–64 | 0.3385 | 0.4733 |
| 65–69 | 0.2698 | 0.4439 |
| 70–74 | 0.1851 | 0.3884 |
| Currently married (yes = 1; no = 0) | 0.5649 | 0.4959 |
| Buddhist (yes = 1; no = 0) | 0.9078 | 0.2891 |
| Educational attainment | | |
| Grade 1–3 | 0.1210 | 0.3262 |
| Grade 4 | 0.2281 | 0.4197 |
| Grade 5 and over | 0.0707 | 0.2564 |
| Other education | 0.0367 | 0.1880 |
| Urban residence (urban = 1; rural = 0) | 0.2554 | 0.4362 |
| Number of consumer durable goods | 3.9480 | 2.5071 |
| Number of living children | 4.8386 | 2.7169 |
| Pension | 0.0303 | 0.1716 |
| (main income source = 1; otherwise = 0) | | |
| Health status | | |
| Healthy (yes = 1; no = 0) | 0.6045 | 0.4890 |
| Excellent (yes = 1; no = 0) | 0.0407 | 0.1976 |
| Good (yes = 1; no = 0) | 0.3194 | 0.4663 |
| Fair (yes = 1; no = 0) | 0.2444 | 0.4298 |

*Note*: Sample size, $N = 2,999$.

The health status variable, which is the principal predictor in the present analysis, has a positive coefficient, thus suggesting that better health facilitates labour force participation. Its impact is substantial. The elderly with good health have a higher probability (0.097) of being in the work-force, compared with those having poor health. Moreover, its impact is much greater in the case of the alternative run. The elderly with excellent health status, compared with those with poor health status, have a much higher probability (0.185) of participating in the workforce. More importantly, the effect of improvements in health status on participation is non-linear, as has been found in the other studies (Stern, 1989). For example, if the health status of the elderly is 'fair' rather than 'poor', their probability of working increases by 0.081. Improved health from 'fair' to 'good' has a much smaller effect (0.018), while the change in health status from 'good' to 'excellent' leads to an increase in their probability by 0.086. These results indicate that the marginal gains are pronounced when the health condition shifts from 'poor' to 'fair' and from 'good' to 'excellent'.

All the coefficients for the age-groups have positive signs, but their size declines with advancing age. This implies that an increase in age leads to a decline in the propensity to participate in the work-force. The elderly aged 60–64, compared with those aged 75 and over, have a higher probability (0.298) of remaining in the labour force. The corresponding figures for the successive five-year age-groups fall to 0.226 for those aged 65–69 and to 0.074 for those aged 70–74. The male elderly are more likely to work than their female counterparts. The older people become, the less likely they are to stay in the labour force. Those who are married, compared with those not married, have a considerably higher probability (0.134) of being in the labour force. The elderly living in urban areas have a substantially lower probability (−0.094) of working than those in rural areas. The larger the number of living children, the less likely their aged parents are to participate in the labour force.

The elderly with a pension as a main income source have a large negative propensity to work, compared with those depending upon other income sources. The probability of the former being in the labour force is lower by 0.367 than that of the latter. It should be noted, however, that because the proportion of those whose main income source is a pension is presently only 3 per cent in the total sample, its impact upon the overall labour force participation rate is virtually negligible. Nevertheless, the pension inducement effect may play an increasingly important role in determining the labour force participation of the Thai elderly as their pension schemes expand and approach maturity in the years to come.

Based upon these estimated results, a profile of the computed age-specific labour force participation rate of the Thai elderly is displayed in Table 12.7. For comparative purposes, the following group of old people have been selected as a reference group: women who are not

TABLE 12.7
Profile of Computed Age-specific Labour Force Participation Rates for the Elderly in Thailand (per cent)

|  | Age-group ||||
| --- | --- | --- | --- | --- |
|  | 60–64 | 65–69 | 70–74 | 75+ |
| Reference group[a] | 30.1 | 23.4 | 12.9 | 9.5 |
| Male | 46.1 | 37.8 | 22.8 | 17.2 |
| Currently married | 46.0 | 37.7 | 22.7 | 17.1 |
| Urban residence | 21.6 | 16.3 | 8.7 | 6.2 |
| No living children | 37.1 | 29.5 | 16.9 | 12.5 |
| Pension | 7.0 | 5.1 | 2.5 | 1.8 |
| Not healthy | 21.3 | 16.1 | 8.5 | 6.2 |

[a] See text.

married, are Buddhists, have no education, live in rural areas, have six living children and two modern consumer durable goods, receive no pension, and are healthy. For each explanatory variable which has a statistically significant effect on participation, a value different from the reference group has been introduced. A close examination of these calculated results reveals that the labour force participation rate for the Thai elderly changed markedly, depending upon their demographic and socio-economic characteristics. It ranged from 1.8 to 46.1 per cent.

Table 12.8 compares the differences in the determinants of labour force participation between old men and women in Thailand. (The means and standard deviations of the explanatory variables are shown in Table 12.9.) Most of the determinants identified in these participation equations are comparable. It should be emphasized, however, that the impact of health status upon participation varies considerably between the sexes. The shift of health status from 'not healthy' to 'healthy' raises the probability of elderly men being in the labour force by 0.155, while the corresponding figure for elderly women is only 0.052. This implies that the effect of health improvements upon overall participation differs substantially, depending upon the extent to which health status improves for each sex.

The pension inducement effect is significant for males, while it is virtually negligible for females, as expected from the earlier discussion. In contrast, the number of modern consumer durable goods affects women's participation considerably, whereas it has no impact on men's. It should be noted that in the women's equation, one of the educational attainment variables (Grade 4) has a negative coefficient that is statistically significant. Nevertheless, the computed value of $-2 \times$ log-likelihood is 7.16, compared with a chi-square critical value of 9.49. Thus, women's educational attainment variables as a group have virtually no impact upon participation.

If these cross-sectional results hold over time, they have some important implications for future changes in labour force participation among the Thai elderly. Demographically, the estimated results for age and sex suggest that because the ageing process of Thai society is expected to accelerate and the feminization of the aged population is likely to become increasingly pronounced in the 1990s and beyond as discussed in the earlier section, the overall labour force participation rate of the elderly may decline substantially as Thailand approaches the end of its demographic transition. Improved mortality, which is projected to continue in Thai society, is likely to contribute to increasing the husband-wife joint survivorship, thus leading to a rise in the labour force participation rate. In addition, declining fertility, which has been under way for some time and is expected to persist in the 1990s and beyond, will reduce the number of living children as well as family structure, which gives rise to a weakening of informal familial support, consequently motivating the Thai elderly to stay in the labour force.

Apart from these various demographic impacts, socio-economic

## TABLE 12.8
### Logit Regressions Coefficients for Labour Force Participation of Old Persons Aged 60 and Over: Thailand, 1986

| Explanatory Variable | Parameter Estimates (t-statistics) Male[a] | Female[b] |
|---|---|---|
| Intercept | −1.6488 | −2.1202 |
|  | (−5.521) | (−7.316) |
| Age-group |  |  |
| 60–64 | 1.3114 | 1.6214 |
|  | (6.658) | (7.271) |
| 65–69 | 0.8365 | 1.3539 |
|  | (4.257) | (6.060) |
| 70–74 | 0.2247 | 0.5567 |
|  | (1.024) | (2.256) |
| Currently married | 0.6222 | 0.6583 |
|  | (3.638) | (5.300) |
| Buddhist | −0.2319 | −0.0834 |
|  | (−1.099) | (−0.406) |
| Educational attainment |  |  |
| Grade 1–3 | −0.0083 | −0.0360 |
|  | (−0.043) | (−0.182) |
| Grade 4 | 0.1791 | −0.4141 |
|  | (1.114) | (−2.437) |
| Grade 5 and over | 0.2321 | −0.0916 |
|  | (0.994) | (−0.212) |
| Other education | 0.2428 | −0.6044 |
|  | (0.917) | (−1.062) |
| Urban residence | −0.4535 | −0.4252 |
|  | (−2.618) | (−2.612) |
| Number of consumer durable goods | 0.0148 | −0.0459 |
|  | (0.522) | (−1.704) |
| Number of living children | −0.0389 | −0.0511 |
|  | (−1.707) | (−2.206) |
| Pension | −2.0129 | −0.9274 |
|  | (−5.180) | (−1.103) |
| Health status |  |  |
| Healthy | 0.6474 | 0.2901 |
|  | (4.880) | (2.334) |
| Log-likelihood | −753.17 | −861.61 |

[a] Sample size, $N = 1,250$.
[b] Sample size, $N = 1,749$.

TABLE 12.9
Means and Standard Deviations of Explanatory Variables Included in Male and Female Participation Equations

| Explanatory Variables | Male[a] Mean | Male[a] Standard Deviation | Female[b] Mean | Female[b] Standard Deviation |
|---|---|---|---|---|
| Age-group | | | | |
| 60–64 | 0.3240 | 0.4682 | 0.3488 | 0.4767 |
| 65–69 | 0.2976 | 0.4574 | 0.2499 | 0.4331 |
| 70–74 | 0.1776 | 0.3823 | 0.1904 | 0.3927 |
| Currently married (yes = 1; no = 0) | 0.7936 | 0.4049 | 0.4014 | 0.4903 |
| Buddhist (yes = 1; no = 0) | 0.9016 | 0.2980 | 0.9125 | 0.2826 |
| Educational attainment | | | | |
| Grade 1–3 | 0.1592 | 0.3660 | 0.0938 | 0.2916 |
| Grade 4 | 0.3096 | 0.4625 | 0.1698 | 0.3756 |
| Grade 5 and over | 0.1328 | 0.3395 | 0.0263 | 0.1601 |
| Other education | 0.0688 | 0.2532 | 0.0137 | 0.1164 |
| Urban residence (urban = 1; rural = 0) | 0.2456 | 0.4306 | 0.2624 | 0.4401 |
| Number of consumer durable goods | 4.0880 | 2.5010 | 3.8479 | 2.5074 |
| Number of living children | 5.1080 | 2.8291 | 4.6461 | 2.6177 |
| Pension (main income source = 1; otherwise = 0) | 0.0608 | 0.2391 | 0.0858 | 0.0922 |
| Health status Healthy (yes = 1; no = 0) | 0.6312 | 0.4827 | 0.5855 | 0.4928 |

[a]Sample size, $N = 1,250$.
[b]Sample size, $N = 1,749$.

developmental factors will affect Thailand's future labour supply among old people. Further improvements in health status, which are closely intertwined with socio-economic development, will lead to a rise in the participation of the elderly in the labour force. This positive effect upon labour force participation among the aged is likely to be offset to some extent by an increase in urbanization and the coverage of pension schemes, both of which are expected to grow rapidly in the 1990s and beyond (Cho and Bauer, 1987; Pernia, 1988; Kiranandana, Wongboonsin, and Kiranandana, 1988). The net effect of these positive and negative impacts on participation is directly dependent upon Thailand's future demographic and socio-economic developments.

For South Korea, parallel to the Thai case, three labour force participation equations have been estimated, that is, one for the whole sample, another for males only, and the other for females only. Because the health status variable has proved to have a significant effect upon participation in only the male equation, the discussion is confined to the estimated results for the male case (Table 12.10). (The means and standard deviations of the explanatory variables are shown in Table 12.11.)

As indicated in Table 12.10, the estimated coefficient for the health status variable has a positive sign, and it is statistically significant at the 10 per cent level with a one-tail test. The elderly with good health status have a higher probability (0.112) of being in the work-force than those with poor health status. Although this computed probability is slightly lower than that for the Thai male case, it is still substantial. Thus, further health investment in the South Korean elderly is likely to lead to a considerable increase in labour supply, all else being equal.

A large impact upon participation is generated by the urban–rural classificatory variable. Those residing in urban areas, compared with their counterparts in rural areas, have a much lower probability (−0.962) of working in the labour force. Similar to the Thai case, both a respondent's age and marital status have a considerable impact on participation. Unlike the results for the Thai analysis, neither the pension variable nor the number of living children has entered into the equation.

Although the female participation equation has been estimated for the

TABLE 12.10
Logit Regressions Coefficients for Labour Force Participation of Old Males Aged 60 and Over: South Korea

|  | Parameter Estimates and Test of Significance | |
| --- | --- | --- |
| Explanatory Variable | Coefficients | t-statistics |
| Intercept | 1.8846 | 2.839 |
| Age-group | | |
| 60–64 | 2.0575 | 3.998 |
| 65–69 | 0.8500 | 1.657 |
| 70–74 | 0.6480 | 1.244 |
| Currently married | 0.6577 | 1.414 |
| Buddhist | 0.3066 | 1.974 |
| Educational attainment | | |
| Primary school | −0.5635 | −1.376 |
| Middle school | −0.5682 | −1.097 |
| High school and over | −0.0456 | −0.110 |
| Urban residence | −4.0595 | −6.949 |
| Pension | −1.4004 | −1.148 |
| Health status | | |
| Healthy | 0.4719 | 1.520 |
| Log-likelihood | −145.43 | |

Note: Sample size, $N = 344$.

## TABLE 12.11
### Means and Standard Deviations of Explanatory Variables Introduced into the Participation Equation: South Korea

| Explanatory Variable | Mean | Standard Deviation |
|---|---|---|
| Age-group | | |
| 60–64 | 0.3314 | 0.4714 |
| 65–69 | 0.2936 | 0.4561 |
| 70–74 | 0.2006 | 0.4010 |
| Currently married (yes = 1; no = 0) | 0.8808 | 0.3249 |
| Buddhist (yes = 1; no = 0) | 0.2791 | 0.4492 |
| Educational attainment | | |
| Primary school | 0.3081 | 0.4624 |
| Middle school | 0.0988 | 0.2989 |
| High school and over | 0.1686 | 0.3750 |
| Urban residence (urban = 1; rural = 0) | 0.6337 | 0.4825 |
| Pension | 0.0145 | 0.1199 |
| (main income source = 1; otherwise = 0) | | |
| Health status | | |
| Healthy (yes = 1; no = 0) | 0.6599 | 0.4744 |

*Note*: Sample size, $N = 344$.

South Korean case, only age and urban–rural residence have shown statistically significant effects. In the case of Thailand, the effect of women's health status variable upon their participation was rather small but statistically significant. In contrast, in the case of South Korea, it was not significantly different from zero. Moreover, the logit regressions have been undertaken for urban and rural samples separately, but the results have remained unchanged.

In addition to these logit regressions, an attempt was made to estimate a few alternative cases for both the Thai and South Korean data sets. For instance, incorporated in the regression was the health status variable that measures a respondent's activities of daily living (ADL), but the computed results are basically the same as those presented. Following some of the earlier studies (Stern, 1989), the presence of interaction between sex and marital status was tested. No significant effect, however, has been detected. It is often hypothesized that the better the income position, the less likely the elderly are to stay in the labour force. To test the validity of this hypothesis, per capita household income has been introduced in an alternative regression, but the estimated results have been different between the two countries: the negative effect for Thailand and the positive effect for South Korea. More importantly, labour force participation and income are endogenous, and directions of causation are difficult to determine. Due to the lack of powerful instrument variables in the data sets at hand, however, the writers could not conduct any endogeneity tests.

## Conclusion

The discussions and analyses presented in this chapter have indicated the predominant role played by families in providing both economic and non-economic support to the elderly in the developing countries along the Asia–Pacific Rim. However, as represented by their high labour force participation rates by international standards, a substantial proportion of old Asians along the Rim support themselves through employment.

The empirical results show that the health status of the elderly is one of the key variables affecting whether or not they participate in the labour force. This impact of the health variable upon participation is particularly pronounced in the case of old men in both Thailand and South Korea. In view of the fact that life expectancy at birth for both sexes combined is 65 years for Thailand and 70 years for South Korea (United Nations, 1989c), both countries are likely to undergo substantial improvements in mortality and morbidity at older ages in the 1990s and beyond. For this reason, the positive impact of the improved health status of the elderly upon their participation will be increasingly important in these countries.

However, the estimated results also show that there are several other factors likely to affect significantly the labour supply of the elderly. These factors include the age and sex compositional shifts of the aged, their marital status, the declining informal family support for the elderly by adult children, urbanization, and the gradual improvements of pension programmes. Because the labour force participation rate of the elderly declines with age, and the ageing process of these countries is expected to accelerate in the 1990s and beyond, the overall labour force participation rate of old persons in each country may decline substantially as each approaches, the end of its demographic transition. Moreover, because old men show a higher participation rate than old women, the projected predominance of the latter relative to the former is likely to further depress the overall labour force participation rate among the elderly. In contrast, both the elderly's marital status and the number of their living children, if their trends persist, are likely to contribute to raising the probability of old people being in the labour force. The last two factors, which are influenced by socio-economic development, generate a positive impact on the labour supply of the elderly. If these cross-sectional results hold over time, the net effect of these variables upon the labour supply of old people is subject to the extent to which each of them will change in the 1990s and in the early part of the twenty-first century.

It is often argued that older individuals have fewer years of life remaining, and thus, less time to enjoy the flow of utility resulting from a health investment (Grossman, 1972). Assuming that the primary effect of health care is to increase the amount of healthy time rather than the total amount of time (that is, the length of life) available to an individual, economic theory predicts, *ceteris paribus*, a smaller investment by older individuals in health care (Clark, Kreps, and Spengler, 1978). In both Thailand and South Korea, however, labour demand has been growing very rapidly due to their remarkable economic growth in the 1980s, and there has been an acute shortage of young workers as a result of expanded enrolment in higher learning and the secular decline of fertility. Although women's increased labour force participation has been substantially alleviating such labour shortage, if rapid economic growth persists in these countries, demand for elderly workers is likely to rise considerably in the 1990s and beyond. For this reason, one can expect that elderly manpower will constitute an increasingly vital component of human resources in these countries, and thus, the importance of medical and health care for the elderly will be enhanced with the passage of time.

In order to maximize the utilization of an old but useful work-force, appropriate policy measures and programmes designed to keep labour force participation among the elderly at a high level should be implemented in the course of future development in the developing countries along the Rim. A gradual shift in retirement age is a salient example. In most of the countries along the Rim, the retirement age in 1990 was 60. As their ageing process advances, it should be raised to a higher age. This shift, however, requires changes in various factors related to the labour market, including the wage system. In view of Japan's experience with the extension of retirement age since the 1960s, however, this is not an easy task (Martin and Ogawa, 1988). In this context, Japanese experiences can be used as a lesson for other Asian countries along the Rim whose populations are expected to age rapidly in the 1990s and beyond.

As mentioned earlier, there are a number of indications that as a consequence of fertility and mortality declines, coupled with rapid industrialization and urbanization, family size and structure have already been shifting in many Asian countries along the Rim, and thus, the pattern of support systems, both personal and public, has been shifting since the 1970s and 1980s. In the 1990s and beyond, the role of public support for the elderly is likely to become increasingly important, relative to family support. However, the availability of resources through the public support system is still severely limited in most of these developing nations. For instance, advocates for the expansion of health and social services for the elderly face tough questioning from those responsible for national budgets, who must weigh many competing claims on scarce budgetary resources (Gibson, 1988). In the case of Malaysia, for instance, owing to the high cost of hospital use and technology in the care of an ever increasing elderly population, the share of total government medical expenditure in GNP increased from 1.51 per cent in 1970 to 3.53 per cent in 1980. As a result, the Malaysian government has recently started exploring the possibility of privatizing medical care services (Ogawa, 1985b). Similarly, the privatization of medical care services is one of the policy options being considered by the Thai government; total government health care expenditures were 1.17 per cent of GNP in 1979, growing to 1.43 per cent in 1983 (Ogawa, Poapongsakorn, and Mason, 1989). Depending upon policies to be adopted by these developing nations along the Rim, further improvement in the health status of the elderly is likely to be seriously affected, which will, in turn, influence the future pattern of their labour supply.

# 13
# Summary and Synthesis: Towards a Model of the Asia–Pacific Rim Success Story and the Role of Human Resources

Warren C. Robinson

THE 'Pacific Century' may or may not be on the verge of dawning but there is no gainsaying the remarkable economic achievements since the 1950s by the nations of the Asia–Pacific Rim—East and South-East Asia. These nations, remarkably diverse in terms of natural endowment, culture, religion, and other factors, have achieved the economic take-off which eludes most of the rest of what used to be called the Third World. What explains this success and what lessons are to be learned from it? This is the basic question which motivates the chapters presented in this volume. They all share an assumption that human resource factors (population size, growth distribution, and health education and utilization) are somehow crucial in the answer to the question.

This chapter will attempt an overview and synthesis of the very diverse material presented in the 12 separate essays presented thus far (excepting, of course, the Introduction). The first section briefly reviews the individual contributions and highlights what each contributes to the cumulative framework of data and ideas which this symposium is attempting to construct. The second section presents the main themes and integrates them into a single general scheme which explains the success stories as well as the failures and which has at least potential application to other regions.

## The Individual Contributions

Part I presents an overview of the trends and major movements of demographic, economic, and human resource-related indicators in the Asia–Pacific Rim countries.

In Chapter 2, Ogawa and Tsuya focus on the relationship between macroeconomic trends and demographic changes. They find a growing diversity and divergence of trends when the four subregions (East Asia,

South-East Asia, South Asia, and Oceania) are compared. Nearly all the nations of the larger region began at about the same economic and demographic position in 1945 at the end of World War II. With the exception of some parts of Oceania, nearly all were poor, technologically-backward, and demographically pre-transition, high-fertility populations. The decades that followed have seen remarkable changes. Considering the region as a whole, mortality has fallen as has fertility. Urbanization and industrialization have proceeded rapidly and per capita incomes have risen sharply.

East Asia led the way in this transition, with South-East Asia a decade or two behind. Both threaten to overtake Australia and New Zealand now. South Asia, on the other hand, has lagged behind the other sub-regions and made much less progress. This then is the first question which emerges from the data: What explains this striking contrast between South Asia and the rest of Asia? The chapter suggests that superior human resource investments going back well before the period of rapid growth since 1960 are a large part of the answer.

Secondly, Ogawa and Tsuya bring into sharp focus the anomalous case of the Philippines. Possessing a superior human resource base and enjoying a favourable growth rate early in the post-World War II period, it has nevertheless fallen behind other South-East Asian countries and stagnated for most of the 1980s. It remains a relatively poor, high-fertility country. Misguided policies and deeply rooted cultural and institutional barriers to change are both presented as possible explanations.

Finally, what is the explanation for the almost unbelievable economic recovery of Japan and its continued economic dominance of the entire region? Ogawa and Tsuya suggest that Japan, indeed, provides a classic example of the overwhelming importance of the human resource factor in explaining growth. But, social, cultural, and institutional factors also seem to be involved.

All in all, Chapter 2 identifies the major questions suggested by a study of the data and guided the discussion of the other chapters throughout the volume.

Campbell's Chapter 3 presents a wealth of data and analytical insights into the way in which economic growth has unfolded in the countries of the Asia–Pacific Rim. While he notes that 'easy generalizations do not seem likely' he nevertheless makes some useful ones.

First, the rapid increase in the labour force in the early decades of development was a positive growth factor for many nations since it meant a dependable supply of labour at relatively low wages. In most of the successful nations the labour force already embodied previous human resource investments (education and health) and hence was flexible and productive.

Secondly, in the most successful cases, as growth occurred the capital per worker, GNP per worker, and also GNP per unit of capital all rose. This can be due only to rapid technological change and/or increasing returns to scale. Campbell suggests that the unevenness of the experience in the region, particularly the poor record of South Asian nations, means that the 'relative effectiveness of economic organization on adaption of technology' is an important qualitative factor.

Thirdly, some old truisms still seem to hold. Governments do seem to respond to the demand for services which rapid population growth helps create and this competes with efficient use of resources. Similarly, further increases in per capita income for the successful nations of the region will still depend upon high savings and investment rates to finance the jump to new high-technology industrial bases.

Campbell also reviews the whole range of government policy interventions which have affected economic performance of the countries in the region. His conclusions are quite consistent with conventional wisdom but worth repeating all the same. The countries with favourable growth records tend to be the ones in which: (i) the government has a small share of GDP and investment; (ii) there are not chronic public budget deficits and public borrowing is a small share of gross domestic investment; (iii) increases in the money supply parallel increases in real output; (iv) the real interest rate is positive and bears at least some relationship to the real scarcity price of capital; (v) the government has attempted to maintain international competitiveness by exchange rate changes as and when needed; and (vi) a generally export-led open economy trade policy has been followed.

In other words, policy has mattered and the laggard cases (most of South Asia and the Philippines) have in retrospect pursued wrong, or at least, different policies than the successful cases of East and South-East Asia. Campbell does not deal with non-economic areas of policy but he could have added that most of the success stories also launched vigorous public sector family planning programmes early in their development which complemented already existing health and education programmes.

Campbell concludes:

In the long run, a country's development history and the contribution of demographic factors to that history depends on the initial resources available, on how technological change affects the relative value of these resources, and on the social and political institutions that shape the way a country utilizes its initial endowments to achieve growth. Within the framework established by these long-run factors, ... it is clear greater openness and less government intervention are positively related to higher economic growth and ... better economic performance....

Part II contains four chapters, each developing different aspects of the theme, human capital formation and labour market interactions.

In Chapter 4, Williamson deals with the issue of human capital deepening, economic inequality, and demographic events in the nations of the region. He begins by relating the issue at hand to the paradigm of endogenous growth theory, formulated in the mid-1980s, which argues that the initial factor endowment (capital–labour ratio) guides all subsequent economic changes. Thus, population size and growth, while endogenous, are important factors structuring the path and pace of economic change. The case of Japan is used as an example. A significant share of its abnormally rapid growth rate in the first several decades after World War II was due to the transitory but highly positive effect of rapid increases in the labour force. The Denison–Chung growth accounting analysis is cited in this connection. Demographic factors impacted on economic growth positively.

Yet labour supply alone was not enough to ensure success. The pointed question is how and why a high-quality labour force was created in Japan and not in, say, India. Williamson asks: 'What attributes of earlier economic and social history explain the above average commitment to human resource development, like schooling, in some countries and the below average in others?'

Williamson next turns to the impact of demographic factors on the savings rate, and looks at two possible linkages. First, he finds that there is evidence that a high dependency ratio, typically the result of high fertility, has been negatively correlated with the savings rate in the countries of the region. This must be taken with caution, however, and related to other factors such as the real interest rate, the demand for investment, and the openness of the economy to foreign capital inflow.

Second, citing earlier work by Schultz and Ram, he notes the possibility that increasing life expectancy could explain the growing propensity of parents to invest in human capital inputs for their children. Thus, improving mortality conditions promotes human capital accumulation, resulting in further improvements in mortality as well as economic growth.

His final theme is the link between growth and economic inequality. He notes the sharp divergence of opinion between the classical (Adam Smith, etc.) model which sees unequal income distribution as the engine of growth (through creation of an investable surplus of savings over consumption needs for the wealthy) and the modern McNamara World Bank School which sees more equal distribution of income as a prerequisite for sustained growth. Without accepting that it is a necessary condition for growth, he finds that for the Asia–Pacific countries, equity and growth have been positively correlated.

Williamson says: 'The four fast growers in East Asia had half the inequality than did the four slow growers in East Asia, and all eight of these East Asian countries had less than half the inequality than did the eight much slower growing Latin American countries.'

Many factors have entered into this greater equity including early land reform measures, the technological bias towards small-scale holdings which rice cultivation seems to display, the losses suffered by entrenched economic interests as a result of World War II, and strong pressures towards representative governments from Western interests.

Most important of all has been the early commitment of these nations to mass education, health, and other human services. The question posed above comes to the fore again. But Williamson does not have an easy answer. He finds that: 'Culture does matter...' particularly in Latin

America and South Asia when compared to East and South-East Asia. Mass education in these areas is not a recent development policy but goes back well before World War II. If these differences are not cultural, what then are they?

Chapter 5, by Pernia examines the growth performance of Indonesia, the Philippines, and Thailand focusing particularly on the human resource inputs. This chapter is, in effect, three case-studies illustrating the relationships sketched out in broad terms in the earlier chapters by Campbell and Williamson.

Generally speaking, Thailand has done well, the Philippines poorly, and Indonesia somewhere in between. All have invested heavily in human resources. The Philippines actually seem to have had a head start in these areas yet the best that Pernia can say is that: 'Without the relatively strong human capital base, the performance of the Philippine economy could in all likelihood have been worse.' The Philippine experience is attributable to 'inappropriate policies and economic mismanagement' which have in turn led to political instability and a hardening of class lines.

Chapter 6 by Lim deals with the special human resource and labour market issues arising from participation by women. She argues that, to an extent not generally recognized, female labour helped fuel the East and South-East Asian economic miracles. This labour—flexible, docile, low cost, and possessing 'unique human resource qualities'—has typically been preferred to males by the employers in the export-oriented light manufacturing, textile, and electronics industries. These industries have been the leading edge of industrial transformation and hence female labour has played a crucial role.

Women have also played a big role in the growth of public services, particularly health and education, and other occupations which were seen as extensions of the traditional nurturing roles, agriculture and services, where they replaced men shifting to other jobs or working abroad. In spite of a lower than average human capital investment per female worker than male, their productivity is comparable. Their wages are lower and this encourages firms to reinvest and grow. Moreover, no cultural bias against female work outside the home has impeded these patterns.

Women have, however, tended to remain marginal workers, with lower average hours of work, uncertain tenure, and poor long-run prospects for retirement. When recession and economic readjustments cause a crunch they get 'crunched' first and hardest. These facts seem beyond dispute.

Since the 1980s, women have also played a dominant role in many of the international streams of labour migration which have provided substantial foreign exchange for the developing countries of South-East Asia. Their conditions in these situations have frequently been even more deplorable yet the volume of migration is growing.

These special vulnerabilities make a powerful case for more special protective legislation and supportive policies by the public sector. However, the current swing towards deregulation and away from public sector interventions make these prospects uncertain at best. Lim proposes that, at the least, encouragement should be given to female-oriented unions, voluntary associations, and self-help groups which can collectively pursue remedies not available to individuals.

From the overall standpoint of human resources and population trends, some of the facets revealed in this chapter are highly interesting. Most countries of East and South-East Asia have always had high female labour force participation (by international standards) and also relatively high female literacy. They were thus better equipped than other groups to enter the labour market in a big way when rising age at marriage, declining fertility, and a growing culture of consumerism made this an easier and more attractive prospect. Which caused which cannot, in all honesty, be sorted out.

The final chapter in Part II, Chapter 7 by Furuya and Clark, is another excellent case-study, this time of Japan.

Clearly, the chapter indicates, human resources must explain a large share of Japanese economic growth. These authors also note the favourable quantitative effects of the large baby boom cohorts from just after World War II in providing a spurt to the labour force just as growth was accelerating. But, the long-standing commitment to education meant that this was a good quality, productive labour force, male and female.

The high levels of productivity attained in Japan are explained to a degree by these overall social investments. But, other more qualitative elements are also explored, including effective management, team work on the job, lower job turnover, and considerable on-the-job training. These last two points interact since the famous lifetime employment agreements between a company and its workers have led companies to make considerable firm-specific investments in their workers, further raising the quality of the human capital and its productivity.

Japan now faces a new challenge, which will soon be faced by other countries of the region—an ageing labour force. In principle, Japanese workers as of the late 1980s retire early (aged 55–60) and contracts could be modified to increase the retirement age. However, wages go up with age and seniority. Hence, older workers are more expensive and typically lower in education and productivity. Hence, the ageing labour force seems certain to increase Japanese labour costs and affect their international competitiveness. The only other solution would appear to be allowing more labour migration from other countries of the region. The chapter does not explore this point.

The final conclusion has an ominous ring to it: 'To a considerable degree, the future economic success of Japan will depend on its ability to adapt to an ageing labour force.'

Part III presents case-studies of the interaction of education with development in two countries of the region—Indonesia (Chapter 8 by Jones), Malaysia (Chapter 10 by Demery and Chesher), and for the region as a whole (Chapter 9 by Mason). All are guided by the theoretical considerations sketched out in the earlier chapters and focus on education, human resource, economic, and demographic interaction.

Jones takes up the interesting but neglected topic of possible overinvestment in education by countries of South-East Asia, focusing particularly on Indonesia. The problem, as he presents it, is that within the region governments and individuals fail to see that what worked in the past may not work in the future. 'A dramatically different age-education profile' labour force is emerging. A person 'leaving the work-force is likely to be illiterate; three of four persons replacing him will have a high school education'. These illustrations are for Indonesia but they fit other countries as well.

The demand for education is very great and it is popular both with the public and with governments. The demand for educated workers is not so great, however, and already is beginning to fall behind supply. The experience of other countries, notably India which is famous for unemployed graduates, is illuminating. Under such labour market conditions, wage differentials by education narrow and long waiting periods between graduation and employment result. So also does a growing upgrading of the credentials required by employers even if the job content remains the same. This is inappropriate utilization of resources and, in effect, a waste of the human capital involved. (It is interesting to recall that the original use of the term 'disguised unemployment' was to describe highly skilled workers doing unskilled jobs due to depressed economic conditions in the Great Depression.)

The chapter illustrates this likely outcome for Indonesia by projecting the labour force by educational attainment, given educational trends of the late 1980s compared to projected employment needs by major industrial and occupational groupings. The results indicate that by the year 2010 some 500,000 workers will have to seek jobs which are below their skill level. Many will have to remain in agriculture and services.

The only solutions, as Jones sees it, are for the professional, managerial, and clerical categories to grow more rapidly and for the real skill content of many jobs to be raised by deliberate adoption of new high-technology methods. There seems no escaping the fact that the flow of graduates will increase and that aspirations will remain high. The trick in policymaking is to see that these relentless forces are channelled into avenues and usages which raise productivity and sustain future growth. Identifying the problem is a start.

Mason's focus in Chapter 9 is the impact of fertility decline on the educational achievement of children. He looks cross-sectionally in particular at Thailand and South Korea for the 1970–80 period using HOMES, a macroeconomic household-based projections model he developed in the mid-1980s. He concludes:

South Korea's and Thailand's experience provides considerable, if not conclusive, support for the view that the fertility declines experienced there have increased the resources available for investment in the human resource development of children. Moreover, in both countries, households with fewer children have apparently been using the increased availability of resources to invest more in the schooling of their children.

But, he cautions that the causation is not established. Perhaps changing economic perceptions lead to a rise in the demand for education which in turn increases the cost of children and leads to a decline in fertility. The result would be the same but the direction of causation and the policy implications would be different.

The final chapter in Part III, Chapter 10 by Demery and Chesher, looks at the private returns to schooling for the male Chinese in Malaysia in 1983. They conclude that: (i) returns rise with the level of schooling; (ii) returns are lower for the self-employed than for paid employees; (iii) returns are lowered by failure to complete final examinations and obtain credentials; and (iv) schooling lowers the probability of self-employment but failure to obtain credentials raises this probability.

Schooling thus seems to serve, among other purposes, as a way of sorting out who will go into which occupations. The writers say: 'These results may be viewed as offering some support for the screening hypothesis of the effect of schooling on earnings.'

Finally, Part IV presents two chapters which explore new health problems which are emerging in the maturing economies of the Asia–Pacific Rim.

Chapter 11, by Tsuya, Ogawa, Chayovan, and Siriboon, deals with the interactions between general socio-economic development, child health care, and infant mortality in Thailand. The chapter is, in effect, a re-examination of the relative importance of general socio-economic development versus specific health interventions in causing decline in infant and child mortality. It uses data from the 1987 Thailand Demographic and Health Survey (TDHS) and data from the 1975 Survey of Fertility in Thailand (SOFT), supplemented with trend data on changes in socio-economic development indicators. The analysis thus was able to deal with a battery of both 'supply-side' variables to measure the strength of health interventions and also a wide range of individual and community development indicators.

This analysis showed that the relative importance of the two sets of forces probably changed during the developments of the mid-1970s to late 1980s. 'The infant mortality effects of mother's age at childbirth and mother's employment status changed significantly under the overall socio-economic development and improvements of health care systems in Thailand during the 1970s and 1980s.' But 'such covariates as breast-feeding, maternal education, and birth order continue to affect infant mortality significantly'.

The final conclusions reinforce anew the conventional wisdom: breast-feeding, maternal education, and birth spacing remain important determinants of infant mortality. However, there is ample scope for public programmes to target particular groups and areas in which infant mortality remains high and where general socio-economic development lags. Effective policy must utilize both approaches.

Finally, Chapter 12, by Ogawa, Tsuya, Wongsith, and Choe, deals with the health status and labour force participation of the elderly in the developing countries of the Asia–Pacific Rim. These writers document anew the rapid increases in the relative proportion of the population aged 65 and over which are expected in these countries up to the year 2020 as a result of the declines in both mortality and fertility. These changes are occurring more rapidly than they did in the West and in some cases at a lower level of overall urbanization and industrialization; both of these factors will make the adjustment process more difficult. Most surveys indicate that the rural elderly tend to work longer, be healthier, and have more access to familial support than their urban Western counterparts.

This chapter also examines the paradigm suggested by Cowgill and Holmes that modernization tends to shift responsibility for care of the elderly from the family to the state. Thus far, little support for this notion has emerged in the Asia–Pacific countries. Most support and most health care are still fully dependent on the elderly themselves and their family. As the ratio of elderly to labour force-aged persons rises within the average household, this may very well require greater public programme supplementation, however.

A careful empirical investigation is undertaken of the interaction between health status and labour force participation in two countries, Thailand and South Korea. As expected, health status of the elderly is one of the key variables affecting whether or not they participate in the labour force. 'However other factors also appear significant, including age and sex composition, marital status, urbanization, growth of public pension programmes, and family support mechanism.'

All in all, the chapter seems to predict a continual high labour force participation by the elderly due to improving health status, rising retirement age, and decline in the relative proportion of younger family members to provide support. The recent push for privatization of such programmes adds an imponderable but potentially significant factor to the future economic status and role of the elderly.

*Proposed Synthesis*

Most authors are cautious about drawing generalizations and that is both understandable and commendable. But, it still seems useful to attempt to step back, as it were, and see if any common elements or factors have emerged from the various historical case-studies.

The success of this region should provide a unique opportunity to test development theories or even to construct a new one. This section does neither but it makes a tentative first step towards the latter.

When one approaches generalizations about the economic and demographic developments in the region one naturally turns to the existing development theories, paradigms, and models for guidance. Without pretending to have conducted an exhaustive search, nevertheless, given the obvious importance of population change and also technological change in these processes, the present writer found the various theoretical propositions advanced by Boserup to be the most helpful.[1]

To recapitulate briefly, Boserup argues that population growth is frequently the driving force behind technological change. More particularly, she says, the 'answer' to population growth can be: (i) emigration and/or foreign conquest of new lands; (ii) fertility control; (iii) technological change; and (iv) no response and hence a declining standard of living. To these, this writer believes a fifth can be added; (v) a rearrangement of distribution so as to squeeze the cultivating worker masses to maintain the standard of living of the élite.

Boserup feels that, by and large, technological change is more likely to be chosen since the others have obvious limitations and drawbacks. On

FIGURE 13.1
The Asia–Pacific Model of Successful Development

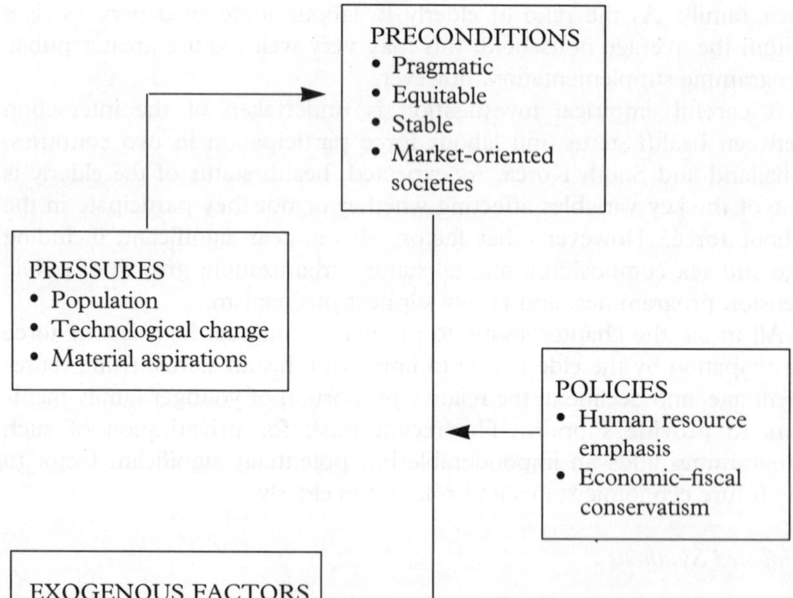

PRECONDITIONS
- Pragmatic
- Equitable
- Stable
- Market-oriented societies

PRESSURES
- Population
- Technological change
- Material aspirations

POLICIES
- Human resource emphasis
- Economic–fiscal conservatism

EXOGENOUS FACTORS
- Economic opportunities and windfalls
- Liberalization of world trade

Sustained socio-economic development and demographic transition the other hand, she is vague about how this works exactly, that is, how at the micro-level the process of technological change occurs or how it is linked to the growing population pressure.

This model can be adapted to the East and South-East Asian experience so as to permit a construction of a tentative general paradigm. Figure 13.1 presents such an effort. Three factors are applying 'pressure': population growth, autonomous technological changes occurring outside the region, and rising consumer aspirations. Two other important parameters also play a role: the favourable external trade regimes and the exogenous 'shocks' which gave further impetus to the forward thrust of the economies.

Two policy variables are also seen as having an input—micro-economic policy and political leadership, and human resource policies. All these variables act upon and interact with the existing socio-cultural setting or preconditions.

*Precondition/Setting Factors*

One important conclusion which emerges is that certain preconditions existed in these countries which made rapid development possible, if not easy, once certain external pressures and forces came to bear. Three such setting factors were identified.

First, there has existed a social consensus such that the various classes and groups within the societies believed there was reciprocity and equity in the overall ordering of things. The societies were highly stratified but clients and patrons found it possible to work together for shared advantage in an atmosphere of mutual respect. Class lines were not rigid and upward economic mobility was possible. The most successful nations have also been the ones with the greatest internal unity and homogeneity, culturally and ethnically.

Women in most of these nations always worked outside the home, had some access to resources, and enjoyed a degree of social equity superior to their sisters in many other parts of the world.

A link between this social consensus and the Confucian ethic, or the alleged Asian instinctive acceptance of authority, is tempting but probably wrong. Such an ethic used to be cited as a reason that Asia could not and would not develop. The message really seems to be that economic development is made easier by social institutions which make for smooth, relatively harmonious day to day relationships among classes and groups, leading everyone to feel a sense of participation.

Policies have also followed this tradition, and have resulted in opening new opportunities and providing new options and not merely redistributing existing wealth. Improvements in the distribution of measured income have lagged but they have occurred. Land reform measures were important in several countries, both substantively to encourage rising output and also as symbols of the government desire for egalitarian development.

Secondly, a tradition of entrepreneurship has existed and the desire for personal and family gain was a legitimate and even praiseworthy motivation. In some cases, this tradition was centred in particular classes, groups, or lines of economic activity. But, 'rational calculation' was widespread and where traditional parasitic nobilities did exist they were swept away quickly by the forces of modernization. The rulers and the élite understood that the commercial and entrepreneurial class was useful and hence this group was a part of the social consensus. Public sector economic ventures tended to be in areas requiring a totally new technology imported from abroad—railways, electrical power, etc., but they never became the preferred way for economic activity.

Thirdly, geographic and historical factors resulted in most of the countries having at least a degree of outward orientation. Early efforts at modernization created a need for imports and an exportable surplus of primary products was called forth in exchange. This early export orientation created experience and skill in dealing with the world market on the part of the traditional entrepreneurial class. The outward orientation also extended to technologies and institutions. Western advisers were accepted, students sent abroad to study Western technology, and local institutions—universities, medical schools, etc.—established to reproduce that education. A pragmatic and flexible approach was evident in dealing with alien ideas and forces.

On balance, these countries were relatively stable politically and economically, had a durable but flexible social hierarchy with an internal consensus, and a higher status for women; had an entrepreneurial tradition and a respect for property; made early commitments to human capital creation and to equitable distribution policies; and had an outward orientation, both in terms of imports and exports and in terms of ideas and technologies. These elements created the potential for rapid development economically, but they did not guarantee it.

*Pressures for Change*

When growth occurred it was in response to what may be called pressures or shocks which called forth a response from these nations.

The first of these pressures was the upsurge of population which occurred as death rates fell sharply after World War II. The traditional rural societies quickly began to run out of land and pressures were felt to transform the economies to urban-based industry.

Secondly, enormous and almost continuous world-wide technological changes began occurring by the 1960s. The nations of the Pacific Rim were beginning almost from scratch with no obsolescent plants to worry about phasing out. (Japan had lost most of its ageing physical capital and was in virtually the same position.) This technology was almost a free good since neither the United States nor Europe took industrial competition from Asia seriously. Later the growth of multinational corporations seeking low-wage labour intensified the technology transfer.

Hence, the late-starters had a distinct advantage.

Thirdly, the revolution of rising expectations and a culture of endless consumerism infected the people of those nations creating a strong motivation for increased money income and material goods. Exposure to Western media—television, movies, advertising—was a major part of this process. Such aspirations resulted in rapid changes in the values of the societies, including a shift to a small-family norm and subsequent declines in fertility.

*Policy Inputs*

Early policy commitment to the development of broadly based education and health programmes paid rich dividends. In most cases, this commitment was not motivated by a conscious economic development thrust but by a much more vague desire to modernize. This policy was in complete accord with a traditional high regard and even veneration of education. By the beginning of the conscious push for economic development in the 1950s and 1960s, a substantial stock of human capital had already been accumulated and literacy and numeracy were widespread.

Public programmes aimed at controlling population growth were adopted early by these nations, leading to declining fertility just as subsequent economic growth became rapid.

Secondly, political, economic, and social stability and conservatism have been an important feature. With one or two exceptions, these nations have avoided prolonged inflation, currency collapses, or systemic budget deficits due to populist economic policies. This has encouraged domestic savings and investment and has also attracted investment from abroad.

This conservatism has also meant tight constraints on wages, making the nations competitive in world market. While these policies have frequently followed from the innate, traditional conservatism of the societies rather than deliberate economic policy, they have, all the same, paid off.

*Exogenous Factors*

Finally, a series of nearly random economic events occurred which offered sudden economic opportunities to these nations. These were: (i) the Korean War which sparked a commodity boom; (ii) the Vietnam War which channelled large amounts of American spending into the region; (iii) the Middle East employment from which resulted large remittances flowing to the nations; and (iv) the enormous expansion in world trade following liberalization by the developed states in the 1970s and 1980s.

All of these events provided opportunities which the countries involved were able to recognize and take advantage of. They were, in effect, windfalls which provided a sudden infusion of foreign exchange, and further opportunities to acquire technological skills. Taken in conjunction with fertility declines, the result was capital deepening and rising labour productivity and profitability of enterprise.

Some of these windfalls were specific to the region, or the location of a given country in the region, but some were not. The Middle East employment—remittance boom presumably should have provided a similar push for the Philippines or Pakistan but has evidently failed to do. Similarly, trade expansion has probably actually harmed, not helped, most Latin American nations.

*Summary*

Thus, it seems that four elements enter into the Asia–Pacific success story. First, a set of favourable preconditions arising from the social, political, and cultural settings; secondly wise (or lucky) early policy decisions which stressed creation of human capital and conservative economic policies; thirdly, a series of pressures or changes which shook up the *status quo* and forced new strategies and new institutions; and fourthly, a series of fortuitous external events which arose and provided windfall opportunities for the nations.

These factors interacted with one another and all were important. Without the favourable preconditions, the pressures and opportunities would lead nowhere. Without pressures, the pre-existing social structure may not feel the need to respond to opportunities. Opportunities may not present themselves or may be insufficient to deal with the pressures. In the Asia–Pacific region these elements combined to lead to success.

The final moral would seem to be the dominant importance of the preconditions. Economically stable, harmonious, productive societies seem to be able to cope and to take advantage of opportunities. This seems to argue for the structural adjustment approach of the International Monetary Fund (IMF) but it also seems that distributional equity and broad participation in growth are important. Market orientation and an acceptance of self-interest as the driving force of growth are the underlying attitudes required, and fertility control is very helpful.

Such a set of factors may or may not be attainable by or acceptable to countries of South Asia, the Middle East, or Africa. But if they wish to learn from Asia's success, this would seem to be the lesson.

## Conclusion: Next Steps in Research

What seems to be called for then is a series of closely linked country case-studies of representative nations in the region looking in greater depth at the dynamics of this growth process. These studies should focus on the issues which emerged in the present symposium including: (i) how and why the early policy commitment to a human resource strategy of development emerged; (ii) how policy managed to achieve rapid technological change and a reasonably equitable growth simultaneously; (iii) why the public sector–private sector co-operation worked so well; (iv) how the export orientation, with its accompanying risks and perils, was managed so well; and (v) the role of external shocks in the whole process.

All the participants in the symposium agreed that the present volume should be viewed as a beginning and that having identified the right questions, more work was needed to get the right answers.

1. Boserup first stated her model in *The Conditions of Agricultural Growth*. She elaborated on the theme in *Population and Technological Change*. A collection of essays and other papers on the same notion has also appeared in Schultz (1990).

# Bibliography

Abella, M. I. (1989), 'Asian Labour Migration: An Overview', *ARPLA Labour Administration Bulletin*, 2.
Adams, N. (1971), 'Dependency Rates and Savings Rates: Comment', *American Economic Review*, 61(3) (June): 472–5.
Ahluwalia, M. (1976), 'Inequality, Poverty and Development', *Journal of Development Economics*, 3: 307–42.
_____ (1980), 'Growth and Poverty in Developing Countries', in H. Chenery (ed.), *Structural Change and Development Policy*, New York: Oxford University Press, pp. 456–95.
Aldrich, John H. and Nelson, Forrest D. (1984), *Linear Probability, Logit, and Probit Models*, Sage University Paper Series No. 45, Beverly Hills: Sage Publications.
Anand, S. (1983), *Inequality and Poverty in Malaysia: Measurement and Decomposition*, Oxford: Oxford University Press.
Anderson, D. and Leiserson, M. W. (1980), 'Rural Nonfarm Employment in Developing Countries', *Economic Development and Cultural Change*, 28(2): 227–48.
Andrews, Gary R., Esterman, Adrian J., Braunack-Mayer, Annette J., and Rungie, Cam M. (1986), *Aging in the Western Pacific: A Four-Country Study*, Manila: World Health Organization Regional Office for the Western Pacific.
Anker, R. and Hein, C. (1985), *Employment of Women outside Agriculture in Third World Countries: An Overview of Occupational Statistics*, Population and Labour Policies Programme Working Paper No. 147, Geneva: International Labour Office.
_____ (eds.) (1986), *Sex Inequalities in Urban Employment in the Third World*, London: Macmillan.
Appleyard, R. T. (1984), 'International Migration in the ESCAP Region', in *Third Asian and Pacific Population Conference*, Bangkok: ESCAP, United Nations, pp. 212–37.
Ariff, M. and Hill, H. (1985), *Export-Oriented Industrialization: The ASEAN Experience*, Sydney: Allen and Unwin.
Ariffin, R. (1985), 'Retrenchment: An Exploratory Study of the Retrenchment Experience of the Textile and Electronics Workers in Penang', Mimeo, Penang, School of Social Sciences, Universiti Sains Malaysia.
Arndt, Heinz W. (1987), *Economic Development: The History of an Idea*, Chicago: University of Chicago Press.
Arnold, Fred and Liu, Zhaoxiang (1986), 'Sex Preference, Fertility, and Family Planning in China', *Population and Development Review*, 12(2): 221–45.

# BIBLIOGRAPHY

Arriaga, E. E. (1970), *Mortality Decline and Its Demographic Effects in Latin America*, Population Monograph Series No. 6, Berkeley: University of California Press.

Arrow, K. J. (1962), 'The Economic Implications of Learning by Doing', *Review of Economic Studies*, 29(3): 155–73.

Asian Development Bank (1983–9), *Asian Development Review*, 1–7, Manila.

⎯⎯⎯ (1986–9), *Key Indicators of Developing Member Countries of ADB*, Manila.

⎯⎯⎯ (1988), *Education and Development in Asia and the Pacific*, Manila.

⎯⎯⎯ (1989, 1990), *Asian Development Outlook*, Manila.

Asian Development Bank, Economics Office (1985), *Improving Domestic Resource Mobilization through Financial Development*, Manila.

Azariadis, C. and Drazen, A. (1990), 'Threshold Externalities in Economic Development', *Quarterly Journal of Economics*, 105(2): 501–26.

Barro, R. J. (1989), 'Economic Growth in a Cross-section of Countries', Paper presented at the Conference on Human Capital and Growth, State University of New York, Buffalo, May.

⎯⎯⎯ (1991), *Economic Growth in a Cross-section of Countries*, NBER Working Paper No. 3120, Cambridge: National Bureau of Economic Research.

Bauer, John (forthcoming), *Children, Living Arrangements, and Female Labor Supply in Korea*, Honolulu: East–West Population Institute, East–West Center.

Bauer, John (1989), *Children, Living Arrangements, and Female Labor Supply in Korea*, Honolulu: East–West Population Institute, East–West Center.

East–West Population Institute, East–West Center.

Baumol, W. J., Blackman, S. A. B., and Wolff, E. N. (1989), *Productivity and American Leadership: The Long View*, Cambridge: MIT Press.

Bautista, Romeo M. (1987), *Production Incentives in Philippine Agriculture: Effects of Trade and Exchange Rate Policies*, Research Report 59, Washington, DC: International Food Policy Research Institute.

⎯⎯⎯ (1988), 'Agricultural Growth as a Development Strategy for the Philippines', *Philippines Economic Journal*, 27(1,2): 9–19.

Bautista, Romeo M. and Naya, S. (eds.) (1984), *Economic and Structural Change in the Asia–Pacific Region*, Manila: Philippine Institute for Development Studies and Asian Development Bank.

Bautista, Romeo M., Power, J. H., and Associates (1979), *Industrial Promotion Policies in the Philippines*, Manila: Philippine Institute for Development Studies.

Becker, Gary (1988), 'Family Economics and Macro Behavior', *American Economic Review*, 78(1): 1–13.

Becker, Gary and Murphy, K. M. (1988), 'Economic Growth, Human Capital, and Population Growth', Mimeo, University of Chicago.

Becker, R. A., Chambers, J. M., and Wilks, A. R. (1988), *The New S Language*, Pacific Grove, California: Wadsworth and Brooks/Cole.

Belassa, Bela (1988), 'The Lessons of East Asian Development: An Overview', *Economic Development and Cultural Change*, 36(3): S273–90.

Belmont, L. and Marolla, F. A. (1973), 'Birth Order, Family Size, and Intelligence', *Science*, 182(4117): 1096–101.

Berndt, E. R., Hall, B. H., Hall, R. E., and Hausman, J. A. (1974), 'Estimation and Inference in Non-linear Structural Models', *Annals of Economic and Social Measurement*, 3(4): 653–65.

Blaug, M. (1972), *An Introduction to the Economics of Education*, Baltimore: Penguin Books.

_____ (1985), 'Where Are We Now in the Economics of Education?', *Economics of Education Review*, 4(1): 17–28.
Blinder, A. S. (1975), 'Distribution Effects and the Aggregate Consumption Function', *Journal of Political Economy*, 83(3): 447–75.
Bongaarts, John (1978), 'A Framework for Analyzing the Proximate Determinants of Fertility', *Population and Development Review*, 4(1): 105–32.
_____ (1980), *The Fertility Inhibiting Effects of the Intermediate Fertility Variables*, Center for Policy Studies Working Paper No. 57, New York: Population Council.
Bongaarts, John and Menken, Jane (1983), 'The Supply of Children: A Critical Essay', in Rodolfo A. Bulatao and Ronald D. Lee (eds.), *Determinants of Fertility in Developing Countries*, Vol. 1, New York: Academic Press, pp. 27–60.
Booth, Anne (1989), 'Repelita V and Indonesia's Medium Term Economic Strategy', *Bulletin of Indonesian Economic Studies*, 25(2): 3–30.
Boserup, Ester (1965), *The Conditions of Agricultural Growth*, Chicago: Aldine.
_____ (1981), *Population and Technological Change*, Chicago: University of Chicago Press.
Boskin, Michael J. (1977), 'Social Security and Retirement Decisions', *Economic Inquiry*, 15: 2–25.
Boswell, J. (1972), *The Rise and Decline of Small Firms*, London: George Allen and Unwin.
Bradford, C. I. and Branson, W. H. (eds.) (1987), *Trade and Structural Change in Pacific Asia*, Chicago: University of Chicago Press.
Cajuguiran-Quiray, M. A. (1989), *Contract Migration of Filipino Women: The Issues and Policy Implications*, Trivandrum, India: Center for Development Studies.
Caldwell, J. C. (1979), 'Education as a Factor in Mortality Decline: An Examination of Nigerian Data', *Population Studies*, 23(3): 395–413.
_____ (1980), 'Mass Education as a Determinant of the Timing of Fertility Decline', *Population and Development Review*, 6(2): 225–55.
_____ (1982), *Theory of Fertility Decline*, London: Academic Press.
Campbell, B. O. (1982), 'Age Structure and Development in ASEAN and Japan, 1950–2015', in J. Encarnacion (ed.), *Growth and Development: Essays In Honor of Harry Oshima*, Manila: University of the Philippines Press.
_____ (1986), 'Trade between Asian Developing Countries: Record and Prospects', *Asian Development Review*, 4(2): 57–92.
_____ (1987), 'Asian and Pacific Developing Economies: Performance and Issues', *Asian Development Review*, 5(1): 1–43.
_____ (1988a), 'The Little Dragons Have Different Tales', *The World Economy*, 11(2): 305–10.
_____ (1988b), 'Increasing Protectionism and Its Implications for Asean–US Economic Relations' (with Dean DeRosa), in *Asean–US Economic Relations 11*, Singapore: Institute of Southeast Asian Studies.
Charlton, S. E. (1984), *Women in Third World Development*, Boulder: Westview Press.
Chayovan, Napaporn, Kamnuansilpa, Peerasit, and Knodel, John (1988), *Thailand Demographic and Health Survey 1987*, Bangkok: Institute of Population Studies, Chulalongkorn University.
Chayovan, Napaporn, Knodel, John, and Wongboonsin, Kua (1989), 'Infant Feeding Practices in Thailand: An Update from the 1987 Demographic and Health Survey', Unpublished manuscript, Institute of Population Studies, Chulalongkorn University.

Chayovan, Napaporn, Wongsith, Malinee, and Saengtienchai, Chanpen (1988), *Socio-Economic Consequences of the Ageing of the Population: Thailand*, Bangkok: Institute of Population Studies, Chulalongkorn University.

Chen, A. J. and Jones, Gavin W. (1989), *Ageing in ASEAN: Its Socio-Economic Consequences*, Singapore: Institute of Southeast Asian Studies.

Chen, E. K. Y. (1976), 'The Role of Women in Economic Development: An Analysis with Special Reference to Hong Kong', in L. Z. Legaspi (ed.), *The Role of Women in Development*, Manila: University of Santa Tomas Press.

Chenery, H. et al. (eds.) (1974), *Redistribution with Growth*, Oxford: Oxford University Press.

Chesnais, Jean-Claude (1989), *Human Investment and Population-related Aspects of Economic Growth in East Asia: A European Perspective*, NUPRI Research Paper Series No. 52, Tokyo: Population Research Institute, Nihon University.

Cheung, Paul P. L. (1989), 'Recent Changes in Population Policies: Malaysia and Singapore', *International Population Conference: New Delhi 1989*, Liège: IUSSP, Vol. 1, pp. 133–41.

Cho, Lee-Jay and Bauer, John G. (1987), 'Population Growth and Urbanization: What Does the Future Hold?' in Roland J. Fuchs, Gavin W. Jones, and Ernesto M. Pernia (eds.), *Urbanization and Urban Policies in Pacific Asia*, Boulder and London: Westview Press, pp. 15–37.

Cho, Lee-Jay and Togashi, Janet Y. (1984), 'Industrial Transition and Demographic Dynamics of the Asian–Pacific Region', in *Proceedings of the International Symposium on the Role of the Asia–Pacific Region in World Economic Development*, Tokyo: College of Economics, Nihon University, pp. 41–59.

Choe, Ehn-Hyun (1988), 'Survey of Population Aging in the Republic of Korea', Paper prepared for ESCAP, Seoul.

Choe, Minja Kim (1981), 'Fitting the Age Pattern of Infant and Child Mortality with the Weibull Survival Distribution', *Asian and Pacific Census Forum*, 4(4): 10–13.

_____ (1987), 'Sex Differentials in Infant and Child Mortality in Korea', *Social Biology*, 34(1–2): 12–25.

Choi, Hoil (1985), 'Selected Characteristics on Population and Aging in the Republic of Korea', Paper presented at the Sixteenth Summer Seminar on Population, Honolulu.

Clark, Robert L. (1991), *Japanese Retirement Systems*, Homewood, Illinois: Irwin.

Clark, Robert L. and Ogawa, Naohiro (1991), 'Reconsidering Tenure and Earnings Profiles of Japanese Men', Unpublished paper, North Carolina State University.

_____ (1992a), 'The Effect of Mandatory Retirement on Earnings Profiles in Japan', *Industrial and Labor Relations Review*, 45(2): 258–66.

_____ (1992b), 'Employment Tenure and Earnings Profiles in Japan and the United States', *American Economic Review*, 82(1): 336–45.

Clark, Robert L., Kreps, Juanita, and Spengler, Joseph (1978), 'Economics of Aging: A Survey', *Journal of Economic Literature*, 16: 919–62.

Cleland, J. and Wilson, C. (1987), 'Demand Theories of the Fertility Transition: An Iconoclastic View', *Population Studies*, 41(1): 5–30.

Cleveland, W. S. (1979), 'Robust Locally Weighted Regression and Smoothing Scatterplots', *Journal of the American Statistical Association*, 74(368): 829–36.

Cline, T. R. (1972), *Potential Effects of Income Redistribution on Economic Growth: Latin American Cases*, New York: Praeger.

Coale, A. J. (1986), 'Population Trends and Economic Development', in J. Menkin (ed.), *World Population and US Policy: The Choices Ahead*, New York: W. W. Norton.

Coale, A. J. and Hoover, E. (1958), *Population Growth and Economic Development in Low-Income Countries*, Princeton: Princeton University Press.

Cochrane, S. H., O'Hara, D. J., and Leslie, J. (1980), *The Effects of Education on Health*, Staff Working Paper No. 405, Washington, DC: World Bank.

Colclough, Christopher (1982), 'The Impact of Primary Schooling on Economic Development: A Review of the Evidence', *World Development*, 10(3): 167–85.

Collins, S. (1989), 'Savings Behavior in Ten Developing Countries', Paper presented at the NBER Conference on Savings, Maui, Hawaii, 6–7 January.

Cowgill, Donald O. and Holmes, Lowell D. (1972), *Aging and Modernization*, New York: Meredith.

Cummings, William K. (1980), *Education and Equality in Japan*, Princeton: Princeton University Press.

DaVanzo, Julie and Habicht, Jean-Pierre (1986), 'Infant Mortality Decline in Malaysia, 1946–1975: The Roles of Changes in Variables and Changes in the Structure of Relationships', *Demography*, 23(2): 143–59.

DaVanzo, Julie, Butz, W. P., and Habicht, Jean-Pierre (1983), 'How Biological and Behavioural Influences on Mortality in Malaysia Vary during the First Year of Life', *Population Studies*, 37(3): 381–402.

David, I. P. and Lee, J. (1989), *A Survey of the External Debt Situation in Asian–Pacific Developing Countries, 1987–88*, Statistical Report Series No. 13, Manila: Asian Development Bank.

Davis, Kingsley and van den Oever, Pietronella (1981), 'Age Relations and Public Policy in Advanced Industrial Societies', *Population and Development Review*, 7(1): 1–18.

Deaton, Angus and Muellbauer, John (1980), *Economics and Consumer Behavior*, Cambridge: Cambridge University Press.

Della Valle, P. A. and Oguchi, N. (1976), 'Distribution, the Aggregate Consumption Function and the Level of Development: Some Cross-country Results', *Journal of Political Economy*, 84(6): 1325–34.

Demeny, Paul (1984), 'A Perspective on Long-term Population Growth', *Population and Development Review*, 10(1): 103–26.

Denison, E. F. (1967), *Why Growth Rates Differ: Post-War Experience in Nine Western Countries*, Washington, DC: Brookings Institution.

Denison, E. F. and Chung, William K. (1976), *How Japan's Economy Grew So Fast: The Sources of Economic Expansion*, Washington, DC: Brookings Institution.

Dick, G. William (1974), 'Authoritarian versus Nonauthoritarian Approaches to Economic Development', *Journal of Political Economy*, 82(4): 817–27.

Dolton, P. J., Makepeace, G. H., and Van Der Klaauw, V. (1989), 'Occupational Choice and Earnings Determination: The Role of Sample Selection and Non-pecuniary Factors', *Oxford Economic Papers*, 41(3): 573–94.

Donaldson, P. J., Nichols, D. J., and Choe, Ehn-Hyun (1982), 'Abortion and Contraception in the Korean Fertility Transition', *Population Studies*, 36(2): 227–35.

Dowling, J. M. and Hiemenz, U. (1983), 'Aid, Saving, and Growth in the Asian Region', *The Developing Economies*, 21(1): 3–13.

D'Souza, Stan and Chen, Lincoln C. (1980), 'Sex Differentials in Mortality in Rural Bangladesh', *Population and Development Review*, 6(2): 257–70.

Duza, M. Badrud (1989), 'The Conditions of Fertility Transition in East and South-East Asia and Prospects for the 1990s', in *International Population Conference: New Delhi 1989*, Liège: IUSSP, Vol. 1, pp. 3–13.

Easterlin, Richard A. (1978), 'The Economics and Sociology of Fertility: A Synthesis', in Charles Tilly (ed.), *Historical Studies of Changing Fertility*, Princeton: Princeton University Press, pp. 57–133.

───── (1981), 'Why Isn't the Whole World Developed?', *Journal of Economic History*, 41(1): 1–19.

───── (1986), 'Economic Preconceptions and Demographic Research: A Comment', *Population and Development Review*, 12(3): 517–28.

East–West Center (1986), *Asia–Pacific Report 1986*, Honolulu.

Economic Planning Agency (1983), *Japan in the Year 2000*, Tokyo: The Japan Times.

Egan, E. L. (1985), 'The Effects of World War II Wealth Destruction on the Saving Rate in Post-War Japan', Seniors Honors Thesis, Harvard.

Eisold, E. (1984), *Young Women Workers in Export Industries: The Case of the Semi-conductor Industry in Southeast Asia*, World Employment Programme Working Paper No. 30, Geneva: International Labour Office.

ESCAP (1982), 'Sources, Availability and Quality of Data for Measuring Mortality Trends and Levels in the ESCAP Region', Appendix in World Health Organization (ed.), *Mortality in South East Asia: A Review of Changing Trends and Patterns, 1950–1975*, Geneva: World Health Organization.

───── (1987), *Women's Economic Participation in Asia and the Pacific*, ESCAP Social Development Division, United Nations, Bangkok.

───── (1989), *1988 ESCAP Population Data Sheet*, United Nations, Bangkok.

Evers, H. D. (1989), 'Urban Poverty and Labour Supply Strategies in Jakarta', in G. Rodgers (ed.), *Urban Poverty and the Labour Market Access to Jobs and Incomes in Asian and Latin American Cities*, Geneva: International Labour Office.

*Far Eastern Economic Review* (1990), various issues.

Fawcett, J. T., Khoo, S. E., and Smith, P. C. (1984), *Women in the Cities of Asia: Migration and Urban Adaptation*, Boulder: Westview Press.

Fei, J. C. H., Ranis, G., and Kuo, S. W. Y. (1979), *Growth with Equity: The Taiwan Case*, New York: Oxford University Press.

Freedman, Ronald and Takeshita, John Y. (1969), *Family Planning in Taiwan: An Experiment in Social Change*, Princeton: Princeton University Press.

Fry, M. J. (1984a), 'Saving, Financial Intermediation and Economic Growth in Asia', *Asian Development Review*, 2(1): 82–91.

───── (1984b), 'Terms of Trade and National Savings Rates in Asia', Mimeo, University of California, Irvine.

Fry, M. J. and Mason, A. (1982), 'The Variable Rate of Growth Effect in the Life-cycle Saving Model,' *Economic Inquiry*, 20(3): 426–42.

Fuchs, V. (1982), 'Self-employment and Labour Force Participation of Older Males', *The Journal of Human Resources*, 17: 339–57.

Galenson, W. (ed.) (1985), *Foreign Trade and Investment: Economic Growth in Newly Industrializing Countries*, Madison: University of Wisconsin Press.

Gannicott, K. (1987), *Education in Papua New Guinea: A Case Study in Wasted Resources*, Islands/Australia Working Paper No. 87/9, Canberra: National Centre for Development Studies, The Australian National University.

Gibson, Mary Jo (1988), 'Public Health and Social Policy', Paper presented at the Expert Group Meeting on the Role of the Family in Care of the Elderly, Mexico City.

Gillis, M., Perkins, D., Roemer, M., and Snodgrass, D. (1983), *Economics of Development*, New York: W. W. Norton.

Gold, Thomas B. (1986), *State and Society in the Taiwan Miracle*, Armank, New York: M. E. Sharpe.

Greene, W. H. (1985), *LIMDEP$^{TM}$*, New York University, New York.

Griffin, K. (1976), *Land Concentration and Rural Poverty*, London: Macmillan.

Grootaert, C. (1986), *The Role of Employment and Earnings in Analyzing Levels of Living*, Living Standards Measurement Study Working Paper No. 27, Washington, DC: World Bank.

Grossman, Michael (1972), 'On the Concept of Health Capital and the Demand for Health', *Journal of Political Economy*, 80(2): 223–55.

Gudgin, G., Brunskill I., and Fothergill, S. (1979), *New Manufacturing Firms in Regional Employment Growth*, Centre for Environmental Studies, Research Series No. 39.

Hackenberg, Robert A. (1980), 'New Patterns of Urbanization in Southeast Asia: An Assessment', *Population and Development Review*, 6(3): 391–419.

Hammer, J. S. (1985), *Population Growth and Savings in Developing Countries*, World Bank Staff Working Paper No. 687, Washington, DC: World Bank.

Hansluwka, H. (1973), 'Health Programmes and the Prospects for Further Reduction of Mortality in Low-mortality Countries', in *IUSSP International Population Conference*, Liège: IUSSP, Vol. 3, pp. 283–300.

Harris, S. E. (1949), *The Market for College Graduates*, Cambridge: Harvard University Press.

Hashimoto, Masanori (1979), 'Bonus Payments, On-the-job Training, and Lifetime Employment in Japan', *Journal of Political Economy*, 87(5/1): 1086–104.

Hauser, Philip M. (1982), 'Labor Force, Urbanization, Migration and Development', Paper presented at the Conference on Urbanization and National Development, Honolulu.

Haveman, Robert H. and Wolfe, Barbara L. (1984), 'Schooling and Economic Well-being: The Role of Non-market Effects', *Journal of Human Resources*, 19(3): 377–407.

Hayami, Yujiro (1987), 'Asian Development: A View from the Paddy-fields', Paper prepared for the Asian Development Bank Distinguished Speaker Program, Manila.

Heckman, J. (1979), 'Sample Bias as a Specification Error', *Econometrica*, 47(1): 153–62.

Herrin, A. N. (1990), *Philippines, Human Resource Policy and Economic Development: Selected Asian Country Studies*, Manila: Asian Development Bank.

Hicks, Norman (1980), *Economic Growth and Human Resources*, World Bank Staff Working Paper No. 408, Washington, DC: World Bank.

Hirashima, S. (1978), *The Structure of Disparity in Developing Agriculture*, Tokyo: Institute of Developing Economies.

Hobcraft, John N., McDonald, J. W., and Rutstein, S. O. (1984), 'Socio-economic Factors in Infant and Child Mortality: A Cross-national Comparison', *Population Studies*, 38(3): 193–223.

Hodge, Robert W. and Ogawa, Naohiro (1991), *Fertility Change in Contemporary Japan*, Chicago: University of Chicago Press.

Hogan, Dennis P. and Frenzen, Paul D. (1981), 'Antecedents to Contraceptive Innovation: Evidence from Rural Northern Thailand', *Demography*, 18(4): 597–614.

Houck, J. P. (1986), *Foreign Agricultural Assistance: Ally or Adversary*, Staff Paper No. P86–50, Minneapolis: Department of Agricultural and Applied

Economics, University of Minnesota.

Howe, Wayne J. (1988), 'Education and Demographics: How Do They Affect Unemployment Rates?', *Monthly Labor Review*, 111(1): 3–9.

Huffman, Sandra L. and Lamphere, Barbara B. (1984), 'Breastfeeding Performance and Child Survival', in W. Henry Mosley and Lincoln C. Chen (eds.), *Child Survival: Strategies for Research, Population and Development Review*, Supplement to Vol. 10: 93–116.

Hugo, G., Hull, T. H., Hull, V. J., and Jones, G. W. (1987), *The Demographic Dimension in Indonesian Development*, Singapore: Oxford University Press.

Husby, R. D. (1971), 'A Nonlinear Consumption Function Estimated from Time-series and Cross-section data', *Review of Economics and Statistics*, 53(1): 76–9.

Ichimura, S. (ed.) (1988), *Challenge of Asian Developing Countries: Issues and Analyses*, Tokyo: Asian Productivity Organization.

Institute for Population and Social Research (1985), *The Secondary Data Analysis of the Morbidity and Mortality Differentials, Thailand 1985*, Bangkok: Institute for Population and Social Research, Mahidol University.

_____ (1988), *The Morbidity and Mortality Differentials, ASEAN Population Programme Phase III, Thailand: Country Study Report*, Bangkok: Institute for Population and Social Research, Mahidol University.

Institute of Population Studies, Chulalongkorn University and Population Survey Division, National Statistics Office (1977), *The Survey of Fertility in Thailand: Country Report*, Vol. 1, Bangkok: Chulalongkorn University and National Statistics Office.

_____ (1989), *Health and Population Studies Based on the 1987 Thailand Demographic and Health Survey*, Bangkok: Chulalongkorn University.

International Center for Research on Women (1980), *Keeping Women Out: A Structural Analysis of Women's Employment in Developing Countries*, Report prepared for the Office of Women in Development, Bureau of Program and Policy Coordination, Agency for International Development, Washington, DC.

International Labour Office (various years), *Yearbook of Labour Statistics*, Geneva.

_____ (1985), *Report of the Director General Growth and Adjustment in Asia Issues of Employment, Productivity, Migration and Women Workers*, Tenth Asian Regional Conference Jakarta Report 1 (Part 1), Geneva.

_____ (1986), *Labour Force Estimates and Projections, 1950–2000*, Geneva.

_____ (1988a), *The Cost of Social Security*, Geneva.

_____ (1988b), *Yearbook of Labour Statistics*, Geneva.

ILO/UNDP (1988), 'Employment Trends and Policy Issues for Repelita V', Unpublished manuscript, UNDP INS/84/006, Jakarta, June–July.

International Monetary Fund (1987–9), *International Financial Statistics Yearbook*, Washington, DC.

James, W. E., Naya S., and Meier, G. M. (1989), *Asian Development: Economic Success and Policy Lessons*, Madison: University of Wisconsin Press.

Japan Ministry of Health and Welfare, Statistics and Information Department, *The 15th Life Table* (Tokyo: Kosei Tokei Kyokai).

Japanese Institute of Labor (1987), Ministry of Labor, 'Survey of Employment Trends', *Japanese Working Life Profile*, Japanese Government, Tokyo.

_____ (1988), *Employment and Employment Policy*, Tokyo.

_____ (1970, 1975, 1980, 1985, 1988), *Basic Survey on Wage Structure*, Tokyo.

Japanese Statistics Bureau, Management and Coordination Agency (1987),

*Rojin no Seikatsu to Ishiki: Kokusai Hikaku Chosa Kekka Hokokusho* [Life and Perceptions of the Elderly: Report of the Results on the International Comparative Survey], Tokyo: Japanese Government Printing Office.

_____ (1960, 1965, 1970, 1975, 1980, 1985, 1988), *Annual Report on the Labor Force Survey*, Tokyo.

_____ (1950, 1960, 1970, 1980, 1985), *Population Census of Japan*, Tokyo.

Joekes, S. (1987), *Women in the World Economy: An INSTRAW Study*, New York: Oxford University Press.

Jones, Gavin W. (1975), *Population Growth and Educational Planning in Developing Nations*, New York: Irvington Publishers.

_____ (1984), 'Economic Growth and Changing Female Employment Structure in the Cities of Southeast and East Asia', in Gavin W. Jones (ed.), *Women in the Urban and Industrial Workforce, Southeast and East Asia*, Development Studies Centre Monograph No. 33, Canberra: Australian National University.

_____ (1987), *The 1985 Intercensal Survey of Indonesia: 5. The Labour Force*, Research Note No. 78, International Population Dynamics Program, Department of Demography, Canberra: Australian National University.

_____ (1988a), 'Consequences of Rapid Fertility Decline for Old Age Security', Paper presented at the IUSSP Seminar on Fertility Transition in Asia: Diversity and Change, Bangkok.

_____ (1988b), *Economic Growth, Changing Employment Structure and Implications for Educational Planning in ASEAN Countries*, NUPRI Research Paper Series No. 47, Tokyo: Nihon University Population Research Institute.

_____ (1990), 'Fertility Transitions among Malay Populations of Southeast Asia: Puzzles of Interpretation', *Population and Development Review*, 16(3): 507–37.

Jones, Gavin W. and Manning, Chris (1992), 'Labour Force and Employment during the 1980s', in Anne Booth (ed.), *The Oil Boom and After: Indonesian Economic Policy and Performance in the Soeharto Era*, Kuala Lumpur: Oxford University Press.

Jorgenson, D. W. and Fraumeni, B. M. (1988), *The Accumulation of Human and Nonhuman Capital, 1943–1984*, HIER Discussion Paper No. 1413, Cambridge, Massachusetts: Harvard University, December.

Kamnuansilpa, Peerasit, Chamratrithirong, Apichat, and Knodel, John (1982), 'Thailand's Reproductive Revolution: An Update', *International Family Planning Perspectives*, 8(2): 51–6.

Katz, E. and Stark, O. (1986), 'Labor Migration and Risk Aversion in Less Developed Countries', *Journal of Labor Economics*, 4(1): 134–49.

Kelley, A. C. (1986), 'The Demise of the Age-dependency Argument: Lessons and Puzzles from Africa', Revised 1987 version of paper presented at the IUSSP Seminar on the Consequences of Population Trends in Africa, Nairobi, 8–10 December.

_____ (1988a), 'Economic Consequences of Population Change in the Third World', *Journal of Economic Literature*, 26: 1685–728.

_____ (1988b), *Australia: The Coming of Age*, Research Paper No. 194, Melbourne: Department of Economics, University of Melbourne.

Keyfitz, Nathan (1989), 'Putting Trained Labour Power to Work: The Dilemma of Education and Employment', *Bulletin of Indonesian Economic Studies*, 25(3): 35–55.

Khoo, S. E. (1987), 'Development and Women's Participation in the Modern Economy: Asia and the Pacific', in *Women's Economic Participation in Asia and the Pacific*, Bangkok: ESCAP, United Nations.

Khoo, S. E., Smith, P. C., and Fawcett, J. T. (1984), 'Migration of Women to Cities: The Asian Situation in Comparative Perspective', *International Migration Review*, 18(4): 1247–63.

Kim, Kwang Woong (1988), *Political Dimension for Economic Development: A Research Design*, NUPRI Research Paper Series No. 48, Tokyo: Nihon University Population Research Institute.

Kiranandana, Thienchay, Wongboonsin, Kua, and Kiranandana, Suchada (1988), *Population Aspects of Development in Thailand: Health/Nutrition, Education and Old Age Security*, Report prepared for ESCAP in connection with the project, Development of Analytical Framework for Population and Development Research and Planning, Bangkok.

Knodel, John and Debavalya, Nibhon (1978), 'Thailand's Reproductive Revolution', *International Family Planning Perspectives and Digest*, 4(2): 34–49.

—— (1980), 'Breast-feeding in Thailand: Trends and Differentials 1969–79', *Studies in Family Planning*, 11(12): 355–77.

Knodel, John, and Prachuabmoh, Visid (1976), 'Preference for Sex of Children in Thailand: A Comparison of Husband's and Wife's Attitudes', *Studies in Family Planning*, 7(5): 137–43.

Knodel, John and Wongsith, Malinee (1989a), 'Educational Expectations and Attainment Patterns for Thai Children', Paper presented at the Seminar on Further Analysis of Demographic, Family Planning and Health Issues Based on Thailand Demographic and Health Survey (TDHS), Bangkok, 26 July.

—— (1989b), 'Monitoring the Education Gap in Thailand: Trends and Differentials in Lower and Upper Secondary Schooling', *Asian and Pacific Population Forum*, 3(4): 25–35.

Knodel, John, Chayovan, Napaporn, and Wongboonsin, Kua (1990), 'Breast-feeding Trends, Patterns and Policies in Thailand', *Asia–Pacific Population Journal*, 5: 135–50.

Knodel, John, Kamnuansilpa, Peerasit, and Chamratrithirong, Aphichat (1985), 'Infant Feeding Practices and Postpartum Amenorrhea in Thailand: Results from the 1984 Contraceptive Prevalence Survey', *Studies in Family Planning*, 16(6): 302–11.

Koo, H. (1984), 'The Political Economy of Income Distribution in South Korea: The Impact of the State's Industrialization Policies', *World Development*, 12(10): 1029–37.

Koo, Sung-Yeal and Mason, Andrew (forthcoming), *Household Factors and School Enrollment in Korea*, Honolulu: East–West Population Institute, East–West Center.

Krugman, P. (1987), 'The Narrow Moving Band, the Dutch Disease and the Competitive Consequences of Mrs Thatcher', *Journal of Development Economics*, 27: 41–55.

Kuznets, P. W. (1988), 'An East Asian Model of Economic Development. Japan, Taiwan, and South Korea', *Economic Development and Cultural Change* (supplement) 36(3): S11–43.

Kuznets, S. (1955), 'Economic Growth and Income Inequality', *American Economic Review*, 45(1): 1–28.

—— (1976), 'Demographic Aspects of the Size Distribution of Income: An Exploratory Essay', *Economic Development and Cultural Change*, 25(1): 1–94.

Lal, Deepak and Myint, Hla (forthcoming), *The Political Economy of Poverty, Equity and Growth*, Washington, DC: World Bank.

Lapham, R. J. and Mauldin, W. P. (1985), 'Contraceptive Prevalence: The

Influence of Organized Family Planning Programs', *Studies in Family Planning*, 16(3): 117–37.

Lau, L. J. (ed.) (1985), *Models of Development: A Comparative Study of Economic Growth in South Korea and Taiwan*, San Francisco: Institute for Contemporary Studies.

Lazear, Edward (1979), 'Why Is There Mandatory Retirement?', *Journal of Political Economy*, 87(6): 1261–84.

Lee, E. (1986), *Economic-restructuring and Human Resource Development*, Occasional Paper Series No. 1, Kuala Lumpur: ADIPA Secretariat Association of Development Research and Training Institute of Asia and the Pacific.

Lee, Jungsoo (1987), *Domestic Adjustment to External Shocks in Developing Asia*, ADB Economic Staff Paper No. 39, Manila: Asian Development Bank.

Lee, Ronald D. and Bulatao, Rodolfo A. (1983), 'An Overview of Fertility Determinants in Developing Countries', in Rodolfo A. Bulatao and Ronald D. Lee (eds.), *Determinants of Fertility in Developing Countries*, New York: Academic Press, Vol. 2, pp. 757–87.

Leete, Richard (1987), 'The Post-demographic Transition in East and South Asia: Similarities and Contrasts with Europe', *Population Studies*, 41(2): 187–206.

_____ (1989), 'Dual Fertility Trends in Malaysia's Multiethnic Society', *International Family Planning Perspectives*, 15(2): 58–65.

Leff, N. (1969), 'Dependency Rates and Savings Rates', *American Economic Review*, 59(5): 886–96.

Leff, N. and Sato, K. (1988), 'Psychocultural Conditions and Economic Development: Saving and Investment Behavior in East Asia and Latin America', Paper presented to the Allied Social Sciences Association Meeting, December.

Lele, U. (1986), 'Women and Structural Transformation', *Economic Development and Cultural Change*, 34(2): 195–221.

Lewis, W. A. (1954), 'Economic Development with Unlimited Supplies of Labor', *Manchester School of Economic and Social Studies* 22, pp. 139–91.

Lim, Lin Lean (1984), 'Towards Meeting the Needs of Urban Female Factory Workers in Peninsular Malaysia', in Gavin W. Jones (ed.), *Women in the Urban and Industrial Workforce Southeast and East Asia*, Development Studies Centre Monograph No. 33, Canberra: Australian National University.

_____ (1986), *Impact of Immigration in Labor Markets in Peninsular Malaysia*, NUPRI Research Paper Series No. 31, Tokyo: Nihon University Population Research Institute.

_____ (1988a), 'International Labour Movements: An Economic Exchanges and Flows Perspective', Paper presented at the IUSSP Seminar on International Migration Systems, Processes and Policies, Kuala Lumpur.

_____ (1988b), 'Economic Dynamism and Structural Transformation in the Asian Pacific Rim Countries—Contributions of the Second Sex', NUPRI Research Paper Series No. 45, Tokyo: Nihon University Population Research Institute.

_____ (1989a), 'Processes Shaping International Migration', in *International Population Conference: New Delhi 1989*, Liège: IUSSP, Vol. 2, pp. 131–44.

_____ (1989b), *Female Migration*, Report submitted to the Economic Planning Unit, Prime Minister's Department Malaysia for the Human Resources Development Plan and the Faculty of Economics and Administration, University of Malaya, Kuala Lumpur.

_____ (1989c), *International Migration*, Report submitted to the Economic Planning Unit, Prime Minister's Department Malaysia for the Human Resources Development Plan and the Faculty of Economics and Administration, University of Malaya, Kuala Lumpur.

──── (1989d), 'The Status of Women and International Migration', Background paper presented at the meeting on International Migration Policies and the Status of Female Migrants, Population Division, United Nations, New York.

Lim, L. Y. C. (1978), 'Multinational Firms and Manufacturing for Export in Less Developed Countries: The Case of Singapore and Malaysia', Ph.D. dissertation, University of Michigan, Ann Arbor.

──── (1986), *Status of Women in Asia and the Pacific Region Series 1, Women in the Economy: Employment*, Bangkok: ESCAP Social Development Division.

Lindert, Peter H. (1983), 'The Changing Economic Costs and Benefits of Having Children' in R. Bulatao and R. Lee (eds.), *Determinants of Fertility in Developing Countries*, New York: Academic Press, pp. 494–516.

Lindert, Peter H. and Williamson, J. G. (1985), 'Growth, Equality and History', *Explorations in Economic History*, 22(4): 341–77.

Livi-Bacci, Massimo (1982), 'Social and Biological Aging: Contradictions of Development', *Population and Development Review*, 8(4): 771–81.

Lo, Fu-Chen and Shinohara, M. (eds.) (1989), *Global Adjustment and the Future of Asian Pacific Economy*, Japan: Institute of Developing Economies and Asian and Pacific Development Centre, PMC Publications.

Lucas, R. E. (1988), 'On the Mechanics of Economic Development', *Journal of Monetary Economics*, 22: 3–42.

McGee, T. G. (1988), 'The Urbanization Transition in Asia: The Emergence of New Regions of Economic Interaction in Asia', *Regional Development Dialogue*, UNCRD, Nagoya.

McGinn, Noel F., Snodgrass, Donald R., Kim, Wung Bong, Kim, Shin-Bok, and Kim, Quee-Yong (1980), *Education and Development in Korea*, Cambridge: Harvard University Press.

McNicoll, Geoffrey (1989), 'Concepts and Frameworks Needed for a Better Understanding of Socio-demographic Processes', *International Population Conference: New Delhi 1989*, Liège: IUSSP, Vol. 3, pp. 423–36.

Maddala, G. S. (1983), *Limited Dependent and Qualitative Variables in Econometrics*, Cambridge: Cambridge University Press.

Maddox, George L. (1982), 'Challenges for Health Policy and Planning', in R. Binstock, W. S. Chow, and J. Schulz (eds.), *International Perspectives on Aging: Population and Policy Challenges*, New York: United Nations Fund for Population Activities, pp. 127–58.

Manning, Chris (1988), 'Rural Employment Creation in Java: Lessons from the Green Revolution and Oil Boom', *Population and Development Review*, 14(1): 47–80.

Manton, K. G., Myers, G. C., and Andrews, R. G. (1987), 'Morbidity and Disability Patterns in Four Developing Countries: Their Implications for Social and Economic Integration of the Elderly', *Journal of Cross-Cultural Gerontology*, 2: 115–19.

Martin, Linda G. (1988), 'The Aging of Asia', *Journal of Gerontology: Social Sciences* (supplement), 43(4): S99–113.

──── (1989a), 'Emerging Issues in Crossnational Survey Research on Aging in Asia', *International Population Conference: New Delhi 1989*, Liège: IUSSP, Vol. 3, pp. 69–80.

──── (1989b), 'Living Arrangements of the Elderly in Fiji, Korea, Malaysia, and the Philippines', *Demography*, 26(4): 627–43.

Martin, Linda G. and Culter, Suzanne (1983), 'Mortality Decline and Japanese Family Structure', *Population and Development Review*, 9(4): 633–50.

Martin, Linda G. and Ogawa, Naohiro (1988), 'The Effect of Cohort Size on Relative Wages in Japan', in Ronald Lee, Brian Arthur, and Gerry Rodgers (eds.), *Economics of Changing Age Distributions in Developed Countries*, Oxford: Clarendon Press, pp. 59–75.

Martin, Linda G., Trussell, L., Salvail, Fiorentina Ryes, and Shah, Nasra M. (1983), 'Covariates of Child Mortality in the Philippines, Indonesia and Pakistan: An Analysis Based on Hazard Models', *Population Studies*, 37(3): 417–32.

Mason, Andrew (1987a), 'National Saving Rates and Population Growth: A New Model and New Evidence', in D. Johnson and R. Lee (eds.), *Population Growth and Economic Development: Issues and Evidence*, Madison: University of Wisconsin Press.

—— (1987b), *HOMES: A Household Model for Economic and Social Studies*, Papers of the East–West Population Institute No. 106, Honolulu: East–West Center, August.

—— (1988), 'Saving, Economic Growth and Demographic Change', *Population and Development Review*, 14(1): 113–44.

Mason, Andrew, Ogawa, Naohiro, and Fukui, Takehiro (1992), *Household Projections for Japan, 1985–2025: A Transition Model of Headship Rates*, Tokyo: Japan Statistical Association, Nihon University Population Research Institute, and Program on Population, East–West Center.

Mason, Andrew, Woramontri, Varai, and Kleinbaum, Robert M. (1987), *Consumer Expenditures in Thailand: An Application of HOMES*, HOMES Research Report 2, Honolulu: East–West Population Institute, East–West Center.

Mason, Andrew, Suits, Daniel B., Koo, Sung-Yeal, Mathana, Phananiramai, and Sigit, Hananto (1986), *Population Growth and Economic Development: Lessons from Selected Asian Countries*, Policy Development Studies No. 10, New York: UN Fund for Population Activities.

Mason, E. S. et al. (1980), *The Economic and Social Modernization of the Republic of Korea*, Cambridge: Harvard University Press.

Massey, D. S. (1988), 'Economic Development and International Migration in Comparative Perspective', *Population and Development Review*, 14(3): 383–413.

Mazumdar, D. (1981), *The Urban Labor Market and Income Distribution: A Study of Malaysia*, Oxford: Oxford University Press.

Meier, G. M. (1984), *Leading Issues in Economic Development*, 4th edn., New York: Oxford University Press.

Mensch, B., Lentzner, H., and Preston, S. H. (1985), *Socio-Economic Differentials in Child Mortality in Developing Countries*, New York: Department of International Economic and Social Affairs, United Nations.

Mincer, J. (1974), *Schooling, Experience and Earnings*, New York: National Bureau of Economic Research.

Mincer, J. and Higuchi, Yoshio (1988), 'Wage Structure and Labor Turnover in the United States and Japan', *Journal of the Japanese and International Economies*, 2(2) (June): 97–133.

Ministry of Education (1962), *Growth and Education in Japan: Development of Education and Economic Growth* (in Japanese), Japan.

—— (1989), *Monbu Tokei Yoran Heisei-Gannen Ban* [Summary of Educational Statistics 1989], Statistics and Planning Department, Minister's Secretariat, Japan Ministry of Education, Tokyo.

Morley, S. A. (1981), 'The Effect of Changes in the Population on Several Measures of Income Distribution', *American Economic Review*, 71: 285–94.

Mosley, W. H. and Chen, L. C. (1984), 'Child Survival: Strategies for Research', *Population and Development Review* (supplement), 10: 25–45.

Mueller, Eva (1976), 'The Economic Value of Children in Peasant Agriculture', in Ronald Ridker (ed.), *Population and Development: The Search for Selective Interventions*, Baltimore: Johns Hopkins University Press, pp. 89–153.

Murakami, Kiyoshi (1991), 'Severance and Retirement Benefits in Japan', in John Turner and Lorna Dailey (eds.), *Pension Policy: An International Perspective*, Washington, DC: US Government Printing Office, p. 133.

Muramatsu, Minoru (1978), 'Estimation of Induced Abortion, Japan, 1975', *Bulletin of the Institute of Public Health*, 27(2): 93–7.

Musgrove, P. (1980), 'Income Distribution and the Aggregate Consumption Function', *Journal of Political Economy*, 88(3): 504–25.

Myers, George C. (1988), 'Demographic Ageing and Family Support for Older People', Paper presented at the Kellogg/WHO Meeting on Family Support and the Elderly, Mexico City.

National Development Planning Agency (1989), *Repelita V: Basic Data and Main Targets*, Jakarta: BAPPENAS.

National Statistical Office (1978), *Report on the Survey of Population Change 1974–1976*, Bangkok.

——— (1989), *Report on the Survey of Population Change 1985–1986*, Bangkok.

Naya, Seiji (1987), 'Economic Performance and Growth Factors of the ASEAN Countries', in Linda G. Martin (ed.), *The ASEAN Success Story*, Honolulu: East–West Center, pp. 47–87.

Naya, Seiji et al. (1982), *Developing Asia: The Importance of Domestic Policies*, Economic Staff Paper No. 9, Manila: Asian Development Bank.

Nilsen, S. E. (1980), 'Microelectronics: Useful for Some, Harmful for Others', *Social Science Information*, 19(2): 423–34.

Ogawa, Naohiro (1981), 'Shussho yokusei no Keizaiteki Gein' [Economic Gains from Fertility Control], *Keizai Shushi*, 50(3): 35–50, Tokyo: College of Economics, Nihon University.

——— (1982), 'Economic Implications of Japan's Ageing Population: A Macroeconomic Demographic Modelling Approach', *International Labour Review*, 121(1): 17–33.

——— (1985a), 'Urbanization and Internal Migration in Selected ASEAN countries: Trends and Prospects', in Philip M. Hauser, Daniel B. Suits, and Naohiro Ogawa (eds.), *Urbanization and Migration in ASEAN Development*, Honolulu: University of Hawaii Press, pp. 83–107.

——— (1985b), *Population Growth and the Costs of Health Care: The Case of Malaysia*, EPU Discussion Paper No. 13, Kuala Lumpur: Prime Minister's Office, Malaysia.

——— (1986a), 'Consequences of Mortality Change on Aging', in *Consequences of Mortality Trends and Differentials*, New York: United Nations, pp. 175–84.

——— (1986b), *Internal Migration in Japanese Postwar Development*, NUPRI Research Paper Series No. 33. Tokyo: Nihon University Population Research Institute.

——— (1988a), 'Population Change and Welfare of the Aged', in *Frameworks for Population and Development Integration*, Asian Population Studies Series No. 92, Bangkok: ESCAP, United Nations, pp. 105–32.

——— (1988b), 'Aging in China: Demographic Alternatives', *Asian–Pacific Population Journal*, 3(3): 21–64.

——— (1989a), 'Population Aging and Household Structural Change in Japan', in John Eekelaar and David Pearl (eds.), *An Aging World: Dilemmas and Challenges for Law and Social Policy*, Oxford: Clarendon Press, pp. 75–98.

—— (1989b), 'Population Aging and Its Impact upon Health Resource Requirements at Government and Familial Levels in Japan', *Ageing and Society*, 9(4): 384–405.

—— (1989c), 'Koreika Shakai no naka ni okeru Hito no Kokusaika' [Internationalization of Human Capital Flows in Aging Society], in *Report on the Community Development in the Era of Internationalization*, Tokyo: National Land Development Agency, pp. 143–60.

—— (1990), 'Economic Factors Affecting the Health of the Elderly', in Robert L. Kane, J. Grimley Evans, and David Macfadyen (eds.), *Improving the Health of Older People: A World View*, Oxford: Oxford University Press, pp. 627–46.

—— (in press), 'Resources for the Elderly in Economic Development', in Hal Kendig, Akiko Hashimoto, and Larry C. Coppard (eds.), *Family Support of the Elderly: The International Experience*, London: Cambridge University Press.

Ogawa, Naohiro and Hodge, Robert W. (1986), *Urbanization, Migration, and Fertility in Contemporary Japan*, NUPRI Research Paper Series No. 28, Tokyo: Nihon University Population Research Institute.

Ogawa, Naohiro and Suits, Daniel B. (1982), 'Lessons on Population and Economic Change from the Japanese Meiji Experience', *Developing Economies*, 20(2): 196–219.

—— (1984), *An Application of the Harris–Todaro Model to Japan*, NUPRI Research Paper Series No. 68, Tokyo: Nihon University Population Research Institute.

Ogawa, Naohiro, Poapongsakorn, Nipon, and Mason, Andrew (1988), *Population Change and the Costs of Health Care in Thailand*, HOMES Research Report 7a, Honolulu: East–West Population Institute, East–West Center.

—— (1989), 'Forecasts of Health Care Cost in Thailand', Paper prepared for the National Economic and Social Development Board of Thailand, Bangkok.

Ogawa, Naohiro, Kondo, Makoto, Sato, Kiichiro, Sadahiro, Akira, Sugihara, Tomoko, Suits, Daniel B., Mason, Andrew, and Feeny, Griffith (1988), *Jinko Keizai Iryo Moderu ni Motozuku Choki Tembo: Feisu III* [Long-term Prospects Based Upon the Population–Economic–Medical Model: Phase III], Tokyo: Nihon University Population Research Institute.

Ohkawa, Kazushi and Rosovsky, H. (1973), *Japanese Economic Growth: Trend Acceleration in the Twentieth Century*, Stanford: Stanford University Press.

Ohkawa, Kazushi and Shinohara, Miyohei (1979), *Pattern of Japanese Economic Development: A Quantitative Appraisal*, New Haven: Yale University Press.

Okita, Saburo, Kuroda, Toshio, Ogawa, Naohiro, and Hauser, Philip M. (1982), *Population, Natural Resources, Environment and Human Resources in Development*, NUPRI Research Paper Series No.11, Tokyo: Nihon University Population Research Institute.

Oshima, Harry T. (1980), 'Manpower Quality in the Differential Economic Growth between East and Southeast Asia', *The Philippines Economic Journal*, 19(3, 4): 380–406.

—— (1982), 'Reinterpreting Japan's Postwar Growth', *Economic Development and Cultural Change*, 31(1): 1–43.

—— (1983a), 'The Industrial and Demographic Transitions in East Asia', *Population and Development Review*, 9: 583–607.

—— (1983b), 'On the Coming Pacific Century: Perspectives and Prospects', Paper presented at the East–West Center, Honolulu.

_____ (1986), 'Human Resources in Asian Development: Trends, Problems and Research Issues', in United Nations ESCAP (ed.), *Human Resources Development in Asia and the Pacific*, Bangkok: ESCAP, United Nations, pp. 56–81.

_____ (1987), *Economic Growth in Monsoon Asia: A Comparative Study*, Tokyo: University of Tokyo Press.

_____ (1988), 'Human Resources in East Asia's Secular Growth', *Economic Development and Cultural Change* (supplement), 36(3): S103–22.

Paglin, M. (1975), 'The Measurement and Trend of Inequality: A Basic Revision', *American Economic Review*, 65(4): 598–609.

Palloni, Alberto and Tienda, Marta (1986), 'The Effects of Breastfeeding and Pace of Childbearing on Mortality at Early Ages', *Demography*, 23(1): 31–52.

Papenek, G. (1985), *Development Strategy, Growth, Equity, and the Political Process in Southern Asia*, Washington, DC: USAID.

Park, Chai Bin (1983), 'Preference for Sons, Family Size, and Sex Ratio: An Empirical Study of Korea', *Demography*, 20(3): 333–52.

Pebley, Anne R. and Millman, Sara (1986), 'Birthspacing and Child Survival', *International Family Planning Perspectives*, 12(3): 71–9.

Pebley, Anne R. and Stupp, Paul W. (1987), 'Reproductive Patterns and Child Mortality in Guatemala', *Demography*, 24(1): 43–60.

People's Republic of China (1987), *Statistical Yearbook*, Beijing.

Perkins, D. H. and Yusuf, S. (1984), *Rural Development in China*, Baltimore: Johns Hopkins University Press.

Pernia, Ernesto M. (1984), 'Implications of Urbanization for Food Policy Analysis in Asian Countries', Paper presented at the Working Group Meeting on Food, Fuel and Urbanization in Asia, Tokyo.

_____ (1988), 'Urbanization and Spatial Development in the Asian and Pacific Region: Trends and Issues', *Asian Development Review*, 6(1): 86–105.

Pernia, Ernesto M. and Wilson, D. N. (1989), *Education and Labor Markets in Indonesia: A Sector Survey*, ADB Economic Staff Paper No. 45, Manila: Asian Development Bank.

Petri, Peter A. (1982), 'Income, Employment, and Retirement Policies', in R. Binstock, W. S. Chow, and J. Schulz (eds.), *International Perspectives on Aging: Population and Policy Challenges*, New York: United Nations Fund for Population Activities, pp. 75–125.

Phananiramai, Mathana and Mason, Andrew (1987), *Enrollment and Educational Cost in Thailand*, HOMES Research Report 4, Honolulu: East–West Population Institute, East–West Center.

Phongpaichit, P. (1982), *From Peasant Girls to Bangkok Masseuses*, Geneva: International Labour Office.

Piampiti, S. (1990), *Women in the Informal Sector in Thailand*, Report prepared for the International Labour Office and National Institute of Development Administration, Bangkok.

Plakiepsombati, Pichit, Knodel, John, and Kasemsook, Raphiphat (1989), 'Child Immunization in Thailand: An Analysis of TDHS Data', Paper presented at the Seminar on Further Analysis of Demographic, Family Planning and Health Issues Based on Thailand Demographic and Health Survey (TDHS), Institute of Population Studies, Chulalongkorn University, Bangkok.

Poapongsakorn, N. (1985), 'Some Problems of Human Resource Development in ASEAN Countries', in Jomo K. S. (ed.), *ASEAN Economies: Crisis and Response*, Kuala Lumpur: Malaysian Economic Association for the Federation of ASEAN Economic Association, pp. 245–77.

Porapakkham, Yawarat (1986), *Mortality and Health Issues: Levels and Trends of Mortality in Thailand*, Asian Population Studies Series No. 77, Bangkok: Economic and Social Commission for Asia and the Pacific.

Postlethwaite, T. N. and Thomas, R. M. (1980), *Schooling in the ASEAN Region*, Oxford: Oxford University Press.

Prachuabmoh, V., Knodel, J., and Alers, J. O. (1974), 'Preferences for Sons, Desire for Additional Children and Family Planning in Thailand', *Journal of Marriage and the Family*, 36(3): 601–14.

Prasithrathsint, Suchart, Sookasame, Kanikar, and Rodmanee, Laddawan (1986), 'Socio-economic Correlates of Mortality in Thailand', in Eng Shui Meng (ed.), *Socio-Economic Correlates of Mortality in Japan and ASEAN*, Singapore: Institute of Southeast Asian Studies, pp. 260–95.

Preston, Samuel H. (1985), 'Mortality in Childhood: Lessons from the WFS', in John Cleland, John Hobcraft, and Betzy Dinesen (eds.), *Reproductive Change in Developing Countries: Insights from the World Fertility Survey*, Oxford: Oxford University Press, pp. 253–72.

Psacharopoulos, George (1973), *Returns to Education: An International Comparison*, Amsterdam: Elsevier Scientific Publishing Company.

_____ (1985), 'Returns to Education: A Further International Update and Implications', *Journal of Human Resources*, 20(4): 583–604.

Psacharopoulos, George and Arriagada, Ana M. (1986), 'The Educational Composition of the Labour Force: An International Comparison', *International Labour Review*, 125(5): 561–74.

Qu, Haibo (1984), 'Analysis of Status of Aged Population', Paper presented at the International Symposium of Population and Development, Beijing.

Rada, J. (1980), 'Microelectronics and Information Technology: A Challenge for Research in the Social Sciences', *Social Science Information*, 19(2): 435–65.

Ram, R. (1982), 'Dependency Rates and Aggregate Savings: A New International Cross-section', *American Economic Review*, 72(3): 537–44.

Ram, R. and Schultz, T. W. (1979), 'Life Span, Health, Savings, and Productivity', *Economic Development and Cultural Change*, 27(3): 399–422.

Ramanamma, A. and Bambawale, U. (1980), 'The Mania for Sons', *Social Science and Medicine*, 14(8): 107–10.

Rana, P. (1983), *The Impact of the Current Exchange Rate System on Trade and Inflation of Selected Developing Member Countries*, Economic Staff Paper No. 18, Manila: Asian Development Bank.

Rees, H. J. B. and Shah, A. (1986), 'An Empirical Analysis of Self-employment in the U.K.', *Journal of Applied Econometrics*, 1(1): 95–108.

Renaud, Bertrand M. (1981), *National Urbanization Policy in Developing Countries*, New York: Oxford University Press.

Republic of China, Taipei (various issues), *Taiwan Statistical Data Book*, Taipei: Council for Economic Planning and Development.

Republik Indonesia (1989), *Rencana Pembangunan Lima Tahun Kelima 1988/89–1993/94*, Jakarta.

Retherford, Robert D. and Sewell, William H. (1991), 'Birth Order and Intelligence: Further Tests of the Confluence Model', *American Sociological Review*, 56(2): 141–58.

Retherford, Robert D., Choe, Minja Kim, Thapa, Shyam, and Gubhaju, Bhakta B. (1989), 'To What Extent Does Breastfeeding Explain Birth-interval Effects on Early Childhood Mortality?' *Demography*, 26(3): 439–50.

Riley, J. G. (1979), 'Testing the Educational Screening Hypothesis', *Journal of Political Economy* (supplement), 87(5/2): S227–51.

Robert, A. (1983), 'The Effects of the International Division of Labour on Female Workers in the Textile and Clothing Industries', *Development and Change*, 4(1): 19–37.

Romer, P. M. (1986), 'Increasing Returns and Long-run Growth', *Journal of Political Economy*, 94(5): 1002–37.

Rosen, S. (1977), 'Human Capital: Relations between Education and Earnings', in M. Intriligator (ed.), *Frontiers of Quantitative Economics*, Vol. 3b, Amsterdam: North Holland.

Rumberger, Russell W. (1981a), 'The Changing Skill Requirements of Jobs in the U.S. Economy', *Industrial and Labor Relations Review*, 34(4): 578–90.

_____ (1981b), *Overeducation in the U.S. Labor Market*, New York: Praeger.

_____ (1987), 'The Impact of Surplus Schooling on Productivity and Earnings', *Journal of Human Resources*, 22(1): 24–50.

Ruzicka, Lado T. and Hansluwka, Harald (1982), 'Mortality Transition in South and East Asia: Technology Confronts Poverty', *Population and Development Review*, 8(3): 567–88.

Sachs, J. D. (1987), *Trade and Exchange Rate Policies in Growth-oriented Adjustment Programs*, NBER Working Paper No. 2226, Cambridge: National Bureau of Economic Research.

Salih, K., Young, M. L., Chan, H. L., Loh, K. W., and Chan, C. K. (1985), *Young Workers and Urban Services: A Case Study of Penang, Malaysia*, Final Report, Participatory Urban Services Project, Universiti Sains Malaysia, Penang.

Saw, Swee-Hock (1990), *Changes in the Fertility Policy of Singapore*, Institute of Policy Studies Occasional Paper No. 2, Singapore: Times Academic Press.

Schultz, T. P. (1961), 'Education and Economic Growth', in N. B. Henry (ed.), *Social Forces Influencing American Education*, Chicago: University of Chicago Press, pp. 46–88.

_____ (1987), 'School Expenditures and Enrollments, 1960–80: The Effects of Income, Prices, and Population Growth', in D. G. Johnson and R. Lee (eds.), *Population Growth and Economic Development: Issues and Evidence*, Madison: University of Wisconsin Press, pp. 413–76.

_____ (ed.) (1990), *Economic and Demographic Relationships in Development: Essays Selected and Introduced by T. Paul Schultz*, Baltimore: Johns Hopkins University Press.

Scitovsky, T. (1985), 'Economic Development in Taiwan and South Korea: 1965–1981', *Food Research Institute Studies*, 19: 215–64.

Shaw, E. S. (1973), *Financial Deepening in Economic Development*, New York: Oxford University Press.

Shimada, Haruo (1989), 'Kyoiku Kunrenmen deno Ukeire o' [Accepting Foreign Workers as Trainees], *Weekly Toyo Keizai*, 8 July, 46–50.

Sieh Lee, M. L. (1988), 'Malaysian Workers in Singapore', *The Singapore Economic Review*, 33(1): (April)

Singelmann, Joachim and Browning, Harley L. (1980), 'Industrial Transformation and Occupational Change in the U.S. 1960–70', *Social Forces*, 59(1): 246–64.

Singh, S. (1975), *Development Economics: Some Findings*, Lexington: D. C. Heath.

Sivamurthy, M. (1981), 'The Deceleration of Mortality Decline in Asian Countries', in International Union for Scientific Study of Population (IUSSP), *International Population Conference, Manila 1981*, Liège: IUSSP, Vol. 2, pp. 51–76.

Speare, Alden, Jr. (1984), 'A Critical Assessment of Urban–Rural Projections with Special Reference to United Nations Methods', in *Population Projections: Methodology of the United Nations*, Population Studies No. 83, New York: United Nations, pp. 75–80.

Spence, M. (1974), *Market Signalling: Informational Transfer in Hiring and Related Screening Processes*, Cambridge: Harvard University Press.

Stahl, Charles W. (1985), 'Labor Migration amongst the ASEAN Countries', in Philip M. Hauser, Daniel B. Suits, and Naohiro Ogawa (eds.), *Urbanization and Migration in ASEAN Development*, Honolulu: University of Hawaii Press, pp. 109–30.

Standing, G. (1989), *Global Feminisation through Flexible Labour*, Labour Market Analysis and Employment Planning Working Paper No. 31, Geneva: International Labour Office.

Stern, Steven (1989), 'Measuring the Effect of Disability on Labor Force Participation', *The Journal of Human Resources*, 24(3): 361–95.

Stewart, Charles T. (1987), 'Structural Change and Intergenerational Occupational Mobility', *Journal of Developing Areas*, 21(2): 141–58.

Stolnitz, George J. (1965), 'Recent Mortality Trends in Latin America, Asia and Africa: Review and Re-interpretation', *Population Studies*, 19(2): 117–38.

_____ (1975), 'International Mortality Trends: Some Main Trends and Implications', in United Nations, *The Population Debate: Dimensions and Perspectives: Papers of the World Population Conference, Bucharest 1974*, New York: United Nations, Vol. 1, pp. 220–36.

Strange, Heather (1981), *Rural Malay Women in Tradition and Transition*, New York: Praeger.

Sun, Te-Hsiung, Lin, Hui-Sheng, and Freedman, Ronald (1978), 'Trends in Fertility, Family Size Preferences, and Family Planning Practice: Taiwan, 1961–76', *Studies in Family Planning*, 9(4): 54–70.

Sussangkarn, Chalongphob (1988), *Production Structures, Labor Markets and Human Capital Investments: Issues of Balance for Thailand*, NUPRI Research Paper Series No 46, Tokyo: Nihon University Population Research Institute.

_____ (1989), 'Human Resource Problems and Priorities for Thailand', Unpublished report prepared for the Asian Development Bank, Bangkok.

Sussangkarn, Chalongphob and Chalamwong, Yongyuth (1989), 'Thailand's Economic Dynamism: Human Resource Contributions and Constraints', Paper presented at the International Symposium on Sources of Economic Dynamism in the Asia and Pacific Region: A Human Resource Approach, Nihon University, Tokyo, 20–3 November.

Takeshita, Yuzuru J. (1987), 'Taminzoku Kokka no Jinkou Mondai to Seisaku: Malaysia no Baai' [Population Problems and Policies in a Multi-ethnic Society: The Case of Malaysia], *Crescent*, Kwansei Gakuin University, Kobe, 11(1): 122–7.

Tan, A. H. H. and Kapur, B. (eds.) (1986), *Pacific Growth and Financial Interdependence*, Sydney: Allen and Unwin.

Thompson, W. S. (1950), 'Population and Resources in Japan: A 1949 Forecast', in *Modernization Programs in Relation to Human Resources and Population Problems*, New York: Milbank Memorial Fund, pp. 142–53.

Trager, L. (1984), 'Family Strategies and the Migration of Women: Migrants to Dagupan City, Philippines', *International Migration Review*, 18(4): 1264–77.

Trussell, James and Hammerslough, C. (1983), 'A Hazard-model Analysis of the Covariates of Infant and Child Mortality in Sri Lanka', *Demography*, 20: 1–26.

Tsuya, Noriko O. and Choe, Minja Kim (1989), 'Trends and Covariates of Infant and Child Mortality in Rural China: The Case of Jilin Province', Paper presented at the Annual Meeting of the Population Association of America, Baltimore.

Tsuya, Noriko O. and Kuroda, Toshio (1989), 'Japan: The Slowing of Urbanization and Metropolitan Concentration', in *Counterurbanization: the Changing Pace and Nature of Population Deconcentration*, London: Edward Arnold, pp. 207–29.

Tsuya, Noriko O. et al. (1989), 'Socio-economic Development, Child Health Care, and Recent Infant Mortality in Thailand', Paper presented at the International Symposium on Sources of Economic Dynamism in the Asia and Pacific Region: A Human Resource Approach, Nihon University, Tokyo, 20–3 November.

United Nations (1976), *Statistical Yearbook 1975*, New York.

—— (1981), *Population and Development Modelling: Proceedings of UN/UNFPA Expert Group Meeting on Population and Development Modelling*, New York.

—— (1985), *Estimates and Projections of Urban, Rural and City Populations, 1950–2025: The 1982 Assessment*, New York.

—— (1986), *World Survey on the Role of Women in Development*, A/CONF.116/4/Rev.1 ST/ESA/180, United Nations Department of International Economic and Social Affairs, New York.

—— (1988a), *Demographic Yearbook*, New York.

—— (1988b), *World Population Trends and Policies, 1987 Monitoring Report*, ST/ESA/SER A/103, New York.

—— (1988c), *The State of the World's Children*, New York.

—— (1988d), *World Demographic Estimates and Projections, 1950–2025*, New York.

—— (1989a), *1989 World Survey on the Role of Women in Development*, ST/CSDHA/6, United Nations Office at Vienna Centre for Social Development and Humanitarian Affairs, New York.

—— (1989b), *Global Estimates and Projections of Population by Sex and Age: The 1988 Revision*, UN ST/ESA/SER.R/93, New York.

—— (1989c), *World Population Prospects 1988*, Population Studies No. 106, New York.

—— (1989d), *Demographic Yearbook 1987*, New York.

United Nations Children's Emergency Fund (UNICEF), The Americas and the Caribbean Regional Office (1987), *The Invisible Adjustment: Poor Women and the Economic Crisis*, Santiago: Alfabeto Impresores.

United Nations Educational, Scientific and Cultural Organization (UNESCO), (various years), *Statistical Yearbook*, Paris.

United Nations and World Health Organization (1982), *Mortality Levels and Trends*, New York and Geneva.

Uzawa, H. (1965), 'Optimum Technical Change in an Aggregative Model of Economic Growth', *International Economic Review*, 6: 18–31.

van de Walle, Etienne and Knodel, John (1967), 'Demographic Transition and Fertility Decline: The European Case', Paper presented at the 1967 Conference of the International Union for the Scientific Study of Population, Sydney, Australia.

—— (1980), 'Europe's Fertility Transition: New Evidence and Lessons for Today's Developing World', *Population Bulletin*, 34(6): 3–43.

Vorapongsathorn, Thavatchai, Athipanykom, Suthi, and Pramanpol, Somjai

(1986), *Socio-economic and Health Service Factors Affecting Infant Mortality in Thailand: Path Analysis*, Bangkok: Department of Biostatistics, Faculty of Public Health, Mahidol University.

Walker, S. H. and Duncan, D. B. (1967), 'Estimation of the Probability of an Event as a Function of Several Independent Variables', *Biometrika*, 54(1–2): 167–79.

Weiner, Myron (1985), 'On International Migration and International Relations', *Population and Development Review*, 11(3): 441–56.

Wheeler, David (1980), *Human Resource Development and Economic Growth in Developing Countries: A Simultaneous Model*, World Bank Staff Working Paper No. 407, Washington, DC.

Williamson, J. G. (1968), 'Personal Saving in Developing Nations: An Intertemporal Cross-section from Asia,' *Economic Record*, 44: 194–210.

_____ (1979a), 'Why Do Koreans Save "So Little"?', *Journal of Development Economics*, 6: 343–62.

_____ (1979b), 'Inequality, Accumulation, and Technological Imbalance: A Growth–Equity Conflict in American History?', *Economic Development and Cultural Change*, 44(3): 231–53.

_____ (1985), *Did British Capitalism Breed Inequality?*, London: Allen and Unwin.

_____ (1989), 'Human Capital Deepening, Inequality, and Demographic Events along the Asian Pacific Rim', Paper presented at the International Symposium on Sources of Economic Dynamism in the Asia and Pacific Regions: A Human Resource Approach, Nihon University, Tokyo, 20–3 November.

_____ (1991), *Inequality, Poverty, and History: The Kuznets Memorial Lectures*, Oxford: Basil Blackwell.

Williamson, J. G. and Lindert, P. H. (1980), *American Inequality: A Macro-economic History*, New York: Academic Press.

Williamson, Nancy (1976), *Sons or Daughters: A Cross Cultural Survey of Parental Preferences*, Beverly Hills: Sage Publications.

Willis, R. J. (1986), 'Wage Determinants: A Survey and Reinterpretation of Human Capital Earnings Functions', in O. Ashenfelter and R. Layard (eds.), *Handbook of Labor Economics*, Vol. 1, Amsterdam: North Holland.

Willis, R. J. and Rosen, S. (1979), 'Education and Self-selection', *Journal of Political Economy* (supplement), 87(5/2): S7–36.

Wirakartakusumah, D. (1990), *Indonesia, Human Resource Policy and Economic Development: Selected Asian Country Studies*, Manila: Asian Development Bank.

Wolpin, K. (1977), 'Education and Screening', *American Economic Review*, 67(5): 949–58.

Wong, Aline K. and Cheung, Paul P. L. (1987), 'Demographic and Social Development: Taking Stock for the Morrow', in Linda G. Martin (ed.), *The ASEAN Success Story*, Honolulu: East–West Center, pp. 17–36.

World Bank (1971–1989), *World Tables 1971, 1976, 1988–1989*, Washington, DC.

_____ (1980–90), *World Development Report*, New York: Oxford University Press.

_____ (1982), 'Urbanization', Sector paper, Washington, DC.

_____ (1986–9), *Research Observer*, Washington, DC, Vols. 1–4.

_____ (1987), *Financing Health Services in Developing Countries*, Washington, DC.

_____ (1987–9), *The World Bank Economic Review*, Washington, DC, Vols. 1–3.

_____ (1989), *Social Indicators of Development*, Washington, DC.
World Health Organization (1974), 'Health Trends and Prospects in Relation to Population and Development', in *The Population Debate: Dimensions and Perspectives: Papers of the World Population Conference, Bucharest, 19–30 August 1974*, United Nations, New York, Vol. 1, pp. 573–97.
Wyngaarde Mahajan, I. (1989), 'International Migration of Asian Women: An Exploration and Overview', Mimeo, Bangkok: ESCAP Social Development Division.
Yamamoto, Takajiro (1987), *Bonyu* [Mother's Milk], Iwanami Shinsho No. 230, Tokyo: Iwanami Shoten.
Yang, Quanhe (1988), 'The Aging of China's Population: Perspectives and Implications', *Asia–Pacific Population Journal*, 3(1): 55–74.
Yang, Shu-O W. and Pendleton, Brian F. (1980), 'Socioeconomic Development and Mortality Levels in Less Developed Countries', *Social Biology*, 27(3): 220–9.
Young, M. L. (1987), 'Industrialization and Its Impact on Labour Migration', Paper presented at the Seminar on Current Issues in Labour Migration in Malaysia, organized by the National Union of Plantation Workers and the Population Studies Unit, University of Malaya, Kuala Lumpur.
Young, M. L. and Salih, K. (1986), 'Industrialization, Retrenchment and Household Processes: Implications of the Recession', Paper presented at the Himpunan Sains Sosial IV, Persatuan Sains Sosial Malaysia, University of Malaya, Kuala Lumpur.
Zabalza, A., Pissarides, C., and Barton, M. (1980), 'Social Security and the Choice between Full-time Work, Part-time Work and Retirement', *Journal of Public Economics*, 14: 245–76.

# Index

AFGHANISTAN, 45
Africa: economic growth, 1; education, 8; income, 66–9; school enrolments, 8; *see also* Egypt; Ghana; Kenya; Nigeria
Age-dependency model, 7
Ageing population, 384; dependency of, 41–5; education of, 362–3; employment of, 370; familial support for, 352–5; index of, 42; health of, 11, 350–60, 381; international comparisons of, 351; labour force participation of, 212, 214–16, 225, 230, 350, 354–5, 358–72, 378, 381; pensions of, 357, 362–9, 381; marital status of, 369; mortality of, 44, 349; retirement of, 10–11, 371; rural, 220, 354, 381; WHO surveys, 352–5, 357
Agriculture, 163–5; changes in, 231–4; female labour in, 196; labour force in, 11, 49, 52–3, 56, 58, 130, 146–7, 180–1, 220; land reforms, 145–7, 376, 383; rural aged, 220, 381
Argentina, 66–8, 147–52
Asia, 373–87; population size, 23; *see also* East Asia; South Asia, South-East Asia
Asian 'socialist economies', *see* Burma; China
Australia: ageing population, 351–2; agriculture, 49, 52–3; demographic transition, 25–30, 374; employment, 234–5, 247, 249, 251; female labour force participation, 49, 52, 219; fertility, 41, 43–5, 201; GNP, 49, 53–4, 235; income, 66–8; labour force, 48, 219; mortality, 35–6; occupation–education matrix, 249; population growth, 24–5; refugees to, 45; school enrolments, 50–3

BALI, 230
Bangkok: health services, 322; infant mortality, 315, 323, 325–8, 336, 342; Labour Force Surveys, 200; wages, 205

Bangladesh: agriculture, 49, 52–3; debts, 92–4; deficits and surpluses, 102–4; demographic transition, 22, 25–30; demographic trends, 115–17; dependency ratio, 41–5, 79, 81, 118; economy, 21, 24, 39–40, 64, 98–113, 119; education, 22, 49–51, 73–5, 124n; exports, 71, 73, 85–8, 109, 120–2, 124n; female labour, 49, 52, 194, 201; fertility, 22, 30–4, 41, 43–5, 49, 201; GDI, 88–92, 99–104, 123; GDP, 83–5, 92–4, 99–104; GDS, 88–92; GNP, 49, 53–4, 76–8, 83–5, 92–4; income, 66–9; inflation, 95–6; labour force, 45–6, 79–81; migration, 40, 45, 195–6; monetary deepening, 96–8, 108; mortality, 22, 34–7, 44, 49, 108; population growth, 22, 25, 40, 79–81, 115–17; school enrolments, 50–3, 73–5; tax ratios, 101–2; technology, 122–4; trade, 21, 64, 71, 73, 85–8, 109, 111–13, 119–22; urbanization, 37–41, 44
Belgium, 45, 219
Brazil, 66–8, 145, 147–53, 156–7
Breast-feeding, 325–9, 346n, 348n, 380
British, *see* United Kingdom
Brunei: economy, 60; migration, 192–3; population size, 23
Buddhism, 156, 360, 369
Burma: debts, 92–4; demographic trends, 115–17; dependency ratios, 79, 81, 118; economy, 98–113, 124; education, 73–5, 124n; exports, 109, 120–2, 124n; finance, 104–11, 119; GDI, 88–92, 99–104, 123; GDS, 88–92; GDP, 83–5, 92–4, 99–104; GNP, 76–8, 83–5, 92–4, 96–7; income, 66–8; inflation, 95–6; labour force, 79–81; population growth, 79–81, 115–17; school enrolments, 73–5, 147–52; tax ratios, 101–2; trade, 85–8, 109, 111–13, 119–22; technology, 122–4

# INDEX

CANADA, 219
Catholicism, 156
Chaebul, 120
Children, *see* Household
China: ageing population, 351–8; agriculture, 49, 52–3, 85; debts, 92, 94; deficits and surpluses, 102–4; demographic transition, 22, 25–30; demographic trends, 115–17, dependency ratio, 6, 41–5, 132–9; economy, 21, 39–40, 92–4, 98–113, 119, 125n, 176; education, 22, 49–51, 73–5, 124n, 147–52; exports, 85–8, 109, 120–2, 124n; female labour, 49, 52, 71–3, 175–91; fertility, 6, 41–5, 201; GDI, 88–92, 99–104, 123; GDP, 83–5, 92–4, 99–104, 176; GDS, 88–92; GNP, 49, 53, 54, 75–8, 83–5, 92–4, 96, 97, 133–5, 176; health care, 357; income, 66–8; inflation, 95–6, 125n; investment, 21, 138; labour force, 45, 48, 79–81, 217, 354–5; migration, 40, 45; monetary deepening, 96–8; mortality, 22, 34–7, 44, 49, 139–40; pensions, 357; policy changes, 45; population growth, 22–5, 40, 79–81, 115–17; school enrolments, 50–3, 73–5, 147–52; structural changes, 69, 70; tax ratios, 101–2; Tiananmen Square, 83, 113, 122; trade, 83, 109, 111–13, 119–22; technology, 122–4; urbanization, 37–41
Chinese in Malaysia, 193, 287–310, 380
Confucianism, 13–14, 60, 156, 196, 383
Costa Rica, 145
Culture, 13–14, 63, 156–7, 374, 376–7

DEMOGRAPHIC: change, 2, 21, 66, 115–19, 373, 379; dynamics, 3, 64; factors, 49, 63, 124, 325–6, 328, 332, 334, 336, 344; status of elderly, 351–2, 362–3, 365–7; structure, 13; transition, 2, 5, 22, 60, 64, 374, 382
Denmark, 219
Dependency ratios, 2, 6–7, 41–5, 132–9, 155–6, 174, 376
Development: cultural factors, 382–3; educational, 15–16; indicators, 380; international trading, 81–3, 88; policies, 13–14; rural, 16; socio-economic, 30, 325–30, 332, 334, 336, 344, 380; strategies, 13, 21, 59–61; urbanization, 16, 37–41; *see also* Economic development
Diseases, *see* Health
Dutch disease, 71

EAST ASIA, 373–87; population size, 23; *see also* China; Hong Kong; Japan; South Korea
East Java, 230
Economic development, 4–5, 12, 17, 44, 64–5, 104–11, 210–11, 215–17, 224, 376–7, 379, 384–5; activity, 384; crises, 22, 81–3; domestic savings, 7, 11; education, 229, 254–7; growth, 3, 7–8, 13–15, 21–3, 63, 83–5, 88, 124, 129–32, 144–7, 159–74, 175–9, 374, 376, 378; inflation, 82–3, 385; investment, 11; mismanagement, 14; performance, 66, 83–5, 375; policies, 12, 375, 382–3, 384; post-war, 1, 5, 12, 23, 210, 376; stagnation, 14; tax ratios, 101–2; trade, 81–8; 109, 111–13; trends, 66, 231, 373; *see also* Development
Education: access to, 17; advanced, 62, 124n; attainment, 2, 379; commitment to, 8, 376, 378, 385; dependency and, 7, 60; development, 16–17, 383; and economic development, 229, 254–7; effect on fertility, 15, 60; effect on growth rates, 166–7; effect on mortality, 15; effect on role of family, 15–16; of elderly, 362–3, 366–9, 371; expenditure, 154–5; female, 14–16, 195, 201, 209, 259, 323–8, 333, 335, 337, 347n, 348n, 377; formal schooling, 3–4, 8, 62; illiteracy, 14, 230, 379; international comparisons, 8, 62; investment in, 4, 7, 8, 11, 14–16, 22; of labour force, 21–2, 221, 230–1, 238–43, 258n; levels of, 17; literacy, 16–17, 170–3; mass, 376–7; overeducation, 255–7, 379; projections, 244–5; public schools, 15, 165–7; rates of expansion, 9, 14–15; return to schooling, 283–8, 301–10; school enrolments, 3, 7–8, 16–17, 50–3, 59, 61, 73–5, 147–52, 166, 236–7, 277–80; system, 14–15
Egypt: education, 149; school enrolments,147–52; income, 66–9
El Salvador, 145
Elderly, *see* Ageing
Employment: in agriculture, 180–1, 220, 231–4, 238–43, 245–8, 251, 377; choice of, 283–7, 309; in construction and shipbuilding, 238–43, 246–7; distribution of, 9; in domestic service, 182; earnings–age profile, 290–4, 310n; in education, 377; in electrical industry, 246–7; female participation in, 175–91, 194–201, 269–73, 377, 383; female

exploitation in, 199–207; in finance, 246–7; in health, 377; in hospitality, 185, 205; growth, 186–7; industry–occupation matrix, 249, 251–4; job tenure, 212–14; male participation in, 83, 85, 177–8, 180–1; in manufacturing, 180–1, 246–7; in migration flows, 192–3, 378–9; in mining, 247; Middle East opportunities, 386; occupational distribution of, 178–82, 221–2, 246; part-time, 200, 223; in production, 180–1, 238–43, 248, 251–2; professional, managerial, and clerical, 9, 180–1, 220, 231–5, 238–43, 246–54, 290–4, 306; projection of, 246, 249–50; prostitution, 185, 205; in public sector, 206; in sales, trade, and services, 178–9, 220, 231–5, 238–43, 246, 248, 252, 284, 289–94, 299–310; seasonal, 45; self-employment, 185, 190–1, 220, 283–7, 294–309; status, 221–2, 270; technical, 16; underemployment, 63; unemployment, 63, 183–6, 251, 255; wage system, 10; *see also* Labour force

Ethiopia: education: 149; school enrolments, 147–52

Europe: dependency rates, 119; economic growth, 21, 82–3, 114–15; exports to, 121; female labour force participation in, 9; industrial competition in, 384; trade, 83

Exports: growth, 1, 171; primary products, 64; processing zones, 176; trade policy, 375; world markets, 384–5

FAMILY PLANNING PROGRAMMES, 33, 40, 201, 269, 375; *see also* Households

Females: conditions, 201–7; discrimination against, 179, 182–4, 202; economic roles, 9, 377; education of, 14–16, 195, 201, 209, 323–6, 330, 333, 335, 337, 347n, 348n; employment, 178, 188–91, 212–13, 215, 217–20, 222–3; exploitation, 179, 201–8; in the home, 209; job skills, 209; labour force participation of, 2, 9, 11–12, 49, 52, 63, 175–81, 186–7, 194–201, 208, 269–73, 377–8; labour migration of, 192–3, 200, 377; literacy of, 378; in occupational groups, 176–82; retirement prospects of, 377; self-employment of, 190–1; social equity of, 383; status of, 16, 384; unemployment of, 183–6, 179, 204–5, 208–9; unions, 179, 204–5, 208–9, 378

Fertility: change, 30–4; control, 5; decline, 2, 6–7, 9, 22, 33, 41, 43–5, 55, 173, 230, 257, 262–5, 273, 280–1, 374, 379, 381, 385; determinants, 15; effect on development, 49; effect on labour supply, 37; high, 374, 376; reduction of, 173; TFR, 30–4, 54, 169–70, 201; transition, 5, 30–4, 42–5, 64, 201

Fiji, 195

Five-year plans, Indonesia: Repelita V, 36, 174, 230, 243–6, 254, 258n; Repelita VI, 243

Five-year plans, Thailand: Third, 322; Fourth, 322; Fifth, 322; Seventh, 8

France: ageing population, 351–2, 356; education, 60; labour force, 219, 354–5; school enrolments, 147–52

GDI, *see* Gross Domestic Investment
GDP, *see* Gross Domestic Product
GDS, *see* Gross Domestic Savings
Germany, 15, 115, 147–52, 219, 351–2
Ghana, 66–9
GNP, *see* Gross National Product
Great Britain, *see* United Kingdom
Great Depression, 379
Gross Domestic Investment (GDI), 88–92, 99–104, 123, 375
Gross Domestic Product (GDP), 10, 84–5, 89, 92–4, 99–104, 125n, 161–4, 170, 176, 356, 375
Gross Domestic Savings (GDS), 88–92, 124n
Gross National Product (GNP), 1, 4–5, 8, 21, 24, 39, 46, 49, 53–4, 76–8, 83–5, 92–4, 133–5, 143, 145, 153–4, 161–4, 166, 176, 258n, 374

HEALTH: care, 17, 357–72, 380, 385; and development, 167–9, 172–3, 376; investment in, 16; maternal and child, 321–2, 326–9, 331–6, 338–45, 347n, 348n; nutrition, 12, 14, 168, 170, 172; public, 36
Hecksher-Ohlin prescription, 13
HOMES model, 261–2, 281n, 379
Hong Kong: ageing population, 351–6; agriculture, 49, 52–3, 146–7; debts, 92–4, 102–4; demographic transition, 22, 25–30, 132–9; demographic trends, 115–17; dependency ratio, 6, 41–5, 79, 81; economic development, 13, 41, 144–7, 159, 175–81; economy, 21, 39, 40, 66–9, 83–5, 92–4, 98–113; education, 7–8, 22, 49–51, 60, 73–5, 124n, 154; employment, 178, 186–91; exports, 71–3, 85–8, 109, 120–2, 124n,

## INDEX

176; female labour, 49, 52, 175–91, 194, 197–9; fertility, 6, 22, 30–4, 41, 43–5, 49, 201; GDI, 88–92, 99–104, 123; GDP, 83–5, 92–4, 99–104, 176; GDS, 88–92, 124n; GNP, 8, 49, 53–4, 76–8, 83–5, 92–4, 133–5, 145, 176; income, 66–8; independence, 120, 123; inflation, 95–6; labour force, 11, 45, 48, 79–81, 177, 218, 354–5; migration, 11, 40, 45, 192–3, 209; monetary deepening, 96–9, 108; mortality, 22, 34–7, 44, 49, 139–40; occupational groups, 176–81, 188–91; policy changes, 45, 108; population growth, 22, 25, 40, 124; school enrolments, 50–3, 74–5; structural change, 69–70, 186–7; tax ratios, 101–2; technology, 122–4; trade, 71–3, 85–8, 109, 111–13; unemployment, 183–6; urbanization, 37–41, 44

Household: child labour in, 10, 61; child rearing, 2, 269–70, 281n; child welfare, 265, 376; divorce, 265–8; drinking water, 327, 343; education costs, 7; elderly in, 10, 41–5, 214–16, 265, 349–72, 378, 381; impact of fertility decline on, 262–5, 269, 280–1; headship, 265–8; income, 270–3; infant and child health, 325, 327, 331, 333–7, 344–5; non-intact, 267–8; labour, 265–8; labour migration from, 265; roles, 14, 16; impact of school enrolment on, 277–80; size, 260, 262–4, 277–80, 385; socio-economic status of, 325, 327, 331, 333, 337; value of children in, 10, 271–3; *see also* Females

Human resources, *see* Education; Health; Labour force

IMF, *see* International Monetary Fund

Imports, 47, 120, 176

Income, 67; distribution, 376, 383; growth, 12, 376; model, 7; per capita, 2; *see also* Wages

India: agriculture, 49, 52–3; debts, 92–4; demographic transition, 22, 25–30; deficits and surpluses, 102–4; demographic trends, 115–17; dependency ratio, 41–5, 79, 81; economic development, 176, 376; economy, 21, 40, 92–113; education, 22, 63, 73–5, 147–52; exports, 71, 73, 85–8, 109, 120–2, 124n; female labour, 175–91, 194–8; fertility, 6, 22, 30–4, 41, 43–5, 49, 201; finance, 104–11; GDI, 88–92, 99–104, 123; GDP, 83–5, 92–4, 99–104, 176; GDS, 88–102; GNP, 76–8, 83–5, 92–4, 96–8, 176; income, 66–9; labour force, 45, 63, 79–81, 376; migration, 45, 195–6, 209; monetary deepening, 96–8, 108; mortality, 22, 34–7, 49; policy changes, 45, 64, 108; population growth, 22, 25, 40, 79–81, 115–17, 124; population size, 23; school enrolments, 50–3, 73–5, 147–52; structural change, 69–70; tax ratios, 101–2; technology, 122–4; trade, 64, 71, 73, 85–8, 109, 111–13, 119–22; unemployment, 379; urbanization, 37–41, 44

Indonesia: ageing population, 351–8; agriculture, 49, 52–3, 146–7, 163–5, 231–4, 254, 238–43, 245–8, 250, 379; debts, 92–4; deficits and surpluses, 102–4; demographic transition, 22, 25–30; demographic trends, 99–104, 115–17, 230, 379; dependency ratio, 79, 81, 118, 132–9, 174; Dutch disease, 71; economic development, 104–11, 144–7, 159–70, 175, 229, 254–7, 377, 379; economy, 21, 40, 92–103; education, 8, 14, 22, 61–3, 73–5, 124n, 147–52, 166–7, 170–3, 231–5, 239–42, 246–57, 379; employment, 6, 8, 178, 186–91, 379; exports, 171; female labour, 175–91, 194–201; fertility, 22, 30–4, 41, 43–5, 49, 168–70, 173, 201, 257; GDI, 88–92, 123; GDP, 83–5, 92–4, 99–104, 124n, 160–4, 170, 176; GDS, 88–92; GNP, 76–8, 83–5, 92–4, 96–7, 133–5, 145, 160–4, 166, 176, 258n; health, 167–70, 172–3; household headship, 265–8; human resources, 165–74; imports, 171; income, 66–8; inflation, 95–6; investment, 138, 171; labour force, 45, 62, 79–81, 163, 175–91, 229–30, 236, 243–5, 354–5, 379; migration, 40, 45, 192, 195–6; monetary deepening, 96–8, 108; mortality, 6, 10, 22, 34–7, 44, 49, 139–40, 167, 170; occupational groups, 176, 188–91, 231–5, 238–43, 246–9; occupation–education matrices, 249–54; pensions, 357; population growth, 22–5, 35, 79–81, 115–17, 124, 169–70, 377; Repelita V, 36, 174, 230, 243–6, 254, 258n; Repelita VI, 243; school enrolments, 8, 61, 50–3, 73–5, 147–52, 166, 236; skill levels, 379; structural change, 69–70, 186–7; tax ratios, 101–2; technology, 122–4; trade, 55, 71–2, 85–8, 109, 111–13, 119–22; unemployment, 184–6; urbanization 37–41, 44

Industry, industrialization, 381; export-led, 12; primary, 231, 374; public sector, 12
Infant mortality rate, *see* Mortality
International labour migration, 12, 45–7, 192–3, 200, 206
International Monetary Fund (IMF), 386
Investment, 11, 376; domestic, 385; in human capital, 5, 171; in infrastructure, 2, 21; public borrowing, 375; savings, 7, 136–8, 375–6; in self-help groups, 378
Iran, 147–52, 194–6
Iraq, 194–6
Italy: education, 149; income, 66–8; labour force, 219; school enrolments, 147–52

JAPAN: abortion, 58; ageing population, 10, 212, 214–16, 225, 351, 356, 378, 384; agriculture, 49, 52–3, 56, 58, 130, 146–7; baby boom, 58, 214, 378; bonus system, 222–3; cultural factors, 374; demographic factors, 376; demographic transition, 22, 25–30, 60; dependency ratio, 6–7, 41–5, 58, 132–9; earnings profile, 214; economic development, 129–32, 144–7, 175, 210–11, 215–17, 224, 374; economy, 1, 2, 9, 15, 21, 39, 40, 55–8, 60, 82, 83, 92–4, 210–11; education, 3, 5, 7, 8, 14, 22, 49, 51, 59, 73–5, 124n, 147–52, 154, 211–12, 221, 224–5, 378; Employees' Pension Insurance, 218–19, 225; employment, 186–91, 221, 234–5, 253; Eugenic Protection Law, 58; female labour, 1, 2, 9, 15, 49, 52, 58, 175–91, 196–7, 212–13, 215, 217–20, 222–3, 378; fertility, 6, 22, 30–4, 41, 43–5, 49, 58, 60, 201, 213, 216, 221; GDP, 356; GNP, 5, 49, 53–4, 92–4, 133–5, 145, 176, 210, 235; household headship, 265–8; household size, 58; human capital, 213–14, 225; human capital deepening, 130; human resources, 210–11, 374; illegal workers, 193; Immigration Control Law 1951, 193; imports, 47; income, 57, 66–8; inflation, 95–6; infant mortality, 318–19, 344; industrial development, 1, 3, 46, 56–60; investment, 138, 378; job tenure, 212–14; labour force, 10–11, 45–8, 55, 57, 130, 177, 212–25, 354–5, 376, 378; labour shortage, 114; Land Reform Act, 56; Meiji Restoration, 2–3, 56, 158; mercantilism, 115; migration, 11, 40, 45, 47, 58, 192–3, 196, 206, 221, 378; Ministry of International Trade and Industry (MITI), 46–7; mobility transition, 58; mortality, 22, 34–7, 44, 49, 216; natural resources, 210; occupational groups, 188–91, 213, 221, 234–5; oil crisis, 210; population growth, 22–5, 55, 215, 376; post-World War II, 22, 55–6, 59, 60, 210, 374, 378; pre-World War II, 5–6, 16, 56; productivity growth, 1, 378; retirement, 214, 216–18, 223–5, 371, 378; rural–urban migration, 221; savings rate, 221; school enrolments, 3, 7–8, 50–3, 59, 73–5, 147–52, 237, 242; societal system, 374; structural changes, 69–70, 186–7; support for elderly, 356; tax ratios, 101; technical expertise, 22, 56, 59–60; technologies, 221; trade, 47, 130; training skills, 59; unemployment, 183–6; urbanization, 37–41, 44, 56; wage system, 10, 46, 59, 378
Johore, 193

KARACHI, 55
Kenya, 66–9
Keynesian inflexibilities, 88
Korean War, 385
Kuala Lumpur, 297–310
Kuznets curve, 59, 142–3

LABOUR FORCE: ageing of, 212, 215–16, 230, 350, 354–5, 358–72, 378; agricultural, 56–7, 245–6; composition of, 217; demand and supply, 8; distribution, 163; educational attainment of, 61, 211–12, 221, 235, 239–42, 379 (*see also* Education); female exploitation, 201–8; discrimination, 179, 182–4, 202; female participation in, 2, 9, 175–91, 194–201, 212–13, 215–17, 219–20, 269–73, 377–8; growth of, 2–3, 12, 48, 115–19, 125, 187, 230, 374; male, 177–8; in manufacturing sector, 11, 246–7, 377; migration, 11, 45–7, 192–3, 377–8; occupational groups, 9, 178–82, 221–2, 246–54; participation rates, 2, 177; productivity, 3–4, 11; projections, 246, 249–50, 379; regional differences, 8; retirement, 7, 214, 216–18, 223–5, 371, 378; return to schooling, 284–7; skill development, 3–4, 11–12, 209, 256, 378–9; structure of, 186–7; technologies, 63, 221; trade unions, 11, 179, 204–5, 208–9; training, 12, 378; unskilled labour, 45–7; wages, 11, 374, 384; *see also* Employment
Land reform, 376, 383
Latin America and the Caribbean: culture, 376–7; economic growth, 1, 102,

144–6, 376; debts, 66; education, 2, 8, 149, 152, 154, 156–8; employment, 386; income, 17, 66–8; labour force, 236; school enrolments, 7–8; *see also* Argentina; Brazil; Mexico; Peru
Lewis's labour-surplus model, 141
Life cycle model, 7
Life expectancy, *see* Mortality
Literacy, *see* Education

MACARTHUR, GENERAL, 55
McNamara World Bank School, 376
Mainichi Newspapers Survey, 47
Malaysia: ageing population, 351–8, 371–2; agriculture, 49, 52–3, 146–7, 231–4, 238–43, 247; Chinese in, 9, 283, 287–310, 380; debts, 62, 92–4; deficits and surpluses, 102–4; demographic transition, 22, 25–30, 41–5; demographic trends, 115–17, 230, 379; dependency ratio, 6, 79, 81, 118, 132–9; earnings–age profiles, 290–4; economic development, 13, 144–7, 175, 229, 254–7, 379; Economic Planning Unit–Department of Statistics Survey, 283, 288; economy, 1, 21, 40, 98–113; education, 7–8, 14, 61–2, 49, 51, 73–5, 124n, 154–8, 229, 235–43, 254–7, 287–8, 297–310, 379; employment, 8–9, 61, 178, 186–91, 200, 231–5, 239–42, 247, 249, 254–7; employment choice, 284–7, 294, 298–310; exports, 1, 71–2, 85–8, 109, 120–2, 124n, 176; female labour, 49, 52, 79–81, 175–91, 196–201; female exploitation, 204; fertility, 6, 22, 30–4, 41, 43–5, 49, 201; GDI, 88–92, 99–104, 123; GDP, 88–92, 176, 356; GDS, 88–92; GNP, 8, 49, 53–4, 76–8, 83–5, 92–4, 96–7, 133–5, 145, 176, 371; health care, 357, 371–2; household headship, 265–8; income, 61, 66–8; investment, 138; labour force, 22, 34–7, 44–9, 175–91, 218, 229–35, 236, 243–4, 254–7, 258n, 354–5; marriage, 201; migration, 192–3, 196, 200; Migration and Employment Survey 1975, 287; 'Mincer' earnings functions, 283, 286–7, 310n; monetary deepening, 96–8, 108; mortality, 6, 139–40; occupational groups, 176–82, 188–91, 231–5, 238–43; pensions, 357; population growth, 22–5, 79–81, 115–17; Rand Corporation Family Life Survey 1976–7, 287; refugees, 45; school enrolments, 8, 50–3, 61, 236–7; structural change, 69–70, 186–7;

support for elderly, 356; tax ratios, 101–2; technology, 122–4; trade, 71–2, 85–8, 109, 111–13, 119–22
Maldives, 23
Malthusian forces, 155–6
Manufacturing, *see* Industry; Labour force
Marriage, *see* Household
Mega-cities, 41
Meiji Restoration, 2, 3, 158; land reforms, 56
Mexico, 66–8, 145–52, 385
Middle East: economy, 119; employment, 385–6; female migrants, 192–3, 207; labour flows, 11, 45; trade, 82
Migration: costs, 206; female, 192–3, 201–7, 377; illegal 45, 206; international, 11, 192–3; 200, 206; labour migration, 377–8; labour migration from household, 265; refugees, 45; restrictions, 4; rural–urban, 195, 221
'Mincer' earnings functions, 283, 286–7, 310n
Ministry of International Trade and Industry (MITI), 46–7
Modernization, 384–5
Monetary deepening, 96, 108
Mortality: changes, 22, 34–7, 376; decline, 6, 44, 371, 374, 381; educational differences, 15; infant, 10, 36, 313–46, 380; life expectancy, 139–41, 167, 170, 370, 376, 380; transition, 6, 34–7, 44–5, 64; trends, 49
MPS (marginal propensity to save), 141
Muslim countries, 195

NATURAL RESOURCES, 3, 22, 47
Nepal: debts, 92–4; deficits and surpluses, 102–4; demographic trends, 22, 115–17; dependency ratio, 79, 81, 118; economic development, 176; economy, 21, 92–4, 104–11, 119; education, 22, 73–5, 124n; exports, 85–8, 109, 120–2, 124n; female labour, 175–91; 198–9; fertility, 22, 201; GDI, 88–92, 99–104, 123; GDP, 83–5, 92–4, 99–104, 176; GDS, 88–92; GNP, 76–7, 83–5, 92–4, 96–7, 176; income, 66–9; inflation, 95–6; labour force, 48, 63, 79–81; monetary deepening, 96–8; mortality, 22; population growth, 22, 79–81, 115–17; school enrolments, 73–5; structural change, 69–70; tax ratios, 101–2; technology, 122–4; trade, 85–8, 109, 111–13, 119–22
Netherlands, 45, 60, 260
New Zealand: ageing population, 351–2;

agriculture, 49, 52–3; demographic transition, 25–30, 374; female labour, 49, 52; fertility, 41, 43–5, 201; GNP, 49, 53–4; income, 66–8; mortality, 35–6; population growth, 24–5; school enrolments, 50–3
NIEs (newly industrialized economies), *see* Hong Kong; Singapore; South Korea; Taiwan
Nigeria, 66–9, 147–52
Niue, 23
North American Region: economic growth comparisons, 1, 21; refugees, 45; *see also* United States
North Sulawesi: labour force, 230
Norway, 351–2
Nutrition, 14; improvement, 12, 168, 170, 172

OCCUPATION–EDUCATION MATRIX, 249–54
Occupations, *see* Employment
Oceania, 374, *see also* Australia; New Zealand
Oil: crisis, 9, 82, 210; exporters, 11, 45, 60, 62, 82, 89, 92, 98; importers, 62, 98; prices, 12, 62, 119, 124n, 161, 165; resources, 92; shocks, 22, 183

'PACIFIC CENTURY', 373
Pakistan: agriculture, 49, 52–3; debts, 92–4; deficits and surpluses, 102–4; demographic transition, 22, 25–30; demographic trends, 115–17; dependency, 41–5, 79, 81; economic policy, 98–113; economy, 21, 104–11, 119; education, 49–51, 73–5, 124n; employment, 386; exports, 71, 73, 85–8, 109, 120–2, 124n; female labour, 49, 52, 175–91, 196–9; fertility, 22, 30–4, 41, 43–5, 49, 201; GDI, 88–92, 99–104, 123; GDP, 83–5, 92–4, 99–104, 176; GDS, 88–92, 99–104, 123; GNP, 49, 53–4, 76–8, 83–5, 92–4, 96–7, 176; income, 66–9; inflation, 95–6; labour force, 45, 48, 79–81; migration, 40, 45; monetary deepening, 96–8, 108; mortality, 22, 34–7, 44, 49; policy change, 45, 64; population growth, 22–5, 79–81, 115–17; school enrolments, 50–3, 73–5; structural changes, 69–70; support for elderly, 356; tax ratios, 101–2; technology, 122–4; trade, 71, 73, 85–8, 109, 111–13, 119–22; urbanization, 37–41, 44
Palm oil, 82

Panama, 145
Pearson correlation coefficients, 53
Peninsular Malaysia, *see* Malaysia
Pensions, 10, 218–19, 356–7, 361–9, 370, 377, 381
Peru, 66–8, 145
Philippines: ageing population, 351–8; agriculture, 49, 52–3, 146–7, 163–5; debts, 92–4, 124n, 165; deficits and surpluses, 102–4; demographic transition, 22, 25–30; demographic trends, 115–17; dependency ratio, 41–5, 132–9, 174; economic development, 144–7, 159–70, 175–91, 225n, 377; economic policy, 99–113; economy, 14–15, 21, 40, 79, 81, 104–11, 118–19, 170, 192–4; education, 8, 22, 49, 52–3, 61–2, 73–5, 124n, 147–52, 154, 166–7, 170–3, 225n; employment, 178, 186–91, 386; exports, 71–2, 85–8, 109, 120–2, 124n, 171, 176; fertility, 22, 30–4, 41, 43–5, 49, 169–70, 173, 201; GDI, 88–92, 99–104, 123; GDP, 83–5, 92–4, 99–104, 161–4, 170, 176; GDS, 188–92; GNP, 49, 53–4, 63, 76–8, 83–5, 92–4, 96–7, 133–5, 145, 161–4, 166, 176; health, 14, 167–70, 172–3, 357; household headship, 265–8; human capital, 165–74; imports, 171; income, 61, 66–9; industrialization, 61; labour force, 14, 45, 48, 79–81, 163, 175–91, 354–5; migration, 40, 45, 192–3, 195–6, 206; monetary deepening, 96–8, 108; mortality, 6, 22, 34–7, 44, 49, 167, 170; occupational groups, 176–82, 188–91; pensions, 357; policy change, 45, 374–5; population growth, 22–4, 79–81, 115–17, 374, 377; school enrolments, 7–8, 50–3, 73–5, 147–52, 166, 236–7; structural changes, 69–71; tax ratios, 101–2; technology, 122–4; trade, 55, 71–2, 85–8, 109, 111–13, 119–22; unemployment, 183–6; urbanization, 37–41, 44
Population: change, 22–3, 64–5, 374; crises, 64; dynamics, 2; explosion, 64; growth, 1–3, 5–7, 14, 22, 24, 40, 115–19, 124, 125n, 169–70, 215, 374–7, 382–3, 385; international comparisons, 21, 23; mobility, 64 (*see also* Migration); policy, 45, 382–3; size, 23; trends, 378; world, 23
Poverty, 23
Public health programmes, *see* Health
Public service: women's role in, 377

REFUGEES: migration, 45

Religion, 63; *see also* Buddhism
Republic of Korea, *see* South Korea
Resources, 88–92, 375
Retirement, 7, 10–11, 214, 216–18, 223–5, 369, 371, 378; female, 377
Romania, 147–52
Rome, 209

SAUDI ARABIA, 192–3
Schools and schooling, *see* Education
Schultz's model, 147, 152–3
Seoul, 196
Singapore: ageing population, 351–6; agriculture, 49, 52–3; Central Provident Fund, 357; debts, 92–4; deficits and surpluses, 102–4; demographic transition, 22, 25–30; demographic trends, 115–17; dependency ratio, 6, 41–5, 79, 81, 118, 132–9; economic development, 13, 159, 211; economy, 21, 40, 92–4, 98–113; education, 7–8, 22, 60–2, 73–5, 124n; employment, 178, 186–91; exports, 71–3, 85–8, 109, 120–2, 124n, 176; female labour, 49, 52, 175–91, 97–9; fertility, 6, 22, 30–4, 41, 43–5, 49, 201; GDI, 88–92, 99–104, 123; GDP, 83–5, 92–4, 99–104, 176, 356; GDS, 88–92; GNP, 8, 49, 53, 54, 76–8, 83–5, 92–4, 96–7, 133–5, 176; health care, 357; housing, 124n; income, 66–8; inflation, 95–6; investment, 138; labour force, 45, 48, 61–2, 177, 354–5; Medisave programme, 357; migration, 40, 45, 192–3, 218; monetary deepening, 96–8, 108; mortality, 6, 22, 34–7, 44, 49, 139–40; occupational groups, 176–82, 188–91; pensions, 357; policy change, 45; population growth, 22–5; resources, 60; school enrolments, 50–3, 73–5, 236–7; structural changes, 69–70, 186–7; support for elderly, 356; tax ratios, 101–2; technology, 122–4; trade, 71–3, 83, 85–8, 109, 111–13, 119–22; unemployment, 183–6; urbanization 37–41, 44
Skill development, *see* Labour force
Smith, Adam, 2, 141–2, 152, 156, 376
Socio-economic: development, 6, 382–3; factors, 325–30, 332, 334, 336, 344; indicators, 17
South America, 95; *see also* Latin America
South Asia, 373–87; population size, 23; *see also* Bangladesh; India; Nepal; Pakistan; Sri Lanka
South Korea: ageing population, 11, 351–72, 381; agriculture, 49, 52–3, 60–1, 146–7, 231; Buddhists, 61, 368–9; census, 279; debt, 92–4; deficits and surpluses, 102–4; demographic trends, 115–17; dependency ratio, 6–7, 41–5, 79, 81, 118, 132–9; economic development, 13, 16, 131, 144–7, 159, 175, 211; development, 379; Economically Active Population Survey 1983, 270; economy, 1, 21, 40, 60, 92–4, 98–113; education, 7–8, 22, 49–51, 60–1, 73–5, 124n, 131, 147–52, 154, 156–7, 273–6, 368–9, 379–80; employment, 178, 186–91, 253; Family Income and Expenditure Survey 1984, 271; export 1, 60, 70–3, 85–8, 109, 120–2, 124n, 176; female labour, 49, 52–3, 175–91, 194, 197, 269–70, 204; fertility, 22, 30–4, 41, 43–5, 49, 273, 280–1, 371, 379–80; financial assistance, 60; GDI, 88–92, 99–104, 123; GDP, 83–5, 92–4, 99–104, 176; GDS, 88–92; GNP, 49, 53–4, 58, 76–8, 83–5, 92–4, 96–7, 133–5, 145, 176; health, 357–61, 367–72, 381; HOMES model, 261–2, 281n, 379; household, 265–8, 271–6, 280, 281n; income, 61, 66–8; industrialization, 1, 60; inflation, 95–6; investment, 138; labour force, 11, 45, 48, 79–81, 175–91, 218, 281n, 354–5, 357–61; migration, 11, 40, 45, 193, 195–6; mobility, 11; monetary deepening, 96–8, 108; morbidity, 370; mortality, 11, 22, 34–7, 44, 49, 139–40, 370–1; occupational groups, 176–82, 188–91; pensions, 361, 370; population growth, 22–5, 79–1, 115–17; post-World War II, 16, 60; SSS (Social Statistical Survey) 1986, 279–80; school enrolments, 7–8, 50–3, 73–5, 147–52, 236–7, 277–80, 371; structural changes, 69–70, 186–7; tax ratios, 101–2; technology, 122–4; trade, 60, 70–3, 83, 85–8, 109, 111–13, 119–22; unemployment, 183–6; urbanization, 37–41, 349–50, 352, 370–1
South-East Asia, 373–87; *see also* Indonesia; Malaysia; Philippines; Singapore; Thailand
Spain, 147–52
Sri Lanka: agriculture, 49, 52–3; debts, 92–4; deficits and surpluses, 102–4; demographic transition, 22, 25–30; demographic trends, 115–17; dependency ratio, 79, 81, 118; economic development, 14–15, 167, 176; economy, 15, 21, 40, 92–113, 119;

education, 14–15, 22, 49–51, 60–3, 73–5, 124n, 167; exports, 71, 73, 85–8, 109, 120–2, 124n; female labour, 49, 52, 175–91, 194–201; fertility, 6, 22, 30–4, 41, 43–5, 49, 201; GDI, 88–92, 99–104, 123; GDP, 83–5, 92–4, 99–104, 176; GDS, 88–92; GNP, 49, 53–4, 63, 76–8, 83–5, 92–4, 176; income, 66–9; inflation, 95–6; labour force, 45, 48, 60, 79–81; migration, 40, 45, 63, 93, 195–6; monetary deepening, 96–8, 108; mortality, 22, 34–7, 44, 49; policy change, 45, 64; population growth, 22–5, 79–81, 115–17; school enrolments, 50–3, 60–1, 73–5; structural changes, 69–70; tax ratios, 101–2; technology, 60, 122–4; trade, 71–3, 85–8, 109, 111–13, 119–22; urbanization, 37–41, 44; welfare subsidies, 63, 167
Suharto, President, 174
Sweden, 219, 351–2, 356
Switzerland, 351–2
Syria, 195

TAIWAN: agriculture, 146–7; debts, 92–4; demographic trends, 115–17; dependency ratio, 79, 81, 118; economic development, 144–7, 211; economy, 1, 104–11, 119, 159; education, 7–8, 73–5, 124n; employment, 178, 251; exports, 1, 71–3, 85–8, 109, 120–2, 124n; GNP, 8, 145; imports, 120; income, 66–8; labour force, 11, 79–81; migration, 11, 193, 196; mortality, 140; occupational groups, 176–82; population growth, 79–81, 115–17; school enrolments, 73–5; structural change, 69–70; trade, 71–3, 83, 85–8, 109, 111–13, 119–22
Technological developments, 2–4, 66, 374–5, 382–3, 384; expertise, 15; imported, 21; progress, 16, 122–4; skills, 386
TFR, *see* Total fertility rate
Thailand: ageing population, 351–72, 381; agriculture, 45, 49, 52–3, 61–2, 146–7, 163–5, 231–4, 238–43; debts, 92–4; deficits and surpluses, 102–4; demographic characteristics, 325–6, 328, 332, 334, 336, 344, 362–3, 365–7; demographic transition, 22, 25–30; demographic trends, 115–17, 230; dependency ratio, 6–7, 31–4, 79, 81, 118, 132–9; economic development, 1, 6, 7–8, 13, 144–7, 159–70, 175–91, 229, 254–7; economy, 1, 21, 40, 98–113, 119, 170; education, 7–8, 14, 16–17, 22, 49–51, 61–2, 73–5, 124n, 147–52, 166–7, 170–3, 229, 236–43, 254–7, 273–6, 325–6, 330, 333, 335, 337, 347n, 348n, 361–3, 379–80; employment, 8–9; exports, 1, 71–3, 85, 88, 109, 120–2, 124n, 325, 327, 330, 333, 335, 337; family size, 260, 262–3; female labour, 49, 52, 175–91, 194–201; fertility, 30–4, 41, 43–5, 168–70, 173, 201, 257, 262–5, 273, 280–1, 317, 371, 379–80; Five-year plans, Third, 322; Fourth, 322; Fifth, 322; Seventh, 8; GDI, 88–92, 99–104, 123; GDP, 83–5, 92–4, 99–104, 356; GDS, 88–92, 161–4, 170, 176; GNP, 49, 53–4, 76–8, 83–5, 92–4, 96–7, 133–5, 145, 161–4, 166, 176, 258n, 314, 321–2; health, 167–70, 172–3, 321–2, 326–9, 331–6, 338–45, 347n, 348n, 359–72, 380–1; HOMES model, 261–2, 281n, 379; household, 262–8, 271–6, 280–1, 325, 327, 331, 333, 337, 344–5; human capital, 165–74, imports, 171; income, 61, 66–9; industries, 8; infant and child mortality, 313–46, 347n; inflation, 95–6; investment, 138; labour force, 8, 45, 48, 62, 79–81, 163, 175–91, 229–35, 236, 243–4, 254–7, 354–5, 358–69, 381; Labour Force Survey 1984, 269; migration, 40, 45, 192–3, 195–6, 206; monetary deepening, 96–8, 108; morbidity, 11, 370; mortality, 6, 10–11, 22, 34–7, 44, 49, 139–41, 167, 170, 370–1, 380; occupational groups, 176–82, 188–91, 231–5, 238–43; pensions, 357, 361–8, 370; policy change, 45; population growth, 22–5, 79–81, 115–17, 169–70, 377; refugees, 45; school enrolments, 7–8, 50–3, 61, 73–5, 147–52, 166, 273, 277–80, 371; socio-economic factors, 325–30, 332, 334, 336, 344, 380; SES (Socio-Economic Survey) 1981, 271, 277; SOFT (Survey of Fertility in Thailand) 1975, 315–17, 325–331, 346n, 380; SPC (Survey of Population Change), 318; structural changes, 69–70, 186–7; support for elderly, 356, 371; tax ratios, 101–2; TDHS (Thailand Demographic and Health Survey) 1987, 314–17, 325–31, 338–9, 346n, 347n, 380; trade, 71–3, 83, 85–8, 109, 111–13, 119–22; technology, 122–4; unemployment, 183–6; urbanization, 37–41, 44, 349–50, 352, 370–1; wages, 205

Thompson, Warren, 55
Total fertility rate (TFR), 32, 30–4, 54, 169–70, 201
Trade, 47, 55, 60, 64, 69–73, 82–3, 85–8, 109, 111–13, 119–22, 130, 386; world markets, 384–5
Trade unions, 11, 179, 204–5
Trengganu, Malaysia, 257
Turkey: education, 149; female labour, 195; labour force growth rates, 48; migration, 195; school enrolments, 147–52

UNITED KINGDOM: ageing population, 351–2, 356; education, 60, 75, 124n, 149; education in employment choice, 283–4; income, 66–8; Industrial Revolution, 141; labour force, 219, 354–5; school enrolments, 147–52
United States: ageing population, 115–19, 351–2; budget deficit, 113–15; economy, 54; education, 75, 124n, 147–54; employment, 234–5, 253–4; exports, 121; Federal Reserve Bank, 114; female labour, 9; financial assistance given, 60; GNP, 1, 235; human capital, 213–14; income, 66–8; industrial competition, 384; inflation, 82–3, 95–6; labour force, 219, 354–5; mortality, 140; overseas spending, 385; productivity growth, 1; Retirement History Survey, 359; school enrolments, 7–8, 73–5, 147–54; structural changes, 69–70; tax ratios, 101; technology, 60; trade, 55, 82–3; unemployment of the educated, 82; *see also* North American Region
Urbanization, 64, 374; effect on ageing population, 349–50, 352, 370–1, 381
USSR, 149

VENEZUELA, 145
Vietnam War, 385; refugees, 45

WEIBULL MODEL, 318–19, 344
Western media, exposure to, 385
Western world: economic interests, 376; industrialized nations, 1, 8, 43
Work-force, *see* Labour force
World Bank, 1

YUGOSLAVIA, 147–52